T0122602

Lecture Notes in Computer Science 1769

Edited by G. Goos, J. Hartmanis and J. van Leeuwen

Springer
Berlin
Heidelberg
New York
Barcelona
Hong Kong
London
Milan
Paris
Singapore
Tokyo

Günter Haring Christoph Lindemann
Martin Reiser (Eds.)

Performance Evaluation: Origins and Directions

Volume Editors

Günter Haring
Universität Wien
Institut für Angewandte Informatik und Informationssysteme
Lenaugasse 2/8, 1080 Wien, Austria
E-mail: haring@ani.univie.ac.at

Christoph Lindemann
Universität Dortmund, Informatik IV
August-Schmidt-Straße 12, 44227 Dortmund, Germany
E-mail: cl@cs.uni-dortmund.de

Martin Reiser
GMD Institut für Medienkommunikation, Schloß Birlinghoven
Postfach 1316, 53754 Sankt Augustin, Germany
E-mail: martin.reiser@gmd.de

Cataloging-in-Publication Data applied for

Die Deutsche Bibliothek -CIP-Einheitsaufnahme

Performance evaluation : origins and directions / Günter Haring ... (ed.). -
Berlin ; Heidelberg ; New York ; Barcelona ; Hong Kong ; London ;
Milan ; Paris ; Singapore ; Tokyo : Springer, 2000
(Lecture notes in computer science ; Vol. 1769)
ISBN 3-540-67193-5

CR Subject Classification (1998): C.4, B.1-4, D.4, C.2, D.2, K.6

ISSN 0302-9743
ISBN 3-540-67193-5 Springer-Verlag Berlin Heidelberg New York

Springer-Verlag is a company in the specialist publishing group BertelsmannSpringer.

Printed in Germany

Typesetting: Camera-ready by author, data conversion by Steingraeber Satztechnik GmbH, Heidelberg
Printed on acid-free paper SPIN: 10719732 06/3142 5 4 3 2 1 0

Foreword

The issue of computer performance evaluation must have concerned computer science and engineering researchers as well as system designers, system operators, and end users ever since computer systems came into existence. But it was not until around 1970 that "performance evaluation", as a clearly identifiable discipline within the computer science/engineering field, established itself. This was the period when IBM introduced its successful 360 series, and time-shared operating systems were the main focus of the computer community.

The IFIP Working Group 7.3 "Computer system modeling" was initiated by Paul Green (IBM Yorktown), Erol Gelenbe (INRIA, France), and myself (IBM Yorktown). The ACM Sigmetrics group was also established around that time. The 1970s was a really exciting period when the new computer performance community played a major role in advancing the state of the art in queuing network models: a major extension of networks was made with "product-form" solutions by Baskett-Chandy-Muntz-Palacios (1975) and a number of other works on related subjects. Len Kleinrock's two volumes *Queuing Systems* (1975, 1976) made major contributions by providing both computer and network communities with the state-of-the-art knowledge in queuing theory. Reiser-Sauer-McNair's efforts at IBM Yorktown in creating QNET and RESQ modeling packages and disseminating them to both industrial and academic communities was a major landmark, and prompted similar efforts undertaken at AT&T, INRIA, and elsewhere. More recently, software packages for the user-friendly specification and automated analysis of stochastic Petri nets like the DSPNexpress package by Christoph Lindemann (1995) made significant impact both in academia and industry.

The MVA algorithm devised by Martin Reiser and Steve Lavenberg (1980) made large scale modeling computationally feasible. Jeff Buzen, who published a seminal paper on the central server model (1973) was among the first successful entrepreneurs to demonstrate a viable business opportunity in performance modeling. The introduction of generalized stochastic Petri nets by Marco Ajmone Marsan, Gianfranco Balbo, and Gianni Conte (1984) allowed the high-level specification of discrete-event systems with exponential events (i.e., Markovian models) and their automated solution process by tool support. A recent landmark in performance modeling of communication networks and the Internet constituted the discovery of self-similar traffic by Walter Willinger and his co-workers at Bellcore (1995). Four personal accounts of these key contributors describing where and how these research results have been discovered are included in this book.

In 1981, an international journal "Performance Evaluation" (North Holland) was created with me as its founding editor-in-chief. Together with the regularly held IFIP WG 7.3's Performance Symposium and ACM's Sigmetrics Conferences, the journal established the identity of our performance community, and thanks to the dedicated efforts by succeeding editors (Martin Reiser, and now

Werner Bux) the journal has maintained its role as a major forum for the archival literature of our research community. Through this journal and the aforementioned symposia and through more recent additions such as Performance Tool Conferences regularly organized by Günter Haring and others, we have been quite successful in embracing our outstanding colleagues from related fields, such as operations research and applied probability.

As the paradigm of computing has changed from time-shared mainframe computers to networks of personal computers and workstations, the focus of performance modeling and evaluation has shifted from CPUs to networks and distributed databases. With the rapidly gaining dominance of the Internet, wireless access networks, and optical network backbones, we will witness profound changes and increasing complexities in associated performance issues. For example, as traffic over the Internet expands exponentially, and end user's desire to access the Web servers from anywhere and at any time grows rapidly, interactions among clients and web proxy servers should present major technical challenges to network service providers, and hence great opportunities for our performance community. Tom Leighton of MIT and his colleagues have seized such an opportunity by developing a network of proxy server's cache called "free flow" and have turned their research project into a rapidly expanding business. I expect similar opportunities will abound in the coming decade, as mobile users and a variety of "information appliances" will be interconnected, forming an ever expanding information network.

It is quite timely that this special volume on "Performance Evaluation" contributed by a number of outstanding colleagues is going to be published at this exciting period, when the complexity and sophistication of information networks continue to multiply and challenge our ability to evaluate, predict, and improve system performance. I congratulate Günter Haring, Christoph Lindemann, and Martin Reiser on their success in compiling these important articles into an archival form.

November 1999 Hisashi Kobayashi

Preface

Performance evaluation has been a discipline of computer science for some thirty years. To us, it seemed to be time to take stock of what we - the performance evaluation community - were doing. Towards this end, we decided to organize a workshop on Performance Evaluation of Computer Systems and Communication Networks, which was held at the international conference and research center for computer science, Schloß Dagstuhl, Germany, September 15-19, 1997. The participants discussed, among other things, the following fundamental questions:

What are the scientific contributions of performance evaluation?
What is its relevance in industry and business?
What is its standing in academia?
Where is the field headed?
What are its success stories and failures?
What are its current burning questions?

During this workshop, working groups focused on areas like performance evaluation techniques and tools, communication networks, computer architecture, computer resource management, as well as performance of software systems (see http://www.ani.univie.ac.at/dagstuhl97/). The participants summarized the past of performance evaluation and projected future trends and needs in the field. It was identified that - as in many other sciences - at the beginning there was the observation of the behavior of systems, generally by measurements, followed by the development of theories to explain the observed behavior. Especially in system modeling, based on these theories, methodologies have been developed for behavior prediction. At that stage, measurement changed its role from pure phenomenological observation to model-driven parameter estimation. Based on a series of highly successful case studies, tool methodology implemented in versatile software packages has been developed to make the theoretical results amenable to practitioners. Originally focused on computer systems and communications, the scope of performance evaluation broadened to include processor architecture, parallel and distributed architectures, operating systems, database systems, client-server computing, fault tolerant computing, and real-time systems.

With the growing size and complexity of current computer and communication systems, both hardware and software, the existing methodologies and software packages for performance modeling seem to reach their limits. It is interesting to observe that for these complex interoperable systems the methodological cycle starts again with measurements to describe the system behavior, and understand it at a qualitative level. High performance parallel processing systems and the Internet traffic are good examples for this pattern of scientific progress. An example is the discovery of self-similar traffic that spurred a large number of observational and empirical studies.

During three decades of research, performance evaluation has achieved a rich body of knowledge. However, the participants of the Dagstuhl workshop felt, that the results are not as crisply focused as those in other prominent fields of computer science. Therefore, the project of writing a monograph on *Performance Evaluation - Origins and Directions* was begun with the following basic ideas. This monograph should document the history, the key ideas and important success stories of performance evaluation and demonstrate the impact of performance evaluation on different areas through case studies. The book should generate interest in the field and point to future trends. It is aimed at senior undergraduate and graduate students (for seminar reading), faculty members (for course development), and engineers (as orientation about available methods and tools). The contributions should be on an academic level, having an essay-character and they should be highly readable. They should also be as lively and stimulating as possible, where the mathematical topics should be presented on the appropriate level, concentrating on concepts and ideas, avoiding difficult technicalities.

As editors we are proud that we have succeeded in recruiting top researchers in the field to write specific chapters. The spectrum of topical areas is quite broad comprising work from an application as well as from a methods point-of-view. Application topics include software performance, scheduling, parallel and distributed systems, mainframe and storage systems, World Wide Web, wireless networks, availability and reliability, database systems, and polling systems. Methodological chapters treat numerical analysis methods, product-form queueing networks, simulation, mean-value analysis and workload characterization. Altogether the volume contains 19 topical chapters. Additionally, it contains one contribution on the role of performance evaluation in industry, and personal accounts of four key contributors describing the genesis of breakthrough results.

We hope that the book will serve as a reference to the field of performance evaluation. For the first time, it presents a comprehensive view of methods, applications, and case studies expressed by authors who have shaped the field in a major way. It is our expectation, that the volume will be a catalyst for the further evolution of performance evaluation and help to establish this exciting discipline in the curriculum, in industry, and in the IT world at large.

October 1999

Günter Haring
Christoph Lindemann
Martin Reiser

Table of Contents

Position Paper

I Topical Area Papers

Position Paper

Performance Evaluation in Industry: A Personal Perspective

Stephen S. Lavenberg and Mark S. Squillante

IBM Research Division, Thomas J. Watson Research Center,
Yorktown Heights NY 10598, USA
{sslaven,mss}@watson.ibm.com

1 Introduction

Performance is one of the fundamental factors in the design, development and configuration of computer and communication systems. Performance evaluation therefore has been and continues to be of great practical importance in the computer industry. Of the two main approaches to performance evaluation, namely measurement and modeling, modeling has received the greatest research attention, both in industry and in universities. Hence, performance modeling is the subject of this paper. The paper is not intended to be a survey of performance modeling in industry. Rather we present our personal perspectives based on the development and application of performance modeling in IBM over the past 30 years.

We will present several success stories of the impact that performance modeling has had on IBM products, and discuss some trends that we have observed over time as technology has advanced and systems have become more complex. Since IBM is a computer company, our focus will be on computer systems and applications and will include computer networks, but will not include telephony systems, applications and networks.

The paper is arranged approximately chronologically. We begin with some early success stories from the late 1960s through the 1980s. We then consider a few success stories from the 1990s that demonstrate somewhat of a shift in performance modeling. We conclude with our observations about some trends in performance modeling research and its practical importance in industry.

2 Early Success Stories

The first two success stories illustrate the use of analytical queueing results to impact product development. The third success story illustrates the development and widespread use of queueing network based performance modeling packages.

2.1 A Simple Queueing Network Model of a Time Sharing System

One of the earliest documented successful applications of analytical computer performance modeling in industry happened in IBM in the late 1960s during the

G. Haring et al. (Eds.): Performance Evaluation, LNCS 1769, pp. 3–13, 2000.

development of IBM's OS/360 Time Sharing Option (TSO). This is described in detail by Lassettre and Scherr [15]. The machine repairman model, originally developed in the operations research literature to model a single repairman servicing machines that break down, was used to represent OS/360 TSO running with a single memory partition and supporting multiple terminal attached users via time sharing the execution of their programs. With a single memory partition, only one user's program could be resident in memory and the system was time shared by swapping programs into and out of memory. The machine repairman model has a very simple analytical solution which was used to estimate the number of users the system could support without exceeding a specified average response time. The model was used in conjunction with measurements. Average program execution time was estimated from measurements on a TSO system with a second computer system simulating the users by running benchmark scripts and generating exponentially distributed user think times. The measured average response time was compared with the mean response time computed using the model under the assumption of exponentially distributed execution times with mean equal to the measured average. It is interesting to note that a substantial difference between the measured and predicted response time was usually due to bugs in the operating system. Once the bugs were removed the measured and predicted results tracked closely. In approximately 75% of the test cases, the prediction error was less than 10% with a maximum error of 24%. This was surprising due to the simplistic model assumptions. In particular, program execution times were assumed to be exponentially distributed, although measurements showed they were not, and programs were assumed to be executed first come first served, rather than via time sharing. Unknown at the time, this queueing model is an example of a product form queueing network. Product form queueing network results of the 1970s showed invariance of performance measures including mean response time when a first-come-first-served queue with exponential service times is replaced by a processor sharing queue with general service times. A processor sharing queue with general service times would have been a more realistic model of the TSO system, but the model's predictions would not have been different, thus helping to explain the model's accuracy.

2.2 The Performance of Token Ring Local Area Networks

One of the most influential analytical performance modeling studies in IBM was done around 1980. The study, which appeared in [6], compared the analytically derived delay-throughput characteristics of local area networks based on ring and bus topologies. Included were the token ring, a ring network with access controlled by a single circulating token that was being built at IBM's Research Lab in Zurich, and the CSMA-CD (carrier sensing, multiple access with collision detection) bus that was the basis of Ethernet, originally developed by Xerox in the 1970s. The study primarily used existing analytical queueing results, modifying them as required to capture the essential characteristics of the networks being modeled. For example, the key to analyzing token ring performance was recognizing that a token ring functioned like a single server that served multiple queues by round robin polling. An elegant discrete time queueing analysis of such a polling system had been obtained by Konheim and Meister [14]. (The discrete time results were converted to continuous time by letting the discrete time interval approach zero.) The study showed that the delay-throughput characteristics of the token ring and CSMA-CD bus were comparable at low transmission speeds, e.g. 1 Mb/sec, but the token ring was superior at higher speeds, e.g. 10 Mb/sec. (The key parameter affecting the relative performance of the token ring and CSMA-CD bus is the ratio of propagation delay to packet transmission time, with higher ratios favoring the token ring.) While many factors influenced IBM's decision to develop a token ring local area network product, the performance of the token ring as demonstrated in this study was a key factor.

2.3 The Research Queueing (RESQ) Package

The discovery of product form queueing networks and their properties and the development of efficient computational algorithms for product form networks was a breakthrough in analytical performance modeling that is covered elsewhere in this volume (see the papers by Buzen, Reiser). Within the computer science literature, the classic paper that first defined product form networks and gave their properties was due to Baskett, Chandy, Muntz and Palacios-Gomez [3]. Researchers in IBM developed the main computational algorithms for solving product form networks, first the convolution algorithm [16], and later the Mean Value Analysis (MVA) algorithm [17], and they incorporated these algorithms in performance modeling software packages to make them available to performance modeling practitioners. The first such package was QNET4, software for specifying and solving closed multichain product form queueing networks. QNET4 provided a textual interface for the user to specify the queues and routing chains and their associated parameter values. Performance measures were computed using the convolution algorithm. Shortly after QNET4 was developed, it was integrated into a more general performance modeling package, the Research Queueing (RESQ) package.

RESQ allowed a user to specify and solve product form networks (initially using the convolution algorithm; the MVA algorithm was added later), but it also allowed a user to specify more general "extended queueing networks" and use discrete event simulation to estimate performance measures. The then recently developed regenerative method for estimating confidence intervals and controlling simulation run length was incorporated in RESQ. A description of extended queueing networks can be found in [18]. One of the key extensions was the inclusion of passive queues, which provide a convenient way to model simultaneous resource possession. QNET4's textual user interface was extended in a natural way to allow specification of extended queueing networks. The modeling level of abstraction provided by extended queueing networks and the implementation in RESQ proved very useful. It allowed the rapid development of simulation models without the programming required with a simulation programming language. It helped guard against the pitfall of developing overly detailed simulation models by forcing a higher level of abstraction. It included modern statistical simulation techniques and made them easy to use. It also helped bridge the gap between analytical modeling and simulation modeling by incorporating both product form networks and extended queueing networks. RESQ was a major success in IBM. Developed by researchers, it began to be widely used in product development groups in IBM in the late 1970s to model computer systems and subsystems and local and wide area computer networks. It was enhanced over time with additional computational algorithms and statistical methods, a graphical user interface, simulation animation and other features, and its widespread use in IBM continued into the 1990s. It was also made available for use in research and teaching at universities.

3 More Recent Success Stories

As computer technology advanced from the late 1960s toward the 1990s and the complexity of computer systems, networks and applications continued to grow, there has been a general shift from fairly simple mathematical methods with broad applicability to either the use of more empirical methods (ranging from experimental tweaking of simple existing models up to building and experimenting with prototype implementations) or simulation or more sophisticated mathematical methods. In the latter case, the focus is often on developing mathematical methods and analysis to investigate a fundamental issue or tradeoff at the core of the real system problem in order to impact the design of complex computer systems, networks and applications. We consider here some success stories that fall into this category. The first two illustrate the use of more advanced mathematical methods to study fundamental problems that arose in computer system scheduling and the exploitation of these results in actual system designs and implementations. The next success story illustrates the use of performance models to evaluate different cluster-based architectures and influence product development. Additional examples are then briefly summarized.

3.1 Computer Scheduling

The performance modeling and related stochastic literature over the past five decades is rich with studies of scheduling optimization problems. This includes optimal scheduling results for minimizing a weighted sum of the per-class mean response times, as well as for achieving a given vector of per-class mean response times, in a single queue or a queueing network, with or without side constraints (i.e., a per-class performance constraint that must be satisfied in addition to the global objective function). These results have basically established that, in many cases, the space of achievable performance measures is a polymatroid, or extended polymatroid, whose vertices correspond to the performance of the system under all possible fixed priority rules. Furthermore, the optimal or desired performance vector is a vertex or an interior point of this performance polytope, and the scheduling strategies which satisfy these classes of objective functions are some form or mixture of fixed priority policies (dynamic priority policies are considered below).

With technology advancements and growing computer system complexities, new customer and/or user requirements arose that were not fully addressed by previous classes of scheduling objective functions. For this reason, research studies at IBM investigated specific scheduling optimization problems to consider the needs of certain IBM computer platforms. We next briefly describe performance modeling research conducted in the early 1990s that is the basis for the processor scheduling algorithms in the Application System/400 (AS/400) and System/390 (S/390) computer systems.

Basis for the AS/400 Processor Scheduler. Much of the previous scheduling research considered scheduling strategies for minimizing a weighted sum of the per-class mean response times. An important additional objective is to maintain a low variance of response times for each class. Two related research studies at IBM that investigated this problem resulted in the concepts of Delay Cost Scheduling, due to Franaszek and Nelson [10], and Time-Function Scheduling, due to Fong and Squillante [9]. These two studies considered different forms of objective functions that are based on minimizing a weighted sum of per-class second moment measures of response time, and they used different approaches to establish certain structural properties for the respective optimal solutions.

One scheduling strategy with the structural properties for a particular instance of the scheduling objectives in [9] is based on the use of general time-based functions to obtain effective and flexible control over the allocation of resources. This scheduling strategy is in part a generalization of the linear time-dependent priority discipline [13,7] in which the priority of each job increases (linearly) according to a per-class function of some measure of time and the job with the highest instantaneous priority value in the queue is selected for execution at each scheduling epoch. In its most general setting, the time parameter for each per-class function can include any measure of the time spent waiting for a resource or set of resources (response mode), any measure of the time spent using a resource or set of resources (usage mode), and any combination of such modes [8]. An adaptive feedback mechanism is used together with mathematical control formulas to adjust these per-class time functions, as well as to migrate each job to a different class upon the occurrence of certain events or upon the job exceeding some criteria, in order to satisfy the scheduling objective function across all and/or varying workloads. These control formulas can also be used to obtain a scheduling strategy that realizes the optimal or desired performance vector which is a (interior) point in the performance space, while providing better per-class response time variance properties. A number of important scheduling issues can be easily accommodated in the per-class time functions and/or addressed by the use of these time functions to control resource scheduling decisions; examples include priority inversion [19] and processor-cache affinities [20]. The theoretical properties of time-function scheduling can be further exploited to obtain very efficient implementations [9].

The above scheduling strategy is a fundamental aspect of the *dynamic priority scheduling* algorithms employed in AS/400 systems. Based on the control formulas mentioned above and a general set of assumptions regarding workloads and performance objectives, this scheduling technology offering has proven to be a great success with AS/400 customers providing efficient and effective control over resource management to address various customer requirements across numerous diverse workloads without any perceived increase in complexity by the system administrator and users.

Basis for the S/390 Processor Scheduler. Instead of minimizing a weighted sum of the per-class mean response times, it can be more natural to associate a mean response time goal with each class and to consider the performance of the class relative to its goal. The corresponding objective function then is to minimize a vector of the per-class ratios of the response time mean to the response time goal. This problem is studied within the context of a multi-class M/GI/1 queue, with and without feedback, by Bhattacharya et al. in [5,4] where adaptive scheduling strategies are presented and shown to lexicographically minimize the vector of per-class performance ratios (exactly or approximately). The results also apply to other systems including certain multi-class Jackson networks and multi-class M/GI/c queues.

Consider a K-class system at a scheduling decision time epoch in which the mean response time for class i realized over the previous scheduling time interval(s) is x_i and the specified mean response time goal for this class is g_i. A fixed scheduling policy that gives priority to jobs of class i over jobs of class j if $x_i/g_i \geq x_j/g_j$ is then used for the next scheduling time interval. In other words, priority is given to the class that has received the worse performance, relative to its goal, over the previous time interval(s). The time intervals between scheduling decision epochs, in which priorities are updated, can be arbitrary provided that they are bounded above by a finite measure. This scheduling strategy is proven optimal in the sense that it converges asymptotically in the number of time intervals to the optimal solution which lexicographically minimizes the vector of ratios x_i/g_i arranged in non-increasing order $x_1/g_1 \geq x_2/g_2 \geq \cdots \geq x_K/g_K$ (with probability 1).

The above scheduling strategy is an important aspect of the processor scheduling algorithms employed in S/390 systems, where x_i and g_i can be functions of performance metrics other than just mean response time – in particular, response time percentiles and/or velocity goals can be used together with or instead of mean response time goals [2]. This S/390 concept is commonly referred to as *goal-oriented scheduling.* It is a key component of the workload management system provided on S/390 computers, which has been a great success for IBM in the control and management of mainframes and mainframe clusters.

3.2 Cluster Architectures and S/390 Parallel Sysplex

As commercial workloads expand and evolve, clusters of multiple computers are required to support high transaction processing rates and high availability in large-scale commercial computing environments, which include on-line transaction processing systems and parallel database systems. The principal cluster architectures proposed to support these scalable commercial application environments are the *shared-nothing* (or partitioned), the *shared-disk*, the *virtual shared-disk*, and the *Parallel Sysplex* models [12]. The shared-nothing architecture consists of partitioning the database and disks among the nodes, where either function-shipping (i.e., a remote function call to be executed by the remote node with the results, if any, returned to the local node) or I/O shipping (i.e., a remote I/O request to fetch the required data from the remote node) is used when a local transaction needs to access data located at a remote node in the cluster. Advantages of this architecture include a higher local buffer hit ratio and no need for global concurrency control, whereas the main disadvantages center around the various additional costs for remote requests to access nonlocal databases and load balancing and availability problems. The shared-disk architecture consists of essentially having all nodes directly access the disks on which shared data is located, where each node has a local database buffer cache and a global concurrency control protocol is used to maintain consistency among the local caches as well as the database. This architecture has advantages with respect to load balancing and availability, but it can suffer from additional overhead to acquire and release global locks, as well as large overhead, latency and increased I/O activity for hot shared data (so-called ping-ponging). The virtual shared-disk architecture is functionally identical to the shared-nothing architecture with I/O shipping, while providing the view of a shared-disk model to the database (i.e., the partitioned disks are transparent to the database). The Parallel Sysplex architecture consists of the shared-disk model together with a shared coupling facility that provides a shared database buffer and highly-efficient support for locking, cache coherency and general-purpose queueing.

Various aspects of each of these principal cluster architecture alternatives have been analyzed with performance models, many of which have been formulated by decomposing the original problem into more tractable parts. The solutions of these hierarchical models have often involved a combination of different methods including analytical, mathematical optimization and simulation. The results of this analysis of the principal cluster architectures by researchers at IBM and elsewhere influenced the design of the IBM S/390 Parallel Sysplex architecture, and was used by IBM to demonstrate the key advantages of this design over alternative cluster architectures. In particular, the Parallel Sysplex architecture provides the benefits of shared-disk architectures and exploits the coupling facility services to obtain very efficient intertransaction concurrency control, buffer cache coherency control, shared buffer management, and shared job queues. This results in transaction rate scaling which is close to linear in the number of nodes, high shared buffer hit ratios which can reduce the I/O rate per node, and excellent dynamic load balancing even in systems with heterogeneous nodes. Additional details on this body of performance modeling research can be found in [12] and the references cited therein.

The Parallel Sysplex technology provides the fundamental infrastructure for IBM's large-scale enterprise server environments, and the above performance modeling studies played a key role in its design.

3.3 Miscellaneous

Network Traffic Management. The allocation and management of shared network resources among different classes of traffic streams with a wide range of performance requirements and traffic characteristics in high-speed packet-switched network architectures, such as ATM, is more complex than in traditional networks. An important aspect of this traffic management problem is to characterize the effective bandwidth requirement of both individual connections and the aggregate bandwidth usage of multiple connections statistically multiplexed on a given network link, as a function of their statistical properties and the desired level of service. These metrics can then be used for efficient bandwidth management and traffic control in order to achieve high utilization of network resources while maintaining the desired level of service for all connections. Guerin et al. [11] proposed a methodology for the computation of the effective bandwidth requirement of individual and multiplexed connections based on a combination of two complementary approaches, namely a fluid model to estimate the bandwidth requirement when the impact of individual connection characteristics is critical, and the stationary bit rate distribution to estimate the bandwidth requirement when the effect of statistical multiplexing is significant. While the fluid model and its extension to capture the impact of multiplexing can be used to obtain an exact computation of the bandwidth requirement, the computational complexity involved is too high in general, and particularly for real-time network traffic management. Guerin et al. therefore used the proposed methodology to develop a computationally simple approximate expression for the effective bandwidth requirement of individual and multiplexed connections, which is shown to have sufficiently good accuracy across the range of possible connection characteristics in comparison with both exact computations and simulation results [11]. This approximation has proven quite successful as one of the key mechanisms used for traffic management in IBM's Networking BroadBand Services (NBBS) architecture [1], as well as in similar offerings from other companies.

Parallel Scheduling. A significant body of the performance modeling research literature has focused on various aspects of the parallel computer scheduling problem – i.e., the allocation of computing resources among the parallel jobs submitted for execution – which is covered elsewhere in this volume (see the paper by Majumdar and Parsons). Several classes of scheduling strategies have been proposed for such computing environments, each differing in the way the parallel resources are shared among the jobs. This includes the class of *space-sharing* strategies that share the processors in space by partitioning them among different parallel jobs, the class of *time-sharing* strategies that share the processors by rotating them among a set of jobs in time, and the class of *gang-scheduling* strategies that combine both space-sharing and time-sharing. The numerous performance modeling and optimization studies in this area have played a fundamental and important role in the design, development and implementation of different forms of space-sharing and gang-scheduling strategies in commercial parallel supercomputing systems. In fact, the IBM SP family of parallel computers supports various forms of space-sharing and gang-scheduling; support for space-sharing and/or gang-scheduling is also included in many other commercial parallel supercomputers, such as the Cray T3E, the Intel Paragon, the Meiko CS-2 and the SGI Origin.

4 Conclusions

In this paper we have illustrated how performance modeling has had an important impact on IBM products. Over time, as computer systems, networks and applications have become more complex, the mathematics required to analyze their performance has become more complex. Breakthrough results in analytical performance modeling that have broad applicability and are widely used by practitioners, as was the case with product form queueing networks (see Sect. 2.3), have been harder to come by and the influence of performance modeling methodology research on performance modeling practice has diminished. Much of the earlier influence was a result of incorporating methodological advances in performance modeling software packages for use by practitioners to model the real system of interest. Performance modeling practitioners then worked directly with system architects and designers to influence products that were being developed. It was not necessary that the modeling researcher work directly with system designers or architects. This has changed in various ways over time. The focus of mathematical performance modeling research has basically shifted towards investigating fundamental issues or tradeoffs at the core of the real system problem. Moreover, in order for this performance modeling research to have an impact on the design and development of better performing products, it is often necessary that performance modeling researchers work closely with system designers and architects. This kind of focus shift and close collaboration underlies most of the success stories in Sect. 3. As a positive side effect, close collaboration allows the performance modeling researcher to better understand the various factors that affect system design and product development and to increase their effectiveness.

Acknowledgements

We thank each of the many colleagues at IBM with whom we spoke throughout the writing of this paper and who made helpful comments on previous drafts, especially Chatschik Bisdikian, Werner Bux, Donna Dillenberger, Phil Emma, Liana Fong, Roch Guerin, Ed MacNair, Sriram Padmanabhan, Nancy Riggs, Chuck Stupca, Asser Tantawi, Brett Tremaine and Li Zhang. Some of our thoughts on the subject of this paper were refined during these discussions.

However, any errors or omissions are the responsibility of the authors, in which cases we will be inclined to invoke the immortal words of Yogi Berra: "I really didn't say everything I said."

References

1. H. Ahmadi, P. F. Chimento, R. A. Guerin, L. Gun, B. Lin, R. O. Onvural, and T. E. Tedijanto. NBBS traffic management overview. *IBM System Journal*, 34(4):604–628, 1995.
2. J. Aman, C. K. Eilert, D. Emmes, P. Yocom, and D. Dillenberger. Adaptive algorithms for managing a distributed data processing workload. *IBM System Journal*, 36(2):242–283, 1997.
3. F. Baskett, K. M. Chandy, R. R. Muntz, and F. Palacios-Gomez. Open, closed and mixed networks of queues with different classes of customers. *Journal of the ACM*, 22:248–260, 1975.
4. P. P. Bhattacharya, L. Georgiadis, and P. Tsoucas. Problems of adaptive optimization in multi-class M/GI/1 queues with Bernoulli feedback. *Mathematics of Operations Research*, 20(2):355–380, 1995.
5. P. P. Bhattacharya, L. Georgiadis, P. Tsoucas, and I. Viniotis. Adaptive lexicographic optimization in multi-class M/GI/1 queues. *Mathematics of Operations Research*, 18(3):705–740, 1993.
6. W. Bux. Local-area subnetworks: A performance comparison. *IEEE Transactions on Computers*, COM-19:1465–1473, 1981.
7. A. Federgruen and H. Groenevelt. M/G/c queueing systems with multiple customer classes: Characterization and control of achievable performance under nonpreemptive priority rules. *Management Science*, 34(9):1121–1138, September 1988.
8. L. L. Fong, R. E. Hough, and M. S. Squillante. Computer resource proportional utilization and response time scheduling. Patent Pending as AT997286, 1997.
9. L. L. Fong and M. S. Squillante. Time-Function Scheduling: A general approach to controllable resource management. In *Proceedings of the Symposium on Operating Systems Principles (SOSP)*, page 230, December 1995.
10. P. A. Franaszek and R. D. Nelson. Properties of delay-cost scheduling in time-sharing systems. *IBM Journal of Research and Development*, 39(3), 1995.
11. R. Guerin, H. Ahmadi, and M. Naghshineh. Equivalent capacity and its application to bandwidth allocation in high-speed networks. *IEEE Journal on Selected Areas in Communications*, 9(7):968–981, September 1991.
12. G. M. King, D. M. Dias, and P. S. Yu. Cluster architectures and S/390 Parallel Sysplex scalability. *IBM System Journal*, 36(2):221–241, 1997.
13. L. Kleinrock. *Queueing Systems Volume II: Computer Applications.* John Wiley and Sons, 1976.
14. A. G. Konheim and B. Meister. Waiting lines and times in a system with polling. *Journal of the ACM*, 21:470–490, 1974.
15. E. R. Lassettre and A. L. Scherr. Modeling the performance of OS/360 Time Sharing Option (TSO). In W. Freiberger, editor, *Statistical Performance Evaluation*, pages 57–72. Academic Press, New York, 1972.
16. M. Reiser and H. Kobayashi. Queueing networks with multiple closed chains: Theory and computational algorithms. *IBM Journal of Research and Development*, 19:283–294, 1975.

17. M. Reiser and S. S. Lavenberg. Mean-value analysis of closed multichain queueing networks. *Journal of the ACM*, 27:313–322, 1980.
18. C. H. Sauer and E. A. MacNair. Extended queueing network models. In S. S. Lavenberg, editor, *Computer Performance Modeling Handbook*, pages 367–393. Academic Press, New York, 1983.
19. L. Sha, R. Rajkumar, and J. P. Lehoczky. Priority inheritance protocols: An approach to real-time synchronization. *IEEE Transactions on Computers*, 39(9):1175–1185, September 1990.
20. M. S. Squillante and E. D. Lazowska. Using processor-cache affinity information in shared-memory multiprocessor scheduling. *IEEE Transactions on Parallel and Distributed Systems*, 4(2):131–143, February 1993.

Part I

Topical Area Papers

Mainframe Systems

Jeffrey P. Buzen

BMC Software, Inc.
880 Winter Street, Waltham, MA 02454-9111, USA
jeff_buzen@bmc.com

1 Introduction

Organizations that depend on mainframes for their mission critical applications have made extensive use of performance modeling for many years. After examining some of the reasons why performance modeling has been so important for mainframes, this article discusses a number of modeling problems that originally arose in the mainframe world, but are now of interest in a broader context. These problems include the analysis of multiprocessing (MPs and SMPs), clustering (shared DASD and parallel sysplex), logical partitioning (PR/SM), I/O subsystems (channels, cache), virtual storage interactions (paging and swapping) and goal mode scheduling.

Until recently, it was very easy to tell the difference between mainframes and other types of computer systems. Mainframes were big, both physically and in terms of their importance to the organizations they served. Mainframes also operated in isolated rooms equipped with heavy duty air-conditioning and special plumbing for the chilled water needed to cool their internal circuits. Finally, mainframes were often positioned behind glass walls so that outsiders could be suitably impressed with the opportunity to peer at these computational wonders.

These days, the distinctions between mainframes and other computer systems are much more difficult to discern. Mainframes have become physically smaller and much less demanding in terms of power consumption and environmental support. Even more important is the fact that non-mainframe systems such as UNIX and Windows NT are closing the performance gap and garnering an increasing share of the mission critical applications that large organizations depend on.

What then are the primary distinguishing features of mainframe systems, especially from the perspective of performance modeling and analysis? In fact, performance modeling never really had anything to do with physical size, environmental requirements, or even the speed of the central processor or the capacity of main memory and channel attached storage devices. However, mainframes have been the subject of a great many performance modeling studies, and most of the lessons learned from those studies carry over to today's smaller systems.

G. Haring et al. (Eds.): Performance Evaluation, LNCS 1769, pp. 17–31, 2000.

2 The Mainframe Environment

Early interest in modeling mainframe systems was motivated primarily by the fact that these systems ran mission critical applications that organizations were absolutely dependent upon. If these applications did not provide satisfactory levels of performance, customers could be lost, and major internal functions could break down. The fact that these mission critical applications used to run almost exclusively on mainframes created the impression that early modeling studies focused on mainframes simply because they were large, complex and expensive. However, the real reason so much effort was devoted to modeling mainframe performance was the importance of the applications that mainframes supported.

Of course, application performance ultimately depends on the processing capacity of the hardware available to support the application. When that hardware is very expensive, there is a strong economic incentive to buy "just enough". Purchasing too much hardware wastes valuable investment capital, while purchasing too little jeopardizes application performance.

Capacity planners using analytic modeling tools such as BEST/1 have been providing guidance to organizations faced with such problems for more than twenty years [4]. The issues these capacity planners deal with while carrying out their work are described in the next few sections.

3 Capacity Planning Objectives

Capacity planners deal primarily with questions about future performance. In particular, they are usually asked to provide hardware upgrade plans that specify how system capacity should be increased to meet growing demand. Obviously, organizations need this type of information for creating annual budgets, so upgrade plans that cover twelve months (with quarter-by-quarter details) are a primary concern. Planning beyond a one year horizon is also important, but those longer range plans involve greater uncertainty, and are subject to revision at the end of each year.

Many capacity planners also focus on short range issues, such as evaluating the benefit a specific hardware upgrade will have on a performance problem that currently exists within a data center. For example, response time for the users of a particular application may have degraded to the point where these users are no longer receiving adequate service, and are expressing their displeasure in various ways.

Management may be under pressure to purchase a faster processor to resolve the problem. However, the real cause of degraded performance may be excessive queuing at a disk containing a critical file needed by the application. In this case, the faster processor will not solve the problem. Instead, the file needs to be moved to a faster I/O device, possibly one that is part of a cached disk subsystem.

Assessing the impact of various upgrade alternatives and deciding which ones provide the most benefit is a critical function for capacity planners. Obviously, hardware vendors perform their own capacity planning studies to support sales efforts for individual customers. While these studies can be valuable, they generally do not include the highly detailed representations of a customer's environment that an in-house capacity planner can provide. This is one of the reasons why most large organizations maintain their own independent capacity planning functions.

Another reason why good management practice requires independent capacity planning is to avoid the possibility of bias in a vendor's recommendations. Management may be concerned that a vendor is proposing a more expensive solution than is really required. However, a far greater concern is that the vendor is proposing an inexpensive solution simply because the solution is attractive for competitive reasons or falls within certain budgetary guidelines. If the proposed solution does not satisfy the organization's performance requirements for the specified planning period, additional unplanned expenditures will be required in the future. From management's perspective, this is a serious problem, and is to be avoided if at all possible.

4 Component vs. System Performance

Note that capacity planners working for commercial organizations are not in a position to design new hardware components to meet their data center's needs. Instead, they can only purchase existing off-the-shelf components that vendors have already designed and manufactured.

Typically, each of these components already has a set of known performance characteristics. For example, a central processor will have a speed rating that indicates how quickly it processes various mixes of instructions.

Similarly, disks will have known performance ratings for seek time, rotational speed, and data transfer rate, while channels will have known transfer rates. The problem faced by the capacity planner is to determine the impact that upgrading one or more individual components within a system will have on overall application performance.

Models perform an essential role by analyzing such problems for the capacity planner. In a large system, components interact in a number of complex ways, and changing the speed of an individual component can often produce unexpected results. The next few sections of this paper describe a number of interactions and analysis problems that have been most important when developing models of mainframe systems.

5 Multiprocessor Performance

With the exception of special purpose scientific computers, mainframes have always represented the fastest computer systems available for general use. Despite this fact, even top of the line mainframes never seem to be fast enough to meet the ever increasing demands that certain users place on them.

There are only a few ways to increase the processing speed of any computer system. One option is to increase the basic speed of the central processing unit within that system. A second is to add more processors to the system. IBM coined the term "tightly coupled multiprocessor" or MP to represent this second option. [These days, MPs are often referred to as symmetric multiprocessors, or SMPs.]

When the applications running on a system start to exceed its processing capacity, it is the job of the capacity planner to recommend an upgrade. Mainframe vendors have traditionally measured the speed of their processors in terms of MIPS (millions of instructions per second). However, there is clearly a difference between a uniprocessor system with one processor rated at 100 MIPS and an MP system with two processors having a combined total of 100 MIPS.

The primary consideration in evaluating these alternatives is the ability of individual applications to effectively exploit the parallel processing capabilities that MP (or SMP) systems provide. In the mainframe world, CICS has been the most widely used transaction processing subsystem for over twenty years. Early versions of CICS were completely unable to use more than one processor at a time, regardless of the number of users who had submitted independent transactions. Even today, CICS applications usually have a limited ability to exploit multiple processors in MP configurations with large numbers of processors.

In contrast, multiple processors can usually be exploited very effectively by multiple batch jobstreams, conventional timesharing (TSO) users, and transaction processing applications that use the IMS transaction manager. Capacity planners using analytic modeling tools have provided valuable analyses of these issues for many years.

6 Clustering, Shared DASD, Parallel Sysplexes

Another way to meet increasing demand for processing capacity is to combine multiple systems into clusters, where systems in the cluster share disks but have their own processors and main memories. IBM uses the term "loosely coupled" to refer to mainframes that share disks, but no other components. [The IBM term for disk is DASD, which stands for "direct access storage device".]

Loosely coupled shared DASD configurations pose special problems for capacity planners. These problems arise in part because the measurement tools residing on each system see only the activity generated by that system. Thus, when these tools report on the utilization of a particular disk, they can only reflect the utilization level generated by their own system.

This suggests that the total utilization of a disk in a shared DASD cluster can be obtained by adding together the utilization measured from each systems. Unfortunately, there is an extra complication that makes this approach unsatisfactory in many cases. To understand this complication, suppose that system A and system B are sharing a disk. If system A attempts to access the disk at a time when system B is using it or has it reserved, the I/O request will not be able to proceed. Instead, the request will be queued in the I/O subsystem and held "pending" until system B relinquishes the device.

The time a request is held pending must be included in the device's service time and utilization when building a queuing model of system A. However, when building a global model [5] that represents both system A and system B, shared DASD contention is represented by ordinary queuing delay rather pending time. Total device utilization must exclude shared DASD pending time in this case.

The complications that arise when analyzing clusters of loosely coupled systems that share disks can be very difficult to deal with [5]. Once again, analytic modeling tools have helped capacity planners understand such configurations and plan effectively for future growth.

Parallel sysplex configurations [13] represent a more advanced form of clustering that is also available for mainframe systems. In a parallel sysplex, an additional hardware component known as a coupling facility is used to coordinate certain activities within the individual systems that are coupled together.

One of the most complex functions performed by the coupling facility is maintaining data integrity when multiple systems within the sysplex are updating the same file or data base. For example, when a particular record is updated by system A, an image of the updated record will usually be retained in system A's main memory. If that record is subsequently updated by system B, the record image in system A's main memory will become invalid. In effect, the coupling facility is responsible for reaching into system A's main memory and invalidating that record image.

Because the coupling facility performs a number of highly critical coordination functions, capacity planners need to be sure that the coupling facility does not become a bottleneck. Once again, models can assist capacity planners with analyzing this issue [8].

7 Logical Partitioning

Another form of clustering that is supported in mainframe environments is known as logical partitioning or multiple domain operation. In these situations, a single mainframe system with a large amount of main memory and a number of tightly coupled multiprocessors is divided into several logical partitions. Each logical partition has its own dedicated region of main memory and runs its own operating system (usually MVS or VM). However, the central processors used by a logical partition may either be dedicated or shared, and the disks may be shared if desired just as they are in any loosely coupled shared DASD configuration [one further complication that arises in logically partitioned systems is that it is possible to share channels as well as disks by utilizing the EMIF facility].

The capacity planner's job in a logically partitioned environment is even more complex. One very difficult problem is determining the optimal number of logical processors per partition. For example, suppose a physical system with eight physical processors is configured to support three logical partitions. Then each logical partition can be assigned from one to eight logical processors. Thus, the total number of logical processors can vary from three to thirty-two.

So long as the total number of logical processors is less than or equal to eight, there will be no extra delays due to contention for physical processors. Above this level, contention delays will arise at times when more than eight logical processors have work to do and are ready to be dispatched to physical processors. While these contention delays are undesirable, configuring a total of exactly eight logical processors is unnecessarily restrictive. Deciding the optimal strategy for configuring logical processors is a difficult problem and requires an appropriate performance analysis tool [6].

8 I/O Subsystem Performance

Another very important application of analytic modeling tools involves the analysis of I/O subsystem performance. Every few years a new generation of disks is introduced which provides substantially more storage capacity per drive than the previous generation. Each new generation also provides substantial economic advantages in terms of cost per megabyte of storage. And each new generation raises the same issue for capacity planners: if more data is stored on a single disk drive, will this cause excessive contention for that larger disk, leading to increased queuing delays and degraded performance.

Analyses of disk performance are invariably complicated by special performance enhancements introduced along with each new disk generation [2,3,15,17]. These enhancements range from direct improvement in basic performance characteristics (seek time, rotational speed, and transfer rate) to subtle improvements such as increasing the number of paths available to the disk (one, two, or four), or providing the ability to dynamically select alternate paths midway through an I/O operation (dynamic path reconnect). In each such case, the capacity planner is responsible for assessing the overall impact that upgrading to the latest generation of disks will have on overall application performance. Once again, analytic modeling tools have provided many capacity planners with valuable information for making their assessments [14], [16].

Another aspect of I/O subsystem architecture that has drawn the attention of capacity planners for a number of years is the use of cached storage devices. Cached devices have completely revolutionized the design of I/O subsystems and now exist in one form or another in almost all large data centers. Capacity planners are responsible for selecting among the alternative cache designs offered by different vendors. Each design typically has certain features that provide it with advantages in some environments and disadvantages in others. Models that reflect differences in cache architecture have proven very useful to capacity planners making recommendations for their own data centers [7].

9 Virtual Storage Interactions

Many of the analyses described above are complicated by interactions introduced by virtual storage mechanisms such as demand paging and physical swapping of interactive users. One example that arose several years ago during a BEST/1 modeling study indicates the degree of complexity that these interactions can attain.

Two systems, A and B, were loosely coupled in a cluster and shared several I/O devices. The arrival rate for one of the applications running on system A was increased. Among the effects that were observed was an increase in CPU utilization for system B. Should this increase have occurred, and if so, why?

A careful analysis of the output of the BEST/1 model provided the answer. Increasing the arrival rate for an application running on system A raised the utilization of a number of system A's resources, including the shared disks. The increased load on these disks resulted in more pending time and higher disk response times for applications which ran on system B and shared these disks.

Since disk response time increased for these system B applications, the transactions associated with these applications required more time to finish. This means they were resident in main memory for a longer time.

Since the throughput rate for the system B applications did not change, more time in main memory per transaction implied (by Little's Law) a higher multiprogramming level (more transactions in main memory at any time).

The higher multiprogramming level implied a reduction in the number of pages that could be maintained in main memory per transaction. This then implied a higher demand paging rate.

Of course, the higher paging rate increased the load on the disks that were part of the paging subsystem. However, each page fault also creates a certain amount of overhead at the central processor. The increase in central processor overhead due to the increased demand paging rate then led to the observed increase in central processor utilization for system B.

Capacity planners and performance analysts who work with modeling tools can become accustomed to thinking about complex interactions such as these. As a result, these individuals can develop powerful intuitions regarding system performance that can be invaluable when dealing with new problems. These intuitions may be the most important byproduct of the use of models for capacity planning.

10 Goal Mode Scheduling

All the examples discussed thus far have involved hardware components such as central processors, disks and main memory. Modeling also plays a vital role in evaluating software scheduling options: in particular, in the assignment of CPU dispatching priorities.

Models have been used for many years to evaluate the impact of increasing the priority of certain applications and lowering the priority of others. Recently, a new scheduling option known as goal mode scheduling [1] has been introduced in MVS mainframe environments.

Goal mode scheduling is based on an appealing concept: system administrators specify the performance goals they wish to achieve, and the system itself automatically adjusts priority levels to meet these goals. Thus, system administrators no longer have to deal with internal, system oriented parameters such as dispatching priority. Instead, they control performance through external, user oriented parameters such as each applications' desired response time.

Although the objectives of goal mode scheduling are easy to describe, there are some obvious complications: for example, how will the system perform when it is given a set of goals that cannot all be satisfied? To deal with this possibility, system administrators specify an additional parameter, importance, along with each goal.

Importance can be completely ignored so long as all goals can be satisfied. In such cases, it is quite possible for a low importance application to be given high priority if this is required to meet its goal.

On the other hand, if all goals cannot be met, the goals for lower importance applications are sacrificed to enable higher importance workloads to satisfy their goals. This means assigning lower priorities to the lower importance applications.

It is not easy for system administrators to know which goals will be satisfied and which will not. Moreover, if the performance of an application proves to be unsatisfactory, the system administrator can either adjust goals or adjust importance levels. Models that will help system administrators understand the tradeoffs involved in these circumstances are not yet available, but the research necessary to develop these models is currently underway [9].

11 Real World Examples

Capacity planners and performance analysts use modeling tools to analyze problems they encounter during their day to day activities. Although they have no need to fully understand the mathematical equations that these modeling tools depend on, practitioners still deal with many subtle and challenging issues that arise when such tools are applied to complex mainframe environments.

A recent paper by Sandro De Santis [10] illustrates several of these issues. The author is affiliated with the TELECOM Italia Data Center in Milan, and is concerned with assessing the impact that new technologies and architectures will have on the operation of that data center.

11.1 Alternative Processor Technologies

The first question discussed by De Santis deals with the deployment of new mainframe systems that utilize processors based on three different technologies (ECL, CMOS and ACE Advanced-CMOS-ECL). The physical differences between these processor technologies are extremely interesting, but they are not important for this particular investigation. What is important is that CMOS technology is least expensive but slowest, while ACE technology is most expensive but fastest. In the particular examples considered by De Santis, three ACE processors provide about 10% more capacity than six ECL processors or eight CMOS processors.

The actual speeds of the CMOS and ECL processors are available from the vendors who manufacture these systems. However, manufacturer's specifications do not consider the relationship between processor speeds and the response times of the particular applications running in TELECOM Italia's Milan Data Center. Since these response times are a critical concern, a modeling tool (BEST/1) was used to analyze this relationship.

The initial step in this analysis was an extensive workload characterization study. In general, workload characterization [19] is the first step in most modeling projects. The objective is to determine which workloads or applications are being processed during periods of primary interest, and what resources these application require. This information is then represented in a baseline model that is used as the starting point for further investigation.

The author focused the workload characterization study on the "daily peak period", which he identified as two hours each morning (10:00 AM to 12:00 noon) plus two hours each afternoon (2:00 PM to 4:00 PM). Measurements collected during the daily peak periods were analyzed over a period of four months.

Ultimately, the author constructed baseline models that represented the most important applications running on each of the two mainframes in the Milan Data Center. He then used these models to predict how workload response times would change if the workloads were moved to systems using each of the three alternative technologies.

The study's conclusions vary by workload and by processor technology. As expected, the ACE technology provided the best overall performance by a substantial margin. However, ACE systems are significantly more costly, and thus any cost/benefit analysis must consider the value of ACE's ability to handle future workload growth. Models play a crucial role in these investigations by allowing the analyst to increase workload arrival rates until response times reach their maximum acceptable values.

The comparison between CMOS and ECL also produced some interesting results. For some of the most critical transaction oriented workloads, the CMOS system with eight (slower) processors provided almost the same response as the ECL system with six (faster) processors. De Santis noted that this is due in part to the fact that the elongation in processing time for the CMOS system is balanced by a reduction in queuing delay resulting from the availability of the two additional CMOS processors. The fact that these workloads are I/O intensive, rather than CPU intensive, is also an important factor.

On the other hand, response times in the CMOS system were 37% longer for the lower priority, more CPU intensive batch workloads. Information such as this is extremely valuable when selecting alternative technologies and negotiating prices with vendors.

11.2 Parallel Sysplex Architectures

The second half of the De Santis paper analyzes a different option for upgrading the capacity of the Milan Data Center. Instead of utilizing faster processors in tightly coupled SMP configurations, several independent mainframe systems can be clustered together in a parallel sysplex. This can be regarded as an architectural, rather than technological, solution to the problem of scalability.

Once again, the author uses a modeling tool to evaluate the impact that migrating to a parallel sysplex architecture would have on the workloads running in the Milan Data Center. However, this analysis requires a number of additional steps that were not needed in the original comparisons between CMOS, ECL and ACE.

Once the baseline model was constructed, the first set of comparisons between CMOS, ECL and ACE processor technologies were very straightforward. Changes in the number of processors in the system being modeled, or in the speed of these processors, are reflected directly in the parameters of the underlying queuing model. It was thus quite easy for De Santis to change these parameters and evaluate the impact of new processor technologies.

On the other hand, migrating from a collection of separate mainframe systems to a parallel sysplex cluster requires more than a simple change in model parameters. The most critical issue is estimating the additional overhead factors that parallel sysplex architectures introduce, and then reflecting these overhead factors in the model.

It is important to note that, if the mainframe systems in the Milan Data Center had already been configured as a parallel sysplex, these overhead factors would be included in the original measurements used to construct the baseline model. This would have substantially reduced the complexity of the analysis.

Since the baseline configuration was not a parallel sysplex, additional research and analysis was required to obtain estimates of the overhead factors. The work that De Santis carried out in this phase of the investigation is representative of the functions that highly skilled users of modeling tools must sometimes perform.

After reviewing the literature on parallel sysplex performance, De Santis located two IBM publications [11], [12] that provide an equation for estimating the required overhead values. This equation incorporates empirical parameters measured at IBM laboratories in an operating environment similar to the environment at the Milan Data Center [CICS transactions accessing a DB2 database]. Essentially, the equation expresses overhead as a function of parameters that are identified as "multi-system management cost, data sharing enablement cost, and incremental data sharing cost per MVS image." Empirical measurements of these parameters are provided together with the equation that can be used to compute total overhead. This equation includes other variables such as the number of MVS images in the parallel sysplex and the percent of I/O operations that involve data sharing.

Unfortunately, the empirical parameters in the IBM documents were not measured under the same hardware configuration that De Santis wished to evaluate. Thus, De Santis had to develop an appropriate way to re-scale the empirically measured parameters, based on the speed differences between the systems measured in the IBM experiments and the systems De Santis wished to evaluate.

Ultimately, De Santis was able to derive overhead values for the processors in each parallel sysplex configuration. He then introduced these overhead loads into the baseline model. This represents an important step in modeling the migration to parallel sysplex.

There are, however, other aspects of parallel sysplex configurations that also need to be modeled. As noted in an earlier section of this paper, parallel sysplex architecture makes use of auxiliary processors known as coupling facilities. Coupling facilities are responsible for handling certain synchronization and data integrity functions that arise when transactions can be routed to any MVS image in a sysplex, and when transactions executing in different images have the ability to share and update the same data. Thus, another important aspect of parallel sysplex modeling is determining the load on each coupling facility, and then relating that load to additional increases in transaction response times.

The BEST/1 modeling tool used by De Santis incorporates equations that calculate coupling facility utilization and determine the effect of coupling facility load on transaction response times. However, these equations require parameters that De Santis had to estimate since his baseline systems were not configured as a parallel sysplex. Once again, De Santis was able to use the empirical measurements from IBM laboratories, plus a number of additional assumptions, to derive estimates of the required parameters.

After this auxiliary analysis, De Santis was able to construct a model that represented the Milan Data Center workloads being processed within a parallel sysplex. De Santis then varied the number of MVS images in the in the sysplex, the number of processors handling each MVS image, the speeds of these processors, and the speed of the processors in the coupling facilities. CMOS, ECL and ACE processors similar to those investigated in the first part of the paper were also used in the parallel sysplex evaluations.

These evaluations produced a number of conclusions. One is that, because of sysplex overhead, the CMOS processors in the study would not be powerful enough to handle many of the applications running in the Milan Data Center. A more general conclusion is that it is better to construct a parallel sysplex from a relatively small number of powerful systems, rather major than a larger number of less powerful systems. Finally, De Santis observed that utilizing a coupling facility that was too slow, relative to the other processors in the sysplex, could have a highly adverse effect on performance.

11.3 Experimental Studies

De Santis based his analysis of parallel sysplex overhead on a combination of experimental results published in IBM reports augmented by his own analytic extrapolations. Sometimes, users of modeling tools cannot obtain the information they need by searching the published literature or conducting theoretical analyses. In such cases, practitioners sometimes carry out empirical experiments to obtain the extra information they need for their modeling studies.

Bryant Osborn of NationsBank in Richmond, Virginia describes such an undertaking [18]. Once again, the issue is estimating the overhead that will arise in the bank's parallel sysplex environment. This time, the critical applications being modeled have been implemented using IBM's IMS transaction manager and VSAM databases, rather than the CICS/DB2 environment used in TELECOM Italia's Milan Data Center. Since the published experimental results that De Santis referred to in his analysis were based on CICS/DB2 environments, Osborn could not apply these results to his case.

Osborn begins his paper with a detailed discussion parallel sysplex architecture and IMS operation in a parallel sysplex environment. Osborn's understanding goes well beyond the level needed to analyze such systems with standard modeling tools. However, it is not unusual for experienced users of modeling tools to become exceptionally knowledgeable about the internal structure and operation of the systems they deal with.

Based on his detailed understanding of parallel sysplex operation in IMS environments, Osborn determined that the overhead factor which is most important to include in his analysis is the increase in processor utilization that arises while transactions wait for the coupling facility to perform certain synchronous operations. [The coupling facility also performs asynchronous operations that do not materially increase processor utilization because the processor can be switched to other transactions or tasks while asynchronous operations are being carried out.]

Osborn identified two major types of synchronous coupling facility operations. The first type, known as VSAM cache structure operations, arise when a record is updated and information must be recorded to prevent out of date copies of that record from being retrieved from local buffers that may exist elsewhere within the sysplex. The second type, known as global IRLM lock structure operations, arise when an area within the database must be locked to prevent a record from being accessed by another system while that record is being updated. Note that these overhead operations are only required when data is shared by an IMS application running on multiple systems within the parallel sysplex.

Osborn conducted a series of experiments to estimate the overhead associated with these operations. He began by analyzing measurements that were already being collected from a system running an actual IMS application at NationsBank. Although this application was moderately large, it was still able to fit on single system within the bank's parallel sysplex environment. Hence, there was no need for this application to incur data sharing overhead.

Osborn then enabled two special IMS data sharing features in succession. Enabling the first feature allowed him to measure the overhead due solely to VSAM cache structure operations. With both features enabled, the combined overhead of VSAM cache structure plus global IRLM lock structure operations could be measured.

By using his detailed knowledge of IMS operation and parallel sysplex architecture, Osborn was able to perform these experiments even though the IMS application was still only running on one system within the sysplex. In effect,

Osborn forced the extra data sharing overhead functions to be carried out, even though they really weren't necessary in his current operating environment. Note that he had to be careful to avoid excessive degradation to the performance of his production system during this experiment. This is why the two overhead functions were introduced progressively.

Osborn then constructed a BEST/1 model of a parallel sysplex with his IMS application now running on two separate systems and sharing a common database. The overhead values obtained in his experiments were incorporated into the model, and the model was then used to estimate how much additional load the parallel sysplex configuration could handle while still providing acceptable response time.

Since the results of the modeling study showed no problems in supporting the anticipated increase in load, the bank proceeded to implement the IMS data sharing/parallel sysplex configuration. Once the IMS application began running on two systems in the sysplex, a large number of new users were allowed to access the application.

After the new users were added, Osborn carried out a follow-up analysis. He compared the overhead values that were estimated in his initial experiment (which only involved a single IMS system) with the overhead values that were actually being experienced in the parallel sysplex configuration with two IMS systems sharing data and handling approximately 55% more transactions per second. Osborn's calculations based on the initial experiment yielded an overhead of 4.0%, while the follow-up measurements showed an overhead of 3.5%. This level of agreement, which is remarkably good, confirmed the validity of the experimental procedure Osborn devised to estimate the overhead values he needed for his modeling study.

When comparing the approaches followed by Osborn and De Santis, it should be noted that Osborn's approach offers certain advantages, even though it is more complex. De Santis was fortunate to find an IBM publication containing experimental results on sysplex overhead in a CICS/DB2 environment that was similar to his own. However, the particular applications that were studied by the IBM researchers could not be identical in all respects to the applications at the Milan Data Center. Thus, De Santis had to make the assumption that the Milan Data Center's applications and the applications in the IBM experiments were sufficiently alike to justify using the published IBM results in his analysis.

Since Osborn was able to measure the actual IMS/VSAM applications running at NationsBank, the overhead values he estimated were more closely related to the values he could expect to encounter when parallel sysplex architecture became fully operational in his data center. As his follow-up study showed, these estimates were extremely accurate.

Of course, both De Santis and Osborn integrated their estimated sysplex overhead values into models that were based on the actual workloads and applications running in their respective data centers. This illustrates the major advantage that models provide over published benchmark results. No matter how much care has been taken to set up and carry out a benchmarking experiment, the benchmark can never fully represent the detailed structure of the applications, data and user behavior that are found in a particular data center. Only a model based on measurements taken within that data center can provide this type of information.

12 Conclusion

In the end, performance modeling for mainframe systems does not differ in any substantial way from performance modeling for non-mainframes. Some of the special topics discussed here in the context of mainframe systems could very will emerge as important issues for UNIX or Windows NT over the next few years. Similarly, certain client-server performance considerations that are not normally regarded as mainframe issues could easily become so as mainframes assume a more central role as ultra-powerful, ultra-reliable servers in client-server architectures.

Practitioners working in the field of mainframe performance do not usually publish their findings in scholarly journals. The best source for papers written by practitioners is the annual proceedings of the Computer Measurement Group, commonly referred to as CMG. Refer to the CMG web site (`www.cmg.org`) for further information.

Text and reference books devoted exclusively to mainframe performance are difficult to find, but a number of books dealing with the general subject of computer performance contain very useful material about mainframe performance [14], [16]. Students who develop expertise in performance modeling in general, including some exposure to mainframe performance issues, will find very stimulating and rewarding career opportunities.

References

1. Aman, J., Eilert, C. K., Emmes, D., Yocom, P., and Dillenberger, D.: Adaptive Algorithms for Managing a Distributed Processing Workload, IBM Systems J., 36, 2, 1997, 242-283.
2. Artis, H. P.: DIBs, Data Buffers and Distance: Understanding the Performance Characteristics of ESCON Links, Proc. CMG '98, December 1998, 617-625.
3. Beretvas, T.: DASD Tuning in the New DASD Environment, Proc. CMG '98, December 1998, 26-38.
4. Buzen, J. P.: A Queuing Network Model of MVS. ACM Computing Surveys 10, 3 (September 1978), 319-331.
5. Buzen, J. P., and Shum, A. S.: Considerations for Modeling Shared DASD. Proc. CMG '88, 298-301.
6. Buzen, J. P., and Shum, A. S.: CPU Contention in Logically Partitioned Systems. Proc. CMG '92, 487-495.
7. Buzen, J. P., and Shum, A. S.: RAID, CAID and Virtual Disks: I/O Performance at the Crossroad. Proc. CMG '93, 658-667.
8. Buzen, J. P., and Shum, A. S.: Architecture and Performance of MVS/390 Parallel Transaction Servers. Proc. CMG '94, 309-316.

9. Bolker, E., and Buzen J. P.: Goal Mode: Part 1 - Theory. CMG Transactions, 99, May 1999, 9-15.
10. De Santis, S.: The Performance Impact of New Technologies (CMOS, ACE) and Architectures (Parallel Sysplex), Proc. CMG '97 December 1997, 954-963.
11. IBM Corporation.: A Comparison of S/390 Configurations - Parallel and Traditional, SG24-4514, 1995.
12. IBM Corporation.: S/390 MVS Parallel Sysplex Performance, SG24-4356, March 1996.
13. King, G. M., Dias, D. M., and Yu, P. S.: Cluster Architectures and S/390 Parallel Sysplex Scalability, IBM Systems J., 36,2,1997, 221-241.
14. Lazowska, E. D., Zahorjan, J., Graham, G. S., and Sevcik, K. C.: Quantitative System Performance. Prentice-Hall, Englewood Cliffs, NJ, 1984.
15. McNutt, B.: Disk Capacity, Performance and Cost: Maintaining the Balance, Proc. CMG '98, December 1998, 106-113.
16. Menasce, D. A., Almeida, V. A. F., and Dowdy, L. W.: Capacity Planning and Performance Modeling. Prentice-Hall, Englewood Cliffs, 1994.
17. Mungal, A. G.: I/O Concurrency, I/O Bandwidth, Access Density and the Like, Proc. CMG '98, December 1998, 518-527.
18. Osborn, B. L.: Parallel Sysplex: An Actual Experience of Capacity Panning for IMS Data Sharing, Proc. Joint SHARE/GUIDE Conf., August 1998, Session 2524.
19. Schwartz, J.: Forecasting Processor Consumption in a Multiple Machine Environment, Proc. CMG '98, December 1998, 842-853.

Performance Analysis of Storage Systems

Elizabeth Shriver, Bruce K. Hillyer, and Avi Silberschatz

Bell Laboratories
Murray Hill, NJ,
{shriver,bruce,avi}@research.bell-labs.com

1 Introduction

By "performance analysis of a storage system," we mean the application of a variety of approaches to predict, assess, evaluate, and explain the system's performance characteristics, along dimensions such as throughput, latency, and bandwidth. Several approaches are commonly used. One approach is analytical modeling, which is the writing of equations that predict performance variables as a function of parameters of the workload, equipment, and system configuration. Another approach is to collect measurements of a running system, and to observe the relationship between characteristics of the workload and the system components, and the resulting performance measurements. A third approach is simulation, in which a computer program implements a simplified representation of the behavior of the components of the storage system, and then a synthetic or actual workload is applied to the simulation program, so that the performance of the simulated components and system can be measured. Trace-driven simulation is an approach that controls a simulation model by feeding in a *trace*—a sequence of specific events at specific time intervals. The trace is typically obtained by collecting measurements from an actual running system.

The value of these performance analysis techniques is that they can give the necessary insight to make purchasing and configuring decisions for disks, disk arrays, and tapes. The performance results are also critical for the design and development of effective storage products and systems.

This chapter is organized as follows. Sect. 2 reviews the elements of storage systems. We describe the basics of disk storage, disk arrays, and tape storage to prepare for the description of performance analysis techniques in later sections. Sect. 3 describes several performance analysis techniques. The techniques are trace analysis, analytic modeling, simulation, benchmarking, and on-line monitoring. The goal of trace analysis is to develop a workload characterization, which can then be used with analytic modeling, simulation, and in developing benchmarks. Both general analytic models and simulators, and specific ones (which only apply to a small subset of possible workloads) are used in the performance analysis of storage systems. Sect. 4 presents a few performance evaluation success stories—the desire is to give the reader a sampling of how performance analysis has played a role in storage system product development. Sect. 5 highlights storage performance topics that deserve future study.

G. Haring et al. (Eds.): Performance Evaluation, LNCS 1769, pp. 33–50, 2000.

2 Types of Storage Systems

This section provides a basic overview of storage devices, to provide the background necessary for the device performance sections that follow. After a brief introduction to the general connection between a computer and a storage device, this section describes disk storage, disk arrays, and tape storage.

2.1 I/O Path

The I/O path between a computer and a storage device consists of device driver software, host adapter hardware, and a bus or network that connects the host adapter to a controller on the storage device. The *device driver* is part of the basic I/O subsystem of the operating system. It handles device-specific interactions, thereby isolating these details from the remainder of the system software. Device drivers usually contain queues that support the reordering of requests to improve response time. The driver interacts with a *host adapter*, which is a circuit board containing hardware to move data to and from the I/O bus or network. On the device side of the bus/network is a controller that operates the device. It handles the communication protocol for data and commands, buffers data to match the speed of the storage device to the speed of the bus/network, and controls the operations of the storage hardware.

2.2 Disks

The disk controller on a disk drive contains a processor, a speed-matching buffer and cache, and a bus/network interface. The controller has many functions. It implements caching policies, maps incoming logical addresses to the corresponding physical disk addresses, and performs error monitoring and recovery. In some disk architectures, the controller maintains a queue of outstanding requests, and computes an efficient order in which to execute the requests. To execute a data transfer, the controller instructs the disk mechanism to transfer data between the disk surface and the speed-matching buffer, and the controller operates the protocol that moves data between this buffer and the bus/network to the host.

The disk mechanism consists of a number of platters that rotate in lockstep on a spindle, and a disk arm that positions a set of read/write heads, one per surface. The heads read and write data by recording and sensing magnetic flux variations on the platter. Typically, the heads all share a single data channel that is switched among them and that is responsible for encoding and decoding the data stream. Only one head can be active with a single data channel.

A platter surface is divided into *tracks*, which are concentric circles, each of a different diameter. A *cylinder* comprises one track from each surface, all having the same diameter. When servicing a request, the disk arm first pivots to the desired cylinder (a *seek*), and than waits until the desired block rotates under the disk head (*rotational latency*).

Each track is divided into fixed-size *sectors* that store data blocks and the headers that hold information such as error-correcting bits. Since the length of the track increases as the radius of the cylinder increases, outer cylinders can hold more sectors. Consequently, the set of cylinders is partitioned into *zones.* Within each zone, all tracks have the same number of sectors. The speed-matching buffer can also be used as a read-ahead cache—after the disk reads data to satisfy a request, it can read additional sectors into the cache in anticipation of future sequential requests. The amount of additional sectors to read is often a user-settable parameter. If the workload contains one or more sequential access streams, a read-ahead strategy can reduce the effective rotational latency and seek time. See [1,2] for additional information about disk storage.

2.3 Disk Arrays

One way to increase the I/O performance of a disk storage system is to use an array of disks. Both the I/O rate and the throughput can be improved by striping the data across a number of disks. The I/O rate increases when multiple disks service independent requests concurrently, and the throughput increases when many disks concurrently service portions of a single request. Redundancy schemes are used to increase the reliability and to protect against data loss. Disk arrays with redundancy are known as *Redundant Arrays of Independent Disks* (RAID). Patterson and colleagues [3] coin the terminology of "RAID levels" that range from RAID1 through RAID5, and describes several schemes. For an extensive survey of RAID technology, see [4].

RAID schemes distribute data files over multiple disks by breaking the file into sets of fixed-size blocks. Each set of blocks is called a *stripe.* Typical schemes use a stripe that consists of N data blocks plus 1 parity block (i.e., the bitwise exclusive-or of the N data blocks) written onto $N+1$ disks. Computing and storing a parity block in each stripe enables the array to tolerate one drive failure without loss of data: the missing block from each stripe can be recreated by calculating the exclusive-or of the remaining $N-1$ data blocks and the parity block. The different RAID levels are distinguished by the size of each data block and the layout of the data and parity blocks on the physical disks.

A disk array is supervised by an array controller. The controller receives requests from the host for I/O transfers of large logical blocks or byte ranges. The array controller translates these requests into individual I/O operations on the physical drives in the array, and performs fragmentation/reassembly of the data blocks, and maintenance of the parity blocks. When a disk in a RAID array fails, the array controller *rebuilds* the array. It uses the redundant information in each stripe to recreate the lost blocks, and it stores the recreated blocks onto a new disk that replaces the failed one. During rebuilding, the controller may also service I/O requests by recreating missing data blocks on the fly. Thus, a disk array progresses from normal mode (all disks operational), to degraded mode (one disk failed, rebuild not yet started), to rebuild mode (broken disk replaced, rebuild in progress), and back to normal mode.

2.4 Tapes

Magnetic tape recording technology is similar in many ways to that of magnetic disks. Analogous to a disk sector, tapes have a *tape block* or *physical record*. Some tape formats use a fixed block size (typically 512 bytes), but many accommodate variable sized records, typically holding 1 to 65535 bytes of data; sometimes much larger. A *tape mark* is a special physical record that contains no user data. It can be written onto a tape to signify the end of a logical *file* (i.e., sequence of records). When reading, the tape controller can be instructed to position the tape to the beginning of the jth file mark or the kth logical record. This *locate* operation is analogous to the seek operation on a disk. It is sometimes implemented by reading the tape from a known location (such as the beginning) and counting the number of tape marks or blocks, but many tape formats maintain directory information to support high-speed positioning.

Tapes make extensive use of error correcting codes to obtain reliable storage. It is typical for 25% of the recorded bits to be used for error correction.

Most tape formats are essentially append-only: updating a block at any point on a tape effectively truncates the tape, rendering any data after that point inaccessible.

The two principal categories of tape drives are termed *serpentine* and *helical-scan*. A serpentine drive operates like an audio cassette, moving a tape linearly past a multi-track tape head. When the end of the tape is reached, the head is shifted sideways to a new set of tracks. This process is repeated many times, creating 10's or 100's of tracks on the tape. By contrast, a helical-scan drive operates like a VCR. It wraps the tape part way around a tilted cylinder. The cylinder rotates at high speed. As the tape moves past the cylinder, heads embedded in the cylinder create diagonal tracks on the tape.

A significant performance parameter for a tape drive is the *loading time*. When a tape is mounted on a drive, a period of time ranging from a few seconds to more than a minute (depending on the particular technology) is required for the tape drive to thread the tape through the tape path, calibrate the tape speed, record usage statistics, retrieve directory information, and position the tape to the beginning of a data block where I/O can commence. In many tape drives the overhead grows further when the tape is removed: the drive rewinds the tape to the beginning and writes error log and block directory information before ejecting the tape. In large systems, tape drives are embedded in robotic tape libraries that switch tapes under computer control, adding additional overhead (the robotic tape switch time).

One clear difference between tape and disk is the tradeoff between storage capacity and positioning time. The surface area of a tape is one or two orders of magnitude larger than the platters of a disk drive, so the storage capacity and cost per bit can be significantly better, and this is magnified by the fact that tape is removable. But the surface area of a tape is hidden, wrapped onto the tape reels, whereas the smaller surface area of a disk drive is all "out in the open", accessible to the heads. This fundamental difference in physical configuration is reflected in significant performance differences. Tape systems incur delays when a new tape is mounted (seconds or tens of seconds), when fast-forwarding or rewinding through a tape to access data far away (tens of seconds to a few minutes), and when performing retry/step-forward cycles to recover from a bad block (tens of seconds). Tape positioning times are two to four orders of magnitude worse than disk. Thus although the transfer rate of tape is comparable to that of disk, tape performs far worse as a random-access medium.

3 Performance Analysis Techniques

This section discusses various performance analysis techniques that have been applied to storage systems. Five common techniques are trace analysis, analytic modeling, simulation, benchmarking, and on-line monitoring. The choice of technique used is determined in part by the intent of the performance analysis; that is, does the system exist, or is the analysis to plan for a future system? How completely is the workload characterized? Are physical implementations available for testing?

3.1 Trace Analysis and Workload Characterization

One step in analyzing the performance of a storage system is to understand the workloads that will be applied. Workload characterization is an important part of analytic modeling, simulation, and benchmarking. It is not always clear what aspects of the workload are important and in what detail the workload needs to be understood. For disk and disk array studies, disk-level *traces* of requests are the most common workload specification (e.g., [5]). Simulators tend to use the traces directly as a faithful workload generator, while analytic models either process traces to extract analytic parameters (e.g., [1]) or make assumptions such as a uniform random spatial distribution of request addresses (e.g., [6,7,8]).

Tape workloads are less well studied, so tape studies often assume either fully sequential I/O, or some simple distribution of random accesses per tape switch.

3.2 Analytic Modeling

Analytic models can approximate values such as the mean service time on a workload-dependent basis for a particular storage system and parameter settings. Below, we describe a number of analytic models for disks, disk arrays, and tapes.

Disks. Key objectives in disk analytic modeling are to approximate the seek time, to determine the cache hit rate, and to approximate the queue delay.

Many disk modeling studies have developed approximations for the seek time, either through functions of the seek distance (e.g., [9,10,2]) or functions of the workload (e.g., [11]). The most common seek time approximation used today is a 3-part function that models (1) the acceleration and deceleration of the disk head, which is proportional to the square root of seek distance, (2) the head coasting time during long moves, which is proportional to the seek distance, and (3) the settling time, during which the head zeroes in on the center of the destination track. The coefficients in the 3-part functions are normally measured experimentally [12].

Some work has been done on approximating the impact of the disk cache. Carson and Setia [13] use queuing models to analyze disk cache write-back policies for workloads having a Poisson arrival process. Solworth and Orji [14] analyze write-only disk caches and derive equations to calculate the cache size needed to enable all writes to use a zero cost piggyback write-back policy. The cache hit and miss ratios are approximated in [1,15] using metrics of workload sequentiality.

Queuing theory is the main analytic approach that has been used for analyzing the effects of request scheduling at the disk. Wilhelm [16] uses an M/G/1 model for the FCFS scheduling algorithm; Hofri [17] extends this by providing a measure of locality of the requests for the FCFS scheduling algorithm, but does not show how to determine the locality measure. The SCAN and LOOK algorithms (which both sort the requests in the order of the physical disk addresses) are analyzed in [18,19,20] for the limited set of Poisson workloads with random uniform accesses.

Shriver [1] presents a validated model of a disk with a read-ahead cache and queuing. The model is validated using a detailed disk simulator and traced and synthetic workloads. The model takes as input a workload specification that includes the mean request size, the fraction of reads, the mean request rate, the spatial locality, and the type of arrival process. The model contains submodels of the request queue, the read-ahead cache, and the disk mechanism. Barve and colleagues [21] present a validated model for multiple disks on a SCSI bus. The workloads that are supported are random reads with zero think time. The model is validated by measurements taken on a variety of operating systems and disks.

Disk Arrays. Many analytic disk array performance models have been developed to model an array in normal mode (e.g., [8,22,23,24,25,26]). (The numerous reliability models fall outside the scope of this chapter.) The performance of a disk array in degraded and rebuilding modes (after a disk has failed) has also been modeled analytically (e.g., [27,28,29]). Analytic models are also used to evaluate potential improvements to disk arrays. For example, [30] uses an analytic model to compare different scheduling policies and data layout schemes.

Most of the disk array models compute service time distributions at the individual disk level using simple disk models that model the request queue. The array models differ in how their disk models capture the disk queuing; for example, [24] has a simple model with an $M/E_k/1$ queuing model and [8] has a simple model with an M/G/1 queuing model.

Early modeling work for mirrored disks (disk systems that implement a logical disk as multiple identical copies of the data on distinct disk drives) assumed that any of the physical disks could service any request. Thus, the analytic models (e.g., [22]) compute the minimum disk service time to approximate the disk array service time. When the requests to the array are split into multiple parallel disk requests (e.g., as when writing a full stripe of data in RAID5), the fork-join synchronization impact on the disk array service time is frequently approximated by computing the maximum of the individual disk service times.

The major drawback of current disk array models lies in the model of the workload experienced by each disk. The models in [8,23,24,26] assume that the workload has a Poisson arrival process, an open queuing model, and random uniform accesses across the cylinders of the disk. If these assumptions do not hold—for example, if the workload is closed, or the arrival process is constant or bursty, or the workload is sequential—the array model can have large errors.

Tapes. Tape I/O scheduling is studied in [31] under the simplifying assumption that the locate time between blocks i and j is proportional to $|j-i|$. Although that assumption works well for the 9-track tapes of that time, it applies less well to modern helical-scan drives that switch to high speed tape motion for long moves, and the assumption is wildly incorrect for serpentine drives. The problem of scheduling the retrieval of a set of overlapping intervals from a tape is studied in [32] assuming that block retrievals for separate intervals cannot be interleaved, that blocks for overlapping intervals are not cached for reuse, and that locate time is proportional to the difference in block numbers.

Striped tape organizations are modeled in [33,34,35,36]. Database algorithms for systems that incorporate both tape and disk are studied in [37], and issues of caching, query optimization, and mount scheduling for relational databases using tape jukeboxes is studied in [38,39].

The problem of optimal data placement for different tape library technologies is studied in [40]. Nemoto and colleagues [41] consider the migration of tapes between robotic libraries for load-balancing purposes. Robotic tape libraries are also modeled in [42,43].

The performance characteristics of a few particular tape drives are modeled in detail in [44,45,46], and the performance of a wider variety of tape drives is described in [47,48].

3.3 Simulation

Simulation has long been a tool for detailed performance analysis on storage devices. Pantheon and DiskSim are two well-known detailed disk simulators [49,50]. These simulators and others like them have been used to support research into various aspects of storage subsystems, such as disk scheduling algorithms [51,52,53], disk array small write performance [54], and disk cache policies [17]. Simulation is a way to get performance predictions for systems that are not available for measurements (e.g., [1,55]). Simulators have also been developed as configuration tools to support the design of disk arrays to meet specific customer requirements (e.g., [56]). Sect. 4.1 gives examples of the impact of simulation results on actual product designs.

Most storage simulators are *trace-driven simulators*, that is, the input consists of a *trace*—a list of {event, timestamp} pairs obtained via instrumentation of a real system. For each event, the simulator executes a model of the actions of the hardware and software of a proposed system.

Simulators can approximate many measurements of storage system performance. For example, Pantheon computes the distributions of the service times and the utilizations of the various components (e.g., the bus and the disk mechanism).

3.4 Benchmarking

A *benchmark* is a set of programs that measure the performance of a computer system under a controlled workload. A good benchmark provides repeatable metrics that support meaningful performance comparisons between systems. A poor benchmark generates "figures of merit" that have little predictive value for system performance under realistic workloads.

In comparing storage systems, benchmarks can be used to study options such as different configurations of hardware, and different devices, algorithms, and parameter settings. Benchmarks also are used by product manufacturers for performance tuning during product development, and for advertising purposes.

Benchmarks vary widely in the detail of results that they give. Some benchmarks compute device-specific values such as zone bandwidths (bandwidth as a function of disk address) and seek times (seek times as a function of seek distance) (e.g., [57]). Others compute just the transfer rates of the storage system (e.g., [58]). A few benchmarks compute detailed characterizations; one example is the *self-scaling* benchmark described in [59,60], which automatically adjusts the workload according to the performance characteristics of the system being measured. The important I/O parameters for this benchmark are the number of unique bytes touched, the percentage of reads, the average request size, the percentage of sequential requests, and the number of processes generating concurrent requests.

Most benchmarks measure the performance of the system when driven by the execution of live code, but a few benchmarks are driven by the replay of traces. For example, RankDisk evaluates specific disk drives by replaying disk-level traces and measuring the service time of each disk access [61].

3.5 On-Line Monitoring

A number of utilities support the on-line monitoring of storage systems. For example, the `sar` (system activity reporter) SysV-derived Unix utility enables one to view the hit rates of the read and write buffer caches, the activity of the storage devices, and the percentage of time that each CPU spends waiting for I/O to complete while there are no runnable processes. If the device performance is found to be unsatisfactory, many corrective actions are available:

- Change when the file system cache is written to disk. If the time interval is increased, the disk will be written to less frequently, and a smaller total volume of data will be written at the cost of increased amounts of data lost on power fail [5].

- Add additional storage, replace current devices with faster ones, or upgrade the host adapter to one that supports caching and command queuing.
- Change the location of files on the storage devices. For example, move frequently accessed disk files to the middle tracks to reduce the average seek distance [62].

Some storage systems dynamically monitor their own performance, and modify their behavior based on the measurements. For example, software in the EMC disk array controller maintains hundreds of counters that are used by the controller to tune its execution strategies under specific workloads.

4 Success Stories

Performance analysis has been necessary in the development of many storage products. But public disclosure of success stories in storage is rare, because the business is highly competitive, and the ideas developed through insightful performance evaluation usually are considered to be trade secrets. This section will discuss a few success stories.

4.1 Disks

Disk Scheduling. Numerous studies have investigated the performance of disk I/O scheduling algorithms involving command queuing (e.g., [18,51,52,63,64,65]), real-time applications (e.g., [66,67,68,69]), and database applications (e.g., [70]). Event-driven simulation studies of disk scheduling algorithms that use rotational position information appear in [52]; these studies were used by Hewlett-Packard's Disk Memory Division in the design of products.

Disk Cache. Performance evaluation methods were used by Quantum during 1996–1998 to develop ATA disks with small caches. The cache algorithms in Quantum disks were tuned to obtain good performance from 128 KB caches, whereas competitors' disks had 512 KB caches. The cost savings attributed to the smaller cache was $1.50 per disk, that is, about $8 million in the bottom line over a product volume of 5.5 million units. To study the strategies for prefetch and segmentation that would be suitable for the smaller cache, a trace-driven disk simulator called Sim-II was used. Ideas for the cache strategies came from the analysis of I/O traces from boot sequences and from popular benchmarks such as WinBench97 from Ziff-Davis. The traces were analyzed both manually and by a tool that computes statistics such as the read percentage and the fraction of sequential requests. The simulation model was validated in two steps. First, the benchmark executions on disks were compared with the simulation results. Second, an abilit y was added to the simulator to enable the actual traces to be replayed on sets of physical disk drives. Both validations showed that the model was accurate to within 2%. As another verification of the model,

Quantum built a small number of drives with the larger caches, and compared their performance measurements with model predictions.

Eventually, market pressure led Quantum to increase the buffer size to match the competitors. With another round of simulation, Quantum improved their cache strategy to obtain a 15% performance improvement in the Fireball EP family.

Multiple Disk Interactions. Analytic modeling has been used to develop a technique to increase I/O bandwidth for heavy disk workloads. Barve and colleagues [21] present a validated model for multiple disks on a SCSI bus under a heavy workload. Two terms in the model reveal opportunities for performance improvement; these opportunities are exploited via user-level software techniques that achieve greater overlap of bus transfers with disk seeks, and that increase the percentage of transfers that occur at the full bus bandwidth rather than at the lower bandwidth of a disk head.

4.2 Disk Arrays

Before RAID systems were built, performance models (e.g., [3,71]) and reliability models (e.g., [72]) were developed. It is accepted that the modeling and simulation work done at Berkeley (and elsewhere) guided the disk array industry and highlighted important issues and insights. For instance, [71] presents a method to determine the stripe unit using the number of outstanding requests in the disk system at any given time, and the average positioning time and the data transfer rate of the disks. Chen and Lee [73] discuss how to choose the stripe unit for RAID5 disk arrays; Ed Lee reports that he received calls from RAID companies about this work. Several performance studies compare mirroring with RAID5 (e.g., [74]). In the beginning, companies built systems that support both mirroring and RAID5, letting the customer decide which option to use. Such decisions were based on tradeoffs between cost/capacity and performance.

Subsequent to the commercial introduction of RAID systems, performance modeling continues to explore variations such as write deferring, parity logging, parity declustering, and log-structured storage.

EMC Symmetrix. At EMC (a RAID vendor), a performance model is developed to study major hardware or software improvement proposals. Using a system-level performance simulation tool calling SES/Workbench, new ideas are evaluated, and current and future bottlenecks in the system are pinpointed. This modeling activity shows where to focus the engineering effort, and supports the evaluation of architectural alternatives. For example, a performance model was developed to examine whether the data and control messages should use separate buses or a common bus. A performance study determined that the ratio of control traffic to data traffic varies widely, so separate buses would incur bottlenecks that a common bus could avoid. The simulation models are commonly evaluated with two sets of workloads: "envelope workloads" that test the extreme cases, and "real workloads" that are synthetic workloads developed from customer traces.

The EMC Symmetrix array performs on-line monitoring to collect measurements that are used for dynamic tuning and for the selection of algorithms in the array controller. For example, the Dynamic Mirror Service Policy algorithm determines from the measurements, every few minutes, from which physical disks to perform the read operations. This allows Symmetrix to balance the load among its different components, and to improve the seek time. The measurements also enable the engineers to verify that the performance of a specific implementation is as expected, for example, the system performs the expected number of data and control transfers and the uses the expected number of locks. Measurements and I/O traces are derived from test systems, and also from live customer systems to obtain a detailed understanding of the Symmetrix array performance under real workloads.

HP AutoRAID. The HP AutoRAID is another success story for performance evaluation [75]. The AutoRAID is a smart disk array that performs automatic migration of data between a higher performance mirrored subsystem and a lower cost RAID5 subsystem. The HP XLR1200 Advanced Disk Array was the first product using this technology. HP's Storage Systems Division in Boise developed analytic performance models of the disk-array controller to support the design and the business case. Their performance predictions were confirmed by an event-driven simulator developed by HP's Storage Systems Program in Palo Alto. The simulator also gave insight into optimizations that fell outside the scope of the analytic performance models. For example, simulation tests of various overwrite policies for the NVRAM write cache were instrumental in selecting the policy that was actually implemented in the product. Subsequent measurements of hardware prototypes confirmed the high accuracy of the analytic performance models and the meri t of the policies identified via simulation.

4.3 Tapes

IBM Magstar. A performance model of the IBM 3570 Magstar MP tape library [76] has been developed that takes as input a description of the workload (e.g., hit rate) and a description of the storage device (e.g., mount time, search time, robot access time) and approximates the mean service time. The model enabled the IBM Tucson Storage Systems Division to quantify the performance tradeoffs for different approaches to increase the capacity. Two of the options are to make a longer and thinner tape, which increases the search time, or to use a higher recording density.

The Magstar MP performance model is also used as a configuration tool to determine the number of tape drives and robotic units required to meet a customer's response time and throughput requirements, given a description of the expected workload.

Performance studies during the development of the IBM Magstar drives resulted in a feature called "capacity scaling" that is available in the firmware of the Magstar 3570 and 3590 tape products. It enables the user to trade off diminished capacity for improved response time. By instructing the drive to use only a fraction of the tape length (25%, 50%, 75%, or 100%) [77] the user thereby reduces the average positioning time for random-access workloads.

4.4 Network-Attached Storage Devices

Analytic models and simulation studies have shown that network-attached storage devices have the potential to improve scalability and bandwidth by providing direct data transfers between storage and clients [78,79]. Experiments on prototype systems have confirmed the model and simulation results [80]. Currently, most of the major storage players participate in the National Storage Industry Consortium, to explore, validate, and document the technological advancements that are prerequisite to the deployment and adoption of network-attached storage devices [81].

4.5 File Systems

Studies on early file systems showed that they were incapable of providing the disk throughput that many applications required [82]. This result was one of the many drivers for the development of the Berkeley FFS. The Berkeley FFS developers capitalized on detailed measurements of the multiuser timeshared Unix I/O workload to develop algorithms, data structures, and policies that obtain high file system performance. For example, trace-driven analysis helped determine the size of the cache to reduce disk traffic. It also led to the the delayed-write scheme that reduces I/O volume by letting files with very short lifetimes die in the cache without ever being written to disk [83]. Ousterhout and colleagues [83] report that about 25% of newly-written blocks are overwritten or deleted within 30 seconds, and about 50% are overwritten or deleted within 5 minutes. Moreover, about 80% of all newly-created files are deleted or overwritten within 3 minutes of creation.

More recently, [60] reports on an I/O benchmark study that compares a number of different hardware configurations. Under some circumstances, the choice of cache size and policy determines whether the processor runs at disk speed or at main memory speed, leading to performance speedups of 10× to 100×. Among the pitfalls identified by the study are file caches that are too small, necessitating frequent disk accesses, and write-through cache policies that cause unnecessary I/Os (i.e., unnecessary because the file will be deleted soon, or because the page will be overwritten soon).

5 Future Work

Performance evaluation methods could help in many areas in the development and use of storage systems. The following are just a few:

- *Workload characterization.* Simulation and benchmarking would be more useful if it were possible to characterize workloads easily, and to create synthetic workloads from such characterizations. In particular, the results of trace-driven simulations are often considered to be more reliable than results derived from synthetic workloads. What, then, are the characteristics of a workload, as represented by a trace, that need to be captured to enable the creation of a faithful synthetic workload? Ganger [84] presents a first step in synthetic workload generation by validating synthetic disk-level traces.
- *Automatic management.* Some disk drives and tape drives monitor their own performance to detect incipient failures, and many disk array controllers tune their behavior based on performance measurements. Nevertheless, current storage systems depend heavily on expert human administrators to monitor performance, to detect and respond to instabilities and bottlenecks, to migrate data for load-balancing and space-balancing purposes, and to plan for system growth to cope with increasing workloads. Opportunities abound for the automation of performance monitoring, performance management, and performance planning. Borowsky and colleagues [85] introduce one approach for automatic storage management.
- *Hierarchical storage management.* Current hierarchical storage systems are designed on the basis of the huge performance gap between disk arrays and tape libraries. It is possible that future tertiary storage may be implemented not with tape, but with ultra high density removable disk storage (evolving from writable DVD, near-field storage, or holographic storage). The use of removable disks could negate critical performance assumptions that underlie current hierarchical storage designs.

Acknowledgements

Many thanks to Greg Ganger, John Gniewek, Andy Hospodor, David Jacobson, Ed Lee, Amnon Naamad, and John Wilkes for supplying success stories.

References

1. E. Shriver, *Performance modeling for realistic storage devices.* PhD thesis, New York University, Department of Computer Science, May 1997. Available at `http://www.bell-labs.com/~shriver/`.
2. C. Ruemmler and J. Wilkes, "An introduction to disk drive modeling," *IEEE Computer*, vol. 27, pp. 17–28, Mar. 1994.
3. D. A. Patterson, G. Gibson, and R. H. Katz, "A case for redundant arrays of inexpensive disks (RAID)," in *Proceedings of 1988 SIGMOD International Conference on Management of Data* (H. Boral and P.-A. Larson, eds.), (Chicago, IL), pp. 109–116, June 1988.
4. P. M. Chen, E. K. Lee, G. A. Gibson, R. H. Katz, and D. A. Patterson, "RAID: high-performance, reliable secondary storage," *ACM Computing Surveys*, vol. 26, pp. 145–185, June 1994.

5. C. Ruemmler and J. Wilkes, "Unix disk access patterns," in *Proceedings of the Winter 1993 USENIX Conference*, (San Diego, CA), pp. 405–420, USENIX Association, Berkeley, CA, Jan. 1993.
6. S. W. Ng, "Improving disk performance via latency reduction," *IEEE Transactions on Computers*, vol. 40, pp. 22–30, Jan. 1991.
7. B. Seeger, "An analysis of schedules for performing multi-page requests," *Information Systems*, vol. 21, pp. 387–407, July 1996.
8. A. Merchant and P. S. Yu, "Analytic modeling of clustered RAID with mapping based on nearly random permutation," *IEEE Transactions on Computers*, vol. 45, pp. 367–373, Mar. 1996.
9. C. C. Gotlieb and G. H. MacEwen, "Performance of movable-head disk storage systems," *Journal of the ACM*, vol. 20, pp. 604–623, Oct. 1973.
10. J. L. Hennessy and D. A. Patterson, *Computer architecture: a quantitative approach.* Morgan Kaufmann Publishers, Incorporated, San Mateo, CA, 1990.
11. A. Hospodor, "Mechanical access time calculation," *Advances in Information Storage Systems*, vol. 6, pp. 313–336, 1995.
12. B. L. Worthington, G. R. Ganger, Y. N. Patt, and J. Wilkes, "On-line extraction of SCSI disk drive parameters," in *Proceedings of ACM SIGMETRICS Conference on Measurement and Modeling of Computer Systems*, (Ottawa, Canada), pp. 146–156, ACM Press, New York, NY, May 1995.
13. S. C. Carson and S. Setia, "Analysis of the periodic update write policy for disk cache," *IEEE Transactions on Software Engineering*, vol. 18, pp. 44–54, Jan. 1992.
14. J. A. Solworth and C. U. Orji, "Write-only disk caches," in *Proceedings of ACM SIGMOD International Conference on Management of Data* (H. Garcia-Molina and H. V. Jagadish, eds.), vol. 19, (Atlantic City, NJ), pp. 123–132, May 1990.
15. E. Shriver, A. Merchant, and J. Wilkes, "An analytic behavior model for disk drives with readahead caches and request reordering," in *Joint International Conference on Measurement and Modeling of Computer Systems (Sigmetrics '98/Performance '98)*, (Madison, WI), pp. 182–191, June 1998. Available at `http://www.bell-labs.com/~shriver/`.
16. N. C. Wilhelm, "An anomaly in disk scheduling: a comparison of FCFS and SSTF seek scheduling using an empirical model for disk accesses," *Communications of the ACM*, vol. 19, pp. 13–17, Jan. 1976.
17. M. Hofri, "Disk scheduling: FCFS vs. SSTF revisited," *Communications of the ACM*, vol. 23, pp. 645–653, Nov. 1980.
18. T. J. Teorey and T. B. Pinkerton, "A comparative analysis of disk scheduling policies," *Communications of the ACM*, vol. 15, pp. 177–184, Mar. 1972.
19. W. Oney, "Queueing analysis of the scan policy for moving-head disks," *Journal of the ACM*, vol. 22, pp. 397–412, July 1975.
20. E. G. Coffman, Jr and M. Hofri, "On the expected performance of scanning disks," *SIAM Journal on Computing*, vol. 11, pp. 60–70, Feb. 1982.
21. R. Barve, E. Shriver, P. B. Gibbons, B. K. Hillyer, Y. Matias, and J. S. Vitter, "Modeling and optimizing I/O throughput of multiple disks on a bus," in *Proceedings of the 1999 ACM SIGMETRICS International Conference on Measurement and Modeling of Computer Systems*, vol. 27, (Atlanta, GA), pp. 83–92, May 1999. Available at `http://www.bell-labs.com/~shriver/`.
22. D. Bitton and J. Gray, "Disk shadowing," in *Proceedings of the 14th International Conference on Very Large Data Bases (VLDB)* (F. Bancilhon and D. J. DeWitt, eds.), (Los Angeles, CA), pp. 331–338, Aug. 1988.

23. S. Chen and D. Towsley, "The design and evaluation of RAID 5 and parity striping disk array architectures," *Journal of Parallel and Distributed Computing*, vol. 17, pp. 58–74, Jan.–Feb. 1993.
24. A. Kuratti and W. H. Sanders, "Performance analysis of the RAID 5 disk array," in *Proceedings of International Computer Performance and Dependability Symposium*, (Erlangen, Germany), pp. 236–245, Apr. 1995.
25. J. Menon, "Performance of RAID5 disk arrays with read and write caching," *Distributed and Parallel Databases*, vol. 2, pp. 261–293, July 1994.
26. A. Thomasian, "RAID5 disk arrays and their performance analysis," in *Recovery in Database Management Systems* (V. Kumar and M. Hsu, eds.), ch. 37, pp. 807–846, Prentice-Hall, 1998.
27. R. R. Muntz and J. C. Lui, "Performance analysis of disk arrays under failure," in *Proceedings of the 16th International Conference of Very Large Databases*, (Brisbane, Australia), pp. 162–173, Aug. 1990.
28. J. Menon and D. Mattson, "Performance of disk arrays in transaction processing environments," in *Proceedings of 12th International Conference on Distributed Computing Systems*, (Yokohama, Japan), pp. 302–309, IEEE Computer Society Press, Los Alamitos, CA, 1992.
29. A. Thomasian and J. Menon, "RAID5 performance with distributed sparing," *IEEE Transactions on Parallel and Distributed Systems*, vol. 8, pp. 640–657, June 1997.
30. S. Chen and D. Towsley, "A performance evaluation of RAID architectures," *IEEE Transactions on Computers*, vol. 45, pp. 1116–1130, Oct. 1996.
31. C. K. Wong, "Minimizing expected head movement in one-dimensional and two-dimensional mass storage systems," *ACM Computing Surveys*, vol. 12, pp. 167–178, June 1980.
32. J. G. Kollias, Y. Manolopoulos, and C. H. Papadimitriou, "The optimum execution order of queries in linear storage," *Information Processing Letters*, vol. 36, pp. 141–145, Nov. 1990.
33. A. L. Drapeau and R. H. Katz, "Striped tape arrays," in *Proceedings of the Twelfth IEEE Symposium on Mass Storage Systems*, (Monterey, CA), pp. 257–265, Apr. 1993.
34. L. Golubchik, R. R. Muntz, and R. W. Watson, "Analysis of striping techniques in robotic storage libraries," in *Proceedings of the Fourteenth IEEE Symposium on Mass Storage Systems*, (Monterey, CA), pp. 225–238, Sept. 1995.
35. T. Chiueh, "Performance optimization for parallel tape arrays," in *Proceedings of the 1995 International Conference on Supercomputing*, (Barcelona, Spain), pp. 385–394, ACM Press, July 1995.
36. A. L. Chervenak, *Tertiary storage: An evaluation of new applications.* PhD thesis, University of California at Berkeley, Computer Science Department, Dec. 1994. Technical Report UCB/CSD 94/847.
37. J. Myllymaki and M. Livny, "Disk-tape joins: synchronizing disk and tape access," in *Proceedings of the 1995 ACM Sigmetrics Conference on Measurement and Modeling of Computer Systems*, (Ottawa, Canada), pp. 279–290, May 1995.
38. S. Sarawagi, "Query processing in tertiary memory databases," in *Proceedings of the 21st International Conference on Very Large Databases*, (Zurich, Switzerland), pp. 585–596, Morgan Kaufmann, San Francisco, Sept. 1995.
39. S. Sarawagi and M. Stonebraker, "Reordering queury execution in tertiary memory databases," in *Proceedings of the 22nd International Conference on Very Large Databases*, (Mumbai, India), pp. 156–167, Morgan Kaufmann, San Francisco, Sept. 1996.

40. S. Christodoulakis, P. Triantafillou, and F. A. Zioga, "Principles of optimally placing data in tertiary storage libraries," in *Proceedings of the 23rd International Conference on Very Large Databases*, (Athens, Greece), pp. 236–245, Morgan Kaufmann, San Francisco, Aug. 1997.
41. T. Nemoto, M. Kitsuregawa, and M. Takagi, "Simulation studies of the cassette migration activities in a scalable tape archiver," in *Proceedings of the Fifth International Conference on Database Systems for Advanced Applications*, (Melbourne, Australia), pp. 461–470, Apr. 1997.
42. T. Johnson, "An analytical performance model of robotic storage libraries," *Performance Evaluation*, vol. 27 and 28, pp. 231–251, 1996. Proceedings of Performance96 (Lausanne, Switzerland).
43. O. Pentakalos, D. Menasce, M. Halem, and Y. Yesha, "Analytical performance modeling of mass storage systems," in *Proceedings of the Fourteenth IEEE Symposium on Mass Storage Systems*, (Monterey, CA), Sept. 1995.
44. B. K. Hillyer and A. Silberschatz, "On the modeling and performance characteristics of a serpentine tape drive," in *Proceedings of the 1996 ACM Sigmetrics Conference on Measurement and Modeling of Computer Systems*, (Philadelphia, PA), pp. 170–179, May 23–26 1996.
45. B. K. Hillyer and A. Silberschatz, "Random I/O scheduling in online tertiary storage systems," in *Proceedings of the 1996 ACM SIGMOD International Conference on Management of Data*, (Montreal, Canada), pp. 195–204, June 3–6 1996.
46. B. K. Hillyer and A. Silberschatz, "Scheduling non-contiguous tape retrievals," in *Sixth Goddard Conference on Mass Storage Systems and Technologies in cooperation with the Fifteenth IEEE Symposium on Mass Storage Systems*, (College Park, MD), pp. 113–123, Mar. 1998.
47. T. Johnson and E. L. Miller, "Benchmarking tape system performance," in *Sixth Goddard Conference on Mass Storage Systems and Technologies in cooperation with the Fifteenth IEEE Symposium on Mass Storage Systems*, pp. 95–112, Mar. 1998.
48. T. Johnson and E. L. Miller, "Performance measurements of tertiary storage devices," in *Proceedings of the 24th International Conference on Very Large Databases*, (New York, NY), pp. 50–61, Aug. 24–27 1998.
49. J. Wilkes, "The Pantheon storage-system simulator," Tech. Rep. HPL–SSP–95–14, Storage Systems Program, Hewlett-Packard Laboratories, Palo Alto, CA, Dec. 1995.
50. G. R. Ganger, B. L. Worthington, and Y. N. Patt, "The DiskSim simulation environment: version 1.0 reference manual," Tech. Rep. CSE-TR-358-98, Department of Electrical Engineering and Computer Science, University of Michigan, Ann Arbor, MI, Feb. 1998.
51. M. Seltzer, P. Chen, and J. Ousterhout, "Disk scheduling revisited," in *Proceedings of Winter 1990 USENIX Conference*, (Washington, DC), pp. 313–323, Jan. 1990.
52. D. M. Jacobson and J. Wilkes, "Disk scheduling algorithms based on rotational position," Tech. Rep. HPL–CSP–91–7, Hewlett-Packard Laboratories, Palo Alto, CA, Mar. 1991.
53. B. L. Worthington, G. R. Ganger, and Y. N. Patt, "Scheduling algorithms for modern disk drives," in *Proceedings of ACM SIGMETRICS Conference on Measurement and Modeling of Computer Systems*, (Santa Clara, CA), pp. 241–251, ACM Press, New York, NY, May 1994.
54. E. Gabber and H. Korth, "Data logging: A method for efficient data updates in constantly active RAIDs," in *Proceedings of the 14th International Conference on Data Engineering*, (Orlando, FL), pp. 144–153, Feb. 1998.

55. K. Keeton, A. Drapeau, D. Patterson, and R. H. Katz, "Storage alternatives for video service," in *Proceedings of the Thirteenth IEEE Symposium on Mass Storage Systems*, (Annecy, France), pp. 100–105, IEEE Computer Society Press, June 1994.
56. P. Zabback, J. Riegel, and J. Menon, "The RAID configuration tool," Research Report RJ 10055 (90552), IBM Research Division, Almaden Research Center, San Jose, CA, Nov. 1996.
57. L. McVoy and C. Staelin, "lmbench: Portable tools for performance analysis," in *Proceedings of Winter 1996 USENIX*, (San Diego, CA), pp. 279–284, Jan. 1996. Lmbench can be found at `http://bitmover.com/lmbench`.
58. "Winbench99," 1999. Available at `http://www.zdnet.com/zdbop/winbench/winbench.html`.
59. P. M. Chen and D. A. Patterson, "A new approach to I/O performance evaluation–self-scaling I/O benchmarks, predicted I/O performance," in *Proceedings of the 1993 ACM SIGMETRICS Conference on Measurement and Modeling of Computer Systems*, (Santa Clara, CA), pp. 1–12, May 1993.
60. P. M. Chen and D. A. Patterson, "Unix I/O performance in workstations and mainframes," Tech. Rep. CSE-TR-200-94, Department of Computer Science and Engineering, University of Michigan, Ann Arbor, MI, Mar. 1994.
61. K. S. Grimsrud, "Rank disk performance analysis tool white paper," Sept. 1997. Avaliable at `http://developer.intel.com/design/ipeak/stortool/index.htm`, Intel Performance Evaluation and Analysis Kit (IPEAK) white papers on Analyze Disk and Rank Disk tools.
62. S. Akyurek and K. Salem, "Adaptive block rearrangement," in *Proceedings of the Ninth International Conference on Data Engineering*, (Vienna, Austria), pp. 182–189, IEEE Computer Society Press, Apr. 1993.
63. S. Daniel and R. Geist, "V-SCAN: an adaptive disk scheduling algorithm," in *Proceedings of International Workshop on Computer Systems Organization*, (New Orleans, LA), pp. 96–103, IEEE, Mar. 1983.
64. K. Bates, *VAX I/O subsystems: optimizing performance*. Professional Press Books, Horsham PA 19044, 1991.
65. R. Geist and J. Westall, "Disk scheduling in Linux," in *Proceedings of International Conference for the Measurement and Performance Evaluation of Computer Systems (CMG '94)*, (Orlando, FL), pp. 739–746, Computer Measurement Group, Dec. 1994.
66. R. Abbott and H. Garcia-Molina, "Scheduling real-time transactions with disk resident data," in *Proceedings of 15th International Conference on Very Large Data Bases*, (Amsterdam, The Netherlands), pp. 385–396, Aug. 1989.
67. S. Chen, J. F. Kurose, J. A. Stankovic, and D. Towsley, "Performance evaluation of two new disk scheduling algorithms for real-time systems," Tech. Rep. UM-CS-1990-077, Department of Computer Science, University of Massachusetts at Amherst, 1990.
68. S. Chen and D. Towsley, "Scheduling customers in a non-removal real-time system with an application to disk scheduling," *Real-Time Systems Journal*, pp. 55–72, June 1994.
69. Y. Li, S.-M. Tan, Z. Chen, and R. H. Campbell, "Disk scheduling with dynamic request priorities," tech. rep., Department of Computer Science, University of Illinois at Urbana-Champaign, IL, Aug. 1995.
70. M. J. Carey, R. Jauhari, and M. Livny, "Priority in DBMS resource scheduling," in *Proceedings of 15th International Conference on Very Large Data Bases*, (Amsterdam, The Netherlands), pp. 397–410, 1989.

71. P. M. Chen and D. A. Patterson, "Maximizing performance in a striped disk array," in *Proceedings of the 17th Annual International Symposium on Computer Architecture (ISCA)*, pp. 322–331, May 1990.
72. G. A. Gibson and D. A. Patterson, "Designing disk arrays for high data reliability," *Journal Parallel and Distributed Computing*, vol. 17, no. 1–2, pp. 4–27, 1993.
73. P. M. Chen and E. K. Lee, "Striping in a RAID level 5 disk array," tech. rep., University of Michigan, Nov. 1993.
74. D. A. Patterson, P. Chen, G. Gibson, and R. H. Katz, "Introduction to redundant arrays of inexpensive disks (RAID)," in *Digest of Papers for 34th IEEE Computer Society International Conference (COMPCON Spring '89)*, (San Francisco, CA), pp. 112–117, Feb. 1989.
75. J. Wilkes, R. Golding, C. Staelin, and T. Sullivan, "The HP AutoRAID hierarchical storage system," *ACM Transactions on Computer Systems*, vol. 14, pp. 108–136, Feb. 1996.
76. J. J. Gniewek, "Evolving requirements for magnetic tape data storage systems," in *Proceedings of the Fifth NASA Goddard Conference on Mass Storages and Technologies* (B. Kobler, ed.), pp. 477–491, Sept. 1996.
77. International Business Machines Corporation, *IBM 3570 tape hardware reference manual, order number GA32-0365-01*, 2 ed., Mar. 1997.
78. G. A. Gibson, D. F. Nagle, K. Amiri, F. W. Chang, E. Feinberg, H. Gobioff, C. Lee, B. Ozceri, E. Riedel, and D. Rochberg, "A case for network-attached secure disks," Tech. Rep. CMU–CS-96-142, Carnegie-Mellon University, June 1996.
79. G. A. Gibson, D. F. Nagle, K. Amiri, F. W. Chang, E. M. Feinberg, H. Gobioff, C. Lee, B. Ozceri, E. Riedel, D. Rochberg, and J. Zelenka, "File server scaling with network-attached secure disks," in *Proceedings of the ACM Sigmetrics Conference on Measurement and Modeling of Computer Systems (Sigmetrics '97)*, vol. 25, (Seattle, WA), pp. 272–284, June 1997.
80. G. A. Gibson, D. F. Nagle, K. Amiri, J. Butler, F. W. Chang, H. Gobioff, C. Hardin, E. Riedel, D. Rochberg, and J. Zelenka, "A cost-effective, high-bandwidth storage architecture," in *Proceedings of the 8th Conference on Architectural Support for Programming Languages and Operating Systems (ASPLOS VIII)*, (San Jose, CA), Oct. 1998.
81. "Mission of the NASD project." `http://www.nsic.org/nasd/goals.html`, Jan. 1997.
82. M. K. McKusick, W. N. Joy, S. J. Leffler, and R. S. Fabry, "A fast file system for UNIX," *ACM Transactions on Computer Systems*, vol. 2, pp.181–197, Aug. 1984.
83. J. K. Ousterhout, H. Da Costa, D. Harrison, J. A. Kunze, M. Kupfer, and J. G. Thompson, "A trace-driven analysis of the UNIX 4.2 BSD file system," in *Proceedings of 10th ACM Symposium on Operating Systems Principles*, vol. 19, (Orcas Island, WA), pp. 15–24, ACM Press, Dec. 1985.
84. G. R. Ganger, "Generating representative synthetic workloads: An unsolved problem," in *Proceedings of the Computer Measurement Group (CMG) Conference*, (Nashville, TN), pp. 1263–1269, Dec. 1995.
85. E. Borowsky, R. Golding, A. Merchant, L. Schreier, E. Shriver, M. Spasojevic, and J. Wilkes, "Using attribute-managed storage to achieve QoS," in *Building QoS into distributed systems* (A. Campbell and K. Nahrstedt, eds.), (Columbia University, NY, NY), pp. 203–206, June 1997. Available at `http://www.bell-labs.com/~shriver/`.

Ad Hoc, Wireless, Mobile Networks: The Role of Performance Modeling and Evaluation

Mario Gerla, Manthos Kazantzidis, Guangyu Pei, Fabrizio Talucci, and Ken Tang

Computer Science Department & Electrical Engineering Department
School of Engineering and Applied Science
University of California, Los Angeles
{gerla,kazantz,pei,talucci,ktang}@cs.ucla.edu

1 The Ad Hoc Network Environment

Consider a networking environment in which the users are mobile, the topology changes, CDMA provides multiple channels, the bandwidth of a given link is unpredictable and possibly very low, the error rates are extremely high and variable, major interference occurs when multiple transmissions take place over (possibly different) links on the same or different codes, real-time multimedia traffic must be supported as well as datagram traffic, there is no stable communication infrastructure, and there is no central control! This is the network environment (often referred to as "Ad Hoc Wireless Network") which we are addressing in this chapter.

We consider the problem of developing performance evaluation techniques and tools in support of networking algorithm development and architecture design. More generally, we are interested in identifying the role played by performance evaluation in the design of efficient ad hoc networks.

To start, we review the unique characteristics of the ad hoc networking environment since these will have direct impact on the models.

First, the network must be capable of providing guaranteed Quality of Service (QoS) to real-time multimedia traffic in a mobile, wireless, multihop, radio network with no fixed infrastructure (e.g., no base stations). This last comment is worth emphasizing since much of the research in wireless communications has exploited the existence of central control emanating from a base station; we deal with no such central system support in this research.

Another element of the environment with which we deal is that of multihop communications. This means that, due to transmitted power constraints, not all radios are within range of each other, and messages may need to be relayed from one radio to another on the way to their intended destinations. One reason for considering multihop communication is that when forced to deploy a radio infrastructure rapidly, it may not be possible to place all radios within range of each other. A second reason is that by carefully limiting the power of radios, we conserve battery power, and cause less interference to other transmissions further away; this gives the additional benefit of "spatial reuse" of channel spectrum,

G. Haring et al. (Eds.): Performance Evaluation, LNCS 1769, pp. 51–95, 2000.

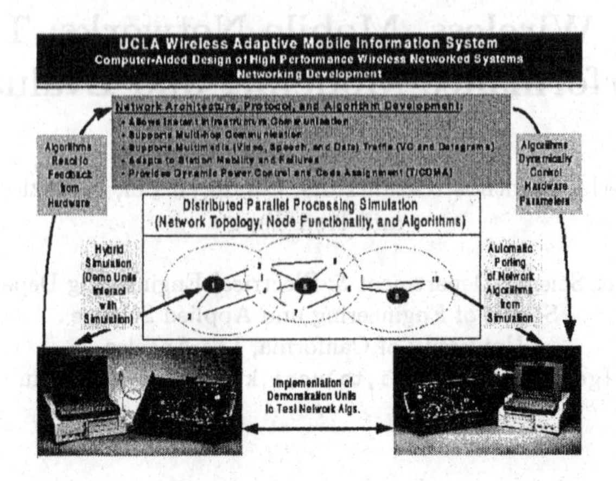

Fig. 1. Simulation Architecture

thus increasing the capacity of the system. Of course, multihop systems are more complex than single-hop centrally controlled systems, and that is part of the challenge we faced in this system design.

The kinds of application scenarios that motivate this research include many that require instant infrastructure network support and multimedia network support. These include military applications (special operations, battlefield scenarios, etc.), disaster relief (fire, earthquake, flood), law enforcement situations, short term scenarios such as public events, etc.

The salient features of this environment may be described as the "3M" environment: real-time Multimedia, Multihop, and Mobile. In the past, there have been studies and implementation of systems that combined any two of these M's, but not all three. For example: real-time Multimedia plus Multihop has been studied in certain satellite systems (e.g., Iridium); real-time Multimedia plus Mobile is pervasive in cellular radio systems and Berkeley's dynamic hand-off with "hints" for multimedia, mobile, cellular (i.e., single hop) networks [32]; and Multihop plus Mobile was well studied in 1970's ARPA packet radio project2. It is the three-way combination that provided the challenges addressed in this paper. Our approach to the "3M" environment has been to address its key systems issues and to provide a methodology for its system performance evaluation (based largely on simulation), development and implementation.

Given the diverse set of factors that can influence the performance of network protocols in this domain, one must adopt an integrated design, evaluation, and prototyping methodology from the outset. The methodology is illustrated in Fig. 1: new protocols are typically simulated prior to implementation. A modular simulation testbed appropriate for mobile systems simulation is described in the next section. In order to preserve the significant investments in model development, the simulation capability must be designed so as to permit the network algorithms to be directly ported from the simulation to the physical domain where the algorithms can be executed on the physical testbed. A capability must also be provided to interface implemented algorithms with the simulation environment so as to permit faithful modeling in the simulation platform.

This chapter addresses the networking issues that arise in such an environment of rapid deployment. The key issues in multimedia digital signal processing revolve around delivering a suitable Quality of Service (QoS) in the face of changing and limited bandwidth as provided by the underlying network. The network focus is on the system design and algorithms that have been developed to cope with changing topology, variable error rate, cross-channel interference, and the requirements of the multimedia traffic. The types of protocols we will describe in this chapter include: Media Access Control; routing and dynamic topology configuration; speech compression. For each protocol we review the performance modeling requirements (performance measures, scaling issues, and other aspects which have impact on the development of an accurate performance model). We describe existing performance models and illustrate these models in representative case studies.

2 Protocol Stack and Simulation Platform

Like other distributed systems, the ad hoc wireless network environment requires performance models which permit to examine tradeoffs and to optimize the relevant parameters for costeffective operation (eg, optimal transmit power, optimal location of base stations, optimal source encoding scheme etc). As a difference from conventional network and distributed system models, however, the appropriate model which must be used to optimize an ad hoc network is much more complex. More precisely, it consists of a moltitude of submodels which are not present in conventional networks (or, at least, which cannot be conveniently abstracted and summarized). These submodels are interacting with eachother at various levels in the protocol architecture and must all be considered in an accurate evaluation of system performance. For example, the fading channel model and the radio model may have profound impact on applications level decisions, such as source coding and task scheduling. The result is that the model cannot be simplified (as it is often done in wired nets) by abstracting the lower layers. Instead, the full complexity must be retained for best performance. This fact has a very important consequence: analytic models are practical only for small scope, microscopic tradeoffs. For more complete studies, simulation is the only viable solution. Moreover, simulation tools must be scalable, so that they can deal with large number of nodes and of parameters.

An example of simulation platform specifically developed at UCLA for an Ad Hoc wireless network environment is GloMoSim [36]. This platform will be extensively used in this chapter to protocol evaluation and comparison. GloMoSim is a library-based sequential and parallel simulator. It is designed as a set of library modules, each of which simulates a specific wireless communication protocol in the protocol stack. The library has been developed using PARSEC, a C-based parallel simulation language [1]. New protocols and modules can be

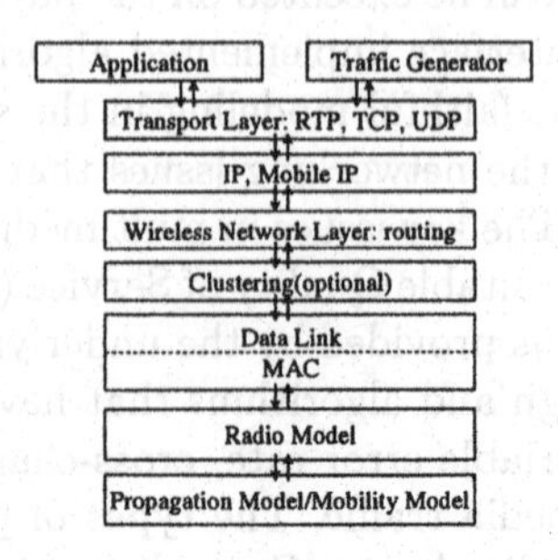

Fig. 2. Simulation Architecture

programmed and added to the library using this language. GloMoSim has been designed to be extensible and composable. It has been implemented on both shared memory and distributed memory computers and can be executed using a variety of synchronization protocols.

As mentioned earlier, the modular structure of GloMoSim reflects the wireless network protocol stack. The most representative layers as shown in Fig. 2. A number of protocols have been developed at each layer. Models for these protocols or layers exist at different levels of granularity.

For example, the channel propagation layer includes: (a) a free space model that calculates signal strength based only on the distance between every source and receiver pair; (b) an analytical model that computes signal attenuation using a log normal distribution; (c) a fading channel model that is computationally much more expensive but incorporates the effect of multi-path, shadowing and fading in calculating signal strength. As an example of alternative protocols, consider the Data Link/MAC layer, where a number of protocols have been proposed in the literature including: carrier sense multiple access (CSMA), multiple access collision avoidance (MACA [19]) and floor acquisition multiple access (FAMA). Each of these has been modeled in the GloMoSim library. At the network layer, flooding protocol, flat distance vector routing protocol DSDV is also contained in the library. Recently, we have modeled a hierarchical routing protocol to handle scaled network routing. At transport layer, a TCP/IP simulator based on Free BSD 2.2.2 implementation has been built into library.

A common API between any two adjacent layers in the protocol stacks is predefined to support their composition. These APIs specify parameter exchanges and services between layers. For example, interfaces between Data Link/MAC layer and network layer are defined as message passing with well specified formats in the simulation library.

The requirements of scalability and modularity make the library design a challenging issue. A straightforward approach is to map each network node to a single simulation object, i.e. a PARSEC entity instance. However, previous experience has indicated that a large number of simulation objects can considerably increase simulation overhead, and such design is not scalable. For example, in order to simulate networks with more than 100,000 mobile nodes, at least 100,000 entity instances have to be created. This was found to be untenable as well as impractical.

Instead, GloMoSim assumes that the network is decomposed into a number of partitions and a single entity is defined to simulate a single layer of the complete protocol stack for all the network nodes that belong to the partition. Interactions among the entities must obey the corresponding APIs described in the previous section. Syntactically, the interactions may be specified using messages, function calls, or entity parameters as appropriate. This method supports modularity because a PARSEC library entity representing a layer of the protocol stack is largely self-contained. It encapsulates the complexity of a specific network behavior independently from other ones. This method also supports scalability because node aggregation inside one entity will be able to reduce the total number of entities which has been found to improve sequential performance even more dramatically than parallel performance.

In summary, the key prerequisites of a simulation platform suitable for large scale wireless ad hoc networks are: modularity; composability; variable degree of course/fine grain in each module; scalability; flexibility; expandibility with user provided modules. These requirements will be verified in many of the applications introduced in the following sections. They are efficiently supported by the parallel GloMoSim platform.

In the following sections, we will examine some of the most critical layers in the wireless network stack, defining performance evaluation issues and challenges, and demonstrating the application of simulation and (when possible) analytic modeling techniques.

3 Wireless MAC: Modeling and Performance Evaluation

3.1 Introduction

An important component of a wireless network design is the MAC (Medium Access Control) layer. CSMA (Carrier Sense Multiple Access) was the MAC layer used in the first generation packet radio networks [22]. CSMA prevents collision by sensing the carrier before transmission. A terminal, however, can sense the carrier only within its transmitting range. Transmissions from terminals out of range cannot be detected. Thus, in spite of carrer sensing a transmission could still collide at the receiver with another transmission from an "out of range" terminal, often referred to as the "hidden terminal".

The Multiple Access with Collision Avoidance protocol (MACA), proposed by Karn [19], solves the hidden terminal problem and outperforms CSMA in a wireless multihop network. Fullmer and Garcia-Luna-Aceves [10] extend MACA by adding carrier sensing. The resulting FAMA-NTR protocol performs almost as well as CSMA in a single-hop wireless network. The same authors propose further improvements (FAMA-PJ [9], CARMA [11]) achieveing even better performance at high loads. In the FAMA-PJ evaluation, an accurate radio model is used to account for the TX-RX turn-around time (the transition time from transmit to receive state). Their study reveals the impact of the turn-around time on performance.

All of these MACA based protocols prepare the data packet transmission, in the sequel referred as the "floor", using different control packets (e.g. RTS). Several modifications have been proposed which suppress RTS, mostly to transmit multipacket messages or to support real time streams. For example, to increase the channel utilization for multipacket message transmissions, Fullmer and Garcia-Luna-Aceves propose in [12] to replace all RTS packets but the first with a MORE flag in the header of the data packet. In [10], the same authors propose to use FAMA-NTR in bulk mode to maximize the throughput. For a multimedia application, Lin and Gerla propose to use RTS/CTS only for the first packet of a real time stream [23]. Subsequent packets are transmitted with a reservation scheme that relies on the periodic nature of the multimedia traffic.

Yet, other extensions to MACA have added even more overhead to the RTS/CTS exchange, mostly for error recovery purposes. For example, in [32] an "invitation minipacket" is introduced to invite the transmitter to retransmit its last packet, in case it has been lost (Negative Acknowledgment). In another case, the three-way handshake is expanded to a five-way handshake (MACAW) with protected ACKs to guarantee transmission integrity in a multihop "nanocell" environment [2]. Unfortunately, each additional pass in the handshake contributes one TX-RX turn-around time plus preamble bits (for synchronization), control bits (e.g. source-destination information) and checksum bits. This overhead clearly reduces the useful throughput.

Recently, the IEEE standards committee has created a working group to develop a standard MAC layer for wireless LANs. The proposed standard, IEEE 802.11, is a derivative of MACAW. It adds, however, the carrier sensing feature. It also allows for centralized MAC layer control from a based station, which in practice corresponds to polling [5].

Let us focus for a moment on the TX-RX turn-around time in order to appraise its impact on performance. According to the standard proposed in [5], the TX-RX turn-around time should be less than 25μs (including radio transients, operating system delays and energy detection). Moreover, every transmission should be delayed by the TX to RX turn-around time (that is, up to 25μs) to give a chance to the previous transmitter to switch to receive mode. This transmit-to-receive transition occurs precisely in the RTS/CTS mechanism of MACA. The higher the channel speed, the higher the turn-around time overhead in terms of bits. Thus, turn-around time will play a key role in future high speed wireless LANs.

The fact that there are so many possible MAC layer options immediately points to the importance of modeling and performance evaluation tools to guide the designer in the selection of the MAC layer which is most appropriate for the configuration at hand. In the sequel, we illustrate the performance modeling

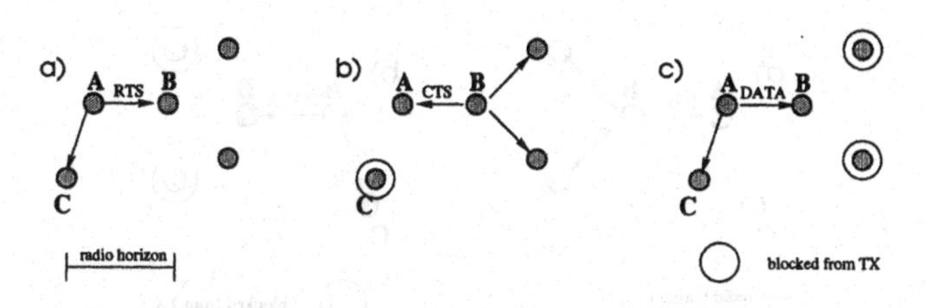

Fig. 3. The three-way handshake of MACA

process for one of the above schemes, MACA-BI. We subsequently compare this scheme with its competitors is some representative network and traffic sessions.

3.2 MACA-BI

Fig. 3 depicts the three basic cycles of the MACA protocol in a typical multi-hop wireless situation. Node A asks for the floor by sending a Request To Send packet (RTS) (Fig. 3a). Node B replies with a Clear To Send packet (CTS) notifying node A that it has acquired the floor (Fig. 3b). Then, node A sends the Data Packet (Fig. 3c).

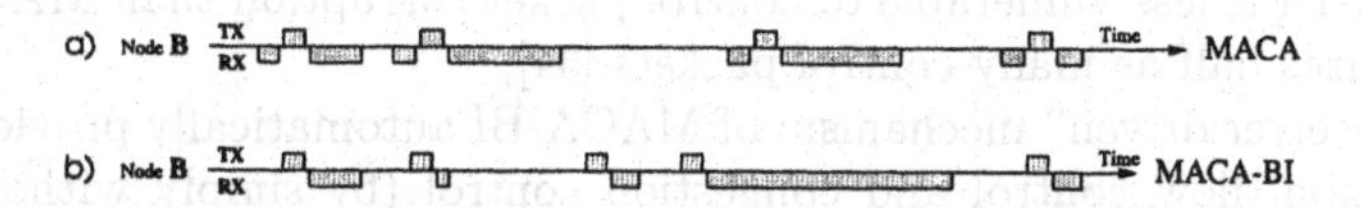

Fig. 4. Two and three-way handshake timing as seen by B

Fig. 4a shows a typical sequence of data packet transmissions as seen by node B, the receiver. This sequence is "driven by the transmitter". That is, node A decides when to start each transmit cycle by issuing RTS. The same result, however, can be achieved with a "receive driven" schedule as shown in Fig. 4b. Namely, we can imagine node B issuing CTS packets at a rate matching the incoming traffic rate, inviting node A to transmit. In this case, RTS packets are suppressed and CTS packets are renamed as RTR (Ready to Receive), indicating the readiness to receive a certain number of packets. The suppression of the CTS packet is the main idea behind MACA-BI (Multiple Access with Collision Avoidance By Invitation) [34] [8].

More precisely, a node ready to transmit, instead of "acquiring" the floor (Floor Acquisition Multiple Access, FAMA) using the RTS (Ready to Transmit) signal, waits for an "invitation" by the intended receiver in the form of an RTR (Ready to Receive) control packet.

The "two pass" handshake of MACA-BI is shown in Fig. 5a and Fig. 5b. Node B does not have the exact knowledge of packet arrival times at node A. Rather, it estimates the average arrival rate. Assuming that each data packet carries the information about the backlog in the transmitter (A in this case), i.e.

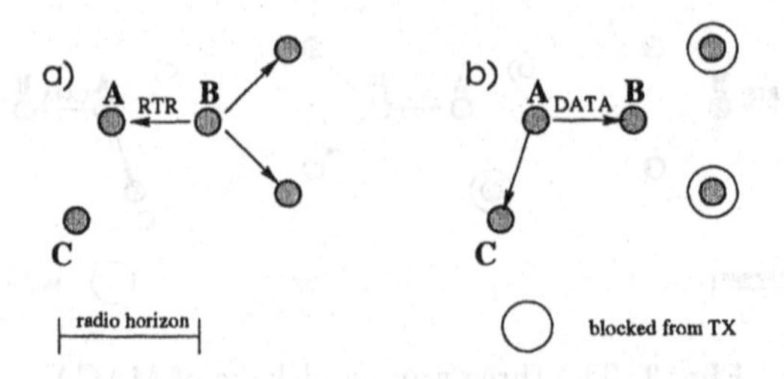

Fig. 5. The two-way handshake of MACA-BI

number of packets and their lengths, the average rate and future backlog can be estimated at B. Thus, B predicts the backlog in A (from previous history) and "prepares the floor" for the predicted number of packets. Node A replies with the transmission of the requested number of packets and with the new backlog information. The reduced "two pass" handshake of MACA-BI exhibits the following features:

- turn-around time overhead is reduced,
- MACA functionality is preserved in MACA-BI [34],
- MACA-BI is data collision free in the same sense as MACA [8],
- MACA-BI is less vulnerable to control packet corruption than MACA, since it requires half as many control packets [34],
- the "receiver driven" mechanism of MACA-BI automatically provides traffic regulation, flow control and congestion control (by simply witholding the "invitation").

3.3 Predicting Traffic

The efficiency of the "invitation" scheme rests on the ability to predict when the neighbours have packets to send. For the receiver it is difficult predict exactly, that is deterministically, the moment in which new data packets will be ready at the transmitter. However deterministic prediction is not necessary, and is not required for each packet. The only information needed is the average rate that can be statistically extimated. To this end, each data packet has an additional field which carries the backlog of the transmitter. This field provides the basic information to estimate the traffic rate. Of course, other parameters can improve the estimate such as derivatives of buffer occupancy or the declared traffic parameters in case of connection oriented services.

Rate estimation is critical in multimedia traffic support, where the task of the multiple access protocol is not simply minimizing the delivery delay but providing periodically and fairly the "floor" required to carry the requested throughput. The period must be selected to optimize the tradeoff between efficient use of node buffers and delay. Whether the transmitter (like in MACA) or receiver (like in MACA-BI) prepares the "floor" is irrelevant. Our choice is the receiver, because the protocol is simplier. In the case of connectionless bursty traffic, prediction and estimation are not very practical. However, the MACA-BI protocol can be extended by allowing nodes to declare their backlog via an RTS control packet if an RTR was not received within a given time out. Thus, RTS is used only to start the flow on link. Subsequent packets are "invited" using RTR. In the limit, MACA-BI reduces to MACA if traffic burstiness prevents timely invitations.

3.4 MACA-BI Performance Evaluation

MACA-BI Analysis for the Single-Hop Case. To evaluate MACA-BI performance, we first develop an analytic model for the single-hop case, using the same approach and assumptions as in [10]. The analysis considers a fully connected single-hop wireless network, which by definition excludes the hidden terminal problem. Briefly, we assume an infinite number of nodes generating Poisson traffic with mean time interval δ between packets. Eache node hears all other nodes (single-hop topology) and the channel is error free. Turn-around time is neglected. We also assume that a floor is suitably prepared each time a packet needs to be transmitted. Hence, we can define:

- λ the aggregate rate of packet generation (new and retransmitted)
- γ the control packet length,
- τ the maximum propagation time,
- $\overline{U}$ the average amount of time during which useful data is sent during a successful busy period,
- $\overline{B}$, $\overline{I}$ the expected duration of busy and idle period,
- P_s the probability of success of an RTR transmission,
- $S = \overline{U}/(\overline{B}+\overline{I})$ the normalized throughput.

A successful transmission consists of an RTR (γ) with one propagation delay (τ), a data packet (δ) followed by another propagation delay:

$$T_s = \gamma + 2\tau + \delta \tag{1}$$

An unsuccesful transmission consists of an RTR followed by one or more RTRs within a time Y ($0 \leq Y \leq \tau$) followed by a propagation delay [22]:

$$T_f = \gamma + \tau + Y = \gamma + 2\tau - \frac{1 - e^{-\tau\lambda}}{\lambda} \tag{2}$$

An RTR is transmitted with success if no other RTRs are transmitted in a the time interval τ that is:

$$P_s = e^{-\tau\lambda}$$

The average busy period is expressed by:

$$\begin{aligned} \overline{B} = T_s P_s + T_f(1 - P_s) = \\ -1/\lambda - e^{-2\tau\lambda}/\lambda + \gamma + 2\tau + (\delta + 2/\lambda)e^{-\tau\lambda} \end{aligned} \tag{3}$$

while the average utilization is:

$$\overline{U} = \delta P_s = \delta e^{-\tau\lambda} \tag{4}$$

Since we assumed that the floor is suitably prepared each time a packet arrives, the average idle period $\overline{I}$ for MACA-BI equals the average arrival time of the floors $1/\lambda$. Finally, the normalized throughput is given by:

$$S = \frac{\delta}{\delta + \frac{2-e^{-\tau\lambda}}{\lambda} + (\gamma + 2\tau)e^{\tau\lambda}} \tag{5}$$

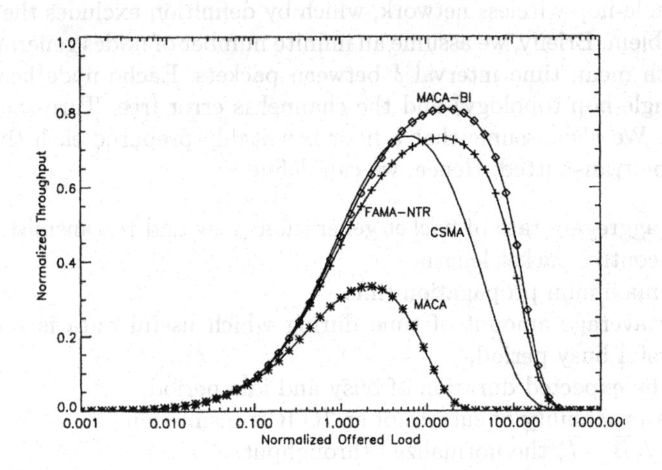

Fig. 6. High Speed channel and SLIP packets

Using data packet length of 296 bytes, control packet length of 20 bytes, a propagation delay of 54 μs (radius 10 miles) and a channel speed of 1Mbps, Fig. 6 reports the normalized throughput for the MACA-BI protocol as well as CSMA non-persistent, FAMA-NTR and MACA protocols taken from [10]. According to the analysis, in a fully connected single hop network MACA-BI performs very well and is comparable with other MACA protocols.

MACA-BI Performance in a Multi-Hop Network. Next, we investigate the performance of MACA-BI in a 9-node multi-hop network via simulation. Three topologies are selected. The Dual Ring with Spokes topology is almost like a single-hop fully connected network with minimal "hidden terminal" situations. The 3x3 Grid topology shows considerably more "hidden terminal" situations. Finally, in the Star topology all the neighbours of the central node are hidden from each other. All the links have a capacity of 1Mpbs and are 10 miles long. Channels are considered error free. Turn-around time (values suggested in [5]) and propagation delay are accounted for.

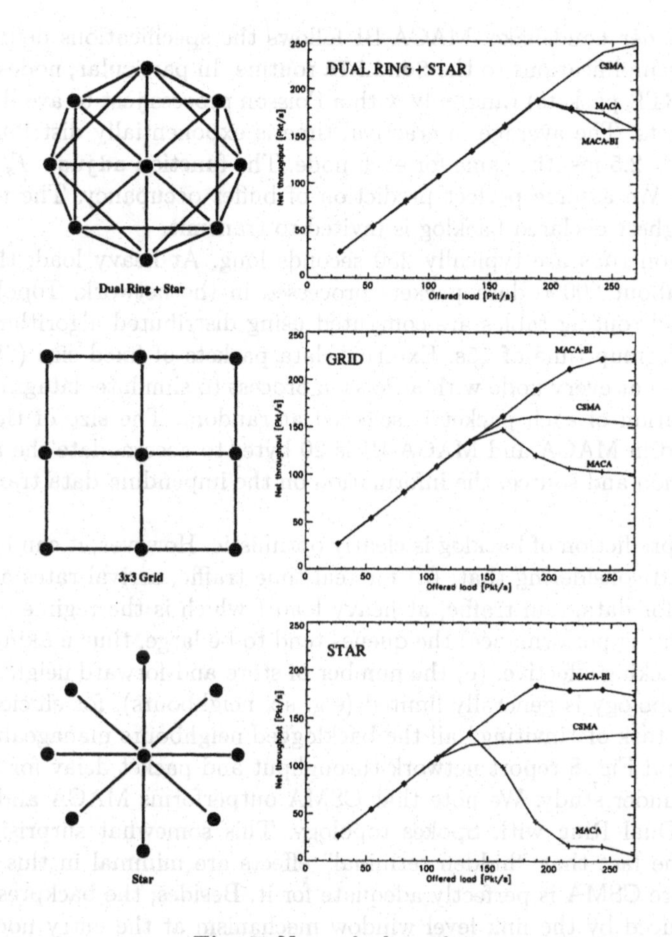

Fig. 7. Network throughput

The simulator implements network, data link and MAC layers. In the network layer, all the basic functionalities are supported. In particular, routing is performed with a Bellman-Ford scheme. Each node has a shared buffer pool of 50 packets. Packets are dropped (at the network layer) when the buffers are full. The data link layer uses a sliding window of size 8 with retransmission timeout of 100ms and selective repeat. The link level protocol recovers from data loss caused by collision not prevented by the MAC layer. This is because, even MACA protocols are not fully protected from packet loss. A separate window is used for each pair of nodes. ACK piggybacking is adopted with a time-out of 20ms.

Separate MAC protocol simulation modules, one for each multiple acces protocol under study, have been developed. CSMA uses a non-persistent access.Our MACA implementation uses the carrier sensing and follows the specifications given in [10], where it is referred to as FAMA-NTR. MACA transmits only one data packet per handshake. MACA-BI follows the specifications defined in [8] with some semplifications to the Send_RTR routine. In particular, nodes reschedule floors (RTR packets) randomly with a Poisson process just to avoid repeated floors conflicts. The average interarrival time is exponentially distributed with mean of $T_s = 2.5$ ms, the same for each node. The function adjust T_s has been suppressed. We assume perfect prediction of buffer occupancy. The neighbour with the highest declared backlog is invited to transmit.

Simulation runs are typically 250 seconds long. At heavy load, this corresponds to about 50000 data packets processed in the network. Topology connectivity and routing tables are computed using distributed algorithms during an initial warmup time of 15s. External data packets of fixed size (256 bytes) are generated at every node with a Poisson process to simulate datagram traffic. The destination of each packet is selected at random. The size of the control packets used in MACA and MACA-BI is 20 bytes to accomodate the addresses for destination and source, the information on the impending data transmission and a CRC.

Perfect prediction of backlog is clearly optimistic. However, it can be reasonably justified considering that: (a) for real time traffic, arrival rates are predeclared, (b) for datagram traffic, at heavy load (which is the regime of interest when evaluating performance) the queues tend to be large, thus making backlog info piggybacking effective, (c) the number of store-and-forward neighbours in a multihop topology is generally limited (e.g. six neighbours), for efficiency, thus making the task of "inviting" all the backlogged neighbours manageable.

Fig. 7 and Fig. 8 report network throughput and packet delay for the three topologies under study. We note that CSMA outperforms MACA and MACA-BI in the Dual Ring with Spokes topology. This somewhat surprising result is due to the fact that "hidden terminal" effects are minimal in this topology and therefore CSMA is perfectly adequate for it. Besides, the backpressure flow control induced by the link level window mechanism at the entry nodes stabilizes CSMA, eliminating the instability problems exhibited in Fig. 6 (where the model did not include the window flow control). MACA and MACA-BI show comparable performance.

As the hidden terminal problem becomes more pronounced, in the Grid and Star topologies, MACA-BI clearly outperforms CSMA, as expected since the latter is adversely affected by the hidden terminal problem. The main surprise here is the poor performance of MACA. A careful examination of the simulation results shows that causes of performance degradation in MACA are the additional turn-around time for each packet and the single packet transmission each floor (which is consistent with the FAMA-NTR model). MACA-BI, instead, can transmit multiple packets per cycle.

3.5 Concluding Remarks

A new multiple access protocol for wireless networks called MACA-BI has been presented. MACA-BI eliminates the need for the RTS packet, thus reducing the

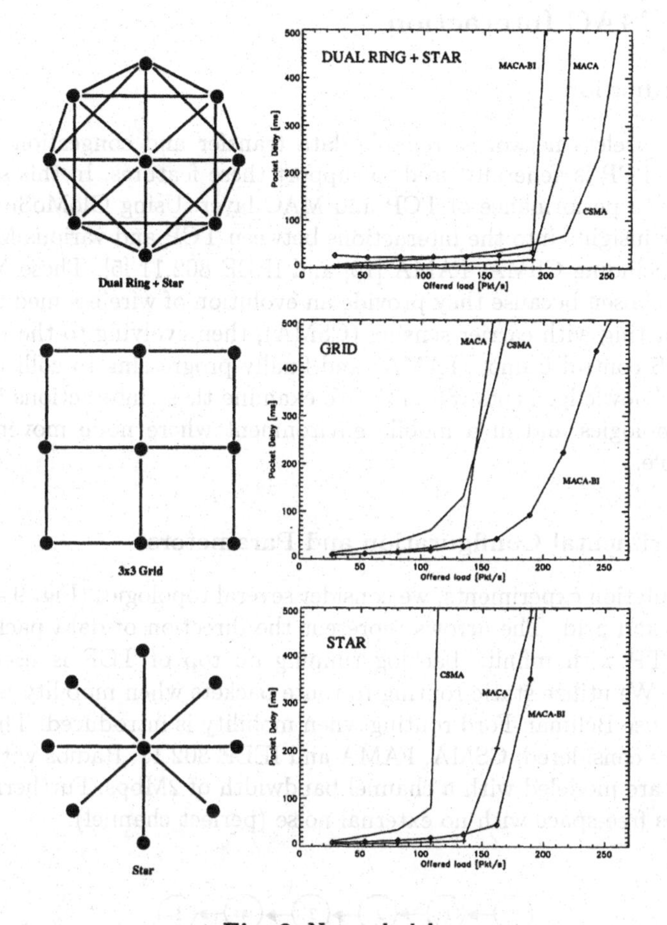

Fig. 8. Network delay

overhead for each packet transmission and simplifying the implementation, yet preserving the data collision free property of MACA. As a result, MACA-BI is more robust to failures such as hidden terminal collision, direct collision or noise corruption. Furthermore, it is less sensitive to the TX-RX turn-around time.

An analyic model for MACA-BI in a single-hop configuration was developed, and was applied to a 1 Mbps wireless network example. A simulation model was also developed to evaluate MACA-BI in multihop environments, and was applied to a 9 node multihop wireless operating at 1 Mbps. Both analytic and simulation results confirm the efficiency of MACA-BI in wireless networks with steady (predictable) traffic. Simulation experiments show its superiority to MACA and CSMA in multihop networks especially when hidden terminal problems are critical. Even better results are expected at higher channel speeds where turn-around times will play a key role.

4 TCP/MAC Interaction

4.1 Introduction

In ad hoc, wireless networks, reliable data transfer and congestion control is paramount. TCP is generally used to support these features. In this section we investigate the performance of TCP and MAC layer. Using GloMoSim [36], we provide new insights into the interactions between TCP and various MAC layer protocols, including CSMA, FAMA [10] and IEEE 802.11 [5]. These MAC protocols were chosen because they provide an evolution of wireless medium access schemes, starting with carrier sensing (CSMA), then evolving to the utilization of RTS/CTS control frames (FAMA) and finally progressing to collision avoidance and acknowledgements (802.11). We examine these interactions in various network topologies and in a mobile environment where node movements are unpredictable.

4.2 Experimental Configuration and Parameters

For our simulation experiments, we consider several topologies (Fig. 9 - Fig. 11): string, ring and grid. The arrows represent the direction of data packet transmissions. FTP with infinite backlog running on top of TCP is used for the application. We utilize static routing to route packets when mobility is not considered and use Bellman-Ford routing when mobility is introduced. Three MAC protocols are considered: CSMA, FAMA and IEEE 802.11. Radios with no capture ability are modeled with a channel bandwidth of 2Mbps. Furthermore, the channel uses free-space with no external noise (perfect channel).

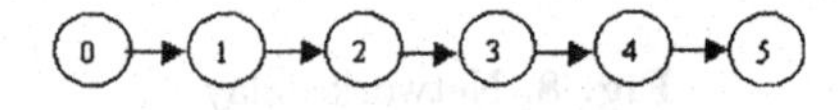

Fig. 9. String Topology

Each node has a 25-packet MAC layer buffer pool. Scheduling of packet transmissions is FIFO. Yield time is defined as the amount of time the sender backs off before sending another data frame after transmitting a data frame. Yield time also refers to the amount of time the receiver backs off before sending a frame after receiving a data frame. 802.11 employs the DCF access method with virtual carrier sense. The TCP simulation code was generated from FreeBSD 2.2.4 code. In particular, window size grows progressively until it reaches the advertised window or until packet loss is detected. In the latter cases, window size is halved (fast retransmission and fast recovery) or abruptly reduced to 1 (slow start). In our experiments, we will "force" the maximum TCP window to take a certain value by setting the advertised window to such value (e.g., 1460B). TCP packet length is assumed fixed at 1460B. TCP connections are started uniformly, distributed between 0 to 10 seconds. Each simulation run is

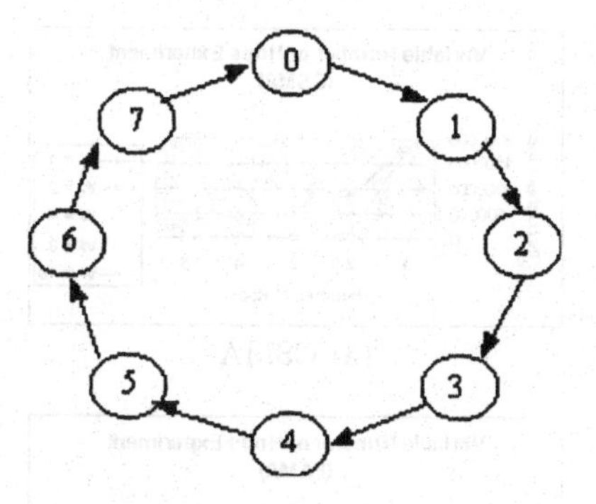

Fig. 10. Ring Topology

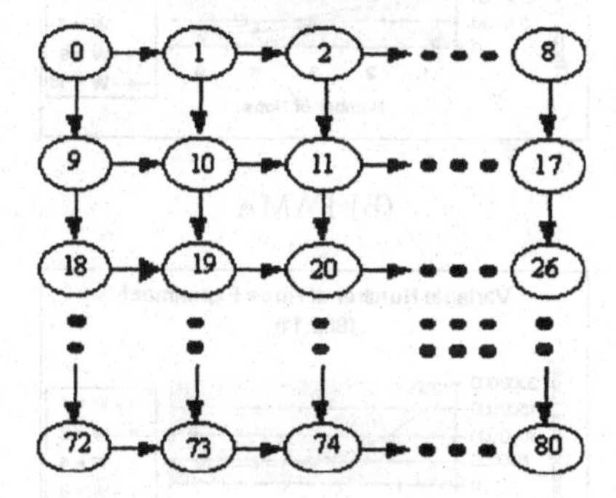

Fig. 11. Grid Topology

executed for 200 simulated seconds except in the grid experiments where the runs last for 400 simulated seconds.

4.3 TCP over MAC Layer

In this study, we introduce the link level ACKs of the IEEE 802.11 MAC layer standard. We argue that increasing the TCP window beyond one packet size has no beneficial impact on network performance. This applies to all three MAC protocols being studied, CSMA, FAMA and 802.11. We then report the results of TCP performance in a wireless ad-hoc network environment under various network configurations. The performance measures of interest are throughput efficiency and fairness.

Variable Number of Hops Experiments. We start by examining the interplay of TCP and MAC layers when there is only one TCP connection present in the network. More precisely, we consider a single TCP connection that covers a variable number of hops, from 1 to 5, as depicted in Fig. 9. Here, the distance between neighbor nodes is equal to the radio transmission range. In the experiment, TCP window (W) varies from 1, 2, 4, 8 and 16 packets, with each

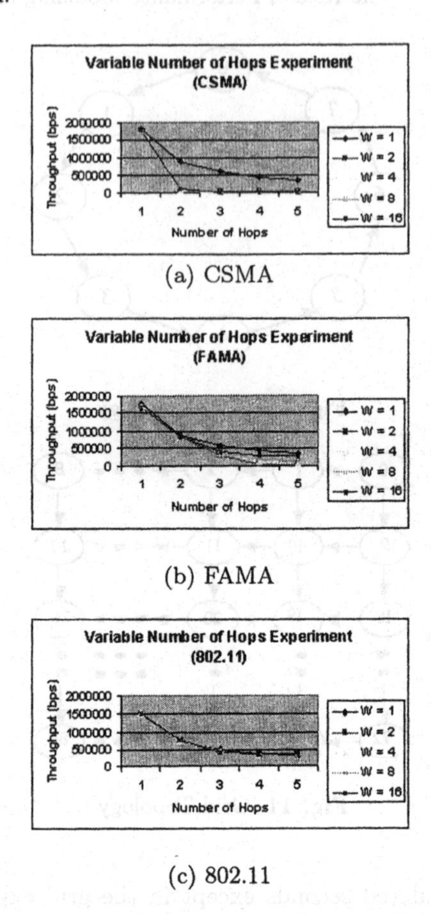

(a) CSMA

(b) FAMA

(c) 802.11

Fig. 12. Single TCP Connection, Variable Number of Hops Experiments

packet being 1460B. The results for CSMA, FAMA and 802.11 throughputs as a function of number of hops (H) and window sizes (W) are reported in Fig. 12a, 12b and 12c. With W = 1 packet, one can verify that throughput values match exactly the analytic predictions for a send-and-wait protocol. The throughput is inversely proportional to the hop distance. CSMA throughput is slightly higher than FAMA because of RTS/CTS overhead in the latter. 802.11 bestows the lowest throughput among the three protocols due to the additional ACK required for each data frame and the collision avoidance scheme.

As we increase the TCP window (up to 16KB), multiple packets and multiple ACKs travel on the path in the opposite direction, creating interference and collisions. We would expect that in balance the window increase improves performance since for 5 hops, for example, analysis shows that the optimal throughput (assuming optimal scheduling of packet and ACK transmissions along the path) is achieved for W = 3 x 1460B. The simulation results in Fig. 12a indicate that this is not true for CSMA. CSMA throughput collapses when H > 2. Hidden terminal losses, which become very substantial for longer paths, cause the loss of TCP ACKs with consequent timeouts and major throughput degradation. FAMA, with a less aggressive yield time, renders better performance compared to that in [25] where FAMA throughput dramatically degrades with H > 3. This can be attributed to the fact that with a less aggressive yield time scheme, the collision between data packets and ACKs dramatically decreases due to the fact that the sender yields for an amount of time that is sufficient for the receiver to respond with ACKs. The performance of 802.11 is comparable to that of FAMA. In addition, the throughput of TCP over 802.11 is consistently comparable to that of W = 1 packet. Note that the throughput tends to become constant as hop distances grow larger - a typical sign of effective pipelining. Moreover, the asymptotic value of 300Kbps is not too far off from the theoretical maximum achievable on a multi-hop wireless path, which is 25% of channel capacity (in our case 0.25 2000Kbps = 500Kbps). The steady performance of 802.11 shown in Fig. 12c is attributed to the fact that 802.11 acknowledges every frame sent and performs local retransmissions if an ACK for a frame is not received. This precludes TCP ACK loss and consequent TCP timeouts.

From the above results we conclude that it is counterproductive to use W larger than single packet size even on connections covering multiple hops due to multiple data packets and multiple ACKs colliding on the opposite path. Therefore, we only consider W = 1460B for the remainder of this paper.

Ring Experiments. To further analyze the interaction of several TCP connections, we consider a ring topology as depicted in Fig. 10. The 8 nodes are engaged in single hop file transfer connections (node 0 to node 1, node 1 to node 2, ... , node 7 to node 0). The results of CSMA, FAMA and 802.11 are illustrated in Fig. 13.

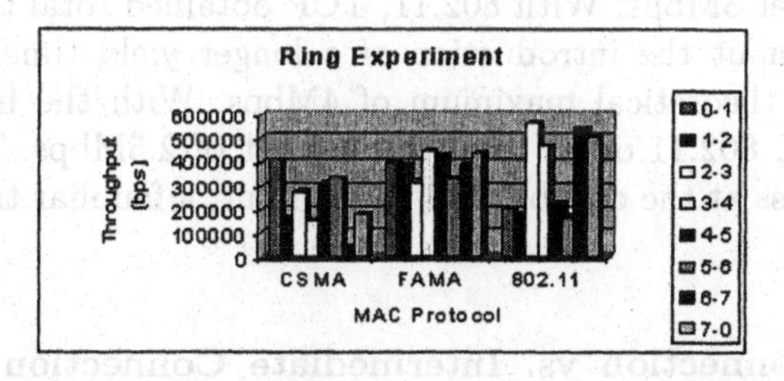

Fig. 13. Throughput (bps), Ring Experiments, W = 1460B

We start with CSMA and note that the behavior reveals some level of capture. The connection from node 0 to node 1 obtains almost ten times the throughput (411Kbps) as that of the connection between node 6 to node 7 (46Kbps). The fairness characteristic is preserved in FAMA, with throughputs ranging from 300Kbps to 400Kbps. This result is in conflict with the result presented in [25] where FAMA demonstrated major capture effects. The discrepancy is explained by the fact that, in this paper, FAMA possesses a fairer yield time. The added yield time permits neighbors of the sender to equally acquire the channel once the sender transmits a packet, thus leading for fairness. Throughput of 802.11 fluctuates from 167Kbps to 566Kbps. We note that the sessions from node 2 to node 3 and from node 3 to node 4 achieve similar throughputs while the throughputs of their neighboring connections (node 1 to node 2, node 4 to node 5) are significantly lower. We witness the same phenomenon with the connections from node 6 to node 7 and from node 7 to node 0. However, by introducing a larger yield time for 802.11 instead of the regular DIFS period, fairness is achieved. Fig. 14 reports the performance of TCP over 802.11 with a larger yield time.

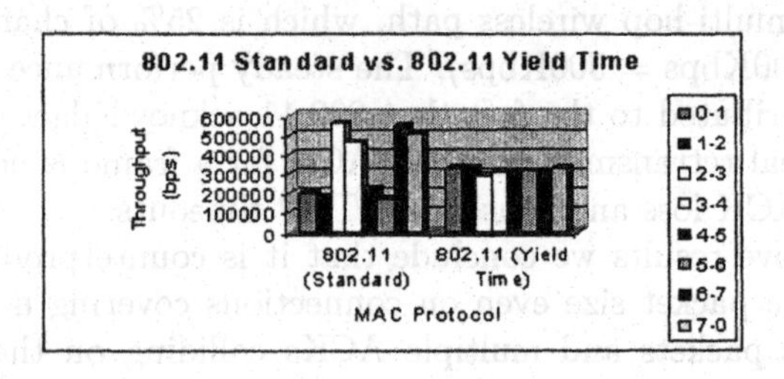

Fig. 14. Throughput (bps), Ring Experiments, 802.11 (Standard) vs. 802.11 (Yield Time), W = 1460B

Fig. 14 leads us to conclude that MAC layer timers are of great importance in terms of achieving equal throughput among node neighbors and needs to be studied in greater detail to understand its impact on network performance. In terms of overall throughput of all nodes, with FAMA, TCP yields aggregate throughput of over 3Mbps. With 802.11, TCP obtained total throughput of almost 3Mbps without the introduction of a longer yield time. This compares favorably to the theoretical maximum of 4Mbps. With the introduction of a longer yield time, 802.11 offers total throughput of 2.5Mbps. Thus, 802.11 accomplishes fairness at the cost of total throughput, a familiar tradeoff discussed earlier.

End-to-End Connection vs. Intermediate Connection Experiments. Next, we wish to examine the behavior of a system that combines end-to-end and intermediate TCP sessions. TCP multi-hop sessions have the tendency to suffer unfair degradation even in wired networks. We expect this unfair treatment to be amplified by the wireless channel. To this end, we consider the case of a TCP connection spanning 5 hops sharing a path with another TCP flow that occupies a shorter number of hops along the same path. Thus, from Fig. 9, we have an end-to-end connection from node 0 to node 5 and a single intermediate flow from either node 2 to node 3, node 2 to node 4 or node 1 to node 4. In other words, the intermediate TCP session varies from one to three hops. Again, each node is only within range of their intermediate neighbors. Table 1a, 1b and 1c report our findings.

Table 1. Throughput (bps) in End-to-End Experiments, W = 1460B

TCP Flow	CSMA	FAMA	802.11
0-5	NE	183459	63
2-3	1819859	809175	15600173

(a) One-Hop Connection

TCP Flow	CSMA	FAMA	802.11
0-5	NE	97131	31719
2-4	908611	625101	672665

(b) Two-Hop Connection

TCP Flow	CSMA	FAMA	802.11
0-5	0	126661	88771
1-4	582346	366257	340292

(c) Three-Hop Connection

Let us first turn our attention to the one-hop intermediate TCP session (Table 1a). NE stands for "Not Established", meaning the TCP connection establishment phase failed. The shorter single hop TCP flow in CSMA dominates the channel and locks out the end-to-end session (TCP was not able to even setup the end-to-end connection) with throughput almost identical to that reported in Fig. 12a with W= 1460B. This is not unexpected since, without link level ACKs, the probability of a packet making it through 5 hops in the face of contention from a single hop connection is indeed slim. FAMA for the first time indicates signs of unfairness with the end-to-end session achieving 183Kbps and the intermediate session attaining 809Kbps. The performance of TCP over 802.11 does not fare any better. The end-to-end connection obtains practically no throughput while the single hop session takes control of the wireless channel. FAMA improves on CSMA and 802.11 in regards to fairness, although still exhibiting capture. As we increase the intermediate connection to two and three hops (Table 1b and 1c), capture still occurs. However, we note that as the source of the intermediate TCP session migrates closer to the source of the end-to-end session (Table 1a, 1c), the degree of fairness increases. This behavior transpires simply because as the source of the intermediate TCP session draws near to the end-to-end session, the source of the end-to-end session is more aware of the intermediate connection and therefore is able to better compete for the channel.

9 X 9 Grid Experiments. In this section we consider a more realistic ad-hoc network environment with larger number of nodes and the inclusion of mobility. To this end, we have selected an 81-node grid topology as shown in Fig. 11. The dimension of the grid is 100 X 100 meters. Each node is 10 meters apart from its horizontal and vertical neighbors. Furthermore, each node has a radio power range of 30 meters. Nodes move at a rate of 10 meters per second in a random direction with a probability of 0.5. When mobility is not considered, static routing is used. When mobility is introduced, Bellman-Ford routing is utilized with routing table updates occurring once every second. FTP connections are established between node 18 to node 26, node 36 to node 44, node 54 to node 62, node 2 to node 74, node 4 to node 76 and node 6 to node 78. Simulation runs with no mobility are executed for 400 simulated seconds. With mobility, simulation runs last for 800 seconds in simulation time with FTP session starting after 400 seconds. We start with the analysis of the experiments with no mobility (Fig. 15).

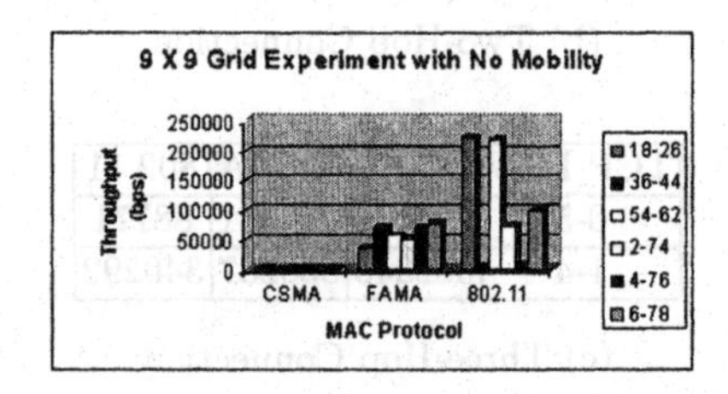

Fig. 15. Throughput (bps), 9 X 9 Grid Experiments, No Mobility, W = 1460B

First, we consider CSMA. Theoretical maximum throughput for an 8-hop connection with W equal to one packet size is 300Kbps. TCP performance under CSMA virtually collapses with maximum throughput of 2.9Kbps from the connection between node 2 to node 74. The average throughput is 1.6Kbps. The horrific performance is due to interference from neighbor FTP connections as well as interference from the three cross traffic connections. Particularly damaging to multi-hop FTP connections in CSMA is the high loss rate on the links and the lack of link loss recovery. Next, we shift our attention to FAMA. FAMA throughput is much higher than CSMA, with average throughput of 59.7Kbps. The improvement of FAMA is credited to the RTS/CTS control frames and the fair yield time. Therefore, FAMA is better protected against hidden terminal losses. Minimum and maximum throughput is 36.6Kpbs and 76.4Kbps, respectively. Compare to the theoretical maximum of 300Kbps, FAMA is still inadequate. With 802.11, the average throughput is 104Kbps. Minimum and maximum are 7.5Kbps and 222.3Kbps, respectively, which measure favorably to the theoretical maximum. The improved throughput is the direct result of the link level ACKs, which help achieve good aggregate throughput in a high loss rate environment. However, capture is not alleviated. We next turn our attention to the same configuration except now nodes move at a rate of 10 meters per second in a random fashion with a probability of 0.5.

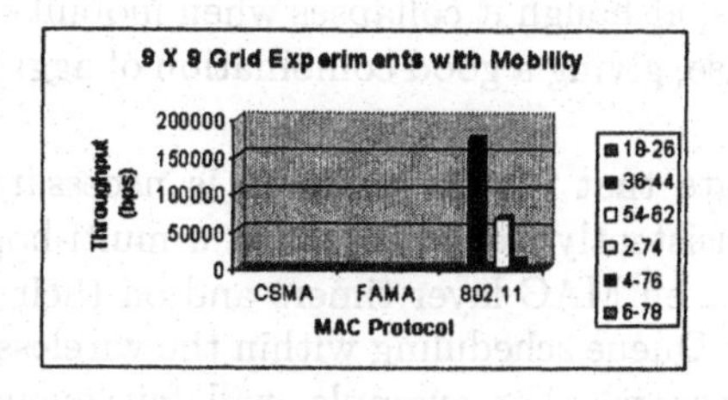

Fig. 16. Throughput (bps), 9 X 9 Grid Experiments, Mobility, W = 1460B

From Fig. 16, CSMA collapses with five out of six sources not being able to establish connection. Furthermore, the lone connection that is able to be established (node 36 to node 44) obtained negligible throughput (381 bps). FAMA improves on CSMA, although not by much. Two connections did not get established and another closed due to too many retransmissions by TCP after the successful connection setup phase. 802.11 performs the best out of the three MAC protocols being studied. Still, two of the sources fail to open the TCP session. TCP sessions from node 36 to node 44 and from node 2 to node 74 obtain throughputs of 172.2Kbps and 67Kpbs, respectively, but the rest show only marginal gain. In summary, the grid experiments confirm the behavior observed in linear topologies. Namely, poor multi-hop connection performance exists under TCP, especially in conjunction with CSMA. FAMA performs better than CSMA, both in absence and in presence of mobility. It is clear, however, that neither FAMA nor CSMA are adequate for ad-hoc network operation without the assistance of link level loss protection and of proper fairness measures. 802.11 is by far superior to both CSMA and FAMA in terms of throughput. However, 802.11 shows evidence of capture effects. When mobility is introduced, CSMA and FAMA collapse. Only 802.11 demonstrates signs of productivity.

4.4 Concluding Remarks

The focus of this section has been the TCP/MAC interaction in a multi-hop radio network. In particular, we focus on TCP performance over CSMA, FAMA and 802.11. We first note that the best performance is achieved with W = 1 packet. With an adaptive window, conflicts between multiple packets and outstanding ACKs arise. We observed capture in 802.11 under the ring experiment but notice that by adjusting the yield time of 802.11, capture is eliminated (at the expense of reduction in aggregate throughput). Furthermore, multi-hop TCP connections in wireless networks are at a clear disadvantage with respect to single hop connections, much more so than in wired networks. Also, we find that if sources in the network are aware of each other's presence, fairness can be achieved. Lack of awareness, however, degrades system performance. Finally, we show that, in the face of mobility, MAC protocols without link loss protection break down. Between the three MAC layer protocols under study, CSMA performs best only when there are no competing TCP streams. FAMA works well in most situations, although it collapses when mobility is introduced. 802.11 shows the most promise, giving a good combination of aggregate throughput and fairness.

The results indicate that further research is necessary to make TCP and MAC layers work consistently well together in a multi-hop environment. More work needs to be done on MAC layer timers and on their interplay with upper layer backoff schemes. Queue scheduling within the wireless node is another area that requires more research. For example, will fair queueing provide fairness in bottleneck links spanning multiple hops? Also, the interplay between backoff policy, link protection scheme and floor acquisition methods must be investigated in greater detail. For example, which of the above features is really responsible for improving performance in any of the situations considered in this study? Finally, more work must be done regarding MAC layer support for mobility.

5 Scalable Routing for Ad-hoc Wireless Networks

5.1 Introduction and Overview

In this section we consider a large population of mobile stations which are interconnected by a multihop wireless network. Key characteristics of the ad hoc system are the large number of users, their mobility and the need to operate without the support of a fixed (wired or wireless) infrastructure. The last feature sets this system apart from existing cellular systems and in fact makes its design much more challenging.

In this environment, we investigate routing strategies which scale well to large populations and can handle mobility. In addition, we address the need to support multimedia communications, with low latency requirements for interactive traffic and Quality of Service (QoS) support for real time streams (voice/video). In the wireless routing area, several schemes have already been proposed and implemented (e.g., flat routing, hierarchical routing, Fisheye state routing, on-demand routing etc). Many flat routing protocols have been proposed to support mobile ad-hoc wireless routing. Some proposals are extensions of schemes previously developed for traditional wired networks. For example, Perkins' Destination-Sequenced Distance Vector (DSDV) [31] is based on Distributed Bellman-Ford (DBF), Garcia's Wireless Routing Protocol (WRP) [26] [27] is based on a loop-free path-finding algorithm, etc. In flat routing schemes each node maintains a routing table with entries for all the nodes in the network. This is acceptable if the user population is small. However, as the number of mobile hosts increases, so does the overhead. Thus, flat routing algorithms do not scale well to large networks.

5.2 Hierarchical State Routing (HSR) Scheme

To permit scaling, hierarchical techniques can be used. The major advantage of hierarchical routing is drastic reduction of routing table storage and processing overhead. In this section we describe two hierarchical schemes proposed for wireless networks.

Partitioning and clustering is common practice in multihop wireless networks both at the MAC layer and at the network layer [13] [4]. Clustering can enhance network performance. For example, at the MAC layer, by using different spreading codes across clusters the interference is reduced and the spatial reuse is enhanced. As the number of nodes grows, there is further incentive to exploit partitions at the network layer in order to implement hierarchical routing and thus reduce routing overhead. In a mobile network, the main drawback of hierarchical routing is mobility and location management as described in [20]. To overcome this problem, in this section, we describe the Hierarchical State Routing (HSR) scheme, which combines dynamic, distributed multi-level hierarchical clustering with an efficient location (membership) management.

HSR maintains a hierarchical topology, where elected cluster heads at the lowest level become members of the next higher level. These new members in turn organize themselves in clusters, and so on. The goals of clustering are the efficient utilization of radio channel resources and the reduction of network-layer routing overhead (i.e., routing table storage, processing and transmission).

In addition to multilevel clustering, HSR also provides multilevel logical partitioning. While clustering is based on geographical (i.e., physical) relationship between nodes, (hence, it will be referred to as **physical** clustering), logical partitioning is based on logical, functional affinity between nodes (e.g., employees of the same company, members of the same family, etc). **Logical** partitions play a key role in location management.

The proposed location (membership) management scheme tracks mobile nodes, while keeping the control message overhead low. It is based on a distributed location server approach which exploits logical partitions. The following sections give more details on both physical and logical partitions.

Physical Multilevel Clustering. Fig. 17 shows an example of physical clustering. At *Level* $= 0$ we have 4 physical level clusters C0-1, C0-2, C0-3, and C0-4. Level 1 and level 2 clusters are generated by recursively selecting cluster heads. Different clustering algorithms can be used for the dynamic creation of clusters and the election of cluster heads [13] [4]. At level 0 clustering, spread-spectrum radios and code division multiple access (CDMA) can be introduced for spatial reuse across clusters. Within a level 0 cluster, the Medium Access Control (MAC) layer can be implemented by using a variety of different schemes (polling, MACA, CSMA, TDMA etc) [23]. Generally, there are three kinds of nodes in a cluster, namely, cluster-head node (e.g., Node 1, 2, 3, and 4), gateway node (e.g., Node 6, 7, 8, and 11), and internal node (e.g., 5, 9, and 10). The cluster-head node acts as a local coordinator of transmissions within the cluster.

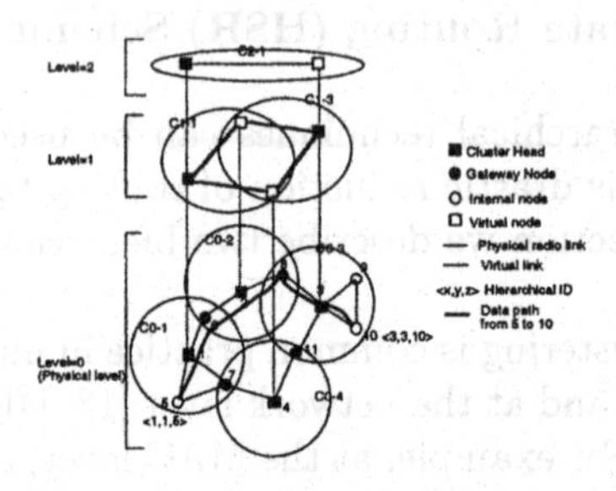

Fig. 17. An example of physical/virtual clustering

The node IDs shown in Fig. 17 (at level = 0) are physical (e.g., MAC layer) addresses. They are hardwired and are unique to each node.

Within a physical cluster, each node monitors the state of the link to each neighbor (i.e., up/down state and possibly QoS parameters such as bandwidth) and broadcasts it within the cluster. The cluster head summarizes link state information within its cluster and propagates it to the neighbor cluster heads (via the gateways). The knowledge of connectivity between neighbor cluster heads leads to the formation of level 1 clusters. For example, as shown in Fig. 17, neighbor cluster heads 1 and 2 become members of the level 1 cluster C1-1. To carry out LS routing at level 1, a link state parameter of the "virtual" link in C1-1 between nodes 1 and 2 (which are neighbor cluster heads) is calculated from the link state parameters of the physical path from cluster head 1 to next cluster head 2 through gateway 6. More precisely, gateway 6 passes the link state update for link (6-2) to cluster head 1. Cluster head 1 estimates the parameters for the path (1-6-2) by using its local estimate for (1-6) and the estimate for (6-2) it just received from gateway 6. The result becomes the link state parameter of the "virtual link" between node 1 and 2 in C1-1. The virtual link can be viewed as a "tunnel" implemented through lower level nodes.

Applying the aforementioned clustering procedure recursively, new cluster heads are elected at each level, and become members of the higher level cluster (e.g., node 1 is elected as a cluster head at level 1 and becomes a member of level 2 cluster C2-1).

Nodes within a cluster exchange virtual link state information as well as summarized lower level cluster information. After obtaining the link state information at this level, each virtual node floods it down to nodes within the lower level cluster. As a result, each physical node has a "hierarchical" topology information, as opposed to a full topology view as in flat LS schemes. The hierarchy so developed requires a new address for each node, the hierarchical address. There are many possible solutions for the choice of the hierarchical address scheme. In HSR, we define the HID (Hierarchical ID) of a node as the sequence of the MAC addresses of the nodes on path from the top hierarchy to the node itself. For example, in Fig. 17 the hierarchical address of node 6, HID(6), is $< 3, 2, 6 >$.

In this example, node 3 is a member of the top hierarchical cluster (level 2). It is also the cluster head of C1-3. Node 2 is member of C1-3 and is the cluster head of C0-2. Node 6 is a member of C0-2 and can be reached directly from node 2. The advantage of this hierarchical address scheme is that each node can dynamically and locally update its own HID upon receiving the routing updates from the nodes higher up in the hierarchy.

The hierarchical address is sufficient to deliver a packet to its destination from anywhere in the network using HSR tables. Referring to Fig. 17, consider for example the delivery of a packet from node 5 to node 10. Note that HID(5)= $< 1, 1, 5 >$ and HID(10)= $< 3, 3, 10 >$. The packet is forward upwards to the top hierarchy by node 5 (i.e., to node 1). Node 1 delivers the packet to node 3, which is the top hierarchy node for destination 10. Node 1 has a "virtual link", i.e. a tunnel, to node 3, namely, the path (1,6,2,8,3). It thus delivers the packet to node 3 along this path. Finally, node 3 delivers the packet to node 10 along the downwards hierarchical path, which in this case reduces to a single hop.

Gateways nodes can communicate with multiple cluster heads and thus can be reached from the top hierarchy via multiple paths. Consequently a gateway has multiple hierarchical addresses, similar to a router in the wired Internet, equipped with multiple subnet addresses.

In order to evaluate the routing table overhead of HSR, let us assume that the average number of nodes in a cluster (at any level) is N, and the number of hierarchical levels is M. Then, the total number of nodes is N^M. A flat link state routing requires $O(N^M)$ entries. The proposed hierarchical routing requires only $O(N \times M)$ entries in the hierarchical map. This maximum occurs in the top hierarchy nodes which belong to M levels (i.e., clusters) simultaneously and thus must store N entries per cluster. Thus, routing table storage at each node is greatly reduced by introducing the hierarchical topology. Of course, there is no "free lunch" in network protocol design. So, the drawbacks of HSR with respect to flat link state routing are the need to maintain a longer (hierarchical) addresses and the cost of continuously updating the cluster hierarchy and the hierarchical address as nodes move. In principle, a continuously changing hierarchical address makes it difficult to locate and keep track of nodes. Fortunately, logical partitioning comes to help, as discussed in the next section.

Logical Partitions and Location (Membership) Management. In addition to MAC addresses, nodes are assigned logical addresses of the type $<$ *subnet*, *host* $>$. These addresses have format similar to IP, and can in fact be viewed as private IP addresses for the wireless network. Each subnet corresponds to a particular user group (e.g., tank battalion in the battlefield, search team in a search and rescue operation, etc). The notion of a subnet is important because each subnet is associated with a home agent, as explained later. Also, a different mobility pattern can be defined independently for each subnet. This allows us to independently define the mobility models for different formations (e.g., members of a police patrol). The transport layer delivers to the network a packet with the private IP address. The network must resolve the IP address into a hierarchical (physical) address which is based on MAC addresses.

A node does not know which cluster a particular destination belongs to, except for those destinations within the same lowest level cluster. The distributed location server assists in finding the destination. The approach is similar to mobile IP, except that here the home agent may also move. Recall that nodes in the same IP subnetwork have common characteristics (e.g., tanks in the same battalion, professionals on the move belonging to the same company, students within the same class, etc). Note that the IP subnetwork is a "virtual" subnetwork which spans several physical clusters. Moreover, the subnet address is totally distinct from the MAC address. Each virtual subnetwork has at least one home agent (which is also a member of the subnet) to manage membership. For simplicity, we assumes that all home agents advertise their HIDs to the top hierarchy. The home agent HIDs are appended to the top level routing tables. Optionally, the home agent HIDs can be propagated downwards to all nodes together with such routing tables.

Each member of a logical subnetwork knows the HID of its home agent (it is listed in the routing table). It registers its own current hierarchical address with the home agent. Registration is both periodic and event driven (e.g., whenever the member moves to a new cluster). At the home agent, the registered address is timed out and erased if not refreshed. Since in most applications, the members of the same subnet move as a group (e.g., tanks in a battalion), they tend to reside in neighboring clusters. Thus, registration overhead is modest.

When a source wants to send a packet to a destination of which it knows the IP address, it first extracts the subnet address field from it. From its internal list (or from the top hierarchy) it obtains the hierarchical address of the corresponding home agent (recall that all home agents advertise their HIDs to the top level hierarchy). It then sends the packet to the home agent using such hierarchical address. The home agent finds the registered address from the host ID (in the IP address) and delivers the packet to destination. Once source and destination have learned each other hierarchical addresses, packets can be delivered directly without involving the home agent.

5.3 Fisheye State Routing (FSR) Scheme

In [21], Kleinrock and Stevens proposed a "fisheye" technique to reduce the size of information required to represent graphical data. The eye of a fish captures with high detail the pixels near the focal point. The detail decreases as the distance from the focal point increases. In routing, the fisheye approach translates to maintaining accurate distance and path quality information about the immediate neighborhood of a node, with progressively less detail as the distance increases. Our Fisheye State Routing (FSR) scheme is built on top of another recently proposed routing scheme called "Global State Routing" (GSR) [33], which is introduced in the following section.

Global State Routing (GSR). GSR is functionally similar to LS Routing in that it maintains a topology map at each node. The key is the way in which routing information is disseminated. In LS, link state packets are generated and flooded into the network whenever a node detects a topology change. In GSR, link state packets are not flooded. Instead, nodes maintain a link state table based on the up-to-date information received from neighboring nodes, and periodically exchange it with their local neighbors only (no flooding). Through this exchange process, the table entries with larger sequence numbers replace the ones with smaller sequence numbers. The GSR periodic table exchange resembles the vector exchange in DBF (or more precisely, DSDV [31]) where the distances are updated according to the time stamp or sequence number assigned by the node originating the update. In GSR (like in LS) link states are propagated, a full topology map is kept at each node, and shortest paths are computed using this map.

In a wireless environment, a radio link between mobile nodes may experience frequent disconnects and reconnects. The LS protocol releases a link state update for each such change, which floods the network and causes excessive overhead. GSR avoids this problem by using periodic exchange of the entire topology map, greatly reducing the control message overhead [33].

The drawbacks of GSR are the large size update message which consumes considerable amount of bandwidth and the latency of the link state change propagation, which depends on the update period. This is where the Fisheye technique comes to help, by reducing the size of update messages without seriously affecting routing accuracy.

The Fisheye State Routing (FSR) Protocol. Fig. 18 illustrates the application of fisheye in a mobile, wireless network. The circles with different shades of grey define the fisheye scopes with respect to the center node (node 11). The scope is defined as the set of nodes that can be reached within a given number of hops. In our case, three scopes are shown for 1, 2 and 3 hops respectively. Nodes are color coded as black, grey and white accordingly.

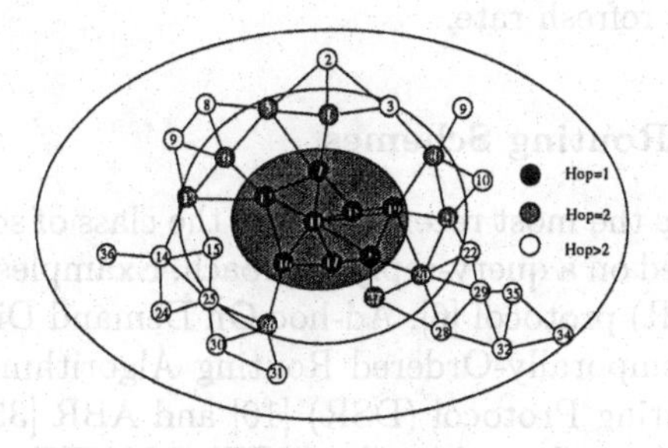

Fig. 18. Scope of fisheye

The reduction of update message size is obtained by using different exchange periods for different entries in the table. More precisely, entries corresponding to nodes within the smaller scope are propagated to the neighbors with the highest frequency. Referring to Fig. 19, entries in bold are exchanged most frequently. The rest of the entries are sent out at a lower frequency. As a result, a considerable fraction of link state entries are suppressed, thus reducing the message size. This strategy produces timely updates from near stations, but creates large latencies that from stations afar. However the imprecise knowledge of the best path to a distant destination is compensated by the fact that the route becomes progressively more accurate as the packet gets closer to destination.

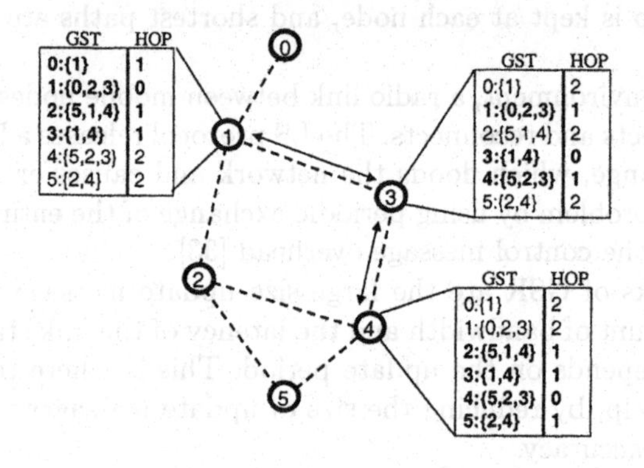

Fig. 19. Message reduction using fisheye

In summary, FSR scales well to large networks, by keeping link state exchange O/H low without compromising route computation accuracy when the destination is near. By retaining a routing entry for each destination, FSR avoids the extra work of "finding" the destination (as in on-demand routing) and thus maintains low single packet transmission latency. As mobility increases, routes to remote destinations become less accurate. However, when a packet approaches its destination, it finds increasingly accurate routing instructions as it enters sectors with a higher refresh rate.

5.4 On-Demand Routing Schemes

On-demand routing is the most recent entry in the class of scalable wireless routing schemes. It is based on a query-reply approach. Examples include Lightweight Mobile Routing (LMR) protocol [6], Ad-hoc On Demand Distance Vector Routing (AODV) [30], Temporally-Ordered Routing Algorithms (TORA) [29] [28], Dynamic Source Routing Protocol (DSR) [16] and ABR [35]. Most of the routing proposals currently evaluated by the IETF's MANET working group for an Ad Hoc Network Standard [30] [28] [16] fall in on-demand routing category.

There are different approaches for discovering routes in on-demand algorithms. Most algorithms employ a scheme derived from LAN bridge routing, i.e. route discovery via backward learning. The source in search of a path floods a query into the network. The transit nodes upon receiving the query "learn" the path to the source (**backward learning**) and enter the route in the forwarding table. The intended destination eventually receives the query and can thus respond using the path traced by the query. This permits establishment of a full duplex path. To reduce new path search overhead, the query packet is dropped on its way to a destination if it encounters a node which already has a route to such destination. After the path has been computed, it is maintained up to date as long as the source uses it. For example, a link failure may trigger another query/response so that the route is always kept up to date.

An alternate scheme for tracing on demand paths (also inspired by LAN bridge routing) is **source routing**. In this case, the query packet reads and stores in its header the IDs of the intermediate nodes. The destination can then retrieve the entire path to the source from the query header. It then uses this path (via source routing) to respond to the source providing it with the path at the same time.

On-demand routing does scale well to large populations as it does not maintain a permanent routing entry to each destination. Instead, as the name suggests, a route is computed only when there is a need. Thus, routing table storage is greatly reduced, if the traffic pattern is sparse. However, on-demand routing introduces the initial search latency which may degrade the performance of interactive applications (e.g., distributed database queries). Moreover, it is impossible to know in advance the quality of the path (e.g., bandwidth, delay etc) prior to call setup. Such a priori knowledge is very desirable in multimedia applications, since it enables call acceptance control and bandwidth renegotiation.

A recent proposal which combines on-demand routing and conventional routing is Zone Routing [14] [15]. For routing operation inside the local zone, any routing scheme, including DBF routing or LS routing, can be applied. For interzone routing, on-demand routing is used. The advantage of zone routing is its scalability, as "global" routing table overhead is limited by zone size. Yet, the benefits of global routing are preserved within each zone.

5.5 Quality of Service Support

In real time applications (e.g., IP telephony) it is beneficial for the source to know, prior to call set up, not only the path to destination but also the average data rate available/achievable on such path. This is important for many reasons, for example: (a) if bandwidth is not available, the call is dropped without congesting the network unnecessarily (i.e., call admission control); (b) if other media (e.g., cellular radio, LEO satellites, UAVs, etc) are available as alternatives to the ad hoc wireless path, this information permits the gateway to make an intelligent routing choice; (c) if bandwidth and/or channel quality is inadequate for full rate transmission, the source may still put the call through by reducing the rate or using a more robust coding scheme; (d) if path bandwidth/quality deteriorates during the call, the source finds out from periodic routing table inspection; it can then modify or drop the call.

In an ad hoc wireless network, the MAC layer is generally responsible for monitoring channel quality and available bandwidth. For example, consider a network with MAC layer clustering and token access protocol [4]. The cluster head can monitor all the traffic in the cluster, both local and transit. It can also monitor channel quality (error rate, etc). It can distinguish between real time and data traffic, and can determine the amount of bandwidth still available for voice (high priority) traffic. In ad hoc networks which do not use clustering, the monitoring of available resources is more complex, but can still be accomplished [24].

In order to include QoS monitoring in the routing process, it suffices to extend the definition of link state by adding to the link entry also bandwidth and channel quality information. In this regard, both FSR and HSR are "QoS ready" in that they are both based on the link state routing model. QoS support can be provisioned also in on-demand routing schemes. However, with on-demand routing the quality of the path is not known a priori. It can be discovered only while setting up the path, and must be monitored by all intermediate nodes during the session, thus paying the related latency and overhead penalty. In AODV for example, the intermediate nodes along a QoS route store state information (e.g., minimum rate) about the session and, upon discovering that the QoS parameters can no longer be maintained, return an ICMP QoS_LOST message back to the source [30].

5.6 Performance Evaluation

The multihop, mobile wireless network simulator was developed on a simulation platform built upon the language Maisie/PARSEC [36]. The simulator is very detailed. It models all the control message exchanges at the MAC layer and the network layer. This is critical in order to monitor and compare the traffic overhead (O/H) of the various protocols. Mobile hosts roaming randomly in all directions at a predefined average speed in a square. A reflecting boundary is assumed. Radio transmission range is 120 meters. A free space propagation channel model is assumed. Data rate is 2Mb/s. Packet length is 10 kbit for data, 2 kbit for cluster head neighbor list broadcast, and 500 bits for MAC control packets. Transmission time is 5 ms for data packet, 1 ms for neighboring list and 0.25 ms for control packet. The buffer size at each node is 15 packets.

The traffic load corresponds to an interactive environment. 100 sessions are established between different source/destination pairs. Within each session, data packets are generated following a Poisson process with an average interval of 2.5 s. For FSR, we use a 2-level fisheye scoping in our experiments. The scope radius is 2 hops i.e. nodes within 2 hops are in-scope. The refresh rate ratio is 1:3 between in-scope nodes and out-scope nodes. This is quite conservative for network sizes larger than 200, we could use multiple level fisheye scoping and refresh the table entries corresponding to nodes in the outmost scope with even lower frequency. Similarly, in HSR we assume only 2 levels. The number of logical

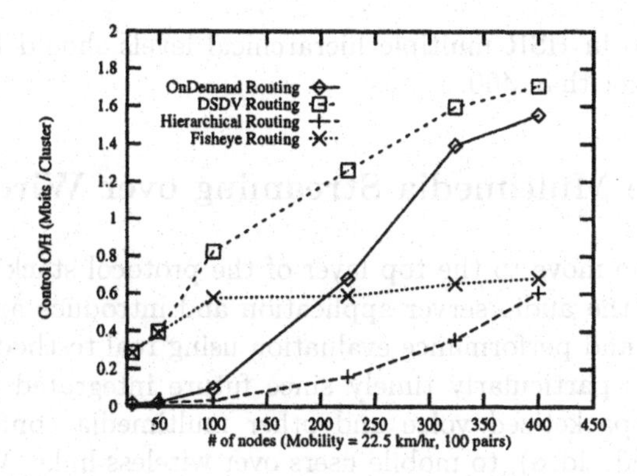

Fig. 20. Control O/H vs. number of nodes

Table 2. Node density (nodes vs. area)

Number of nodes	Simulation area
25	500x500
49	700x700
100	1000x1000
225	1500x1500
324	1800x1800
400	2000x2000

partitions (i.e., IP subnets) in HSR varies depending on network size. Namely, it is 1, 2, 4, 8, 12, 16 for 25, 49, 100, 225, 324 and 400 nodes respectively.

Fig. 20 shows the increase of the control O/H as function of number of nodes. Geographical node density is kept the same for all runs as shown in Table 2. When the network size is small (say less than 50 nodes), 2-level fisheye scoping does not significantly reduce O/H with respect to DSDV. However, as network size grows larger, the fisheye technique aggressively reduces the O/H. In fact, O/H is almost independent of size beyond 100 nodes. For larger network sizes, further improvements in performance may be achieved by using more than 2 levels of scoping. On-demand routing performs well in a small network since most routes are reusable (we assume up to 100 active node pairs). For large networks, however, on-demand routing generates considerable O/H. This is because the chance of finding precomputed (and thus reusable) routes decreases. Note that the control O/H of on-demand routing increases linearly as the number of nodes increases. For HSR as the network size grows, the control O/H also increases due to the growth in number of clusters and logical subnets. However the growth slope is less than in DSDV because the routing information exchange is done in a hierarchical fashion (i.e., only cluster heads exchange the routing information).

As for FSR, also in HSR multiple hierarchical levels should be considered for network size larger than 400.

6 Adaptive Multimedia Streaming over Wireless Links

In this section we move to the top layer of the protocol stack - the application layer. We study the audio server application and introduce an adaptive audio-on-demand tool and performance evaluation using real testbed experiments.

This study is particularly timely since future integrated networks are expected to offer packetized voice and other multimedia conferencing services (data, images and video), to mobile users over wireless links. Wireless networks cannot easily support multimedia applications due to the media high loss probability, burstiness, persistence of errors and delay jitter suffered by packets.

This is not only attributed to traditional variability in queuing delays due to connection multiplexing. The air interface is a channel extremely susceptible to noise, fading and interference effects and presents lower bandwidth limits than those seen on wired links. The broadcast nature of the wireless link, transient service outage, high error rates, burst error patterns demands LLC/MAC layer protocol retransmissions in order to provide the required services to the upper layers. Node mobility imposes extra requirements on routing introducing handovers, motion-induced effects, and heavy routing overhead. At the transport layer lower level services must be utilized, under minimum protocol overhead, in order to provide end-to-end QoS guarantees. Applying congestion and flow control is inherently more difficult when wireless links are used not only at end nodes, as in a multi-hop network. In this environment, the transport will need to be presented with a compressed form of the multimedia data, and thus will need to present to the upper layers a reliable service. Furthermore, seamless interaction with wired peers is generally required. Widely accepted transport protocols have been written for wired networks and will need middleware to achieve acceptable performance.

Through this saga, the level of quality of service delivered to the application cannot be expected to be stable. To cope with this highly variable behavior associated with the wireless environment, it is widely recognized that protocols across layers should be able to adapt to a wide variety of situations.

In supporting multimedia traffic at the application level, even though it is recognized that the details of the infrastructure support should be hidden from the user applications, the application needs to negotiate resource allocation with the network and adapt to the changing network condition by using adaptive compression. The QoS information fed back to the multimedia layer permits dynamic renegotiations of parameters so as to adjust to these changes.

In this paragraph, after describing metrics and techniques that must be incorporated for enabling this kind of QoS adaptation, we proceed by describing and showing performance evaluation experiments on adaptive multimedia run on a real all-wireless (multi-hop test-bed). Such test-beds are very useful for performance evaluations. Even though large-scale experiments become very costly, smaller scale experiments are of great value since they are performed at the natural full complexity. Furthermore, the results can be used to validate and direct performance evaluation based on simulation.

These simple experiments, presented in the case study, reveal the potential in perceptual improvement of a wireless multimedia conference, by applying application level monitoring and adapting to QoS techniques. The perceptual improvement is sketched in loss rate improvements combined with a graphical visualization of the possible thrashing from frequent layer switching.

6.1 How to Be Adaptive

As mentioned in the opening paragraph the application needs to negotiate resource allocation with the network and adapt to the changing network condition by using adaptive compression. The QoS information fed back to the multimedia layer permits dynamic renegotiations of parameters so as to adjust to these changes. This may be hidden from user applications by use of agent software or any other middle-ware e.g. in the form of an API.

Adapting to layers starts at the application's flexibility to carry on its useful task (i.e. meaningful communication in a multimedia conference) in different grades of service. The network is assumed able to support the application's highest demand on light load.

In a multimedia application one or more encoders may define the different grades of service, for example. CODEC technology has seen rapid development in recent years mainly due to the demand to deliver multimedia content to the personal computer through some storage media or a wired network. Current well-defined and highly used CODECs are defined in MPEG-3 (4 to be published December 1999) standards, for entertainment purposes since the compromise in quality for compression is not very obvious, and H.2/3XX for video/telephony. Future wireless mobile communication systems and networks present a different substrate under which such layering schemes may be redesigned. Important differences are: the invalidation of the assumption of a more or less reliable substrate, a much lower acceptable bit rate, and finally a stronger demand for multi-resolution (the ability to reproduce lower bit-rate streams from the original stream on the fly) and aggressive and finer layering. The latter will enable the flexibility to request different QoS support from the network, based on a compromise between the user perception and a reasonable future expectation from the network. If the application (or middleware) is to be able to switch between layers at any time, extra information need to be maintained, either encapsulated in an RTP-type packet or in a separate packet (even stream) indexed or synchronized to the data packet (or stream). This is because the application needs to be aware of the received stream characteristics. This required extra information introduces overhead which may prove damaging to performance. By combining the ability to switch between different streams (using one or more encoders) of different QoS requirements with monitoring and quantifying the underlying network conditions an adaptation strategy can be developed that will incorporate experience on how and when to choose layers.

Quantifying and Monitoring the Network Conditions. Quantification of the network conditions is performed by defining metrics that can adequately describe the QoS provided by the network. The decision of switching will be based solely on their value.

Multimedia applications are sensitive to lost packets, delayed packets and jitter. Fortunately, in multimedia streaming it is easy to measure the loss rate, since the expected bit rate is known a priori. Jitter can be sampled by keeping information to perform an RTP-like measurement. Monitoring of these conditions is done along the path from the sender to the receiver, usually where the ability of changing layers is desired (at end-points for application level adaptation). The sampling is done periodically, and the quantification corresponds to a past interval. This past interval will be used to predict the near future. In essence, the underlying assumption here is usually that, in the near future, the QoS to be provided by the network can be anticipated to be similar to the QoS provided in the near past. This implies that older QoS information must be given decreasing importance. Due to the high variability of the wireless link this implies in turn that the QoS information is very time-sensitive. Furthermore, since QoS information is generally quantified in a different node than the QoS user node, feedback delays imply different importance too. Another realization related to the feedback path delay is that, sadly, when we need the QoS information the most -that is when the network conditions are highly adverse- is exactly when they are usually received late, errored or lost altogether (near symmetric links assumed.)

Let us now look at evaluating performance gain by using a simple adaptation strategy built from scratch on a audio on demand server/client application.

6.2 Experiments on an Audio on Demand System Using Application Layer Adaptation over Ad-hoc, Multi-hop Networks

An adaptation scheme for audio applications based on a QoS Notification Programming Model is described, in which senders use QoS feedback information from the receivers to dynamically select audio encoding parameters most appropriate to the reported network conditions. The selection of audio encoding is based on the principle of media scaling. By this principle, the bit-rate (and, hence, the quality) of an audio or a video stream is varied to be consistent with the available bandwidth. The effectiveness of this tool in enhancing end user perception is based on using QoS adaptation strategies and aggressive speech layering ideas like captioning.

In order to improve end user perception, even at the face of extremely adverse network conditions (as reported in [3], the perceived audio quality drops sharply as packet loss reaches 20%), an ultimate encoding layer is introduced. A text transcription is associated with the speech stream, either real-time using a speech recognition engine or from a caption file. The text traverses the path easier (smaller packets, very low bit rate) and more reliably (e.g. using redundancy). The data can be displayed at the receiver side in a caption window or, more importantly, when the QoS information suggests switching to this bottom layer, the speech can be reproduced using the transcription with a text-to-speech synthesizer. In this way the speech stream can still be comprehensible at the receiver. Switching into this layer must be properly indicated, so that it is triggered at the point where the layer above it, would not produce comprehensible speech. Switching to this "ultimate" layer is a local decision and is inherently different with decisions based on QoS information that have traveled through the reverse path. The QoS is measured at the receiver, exactly where the decision to use the synthesizer or the received audio stream is made.

By running experiments in our wireless multi-hop testbed and reporting the measured QoS provided by the network we show that the communication quality is substantially upgraded even when adverse network conditions persist for a long time. As performance metrics we define the very same metrics monitored and used in the adaptation process.

Application Architecture. The application follows the principles of Application Level Framing (ALF) [7]. This way, the application can take advantage of the QoS parameter information provided by the network to adapt to changes in network's behavior [17].

A network-independent QoS notification programming model is implemented to provide the audio server with the ability to monitor network conditions at the client end and react adequately when congestion occurs. The model is designed so that future evolution of network layer services will not affect its generality and is comprised of three main parts: 1) the network layer API which provides the interface to network services; 2) the Network Monitor module which collects and analyses QoS information from the network, and 3) the Application QoS Notification API which accepts this QoS information from the Network Monitor and processes it. Such separation of the model into three modules allows the application to achieve the desired network independence.

The Network Monitor provides a quality of service abstraction for the application, so that it can always assume that the network provides QoS support, while in reality it may not. Its activity consists of the following three parts: 1) it monitors the multimedia stream from the server to the receiver; 2) it measures QoS parameters of this stream; and 3) it reports this QoS information to the application.

The protocol used to stream data to the receiver is similar to RTP but contains only the necessary functionality. The server generates the sequence number and timestamp information when it sends a packet over to the client. It stores the two numbers in the audio packet's transport header. When the packet arrives to the destination, the receiver extracts these parameters from the header and passes them to the Network Monitor.

The Network Monitor uses the sequence number, the timestamp, and the local time information to determine two QoS parameters of the stream: packet loss rate lr and delay jitter jt. It divides time into measuring periods of duration $t_{mp} = 1$ sec. During each measuring period, it counts the total number of packets received n_{total}, and the number of packets lost nlost. It also records the arrival and send times of the last packet in the measuring period: $t_{LastArrival}$ and $t_{LastSend}$. The arrival time is taken to be the system time when the packet arrives to the receiver, while the send time is extracted from the packet header. At the end of every period k, the Network Monitor computes the two QoS parameters with the following simple calculations:

$$l_r(k) = \frac{n_{lost}(k)}{n_{total}(k)} \quad (6)$$

$$j_t(k) = \frac{[InterArrivalTime(k) - InterSendTime(k)]}{InterSendTime(k)} \quad (7)$$

where

$$InterArrivalTime(k) = t_{LastArrival}(k) - t_{LastArrival}(k-1) \quad (8)$$

$$InterSendTime(k) = t_{LastSend}(k) - t_{LastSend}(k-1) \quad (9)$$

In order to de-couple the jitter measurement from packet losses alternative metrics may be assumed. For example, difference in amount of playing time queued as seen by 2 chosen packets. The two parameters are then reported to the receiver application. A structural representation of the application objects and the data QoS paths can be seen in Fig. 21.

Source Adaptation to QoS Change. Upon receiving a QoS update, the server makes a decision on whether to change the current audio sampling rate or leave it intact. This decision is based upon the following heuristics:

If $lr > LR_{UpperThreshold}$ then
$SamplingRate_{Current} =$
$OneStepDownSamplingRate(SamplingRate_{Current})$
$PacketSize_{Current} =$
$OneStepDownPacketSize(PacketSize_{Current})$
If $lr \geq LR_{LowerThreshold}$ then
$SamplingRate_{Current} =$
$OneStepUpSamplingRate(SamplingRate_{Current})$
$PacketSize_{Current} =$
$OneStepUpPacketSize(PacketSize_{Current})$
If $jt > JT_{UpperThreshold}$ then
$SamplingRate_{Current} =$
$OneStepDownSamplingRate(SamplingRate_{Current})$
If $jt \leq JT_{LowerThreshold}$ then
$SamplingRate_{Current} =$
$OneStepUpSamplingRate(SamplingRate_{Current})$

where lr is the loss rate , jt is the jitter, $LR_{UpperThreshold}$ and $LR_{LowerThreshold}$ and $JT_{UpperThreshold}$ and $JT_{LowerThreshold}$ are threshold values, and $OneStep[Down/Up][SamplingRate/PacketSizze]()$ are functions that take a current parameter and returns the next lower/upper value of the parameter.

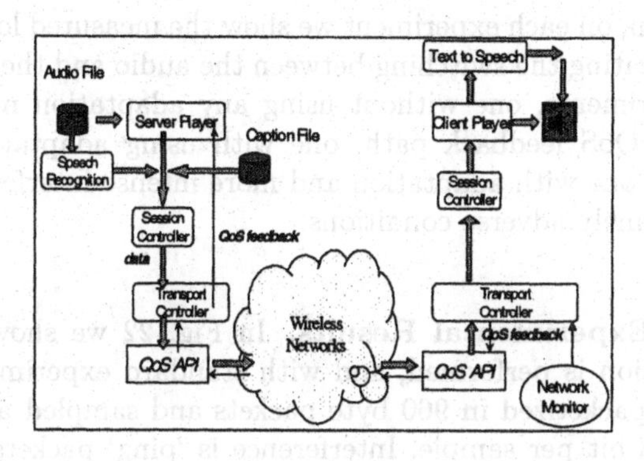

Fig. 21. Application objects and paths

This heuristic is based on the assumption that the primary cause of packet loss is congestion. Hence, when the audio server decreases the audio sampling rate, and therefore, its transmission rate, the packet loss should decrease and the perceived speech quality should increase. Similarly, the audio packet is decreased in size, in order improve packet loss characteristics of the channel.

Testbed. The multi-hop testbed used for the experiments consists of a server, a client, a gateway and a (packet level) interfering station. A Wavelan I [18] is used for wireless networking, which has a closed configuration range of a 100 feet, works at 915Mhz and uses a CSMA/CA MAC protocol.

Performance Evaluation Based on Experimental Results. Our goal is both to show that by adapting to network conditions the application will have on average a higher quality of perception and that by introducing an ultimately compressed layer perception can be improved more even at most adverse network conditions. In the lab we can hear the differences. We may quantify the quality of the audio delivered in the different experiments by using two facts:

1. The loss rate (meaning both actually lost and packets that arrived after the playback point) is a good indication of perception. Theoretically, if the stream could be finely layered, the QoS directed exactly on time switching to

the appropriate layer -assuming that the lower layer is an ultimate compression that will go through even at most adverse conditions- then by adapting we would achieve the highest quality possible, and an insignificant loss rate.
2. However, anomalies from frequent switching in and out of different layers would limit perception. Consequently, we move to the second fact. In order to evaluate perception a visualization of the layer switching is needed.

For this reason, on each experiment we show the measured loss rate over time and a graph indicating the switching between the audio and the text stream. We show three experiments, one without using any adaptation mechanism which would require a QoS feedback path, one with using adaptation in the same environment and one with adaptation and more intense interference to emulate behavior in extremely adverse conditions.

Discussion of Experimental Results. In Fig. 22 we show the loss Rates when no adaptation is performed, and with standard experiment interference. Audio stream is packetized in 960 byte packets and sampled at 22000 samples per second and 8 bit per sample. Interference is 'ping' packets of 40 bytes attempting to fill the channel. In 23 we show loss rates when adapting to QoS, and with standard experiment interference. Audio stream is packetized in 240-960 byte packets and sampled at 8-22Khz . Interference is 'ping' packets of 40 bytes attempting to fill the channel. 24 shows loss rates when adapting to QoS with extremely adverse network conditions. Interference is 'ping' packets of 160 bytes attempting to fill the channel The distance between the stations here is larger and the larger propagation delays result in higher loss rates due to the MAC protocol. In 25, 26 and 27 a visualization of text synthesizer use i.e. switching between audio (even number) and text stream (odd number) with different TTS-thresholds in first, second and third experiment is presented resectively.

In Fig. 22 we can observe the loss rates measured by the application QoS monitor at the receiver side. The MAC (CSMA/CA) layer prevents any node from constantly transmitting, resulting in a highly variable and oscillatory loss rate for our real-time application as expected from a highly utilized wireless channel. In Fig. 23 it is clear that by employing adaptation the loss rates are reduced (averaging 13% as opposed to 40%) and a more stable channel is seen by the application (notice also the difference in scale). In Fig. 24 we show the loss rate the application suffers with very intense (packet level) interference. The audio stream is corrupted at these high loss rates averaging 77%. In this environment the ultimately compressed layer takes over. With almost cut-off loss rates of 99%, as long one packet goes through in the 2-second predefined time window and the transcription is delivered, with the redundant scheme used, and the conference is kept alive.

The remaining graphs (Figs. 24, 25, 26 contain the same information. They show clearer the switching between the audio and the text stream for different threshold values. A 'high; on each line indicates that the speech is reproduced from the TTS synthesizer. Different lines are shown corresponding to different

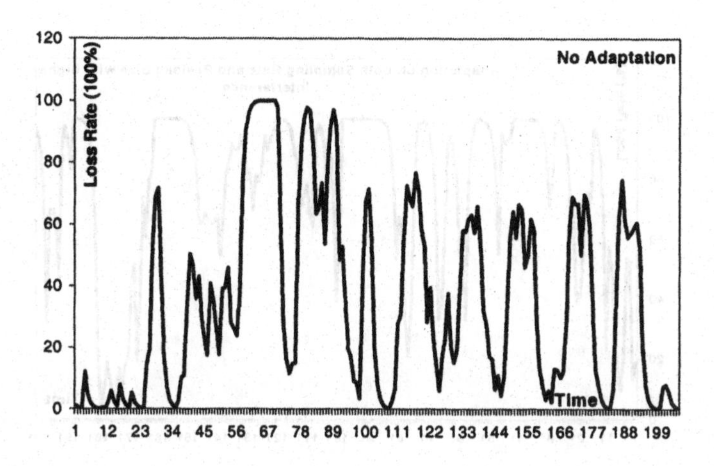

Fig. 22. Experiment 1 loss rates.

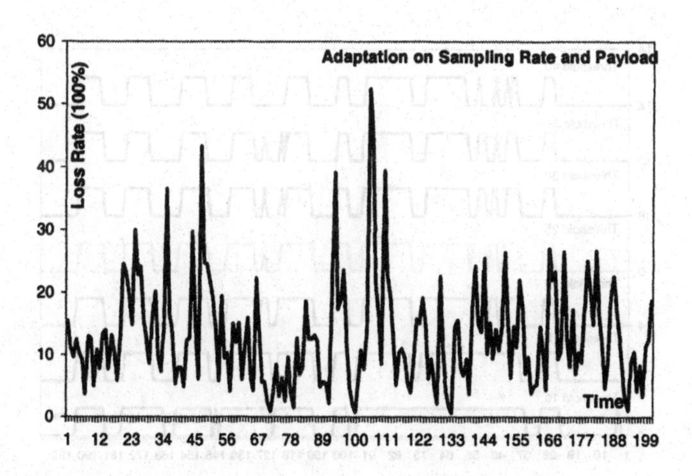

Fig. 23. Expreriment 2 loss rates.

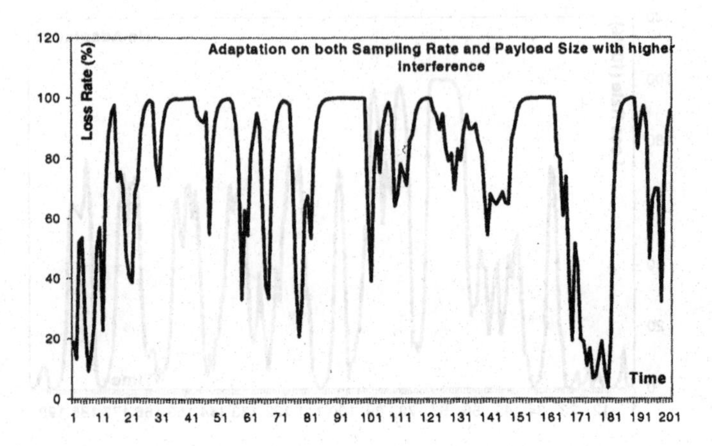

Fig. 24. Experiment 3 loss rates

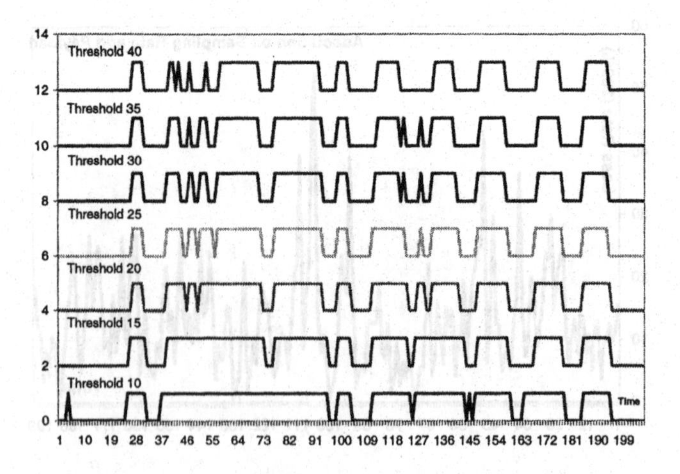

Fig. 25. Visualization of TTS use in experiment 1

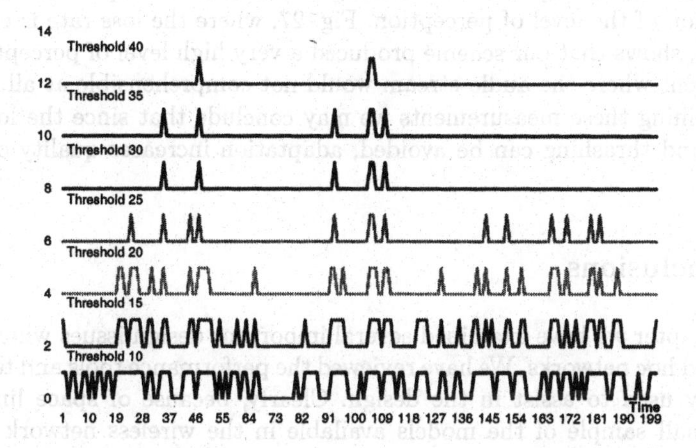

Fig. 26. Visualization of TTS use in experiment 2

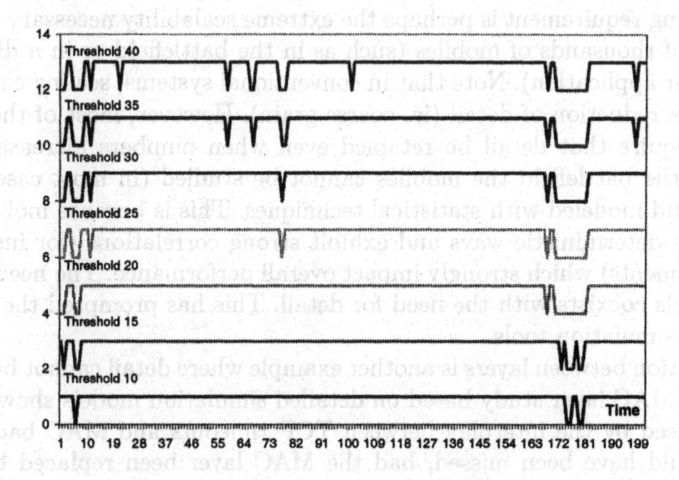

Fig. 27. Visualization of TTS use in experiment 3

thresholds from 10% (lower line) to 40%. In Fig. 26 we can observe the behavior of multiplexing the layers when the loss is oscillatory (experiment with no adaptation). In Fig. 26 the switching is much more frequent resulting in a degradation of the level of perception. Fig. 27, where the loss rate is constantly very high, shows that our scheme produced a very high level of perception in an environment where the audio stream would not comprehensible at all.

Combining these measurements we may conclude that since the loss rate is reduced and thrashing can be avoided, adaptation increases quality of perception.

7 Conclusions

In this chapter we have examined several important design issues which arise in wireless ad hoc networks. We have reviewed the performance tools and techniques commonly used to assist in the design. Clearly, because of space limitations, only a small sample of the models available in the wireless network repertoir was demonstrated. The bias here has been in favor of network type models and protocols, from link to application layer. We have not addressed a very large body of (highly specialized) models available for the study of radio propagation effects; likewise, the pluritude of models and tools which have been developed to evaluate the efficiency of modulation and coding techniques in the presence of different types of interference.

The examples reported in his chapter, albeit limited, are more than sufficient, however, to expose the complexity of ad hoc wireless systems. There are several dimensions of complexity which require unique modeling features. The most striking requirement is perhaps the extreme scalability necessary to handle hundreds of thousands of mobiles (such as in the battlefield or in a distributed microsensor application). Note that in conventional systems, scaling can be handled with a reduction of detail (ie, coarse grain). However, most of the wireless systems require that detail be retained even when numbers increase. For example, in the battlefield the mobiles cannot be studied (in most cases) as gas particles and modeled with statistical techniques. This is because mobiles interact in very deterministic ways and exhibit strong correlations (for instance, in their movements) which strongly impact overall performance. The need for large scale models coexists with the need for detail. This has prompted the adoption of parallel simulation tools.

Interaction between layers is another example where detail cannot be ignored. The TCP/MAC layer study based on detailed simulation models shows capture effects caused by the interplay between TCP timeouts and MAC backoff. The effects would have been missed, had the MAC layer been replaced by an abstracted, oversimplified model (as it had been the case in previous wireless TCP studies).

Efficiency of the simulation is another key requirement. Network analysts are relying more and more on simulation graphic interfaces to debug their code. The faster the processing, the faster the debugging. In other cases, simulation is embedded in the network management system, and run in real time in order to answer what-if questions.

The integration of real and simulated components in a hybrid testbed is another emerging modeling technique which can enhance the realism of experiments. With reference to the audio server application, we have used hybrid simulation to study the impact of different wireless network architectures and sytems configurations on particular audio encoding schemes. In our case, a real audio stream was injected in a GloMoSim platform. The output was then converted again to audio, to perceptually evaluate output speech quality.

In this chapter we have introduced and demonstrated only one simulation platform - GloMoSim. Yet many exist (eg, OPNET, VINT etc) and are routinely used to evaluate wireless architectures. One critical issue is the consistency of different platforms (eg, performance measures, protocol implementations, propagation model assumptions) and the ability to compare results obtained from different platforms. To illustrate the importance of such consistency, standard committees place considerable weight on performance comparisons in deciding which standard protocol, say, to adopt. There should be a way to "validate" the assumptions/methodology/ protocol implementations/performance measures of a platform. Yet, no such methodology exists today.

In summary, there have been important recent advances in the state of the art in performance evaluation (in particular, simulation) of ad hoc wireless systems. There are still directions which require further research, such as efficient hybrid modeling/simulation, validation/certification of different modeling platforms and portability of simulation code into an operational system and viceversa.

References

1. R. Bagrodia and R. Meyer et al. Parsec: A parallel simulation enviroment for complex system. Technical report, UCLA, 1997.
2. V. Bharghavan, A. Demers, S. Shenker, and L. Zhang. Macaw: A media access protocol for wireless lan's. In *SIGCOMM '94*, pages 212–225. ACM, 1994.
3. J.-C. Bolot and A. Vega-Garcia. The case for fec-based error control for packet audio in the internet. *ACM Multimedia Systems*, 1998.
4. Ching-Chuan Chiang, Hsiao-Kuang Wu, Winston Liu, and Mario Gerla. Routing in clustered multihop, mobile wireless networks with fading channel. In *The IEEE Singapore International Conference on Networks*, pages 197–211, 1997.
5. IEEE Computer Society LAN MAN Standards Committee. Wireless lan medium access control (mac) and physical layer (phy) specifications. IEEE Std 802.11-1997, June 1997.
6. M. Scott Corson and A. Ephremides. A distributed routing algorithm for mobile wireless networks. *ACM/Baltzer Journal of Wireless Networks*, 1(1):61–81, February 1995.
7. D.Clark and D. Tennenhouse. Architectural considerations for a new generation of protocols. *Computer Communication Review*, 20(4):200–208, Sep. 1990.

8. M. Gerla F. Talucci and L. Fratta. Maca-bi (maca by invitation): A receiver oriented access protocol for wireless multihop networks. In *The 8th International Symposium on Personal, Indoor and Moile Radio Communications*, pages 435–439. IEEE, September 1997. Helsinki, Finland.
9. Chane L. Fullmer and J.J. Garcia-Luna-Aceves. Fama-pj: A channel access protocol for wireless lans. In *Mobile Computing and Networking '95*, pages 76–85. ACM, November 1995. Berkley, CA (USA).
10. Chane L. Fullmer and J.J. Garcia-Luna-Aceves. Floor acquisition multiple access (fama) for packet-radio networks. In *SIGCOMM '95*, pages 262–273. ACM, August 1995. Cambridge, MA (USA).
11. Rodrigo Garces and J.J. Garcia-Luna-Aceves. Floor acquisition multiple access with collision resolution. In *Mobile Computing and Networking '96*, pages 187–197. ACM, 1996.
12. J.J. Garcia-Luna-Aceves and Chane L. Fullmer. Floor acquisition multiple access (fama) in single-channel packet-radio networks. Technical report, UCSC, Sept. 1996.
13. M. Gerla and J.T.-C. Tsai. Multicluster, mobile, multimedia radio network. *ACM/Baltzer Journal of Wireless Networks*, 1(3):255–265, 1995.
14. Z. J. Haas. A routing protocol for the reconfigurable wireless networks. In *IEEE International Conference on Universal Personal Communications (ICUPC'97)*, 1997.
15. Z. J. Haas and M. R. Pearlman. *The Zone Routing Protocol (ZRP) for Ad Hoc Networks.* IETF, Internet Draft: draft-zone-routing-protocol-00.txt, November 1997.
16. D. Johnson J. Broch and D. Malts. *The Dynamic Source Routing Protocol for Mobile Ad Hoc Networks.* IETF, Internet Draft: draft-ietf-manet-dsr-00.txt, March 1998.
17. J.Du and et al. An extensible framework for rtp-based multimedia applications. Network and Operating System support for Digial Audio and Video, May 1997.
18. Ad Kamerman and Leo Monteban. Wavelan -ii: A high-performace wireless lan for the unlicensed band. Technical report, Bell Labs Technical Journal, 1997.
19. P. Karn. Maca: a new channel access method for packet radio. In *9th Computer Networking Conference*, pages 134–140. ARRL/CRRL Amateur Radio, 1990.
20. K.K. Kasera and R. Ramanathan. A location management protocol for hierarchically organized multihop mobile wireless networks. In *IEEE International Conference on Universal Personal Communications (ICUPC'97)*, 1997.
21. L. Kleinrock and K. Stevens. Fisheye: A lenslike computer display transformation. Technical report, UCLA, 1971.
22. L. Kleinrock and F. Tobagi. Packet switching in radio channels: Part i - carrier sense multiple-access modes and their throughput-delay characteristic. *IEEE Trans. Comm.*, COM-23 n 12:1400–1416, 1975.
23. Chunhung Richard Lin and Mario Gerla. Maca/pr: An asynchronous multimedia multihop wireless network. In *INFOCOM*. IEEE, 1997.
24. C.R. Lin and M. Gerla. Adaptive clustering for mobile wireless networks. *IEEE JSAC*, 15(7):1265–75, Sept. 1997.
25. Ken Tang Mario Gerla and Rajive Bagrodia. Tcp performance in wireless multihop networks. In *Proceedings of IEEE WMCSA '99*, Feb 1999.
26. S. Murthy and J.J. Garcia-Luna-Aceves. A routing protocol for packet radio networks. In *Proceeding of IEEE Mobicom*, pages 86–95, Nov 1995.
27. S Murthy and J.J. Garcia-Luna-Aceves. An efficient routing protocol for wireless networks. *ACM Mobile Networks and Applications Journal, Special Issue on Routing in Mobile Communication Networks*, 1996.

28. V. Park and S. Corson. *Temporally-Ordered Routing Algorithms (TORA) Version 1 Functional Specification.* IETF, Internet Draft: draft-ietf-manet-tora-spec-00.txt, November 1997.
29. V.D. Park and M.S. Corson. A highly adaptive distributed routing algorithm for mobile wireless networks. In *IEEE Infocom*, 1997.
30. C. Perkins. *Ad Hoc On Demand Distance Vector (AODV) Routing.* IETF, Internet Draft: draft-ietf-manet-aodv-00.txt, November 1997.
31. C.E. Perkins and P. Bhagwat. Highly dynamic destination-sequenced distance-vector routing (dsdv) for mobile computers. In *ACM SIGCOMM*, pages 234–244, 1994.
32. J. L. Sobrinho and A. S. Krishnakumar. Distributed multiple access procedures to provide voice communications over ieee 802.11 wireless networks. In *GLOBECOM '96*, pages 1689–1694. IEEE, 1996.
33. M. Gerla T.-W. Chen. Global state routing: A new routing schemes for ad-hoc wireless networks. In *IEEE ICC'98*, June 1998.
34. F. Talucci and M. Gerla. Maca-bi (maca by invitation): A wireless mac protocol for high speed ad hoc networking. In *6th International Conference on Universal Personal Communications Record*, pages 913–917. IEEE, October 1997. San Diego (CA).
35. C.-K. Toh. Associativity based routing for ad hoc mobile networks. *Wireless Personal Communications Journal, Special Issue on Mobile Networking and Computing Systems*, 4(2):103–139, March 1997.
36. R. Bagrodia X. Zeng and M. Gerla. Glomosim: a library for the parallel simulation of large-scale wireless networks. In *Proceedings of the 12th Workshop on Parallel and Distributed Simulations*, 1998.

Trace-Driven Memory Simulation: A Survey

Richard A. Uhlig[1] and Trevor N. Mudge[2]

[1] Intel Microcomputer Research Lab (MRL), Hillsboro, Oregon
richard.a.uhlig@intel.com

[2] Advanced Computer Architecture Lab (ACAL), Electrical Engineering and Computer Science Department, The University of Michigan, Ann Arbor, Michigan
tnm@eecs.umich.edu

1 Introduction

It is well known that the increasing gap between processor and main-memory speeds is one of the primary bottlenecks to good overall computer-system performance. The traditional solution to this problem is to build small, fast memories (caches) to hold recently-used data and instructions close to the processor for quicker access (Smith [64]). During the past decade, microprocessor clock rates have increased at a rate of 40% per year, while main-memory (DRAM) speeds have increased at a rate of only about 11% per year (Upton [76]). This trend has made modern computer systems increasingly dependent on caches. A case in point: disabling the cache of the VAX 11/780, a machine introduced in the late 1970's, would have increased its workload run times by a factor of only 1.6 (Jouppi [32]), while disabling the cache of the HP 9000/735, a more recent machine introduced in the early 1990's, would cause workloads to slow by a factor of 15 (Upton [76]).

It is clear that these trends are making overall system performance highly sensitive to even minor adjustments in cache designs. As a result, memory-system designers are becoming increasingly dependent on methods for evaluating design options before having to commit them to actual implementation. One such method is to write a program that simulates the behavior of a proposed memory-system design, and then to apply a sequence of memory references to the simulation model to mimic the way that a real processor might exercise the design. The sequence of memory references is called an address trace, and the method is called trace-driven memory simulation. Although conceptually simple, a number of factors make trace-driven simulation difficult in practice. Collecting a complete and detailed address trace may be hard, especially if it is to represent a complex workload consisting of multiple processes, the operating system, and dynamically-linked or dynamically-compiled code. Another practical problem is that address traces are typically very large, potentially consuming gigabytes of storage space. Finally, processing a trace to simulate the performance of a hypothetical memory design is a time-consuming task.

During the past ten years, researchers working on these problems have made a number of important advances in trace collection, trace reduction and trace processing. This survey documents these developments by defining various criteria

G. Haring et al. (Eds.): Performance Evaluation, LNCS 1769, pp. 97–139, 2000.

for judging and comparing these different components of trace-driven simulation. We consider accuracy, speed, memory usage, flexibility, portability, expense and ease-of-use in an analysis and comparison of over 50 actual implementations of recent trace-driven simulation tools. We discuss which methods are best under which circumstances, and comment on fundamental limitations to trace-driven simulation in general. Finally, we conclude this survey with a description of recent developments in memory-system simulation that may overcome fundamental bottlenecks to strict trace-driven simulation. This chapter is an abridged version of Uhlig and Mudge ([75]).

2 Scope, Related Surveys and Organization

Trace-driven simulation has been used to evaluate memory systems for decades. In his 1982 survey of cache memories, A. J. Smith gives examples of trace-driven memory-system studies that date as far back as 1966 (Smith [64]), and several surveys of trace-driven techniques have been written since then (Holliday [30]; Kaeli [33]; Stunkel et al. [69]; Cmelik and Keppel [15]). Holliday examined the topic for uniprocessor and multiprocessor memory-system design (Holliday [30]) and Stunkel et al. studied trace-driven simulation in the specific context of multiprocessor design (Stunkel et al. [69]). Pierce et al. surveyed one aspect of trace collection based on static code annotation techniques (Pierce et al. [54]), while Cmelik and Keppel surveyed trace collectors based on code emulation (Cmelik and Keppel [15]).

This survey distinguishes itself from the others in that it is more up-to-date, and in its scope. Numerous developments in trace-driven simulation during the past five years warrant a new survey of tools and methods that have not been reviewed before. This survey is broader in scope than the surveys by Pierce et al. and Cmelik et al., in that it considers all aspects of trace-driven simulation, from trace collection and trace reduction to trace processing. On the other hand, its scope is more limited, yet more detailed than the surveys by Holliday and Stunkel et al. in that it focuses mainly on uniprocessor memory simulation, but pays greater attention to tools capable of tracing multi-process workloads and the operating system.

We do not examine analytical methods for predicting memory-system performance. A good starting point for study of these techniques is (Agarwal et al. [2]). Although trace-driven methods have been successfully applied to other domains of computer architecture, such as the simulation of super-scalar processor architecture, or the design of I/O systems, this survey will focus on trace-driven memory-system simulation only. Memory performance can also be measured with hardware-based counters that keep track of events such as cache misses in a running system. While useful for determining the memory performance of an existing machine, such counters are unable to predict the performance of hypothetical memory designs. We do not study them here, but several examples can be found in Emer and Clark ([21]), Clark et al. ([13]), IBM ([31]), Nagle et al. ([50]), Digital ([19]), and Cvetanovic and Bhandarkar ([16]).

We begin this survey by establishing several general criteria for evaluating trace-driven simulation tools in Section 3. Sections 4 through 7 examine the different stages of trace-driven simulation, and Section 8 studies some new methods for memory simulation that extend beyond the traditional trace-driven paradigm. Section 9 concludes the survey with a summary.

This survey makes frequent use of tables to summarize the key features, performance characteristics, and original references for each of the trace-driven simulation tools discussed in main body of text. This organization enables a reader to approach the material at several levels of detail. We suggest a reading of Section 3, the opening paragraphs of Sections 4 through 7, and an examination of each of the accompanying tables to obtain a good cursory introduction to the field. A reader desiring further information can then read the remainder of the body text in greater detail. The original papers themselves, of course, offer the greatest level of detail, and their references can be found quickly in the summary tables and the bibliography at the end of the survey.

3 General Evaluation Criteria and Metrics

A trace-driven memory simulation is sometimes viewed as consisting of three main stages: trace collection, trace reduction and trace processing (Holliday [30]) (see Fig. 1). Trace collection is the process of determining the exact sequence of memory references made by some workload of interest. Because the resulting address traces can be very large, trace-reduction techniques are often used to remove unneeded or redundant data from a full address trace. In the final stage, trace processing, the trace is fed to a program that simulates the behavior of a hypothetical memory system. To form a complete trace-driven simulation system, the individual stages of trace-driven simulation must be connected through trace interfaces so that trace data can flow from one stage to the next.

In Sections 3–7, we shall examine each of the above components in greater detail, but it is helpful to define, at the outset, some general criteria for judging and comparing different trace-driven simulation tools.[1] Perhaps the most important criterion is accuracy, which we loosely define in terms of percent error in some performance metric such as miss ratio or misses per instruction:

$$\text{Error} = \left[\frac{(\text{True Performance} - \text{Simulated Performance})}{(\text{True Performance})}\right] \cdot 100\% \ . \qquad (1)$$

Error is often difficult to determine in practice because true performance may not be known, or because it may vary from run to run of a given workload. Furthermore, accuracy is affected by many factors, such as the "representativeness" of the chosen workload, the quality of the collected address trace, the way that the trace is reduced, and the level of detail modeled by the trace-driven memory simulator. Although it may be difficult to determine from which of these factors

[1] Some evaluation criteria apply to only a specific stage of trace-driven simulation, so we shall cover them in future sections where the details are more relevant.

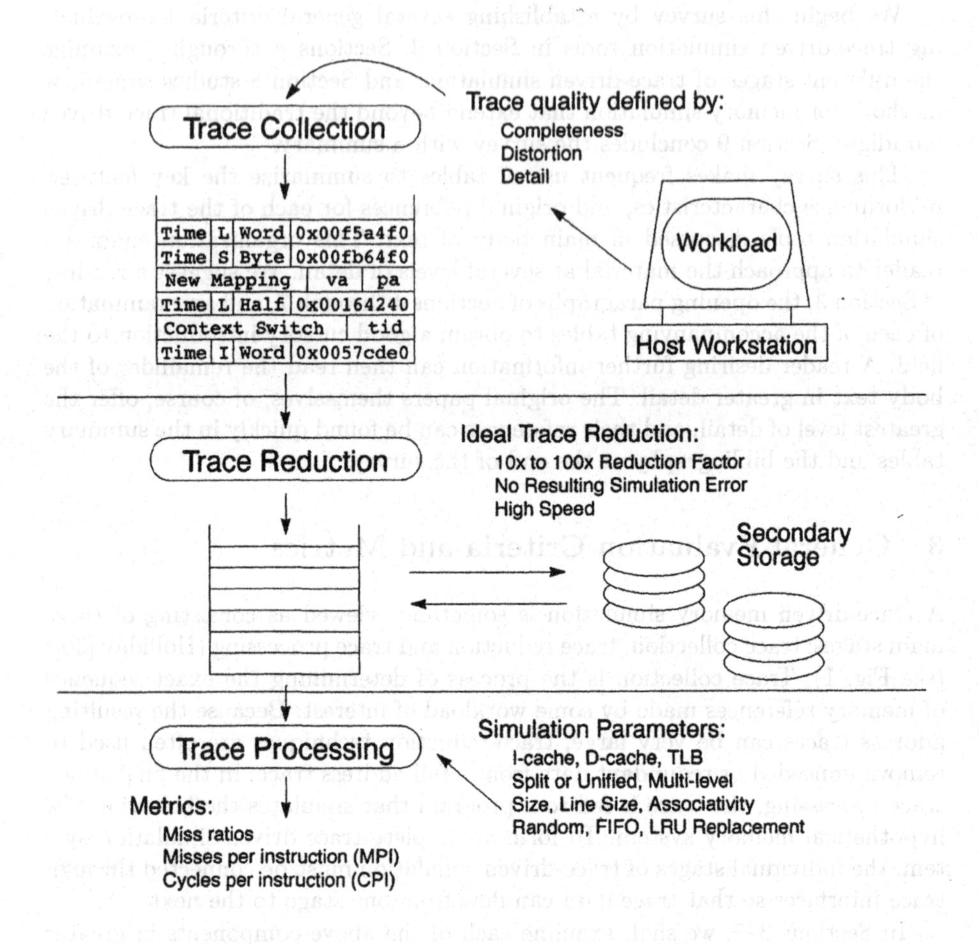

Fig. 1. The three stages of trace-driven simulation

some component of error originates, it is important to understand the nature of these errors, and how they can be minimized:

Ideally, a workload suite should be selected in a way that represents the environment in which the memory system is expected to perform. The memory system might be intended for commercial applications (database, spreadsheet, etc.), for engineering applications (computer-aided design, circuit simulation, etc.), for embedded applications (e.g., a postscript interpreter in a laser printer), or for some other purpose. Studies have shown that the differences between these types of workloads are substantial (Gee et al. [24]; Maynard et al. [47]; Uhlig et al. [74]; Romer et al. [59]), so good workload selection is crucial – even the most perfect trace acquisition and simulation tools cannot overcome the bias in predicted performance that results if this stage of the process is not executed with care.

We shall explore, in the next sectio, some reasons why a collected trace might differ from the actual stream of memory references generated by a workload, but it is easy to see at this point in the discussion why differences are important. Many trace-collection tools exclude, for example, memory references made by the operating system. Excluding the OS, which may constitute a large fraction of a workload's activity, is bound to affect simulation results (Chen and Bershad [11]; Nagle et al. [51]; Nagle et al. [52]).

When we look at trace reduction in Section 5 we will see that some methods achieve higher degrees of reduction at the expense of lost trace information. When this happens, we can use a modified form of (1) to measure the effects:

$$\text{Error} = \left[\frac{(\text{Measurements with Full Trace} - \text{Measurements with Reduced Trace})}{(\text{Measurements with Full Trace})}\right] \cdot 100\% \ . \tag{2}$$

Errors can also come from the final, trace-processing stage, where a memory system's behavior is simulated. Such errors arise whenever the simulator fails to model the precise behavior of the design under study, a task that is becoming increasingly difficult as processors move to memory systems that support features such as prefetching and non-blocking caches.

A second criterion by which each of the stages of trace-driven simulation can be evaluated is *speed*. The rate per second at which addresses are collected, reduced or processed is one natural way to measure speed, but this metric makes it difficult to compare trace collectors or processors that have been implemented on different hardware platforms. Because the number of addresses processed per second by a particular trace processor is a function of the speed of the host hardware on which it is implemented, it is not meaningful to compare this rate against a different trace-processing method implemented on older or slower host hardware. To overcome this difficulty, we report all speeds in terms of *slowdown* relative to the host hardware from which traces are collected from or processed on. Depending on the context, we compute slowdowns in a variety of ways:

$$\text{Slowdown} = \frac{\text{Address Collection Rate}}{\text{Host System Address Generation Rate}} \ , \tag{3}$$

$$\text{Slowdown} = \frac{\text{Address Processing Rate}}{\text{Host System Address Generation Rate}} \ , \tag{4}$$

$$\text{Slowdown} = \frac{\text{Total Simulation Time}}{\text{Normal Host System Execution Time}} \ . \tag{5}$$

Because each of these definitions divide by the speed of the host hardware, they enable an approximate comparison of two methods implemented on different hosts.

Some of the trace-driven simulation techniques that we will examine can reduce overall slowdowns. We report their effectiveness in terms of *speedups*, which divide slowdowns to obtain overall slowdowns:

$$\text{Overall Slowdown} = \frac{\text{Slowdown}}{\text{Speedup}} \ . \tag{6}$$

A third general evaluation criterion is the amount of extra memory used by a tool. Depending on the circumstances, memory can refer to secondary storage (disk or tape), as well as primary storage (main memory). As with speed, it is often not meaningful to report memory usage in terms of bytes because different workloads running on different hosts may have substantially different memory requirements to begin with. Therefore, whenever possible, we report memory usage as an expansion factor or *overhead* based on the usual memory required by the workload running on the host machine:

$$\text{Memory Overhead} = \frac{\text{Additional Memory Required}}{\text{Normal Host Memory Required}} . \tag{7}$$

Additional memory can be required at each stage. Some trace-collection methods annotate or emulate workloads, causing them to expand in size, some trace-processors use complex data structures that are memory intensive, and trace interfaces use additional memory to buffer trace data as it passes from stage to stage. The purpose of the second stage, trace reduction, is to reduce these memory requirements. We measure the effectiveness of trace reduction in terms of a memory *reduction factor*:

$$\text{Reduction Factor} = \frac{\text{Full Address Trace Size}}{\text{Reduced Address Trace Size}} . \tag{8}$$

In additional to *accuracy*, *speed* and *memory*, there are other general evaluation criteria that recur throughout this survey. A tool has high *portability* if it is easy to re-implement it on different host hardware. It has *flexibility* if it is able to be used for the simulation of a wide range of memory parameters (cache size, line size, associativity, replacement policy, etc.) and for collecting a broad range of performance metrics (miss ratio, misses per instruction, cycles per instruction, etc.). By *expense* we mean the cost of any hardware or special monitoring equipment required solely for the purposes of conducting simulations. Finally, *ease-of-use* refers to the amount of effort required of the end user to learn and to operate the trace-driven simulator once it has been developed.

4 Trace Collection

To ensure accurate simulations, collected address traces should be as close as possible to the actual stream of memory references made by a workload when running on a real system. Trace quality can be evaluated based on the *completeness* and *detail* in a trace, or on the degree of *distortion* that it contains. A *complete* trace includes all memory references made by each component of the system, including all user-level processes and the operating system kernel. User-level processes include not only applications, but also OS server and daemon processes that provide services such as a file system or network access. Complete traces should also include dynamically-compiled or dynamically-linked code, which is becoming increasingly important in applications such as processor or operating-system emulation (Nagle et al. [52]; Cmelik and Keppel [15]).

An ideal *detailed* trace is one that is annotated with information beyond simple raw addresses. Useful annotations include changes in VM page-table state for translating between physical and virtual addresses, context switch points with identifiers specifying newly-activated processes, and tags that mark each address with a reference type (read, write, execute), size (word, half word, byte) and a timestamp. Traces should be *undistorted* so that they do not include any additional memory references, or references that appear out of order relative to the actual reference stream of the workload had it not been monitored. Common forms of distortion include *trace discontinuities*, which occurs when tracing must stop because a trace buffer is not large enough to continue recording workload memory references, and *time dilation* and *memory dilation*, which occur when the tracing method causes a monitored workload to run slower, or to consume more memory than it normally would.

In addition to the three aspects of trace quality described above, a good trace collector exhibits other characteristics as well. In particular, *portability*, both in moving to other machines of the same type and to machines that are architecturally different is important. Finally, an ideal trace collector should be *fast*, *inexpensive* and *easy to operate*.

Address traces have been extracted at virtually every system level, from the circuit and microcode levels to the compiler and operating-system levels (see Fig. 2). We organize the remainder of this section accordingly, starting at instruction-set emulation. For more details on microcode modification and external hardware probes see Uhlig and Mudge ([75]).

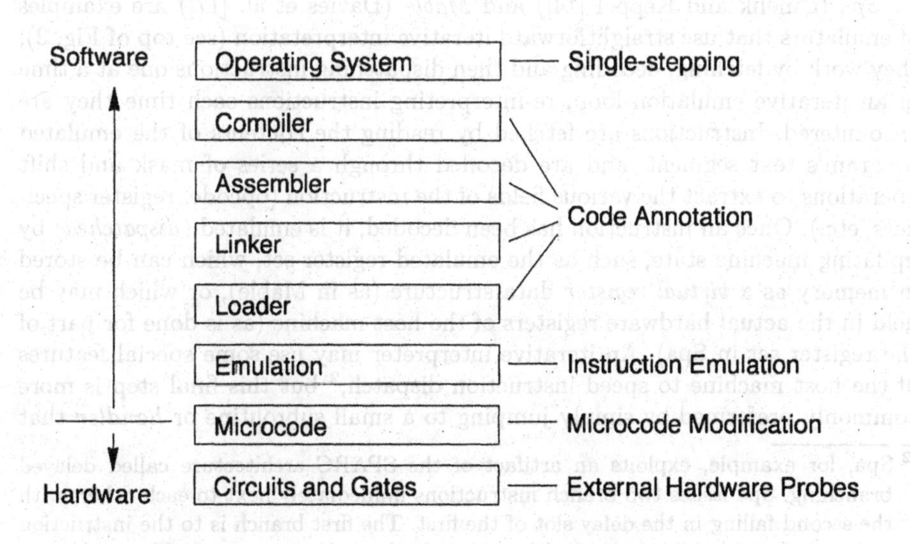

Fig. 2. Levels of system abstraction and trace collection methods

4.1 Instruction-Set Emulation

An instruction-set architecture (ISA) is the collection of instructions that defines the interface between hardware and software for a particular computer system. A microcode engine, as described in the previous section, is an ISA interpreter that is implemented in hardware. It is also possible to interpret an instruction set in software through the use of an *instruction-set emulator.* Emulators typically execute one instruction set (the *target* ISA) in terms of another instruction set (the *host* ISA) and are usually used to enable software development for a machine that has not yet been built, or to ease the transition from an older ISA to a newer one (Sites et al. [62]). As with microcode, an instruction-set emulator can be modified to cause an emulated program to generate address traces as a side-effect of its execution.

Conventional wisdom holds that instruction-set emulation is very inefficient, with slowdowns estimated to be in the range of 1,000 to 10,000 (Agarwal [1]; Wall [78]; Borg et al. [8]; Stunkel et al. [69]; Flanagan et al. [23]). The degree of slowdown is clearly related to the level of emulation detail. For some applications, such as the verification of a processor's logic design, the simulation detail required is very high and the corresponding slowdowns may agree with those cited above. In the context of this review, however, we consider an instruction-set emulator to be sufficiently detailed for the purposes of address-trace collection if it can produce an accessible trace of memory references made by the instructions that it emulates. Given this minimal requirement, there are several recent examples of instruction-set emulators that have achieved slowdowns much lower than 1,000 (see Table 1).

Spa (Cmelik and Keppel [14]) and *Mable* (Davies et al. [17]) are examples of emulators that use straightforward iterative interpretation (see top of Fig. 3); they work by fetching, decoding and then dispatching instructions one at a time in an iterative emulation loop, re-interpreting instructions each time they are encountered. Instructions are fetched by reading the contents of the emulated program's text segment, and are decoded through a series of mask and shift operations to extract the various fields of the instruction (opcode, register specifiers, etc.). Once an instruction has been decoded, it is emulated (*dispatched*) by updating machine state, such as the emulated register set, which can be stored in memory as a *virtual register* data structure (as in Mable), or which may be held in the actual hardware registers of the host machine (as is done for part of the register set in Spa). An iterative interpreter may use some special features of the host machine to speed instruction dispatch,[2] but this final step is more commonly preformed by simply jumping to a small subroutine or *handler* that

[2] Spa, for example, exploits an artifact of the SPARC architecture called delayed branching. Spa issues two branch instructions immediately next to each other, with the second falling in the delay slot of the first. The first branch is to the instruction to be emulated, while the second branch is back to the interpreter. This technique enables Spa to "emulate" the instructions from a program's text segment via direct execution, while at the same time allowing the interpreter loop to maintain control of execution.

Table 1. Instruction-Set Emulators that Support Trace Collection. An instruction-set emulator is a program that directly reads executable images written in one ISA (the *target*) and emulates it using another ISA (the *host*). In general, the target and host ISAs need not be the same, although they may be. We only consider instruction-set emulators that also generate address traces (for a more complete survey of instruction-set emulators in general, see Cmelik and Keppel ([14]) and Cmelik and Keppel ([15]). The leftmost column (*Method*) indicates the general method used by the emulator (see Fig. 3), but it should be noted that not all emulators fit neatly into one category or the other. The table includes additional characteristics that help to define the methods used by these emulators. *Register State*, for example, can be held either by the registers of the host machine, in memory (as part of the emulator's data structures), or in both places via a *hybrid* scheme. When emulators predecode or translate target instructions, some do so *all-at-once*, when the workload begins executing, while others use a *lazy* policy, predecoding or translating when an instruction is first executed. Finally, some emulators attempt to reduce the overhead of the dispatch loop by clustering groups of instructions together by *chaining* or *threading* individual instructions together. The same effect can be achieved by translating entire *blocks* of instructions at a time. *Note:* slowdowns may include additional overhead that is not strictly required for collecting address traces.

Method	Reference	Name	Target(s)	Host(s)	Other Characteristics			Slowdown
					Register State Held In	Predecode/ Translation Policy	Chain, Thread or Block	
Iterative Interpretation	Cmelik & Keppel ([14])	Spa (Spy)	SPARC	SPARC	Host Registers	N/A	No	40–600
	Davies et al. ([17])	Mable	MIPS-I, MIPS-III	MIPS-I	Memory	N/A	No	20–200
Predecode Interpretation	Larus ([37])	SPIM	MIPS-I	SPARC, 680x0, MIPS, x86, HP-PA	Memory	All-at-once	No	25
	Magnusson ([43])	gsim	88100	HP-PA, SPARC	Memory	Lazy	Threading	45–75
	Bedichek ([7])	Talisman	88100	SPARC	Memory	Lazy	Threading	100–150
	Veenstra & Fowler ([77])	MINT	R3000	R3000	Hybrid	All-at-once	Block	20–70
Dynamic Translation	Cmelik and Keppel ([15])	Shade	SPARC-V8, SPARC-V9, MIPS	SPARC-V8	Memory	Lazy	Chaining	9–14

updates machine state as dictated by the instruction's semantics (e.g., updating a register with the results of an add or load operation). The reported slowdowns for iterative emulators such as Spa and Mable range from 20 to about 600, but these figures should be interpreted carefully because larger slowdowns may represent the time required to emulate processor activity that is not strictly required to generate address traces. The range of Mable slowdowns, for example, includes the additional time to simulate the pipeline of a dual-issue superscalar processor.

Some interpreters avoid the cost of repeatedly decoding instructions by saving *predecoded* instructions in a special table or cache (see middle of Fig. 3). A predecoded instruction typically includes a pointer to the handler for the instruction, as well as pointers to the memory locations that represent the registers on which the instruction operates. The register pointers save both decoding time as well as time in the instruction handler, because fewer instructions are required to compute the memory address of a virtual register. An example of such an emulator is *SPIM*, which reads and translates a MIPS-I executable, in its entirety, to an intermediate representation understood by the emulation engine (Larus [37]). After translation, SPIM can lookup and emulate predecoded instructions with a slowdown factor of approximately 25. *Talisman* (Bedichek [7]) and *gsim* (Magnusson [43]) also use a form of instruction predecoding, but instead of decoding all instructions of a workload before it begins running, these emulators predecode instructions lazily, as they are executed for the first time. By caching the results, these emulators can benefit from predecoding without the initial start-up delay exhibited by SPIM. Both Talisman and gsim implement a further optimization, called *code threading*, in which the handler for one instruction directly invokes the handler for the subsequent instruction, without having to pass through the dispatch loop. The slowdowns of Talisman and gsim are higher than those of SPIM, but it should be noted that they are complete system simulators that model caches, memory-management units, as well as I/O devices. *MINT*, a trace generator for shared-memory multiprocessor simulation, also uses a form of predecoded interpretation in which a handlers for sequential blocks of code that do not contain memory references or branches are formed in native host code, which can then be quickly dispatched via a function pointer (Veenstra and Fowler [77]). Veenstra reports slowdowns for MINT in the range of 20–70 for emulation of a single processor, which is comparable to the slowdowns of SPIM.

Shade takes instruction decoding a step further by dynamically compiling target instructions into equivalent sequences of host instructions (Cmelik and Keppel [15]). As each instruction is referenced for the first time, Shade compiles it into an efficient sequence of native instructions that run directly on the host machine (see bottom of Fig. 3). Shade records compiled sequences of native code in a lookup table, which is checked by its core emulation loop each time it dispatches a new instruction. If a compiled translation already exists, it is found through the lookup mechanism and the code sequence need not be recompiled. Like gsim and Talisman, Shade's compile-and-cache method enables it to translate source instructions lazily, only as needed. Shade implements an optimization

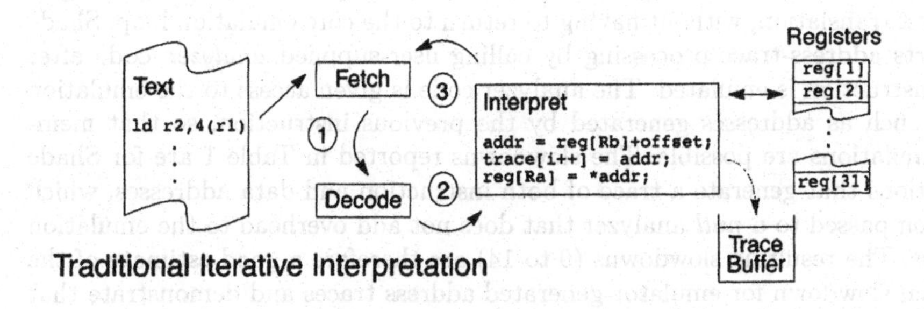

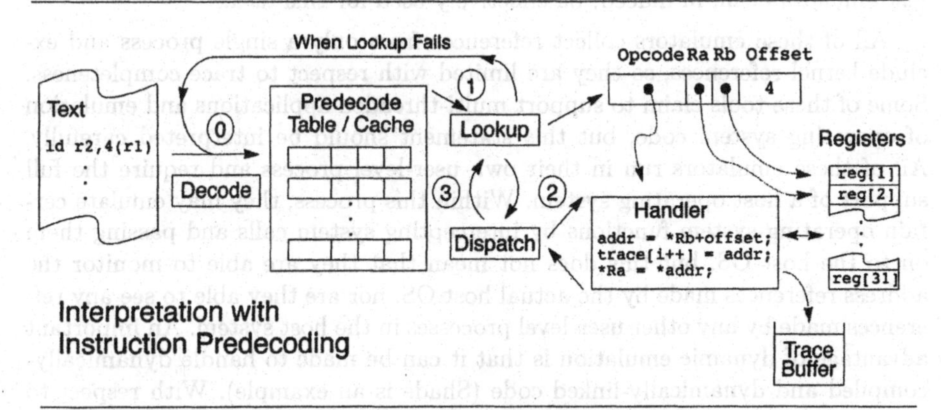

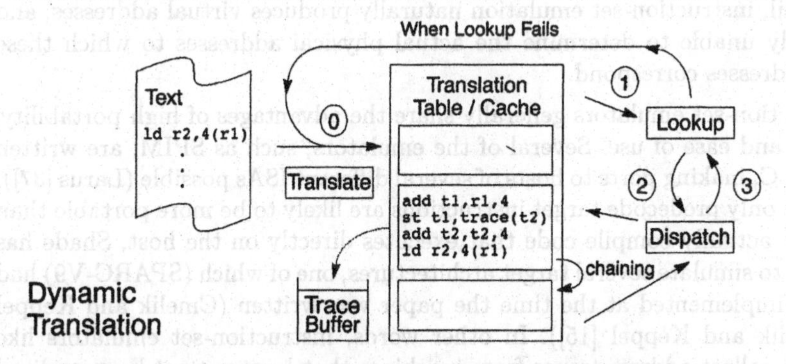

Fig. 3. Some emulation methods. Traditional emulators fetch, decode and interpret each instruction from a workload's text segment in an iterative loop (top figure). To avoid the cost of re-decoding instructions each time they are encountered, some faster emulators pre-decode instructions and store them in a table for rapid lookup and dispatch (middle figure). A further optimization is to translate target instructions from the emulated workload into equivalent sequences of host instructions that can be executed directly (bottom figure). In all three cases, code can be added to emit addresses into a trace buffer as the workload is emulated

similar to code threading, in which two consecutive translations are *chained* together so that the end of one translation can directly invoke the beginning of the next translation, without having to return to the core emulation loop. Shade supports address-trace processing by calling user-supplied *analyzer* code after each instruction is emulated. The analyzer code is given access to the emulation state, such as addresses generated by the previous instruction, so that memory simulations are possible. The slowdowns reported in Table 1 are for Shade emulations that generate a trace of both instruction and data addresses, which are then passed to a *null* analyzer that does not add overhead to the emulation process. The resulting slowdowns (9 to 14) are therefore a good estimate of the minimal slowdown for emulator-generated address traces and demonstrate that fast emulators can, in indeed, be effectively used for this task.

All of these emulators collect references from only a single process and exclude kernel references, so they are limited with respect to trace completeness. Some of these tools claim to support multi-threaded applications and emulation of operating system code, but this statement should be interpreted carefully. All of these emulators run in their own user-level process and require the full support of a host operating system. Within this process, they may emulate certain operating-system functions by intercepting system calls and passing them on to the host OS, but this does not mean that they are able to monitor the address references made by the actual host OS, nor are they able to see any references made by any other user-level processes in the host system. An important advantage of dynamic emulation is that it can be made to handle dynamically-compiled and dynamically-linked code (Shade is an example). With respect to trace detail, instruction-set emulation naturally produces virtual addresses, and is generally unable to determine the actual physical addresses to which these virtual addresses correspond.

Instruction-set emulators generally share the advantages of high portability, flexibility and ease of use. Several of the emulators, such as SPIM, are written entirely in C, making ports to hosts of several different ISAs possible (Larus [37]). Tools that only predecode target instructions are likely to be more portable than those that actually compile code that executes directly on the host. Shade has been used to simulate several target architectures, one of which (SPARC-V9) had yet to be implemented at the time the paper was written (Cmelik and Keppel [14]; Cmelik and Keppel [15]). In other words, instruction-set emulators like Shade can collect address traces from machines that have not yet been realized in hardware. Some of these emulators are very flexible in the sense that the analyzer code can specify the level of trace detail required. Shade analyzers, for example, can specify that only load data addresses in a specific address range should be traced (Cmelik and Keppel [15]). Ease-of-use is enhanced by the ability of these emulators to run directly on executable images created for the target architecture, with no prior preparation or annotation of workloads required.

A major disadvantage of instruction-set emulators is that they build up a large amount of state. Instructions that have been translated to an intermediate representation, or to equivalent host instructions, can use an order of magnitude more memory than equivalent native code (Cmelik and Keppel [15]). Other auxiliary data structures, such as tables that accelerate the lookup of translated instructions, boost memory usage even higher. Actual measurements of memory usage are unavailable for most of the emulators in Table 1, but for Shade they are reported to be in the range of 4 to 40 times the usual memory required by normal, native execution (Cmelik and Keppel [14]; Cmelik and Keppel [15]). Increased memory usage means that these systems must be equipped with additional physical memory to handle large workloads.

4.2 Static Code Annotation

The fastest instruction-set emulators *dynamically* translate instructions in the target ISA to instructions in the host ISA, and optionally annotate the host code to produce address traces. Because these emulators perform translation at run time they gain some additional functionality, such as the ability to trace dynamically-linked or dynamically-compiled code. This additional flexibility comes at some cost, both in overall execution slowdown and in memory usage. For the purposes of trace collection, it is often acceptable to trade some flexibility for increased speed. If the target and host ISAs are the same and if dynamically-changing code is not of interest, then a workload can be annotated *statically*, before run time. With this technique, instructions are inserted around memory operations in a workload to create a new executable file that deposits a stream of memory references into a trace buffer as the workload executes (see Fig. 4). Static code annotation can be performed at the source (assembly) level, the object-module level, or the executable (binary) level (see Fig. 2 and Table 2), with different consequences for both the implementation and the end user (Stunkel et al. [69]; Wall [79]; Pierce and Mudge [53]).

The main advantage of annotating code at the source level is ease of implementation. At this level, the task of relocating the code and data of the annotated program can be handled by the usual assembly and link phases of a compiler, and more detailed information about program structure can be used to optimize code-annotation points. Unfortunately, annotation at this level may render the tool unusable in many situations because the complete source code for a workload of interest is often not available. An early example of code annotation performed at the source level is the *TRAPEDS* system (Stunkel and Fuchs [68]). TRAPEDS adds trace-collecting code and a call to an analyzer routine at the end of each basic block in an assembly source file. The resulting program expands in size by a factor of about 8 to 10, and its execution is slowed by about 20 to 30. Some other tools take greater advantage of the additional information about program structure available at the source level. Both *MPtrace* (Eggers et al. [20]) and *AE* (Larus [36]) use control-flow analysis to annotate programs in a minimal way so that they produce a trace of only significant dynamic events. AE, for example, analyzes a program to find those instructions that contribute to address calculations. It then determines which addresses are easy to reconstruct, and which addresses depend on values that are difficult or impossible to determine through static analysis. Larus gives an example annotation of a simple subroutine that

Table 2. Static code annotators. Code-annotation tools add instructions to a program at the *Source, Object* or *Binary* level to create an *annotated* program executable file that outputs address traces as a side effect of its execution. In the table below, *Slowdown* refers to the time it takes both to run the annotated program and to produce the full address trace, while *Time Dilation* refers only to the time it takes to run the annotated program. Usually these are the same, but some annotated programs generate only a minimal trace of significant events which must be post-processed to reconstruct the full trace. *Memory Dilation* refers to the additional space used by the annotated program relative to an un-annotated program.

Method	Reference	Name	Slow-down	Time Dilation	Memory Dilation	Completeness		Processor	Analyzer Interface
						Multi-process	OS Kernel		
Source	Stunkel & Fuchs ([68])	TRAPEDS	20–30	20–30	8–10	No	No	iPSC/2	Linked into Process
	Eggers et al. ([20])	MPtrace	1,000+	2–3	4–6	No	No	i386	File + Post Process
	Larus ([36])	AE	20–65	2–5	—	No	No	MIPS, SPARC	File + Post Process
	Goldschmidt & Hennessy ([26])	TangoLite	45	45	4	No	No	MIPS	Memory Buffers
Object	Borg et al. ([8])	Epoxie	8–12	8–12	5	Yes	No[a]	Titan	Global Buffer
	Chen ([10])	Epoxie2	15	15	2	Yes	Yes	R3000	Global Buffer
	Srivastava & Eustace ([66]); Eustace & Srivastava ([22])	ATOM	6–13	6–13	—	No	Yes	Alpha	Linked into Process
Binary	Smith ([65])	Pixie	10	10	4–6	No	No	MIPS	File / Pipe
	Stephens et al. ([67])	Goblin	20	20	10	No	No	RS/6000	Linked into Process
	Pierce & Mudge ([53])	IDtrace	12	12	12	No	No	i486	File / Pipe
	Larus ([38])	Qpt	10–60	2-5	3	No	No	MIPS, SPARC	File + Post Process
	Larus ([39])	EEL	—	—	—	No	No	MIPS, SPARC	—

[a] Kernel tracing was implemented, but was not fully debugged.

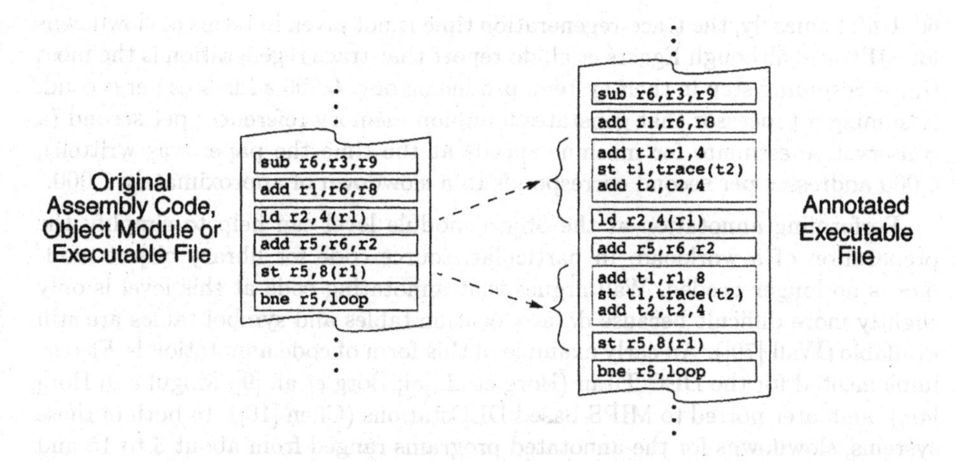

Fig. 4. Static code annotation. In this example, memory references made by a workload are traced by inserting instructions ahead of each load and store operation in the annotated executable file. The inserted code computes the load or store address in register `t1`, saves it in a trace buffer, and then increments the trace buffer index, which is held in register `t2`. Notice that registers `t1` and `t2` are assumed to be not live during this fragment of code. If the code annotator is unable to determine, via static analysis, whether this assumption is true, then it may be forced to temporarily save and restore these registers to memory, thus increasing the size of the annotation code. Annotations can also be inserted at the beginnings of basic blocks to trace instruction-memory references

initializes 100 elements in an array structure starting from a location specified as a parameter to the procedure. The starting address is a value that cannot be known statically, so it is considered to be a *significant event*, and the program is annotated to emit this value to a trace file. The remaining addresses, however, can easily be reconstructed later, given the starting address and a description of the striding pattern through the array, which AE specifies in a program *schema*. Given a trace of significant events, along with the program schema, Larus describes how to construct a post-processing program that reconstructs the full trace. Tracing only significant events reduces both the size and execution time of the annotated program. Programs annotated by MPtrace, for example, are only about 4 to 6 times larger than usual, and exhibit slowdowns of only 2 to 3, not including the time to regenerate the full trace. Eggers et al. argue that it is useful to postpone full-trace reconstruction until after the workload runs because this minimizes trace distortion due to time dilation, a source of error that can be substantial in the case of multi-processor memory simulation. *TangoLite* (Goldschmidt and Hennessy [26]), a successor to *Tango* (Davis et al. [18]), minimizes the effects of time dilation in a different way by determining event order through event-driven simulation. It is important to include the time to regenerate the full address trace when considering the speed of these methods. In the case of AE, trace regeneration increases overall slowdowns to about 20 to

60. Unfortunately, the trace-regeneration time is not given in terms of slowdowns for MPtrace, although Eggers et al. do report that trace regeneration is the most time-consuming step in their system, producing only 6,000 addresses per second. Assuming a processor that generates 6 million memory references per second (a conservative estimate for machine speeds at the time the paper was written), 6,000 addresses per second corresponds to a slowdown of approximately 1,000.

Performing annotation at the object-module level can help to simplify the preparation of a workload. In particular, source code for library object modules is no longer needed. Wall argues that annotating code at this level is only slightly more difficult because data-relocation tables and symbol tables are still available (Wall [79]). An early example of this form of code annotation is *Epoxie*, implemented for the DEC Titan (Borg et al. [8]; Borg et al. [9]; Mogul and Borg [49]), and later ported to MIPS-based DECstations (Chen [10]). In both of these systems, slowdowns for the annotated programs ranged from about 8 to 15 and code expansion ranges from 2 to 5.

Code annotation at the executable level is the most convenient to the end user because it is not necessary to annotate a collection of source and/or object files to produce the final program. Instead, a single command applied to one executable file image generates the desired annotated program. Unfortunately annotation at this level is also the most difficult to implement because executable files are often stripped of symbol-table information. A significant amount of analysis may be required to properly relocate code and data after trace-generating instructions have been added to the program (Pierce and Mudge [53]). Despite these difficulties, there exist several program-annotation tools that operate at the executable level. An early example is *Pixie*, which operates on MIPS executables (MIPS [48]; Smith [65]). The popularity of Pixie has prompted the development of several similar programs that work on other instruction-set architectures. These include *Goblin* (Stephens et al. [67]) and *IDtrace* (Pierce and Mudge [53]), which operate on RS/6000 and i486 binaries, respectively. A second generation of the AE tool, called *Qpt*, can operate on both MIPS and SPARC binaries (Larus [38]). The slowdowns and memory overheads for each of these static annotators compares favorably with the best dynamic emulators discussed in the previous section.

A common problem with many code annotators is that they produce traces with an inflexible level of detail, requiring a user to select the monitoring of either data or instruction references (or both) with an all-or-nothing switch. Many tools are similarly rigid in the mechanism that they use to communicate addresses, typically forcing the trace through a file or pipe interface to another process containing the trace processor. Some more recent tools, such as *ATOM* (Srivastava and Eustace [66]; Eustace and Srivastava [22]) and *EEL* (Larus [39]) overcome these limitations. ATOM offers a flexible interface that enables a user to specify how to annotate each individual instruction, basic block and procedure of an executable file; at each possible annotation point the user can specify the machine state to extract, such as register values or addresses, as well as an analysis routine to process the extracted data. If no annotation is desired at a given location, ATOM does not add it, thus enabling a minimal degree of annotation to be specified for a given application. For I-cache simulation, for example, a simulator writer can specify that only instruction references be annotated, and that a specific I-cache analysis routine be called at these points. Eustace and Srivastava report that addresses for cache simulation can be collected from ATOM-annotated SPEC92 benchmarks with a slowdowns of between 6 and 13 (Eustace and Srivastava [22]). EEL is a similarly-flexible executable editor that is the basis of a new version of qpt as well a high-speed cache simulator named Fast-cache (Lebeck and Wood [41]), which we will discuss in Section 8.

In general, code annotators are not capable of monitoring multi-process[3] workloads or the operating system kernel, but there are some exceptions. Borg and Mogul describe modifications to the Titan operating system, Tunix, that support tracing of multiple workload processes by *Epoxie* (Borg et al. [8]; Borg et al. [9]; Mogul and Borg [49]). Tunix interleaves the traces generated by multiple processes into a global trace buffer that is periodically emptied by a trace-processing program. These researchers also experimented with annotating the Tunix kernel itself, although they do not report any results obtained from these traces (Mogul and Borg [49]). Chen continued this work by porting a version of Epoxie to a MIPS-based DECstation running both Ultrix and Mach 3.0 to produce traces from single-process workloads including the user-level X and BSD servers, and the kernel itself (Chen [10]; Chen [12]). Recent version of ATOM can annotate OSF/1 kernels, but because ATOM analyzer routines are linked into each annotated executable, there is no straightforward way to capture system-wide, multi-process activity. For example, ATOM cannot easily simulate a cache that is shared among several processes and the kernel because the analyzer routines for each executable have no knowledge of the memory references made in other executables.

By definition, static code annotation does not handle code that is dynamically compiled at run time. Dynamically-linked code also poses a problem although some systems, such as Chen's, treat this problem in special cases (he modified the BSD server to cause it to dynamically map a special annotated version of the BSD emulation library into user-level processes that require a BSD API).

With respect to trace detail, these methods naturally produce virtual addresses tagged by access type and size, and some of the systems that can annotate multi-process workloads are also able to tag references with a process identifier (Borg et al. [8]). Associating a true physical address with each virtual address is, however, very difficult because an annotated program is expanded in size and therefore utilizes virtual memory very differently than an unannotated workload would.

[3] Many of the tracing tools discussed on this section were designed to monitor multi-threaded workloads running on a multi-processor memory system (e.g., MPtrace, TRAPEDS, TangoLite). However, the multiple threads in these workloads run in the same protection domain (process), so we consider them to be single-process workloads.

The tools that include multi-process and kernel references are subject to several forms of trace distortion. Trace discontinuities occur when the trace buffer is processed or saved to disk and time-dilation distortion occurs because the annotated programs run 10 to 30 times slower than they normally would. Chen and Borg et al. note that the effects of these distortions on clock-interrupt frequency and the CPU scheduler can be countered by reprogramming the clock-generation chip (Borg et al. [8]; Chen [10]). However, a solution to the problem of apparent I/O device speedup is not discussed. Borg et al. discuss a third form of trace distortion due to annotated-code expansion called *memory dilation*. This effect can lead to increased TLB misses and paging activity. The impact of these effects can be minimized by adding additional memory to the system (to avoid paging), and to emulate, rather than annotate, the TLB miss handlers (to account for increased TLB misses) (Borg et al. [8]; Chen [10]).

These tools share a number of common characteristics. First, they are on average about twice as fast as instruction-set emulation techniques, although some of these tools are outperformed by very efficient emulators, like Shade. Second, all of these tools suffer from the disadvantage that all workload components must be prepared prior to being run. Usually this is not a major concern, but it can be a time-consuming and tedious process if a workload consists of several source or object files. Even for the tools that avoid source or object-file annotation, it can be difficult to locate all of the executables that make up a complex multi-process workload. Portability is generally high for the source-level tools, such as AE, but decreases as code modification is postponed until later stages of the compilation process. Portability is hampered somewhat in the case of Chen's system, where several workload components in the kernel must be annotated by hand in assembly code. Note that static annotation must annotate all the code in a program, whether it actually executes or not. This is not the case with the instruction-set emulators, which only need to translate code that is actually used. This is an important consideration for very large executables, such as X applications, which are often larger than a megabyte, but only touch a fraction of their text segment (Chen [12]).

4.3 Summary of Trace Collection

Table 3 summarizes the general characteristics of each of the trace-collection methods examined in this section. Because of the range of capabilities of tools within each category, and because of the subjective nature of some of the characteristics (e.g., ease-of-use), it is difficult to accurately and fairly summarize all considerations in a single table. It is nevertheless worthwhile to attempt to do so, so that some general conclusions can be drawn. We begin by describing how to interpret the table:

For descriptions of trace quality (*completeness*, *detail* and *distortion*), a *Yes* entry means that most existing implementations of the method naturally provide trace data with the given characteristics. A *Maybe* entry means that the method does not easily provide this form of trace data, but there are nevertheless a few existing tools that overcome these limitations. A *No* entry means that there are

Table 3. Summary of Trace-Collection Methods. This table summarizes the characteristics of five common methods for collecting address traces. For the descriptions of trace quality (*completeness, detail* and *distortions*) a *Maybe* entry means that the method has inherent difficulty providing data with the given characteristics, but there are examples of tools in the given category that overcome these limitations. The ranges given in the *slowdown* row exclude times for excessively bad implementations.

Characteristics		External Probe-Based	Microcode Modification	Instruction-Set Emulation	Static Code Annotation	Single-Step Execution
Completeness	Multi-process Workloads	Yes	Yes	Maybe	Maybe	No
	OS Kernel Code	Yes	Yes	Maybe	Maybe	No
	Dynamically-Compiled Code	Yes	Yes	Yes	No	No
	Dynamically-Linked Code	Yes	Yes	Yes	Maybe	No
Detail	Tags (R / W / X / Size)	Yes	Yes	Yes	Yes	Yes
	Virtual Addresses	Maybe	Yes	Yes	Yes	Yes
	Physical Addresses	Yes	Yes	Emulated	No	Yes
	Process Identifiers	Maybe	Yes	Emulated	Maybe	N/A
	Time Stamps	Yes	No	Maybe	No	No
Distortions	Discontinuities	Yes	Yes	No	Maybe	N/A
	Time Dilation	No	10–20	No	2–30	N/A
	Memory Dilation	No	No	No	4–10	N/A
Speed (Slowdown)		1,000+	10–20	15–70	10–30	100–10,000
Memory (Workload Expansion + Buffers)		External Buffer	Buffer	4–40	10–30 + Buffer	Buffer
Portability		Low	Very Low	High-Medium	Medium	High
Expense		High	Medium	Medium-Low	Medium-Low	Low
Ease-of-Use		Low	High	High	High-Low	High

no existing examples of a tool in the given category that provide trace data of the type in question, usually because the method makes it difficult to do so. To make the comparisons fair, trace-collection slowdowns include any additional overhead required to produce a complete, usable address trace. This may include the time required to unload an external trace buffer (in the case of the probe-based methods), or to regenerate a complete address trace from a significant-events file (in the case of certain code-annotation methods). Slowdowns do not include the time required to process the trace, nor the time to save it to a secondary storage device. We give a range of slowdowns for each method, removing any excessively bad implementations in any category. Additional *Memory* requirements include external trace buffers and memory from the simulator host machine that is consumed either by trace data or by a workload expanded in size due to annotation. Factors that determine the *Expense* of the method include the purchase of special monitoring hardware, or any necessary modifications to the host hardware, such as changes to the motherboard to make CPU pins accessible by external probes, or the purchase of extra physical memory for the host to satisfy the memory requirements of the method. *Portability* is determined both by the ease with which the tool can be moved to other machines of the same type, and to machines that are architecturally different. Finally, *Ease-of-Use* describes the amount of effort required of the end user to operate the tool once it has been developed. These last few characteristics require a somewhat subjective evaluation which we provide with a rough *High*, *Medium*, or *Low* ranking.

Despite these qualifications, it is possible to draw some general conclusions about how the different trace-collection methods compare. A first observation is that high-quality traces are still quite difficult to obtain. Methods that by their nature produce complete, detailed and undistorted traces (e.g., the probe-based or microcode-based techniques) are either very expensive, hard to port, hard to use or outdated. On the other hand, the techniques that are less expensive and easier to use and port (e.g., instruction-set emulation and code annotation) generally have to fight inherent limitations in the quality of traces that they can collect, particularly with respect to completeness (multi-process and kernel references). Second, none of the methods are able to collect complete traces with a slowdown of less than about 10. Finally, when all the factors are considered, no single method for trace collection is a clear winner, although some, such as single-step execution, have clearly dropped from favor. The probe-based and microcode-based methods probably produce the highest quality traces as measured by completeness, detail and distortion, but their applicability could be limited if designers fail to provide certain types of hardware support or greater accessibility in future machines. Code annotation is probably the most popular form of trace collection because of its low cost, relatively high speed, and because of recent developments that enable it to collect multi-process and kernel references. However, advances in instruction-set emulation speeds and the greater flexibility of this method may lead to the increased use of this alternative to static code annotation in the future.

5 Trace Reduction

Once an address trace has been collected, it is input to a trace-processing simulator or stored on disk or tape for processing at a later time. Considering that a modern uniprocessor operating at 100 MHz can easily produce half a gigabyte of address-trace data every second, there has been considerable interest in finding ways to reduce the enormous size of traces to minimize both processing and storage requirements. Fortunately address traces exhibit high spatial and temporal locality, so there are many opportunities for achieving high factors of trace reduction. Several studies have, in fact, shown that the information content of address traces tends to be very low, suggesting that trace compaction or compression techniques could be quite effective (Hammerstrom and Davidson [27]; Becker and Park [5]; Pleszkun [55]).

There are several criteria for evaluating and comparing different methods of trace reduction (see Table 4). The first, of course, is the trace *reduction factor.* The time required to reconstruct or decompress a trace is also important because it directly affects simulation times. Ideally, trace reduction achieves high factors of compression without reducing the accuracy of simulations performed by the reduced traces. It may, however, be acceptable to relax the constraint of exact trace reduction if higher factors of compression can be attained and if the resulting simulation error is low. If results are not exact, Table 4 shows the amount of error and its relationship to the parameters of the memory structure being simulated. Many trace reduction methods make assumptions about the type of memory simulation that will be performed using the reduced trace. Table 4 shows when and how these assumptions imply restrictions on the use of the reduced trace. For more details see Uhlig and Mudge ([75]).

6 Trace Processing

The ultimate objective of trace-driven simulation is, of course, to estimate the performance of a range of memory configurations by simulating their behavior in response to the memory references contained in an input trace. This final stage of trace-driven simulation is often the most time consuming component because a designer is typically interested in hundreds or thousands of different memory configurations in a given design space. As an example, the space of simple caches defined by sizes ranging from 4 K-bytes to 64 K-bytes (in powers of two), line sizes ranging from 1 word to 16 words (in powers of two), and associativities ranging from 1-way to 4-way, contains 100 possible design points. Adding the choice of different replacement policies (LRU, FIFO, Random), different set-indexing methods (virtually- or physically-indexed) and different write policies (write-back, write-through, write-allocate) creates thousands of additional possibilities. These design options are for a single cache, but actual memory systems are typically composed of multiple caches that cooperate and interact in a multi-level hierarchy. Because of these interactions and because different memory components often compete for scarce resources such as chip-die area, the

Table 4. Methods for Address Trace Reduction. The trace reduction factor is the ratio of the sizes of the reduced trace and the full trace. *Decompression Slowdown* is only relevant to methods that reconstruct the full trace before it is processed. Most of these methods pass the reduced trace directly to the trace processor which is able to process this data much faster than the full trace (see *Simulation Speedup*). Simulations with a reduced trace usually result in some simulation error and can be performed only in a restricted design space (see *Exact, Error* and *Restrictions*).

Method	Reference	Reduction Factor	Decompression Slowdown	Simulation Speedup	Exact?	Error	Restrictions
Trace Compression	Samples ([61])	10–100	100–200	1	Yes	N/A	None
Significant-Event Traces	Larus ([36]); Larus ([38])	10–40	20–60	1	Yes	N/A	None
	Eggers et al. ([20])	—	1,000+	1	Yes	N/A	None
Stack Deletion Filter	Smith ([63])	5–100	0	4–50	No	< 4–5%	Fully-associative Memories
Snapshot Filter	Smith ([63])	5–100	0	4–50	No	< 4–5%	Fully-associative Memories
Cache Filter	Puzak ([56])	10–20	0	—	Yes	N/A	Fixed-line-size Caches
	Wang and Baer ([80])	10–20	0	7–15	Yes	N/A	Fixed-line-size Caches
Block Filter	Agarwal and Huffman ([3])	50–100	0	—	No	< 12%	Fixed-line-size Caches
Time Sampling	Laha et al. ([35])	5–20	0	< 5–20	No	< 5%	Small Caches (< 128 K-byte)
	Kessler ([34])	10	0	< 10	No	< 10%	Small Caches (< 1 M-byte)
Set Sampling	Puzak ([56])	5–10	0	< 10	No	< 2%	Set Sample Not General
	Kessler ([34])	10	0	< 10	No	< 10%	Constant-bits Set Sample

different components cannot be considered in isolation. This leads to a further, combinatorial expansion of the design space. Researchers have explored two basic approaches to dealing with this problem: (1) parallel distributed simulations, and (2) multi-configuration simulation algorithms.

The first approach exploits the trivially-parallelizable nature of trace-driven simulations and the abundance of unused computing cycles on networks of workstations; each memory configuration of interest can be simulated completely independently from other configurations, so it is a relatively simple matter to distribute multiple simulation jobs across the under-utilized workstations on a network. In practice, there are some complications with this approach. If, for example, the "owner" of a workstation wants to reclaim the resources of the computer sitting on his desk, it is useful to have a method for suspending or moving a compute-intensive simulation task that has been started on his machine. Another problem is that networks of workstations are notoriously unreliable, so keeping track of which simulation configurations have successfully run to completion can be an unwieldy task. Several software packages for workstation-cluster management, which offer features such as process migration, load balancing, and checkpointing of distributed batch simulation jobs, help to solve these problems. These systems are well-documented elsewhere (see Baker ([4]) for a survey), so we discuss them no further here.

Algorithms that enable the simulation of multiple memory configurations in a single pass of an address trace offer another solution to the compute-intensive task of exploring a large design space. We use several criteria to judge a multi-configuration simulation algorithms in this survey (see Table 5). First, it is desirable that the algorithm be able to vary several simulation *parameters* (cache size, line size, associativity, etc.) at a time and, second, that it be able to produce any of several different *metrics* for performance, such as miss counts, miss ratios, misses per instruction (MPI), write backs and cycles per instruction (CPI). The *overhead* of performing a multi-configuration simulation relative to a single-configuration simulation is also of interest because this value can be used to compute the effective simulation speedup relative to the time that would normally be required by several single-configurations simulations.

6.1 Stack Processing

Mattson et al. were the first to develop trace-driven memory simulation algorithms that are able to consider multiple configurations in a single pass of an address trace (Mattson et al. [46]). In their original paper they introduced a method, called *stack processing*, which determines the number of memory references that hit in any size of fully-associative memory that uses a *stack algorithm* for replacement. Their technique relies on the property of *inclusion*, which is exhibited by certain classes of caches with certain replacement policies. Mattson et al. show, for example, that an n-entry, fully-associative cache that implements an least-recently-used (LRU) replacement policy includes all of the contents of a similar cache with only $(n-1)$ entries.

Table 5. Multi-configuration Memory Simulators. Multi-configuration memory simulators can determine the performance for a range of memory configurations in a single pass of an address trace. Each of these simulators is, however, limited in the way that memory-configuration parameters can be varied (see *Range of Parameters*) or in the performance metrics that they can produce (see *Metrics*). Most multi-configuration algorithms cannot vary total cache size directly. Instead, they vary the number cache sets or associativity, and thus vary total cache size as determined by the equation: $Size = Sets * Assoc * Line$. *Overhead* is the extra time that it takes to perform a multi-configuration simulation relative to a single-configuration simulation (as reported by the authors of each simulator). This overhead is usually an underestimate of the true processing overhead because values reported in papers typically do not include the time to read input traces from a file.

Reference	Name	Range of Parameters					Metrics	Overhead
		Sets	Line	Assoc	Write Policy	Sector		
Mattson et al. ([46])	Stack Processing	Fixed	Fixed	Vary	None	No	Misses, Miss Ratio, MPI	—
Hill ([28])	Forest Simulation	Vary	Fixed	1-way	None	No	Misses, Miss Ratio, MPI	< 5%
Hill ([28])	All-Associativity	Vary	Fixed	Vary	None	No	Misses, Miss Ratio, MPI	< 30%
Thompson and Smith ([72])	—	Fixed	Fixed	Vary	W-back	Yes	Misses, Write Backs	< 100%
Wang and Baer ([80])	—	Vary	Fixed	Vary	W-back	No	Misses, Write Backs	< 65%
Sugumar ([70])	Cheetah	Fixed	Vary	1-way	W-thru	No	Misses, WB Stalls	< 120%

When inclusion holds, a range of different-sized, fully-associative caches can be represented as a stack as shown in Fig. 5. The figure shows that a one-entry cache holds the memory line starting at 0x700A, a two-entry cache holds the lines starting at 0x700A and 0x5000, and so on. Trace addresses are processed, one at a time, by searching the stack. Either the address is found (i.e., *hits*) in the stack at some *stack depth* (Case I), or it is not found (Case II). In the first case, the entry is pulled from the middle of the stack and pushed onto the top to become the most-recently-used entry; other entries are shifted down until the vacant slot in the middle of the stack is filled. In the second case, the missing address is pushed onto the top of the stack and all other entries are shifted down.

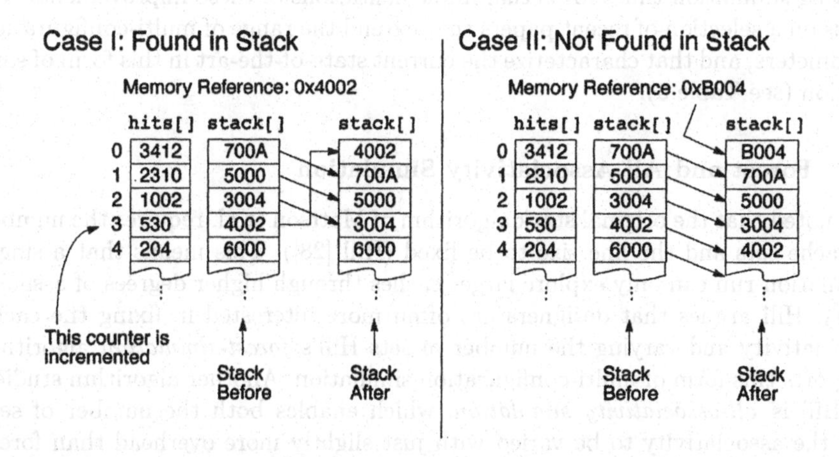

Fig. 5. Data structures for stack simulation. In Case I, the address is found at stack depth 3, so the hits[3] counter is incremented, and the entry at this depth is pulled to the top of the stack. In Case II, the address is not in the stack, so it is pushed onto the top, and no counter is incremented

To record the performance of different cache sizes, the algorithm also maintains an array that counts the number of hits at each stack depth. As a consequence of the inclusion property, the number of hits in a fully-associative cache of size n (hits_n) can be computed from this array by adding all the hit counts up to a stack depth of $(n-1)$ as follows:

$$\text{hits}_n = \sum_{i=0}^{n-1} \text{hits}[i] \ . \tag{9}$$

Further metrics, such the number of misses, the miss ratio, or the MPI in a cache of size n can then be computed as follows:

$$\text{misses}_n = \text{totalReferences} - \text{hits}_n \ , \tag{10}$$

$$\text{missRatio}_n = \text{misses}_n / \text{totalReferences} \ , \tag{11}$$

$$\text{MPI}_n = \text{misses}_n / \text{totalInstructions} . \quad (12)$$

Mattson et al. give other examples of stack replacement algorithms (such as OPT), and also note that some replacement policies, such as FIFO, are not stack algorithms. In their original paper, and in a collection of other follow-on reports (see Sugumar [70] or Thompson and Smith [72] for a more complete description), Mattson et al. described extensions to the basic stack algorithm to handle different numbers of cache sets, lines sizes and associativities. In their early work, Mattson et al. did not report on the efficiency of actual implementations of their multi-configuration simulation algorithms. Many researchers have advanced multi-configuration simulation by proposing various enhancements and by reporting simulation times for actual implementations of these improvements. We focus on a selection of recent papers that extend the range of multi-configuration parameters, and that characterize the current state-of-the-art in this form of simulation (see Table 5).

6.2 Forest and All-Associativity Simulation

Hill noted that the original stack algorithm of Mattson et al. requires the number of cache sets and the line size to be fixed (Hill [28]). This means that a single simulation run can only explore larger caches through higher degrees of associativity. Hill argues that designers are often more interested in fixing the cache associativity and varying the number of sets Hill's *forest-simulation* algorithm supports this form of multi-configuration simulation. Another algorithm studied by Hill is *all-associativity simulation*, which enables both the number of sets and the associativity to be varied with just slightly more overhead than forest simulation. Thompson and Smith developed extensions that count the number of writes to main memory for different-sized caches that implement a write-back write policy (Thompson and Smith [72]). They also studied multi-configuration algorithms for sector or sub-block caches. Wang and Baer combined the work of Mattson et al. ([46]), Hill ([29]) and Thompson and Smith ([72]) to compute both miss ratios and write backs in a range of caches where the both the number of sets and the associativity is varied. In his dissertation, Sugumar developed algorithms for varying line size with direct-mapped caches of a fixed size, and also for computing write-through stalls and write traffic in a cache with a coalescing write buffer (Sugumar [70]).

6.3 Summary of Trace Processing

There are several points to be made about multi-configuration algorithms in general. First, for all of the examples considered, the overhead of simulating multiple configurations in one trace pass is reported to be less than 100%, which means that one multi-configuration simulation of two or more configurations would perform as well as or better than collections of two or more single-configuration simulations. These results should, however, be interpreted with care because these overheads are reported relative to the time to read *and* to process traces.

When the time to read an input trace is high, as is often the case when the trace comes from a file, the overhead of multi-configuration is very low. If, however, the trace input times are relatively low, then the multi-configuration overheads will be much higher. This is the case with the Sugumar's *Cheetah* simulator which appears to have very high overheads relative to Hill's *Tycho* simulator (Hill [28]; Sugumar [70]) (see Table 5). Cheetah's overall simulation times are, however, approximately eight times faster than Tycho because its input processing is more optimized (Sugumar [70]).

A second point is that even though multiple configurations can be simulated with one trace pass, it is often still necessary to re-apply multi-configuration algorithms several times to cover an entire design space. Hill gives an example design space of 24 caches, with a range of sizes, line sizes and associativities where the minimal number of trace passes required by stack simulation is 15 (Hill [28]). For the same example, forest simulation still requires 3 separate passes but can cover only half of the space. Hill argues that all-associativity simulation is the best method in this case because although it also requires 3 separate passes, it can cover the entire design space.

Finally, despite many advances in multi-configuration simulation, there are many types of memory systems and performance metrics that cannot be evaluated in a single trace pass. Most of these algorithms restrict replacement policies to LRU, which is rarely implemented in actual hardware. Similarly, performance metrics that require very careful accounting of clock cycles, such as CPI, generally cannot be computed for a range of configurations in a single simulation pass (e.g., simulating contention for a second-level cache between split primary I- and D-caches requires a careful accounting of exactly when cache misses occur in each cache).

7 Complete Trace-Driven Simulation Systems

Until now, we've examined the three components of trace-driven simulation in isolation. In this section we examine some of the ways that these components can be combined to form a complete simulation system. Fig. 1 suggests a natural composition of the three components in which they communicate through a simple linear interface of streaming addresses that may or may not include some form of buffering between the components. Because of the high data rates required, the selection of mechanisms used to transfer and buffer trace data is crucial to the overall speed of a trace-driven system. A bottleneck anywhere along the path from trace collection to trace processing can increase overall slowdowns. In this section we examine the pros and cons of different interfacing methods and summarize some overall simulation slowdowns as reported in the literature, as well as those measured by our own experiments.

7.1 Trace Interfaces

Because address traces conform to a simple linear-data-stream model, there are several options available for communicating and buffering them (see Fig. 6).

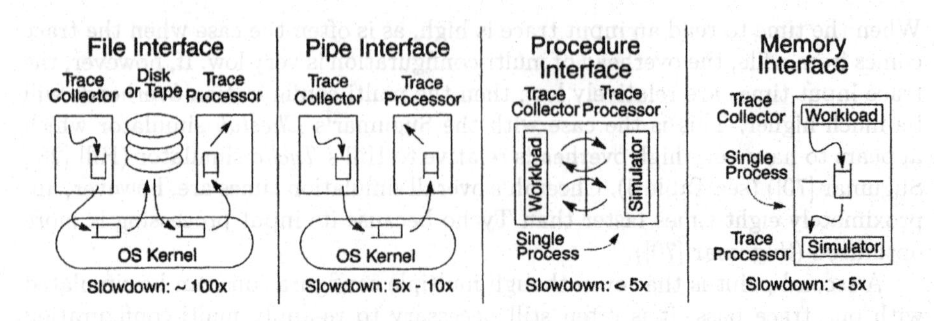

Fig. 6. Trace interfaces. The slowdowns for each of these trace-interface options were estimated by measurements performed on a DECstation 5000/133 with a 33-MHz processor and a SCSI-connected disk running Ultrix

Some simulators rely on mechanisms provided by the host operating system (*files* or *pipes*), while others implement communication on their own using standard procedure calls or regions of memory shared between the trace collector and the trace processor. We shall examine each of the possibilities in turn.

Because they are backed by secondary storage devices, files provide the advantages of deep and non-volatile buffering. These capabilities enable the postponement of trace processing as well as the ability to repeatedly use the same traces to obtain reproducible simulation results. Unfortunately, files suffer some important disadvantages, the first of which is speed. Assuming disk bandwidth of 1 MB/sec and an address-generation rate of 100 MB/sec by the host, a file stored on disk can slow both trace collection and trace processing by a factor of 100 or more. A second disadvantage of files is that they are simply never large enough. Assuming again a host address-generation rate of 100 MB/sec, a one gigabyte hard disk would be filled to capacity in about 10 seconds of real-time execution. This underscores the importance of the trace-reduction methods, described in Section 5, which can improve effective file capacity and bandwidth by one to two orders of magnitude.

Pipes, which establish a one-way channel for the flow of sequential data from one process to another, are another communication abstraction that can sometimes overcome the limitations of files. Pipes use only a moderate amount of memory (on the order of kilobytes) to buffer the data flowing between the two processes, which implies that both a trace collector and trace processor must be running at the same time to prevent buffer overflow. With this approach, which is often called *on-the-fly* simulation, traces are discarded just after they are processed. Because traces must be re-collected for each new simulation run, this technique is most effective when the trace collector is able to produce traces faster than can be read from a file. In the case of instruction-set emulators and code annotators, where slowdowns range from 10 to 70, this requirement is usually met. Communication via pipes is substantially faster than via files, with overheads typically adding 5 to 10 to overall simulation slowdown. Note that when pipes are used, trace-reduction methods are less attractive because they must be re-applied during each simulation run and thus provide little or no advantage over simply processing the full address trace.

Both files and pipes are inter-process communication mechanisms provided by an OS filesystem. As such, their use incurs a certain amount of operating system overhead for copying or mapping data from one address space to another, and from context switching between processes. These overheads can be avoided if a trace collector and trace processor run in the same process and arrange communication and buffering without the assistance of the OS. Several of the instruction-set emulation and code-annotation tools support trace collection and trace processing in the same process address space (see Table 2). In these systems, two different approaches to communicating and buffering trace data are commonly used. The first method is to make a *procedure call* to the trace processor after each memory reference. In this case, trace collection and processing are very tightly coupled and thus no trace buffering is required. A disadvantage is that procedure-call overhead, such as register saving and restoring, must be paid after each memory reference. With the second method, a region of *memory* in a process's address space is reserved to hold trace data. Execution begins in a trace-collecting mode, which continues until the trace buffer fills, and then switches to a trace-processing mode which runs until the trace buffer is again empty. By switching back and forth between these two modes infrequently, this method helps to amortize the cost of procedure calls over many addresses. By bringing communication slowdowns under a factor of 5, both of these methods improve over files and pipes, but it should be noted that placing a simulator in the same process as the monitored workload can complicate the monitoring multi-process workloads.

7.2 Complete Trace-Driven Simulation Slowdowns

Because of the variety of trace-driven simulation techniques and the ways to interconnect them, overall trace-driven simulation slowdowns range widely. Unfortunately, very few papers report overall slowdowns because most tend to focus on just one component or aspect of trace-driven simulation, such as trace collection. Researchers that do assemble complete trace-driven simulation environments tend to report the results, not the speed of their simulations. There are, however, a few exceptions, which we summarize in this section and augment with our own measurements.

Table 6 lists several complete trace-driven simulators composed of many different types of trace-collection and trace-processing tools. As such, these systems are fairly representative of the sort of simulators that can be constructed with state-of-the-art methods. We must be careful when comparing the different slowdowns reported in Table 6 because each corresponds to the simulation of different memory configurations[4] at different levels of detail, running different workloads

[4] For tools that enable multiprocessor memory simulations we report the slowdowns for one processor only to enable more meaningful comparisons with the uniprocessor-only simulators.

and using different instruction-set architectures. The table does, however, enable us to draw some general conclusions about the achievable speed of standard trace-driven simulation systems.

As Table 6 shows, complete simulators rarely exhibit slowdowns of less than about 100, with a few rare exceptions that are able to achieve slowdowns of around 50. The fastest integrated simulator was gsim, with reported slowdowns in the range of 45–75 for a relatively simple workload (an optimized version of the Drystone benchmark). The fastest composed simulator, constructed by driving Pixie traces through a pipe to the Cache2000 (MIPS [48]) trace processor, exhibits slowdowns in the range of about 60–80. The workload in this case is more substantial: an MPEG video decoder. By comparing the slowdowns for Cheetah driven by traces coming from a file (Monster traces) versus coming from a pipe (Pixie traces) we can see the benefits of on-the-fly trace generation and processing; the Pixie + Cheetah combination is more than two times faster than the Monster + Cheetah system, despite the fact that a greater number of configurations (44 versus 8, respectively) is being simulated. Note that the overheads of the two multi-configuration simulators (Tycho and Cheetah) cause their overall slowdowns, relative to single-configuration simulation with Cache2000, to be much higher than the values reported in Section 6. For Cheetah, the overheads are at least 300%, and for Tycho they are an order of magnitude higher. Given the degree of their simulation detail, the integrated simulators Talisman and gsim, which are based on emulation techniques similar to those described in Section 4.1, perform quite well, providing further evidence than instruction-set emulation is a very viable technique for memory-system evaluation.

To better understand the sources of trace-driven slowdown, we measured the speed of the Cache2000 + Pixie combination over a range of instruction- and data-cache sizes. The results, shown in Fig. 7, illustrate that most of the slowdowns are due to trace processing. This observation is supported by reported experiences with other tools as well. Goldschmidt reports that trace processing in TangoLite slows a system by an additional factor 17 relative to a workload that is annotated to produce address traces only (Goldschmidt and Hennessy [25]) (compare the TangoLite entries in Table 2 with those of Table 6). Borg et al. report a similar observation, noting that their Epoxie-driven Panama simulations spend far more time processing address references than collecting them (Borg et al. [8]).

7.3 Summary of Complete Trace-Driven Simulation Systems

As Table 6 and Fig. 7 show, the generation, transfer and processing of trace data for memory-system simulation is extremely challenging – few traditional trace-driven simulators achieve slowdowns much lower than about 50, with the main bottleneck being the time required to process address traces. These results suggest that the biggest gains in overall trace-driven simulation speed are likely to come either from methods that speed-up trace processing, or from techniques that can avoid invoking the trace processor altogether. The latter strategy is the subject of our next section.

Table 6. Slowdowns for Some Complete Trace-Driven Memory Simulation Systems. This table gives some typical slowdowns for a complete trace-driven simulation system. The number of configurations considered in a single pass of the trace are given under the *Trace Processing* column. *Slowdowns* are for a single simulation run, while *Effective Slowdowns* are computed by dividing by the number of configurations (given in parenthesis) simulated during that run. In each row, slowdowns were taken (or computed) directly from the referenced paper. For entries that have an asterisk by the reference, slowdowns do not come from the paper, but were determined by our experiments on a DECstation 5000/240.

Sets	Reference	Trace Collection	Trace Reduction	Trace Processing	Interface Method	Slowdown	Effective Slowdown
Pixie + Cache2000	MIPS ([48])*	Annotation	None	Single Config	Pipe	60–80	60–80
Monster + Cheetah	—	Probe-based	Time Sample	Multi (8)	File	419	52
Pixie + Cheetah	Sugumar ([70])*	Annotation	None	Multi (44)	Pipe	183	4
Pixie + Tycho	Gee et al. ([24])	Annotation	None	Multi (44)	Pipe	6250	142
gsim	Magnusson ([43])	Emulation	None	Single Config	Procedure	45–75	45–75
Talisman	Bedichek ([6], [7])	Emulation	None	Single Config	Procedure	100–150	100–150
TangoLite	Goldschmidt & Hennessy ([25], [26])	Annotation	None	Single Config	Memory	765	765
Epoxie + Panama	Borg et al. ([8])	Annotation	None	Single Config	Memory	100	100

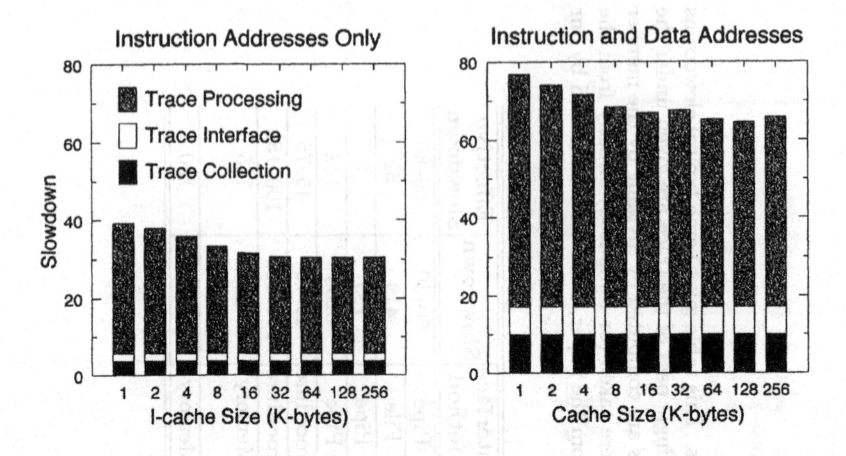

Fig. 7. The components of trace-driven simulation slowdowns. These two plots show the components of trace-driven slowdowns for a complete trace-driven memory simulator constructed by driving the Cache2000 trace processor with Pixie-generated traces via the pipe interface under Ultrix. The left plot shows slowdowns for I-cache simulations, while the right plot shows the slowdowns when simulating both I- and D-caches concurrently

8 Beyond Trace-Driven Simulation

Strict adherence to the trace-driven simulation paradigm is likely to limit further substantial improvements in memory-simulation speeds. The primary bottleneck in trace-driven simulation comes from collecting and processing *each* memory reference made by a workload, whether or not it changes the state of a simulated memory structure. Several researchers, noting this bottleneck to trace-driven simulation, have developed innovative methods for eliminating or reducing the cost of processing memory references (see Table 7). Although the mechanisms that they use differ, each of these tools works by finding special cases where a memory reference has no affect on simulated memory state. A common example is a cache hit which, unlike a cache miss, typically does not require any updates to a cache's contents.

8.1 Software-Based Miss Detection

MemSpy (Martonosi et al. [44]) is a memory simulation and analysis tool built on top of the TangoLite trace collector discussed in Section 4.2. Original implementations of MemSpy, which annotated assembly code to call a simulation routine after each heap or static-data reference, exhibited typical trace-driven slowdowns in the range of 20 to 60 when performing simulations of a 128-KB, direct-mapped data cache. Each call to the MemSpy simulator incurred overheads for saving and restoring registers, simulating the cache, and updating statistics. Martonosi

Table 7. Beyond Traces: Some Recent Fast Memory Simulators. Each of the simulators in this table improve performance by reducing or eliminating the cost of processing memory references that do not cause a change of cache state (e.g., cache hits). The cost of cache or TLB hits (*Cycles per Hit*) and misses (*Cycles per Miss*), as well as their relative numbers determine *Overall Slowdown*. Because cache misses are dependent on the configuration (size, associativity) of the cache or TLB being simulated, overall slowdowns can vary widely, so we report them as ranges of values. *Type of Simulation* and *Completeness* summarize the range of simulations supported. Although some systems (e.g., SimOS and WWT) support simulation of multiprocessor memory systems, we report only their uniprocessor slowdowns here.

Method	References	Name	Cycles per Hit	Cycles per Miss	Overall Slowdown	Miss-Detection Mechanism	Type of Simulation	Completeness: Multi Process	Completeness: OS Kernel
Software-Based	Martonosi et al. ([44],[45])	MemSpy	25	320–510	10–20	Annotation	D-cache	No	No
	Lebeck & Wood ([41])	Fast-Cache	4	55	2–7	Annotation	D-cache	No	No
	Rosenblum et al. ([60]); Witchel & Rosenblum ([81])	SimOS + Embra	10	—	7–21	Emulation	D-cache, I-cache, TLB	Yes	Yes
Hardware-Based Miss Detection	Nagle et al. ([51])	Tapeworm	1–2	100–650	0.5–4.5	TLB Miss	TLB	Yes	Yes
	Reinhardt et al. ([57])	WWT	1–2	2,500[a]	1.4–46[a]	ECC	D-cache	No	No
	Uhlig et al. ([73])	Tapeworm II	1–2	300	0–10	ECC	I-cache, TLB	Yes	Yes
	Lee ([42])	Tapeworm486	1–2	3,600–4,000	0–14	Page Fault	TLB	Yes	Yes
	Talluri & Hill ([71])	Foxtrot	1–2	1,500–4,000	—	TLB Miss	TLB	No	No

[a] Miss costs and slowdowns for WWT are from Lebeck and Wood ([40]).

et al. observed that in the case of a cache hit, memory state need not be updated, and the call to the cache simulator can be avoided altogether. To exploit this fact, Martonosi et al. modified the annotations around each memory reference to test for a cache hit before invoking the full cache simulator. When hit occurs, the MemSpy simulator code is *bypassed* and execution continues to the next instruction. This *hit-bypassing* code requires about 25 instructions, compared with the 320 to 510 cycles for a full call into the MemSpy simulator on a cache miss. Because cache hits are far more common than misses, the long path is infrequently invoked, and the MemSpy slowdowns were effectively reduced to the range of 10 to 20.

Fast-cache (Lebeck and Wood [41]) is another example of a simulator that optimizes for the common case of cache hits. Fast-cache is based on an abstraction called *active memory*, which is a block of memory with a pointer to an associated *handler* routine that is called whenever memory locations in the block are referenced. During a cache simulation, these handlers are changed dynamically to detect when cache misses occur. At the beginning of a simulation, all Fast-cache memory blocks point to a handler for cache misses. As the blocks of memory are accessed for the first time, the miss handler is invoked, it counts the miss and then sets the handler for the missing memory block to point to a NULL routine. Future accesses to these memory blocks (which are now resident in the simulated cache) are processed much more quickly because the NULL routine simply returns to the workload without invoking the complete cache simulator. As the simulated cache begins to fill, the miss handler will eventually begin loading newly-referenced memory blocks into the cache at locations that are already occupied by other memory blocks. These cache conflict misses are modeled by resetting the handler for the displaced memory blocks to point back to the miss handler again so that future references to the displaced block will register a miss. *Fast-cache* implements active memory blocks by using the EEL executable editor, described in Section 4.2, to annotate each workload instruction that makes a memory reference with 9 additional instructions that lookup the state of an active memory block and invoke the appropriate handler. In the case of a NULL handler, only 5 additional instructions are required per memory reference. Depending on the workload, Fast-cache achieves overall slowdowns in the range of about 2 to 7 for the simulation of direct-mapped data caches ranging in size from 16 KB to 1 MB. Like MemSpy, Fast-cache simulates only data caches for single process workloads (i.e, it does not monitor instruction or operating-system references).

Embra (Witchel and Rosenblum [81]) uses dynamic compilation techniques similar to those of Shade (see Section 4.3) to generate code sequences that test for simulated TLB and cache hits before invoking slower handlers for misses in these structures. Embra's overall slowdowns (7–21) compare very favorably with those of MemSpy and Fast-cache, given that it simulates a more complete memory system consisting of TLB, I-cache and D-cache. Embra runs as part of the *SimOS* (Rosenblum et al. [60]) simulation environment, which enables it to fully emulate multi-process workloads as well as operating-system kernel code.

8.2 Hardware-Based Miss Detection

Simulators like Memspy, Fast-cache, and Embra reduce the cost of processing cache hits, but because they are based on code annotation or emulation, they always add a minimal base overhead to the execution of every memory operation. One way around this problem is to use the host hardware to assist in the detection of simulated misses. This can sometimes be accomplished by using certain features of the host hardware, such a memory-management units or error-correcting memory, to constrain access to the host's memory and cause kernel traps to occur whenever a workload makes a memory access that would cause a simulated cache or TLB miss. If implemented properly, this method requires no instructions to be added to a workload, enabling simulated hits to proceed at the full speed of the underlying host hardware. Trap-driven simulations can thus, in principle, achieve near-zero slowdowns when the simulated miss ratio is low.

Tapeworm is an early example of a trap-driven TLB simulator that relies on the fact that all TLB misses in its host machine (a MIPS-based DECstation) are handled by software in the operating-system kernel (Nagle et al. [51]). Tapeworm works by becoming part of the operating system of the host machine that it runs on – the usual software handlers for TLB misses are modified to pass the relevant information about all user and kernel TLB misses directly to the Tapeworm simulator after each miss. Tapeworm then uses this information to maintain its own data structures for simulating other possible TLB configurations, using algorithms similar to the software-based tools described in the previous section. There are two principal advantages to compiling the Tapeworm simulator into the host operating system to intercept TLB miss traps. First, by being in the kernel, Tapeworm can capture TLB misses from all user processes, as well as the OS kernel itself. Second, because Tapeworm doesn't add any instructions to the workload that it monitors, non-trapping memory references proceeded at the full speed of the underlying host hardware, which results in zero-slowdown processing of simulated TLB hits. On the other hand, a simulated TLB miss incurs the full overhead of a kernel trap and the simulator code, which varies from 100 to 650 host cycles. Fortunately, TLB hits are far more frequent than TLB misses, outnumbering them by more than 300 to 1 in the worst case (Nagle et al. [51]). The result is that Tapeworm TLB simulation slowdowns range from about 0.5 to 4.5.

Trap-driven TLB simulation has recently been implemented on other architectures with similar success. Lee has implemented a trap-driven TLB simulator on a 486-based PC running Mach 3.0 (Lee [42]). Because the i486 processor has hardware-managed TLBs, Lee's simulator uses a different mechanism for causing TLB miss traps, one that is based on page-valid bits. By manipulating the valid bit in a page-table entry, Lee's simulator causes TLB misses to result in kernel traps in the same way that they do in a machine with software-managed TLBs. Talluri et al. uses similar techniques in a trap-driven TLB simulator that runs on SPARC-based workstations under the *Foxtrot* operating system to study architectural support for superpages (Talluri and Hill [71]). Talluri and Lee both report that the overall slowdowns for their simulators are comparable to those of Tapeworm.

A limitation of the trap-driven simulators described above is that they are not easily extended to cache simulation. This is because the mechanisms that they use to cause kernel traps operate at the granularity of a memory page. The first trap-driven simulator that overcame this limitation is the *Wisconsin Wind Tunnel* (*WWT*), which caused kernel traps by modifying the error-correcting code (ECC) check bits in a SPARC-based CM-5 (Reinhardt et al. [57]). Because each memory location has ECC bits, this method enables traps to be set and cleared with a much finer granularity, enabling cache simulation. As with the trap-driven TLB simulators noted above, a simulated cache hit in WWT runs at the full speed of the host machine, and for caches with low miss ratios, overall slowdowns are measured to be as low as 1.4. However, in a comparison with Fast-cache, Lebeck et al. reports that WWT exhibits slowdowns of greater than 30 or 40 for caches smaller than 32KB (Lebeck and Wood [40]). These slowdowns are much higher than those reported for TLB simulation, both because cache misses occur much more frequently than TLB misses, and because a WWT trap requires about 2,500 cycles to service.

Tapeworm II, a second-generation Tapeworm simulator which also uses ECC-bit modification to simulated caches, improves on the speed of WWT by showing that trap-handling times can be reduced by nearly an order of magnitude to about 300 cycles, bringing overall simulation slowdowns for instruction caches into the range of 0 to 10 (Uhlig et al. [73]). Tapeworm II, like the original Tapeworm, also demonstrates that trap-driven cache simulation is capable of complete monitoring multi-process and operating-system workloads. Experiments performed with Tapeworm II show that trap-driven simulation slowdowns are highly dependent on the memory structure being simulated, with the relationship between slowdown and configuration parameters often being quite different than with trace-driven simulation. Trace-driven simulations of associative caches, for example, are typically slower than direct-mapped cache simulations because of the extra work required to simulate an associative search. With trap-driven simulations, however, the opposite is true: Tapeworm's associative-cache simulations are faster because there is a lower ratio of misses (and thus traps) to total memory references relative to simulations of direct-mapped caches of the same size. Other experiments with Tapeworm II have examined sources of measurement and simulation error of trap-driven simulation compared with those of trace-driven simulation. Many sources of error are the same (e.g., time dilation), but some were found to be unique to trap-driven simulation. In particular, because Tapeworm II becomes part of its running host system, it is more sensitive to dynamic system effects, such as virtual-to-physical page allocation and memory fragmentation in a long-running system. Although Tapeworm's sensitivity to these effects may necessitate multiple experimental trials, this should not be viewed as a liability; a trap-driven simulator that becomes part of a running system can give insight into real, naturally-occurring system effects that are beyond the scope of static traces.

8.3 Summary of New Memory Simulation Methods

With slowdowns commonly around 10, and in some cases approaching 0, the new simulators discussed in this section show that memory-simulation speeds can be improved dramatically by rejecting the traditional trace-driven simulation paradigm of collecting and processing each and every memory reference made by a workload. There are substantial performance gains to be had by optimizing for the common case of cache or TLB hits.

The three software-based systems (MemSpy, Fast-cache, and Embra/SimOS) share a number of important advantages. They are flexible, low in cost, and relatively portable because they do not rely on special hardware support. Because they are based on the same basic techniques as trace collectors that use code annotation or emulation, these three tools suffer from some of the same disadvantages, such as memory overheads as high as 5 to 10 due to added instructions and/or emulation state. Code expansion may not be a concern for applications with small text segments, but annotating larger, multi-process workloads along with the kernel, can cause substantial expansion.

The hardware-based trap-driven simulators, such as Tapeworm II and WWT, avoid the problems of code expansion, and they are also able to achieve near-zero slowdowns when miss ratios are small. The main weakness of trap-driven simulation is low flexibility and portability – all of the trap-driven simulators that we examined were limited in the simulations that they could perform, and all rely on ad-hoc methods to cause OS kernel traps.

While hit overheads are zero with the hardware-based methods, their miss costs are on average much higher than those for the software-based techniques. This suggests that the fastest method depends highly on the ratio of hits to misses for a given workload and memory configuration. Lebeck studied this issue and concluded that a hardware-based approach is better for miss ratios up to about 5%, at which point the high cost of servicing miss traps begins to make a software-based approach more attractive (Lebeck and Wood [41]). Given this, the software-based methods are probably the better choice for simulating small on-chip caches with their higher miss ratios, but the trap-driven methods are more effective for simulating large off-chip caches, which have traditionally been difficult to manage with standard trace-driven simulation because of the time it takes to overcome cold-start bias (Kessler [34]).

Both the hardware- and software-based techniques have been shown capable of monitoring complete OS and multi-task workloads (e.g., SimOS, Tapeworm II). The Tapeworm II approach of compiling the trap handlers directly into the kernel of the host system enables it to benefit from much of the existing host infrastructure. SimOS, by contrast, must develop detailed simulation models of several system components (such as network controllers, disk controllers, etc.) to achieve the same effect. Although more work is required to establish these models, SimOS, in the end, is able to account for effects such as time dilation, a form of distortion that Tapeworm II has difficulty compensating for.

When hit-bypassing is implemented in software, it limits the effectiveness of techniques such as time sampling (Laha et al. [35]) and set sampling (Puzak

[56]). Martonosi investigated time sampling by adding an additional check to MemSpy's annotations that enabled and disabled monitoring at regular intervals (Martonosi et al. [45]). When enabled, annotation overheads are similar to those cited previously (25 instructions per hit), but when disabled, an annotated reference executes only 6 extra instructions. When trapping is enabled for 10% of the entire execution time, MemSpy slowdowns dropped to about 4 to 10, a factor of two improvement over simulations without sampling. Ideally 10% sampling would result in a factor of 10 speedup, but in this case, code annotation adds an unavoidable base overhead; even when trapping is turned off, each annotated memory reference still results in the execution of 6 extra instructions. In contrast, experiments with Tapeworm II show that the trap-driven approach lends itself well to sampling (Uhlig et al. [73]) – when Tapeworm samples $1/N$th of all references, slowdowns are reduced in direct proportion, by a factor of N. This is true because unsampled references, like simulated cache hits, can run at the full speed of the host hardware.

The trade-offs between these new memory-system simulators are complex, and neither the software-based or hardware-based approaches are clear winners in every situation. The reliance on ad-hoc trapping mechanisms is a considerable disadvantage for the trap-driven simulators, so the software-based tools are likely to be more popular in the immediate future. If, however, future machines begin to provide better support for controlling memory access in a fine-grained manner, trap-driven simulation could become more attractive. Such support is not necessarily expensive, and could be useful for other applications as well, such as distributed shared memory (Reinhardt et al. [58]).

9 Summary

Trace-driven simulation has played an important role in the design of memory systems in the past, and because of the increasing processor-memory speed gap its usefulness is likely to continue growing in the future. This survey has defined several criteria to use when judging the features of a trace-driven simulation system, and has come to several conclusions contrary to the conventional wisdom. In particular, instruction-set emulation is faster than commonly believed, probe-based trace collection is slower than commonly believed, and multi-configuration simulations include more overhead than typically reported. Most importantly, no single method is best when all points of comparison, including speed, accuracy, flexibility, expense, portability and ease-of-use, are taken into consideration.

Perhaps the most important factor to keep in mind when selecting the components of a complete trace-driven memory simulator is balance. Research in trace-driven simulation frequently places too much emphasis on one aspect of the process (e.g., speed) at the expense of others (e.g., completeness or portability). In the quest for raw speed, a simulator writer might, for example, be tempted to select a static code annotator over an instruction-set emulator because the former is typically twice as fast as the latter for collecting addresses traces. When trace-processing times are taken into account, however, this difference may make a negligible contribution to overall slowdowns and may not be worth the flexibility and ease-of-use that annotators sacrifice to obtain their speed advantage over emulators. Similarly, the results obtained from fastest known cache simulator may not be of much value if it can only be used to study single-process workloads. A slower, but more complete system, capable of capturing multi-process and operating-system activity, may often be the better choice.

Looking forward, we can expect to see continued changes in the way that memory-system simulation is performed. The biggest change is likely to come in the contents of the traces themselves. As we saw in Section 8, there is much to be gained by moving beyond a simple sequential trace interface in which each and every memory reference is passed from trace collector to trace processor. Richer trace interfaces will result not only in faster simulation times, but may become a necessity to enable accurate simulations of tomorrow's complex microprocessors, which will be capable of making out-of-order, non-blocking accesses to the memory system.

Acknowledgements

This work was supported by ARPA Contract #DAAH04-94-G-0327, by NSF Contract #CISE9121887, by an NSF Graduate Fellowship and by a European Research Consortium for Informatics and Mathematics (ERCIM) Postgraduate Fellowship.

Many thanks to Stuart Sechrest, Peter Bird, Peter Honeyman and Mike Smith, as well as the anonymous reviewers from *Computing Surveys* for their helpful comments on earlier versions of this paper. A special thanks to Andre Seznec and IRISA for supporting this work during its final stages.

References

1. Agarwal, A.: Analysis of cache performance for operating systems and multiprogramming. Ph.D. dissertation, Stanford. 1989
2. Agarwal, A., Horowitz, M., and Hennessy, J.: An analytical cache model. ACM Transactions on Computer Systems **7** (2): 184–215, 1989
3. Agarwal, A. and Huffman, M.: Blocking: Exploiting spatial locality for trace compaction. In Proc. of the 1990 SIGMETRICS Conf. on Measurement and Modeling of Computer Systems, Boulder, CO, ACM, 48–57, 1990.
4. Baker, M.: Cluster Computing Review. Northeast Parallel Architectures Center (NPAC) Technical Report SCCS–748, November, 1995
5. Becker, J. and Park, A.: An analysis of the information content of address and data reference streams. In Proc. of the 1993 SIGMETRICS Conf. on the Measurement and Modeling of Computer Systems, Santa Clara, CA, 262–263, 1993
6. Bedichek, R.: The Meerkat multicomputer: Tradeoffs in multicomputer architecture. Ph.D. dissertation, University of Washington Department of Computer Science Technical Report 94–06–06, August 1994
7. Bedichek, R.: Talisman: fast and accurate multicomputer simulation. In Proc. of the 1995 SIGMETRICS Conf. on Measurement and Modeling of Computer Systems, 14–24, 1995

8. Borg, A., Kessler, R., Lazana, G., and Wall, D.: Long address traces from RISC machines: generation and analysis. DEC Western Research Lab Technical Report 89/14, 1989
9. Borg, A., Kessler, R., and Wall, D.: Generation and analysis of very long address traces. In Proc. of the 17th Ann. Int. Symp. on Computer Architecture, IEEE, 1990
10. Chen, B.: Software methods for system address tracing. In Proc. of the Fourth Workshop on Workstation Operating Systems, Napa, California, 1993
11. Chen, B. and Bershad, B.: The impact of operating system structure on memory system performance. In Proc. of the 14th Symp. on Operating System Principles, 1993
12. Chen, B.: Memory behavior of an X11 window system. In Proc. of the USENIX Winter 1994 Technical Conf., 1994
13. Clark, D. W., Bannon, P. J., and Keller, J. B.: Measuring VAX 8800 performance with a histogram hardware monitor. In Proc. of the 15th Ann. Int. Symp. on Computer Architecture, Honolulu, Hawaii, IEEE, 176–185, 1985
14. Cmelik, R. and Keppel, D.: Shade: A fast instruction-set simulator for execution profiling. University of Washington Technical Report UWCSE 93-06-06. 1993
15. Cmelik, B. and Keppel, D.: Shade: A fast instruction-set simulator for execution profiling. In Proc. of the 1994 SIGMETRICS Conf. on Measurement and Modeling of Computer Systems, Nashville, TN, ACM, 128–137, 1994
16. Cvetanovic, Z. and Bhandarkar, D.: Characterization of Alpha AXP performance using TP and SPEC Workloads. In Proc. of the 21st Ann. Int. Symp. on Computer Architecture, Chicago, IL, IEEE, 1994
17. Davies, P., Lacroute, P., Heinlein, J., Horowitz, M.: Mable: A technique for efficient machine simulation. Stanford University Technical Report CSL–TR–94–636, October, 1994
18. Davis, H., Goldschmidt, S., and Hennessy, J.: Multiprocessor simulation and tracing using Tango. In Proc. of the 1991 Int. Conf. on Parallel Processing, 99–107, 1991
19. Digital: Alpha Architecture Handbook. USA, Digital Equipment Corporation, 1992
20. Eggers, S., Keppel, D., Koldinger, E., and Levy, H.: Techniques for efficient inline tracing on a shared-memory multiprocessor. In Proc. of the 1990 SIGMETRICS Conf. on Measurement and Modeling of Computer Systems, Boulder, CO, 37–47, 1990
21. Emer, J. and Clark, D.: A characterization of processor performance in the VAX-11/780. In Proc. of the 11th Ann. Symp. on Computer Architecture, Ann Arbor, MI, 301–309, 1984
22. Eustace, A. and Srivastava, A.: ATOM: a flexible interface for building high performance program analysis tools. In Proc. of the USENIX Winter 1995 Technical Conf. on UNIX and Advanced Computing Systems, New Orleans, Louisiana, 303–314, January, 1995
23. Flanagan, J. K., Nelson, B. E., Archibald, J. K., and Grimsrud, K.: BACH: BYU address collection hardware, the collection of complete traces. In Proc. of the 6th Int. Conf. on Modelling Techniques and Tools for Computer Performance Evaluation, 128–137, 1992
24. Gee, J., Hill, M., Pnevmatikatos, D., and Smith, A. J.: Cache performance of the SPEC92 benchmark suite. IEEE Micro (August): 17–27, 1993
25. Goldschmidt, S. and Hennessy, J.: The accuracy of trace-driven simulation of multiprocessors. Stanford University Technical Report CSL–TR–92–546, September 1992

26. Goldschmidt, S. and Hennessy, J.: The accuracy of trace-driven simulation of multiprocessors. In Proc. of the 1993 ACM SIGMETRICS Conf. on Measurement and Modeling of Computer Systems, 146–157, May 1993
27. Hammerstrom, D. and Davidson, E.: Information content of CPU memory referencing behavior. In Proc. of the 4th Int. Symp. on Computer Architecture, 184–192, 1977
28. Hill, M.: Aspects of cache memory and instruction buffer performance. Ph.D. dissertation, The University of California at Berkeley. 1987
29. Hill, M. and Smith, A.: Evaluating associativity in CPU caches. IEEE Transactions on Computers **38** (12): 1612–1630, 1989
30. Holliday, M.: Techniques for cache and memory simulation using address reference traces. Int. Journal in Computer Simulation **1**: 129–151, 1991
31. IBM: IBM RISC System/6000 Technology. Austin, TX, IBM, 1990
32. Jouppi, N.: Improving direct-mapped cache performance by the addition of a small fully-associative cache and prefetch buffers. In Proc. of the 17th Ann. Int. Symp. on Computer Architecture, Seattle, WA, IEEE, 364–373, 1990
33. Kaeli, D.: Issues in trace-driven simulation. In Proc. of the 22rd Ann. Pittsburgh Modeling and Simulation Conf., Vol. **22**, Part 5, May, 2533–2540, 1991
34. Kessler, R.: Analysis of multi-megabyte secondary CPU cache memories. Ph.D. dissertation, University of Wisconsin-Madison. 1991
35. Laha, S., Patel, J., and Iyer, R.: Accurate low-cost methods for performance evaluation of cache memory systems. IEEE Transactions on Computers **37** (11): 1325–1336, 1988
36. Larus, J. R.: Abstract execution: A technique for efficiently tracing programs. Software Practice and Experience, **20** (12):1241–1258, December, 1990
37. Larus, J.: SPIM S20: A MIPS R2000 Simulator. University of Wisconsin-Madison Technical Report, Revision 9. 1991
38. Larus, J. R.: Efficient program tracing. IEEE Computer, May: 52–60, 1993
39. Larus, J. R. and Schnorr, E.: EEL: Machine independent executable editing. In Proc. SIGPLAN Conf. on Programming Language Design and Implementation, June, 1995
40. Lebeck, A. and Wood, D.: Fast-Cache: A new abstraction for memory-system simulation. University of Wisconsin-Madison Technical Report 1211, 1994
41. Lebeck, A. and Wood, D.: Active Memory: A new abstraction for memory-system simulation. In Proc. of the 1995 SIGMETRICS Conf. on the Measurement and Modeling of Computer Systems, May, 220–230, 1995
42. Lee, C.-C.: A case study of a hardware-managed TLB in a multi-tasking environment. University of Michigan Technical Report. 1994
43. Magnusson, P.: A design for efficient simulation of a multiprocessor. In Proc. of the 1993 Western Simulation Multiconference on Int. Workshop on Modeling, Analysis and Simulation of Computer and Telecommunication Systems, 69–78, La Jolla, California, 1993
44. Martonosi, M., Gupta, A., and Anderson, T.: MemSpy: Analyzing memory system bottlenecks in programs. In Proc. of the 1992 SIGMETRICS Conf. on the Measurement and Modeling of Computer Systems, ACM, 1992
45. Martonosi, M., Gupta, A., and Anderson, T.: Effectiveness of trace sampling for performance debugging tools. In Proc. of the 1993 SIGMETRICS Conf. on the Measurement and Modeling of Computer Systems, Santa Clara, California, ACM, 248–259, 1993
46. Mattson, R. L., Gecsei, J., Slutz, D. R., and Traiger, I. L.: Evaluation techniques for storage hierarchies. IBM Systems Journal **9** (2): 78–117, 1970

47. Maynard, A. M., Donnelly, C., and Olszewski, B.: Contrasting characteristics and cache performance of technical and multi-user commercial workloads. In Proc. of the Sixth Int. Conf. on Architectural Support for Programming Languages and Operating Systems, San Jose, CA, ACM, 145–156, 1994
48. MIPS: RISCompiler Languages Programmer's Guide. MIPS, 1988
49. Mogul, J. C. and Borg, A.: The effect of context switches on cache performance. In Proc. of the 4th Int. Conf. on Architectural Support for Programming Languages and Operating Systems, Santa Clara, California, ACM, 75–84, 1991
50. Nagle, D., Uhlig, R., and Mudge, T.: Monster: A tool for analyzing the interaction between operating systems and computer architectures. University of Michigan Technical Report CSE–TR–147–92. 1992
51. Nagle, D., Uhlig, R., Stanley, T., Sechrest, S., Mudge, T., and Brown, R.: Design tradeoffs for software-managed TLBs. In Proc. of the 20th Ann. Int. Symp. on Computer Architecture, San Diego, California, IEEE, 27–38, 1993
52. Nagle, D., Uhlig, R., Mudge, T., and Sechrest, S.: Optimal allocation of on-chip memory for multiple-API operating systems. In Proc. of the 21st Int. Symp. on Computer Architecture, Chicago, IL, 1994
53. Pierce, J. and Mudge, T.: IDtrace – A tracing tool for i486 simulation. University of Michigan Technical Report CSE–TR–203–94. 1994
54. Pierce, J., Smith, M. D., and Mudge, T.: "Instrumentation tools," in Fast Simulation of Computer Architectures (T. M. Conte and C. E. Gimarc, eds.), Kluwer Academic Publishers: Boston, MA, 1995
55. Pleszkun, A.: Techniques for compressing program address traces. Technical Report, Department of Electrical and Computer Engineering, University of Colorado-Boulder. 1994
56. Puzak, T.: Analysis of cache replacement algorithms. Ph.D. dissertation, University of Massachusetts. 1985
57. Reinhardt, S., Hill, M., Larus, J., Lebeck, A., Lewis, J., and Wood, D.: The Wisconsin Wind Tunnel: Virtual prototyping of parallel computers. In Proc. of the 1993 SIGMETRICS Int. Conf. on Measurement and Modeling of Computer Systems, Santa Clara, CA, ACM, 48–60, 1993
58. Reinhardt, S., Pfile, R., and Wood, D.: Decoupled hardware support for distributed shared memory. To appear in Proc. of the 23rd Ann. Int. Symp. on Computer Architecture, 1996
59. Romer, T., Lee, D., Voelker, G., Wolman, A., Wong, W., Baer, J., Bershad, B., and Levy, H.: The structure and performance of interpreters. To appear in the Proc. of the 7th Int. Conf. on Architectural Support for Programming Languages and Operating Systems, Cambridge, MA, October, 1996
60. Rosenblum, M., Herrod, S., Witchel, E., and Gupta, A.: Complete computer simulation: the SimOS approach, In IEEE Parallel and Distributed Technology, Fall 1995
61. Samples, A.: Mache: no-loss trace compaction. In Proc. of 1989 SIGMETRICS Conf. on Measurement and Modeling of Computer Systems, ACM, 89–97, 1989
62. Sites, R., Chernoff, A., Kirk, M., Marks, M., and Robinson, S.: Binary translation. Digital Technical Journal **4** (4): 137–152, 1992
63. Smith, A. J.: Two methods for the efficient analysis of memory address trace data. IEEE Transactions on Software Engineering SE-3 (1): 94–101, 1977
64. Smith, A. J.: Cache memories. Computing Surveys **14** (3): 473–530, 1982
65. Smith, M. D.: Tracing with pixie. Technical Report, Stanford University, Stanford, CA. 1991

66. Srivastava, A. and Eustace, A.: ATOM: A system for building customized program analysis tools. In Proc. of the SIGPLAN '94 Conf. on Programming Language Design and Implementation, 196–205, June 1994
67. Stephens, C., Cogswell, B., Heinlein, J., Palmer, G., and Shen, J.: Instruction level profiling and evaluation of the IBM RS/6000. In Proc. of the 18th Ann. Int. Symp. on Computer Architecture, Toronto, Canada, ACM, 180–189, 1991
68. Stunkel, C. and Fuchs, W.: TRAPEDS: producing traces for multicomputers via execution-driven simulation. In Proc. of the 1989 SIGMETRICS Conf. on Measurement and Modeling of Computer Systems, Berkeley, CA, ACM, 70–78, 1989
69. Stunkel, C., Janssens, B., and Fuchs, W. K.: Collecting address traces from parallel computers. In Proc. of the 24th Ann. Hawaii Int. Conf. on System Sciences, Hawaii, 373–383, 1991
70. Sugumar, R.: Multi-configuration simulation algorithms for the evaluation of computer designs. Ph.D. dissertation, University of Michigan. 1993
71. Talluri, M. and Hill, M.: Surpassing the TLB performance of superpages with less operating system support. In Proc. of the 6th Int. Conf. on Architectural Support for Programming Languages and Operating Systems, San Jose, CA, ACM, 1994
72. Thompson, J. and Smith, A.: Efficient (stack) algorithms for analysis of write-back and sector memories. ACM Transactions on Computer Systems **7** (1): 78–116, 1989
73. Uhlig, R., Nagle, D., Mudge, T., and Sechrest, S.: Trap-driven simulation with Tapeworm II. In Proc. of the Sixth Int. Conf. on Architectural Support for Programming Languages and Operating Systems, San Jose, California, ACM Press (SIGARCH), 132–144, 1994
74. Uhlig, R., Nagle, D., Mudge, T. Sechrest, S., and Emer, J.: Instruction fetching: coping with code bloat. To appear in Proc. of the 22nd Int. Symp. on Computer Architecture, Santa Margherita Ligure, Italy, June, 1995
75. Uhlig, R., and Mudge, T.: Trace driven memory simulation: A survey. Computing Surveys **29** (2) 128–170, 1997.
76. Upton, M. D.: Architectural trade-offs in a latency tolerant gallium arsenide microprocessor. Ph.D. Dissertation, The University of Michigan, 1994
77. Veenstra, J. and Fowler, R.: MINT: A front end for efficient simulation of shared-memory multiprocessors. In Proc. of the 2nd Int. Workshop on Modeling, Analysis, and Simulation of Computer and Telecommunication systems (MASCOTS), 201–207, 1994
78. Wall, D.: Link-time code modification. DEC Western Research Lab Technical Report 89/17. 1989
79. Wall, D.: Systems for late code modification. DEC Western Research Lab Technical Report 92/3. 1992
80. Wang, W.-H. and Baer, J.-L.: Efficient trace-driven simulation methods for cache performance analysis. In Proc. of the 1990 SIGMETRICS Conf. on Measurement and Modeling of Computer Systems, Boulder, CO, ACM, 27–36, 1990
81. Witchel, E. and Rosenblum, M.: Embra: fast and flexible machine simulation, In Proc. of the 1996 SIGMETRICS Conf. on Measurement and Modeling of Computer Systems, Philadelphia, May, 1996

Performance Issues in Parallel Processing Systems

Luiz A. DeRose, Mario Pantano, Daniel A. Reed, and Jeffrey S. Vetter

Department of Computer Science,
University of Illinois, Urbana, Illinois 61801 USA
{derose,pantano,reed,jsv}@cs.uiuc.edu

1 Introduction

Simply put, the goal of performance analysis is to provide the data and insights required to optimize the execution behavior of application or system components. Using such data and insights, application and system developers can choose to optimize software and execution environments along many axes, including execution time, memory requirements, and resource use. Given the diversity of performance optimization goals and the wide range of possible problems, a complete performance analysis toolkit necessarily includes a broad range of techniques. These range from mechanisms for simple code timings to multi-level hardware/software measurement and correlation across networks, system software, runtime libraries, compile-time code transformations, and adaptive execution.

High-performance parallel systems exacerbate already difficult performance-optimization problems. Although performance is the *raison detre* for parallel computing, subtle interactions among parallel software components can easily lead to unexpected bottlenecks. More perniciously, Amdahl's law shows that serialization of even a small fraction of a code can have dramatic effects on overall performance. Consequently, the history of parallel computing is replete with stories of application and system designs that failed to meet expected performance goals.

For example, preliminary experiences with terascale systems (i.e., thousand processor systems capable of more than 10^{12} operations per second), suggest that the fraction of achieved performance can actually decline as one adds processors. These systems are so complex that the resource demands of each large-scale, multidisciplinary application can expose portions of the behavioral-execution space never before tested or explored. It is these unanticipated patterns of hardware, system software, and application interaction that cause poor performance.

To understand and master the complexity of large-scale parallel systems, a plethora of performance-analysis tools and techniques have been proposed and developed. Despite their number and diversity, most tools and techniques lie in one of three broad categories: analytic modeling, simulation, or empirical performance measurement.

G. Haring et al. (Eds.): Performance Evaluation, LNCS 1769, pp. 141–159, 2000.

The attraction of analytic models (e.g., Petri nets, queueing networks, or Markov models) lies in their ready parameterization and rapid solution, allowing one to quickly predict performance over a broad range. Their major liability is that tractability requirements often dictate restrictive assumptions (e.g., service times with negative exponential distributions) that are violated in practice, lessening accuracy.

In contrast, the flexibility of discrete event simulation enables construction of detailed, highly accurate models of system components. Furthermore these models can be evaluated using realistic workloads. This flexibility is not without price — simulations must be carefully validated against empirical data, lest generalizations from parametric simulation studies be based on faulty models. Moreover, the time and computational cost demanded by detailed simulations, particularly for large-scale systems, often precludes their use.

Given these constraints, experimental performance analysis remains the method of choice for tuning large-scale, parallel systems. In this chapter, we begin by discussing the typical cycle of performance analysis, emphasizing measurement, data analysis and visualization, and system tuning.

The remainder of this chapter is structured as follows. In Sect. 3, we begin with a detailed description of the range of basic instrumentation and measurement techniques for parallel systems, followed in Sect. 4 by an assessment of more sophisticated approaches to reducing and analyzing performance data sets. In Sect. 5, we discuss a suite of performance visualization and presentation techniques for parallel systems. This is followed in Sect. 6 by an assessment of integrated methodologies for instrumentation, analysis, and visualization, including analysis of the costs for each. Finally, we conclude in Sect. 7 with a few observations on the performance analysis process.

2 The Performance Analysis Cycle

The most common approach to experimental performance analysis relies on a five phase cycle of instrumentation, measurement, analysis, presentation, and optimization. At present, the phases of this cycle span code preparation, execution, and post-mortem analysis and optimization.

Instrumentation. Performance instrumentation can be either implicit or explicit. Implicit instrumentation relies on monitoring daemons to capture performance data; most profiling tools [20] rely on some variation of this approach. In contrast, explicit instrumentation modifies software by directly inserting measurement code. For application or system software, this explicit instrumentation can be inserted automatically (e.g., via object code patching [32] or via instrumenting parsers or compilers [1]) or manually by including calls to instrumentation library routines. For hardware instrumentation, one needs either specialized probes or software accessible counters or registers (e.g., the hardware counters now embedded on most commodity microprocessors [48]).

Measurement. To capture performance data, one then observes the instrumented system during execution, while the instrumentation software and hardware records pertinent performance data. For application software instrumentation, this typically includes procedure, loop, and basic block execution counts and times, communication (i.e., message passing or shared memory references) and synchronization costs, I/O patterns and system calls. System software measures often include network traffic, virtual memory overhead, context switches and task scheduling patterns, and disk traffic. Finally, common hardware measures include instruction mixes and stalls, as well as cache misses.

Data Reduction and Correlation. Following measurement, the resulting performance data must be processed to yield compact and easily interpretable results. If event tracing [36] was used to capture the pattern of software component interactions (e.g., message passing, I/O, or procedure calls), statistical summarization can transform large, unwieldy masses of raw data into succinct descriptions. Alternatively, it may be necessary to relate measurements of executable code to source code by inverting key compile-time code transformations (e.g., when high-level data parallel code was translated to message passing code during compilation [1]).

Analysis and Presentation. The goal of instrumentation and measurement is insight. Hence, one must present data in meaningful and intuitive ways. For simple profiles, standard tabular mechanisms suffice. For more complex measurements and subtle performance problems where one must trace problems from proximate to root causes, more powerful data analysis and presentation techniques are required. Static color graphics, workstation animations, and immersive virtual environments have all been used to visualize performance data [19].

System Optimization. Given an understanding of the causes of performance problems, the final step is remediation. This requires either modifying the application or system software, reconfiguring or adding hardware, or changing application or system parameters. Realizing these changes can be either trivial or extraordinarily difficult. Moreover, one must weigh the intellectual and labor costs of optimization against the perceived rewards. Rarely is *optimizing* execution time or system resource use the true goal. Instead, one seeks to reduce execution time or resource use subject to some constraints.

2.1 Measurement Constraints

Within this five step cycle, users and performance analysts are free to choose instrumentation, measurement, analysis, and presentation techniques that balance

- *resolution*, the level of detail (e.g., profiling or tracing) and granularity (e.g., loop nest or procedure call) of measurements,
- *perturbation*, the change in observed behavior from that when no instrumentation is present,

– *flexibility*, the ability to apply performance tools in multiple contexts and applications in configurable ways, and
– *accuracy*, capturing the true behavior of the observed system, subject to errors induced by perturbation.

Because many of these attributes are inimical (.e.g., high resolution is rarely possible without substantial perturbation), no single set of options is appropriate for all performance optimization scenarios. For example, some techniques minimize measurement perturbation by dynamically enabling instrumentation only when needed [32], while other techniques attempt to estimate and remove perturbation from measurements during analysis [29]. Both of these perturbation choices affect accuracy and resolution.

2.2 *In Vivo* Optimization

The classic cycle of instrumentation, measurement, reduction, analysis, and optimization described above presumes that observed behaviors are repeatable, namely that subsequent executions based on post-mortem optimization will yield performance improvement because similar behavior will accrue. For the common case of application program tuning on an otherwise quiescent sequential or parallel system, this assumption holds.

However, emerging applications are increasingly dynamic and adaptive and execute on heterogeneous collections of distributed, shared resources. In such an environment, the execution context is rarely repeatable, making post-mortem tuning problematic. Instead, the conventional *in vitro* cycle of instrumentation, measurement, assessment, and tuning must be replaced with *in vivo* optimization techniques that instrument, measure, and tune software during its execution. We will return to this topic in Sect. 4.

3 Instrumentation and Measurement Techniques

One can instrument systems at many levels, though the four most common are hardware, system software, runtime systems, and application code. Given the complexity of parallel systems and their sensitivity to small changes in component interactions, correlating performance data across two or more of these levels is normally required to understand the actual causes of performance problems.

Software instrumentation, for example, can capture the interaction of compiler-synthesized code with runtime libraries and system software. However, to understand the effects of superscalar instruction scheduling or cache hierarchies in a distributed shared memory (DSM) system, one must capture and correlate both software and hardware performance metrics.

Fortunately, new microprocessors commonly provide a set of performance registers for low-overhead access to hardware performance data. For example, the MIPS R10000 [33] includes registers that count hardware events, including cycles, instruction and data cache misses, floating point instructions, and branch mispredictions. Similar counters exist on other architectures.

These different levels of instrumentation can be realized via several methods. First, instrumentation can be inserted either statically, during code development or compilation, or dynamically, during execution. Second, instrumentation can be inserted manually or automatically. Finally, the nature of the data gathered (e.g., hardware, application, or system software) depends on the measurement technique.

3.1 Static and Dynamic Instrumentation

The most common instrumentation approach augments source code with calls to specific instrumentation libraries. During execution, these library routines collect behavioral data. Examples of static instrumentation systems include the widely used UNIX `prof` and `gprof` [20], the Automated Instrumentation and Monitoring System (AIMS) [47], the Executable Editing Library (EEL) [27], and the Pablo performance environment toolkit [38].

The primary drawback of static instrumentation is its lack of flexibility — it cannot be modified during program execution. Thus, changing the types of data collected typically requires application re-instrumentation, recompilation, and a new execution.

In contrast, dynamic instrumentation allows users to interactively change instrumentation points, focusing measurements on code regions where performance problems have been detected. Paradyn [32] is the exemplar of such dynamic instrumentation systems. The drawback of dynamic instrumentation is that the application must execute long enough for users or performance runtime systems to find performance problems by incrementally modifying the instrumentation.

3.2 Interactive and Automatic Insertion

As we noted earlier, performance analysis tools can insert instrumentation either automatically or interactively. The strength of interactive instrumentation is its flexibility; users can insert instrumentation library calls at arbitrary code points. However, naive or excessive instrumentation can excessively perturb execution behavior (e.g., by inhibiting compiler optimizations or by instrumenting frequently executed inner loops). Conversely, automatic instrumentation relies on the compiler or the runtime system to insert measurement code. This approach reduces the risk of perturbation, but sacrifices user control over instrumentation points.

3.3 Instrumentation Methods

Regardless of the instrumentation level, there are four main approaches to performance data capture: sampling, counting, timing, and tracing. Each reflects a different balance among data volume, potential instrumentation perturbation, accuracy, and implementation complexity. In addition, each can be implemented in a variety of ways, ranging from extrinsic (e.g., an external hardware monitor that counts data cache misses) to intrinsic (e.g., inserted code that computes a histogram of procedure activation lifetimes).

Program Counter Sampling. By far the most common instrumentation method is program counter sampling. The prof and gprof utilities [20] periodically sample the program counter and compute a histogram of program counter locations. Profiling depends on an external sampling task, leading to coarse granularity and requiring the total program execution time to be long enough to accumulate a statistically meaningful sample set. Moreover, as discussed in Sect. 6.1, profilers often assume a simple mapping from object code to the original source code, which is rarely true on parallel systems with aggressive restructuring compilers.

Event Counting. Event counting eliminates some of sampling's limitations, albeit with possibly increased perturbation for frequent events. Because counting is not a statistical measure, the observed frequencies are accurate even for short executions.

Some performance data capture toolkits combine sampling and counting. For instance, the MIPS R10000 microprocessor includes two hardware performance counters, each able to track one of 16 events per cycle. To capture more than one event per counter, the operating system maintains a set of 32 virtual counters, multiplexing (sampling) the physical counters across these. This multiplexing mechanism sacrifices accuracy but increases coverage, allowing a single program execution to acquire data for all the desired counters.

Interval Timing. Interval timing combines counting with elapsed-time measurements. Rather than simply sampling the program counter, interval timing surrounds code fragments with calls to timing routines, accumulating cumulative data and counts of code fragment execution time. This requires software access to high-resolution, low overhead clock.

With increasing processor speeds, the standard UNIX timing facility, often with 50 or 60 Hz resolution, is unacceptably coarse. Only with microsecond resolution (or better) clocks and low overhead access routines can one accurately measure small code fragments.

Event Tracing. Event tracing is the most general of instrumentation techniques — from an event trace, one can compute counts or times; the converse is not true. The primary disadvantages of tracing are the large data volume and the potential instrumentation perturbation. For example, instrumenting procedures to record entry and exit can easily generate 16 KB/second on a single processor if the mean procedure activation lifetime is 500 microseconds and the data associated with each event includes only a four-byte event identifier and a four-byte time stamp. On a parallel system with hundreds or thousands of processors, the data volume can be many megabytes/second.

Runtime summarization can reduce event tracing's data volume by trading computation overhead for data volume. Rather than generating trace files, the instrumentation system computes metric values during execution, generating periodic statistical summaries. In Sect. 4, we discuss summarization techniques in more detail.

In general, perturbation, resolution, and accuracy are dependent on the instrumentation method; no single instrumentation approach is appropriate for all cases. The choice of a particular method is dictated by the desired information and the constraints of the available instrumentation — some measurements may not be possible in a particular environment.

4 Performance Data Analysis

The main goal of performance analysis is identifying bottlenecks or sources of poor performance. However, with increased software and parallel system complexity, identifying these bottlenecks becomes commensurately more difficult.

Performance bottlenecks may lie in instruction schedulers, memory-hierarchy management, wide-area or local communication protocols, scheduling algorithms, or application load balance. Consequently, the metrics that highlight performance problems are highly dependent on the execution context; determining appropriate metrics and assessing the resulting data is the goal of performance analysis.

4.1 Data Management Techniques

The simplest form of analysis filters data that do not meet user-specified, criteria, retaining and computing metrics from only the pertinent data (e.g., standard statistical metrics such as the mean, minimum, maximum, percentiles, variance, and coefficient of variation). Often, these metrics suffice — the causes of performance problems are obvious once even simple measurements are examined.

For more complex performance problems, detailed analysis based on event traces may be required. However, the potentially large volume of event trace data, the large number of possible performance metrics, and consequent behavioral perturbations make this approach impractical for large, long-running applications. To retain the advantages of event tracing while minimizing data volume and intrusion, analysts must reduce both the number of metrics that are needed to identify bottlenecks (metric dimensionality) and the number of locations where data must be captured (metric plurality).

As a basis for discussing event trace reduction, consider a set of n dynamic performance metrics, each measured on a set of P parallel tasks. Conceptually, an event trace defines a set of n dynamic performance metrics, $m_i(t)$, on each of P tasks

$$(m_1(t), m_2(t), ..., m_n(t))_p \qquad p \in [1..P]$$

that describe parallel system characteristics as a function of time t. Following [35], if R_i denotes the range of metric $m_i(t)$, we call the Cartesian product

$$M = R_1 \times R_2 \times ... \times R_n$$

a performance metric space. Thus, the ordered n-tuples

$$(m_1(t) \in R_1; m_2(t) \in R_2; ...; m_n(t) \in R_n)$$

are points in $M(t)$, and the event trace defines the temporal evolution of these P points in an n dimensional space.

There are several possible approaches to reducing metric dimensionality and plurality. Below, we describe two — statistical clustering and projection pursuit. Statistical clustering reduces the number of measurement points (i.e., P) by eliding data from groups of processors with similar behavior. Conversely, projection pursuit reduces the dimensionality of the metric space (i.e., n) by identifying "important" metrics.

Statistical Clustering. Programs for parallel systems generally use the Single Process Multiple Data (SPMD) model (e.g., using MPI), the data-parallel or object-parallel models (e.g., using HPF or parallel C++), or simple functional decompositions. In the first three models, the same code executes on all processors, with behavior differentiated by data-dependent control flow. In the functional decompositions, similar code executes on several processor groups.

Regardless of the programming model, tasks executing the same code with similar data form behavioral equivalence classes with comparable trajectories in the metric space. Statistical clustering groups processors (or tasks) in equivalence classes whose performance metrics trace similar trajectories in the metric space and chooses one member of each grouping as a representative of the others.

As an example, consider an SPMD code that relies on a master task to read initialization data and allocate work to a set of N worker tasks. If all workers behave similarly, clustering identifies two clusters, the first with cardinality one, the master, and a second with cardinality N, the workers. Only two tasks, the master and any one of the remaining tasks, fully represent the range of application behavior. By periodically computing clusters using real-time data, an event tracing system need record data only for the representatives of each cluster, dramatically reducing the total data volume [35].

Projection Pursuit Statistical clustering reduces the number of processors (or tasks) P from which event data must be recorded, but it does not reduce the number of metrics n, the dimensionality of the metric space. Projection pursuit [25], a statistical variant of principal component analysis, identifies a subset of the metrics that captures most of the statistical variation.

Conceptually, at any time t, many of the n metrics are highly correlated. Multidimensional projection pursuit selects the least correlated k metrics from the multidimensional metric space; typically, k is two or three (i.e., two or three-dimensional projection pursuit). Using projection pursuit, real-time event tracing need record only that subset of the metrics deemed "important" by the projection.

As Fig. 1 suggests, combining statistical clustering and projection pursuit can potentially reduce both the number of processors and the number of metrics

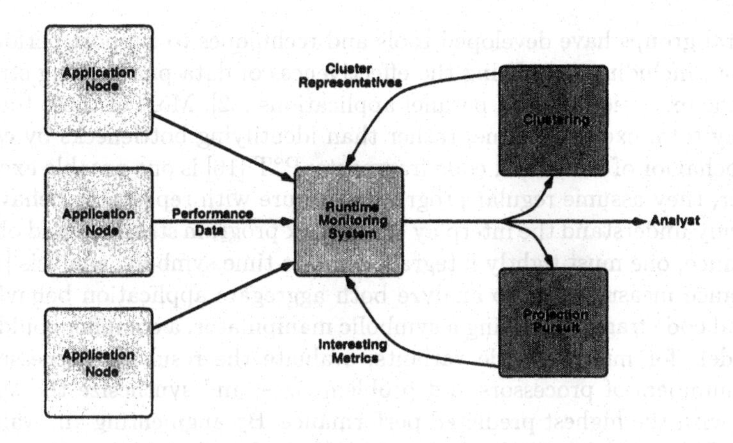

Fig. 1. Integrated Clustering and Projection Pursuit

that an event tracing system must record during program execution [41]. However, the possible data reduction from clustering and projection pursuit must be balanced against the additional computational overhead and decreased measurement accuracy.

Between successive application of clustering and projection pursuit, only data from the representative processors and metrics is recorded. If the algorithms are applied too infrequently, application phase changes may be missed (i.e., the recorded data may no longer be representative). Conversely, if applied too frequently, the computational overhead may excessively perturb application behavior. Hence, developing adaptive windowing algorithms for triggering clustering and projection pursuit remains a key research problem.

4.2 Performance Prediction

In standard practice, performance analysis is remedial, identifying problems created earlier, during design of hardware, application or system software. However, if it were possible to estimate application or system performance *during* rather than after design, performance analysis tools could lessen the high intellectual cost of developing and optimizing parallel applications. This would allow developers to understand the interactions of architectural parameters, problem size, application structure, and number of processors, identifying and eliminating potential bottlenecks during design.

Because performance bottlenecks may shift as these values change, a broad characterization of the parameter space would both enable creation of applications with portable performance and place system design on a solid performance engineering foundation. These characterizations need not be quantitatively exact, only qualitatively correct. Thus, large performance prediction errors are acceptable if the predictions accurately identify bottlenecks and track their movement with changing assumptions and parameters.

Several groups have developed tools and techniques to support performance prediction, including estimating the effectiveness of data partitioning strategies [3] and the execution time of parallel applications [22]. Most of these tools estimate only total execution time, rather than identifying bottlenecks by estimating the behavior of individual code fragments; P^3T [16] is one notable exception. Moreover, they assume regular program structure with repeatable behavior.

To truly understand the interplay of complex program structure and observed performance, one must tightly integrate compile-time symbolic analysis [17] and performance measurement to analyze both aggregate application behavior and individual code fragments Using a symbolic manipulator, a compiler could create cost models for multiple code variants, evaluate the resulting expressions for specific numbers of processors and problem sizes, and synthesize the the code variants with the highest predicted performance. By augmenting and validating these symbolic models with dynamic performance data from program executions, the compiler could incrementally refine the quality of its predictions and code generation choices.

In this model, compilation and performance analysis are a closed loop, with both symbolic performance predictions and quantitative measurements guiding the compilation process [30]. However, for symbolic control flow analysis to be broadly effective, it must be extended to include both linear and non-linear expressions, more powerful simplification mechanisms, and relations between input data and output information.

4.3 Scalability Analysis

Assessing the scalability of algorithms, applications, and architectures is a specific aspect of performance prediction. Like symbolic analysis, most automated scalability techniques require deep compiler/performance tool integration.

As a feasibility test of performance scalability analysis, Mendes extended the Rice Fortran D95 compiler to predict the scalability of regular data parallel codes [31,1]. The extended compiler translated data parallel code and generated a symbolic cost model for the execution time of each code fragment in the original data parallel source code. The scalability of these fragments could then be evaluated as a function of program size and number of processors.

In a similar effort, Sun *et al* extended the Vienna Fortran Compilation System (VFCS) [4] for scalability prediction [45]. The integrated system combines performance data from measurements on a small number of processors with a cost model of the application. The scalability is then automatically predicted as the number of processors varies in proportion to the problem size.

These experiments have shown that the automatic scalability prediction is feasible for small, regular codes. However, general techniques are needed that can predict performance scaling for large, irregular applications.

5 Performance Visualization

Because it allows users to grasp essential features of large, complex data sets, visualization is now a standard part of the scientific process. These same qualities also make visualization highly attractive for performance data analysis [24,26,44,39], especially on parallel systems where data collections grow very large.

Scientific and performance data visualization share many features and design goals, though they also differ in important, though subtle ways.

- *Flexibility.* Given the diversity of performance data, visualization systems must allow users to bind data to those graphical representations the users find useful and intuitive (e.g., it should be possible to represent the same data multiple ways and different data using the same representations). Further, when a binding is not obvious, visualizations should allow users to explore a variety of bindings and data perspectives [40].
- *Multiple levels of detail.* Because performance problems can arise at every hardware and software level, visualizations must enable users to focus on interesting yet complex behavior while eliding irrelevant or tedious details. Consider a distributed computation that spans several geographically distributed sites. A performance analyst might wish to view the wide-area communication traffic and aggregate performance at each site, examine the task scheduling on one node, or, explore the data locality of a code fragment. Visualization techniques should encourage users to freely navigate among the many levels of performance data associated with such a distributed computation.
- *Data management.* As we have discussed, detailed event tracing of large parallel or distributed systems can quickly produce large volumes of data. Unlike traditional scientific data, performance data is often of high dimension, and very sparse — it contains multiple, time varying metrics captured on each of hundreds or thousands of processors. Performance data management systems must filter, extract, and correlate data subsets in response to user queries. Clustering, statistical summarization, projection pursuit, binning, surface contouring, and volume visualization [43] all reduce the data management burden by extracting important features from the data set while discarding repetitive or uninteresting data.
- *User interfaces and interaction.* Visualizations should provide natural and intuitive user interfaces and methods for users to manipulate large data collections. Although static visualizations of data collections are useful and common, comprehension generally improves when users can interactively explore their data [42].
- *Scalability.* Given the volume of performance data generated by parallel systems, visualizations must scale to large numbers of processors and support analysis of codes that run hours or days. For very large executions, this mandates real-time measurement and display.

Attempts to satisfy these conflicting goals have resulted in large numbers of performance analysis and visualization systems for high-end computers. Notable examples include the seminal Seecube toolkit [14], ParaGraph [23], Medea [9], and Pablo [38]. Despite the diversity of tools, their displays can be broadly classified along five axes.

- *Statistical visualizations.* Because many performance metrics are statistical measures, a large class of performance displays are variants of common statistical data visualizations [12] (e.g., scatterplots or histograms). The generality of these displays is both a strength and a weakness. They can represent virtually any performance metric. However, they do not easily scale to large numbers of metrics nor do these simple animations readily convey evolutionary behavior.
- *Specialized performance visualizations.* In contrast to generic statistical data displays, several research groups have developed domain-specific performance displays that directly represent some important feature of parallel hardware or software. Among the best known of these are procedure call graph displays [37], network topologies [23], and geographic traffic displays [19]. Many of these domain-specific displays are tightly coupled to specific programming models (e.g., message passing with PVM or MPI). For example, ParaGraph [23] includes a wide variety of hypercube topology projections, each animated with message traffic patterns.
- *Animations.* Because the majority of performance data consists of time series, animation is often used to represent evolutionary behavior. For large data volumes and long-running computations, animation is often the only practical method to create scalable displays — displays lack sufficient resolution to display entire execution lifetimes without abstracting detail.
- *Source code browsers.* As noted in Sect. 6, with increasingly sophisticated compilers, the behavior of compiler-synthesized code may differ dramatically from that written by the user (e.g., by transforming data parallel code into message passing code for a distributed memory parallel system). For users to optimize their code, performance measurement and display systems must relate dynamic performance data to the original source code. Not only does this require deep integration of compilers and performance tools, it encourages creation of source code browsers that display both source code and performance data. Source code browsers like SvPablo [15] display hardware metrics (e.g., cache behavior and instruction mixes) beside lines of source code, allowing users to explore performance within the context of their source code.
- *Immersive environments.* With high-end systems emerging with thousands of processors, performance presentation systems must either elide increasing detail to represent aggregate performance on workstation displays or adopt new, high resolution, high modality systems that can display more data. Immersive virtual environments not only have multi-megapixel resolution, they exploit sound and haptics to create immersive experiences — one is surrounded by dynamic performance data. As an example, Virtue [37] sup-

ports collaborative, immersive performance analysis and real-time display. Real-time data streams are mapped to a hierarchy of displays, ranging from geographic representations of wide-area traffic, through "time tunnel" representations of parallel system behavior, to dynamic call graphs of execution on a single tasks. By touching graph components, users can expand or contract subgraphs and change the behavior of executing software.

With a brief description of performance instrumentation, analysis, and display techniques, we turn now to integration of the components.

6 Deeply Integrated Performance Environments

For performance evaluation tools to be truly effective, they must integrate measurement, data analysis, visualization, and performance remediation. Ideally, they should also scale to thousands of processors, support analysis of distributed computations, and be portable across a wide variety of parallel systems. As we noted earlier, scalability means that the tools must not only capture and analyze data from large numbers of processors or tasks but also present the data in ways that are intuitive and instructive.

Early performance visualization systems focused on single architectural and programming models (e.g., message passing) and represented the states of individual processors (e.g., by a colored square for each processor) and communication links (e.g., by communication network animations). In consequence, workstation screen real estate limited these displays to a few hundred processors.

Complex applications now involve code written in a variety of languages and programming models, all executing on multiple parallel architectures. Without performance tool portability and flexibility, users must learn a new tool each time the programming model or parallel architecture changes.

Today, the *de facto* standard for performance instrumentation and analysis remains application profiling with post-mortem analysis of performance bottlenecks. This model was adequate for parallel codes written in sequential languages for homogeneous parallel systems and for compiler-generated object code that directly reflects source code control. However, sophisticated parallelizing compilers, high-level languages like HPF, and object-parallel models like parallel C++ mean that an application software developer's mental model of a program and the actual code that executes on a particular parallel system can be quite different. Concurrently, execution environments have expanded to include heterogeneous collections of parallel systems with time-varying resource availability.

New performance tools must guide optimization at the semantic level where code is developed. Thus, they must integrate dynamic performance data with compile-time data that describes the mapping from the high-level source to the low-level, explicitly parallel code, minimizing total performance data volume while still enabling users to interactively drill down to identify performance problems on remote systems. Moreover, they must accommodate execution heterogeneity and non-reproducible behavior, replacing *post-mortem* analysis with real-time analysis and optimization. Below, we outline the challenges inherent in integrating compilers and performance tools.

6.1 Integrated Compiler Support

To support source-level performance analysis of transformed programs, compilers must share data on the mapping from the low-level, executable code to the original source [1]. Conversely, a restructuring compiler should exploit dynamic performance data code generation during subsequent recompilation.

Compiler Data Sharing. Several academic and vendor groups have developed integrated compilation and performance analysis systems. For example, we integrated Pablo with the Rice Fortran D restructuring compiler to create an integrated system that could relate the performance of measured object code to regular data parallel source [1,2]. During compilation, the Fortran D compiler emitted both instrumented code and the sequence of source code transformations applied, tying each synthesized code fragment to a portion of the original data parallel source code. Later, during program execution, the instrumentation system captured data from the compiler-synthesized code. Finally, a post-processing phase exploited the program transformation data to map performance metrics to the original data parallel source code. These metrics included both execution times and array reference data locality.

In a related effort, Calzarossa *et al* [10] integrated Medea [9] with the VFC compiler's instrumentation system [6]. This integration provides a comprehensive view of the performance of irregular applications written in HPF+ [5]. For independent loops, each individual phase (work distribution, inspector, gather, executor, and scatter) is automatically instrumented by the compiler during the code transformation. Medea analyzes the collected performance data and presents a detailed assessment of the performance in each phase.

Finally, Malony *et al* [34] have developed complementary approaches for parallel, object-oriented pC++ [8], capturing data on object method invocations. Building on the Sage's [7] support for pC++, TAU includes routine and data access profile and parallel execution extrapolation displays.

Although promising, all of these are research efforts. Robust integration of performance measurement and compilers will require new committments from vendors to expose software interfaces and exchange performance data.

Performance-Directed Code Optimization. The compiler-performance tool partnership can aid compilers as well as performance tools by providing compilers with data not available from code analysis (e.g., likely loop bounds or branch directions). For example, trace scheduling for very long instruction word (VLIW) processors [18,13] can use profile data to optimize execution of the most probable code execution paths. Commercially, Silicon Graphics compilers use *prof* or *gprof* data to order procedure object code, based on procedure invocation frequencies, to reduce page faults and instruction cache misses.

More recently, Hwu *et al* [11] have developed even more aggressive profile-based optimization techniques for superscalar and VLIW code generation. These approaches are an integral part of the code generator for the new HP/Intel Merced processor.

For data parallel and object parallel codes, it is also possible to exploit data on interprocessor communication frequencies and method invocations to choose or optimize data distributions [3]. However, this and other performance-directed optimizations require concurrent, coordinated development of compilers and performance tools; market pressures often make this impractical. Simply put, despite the great promise of performance-directed code generation, much work remains to balance ease of use and possible performance gains.

6.2 Dynamic Resource Management

Although post-mortem performance analysis remains the method of choice, it is ill-suited to emerging multidisciplinary applications with time-varying resource demands that execute on heterogeneous collections of geographically distributed computing resources. Not only may the execution context not be repeatable *across* program executions, resource availability may change *during* execution. In such chaotic environments, only real-time measurement and dynamic optimization can adapt to changing application resource demands and system resource availability.

Dynamic optimization can be either interactive, based on real-time visualization and human-in-the-loop adaptation, or software-mediated by an intelligent decision support system. In both cases, the performance analyst must formulate general-purpose, performance-optimization rules that can be applied by the adaptive infrastructure.

Several groups have built interactive or software-mediated adaptive control systems [46]. Notable examples include Leblanc's [28] adaptive real-time system for robotic control, Schwan *et al*'s Falcon adaptive control toolkit [21], and our own Autopilot distributed control system [41].

Autopilot, built atop the Globus wide-area communication system [19], includes a set of configurable performance sensors and resource policy actuators. These sensors and actuators are managed by a fuzzy logic control system whose rules are triggered by sensor data. Rule outputs activate remote policy actuators to adjust application or system behavior for maximal performance. For interactive visualization and control, the fuzzy logic rule system can be replaced with our Virtue immersive visualization system [37].

7 Conclusions

As the space of high-performance computing evolves to include ever more complex, distributed collections of parallel systems, analyzing and tuning application, system software, and architecture designs becomes increasingly difficult.

To understand and master the complexity of these systems, a plethora of performance analysis tools and techniques have been proposed and developed. Although great progress has been made, many open problems remain, including accurate performance prediction for large-scale applications, real-time adaptive control for wide-area computations, and visualizations that highlight important performance problems.

Acknowledgements

This work was supported in part by the Defense Advanced Research Projects Agency under DARPA contracts DABT63-94-C0049 (SIO Initiative), F30602-96-C-0161, DABT63-96-C-0027, and N66001-97-C-8532 by the National Science Foundation under grants NSF CDA 94-01124 and ASC 97-20202, and by the Department of Energy under contracts DOE B-341494, W-7405-ENG-48, and 1-B-333164.

References

1. ADVE, V., MELLOR-CRUMMEY, J., WANG, J.-C., AND REED, D. Integrating Compilation and Performance Analysis for Data-Parallel Programs. In *Proceedings of Supercomputing'95* (November 1995).
2. ADVE, V. S., MELLOR-CRUMMEY, J., ANDERSON, M., KENNEDY, K., WANG, J., AND REED, D. A. Integrating Compilation and Performance Analysis for Data-Parallel Programs. In *Proceedings of the Workshop on Debugging and Performance Tuning for Parallel Computing Systems*, M. L. Simmons, A. H. Hayes, D. A. Reed, and J. Brown, Eds. IEEE Computer Society Press, 1994.
3. BALASUNDARAM, V., FOX, G., KENNEDY, K., AND KREMER, U. A Static Performance Estimator to Guide Data Partitioning Decisions. In *3rd ACM Sigplan Symposium on Principles and Practice of Parallel Programming (PPoPP)* (April 1991).
4. BENKNER, S. Vienna Fortran Compilation System - Version 2.0 - User's Guide. Tech. rep., University of Vienna, 1995.
5. BENKNER, S., AND PANTANO, M. HPF+: Optimizing HPF for Advanced Applications. *Supercomputer 13*, 2 (1997), 31–43.
6. BENKNER, S., SANJARI, K., SIPKOVA, V., AND VELKOV, B. Parallelizing Irregular Applications with the Vienna HPF+ Compiler VFC. In *HPCN Europe* (April 1998), Lecture Notes in Computer Science, Springer-Verlag.
7. BODIN, F., BECKMAN, P., GANNON, D., GOTWALS, J., NARAYANA, S., SRINIVAS, S., AND WINNICKA, B. Sage++: An Object-Oriented Toolkit and Class Library for Building Fortran and C++ Restructuring Tools. In *OON-SKI'94 Proceedings of the First Annual Object-Oriented Numerics Conference* (April 1993), pp. 122–138.
8. BODIN, F., BECKMAN, P., GANNON, D., NARAYANA, S., AND YANG, S. Distributed pC++: Basic Ideas for an Object Parallel Language. In *OON-SKI'93 Proceedings of the First Annual Object-Oriented Numerics Conference* (April 1993), pp. 1–24.
9. CALZAROSSA, M., MASSARI, L., MERLO, A., PANTANO, M., AND TESSERA, D. Medea: A Tool for Workload Characterization of Parallel Systems. *IEEE Parallel and Distributed Technology 3*, 4 (November 1995), 72–80.

10. Calzarossa, M., Massari, L., Merlo, A., Pantano, M., and Tessera, D. Integration of a Compilation System and a Performance Tool: The HPF+ Approach. In *HPCN Europe* (April 1998), Lecture Notes in Computer Science, Springer-Verlag.
11. Chang, P. P., Mahlke, S. A., and Hwu, W. W. Using Profile Information to Assist Classic code Optimization. *Software - Practice & Experience* (to appear).
12. Cleveland, W. S., and MiGill, M. E., Eds. *Dynamic Graphics for Statistics.* Wadsworth & Brooks/Cole, 1988.
13. Colwell, R., Nix, R., O'Donnell, J., Papwoth, D., and Rodman, P. A VLIW Architecture for a Trace Scheduling Compiler. In *Proceedings of the Second International Conference on Architectural Support for Programming Languages and Operating Systems* (October 1987).
14. Couch, A. *Graphical Representations of Program Performance on Hypercube Message-Passing Multiprocessors.* PhD thesis, Tufts University, Department of Computer Science, 1988.
15. DeRose, L., Zhang, Y., and Reed, D. Svpablo: A Multi-Language Performance Analysis System. In *Computer Performance Evaluation Modelling Techniques and Tools* (September 1998), R. Puigjaner, N. Savino, and B. Serra, Eds., Lecture Notes in Computer Science, vol. 1469, Springer-Verlag, pp. 352–355.
16. Fahringer, T. Estimating and Optimizing Performance for Parallel Programs. *IEEE Computer 28*, 11 (November 1995), 47–56.
17. Fahringer, T. Effective Symbolic Analysis to Support Parallelizing Compilers and Performance Analysis. In *HPCN Europe* (April 1997), Lecture Notes in Computer Science, Springer-Verlag.
18. Fisher, J. Trace Scheduling: A Technique for Global Microcode Compactation. *IEEE Tranactions on Computers* (July 1981), 478–490.
19. Foster, I., and Kesselman, C., Eds. *The Grid: Blueprint for a New Computing Infrastructure.* Morgan-Kaufmann, 1998.
20. Graham, S., Kessler, P., and McKusick, M. gprof: A Call Graph Execution Profiler. In *Proceedings of the SIGPLAN '82 Symposium on Compiler Construction* (Boston, MA, June 1982), Association for Computing Machinery, pp. 120–126.
21. Gu, W., Eisenhauer, G., Schwan, K., and Vetter, J. Falcon: On-line monitoring and steering of parallel programs. *Concurrency: Practice and Experience 10*, 9 (1998), 699–736.
22. Hartleb, F., and Mertsiotakis, V. Bounds for the Mean Runtime of Parallel Programs. In *Computer Performance Evaluation '92: Modeling Techniques and Tools* (1992), R. Pooley and J. Hillston, Eds., pp. 197–210.
23. Heath, M. T., and Etheridge, J. A. Visualizing the Performance of Parallel Programs. *IEEE Software* (Sept. 1991), 29–39.
24. Heath, M. T., Malony, A. D., and Rover, D. T. The Visual Display of Parallel Performance Data. *Computer 28*, 11 (1995), 21–8.
25. Hurley, C., and Buja, A. Analyzing High-dimensional Data with Motion Graphics. *SIAM Journal of Scientific and Statistical Computing 11*, 6 (Nov. 1990), 1193–1211.
26. Kraemer, E., and Stasko, J. T. The Visualization of Parallel Systems: An Overview. *Jour. Parallel and Distributed Computing 18*, 2 (1993), 105–17.
27. Larus, J. R., and Schnarr, E. EEL: Machine-Independent Executable Editing. In *Proceedings of the SIGPLAN '95 Conference on Programming Languages Design and Impelementation (PLDI)* (June 1995).

28. LEBLANC, T. J., AND MARKATOS, E. P. Operating System Support for Adaptive Real-time Systems. In *Proceedings of the Seventh IEEE Workshop on Real-Time Operating Systems and Software* (May 1990), pp. 1–10.
29. MALONY, A. D., REED, D. A., AND WIJSHOFF, H. Performance Measurement Intrusion and Perturbation Analysis. *IEEE Transactions on Parallel and Distributed Systems 3*, 4 (July 1992), 433–450.
30. MENDES, C. L. *Performance Scalability Prediction on Multicomputers.* PhD thesis, University of Illinois at Urbana-Champaign, May 1997.
31. MENDES, C. L., WANG, J.-C., AND REED, D. A. Automatic Performance Prediction and Scalability Analysis for Data Parallel Programs. In *Proceedings of the CRPC Workshop on Data Layout and Performance Prediction* (Houston, April 1995).
32. MILLER, B. P., CALLAGHAN, M. D., CARGILLE, J. M., HOLLINGSWORTH, J. K., IRVIN, R. B., KARAVANIC, K. L., KUNCHITHAPADAM, K., AND NEWHALL, T. The Paradyn Parallel Performance Measurement Tools. *IEEE Computer 28*, 11 (November 1995), 37–46.
33. MIPS TECHNOLOGIES INC. *MIPS R10000 Microprocessor User's Manual*, 2.0 ed., 1996.
34. MOHR, B., MALONY, A., AND CUNY, J. Tau Tuning and Analysis Utilities for Portable Parallel Programming. In *Parallel Programming using C++*, G. Wilson, Ed. M.I.T. Press, 1996.
35. NICKOLAYEV, O. Y., ROTH, P. C., AND REED, D. A. Real-time Statistical Clustering for Event Trace Reduction. *International Journal of Supercomputer Applications and High Performance Computing* (1997).
36. REED, D. A. Experimental Performance Analysis of Parallel Systems: Techniques and Open Problems. In *Proceedings of the 7th International Conference on Modelling Techniques and Tools for Computer Performance Evaluation* (May 1994), pp. 25–51.
37. REED, D. A., AYDT, R. A., DEROSE, L., MENDES, C. L., RIBLER, R. L., SHAFFER, E., SIMITCI, H., VETTER, J. S., WELLS, D. R., WHITMORE, S., AND ZHANG, Y. Performance Analysis of Parallel Systems: Approaches and Open Problems. In *Proceedings of the Joint Symposium on Parallel Processing (JSPP)* (June 1998), pp. 239–256.
38. REED, D. A., AYDT, R. A., NOE, R. J., ROTH, P. C., SHIELDS, K. A., SCHWARTZ, B., AND TAVERA, L. F. Scalable Performance Analysis: The Pablo Performance Analysis Environment. In *Proceedings of the Scalable Parallel Libraries Conference* (1993), A. Skjellum, Ed., IEEE Computer Society.
39. REED, D. A., ELFORD, C. L., MADHYASTHA, T., SCULLIN, W. H., AYDT, R. A., AND SMIRNI, E. I/O, Performance Analysis, and Performance Data Immersion. In *Proceedings of MASCOTS '96* (Feb. 1996), pp. 1–12.
40. RIBARSKY, W., AYERS, E., EBLE, J., AND MUKHERJEA, S. Using Glyphmaker to Create Customized Visualizations of Complex Data. *IEEE Computer*, July (1994), 57–64.
41. RIBLER, R., VETTER, J., SIMITCI, H., AND REED, D. Autopilot: Adaptive Control of Distributed Applications. In *Proc. Seventh IEEE Int'l Symp. High Performance Distributed Computing (HPDC)* (1998), pp. 172–9.
42. ROBERTSON, G. G., CARD, S. K., AND MACKINLAY, J. D. Information Visualization using 3D Interactive Animation. *Communications of the ACM 36*, 4 (1993), 56–71.
43. ROSENBLUM, L. J. Research Issues in Scientific Visualization. *IEEE Computer Graphics and Applications 14*, 2 (1994), 61–3.

44. Stasko, J., Domingue, J., Brown, M. H., and Price, B. A., Eds. *Software Visualization: Programming as a Multimedia Experience,*. MIT Press, Cambridge, MA, 1998.
45. Sun, X. H., Pantano, M., and Fahringer, T. Performance Range Comparison for Restructuring Compilation. In *IEEE International Conference on Parallel Processing* (Minneapolis, August 1998), pp. 595–602.
46. Vetter, J. S. Computational Steering Annotated Bibliography. *SIGPLAN Notices 32*, 6 (1997), 40–4.
47. Yan, J. C., Sarukkai, S. R., and Mehra, P. Performance Measurement, Visualization and Modeling of Parallel and Distributed Programs using the AIMS Toolkit. *Software Practice & Experience 25*, 4 (April 1995), 429–461.
48. Zagha, M., Larson, B., Turner, S., and Itzkowitz, M. Performance Analysis Using the MIPS R10000 Performance Counters. In *Proceedings of Supercomputing'96* (November 1996).

Measurement-Based Analysis of Networked System Availability

Ravishankar K. Iyer, Zbigniew Kalbarczyk, and Mahesh Kalyanakrishnan

Center for Reliable and High-Performance Computing
University of Illinois at Urbana-Champaign
1308 W. Main St., Urbana, IL 61801-2307 USA
{iyer,kalbar,mahesh}@crhc.uiuc.edu

1 Introduction

The dependability of a system can be experimentally evaluated at different phases of its life cycle. In the *design phase*, computer-aided design (CAD) environments are used to evaluate the design via simulation, including simulated fault injection. Such fault injection tests the effectiveness of fault-tolerant mechanisms and evaluates system dependability, providing timely feedback to system designers. Simulation, however, requires accurate input parameters and validation of output results. Although the parameter estimates can be obtained from past measurements, this is often complicated by design and technology changes. In the *prototype phase*, the system runs under controlled workload conditions. In this stage, controlled physical fault injection is used to evaluate the system behavior under faults, including the detection coverage and the recovery capability of various fault tolerance mechanisms. Fault injection on the real system can provide information about the failure process, from fault occurrence to system recovery, including error latency, propagation, detection, and recovery (which may involve reconfiguration). But this type of fault injection can only study artificial faults; it cannot provide certain important dependability measures, such as mean time between failures (MTBF) and availability. In the *operational phase*, a direct measurement-based approach can be used to measure systems in the field under real workloads. The collected data contain a large amount of information about naturally occurring errors/failures. Analysis of this data can provide understanding of actual error/failure characteristics and insight into analytical models. Although measurement-based analysis is useful for evaluating the real system, it is limited to detected errors. Further, conditions in the field can vary widely, casting doubt on the statistical validity of the results. Thus, all three approaches - simulated fault injection, physical fault injection, and measurement-based analysis - are required for accurate dependability analysis.

In the design phase, simulated fault injection can be conducted at different levels: the electrical level, the logic level, and the function level. The objectives of simulated fault injection are to determine dependability bottlenecks, the coverage of error detection/recovery mechanisms, the effectiveness of reconfiguration schemes, performance loss, and other dependability measures. The feedback from simulation can be extremely useful in cost-effective redesign of the system. For

G. Haring et al. (Eds.): Performance Evaluation, LNCS 1769, pp. 161–199, 2000.

thorough discussion of different techniques for simulated fault injection can be found in [15].

In the prototype phase, while the objectives of physical fault injection are similar to those of simulated fault injection, the methods differ radically because real fault injection and monitoring facilities are involved. Physical faults can be injected at the hardware level (logic or electrical faults) or at the software level (code or data corruption). Heavy-ion radiation techniques can also be used to inject faults and stress the system. The detailed treatment of the instrumentation involved in fault injection experiments using real examples, including several fault injection environments is given in [15].

In the operational phase, measurement-based analysis must address issues such as how to monitor computer errors and failures and how to analyze measured data to quantify system dependability characteristics. Although methods for the design and evaluation of fault-tolerant systems have been extensively researched, little is known about how well these strategies work in the field. A study of production systems is valuable not only for accurate evaluation but also for identifying reliability bottlenecks in system design. In [15] the measurement-based analysis is based on over 200 machine-years of data gathered from IBM, DEC, and Tandem systems (note that these are not networked systems).

In this chapter we discuss the current research in the area of experimental analysis of computer system dependability in the context of methodologies suited for measurement-based dependability analysis of networked systems. We use examples of LAN of UNIX-based workstations, LAN of Windows NT based computers, and Internet to present methods for collecting and analyzing failure data to obtain dependability characterization of the network.

2 Measurement-Based Studies of Computer System Availability

There are many possible sources of errors, including untested manufacturing faults and software defects, transient errors induced by radiation, power surges, or other physical processes, operator errors, and environmental factors. The occurrence of errors is also highly dependent on the workload running on the system. A distribution of operational outages from various error sources for several major commercial systems are reported in [35].

There is no better way to understand dependability characteristics of computer systems (including networked systems) than by direct measurements and analysis. Here, measuring a real system means monitoring and recording naturally occurring errors and failures in the system while it is running under user workloads. Analysis of such measurements can provide valuable information on actual error/failure behavior, identify system bottlenecks, quantify dependability measures, and verify assumptions made in analytical models. Given field error-data collected from a real system, a measurement-based study consists of four steps, as shown in Fig. 1: 1) data processing, 2) model identification and parameter estimation, 3) model solution if necessary, and 4) analysis of models and measures.

Step 1 consists of extracting necessary information from field data (the result can be a form of compressed data or flat data), classifying errors and failures, and coalescing repeated error reports. In a computer system, a single problem commonly results in many repeated error observations occurring in rapid succession. To ensure that the analysis is not biased by these repeated observations of the same problem, all error entries that have the same error type and occur within a short time interval (e.g., 5 minutes) of each other should be coalesced into a single record. The output of this step is a form of coalesced data in which errors and failures are identified. This step is highly dependent on the measured system. Coalescing algorithms have been proposed in [46], [13], [8].

Step 2 includes identifying appropriate models (such as Markov models) and estimating various measures of interest (such as MTBFs and TBF distributions) from the coalesced data. Several models have been proposed and validated using real data. These include workload-dependent cyclostationary models [3], a workload hazard model [10], and error/failure correlation models [41]. Statistical analysis packages such as SAS [33] or measurement-based dependability analysis tools such as MEASURE+ [44] are useful at this stage.

Step 3 solves these models to obtain dependability measures (such as reliability, availability, and transient reward rates). Dependability and performance modeling and evaluation tools such as SHARPE [32] can be used in this step. Step 4, the most creative part of this study, involves a careful interpretation of the models and measures obtained from the data; for example, the identification of reliability bottlenecks and the impact on availability of design enhancement. The analysis methods can vary significantly from one study to another, depending on project goals.

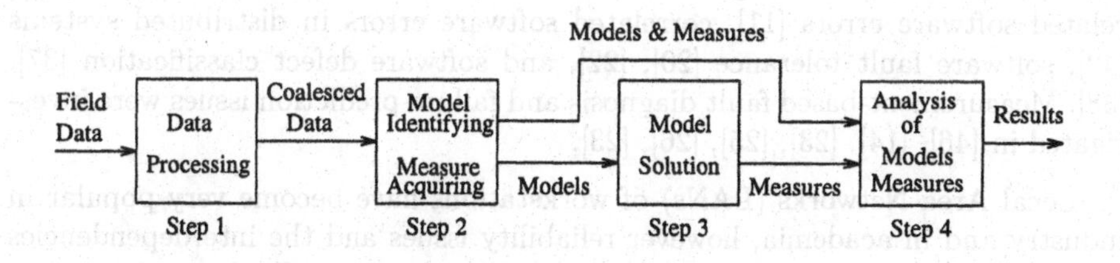

Fig. 1. Measurement-based Analysis

Measurement-based dependability analysis of operational systems has evolved significantly over the past 15 years. These studies have addressed one or more of the following issues: basic error characteristics, dependency analysis, modeling and evaluation, software dependability, and fault diagnosis. Table 1 provides a quick overview of the issues addressed in the literature.

Early studies in this field investigated transient errors in DEC computer systems and found that more than 95% of all detected errors are intermittent or transient errors [34], [28]. The studies also showed that the inter arrival time of transient errors follows a Weibull distribution with a decreasing error rate. This distribution was also shown to fit the software failure data collected from an IBM operating system [12]. A recent study of failure data from three different operating systems showed that time to error (TTE) can be represented by a multistage gamma distribution for a single- machine operating system and by a hyperexponential distribution for the measured distributed operating systems [21].

Several studies have investigated the relationship between system activity and failures. In the early 1980s, analysis of measurements from IBM [2] and DEC [3] machines revealed that the average system failure rate was strongly correlated with the average workload on the system. The effect of workload-imposed stress on software was investigated in [4] and [12]. Analyses of DEC [39], [48], and Tandem [19] multicomputer systems showed that correlated failures across processors are not negligible, and their impacts on availability and reliability are significant [6], [40], [41].

In [9], analytical modeling and measurements were combined to develop measurement-based reliability/performability models using data collected from an IBM mainframe. The results showed that a semi-Markov process is better than a Markov process for modeling system behavior. Markov reward modeling techniques were further applied to distributed systems [43] and fault-tolerant systems [20] to quantify performance loss due to errors/failures for both hardware and software.

A census of Tandem system availability indicated that software faults are the major source of system outages in the measured fault-tolerant systems [7]. Analyses of field data from different software systems investigated several dependability issues including the effectiveness of error recovery [47], hardware-related software errors [11], correlated software errors in distributed systems [42], software fault tolerance [20], [22], and software defect classification [37], [38]. Measurement-based fault diagnosis and failure prediction issues were investigated in [46], [14], [23], [25], [26], [23].

Local Area Networks (LANs) of workstations have become very popular in industry and in academia, however reliability issues and the interdependencies of failures in such networks are still not well understood. Studies presented in [45] and [18] are a step in the direction of understanding of the nature of failures in networked systems. Thakur [45] presented a simple yet effective methodology for collecting and analyzing failures in a network of UNIX-based workstations. The majority of observed failures (68%) encountered were network related. Kalyanakrishnam [18] analyzed machine reboots collected in a network of Windows NT-based servers. This study investigated the major causes of reboots and obtained quantitative measures of machine up-times and down-times. The failure behavior of a typical machine and of the network as a whole was modeled in terms of a finite state machine, providing insights into the typical problems encountered and their dynamics.

Table 1. Measurement-Based Studies of Computer-System Dependability

Category	Issues	Studies
Data coalescing	Analysis of time-based tuples	[46], [8]
	Clustering based on type and time	[13], [19], [43]
Basic Error Characteristics	Transient faults/errors	[34], [28], [13]
	Error/failure bursts	[13], [43]
	TTE/TTF distributions	[28], [12], [21]
Dependency Analysis	Hardware failure/workload dependency	[2], [4], [10]
	Software failure/workload dependency	[4], [12]
	Correlated failures and impact	[39], [48], [41]
Modeling and Evaluation	Two-way and multiway failure dependency	[6], [19], [40]
	Performability model for single machine	[9]
	Markov reward model for distributed system	[43]
	Two-level models for operating systems	[21]
Software Dependability	Error recovery	[47]
	Hardware-related & correlated software errors	[11], [42], [21]
	Software fault tolerance	[7], [20], [22]
	Software defect classification	[37], [38]
Fault Diagnosis	Heuristic trend analysis	[46], [23]
	Statistical analysis of symptoms	[14]
	Network fault signature	[25], [26] [27]
Network availability	Failure behavior of LANs of machines	[45], [18]
	Internet host behavior	[16], [36], [24], [1], [29], [30], [17]

The issue of Internet host behavior has been the focus of active research. Kalyanakrishnam [17] studied reliability of Internet hosts from the user perspective. Long et al. [24] evaluated mean time to failure (MTTF), mean time to repair (MTTR), availability, and reliability for a sample of hosts on the Internet by repeatedly polling the hosts from different sites at exponentially distributed time intervals. Paxson [30] described in great detail the vagaries of end-to-end Internet routing. The traceroute [36], [16] program (which traces the probable route of data from a remote host to the user site) was extensively used to study, in detail, routing behavior in the Internet. Major routing pathologies and properties were identified.

Chimoy [5] examined NSFNET backbone routing. The study was based on the trace information collected over a 12-hour period on all the NSFNET nodes on the T1 backbone. The backbone was evaluated with respect to parameters such as Update Propagation Time (the time taken to propagate update information from one router to another) and Unreachability Cycle Distribution (the time during which a network is unreachable from the backbone. It was shown that only a small number of networks have a highly volatile connectivity to the NSFNET backbone; most networks have a fairly stable connectivity. Paxson [30] obtained metrics that could characterize Internet performance. Arlitt et al. [1] studied Web server workloads and obtained invariants that characterize it. In this study, the access logs of six different Web servers were evaluated in terms of Success Rate, Mean Transfer Size, and Inter-Reference Time. It was found that most of the Web server traffic consisted of HTML and image files.

In the following sections, we discuss issues and representative studies involved in measurements, data processing, error and failure analysis, dependency analysis, and the modeling and evaluation of dependability.

3 Measurements

The question of what and how to measure is difficult one. A combination of installed and custom instrumentation is typically used in most studies. From a statistical point of view, sound evaluations require a considerable amount of data. In modern computer systems, failures are infrequent and, in order to obtain meaningful data, measurements must be taken over a long period of time. Also, the measured system must be exposed to a wide range of usage conditions for the results to be representative. In an operational system, only detected errors can be measured.

There are two ways to take measurements: on-line automated logging and human manual logging. Many large computer systems, such as IBM and DEC mainframes, provide error-logging software in the operating system. Similarly, commercial operating systems such as UNIX and Windows NT offer capabilities for error logging. This software records information on errors occurring in the various subsystems, such as the memory, disk, and network subsystems, as well as other system events, such as reboots and shutdowns. The reports usually include information on the location, time, and type of the error, the system state at the time of the error, and sometimes error recovery (e.g., retry) information. The reports are stored chronologically in a permanent system file. As failures are relatively rare events, it is necessary to meticulously collect and analyze error data for many machine months before the results of the data analysis can be considered statistically valid. Such regular and prolonged data acquisition is possible only through automated event logging. Hence most studies of failures in single and networked computer systems are based on the error logs maintained by the operating system running on those machines. The main advantage of on-line automatic logging is its ability to record a large amount of information about transient errors and to provide details of automatic error recovery processes, which cannot be done manually. Disadvantages are that an on-line log does not usually include information about the cause and propagation of the error or about off-line diagnosis. Also, under some crash scenarios, the system may fail too quickly for any error messages to be recorded.

Before we explore how event logs can be used in analyzing behavior of networked systems, we illustrate how events are generated and logged in the Windows NT operating system. We also show the format and particulars of the event log created by the operating system.

3.1 Event Logging Mechanism in Windows NT Operating System

Event logging in the Windows NT operating system is provided through a dedicated *Event Logging Subsystem.* This subsystem consists of multiple execution threads each carrying out part of the event logging functionality. Some threads are dedicated to receiving event log requests through transport layer *ports*, whereas other threads actually write the event to the event log.

The mechanism of event logging is slightly different for different types of events. For events that are logged by applications or other subsystems, the Event Logging Subsystem provides an API (Application programmer interface) to log events. For events that are generated within the *Executive*[1] (e.g., device drivers), the events are directly written to the event log file by the *I/O Manager*, which is a part of the Windows NT Executive.

3.2 Event Log Format

The event logs conform to a specific format employed by the Windows NT operating system. Events on Windows NT machines fall into one of three types:

- *Application events* are those that are logged by applications running on NT machines (e.g., error logged by MSExchange MTA (Message Transfer Agent)).
- *System events* are those that are reported by components of the Windows NT operating system (e.g., Server, Redirector, NETLOGON service, etc.).
- *Security events* are those that relate to user authentication or verification of access permissions.

A sample event log is shown below, the format of the log may not be universal, but the fields in it are.

```
1997/09/11 15:02:53 4 0 5715 NETLOGON N/A EXCHOU-CA0201 LSA EXCHOU-CONN02 1
```

The fields in the event log are:

1. *Date* and *time* of the event
2. *Severity* of the event (4) (1 indicates an Error, 2 indicates a Warning, 4 indicates an Information message)
3. Event *id* (5715)
4. The *source* that logs that event (NETLOGON)
5. The *machine* on which the event was logged (EXCHOU-CA0201)
6. *Event-specific information* (EXCHOU-CONN02 1)

[1] *Kernel* and *Executive* are two basic components of the Windows NT operating system. The two components run in *kernel* (privileged) *mode*.

Typically, each source that logs an event provides a "message" file that contains a description of the event. So further information about the event can be obtained by looking at the text description in the message file. All Windows NT systems have a built-in Event Viewer, a tool used to examine events logged on a given machine. The Event Viewer uses the message files provided by the system component or application in order to provide a textual description of the event. This particular method of displaying events pose quite a few problems, which are listed below:

- The message files ship with the respective application. In order to interpret the event, the application that logged the message must be running on the machine performing the analysis. Because this is impractical, it is not possible to obtain the textual description of most application events.
- Even for system events, not all message files are accessible. The Windows NT event logging source code contains message files for some, but not all, system components.
- Windows NT stores the event logs in a file on the local machine. Depending on the system configuration, the old event logs get overwritten regularly so that the number of logs collected does not increase without bound. For this reason, it is necessary to retrieve event logs before they are over-written.

4 Data Processing

Usually, online logs contain a large amount of redundant and irrelevant information in various formats. Thus, data processing must be performed to classify this information and to put it into a flat format to facilitate subsequent analyses. The first step in data processing is error classification. This process classifies errors in the measured system into types based on the subsystems and components in which they occur. There is no uniform or best error classification, because different systems have different hardware and software architectures. Moreover, the error categories depend on the criteria used to classify errors.

4.1 Measurement Overview

As we focus on the network systems, a basic yet useful classification is based on the fault origin. A networked computing environment has two major types of faults based on their source:

- *Machine-related.* A computation node (workstation) encounters failure conditions because of problems that are local to that workstation.
- *Network-related.* A computation node encounters a failure because of a problem in a network component. For example, a failure condition encountered on a client due to a failed server would be classified as a network-related failure.

Table 2 summarizes the classification of errors collected for a LAN of UNIX workstations [45], a LAN of Windows NT machines [18], and Internet [17]. Table 2 should not be used to make a direct comparison between these networks because they are vastly different systems, measured over different periods and operating under different conditions. The data are, however, useful to provide insight into the type of failures encountered in different environments. For example, Table 2 indicates that most of the problems in a LAN of UNIX workstations and on the Internet are network-related. The data for the Windows NT-based network show opposite tendency, i.e., most of the problems are machine-related. The reason is that for the Windows NT based system we analyze only machine reboots, and most of these can be attributed to machine-related problems. The above classification is very generic and does not provide enough insight into the real nature of failures observed in the network system. More detailed analysis is needed to identify weak points in the system.

Table 2. Network-related and Machine-related Problems in Three Different Network Systems

	LAN of UNIX Workstations	LAN of Windows NT Machines	Internet
Type of environment	Academic environment	Commercial environment	N/A
Type and number of machines	69 SunOS-based workstations	68 Windows NT 4.0 based mail servers	97 most popular Web sites
Period for data collecting	32 weeks	6 months	40 weeks
Failure context	All types of failures logged in a workstation's system log.	Machine reboots logged in a server system log.	Inability to contact a host and fetch an HTML file from it.
Machine-related failures	32%	69%	47%
Network-related failures	68%	31%	53%

In the following discussion, failure data collected from a LAN of UNIX-based workstations and a LAN of Windows NT-based servers are used to illustrate analysis methods for obtaining detailed failure characterization of the system behavior. In the case of Internet, the process of collecting and analyzing data is significantly different that used for the two LANs. Therefore, the Internet related analysis is presented separately, in Section 10 of this chapter.

4.2 Data Extraction and Data Entry

The data processing that follows error classification consists of two steps: *data extraction* and *data coalescing.* Data extraction consists of selecting useful entries, such as error and reboot reports from the log file (throwing away uninteresting entries such as disk volume change reports) and transforming the data set into a flat format. The design of the flat format depends on the necessity of the subsequent analyses. The following is a possible format:

entry number | logging time | error type | device id | error description fields

In on-line error logs, a single fault in the system can result in many repeated error reports in a short period of time. To ensure that the subsequent analyses will not be distorted by these repeated reports, entries that correspond to the same problem should be coalesced into a single event, or *tuple* [46]. A typical data-coalescing algorithm merges all error entries of the same error type that occur within a ΔT interval of each other into a tuple. A tuple reflects the occurrence of one or more errors of the same type in rapid succession. It can be represented by a record containing information such as the number of entries in the tuple and the time duration of the tuple.

Different systems may require different time intervals to data coalesce. A recent study [8] defined two kinds of mistakes that can be made in data coalescing: *collision* and *truncation*. A collision occurs when the detection times of two faults are close enough (within ΔT) that they are combined into a tuple. A truncation occurs when the time between two reports caused by a single fault is greater than ΔT, so that the two reports are split into different tuples. If ΔT is large, collisions are likely to occur. If ΔT is small, truncations are likely to occur. The study found that there is a time-interval threshold beyond which collisions rapidly increase. Based on this observation, the study proposed a statistical model that can be used to select an appropriate time interval. In our experience, collision is not a big problem if the error type and device information is used in data coalescing, as shown in the above coalescing algorithm. Truncation is usually not considered to be a problem [8]. Also, there are techniques [14], [23] to deal with truncation which have been used for fault diagnosis and failure prediction.

4.3 Error and Failure Analysis

Once coalesced data is obtained, the basic dependability characteristics of the measured system can be identified by a preliminary statistical analysis. Commonly used measures in the analysis include error/failure frequency, TTE or TTF distribution, and system availability. These measures provide an overall picture of the system and help to identify dependability bottlenecks.

Initial Classification of Data Collected from a LAN of UNIX-Based Workstations. To better understand real failure nature, the machine-related and network-related failures are classified into two groups based on the effect they have on the network components [45]. This kind of analysis helps in focusing resources to the major failure points in the system. Two basic classes are identified:

- *Hard failure.* A failure state, in which a machine becomes unusable. An unresponsive server, a loose cable, or even a keyboard error can cause a hard failure.
- *Soft failure.* A failure in which a system is affected in such a way that it does not become unusable. In most cases, this effect manifests as a performance loss. Failures such as disk errors and delayed responses from the server, are examples of soft failures.

In [45], it was observed that, on a system-wide basis, 72% of the failures are hard failures and 28% are soft failures. Further analysis of these failures shows that: (1) out of the 28% soft failures, 61% are network related, (2) machine-related failures constitute only 25% of the hard failures. With 75% of the hard failures related to the network, it is obvious that network components are the major cause of failures in a network of workstations. Note that by the hard network failure we understand a failure, a workstation encounters due to a failure (hard or soft) in another network component.

Types of Network and Machine Related Failures. Having established that network- related failures are the primary cause of problems in a network of workstations, we look at the types of network-related failures.

Network-related soft failures include:

- errors in remote procedure calls 0% (RPC errors, not important),
- network file-write errors 3% (NFS errors),
- delayed responses from the server due to an excessive load on the server 27% (performance-related),
- overflowing network buffers 3%.

Thus, soft failures account for approximately 30% of all network-related failures. A vast majority of network-related soft failures are performance related (failures due to inadequate performance response).

Network-related hard failures include:

- cable errors 4% (loose cable wire, unplugged transceiver),
- portmapper errors 1% (portmapper stops responding),
- Ethernet jamming due to hardware failure, buffer overflowing 6%, and
- network server unresponsiveness to a client's request 56%.

Thus, approximately 80% (56% of [4+1+6+56]%) of the network hard failures can be attributed to a failure due to an unresponsive server. In our measurement, in 48% of cases of an unresponsive server, a single client failed and identified a healthy server as unresponsive. In 22% of the cases, the client identified a wrong server as the problem source. For example, a client X says that server Y has failed; however, at that time server Z was the one that failed. In the remaining 30% of the cases, the right server was identified, but the cause for the server's hand/halt service could not be ascertained.

Machine-related soft failures, which account for a third of the machine-related failures, include:

- memory errors 32% (both system memory errors and disk errors) and
- kernel errors 5% (errors in any kernel structure, such as the signal stack or the process table).

Machine-related hard failures include:

- machine reboots 62% (reboot of a machine because of a local fault) including:
  1. halts due to impatient users 13% (user reboots local machine to remove a server problem),
  2. machine service by the system administrator 12%, and
  3. other machine problems that need reboot 75%.
- keyboard errors 1% (unresponsive keyboard makes a machine unusable).

We observed that there are at least twice as many machine-reboots (62%) as disk and memory errors together (32%). This is contrary to the VAXcluster data reported in [15], which indicates dominance of memory and disk errors.

Initial Classification of Data Collected from a LAN of Windows NT-Based Servers. The initial breakup of the data on a system reboot is primarily based on the events that preceded the current reboot by no more than an hour (and that occurred after the previous reboot). For each instance of a reboot, the most severe and frequently occurring events (hereafter referred to as prominent events) are identified. The corresponding reboot is then categorized based on the source and the id of these prominent events. In some cases, the prominent events are specific enough to identify the problem that caused the reboot. In other cases, only a high-level description of the problem can be obtained based on the knowledge of the prominent events. Table 3 shows the breakup of the reboots by category. (This data pertains to reboots in the domain over a period of six months.)

The categories in Table 3 should be interpreted as follows:

- *Hardware or firmware related problems*: This category includes events that indicate a problem with hardware components (network adapter, disk, etc.), their associated drivers (typically drivers failing to load because of a problem with the device), or some firmware (e.g., some events indicated that the Power On Self Test had failed).
- *Connectivity problems*: This category denotes events that indicated that either a system component (e.g., Redirector, Server) or a critical application (e.g., MSExchange System Attendant) could not retrieve information from a remote machine. In these scenarios, it is not possible to pinpoint the actual cause of the connectivity problem. Some of the connectivity failures result from network adapter problems and hence are categorized as hardware related.
- *Crucial application failure*: This category encompasses reboots, which are preceded by severe problems with, and possibly shutdown of, critical application software (such as Message Transfer Agent). In such cases, it wasn't

Table 3. Breakup of Reboots Based on Prominent Events

Category	Frequency	Percentage
Total reboots	1100	100
Hardware or firmware problems	105	9
Connectivity problems	241	22
Crucial application failures	152	14
Problems with a software component	42	4
Normal shutdowns	63	6
Normal reboots/power-off (no indication of any problems)	178	16
Unknown	319	29.00

clear why the application reported problems. If an application shutdown occurs as a result of connectivity problem, then the corresponding reboot is categorized as connectivity- related.

– *Problems with a software component*: Typically these reboots are characterized by startup problems (such as a critical system component not loading or a driver entry point not being found). Another significant type of problem in this category is the machine running out of virtual memory, possibly due to a memory leak in a software component. In many of these cases, the component causing the problem is not identifiable.
– *Normal shutdowns*: This category covers reboots, which are not preceded by warnings or error messages. Additionally, there are events that indicate shutting down of critical application software and some system components (e.g., the BROWSER). These represent shutdowns for maintenance or for correcting problems not captured in the event logs.
– *Normal reboots/power-off*: This category covers reboots which are typically not preceded by shutdown events, but do not appear to be caused by any problems either. No warnings or error messages appear in the event log before the reboot.

Based on data in Table 3, the following observations can be made about the failures:

1. 28% of the reboots cannot be categorized. Such reboots are indeed preceded by events of severity 2 or lesser, but there is not enough information available to decide (a) whether the events were severe enough to force a reboot of the machine or (b) the nature of the problem that the events reflect.
2. A significant percentage (22%) of the reboots have reported connectivity problems. This is not surprising considering that the workload on the machines is network I/O intensive.
3. Only a small percentage (10%) of the reboots can be traced to a system hardware component. Most of the identifiable problems are software related.
4. Nearly 50% of the reboots are abnormal reboots (i.e., the reboots were due to a problem with the machine rather than due to a normal shutdown).

5. In nearly 15% of the cases, severe problems with a crucial mail server application force a reboot of the machine.
6. Some of the reboots due to connectivity problems might be the result of propagated failures in the domain. Furthermore, it is possible that the machines functioning as the master browser and the Primary Domain Controller (PDC)[2], respectively are potential reliability bottlenecks of the domain.

5 Analysis of Failure Behavior of Individual Machines

After the preliminary investigation of the causes of failures, we probe failures from the perspective of an individual machine as well as the whole network. First we focus on the failure behavior of individual machines in the domain to obtain (1) estimates of machine up-times and down-times, (2) an estimate of the availability of each machine, and (3) a finite state model to describe the failure behavior of a typical machine in the domain. The discussion in Sections 5 to 9 is based on the results from the analysis of failure data collected from LAN of Windows NT based servers. Machine up-times and down-times are estimated as follows:

- For every reboot event encountered, the timestamp of the reboot is recorded.
- The timestamp of the event immediately preceding the reboot is also recorded. (This would be the last event logged by the machine before it goes down.)
- A smoothing factor of one hour is applied to the reboots (i.e., for multiple reboots that occurred within an period of one hour, except the last one, are disregarded). (Since the intermediate reboots indicate an incomplete recovery from the failure, the machine would have to be considered as being down until the last of such reboots occurs.)
- Each up-time estimate is generated by calculating the time difference between a reboot timestamp and the timestamp of the event preceding the next reboot.
- Each down-time estimate is obtained by calculating the time difference between a reboot timestamp and the timestamp of the event preceding it.

Machine up-times are presented in Table 4 (the numbers pertain to analysis of 5 months of data.)

As the standard deviation suggests, there is a great degree of variation in the machine up-times. The longest up-time was nearly three months. The average is skewed because of some of the longer up-times. The median is more representative of the typical up-time.

Machine down-times are provided in Table 5 (the numbers pertain to analysis of 5 months of data.).

As the table clearly shows, 50% of the down-times last about 12 minutes. This is probably too short a period to replace hardware components and reconfigure

[2] In the analyzed network, the machines belonged to a common Windows NT domain. One of the machines was configured as the Primary Domain Controller (PDC). The rest of the machines functioned as Backup Domain Controllers (BDCs).

Table 4. Machine Up-Time Statistics

Item	Value
Number of entries	616
Maximum	85.2 days
Minimum	1 hour
Average	11.82 days
Median	5.54 days
Standard Deviation	15.656 days

Table 5. Machine Down-Time Statistics

Item	Frequency
Number of entries	682
Maximum	15.76 days
Minimum	1 second
Average	1.97 hours
Median	11.43 minutes
Standard Deviation	15.86 hours

the machine. The implication is that majority of the problems are software related (memory leaks, misloaded drivers, application errors etc.). The maximum value is unrealistic and might have been due to the machine being temporarily taken off-line and put back in after a fortnight.

Discussion of up-times and down-times. Since the machines under consideration are dedicated mail servers, bringing down one or more of them would potentially disrupt storage, forwarding, reception, and delivery of mail. The disruption can be prevented if explicit rerouting is performed to avoid the machines that are down. But it is not clear if such rerouting was done or can be done. In this context the following observations would be causes for concern: (1) average down-time measured was nearly 2 hours or (2) 50% of the measured up-time samples were about 5 days or less.

6 Availability

Having estimated machine up-time and down-time, we can estimate the availability of each machine. The availability is evaluated as the ratio:

```
[<average up-time> / (<average up-time> + <average down-time>)] * 100
```

Table 6 summarizes the availability measurements. As it depicts, the majority of the machines have an availability of 99.7% or higher. Also there is not a great deal of variation among the individual values. This is surprising considering the rather large degree of variation in the average up-times. It follows that machines with smaller average up-times also had correspondingly smaller average down-times, so that the ratios are not very different. Hence, broadly speaking, the

Table 6. Machine Availability

Item	Value
Number of machines	66
Maximum	99.99
Minimum	89.39
Median	99.76
Average	99.35
Standard Deviation	1.52

domain has two types of machines: those that reboot often but recover quickly and those that stay up relatively longer but take longer to recover from a failure.

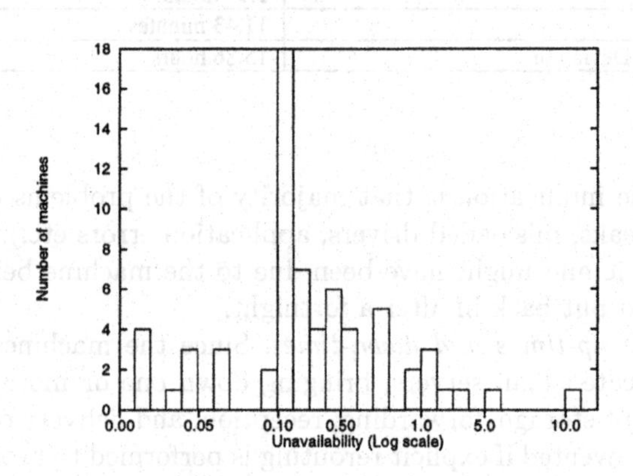

Fig. 2. Unavailability Distribution

Fig. 2 shows the *unavailability distribution* across the machines (unavailability was evaluated as: *100 - Availability*). Less than 20% of the machines had an availability of 99.9% or higher. However, nearly 90% of the machines had an availability of 99% or higher. It should be noted that these numbers indicate the fraction of time the machine is alive. They do not necessarily indicate the ability of the machine to provide useful service because the machine could be alive but still unable to provide the service expected of it. To elaborate, each of the machines in the domain acts as a mail server for a set of user machines. Hence, if any of these mail servers has problems that prevent it from receiving, storing, forwarding, or delivering mail, then that server would effectively be unavailable to the user machines even though it is up and running. Hence, to obtain a better estimate of machine availability, it is necessary to examine how long the machine is actually able to provide service to user machines.

Table 7. Machine States

State Name	Main Events (id/source/severity)	Explanation
Reboot	6005/EventLog/4	Machine logs reboot and other initialization events
Functional	5715/NETLOGON/4 1016/MSExchangeIS Private/8	Machine logs successful communication with PDC
Connectivity problems	3096/NETLOGON/1 5719/NETLOGON/1	Problems locating the PDC
Startup problems	7000/Service Control Manager/1 7001/Service Control Manager/1	Some system component or application failed to startup
MTA problems	2206/MSExchangeMTA/2 2207/MSExchangeMTA/2	Message Transfer Agent has problems with some internal databases
Adapter problems	4105/CpqNF3/1 4106/CpqNF3/1	The NetFlex Adapter driver reports problems
Temporary MTA problems	9322/MSExchangeMTA/4 9277/MSExchangeMTA/2 3175/MSExchangeMTA/2 1209/MSExchangeMTA/2	Message Transfer Agent reports problems of a temporary (or less severe) nature
Server problems	2006/Srv/1	Server component reports having received badly formatted requests
BROWSER problems	8021/BROWSER/2 8032/BROWSER/1	Browser reports inability to contact the master browser
Disk problems	11/Cpq32fs2/1 5/Cpq32fs2/1 9/Cpqarray/1 11/Cpqarray/1	Disk drivers report problems
Tape problems	15/dlttape/1	Tape driver reports problems
Snmpelea problems	3006/Snmpelea/1	Snmp event log agent reports error while reading an event log record
Shutdown	8033/BROWSER/4 1003/MSExchangeSA/4	Application/machine shutdown in progress

7 Modeling Machine Behavior

To obtain more accurate estimates of machine availability, we modeled the behavior of a typical machine in terms of a *finite state machine.* The model was based on the events that each machine logs. In the model, each state represents a level of functionality of the machine. A machine is either in a fully functional state, in which it logs events that indicate normal activity, or in a partially functional state, in which it logs events that indicate problems of a specific nature.

Selection and assignment of states to a machine was performed as follows. The logs were split into time-windows of one hour each. For each such window, the machine was assigned a state, which it occupied throughout the duration of the window. The assignment was based on the events that the machine logged in the window. Table 7 describes the states identified for the model.

Each machine (except the Primary Domain Controller (PDC) whose transitions were different from the rest) in the domain was modeled in terms of the states mentioned in the table. A hypothetical machine was created by combining the transitions of all the individual machines and filtering out transitions that occurred less frequently. Fig. 3 describes this hypothetical machine. In the figure, the weight on each outgoing edge represents the fraction of all transitions from the originating state (i.e., tail of the arrow) that end up in a given terminating state (i.e., head of the arrow). For example, if there is an edge from state A to state B with a weight of 0.5, then it would indicate that 50

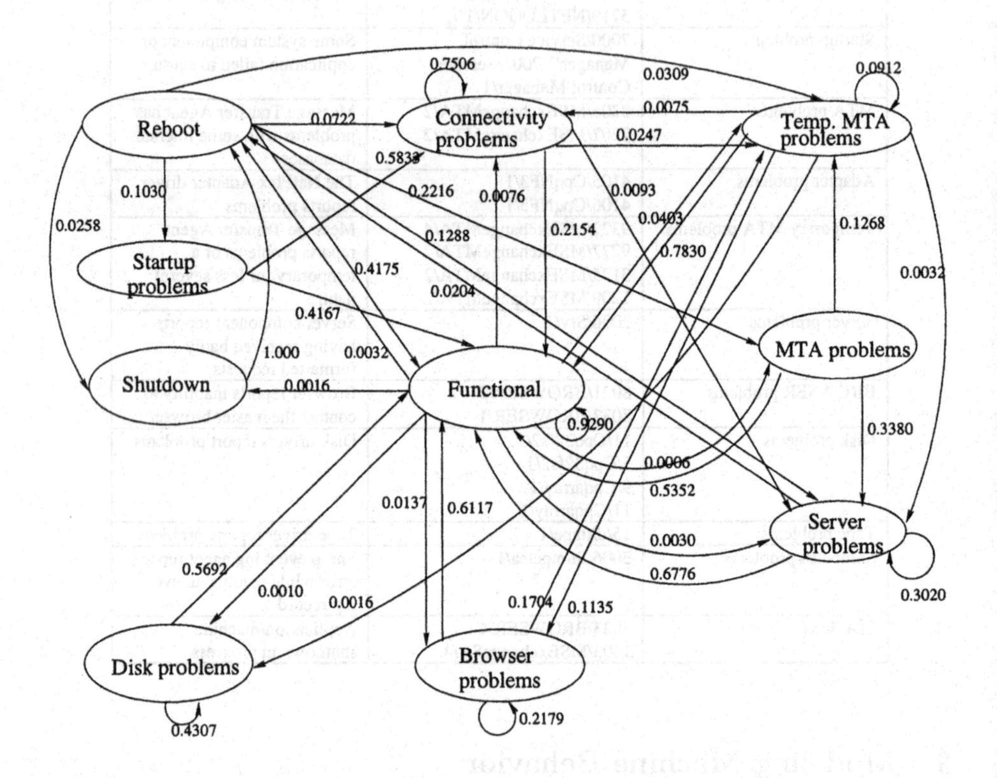

Fig. 3. State Transitions of a Typical Machine

From Fig. 3 the following observations can be made:

- Only about 40% of the transitions out of the *Reboot* states are to the *Functional* state. This indicates that in the majority of the cases, either the reboot is not able to solve the original problem, or it creates new ones.
- More than half of the transitions out of the *Startup problems* are to the *Connectivity problems* state. Thus, the majority of the startup problems are related to components that participate in network activity.
- Most of the problems that appear when the machine is functional are related to network activity. Problems with the disk and other components are less frequent.

– The self loops on states *Connectivity problems, Disk problems, Browser problems*, and *Server problems* indicate that these problems might be more persistent than others.
– More than 50% of the transitions out of *Disk problems* state are to the *Functional* state. Also, we do not observe any significant transitions from the *Disk problems* state to other states. This could be due to one or more of the following:
  1. The machines are equipped with redundant disks so that even if one of them is down, the functionality is not disrupted in a major way.
  2. The disk problems, though persistent, are not severe enough to disrupt normal activity (maybe retries to access the disk succeed).
  3. The activities that are considered to be representative of the *Functional* state may not involve much disk activity.
– Over 11% of the transitions out of the *Temporary MTA problems* state are to the *Browser problems* state. We suspect that there was a local problem that caused RPCs to timeout or fail and caused problems for the MTA and BROWSER. Another possibility is that, in both cases, it was the same remote machine that could not be contacted. Based on the available data, it was not possible to determine the real cause of the problem.

To view the transitions from a different perspective, we computed the weight of each outgoing edge as a fraction of all the transitions in the finite state machine. Such a computation provided some interesting insights, which are enumerated below:

1. Nearly 10% of all the transitions are between the *Functional* and *Temporary MTA* problems states. These MTA problems are typically problems with some RPC calls (either failing or being canceled).
2. About 0.5% (1 in 200) of all transitions are to the *Reboot* state.
3. The majority of the transitions into the *MTA problems* state are from the *Reboot* state. Thus, MTA problems are primarily problems that occur at startup. In contrast, the majority of the transitions into the *Server problems* state and the *Browser problems* state (excluding the self loops) are from the *Functional* state. So, these problems (or at least a significant fraction of them) typically appear after the machine is functional.
4. 92.16% of all transitions are into the *Functional* state. This figure is approximately a measure of the average time the hypothetical machine spends in the functional state. Hence it is a measure of the average availability of a typical machine. In this case, availability measures the ability of the machine to provide service, not just to stay alive.

In summary, a detailed examination of the behavior of the individual machines in the domain revealed:

– There is an average up-time of over 11 days and an average down-time of about 2 hours.

– There is a great degree of variation in the average up-time and down-time exhibited by each machine. Some machines stay up for over a month on the average, whereas more than 50% of the machines stay up for less than 2 weeks.
– The behavior of a majority of the machines can be characterized by a finite state model. Examination of the model indicates that problems related to connectivity appear frequently and might be persistent. It also indicates that temporary RPC problems or non-severe problems appear to be dominant.
– About 92% of all transitions are into the *Functional* state. Thus, a typical machine on an average would be able to provide useful service about 92% of the time.
– Average availability (measured as ratio involving up-time and down-time) was estimated to be 99.35%.

8 Modeling Domain Behavior

Analyzing system behavior from the perspective of the whole domain (1) provides a macroscopic view of the system rather than a machine-specific view, (2) helps to characterize the nature of interactions in the network, and (3) aids in identifying potential reliability bottlenecks and suggests ways to improve resilience to operational faults.

Table 8. Inter-reboot Time Statistics for the Domain

Item	Value
Number of samples	882
Maximum	2.46 days
Minimum	Less than 1 second
Median	2402 seconds
Average	4.09 hours
Standard Deviation	7.52 hours

Inter-reboot Times. An important characteristic of the domain is how often reboots occur within it. To examine this, the whole domain is treated as a black box, and every reboot of every machine in the domain is considered to be a reboot of the black box. Table 8 shows the statistics of such inter-reboot times measured across the whole domain.

Fig. 4 shows the distribution of inter-reboot times across the domain. Over a third of the reboots in the domain occur within 1000 seconds of each other. Probing these reboots further, about 25% of them (about 8% of the total) are due to the same machine being rebooted multiple times. Also, only about 43% of them occur during the working hours. So, it appears that the majority of such reboots are primarily due to planned shutdowns for maintenance. However, it is also possible that some of the reboots are correlated and that they are due

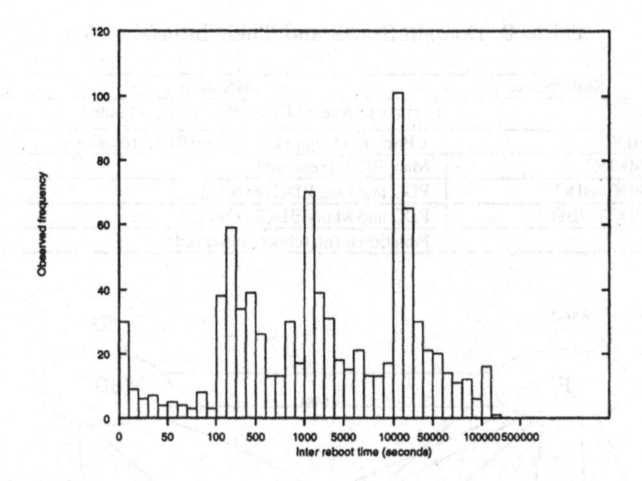

Fig. 4. Inter-reboot Time Distribution for the Domain

to common cause. Such reboots are indications of propagated failures across the domain.

8.1 Finite State Model of the Domain

The proper functioning of the domain relies on the proper functioning of the PDC and its interactions with the Backup Domain Controllers (BDCs). Thus it would seem useful to represent the domain in terms of how many BDCs are alive at any given moment and also in terms of the PDC being functional or not. Accordingly, a finite state model was constructed as follows:

1. The data collection period was broken up into time windows of a fixed length,
2. For each such time window, the state of the domain was computed, and
3. A transition diagram was constructed based on the state information.

The state of the domain during a given time window was computed by evaluating the number of machines that rebooted during that time window. More specifically, the states were identified as shown in Table 9.

Fig. 5 shows the transitions in the domain. The results are based on the analysis of event logs spanning a 6-month period. Each time window was one hour long.

Fig. 5 reveals some interesting insights.

1. Nearly 77% of all transitions from the F state, excluding the self-loops, are to the BDC state. If these transitions do indeed result in disruption in service, then it is possible to improve the overall availability significantly just by tolerating single machine failures.

Table 9. Domain States and Their Interpretation

State Name	Meaning
PDC	Primary Domain Controller (PDC) rebooted
BDC	1 Backup Domain Controller (BDC) rebooted
MBDC	Many BDCs rebooted
PDC+BDC	PDC and One BDC rebooted
PDC+MBDC	PDC and Many BDCs rebooted
F	Functional (no reboots observed)

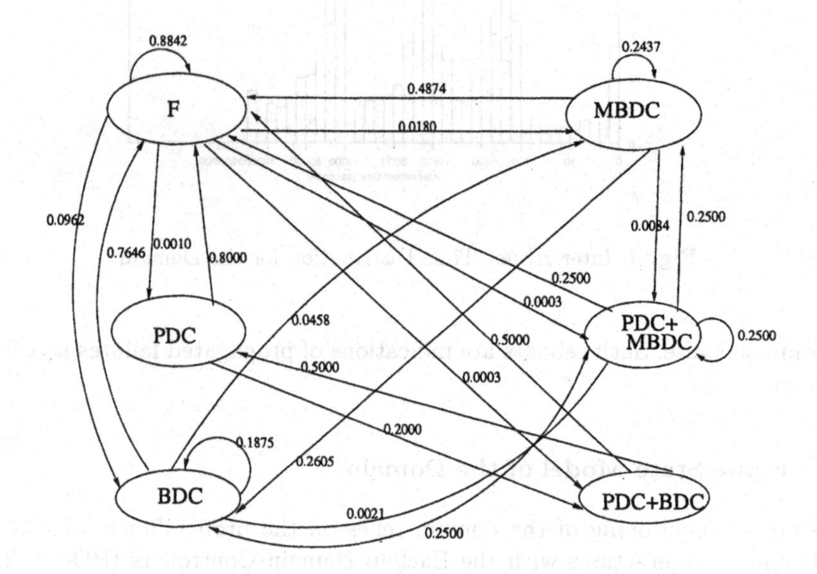

Fig. 5. Domain State Transitions

2. A non-negligible number of transitions are between the F state and the MBDC state. This would potentially indicate correlated failures and recovery among BDCs. (These transitions are explored in detail later.)
3. Again, a non-negligible fraction of transitions are between states BDC and MBDC. This would indicate potentially correlated failures and recovery (explored in detail later).
4. Majority of transitions from state PDC are to state F. This could be explained by one of the following:
   - Most of the problems with the PDC are not propagated to the BDCs,
   - The PDC typically recovers before any such propagation takes effect on the BDCs, or
   - The problems on the PDC are not severe enough to bring it down, but they might worsen as they propagate to the BDCs and force a reboot.

However, 20% of the transitions from the PDC state are to the PDC+BDC state. So there is a possibility of the propagation of failures. We obtain further useful insights into the dynamics of the domain by considering what percentage of the total transitions of the domain go into each state. Table 10 shows the details.

Table 10. Domain Transitions by State

Target state	Percentage of total transitions
F	85.68
PDC	0.11
BDC	11.04
MBDC	2.74
PDC+BDC	0.04
PDC+MBDC	0.08

From Table 10 we observe the following:

- Less than 1% of all transitions involve the reboot of the PDC. So the PDC exhibits a higher availability than the BDCs.
- Over 11% of all transitions are into the BDC state. If the domain is configured to tolerate the failure of a single BDC, then disruption of mail service could be reduced significantly.
- A non-negligible percentage (2.74%) of transitions end in MBDC state. Since each BDC is responsible for handling part of the mail service, the MBDC state represents a potentially serious disruption of service.

In summary, we conclude the following:

- Of the reboots in the domain 50% occur within 40 minutes of each other. Moreover, about 30% of them occur within 15 minutes of each other. Thus, there exists the possibility of correlated/propagated failures.
- The domain is in the MBDC state for about 3% of the time, on average. Since each machine contributes to the mail delivery, this represents a potentially serious disruption of service.
- About 77% of the transitions from the F state (excluding the self-loop) are due to the rebooting of a single machine. Thus, providing single-machine failure tolerance could significantly improve the overall availability of the domain.
- A non-negligible fraction of the domain transitions are between states BDC and MBDC. These transitions suggest the possibility of correlated failures and recovery.

9 Error Propagation

Examination of the domain-wide behavior suggests the possibility of correlated/ propagated failures. Below, we examine indications of propagation of problems within the domain. It should be noted that the networked-based systems are usually loosely coupled; consequently the propagation of failures may not be as strong or easily identifiable as in tightly coupled systems.

Classification of prominent events. An approach to studying propagation of failures in the domain is to classify each occurrence of the prominent events (i.e., the events upon which reboots in our target system were categorized) as caused by one of the following:

1. a problem specific to the local machine (i.e., the machine on which the event was observed),
2. a problem related to a remote machine (this could be true in case of connectivity problems), or
3. a general, network-related problem.

Each occurrence of a prominent event that was caused by a remote-machine problem would indicate propagation of failure.

Approach to classifying prominent events. Classification of the occurrences of prominent events was based on tests designed using event-specific information. These tests were designed as follows. Essentially, for each event occurrence, the entire set of events occurring in the domain around that event (e.g., within an hour of it) was obtained. Based on the events that were found in this *event window*, the current occurrence of the event was classified into one of the above-mentioned categories.

The anatomy of a test. The tests were generated based on manual analysis of events. However, they were applied to events in an automated fashion. Thus, the test had to be specified in a format conducive to interpretation by a script. A sample test is shown below.

```
Event 2006 Srv
MP_test_begin
   4320  NetBT 7200 7 local-machine yes 1 1
   3013  Rdr   3600 8 local-machine 7 !local-machine yes 3 1
   5711  NETLOGON +3600 7 local-machine yes 1 2
   5715  NETLOGON +3600 7 local-machine yes 1 2
   6005  EventLog +3600 7 local-machine yes 1 1
   2006  Srv 3600 7 local-machine yes 3 3
MP_test_end
```

The first line indicates the *event id* and the *source* of the event for which the test is applicable. The keywords *MP_test_begin* and *MP_test_end* denote that the set of entries in between comprise a test for a local machine problem (MP). Each line between these two keywords corresponds to a *test event.* A typical test event description contains the following fields:

- event id (4320),
- source logging the event (NetBT),
- time window within which the event should occur relative to the event being tested (7200) (a plus sign before the number indicates that the test event should occur after the event being tested), and
- other constraints on the test event observed.

The constraints on the test event are better understood with an example. Let us consider the first test event in the sample shown above.

1. The entries *7 local-machine*, indicate that the test will be passed only if an occurrence of the test event is found whose 7th field matches the local machine on which the event being tested was logged. If the same entries read *7 !local-machine*, then the test would be passed only if the 7th field did *not* match the machine name.
2. The field *yes* indicates that if a test event satisfying all the constraints is found in the event window, then that test is considered passed. A *No* for that field would indicate that the test would pass if no such test event was found.
3. The last two fields in the test event indicate, respectively, the *number of times* the event must occur (for the test to be passed) and the *group* to which the test event belongs.

Application of the test. A specific instance of a prominent event is considered to be due to a local machine problem if it passes the test designed for that purpose. The tests are applied in *groups.* If any one test in a group is passed by the given event instance, then the whole group is considered to be passed. If the majority of the groups are passed, then the test itself is considered to have passed. The tests for a remote machine problem and a network problem are performed in a similar manner.

Designing a test. The test events are framed based on manual analysis of the events. It is instructive to explore in detail the sample test event depicted above. The event to be tested has an *event id* of 2006 and is logged by the *Srv* (server). The text description for this event states that the *server received an incorrectly formatted request from an unknown source.* To evaluate if a given occurrence of this event represents a problem specific to the local machine, we perform the following tests:

1. Do we observe a problem with the transport service in the local machine? (This corresponds to event 4320.)
2. Do we observe at least three instances of the Redirector service on a remote machine trying to contact the Server on the local machine and reporting a failure? (This corresponds to event 3013.)
3. Does the local machine show evidence of normal network activity within an hour of the 2006 event? (This is indicated by the 5711/5715 event.)
4. Do we observe a reboot of the local machine within one hour of the 2006 event? (This corresponds to event 6005.) The reasoning behind this is that the system administrator might have suspected a problem with the local machine and attempted to solve it by rebooting the machine (possibly after some maintenance).
5. Do we observe at least three instances of 2006 from the same machine in a 1-hour period? (This corresponds to event 2006.)

As evident from the explanation, designing test events involves a heuristic approach. However, in the absence of more specific event descriptions, this seems to be reasonable. In an ideal situation, the accuracy of these tests could be improved by validating the predictions against operator logs that report the actual cause of the problem. However, in the data that was analyzed, no operator log was available.

Results of the tests. Table 11 summarizes the results obtained on selected events.

Table 11. Breakup of Selected Events

Event	Source	Severity	Number	Local Machine Problem	Remote Machine Problem	Unknown
3012	Redirector	1	218	218	0	0
8021	Browser	1	790	261	0	509
2006	Server	1	19586	9907	0	9679

It is observed that most of the identifiable problems seem to be local machine related. This would suggest that propagation of failures is not observed on a regular basis. However, in quite a few cases, the tests were not able to classify the event one way or another. It is possible that some of these unknowns represent propagated failures. Besides, designing such tests requires a fair amount of operating-system- specific knowledge, which is not easy to obtain. However, the idea of designing event-specific tests and using them does appear to be a reasonable approach to implementing automated propagation detection.

10 Reliability of Internet Hosts

The previous sections used examples of failure data collected from networked systems configured as Local Area Networks. With the ever-increasing use and rapid expansion of the Internet, connection to a host from a user site, and the reliability of this connection are becoming increasingly important. The key question is whether the approaches to collecting and analyzing failure data discussed here are applicable in assessing the availability of Wide Are Networks such as Internet. From the perspective of an *average Internet user* (i.e., the majority of users that access various Web sites to obtain information from them) how can we address issues such as:

1. What is the (stationary) probability that a user request to access an Internet host succeeds?
2. On an average, what percentage of hosts might remain accessible to the user at a given moment?
3. What are the major causes of access failures as seen by the user?
4. Typically, how long could a host be unavailable to the user?

To answer these questions, we will use the results of a 40-day availability study of Internet hosts for the 97 most popular Web sites [17]. The term *failure*, in this context, refers to the inability to contact a host and fetch an HTML file from it. The failure might be due to problems with the host (e.g., the host is too busy handling other requests) or problems with the underlying network (e.g., no proper route to the host exists). Thus, the failure is an integration of the behavior of the remote host, the intermediate routers, and the local network at the user site. We believe that this corresponds well to the reliability of the "black box" between a user's local machine and a remote host. Although network instability and absolute failures of remote hosts are individually important, it is the combined impact of these failures that is critical for the end user.

10.1 Data Collection

We selected 97 of the top 100 Web sites, as rated by the PC Magazine [31], for the study. The data collected during our study consists of success/failure logs corresponding to attempts to connect to and fetch an HTML file from a Web site. On a failure, the cause of the failure, if recognizable, was also recorded. A sample of the logs is shown below:

```
Server www.cnn.com time: 5-3-97 : 7:48:23;
Downloaded 22009 bytes successfully

Server www.columbiahouse.com time : 5-3-97 : 7:48:24;
server returned error 302, Trying with new URL:
http://www.columbiahouse.com/?86264561812817419329132317
Downloaded 11260 bytes successfully

Server www.americangreetings.com time : 5-3-97 : 7:48:35;
Connection failed with error code Connection timed out

Server www.egghead.com time : 5-6-97 : 6:17:25;
server returned error 500
```

The logs include the following information: (1) server (Web site) name, (2) date and time of the attempt, and (3) result of the attempt. The sample above depicts the outcome of four separate access (the term *access* refers to the process of connecting to a Web site and fetching a HTML file from it) attempts, each to a different Web site. The first attempt (www.cnn.com) was a success. The second attempt (www.columbiahouse.com), though successful, required a re-attempt as the HTTP server first returned an error response. The third attempt (www.americangreetings.com) was a failure due to a problem with connection establishment. The last entry in the sample depicts another failure (www.egghead.com), which was due to an error response from the HTTP server at the Web site.

The data collection was performed by a tool (a Perl script) that ran continuously at the test site. The tool maintains a list of the Web sites under study. It periodically iterates through the list. During an iteration, the tool attempts to access each of the Web sites, one after the other. Web sites that are found to be inaccessible during a regular iteration are handled by the tool as follows. Initially, the tool attempts to access each of these sites once every five minutes. If such an attempt succeeds, the frequency of access attempts to that Web site is reduced to the default rate (once every two hours). However, if failures continue, the frequency of attempts to access that particular Web site is gradually reduced until it reaches the original rate of once every two hours, and then the whole process repeats. In addition, the first few re- attempts to access a Web site (i.e., after a failure has been encountered) are supplemented by simultaneous runs of the traceroute program on the same site. This aids in detecting routing problems that might be the cause of the problem. The default period of a single iterations is two hours. This value was determined by considering the following: (a) requirements on the sample frequency should be high enough to provide insights into the daily behavior of the servers, but (b) it should not be so high that it would artificially increase the workload on the Web sites significantly and cause congestion at the test site. Such a scenario would bias the results and possibly lead to an underestimation of the accessibility and availability of the Web sites. The motivation behind this variation of the rate of access attempts is to get a tight upper bound for the duration of the failure and to progressively "back off" if the failure seems to be of long duration.

10.2 Identification of Internet Hosts Accessibility Parameters

We commence the discussion with a brief examination of the parameters that, we believe, reflect the accessibility and reliability of Internet hosts as seen from the user's perspective. Table 12 lists these parameters and their corresponding measured (mean).

Table 12. Parameters to Describe Accessibility/Availability of Internet Hosts

Parameter	Value
Average success frequency	94.4
Failure duration	43.022 min (mean)
Interfailure time	4.016 days (mean)
Hourly failure rate	2.16 (mean)
Modes of failure	Connection Timeouts (42.8%) Connection Refusals (27.0%)
Mean availability	0.993

The *average success frequency* (ASF) for a Web site is defined as the percentage of HTML file-fetch attempts to that Web site that are successful. It functions as an indicator of host accessibility, since the greater the ASF, the more accessible the host. We obtained a high mean ASF indicating that, on an average, host accessibility is high.

The *failure duration* is the amount of time for which a particular remote host is inaccessible to the user. It represents the collective failure of the host and the network and is a measure of the ability of the host/network to recover. Though we observed the mean failure duration to be around 43 minutes, most (70%) of the failures lasted less than 15 minutes.

The *interfailure time* is the time period between two consecutive instances of failure of the same remote host. It provides an estimate of the degree of nonstop operation of the host. Though the mean value was around 4 days, individual sites differed greatly in their mean interfailure time.

The *hourly failure rate* is the percentage of Web sites that fail at least once during any given hour interval. It is a measure of the fraction of the network unavailable to the user at any time (the granularity being an hour). We observed that, on average, only 2% of the hosts are unavailable at any time.

The *modes of failure* provide insights into the actual causes of the failures. Our study found that failures due to connection timeouts and connection refusals are the two most frequently observed failure modes. Also, the majority of connection timeout failures appear to be network related.

The *mean availability* is defined as the ratio of interfailure time (mean) to the sum of the failure duration (mean) and the interfailure time (mean). It denotes, on average, what fraction of the time a remote host is available. The data showed that the mean availability was very high, with a small variation.

10.3 Average Success Frequency (ASF)

The ASF is a measure of the stationary probability of the success of a given file-fetch request to a host. The average success frequency for 86 servers[3] is given in Table 13.

Table 13. Measured ASF

Parameter	Value
mean	94.4 ± 6.3 (90%)
median	95.8
standard deviation	5.6

The stationary probability of an HTML file-fetch attempt being successful is 0.944. Fig. 6 shows the distribution of ASF for this reduced set. The distribution appears highly skewed, with most of the Web sites (95.3%) showing an ASF of 80 or more. A high percentage (83.7%) of the sites showed an ASF of 90 or more. A small fraction (about 4.7%) exhibited a lower ASF (less than 80) and were consequently less accessible than the rest. We also examined the distribution of

[3] Eleven of the Web sites almost always responded with error codes 302/404 (which are HTTP-specific errors) or with a connection refused error message; hence they were excluded from further analysis.

the average failure frequency, defined as [(1-ASF)/100]. The distribution fitted an exponential distribution at a significance level of 0.05.

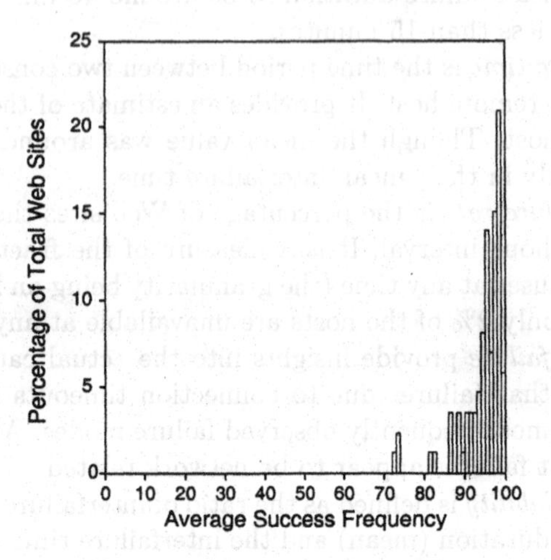

Fig. 6. Distribution of ASF

10.4 Failure Duration

The failure-duration parameter is an upper bound on the duration of an instance of failure. As discussed earlier, this parameter indicates the ability of the network/remote host to recover from a failure.

In this context, each instance of failure represents the string of consecutive unsuccessful attempts to access the same Web site (i.e., successive failed attempts were coalesced into a single instance of failure). Thus the failure duration truly represents the time period for which the host is inaccessible. Table 14 summarizes the results for the measured failure duration. The observed mean failure duration (MFD) is distorted somewhat by a small fraction of failures that lasted much longer (a day or more) than the rest. The median however, is only slightly greater than 5 minutes. On closer examination, we found that most of the failures had a much shorter duration than the MFD. Fig. 7 shows the distribution of the failure duration. More than a third (37.2%) of the failures lasted less than 5 minutes. Nearly a third (33.3%) of the failures lasted between 5 and 15 minutes. Approximately 18% of the failures lasted longer than 30 minutes. There were only 3 instances of failure that lasted longer than a day. The longest failure recorded lasted 3.375 days. The peak at the 5-6 minute range was predominantly due to two kinds of failures: failures due to a connection refusal by the server, and failures due to a timeout[4] while reading the HTTP header that precedes the HTML file.

Table 14. Measured Failure Duration

Failure Instances	Mean(min)/ Confidence	Standard Deviation	Median (min)
783	43.022 ± 41.990 (75%)	233.504 min	6.667

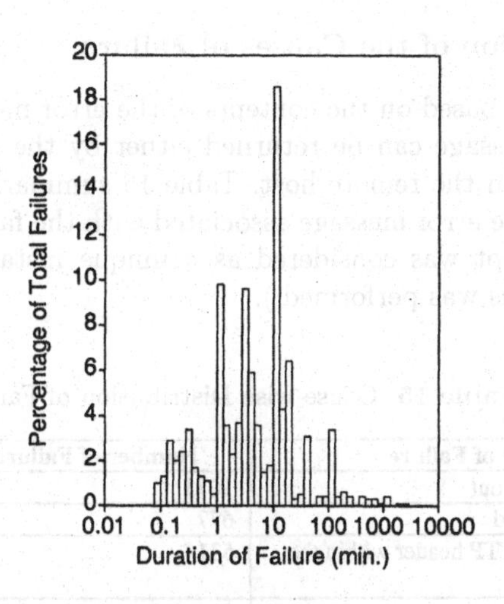

Fig. 7. Duration of Failure (min.)

In order to understand the failures better, we further categorized them based on the number of unsuccessful access attempts made during the failure period. Specifically a *one-time failure* is defined as an instance of failure that involves only one unsuccessful access attempt. On the other hand, a *multiple failure* is defined as an instance of failure that involves two or more unsuccessful access attempts.

We observed that 44.8% of the failures were multiple failures. This would suggest that, once a failure is encountered, the probability of an immediate re-attempt being a success is not high. We examined the results of all re-attempts (on encountering a failure) made within five minutes of encountering a failure. Out of the 1268 such re- attempts, only 38.2% succeeded, indicating that the probability that an immediate re- attempt will succeed is very low. The value

[4] Once the tool successfully establishes connection with the HTTP server process on the remote host, it waits for a predefined timeout interval to receive the HTTP header from the server.

for MFD obtained in our study is significantly different from the values for the mean time to repair (MTTR) obtained in [24]. The discrepancy, we feel, is due to the difference in the types of hosts evaluated. In [24] the sample included hosts with a widely varying degree of reliability. Many of these hosts used to be shutdown nightly or weekly for maintenance purposes (which would significantly increase MTTR). In our study, however, the hosts were dedicated Web sites that receive millions of hits every day and are designed to stay up most of the time (i.e., shutdowns are very minimal. This is reinforced by the fact that most of the failures lasted only 15 minutes or less, which is too short for a regular shutdown. Hence we observed a lower MFD.

10.5 Classification of the Causes of Failure

We classify failures based on the contents of the error messages associated with them. An error message can be returned either by the connect system call or the HTTP server on the remote host. Table 15 summarizes the distribution of failures based on the error message associated with the failure. In this case, each failed access attempt was considered as a unique instance of failure (i.e., no coalescing of failures was performed.).

Table 15. Cause-wise Distribution of Failures

Cause of Failure	Number of Failures	Percentage
Connection timed out	1073	42.8
Connection refused	677	27.0
Could not read HTTP header within the timeout interval	531	21.2
No route to host	92	3.7
Server returned error 500	76	3.0
Server returned error 401	51	2.0
Network is unreachable	1	0.0

The following error categories are related to the host: (1) connection refused (the network was able to reach the host but the host did not respond favorably to the request) and (2) server returned error 500/401. Errors 500 (internal error) and 401 (unauthorized request) indicate a problem with the HTTP server on the host.

The following error categories are related to the network: (1) no route to host and (2) network is unreachable. Connection timeout failures and failures due to timeout while reading the header could be due to either the host or the network.

10.6 Connection Timeouts and Timeouts While Reading Header

Connection timeouts can arise due to (among other factors) a route establishment problem, the server having too many pending connect requests at that time, or congestion along the route to the server. Timeouts while reading the header can occur due to sudden failure of the host/network or (more plausibly) temporary congestion along the route. To categorize these failures as network-related problems or host- related problems, we use the results of the traceroute runs. Specifically, we examine all traceroute runs to each Web site that were executed within five minutes before/after facing a connection timeout or a timeout while reading header. Table 16 shows the results of such traceroutes.

Table 16. Summary of Traceroute Runs Made While Experiencing Timeouts

Parameter	Connection Timeout	Header-Read Timeout
Total instances of failure	1073	531
Total traceroutes executed within 5 minutes of failure	659	436
Number of such traceroutes that failed to reach the host	434 (66%)	100 (23%)

Evidently, the majority of the traceroute runs executed on facing connection timeouts failed. Moreover, most such failures occurred at one of the intermediate routers, (i.e., not near the host) clearly indicating a network problem. Thus the majority of these traceroutes failed due to network-related problems. Since each such traceroute was executed within minutes of a connection timeout failure, we can conclude that the corresponding connection timeout also failed due to a network problem. If we extrapolate this result to cover all the connection timeouts, about 66% of the connection timeouts are network related.

For the timeouts while reading the header, however, most traceroute runs reached the host. Since a successful traceroute run implies proper functioning of both the host and the network, the actual cause of failure is not evident. However, since the host did respond favorably to a connection request a few seconds before the failure (the tool waits for the header only if it is able to successfully connect to the HTTP server), and since such hosts (dedicated to maintaining the Web site) typically have some built-in fault-tolerance, a sudden host failure seems unlikely. A more plausible explanation is a temporary network problem, such as congestion along the route to the host, that might have delayed the reception of the header. Thus, with a small margin of error, we can conclude that almost all of these failures were due to network problems (though the problem may not be as severe as in the case of connection timeouts, which lasted much longer). Thus, approximately 53% (42.8 * 0.66 +21.2 + 3.7) of the failures are network related.

10.7 Comparing of the Major Classes of Failure

A comparative study of the three major classes of failure (i.e. connection timeouts, connection refusals and timeouts while reading header) yields useful insights. We focus on the failure duration and the inter-failure time for each class of failure. For this study, all consecutive access attempts that failed with the same error message are coalesced into a single instance of failure. Table 17 and Table 18 summarize the failure duration and the inter-failure time, respectively.

Table 17. Comparison of Failure Duration for Different Classes of Failures

Cause of Failure	Mean (min)	Median (min)	Standard Deviation (min)
Connection timeout	46.558	12.117	134.106
Connection refused	30.259	6.742	191.815
Timeout while reading header	17.486	2.725	76.714

Table 18. Comparison of Interfailure Time for Different Classes of Failures

Cause of failure	Mean (days)	Median (days)	Standard Deviation (days)
Connection timeout	5.652	4.002	6.077
Connection refused	7.274	4.076	7.980
Timeout while reading header	2.695	1.080	3.882

These tables reveal the following:

1. Connection timeouts last longer than most other failures. Since majority of the connection timeouts are network related, it appears that the network is relatively slow in recovering from failures as compared to the remote host.
2. Timeouts while reading the header lasted for a much shorter period than the other failures. (In fact nearly 37% of these failures lasted less than a minute.)
3. Connection refusals occur less frequently than the other two classes.

In summary, we observe the following: (1) connection timeouts (majority of which are network related) and connection refusals (which are host related) account for nearly 70% of the failures, (2) network related failures marginally outnumber host- related failures, and (3) network related failures last longer than host related ones.

10.8 Mean Availability

To quantitatively describe the behavior of the hosts from the user's perspective, we evaluated the *mean availability* of the hosts. The mean availability is defined as this ratio:

(Mean Inter-Failure Time)/(Mean Failure Duration + Mean Inter-Failure Time)

The mean availability evaluates to 0.993. To obtain a range for this parameter, we calculate the availability for each Web site using the corresponding mean values of failure duration and inter-failure time for that Web site. The results of this computation are shown in Table 19[5].

Table 19. Measured Availability

Parameter	Value/Confidence Interval
Mean	0.993 ± 0.067 (99%)
Standard Deviation	0.013
Median	0.997

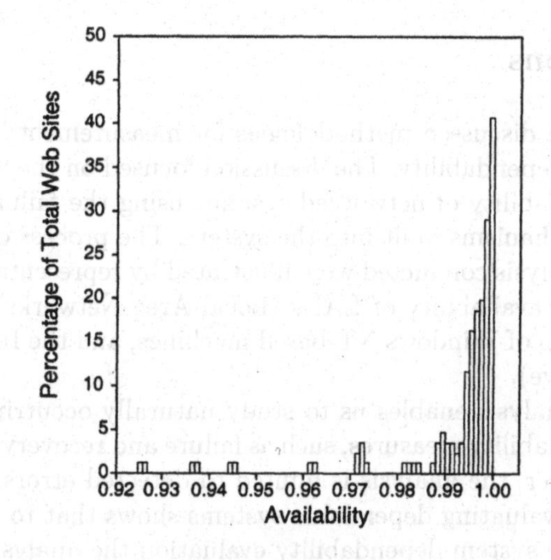

Fig. 8. Availability

Fig. 8 shows a histogram of the availability distribution over all 86 participant sites. The distribution is skewed, with all the sites having an availability of at least 0.92. A significant percentage (40%) of the sites exhibited an availability of 0.99 or more. However, there was no site that had an availability of 1.00. Comparing the results obtained here with the results obtained in [24], the hosts in our study exhibit a higher availability than the hosts in [24] (where the mean availability was 0.926). In summary, this study of the Internet hosts reveals:

1. Most of the user requests to the Web servers are successful, hence there is a high stationary probability (0.94) that a given request goes through successfully.

[5] The mean of the availability of individual sites has the same value as the overall mean availability (computed using MFD and the mean inter-failure time).

2. On an average, only about 2% of the servers fail within a given one hour interval.
3. Connectivity problems play a major role in determining the accessibility of the hosts. Network-related failures tend to outnumber host-related failures. Also, the network appears to be slower in recovering from failures than the hosts.
4. The majority (70.5%) of the failures are short (less than 15 minutes). However, a few failures spanned several days.
5. On average, Web sites stay up for over four days without any failures, though a good fraction of them fail at least once a day.
6. Connectivity to the hosts seems to be good on average. However, we did observe a few major network-related failures that rendered nearly 70% of the hosts inaccessible for a significant period of time.
7. The mean availability of the hosts is very high (0.993).

11 Conclusions

In this chapter, we discussed methodologies for measurement-based analysis of computer system dependability. The discussion focused on the issues involved in analyzing the availability of networked systems using the failure data collected by the logging mechanisms built into the system. The process of collecting data and the type of analysis conducted were illustrated by representative studies that include analysis of availability of LANs (Local Area Networks) of UNIX-based workstations, LANs of Windows NT-based machines, and the Internet (from the end-user perspective).

This type of analysis enables us to study naturally occurring errors and all measurable dependability measures, such as failure and recovery rates, reliability, availability. However, the analysis is limited to detected errors. Our experience in designing and evaluating dependable systems shows that to achieve accurate and comprehensive system dependability evaluation the analysis must span the three phases of system life: design phase, prototype phase, and operational phase (which is covered in this chapter). The thorough discussion of techniques suited for conducting dependability evaluation during the system design phase (simulated fault injection) and the system prototype phase (physical fault injection) the reader is referred to [15].

Significant progress has been made in all the three fields over the past 15 years, Increasing attention is being paid to 1) combining analytical modeling and experimental analysis and 2) combining system design and evaluation. In the first area, state-of-the-art analytical modeling techniques are being applied to real systems to evaluate various dependability and performance characteristics. Results from experimental analysis are being used to validate analytical models and to reveal practical issues that analytical modeling must address to develop more representative models. In the second area, dependability analysis tools are being combined with each other and with other CAD tools to provide an automatic design environment that incorporates multiple levels of joint evaluation of functionality, performance, dependability, and cost. Software failure data from the testing and operational phases are also providing feedback to software designers for improving software reliability.

For example, the presented study of the various kinds of failures in a network of Windows NT machines reveals useful and interesting insights into network system failure behavior.

1. Most of the problems that lead to reboots are software related. Only 10% are attributable to specific hardware components.
2. Connectivity problems contribute most to reboots.
3. Rebooting the machine does not appear to solve the problem in many cases. In about 60% of the reboots, the rebooted machine reported problems within a hour or two of the reboot.
4. Though the average availability evaluates to over 99%, a typical machine in the domain, on average, provides acceptable service only about 92% of the time.
5. About 1% of the reboots indicate memory leaks in the software.
6. There are indications of propagated or correlated failures. Typically, in such cases, multiple machines exhibit identical or similar problems at almost the same time.

Acknowledgements

This manuscript is based on a research supported in part by the US National Aeronautic and Space Administration (NASA) under grant NAG-1-613, in cooperation with the Illinois Computer Laboratory for Aerospace Systems and Software (ICLASS), by the Defense Advanced Research Project Agency (DARPA) under contract DABT63-94-C-0045 and by Tandem (now Compaq) Computers. The findings, opinions, and recommendations expressed herein are those of the authors and do not necessarily reflect the position or policy of the United State Government and no official endorsement should be inferred. We are pleased to thank Fran Baker for her assistance in editing this manuscript.

References

1. Arlitt, M.F., Williamson, C. L.: Web Server Workload Characterization: The Search for Invariants. SIGMETRICS '96. (1996) 126–137
2. Butner, S.E., Iyer R.K.: A Statistical Study of Reliability and System Load at SLAC. Proc. 10th Int. Symp. Fault-Tolerant Computing. (1980) 207–209
3. Castillo, X., Siewiorek, D.P.: Workload, Performance, and Reliability of Digital Computer Systems. Proc. 11th Int. Symp. Fault-Tolerant Computing. (1981) 84–89
4. Castillo, X., Siewiorek, D.P.: Workload Dependent Software Reliability Prediction Model. Proc. 12th Int. Symp. Fault-Tolerant Computing. (1982) 279–286
5. Chimoy, B.: Dynamics of Internet Routing Information. Proc. SIGCOMM '93. (1993) 45–52

6. Dugan, J.B.: Correlated Hardware Failures in Redundant Systems. Proc. 2nd IFIP Working Conf. Dependable Computing for Critical Applications. (1991)
7. Gray, J.: A Census of Tandem System Availability Between 1985 and 1990. IEEE Trans. Reliability. **39** (1990) 409–418
8. Hansen, J.P., Siewiorek, D.P.: Models for Time Coalescence in Event Logs. Proc. 22nd Int. Symp. Fault-Tolerant Computing. (1992) 221–227
9. Hsueh, M.C., Iyer, R.K., Trivedi, K.S.: Performability Modeling Based on Real Data: A Case Study. IEEE Trans. Computers. **37** (1988) 478–484
10. Iyer, R.K., Rossetti, D.J.: A Statistical Load Dependency Model for CPU Errors at SLAC. Proc. 12th Int. Symp. Fault-Tolerant Computing. (1982) 363–372
11. Iyer, R.K., Velardi, P.: Hardware-related Software Errors: Measurement and Analysis. IEEE Trans. Software Engineering. **SE-11** (1985) 223–231
12. Iyer, R.K., Rossetti, D.J.: Effect of System Workload on Operating System Reliability: A Study on IBM 3081. IEEE Trans. Software Engineering. **SE-11** (1985) 1438–1448
13. Iyer, R.K., Rossetti, D.J., Hsueh, M.C.: Measurement and Modeling of Computer Reliability as Affected by System Activity. ACM Trans. Computer Systems. **4** (1986) 214–237
14. Iyer, R.K., Young, L.T., Iyer, P.V.K.: Automatic Recognition of Intermittent Failures: An Experimental Study of Field Data. IEEE Trans. Computers. **39** (1990) 525–527
15. Iyer, R.K., Tang D.: Experimental Analysis of Computer System Dependability. Chapter 5 in Fault Tolerant Computer Design, D.K. Pradhan, Prentice Hall. (1996) 282–392
16. Jacobson, V.: traceroute, ftp://ftp.ee.lbl.gov/traceroute.tar.Z. (1989)
17. Kalyanakrishnam, M., Iyer, R.K., Patel, J.: Reliability of Internet Hosts: A Case Study from End User's Perspective. Proc. 6th Int. Conf. on Computer Communications and Networks. (1996) 418–423
18. Kalyanakrishnam, M.: Analysis of Failures in Windows NT Systems. Master Thesis, Technical Report CRHC 98-08, University of Illinois at Urbana-Champaign. (1998)
19. Lee, I., Iyer, R.K., Tang, D.: Error/Failure Analysis Using Event Logs from Fault Tolerant Systems. Proc. 21st Int. Symp. Fault-Tolerant Computing. (1991) 10–17
20. Lee, I., Iyer, R.K.: Analysis of Software Halts in Tandem System. Proc. 3rd Int. Symp. Software Reliability Engineering. (1991) 227–236
21. Lee, I., Tang, D., Iyer, R.K., Hsueh, M.C.: Measurement-Based Evaluation of Operating System Fault Tolerance. IEEE Trans. Reliability. **42** (1993) 238–249
22. Lee, I., Iyer, R.K.: Faults, Symptoms, and Software Fault tolerance in the Tandem GUARDIAN90 Operating System. Proc. 23rd Int. Symp. Fault-Tolerant Computing. (1993) 20–29
23. Lin, T.T., Siewiorek, D.P.: Error Log Analysis:Statistical Modeling and Heuristic Trend Analysis. IEEE Trans. Reliability. **39** (1990) 238–249
24. Long, D., Muir, A., Golding, R.: A Longitudinal Survey of Internet Host Reliability. Proc. Symposium on Reliable Distributed Systems. (1995) 2–9
25. Maxion,, A.: Anomaly Detection for Diagnosis. Proc. 20th Int. Symp. Fault-Tolerant Computing. (1990) 20–27
26. Maxion, R.A., Feather, F.E.: A Case Study of Ethernet Anomalies in a Distributed Computing Environment. IEEE Trans. Reliability. **39** (1990) 433–443
27. Maxion, R.A., Olszewski, R.T.: Detection and Discrimination of Injected Network Faults. Proc. 23rd Int. Symp. Fault-Tolerant Computing. (1993) 198–207

28. McConnel, S.R., Siewiorek, D.P., Tsao, M.M.: The Measurement and Analysis of Transient Errors in Digital Computer Systems. Proc. 9th Int. Symp. Fault-Tolerant Computing. (1979) 67–70
29. Paxson, V.: Towards a Framework for Defining Internet Performance Metrics. Proc. INET '96.
30. Paxson, V.: End-to-End Routing Behavior in the Internet. SIGCOMM "96. (1996)
31. PC Magazine. **16** (1997) 101–124
32. Sahner, R.A., Trivedi, K.S.: Reliability Modeling Using SHARPE. IEEE Trans. Reliability. **R-36** (1987) 186–193
33. SAS User's Guide: Basics. SAS Institute. (1985)
34. Siewiorek, D.P., Kini, V., Mashburn, H., McConnel, S.R., Tsao, M.: A Case Study of C.mmp, Cm, and C.vmp: Part I - Experience with Fault Tolerance in Multiprocessor Systems. Proc. of IEEE. **66** (1978) 1178–1199
35. Siewiorek, D.P., Swarz. R.W.: Reliable Computer Systems: Design and Evaluation. Digital Press. (1992)
36. Stevens, W.R.: TCP/IP Illustrated, Volume 1: The Protocols. Addison-Wesley. (1994)
37. Sullivan, M.S., Chillarege, R.: Software Defects and Their Impact on System Availability-A Study of Field Failures in Operating Systems. Proc. 21st Int. Symp. Fault-Tolerant Computing. (1991) 2–9
38. Sullivan, M.S., Chillarege, R.: A Comparison of Software Defects in Database Management Systems and Operating Systems. Proc. 22nd Int. Symp. Fault-Tolerant Computing. (1992) 475–484
39. Tang, D., Iyer, R.K., Subramani, S.: Failure Analysis and Modeling of a VAXcluster System. Proc. 20th Int. Symp. Fault-Tolerant Computing. (1990) 244–251
40. Tang, D., Iyer, R.K.: Impact of Correlated Failures on Dependability in a VAXcluster System. Proc. 2nd IFIP Working Conf. Dependable Computing for Critical Applications. (1991)
41. Tang, D., Iyer, R.K.: Analysis and Modeling of Correlated Failures in Multicomputer Systems. IEEE Trans. Computers. **41** (1992) 567–577
42. Tang, D., Iyer, R.K.: Analysis of the VAX/VMS Error Logs in Multicomputer Environments-A Case Study of Software Dependability. Proc. 3rd Int. Symp. Software Reliability Engineering. (1992) 216–226
43. Tang, D., Iyer, R.K.: Dependability Measurement and Modeling of a Multicomputer System. IEEE Trans. Computers. **42** (1993) 62–75
44. Tang, D., Iyer, R.K.: MEASURE+-A Measurement-Based Dependability Analysis Package. Proc. ACM SIGMETRICS Conf. Measurement and Modeling of Computer Systems. (1993) 110–121
45. Thakur, A., Iyer, R.K.: Analyze-NOW-An Environment for Collection and Analysis of Failures in a Network of Workstations. IEEE Trans. Reliability. **R-46** (1996) 561–570
46. Tsao, M.M., Siewiorek, D.P.: Trend Analysis on System Error Files. Proc. 13th Int. Symp. Fault-Tolerant Computing. (1983) 116–119
47. Velardi, P., Iyer, R.K.: A Study of Software Failures and Recovery in the MVS Operating System. IEEE Trans. Computers. **C-33** (1984) 564–568.
48. Wein, A.S., Sathaye, A.: Validating Complex Computer System Availability Models. IEEE Trans. Reliability. **39** (1990) 468–479

Performance of Client/Server Systems

Daniel A. Menascé[1] and Virgilio A. F. Almeida[2]

[1] George Mason University, Fairfax, VA, USA,
menasce@cs.gmu.edu
[2] Federal University of Minas Gerais, MG, Brazil,
virgilio@dcc.ufmg.br

1 Introduction

Client/server (C/S) systems are composed of client processes that submit requests to one or more server processes. Servers passively await for client requests and may enlist other servers in order to reply to a request originating from a client. These processes, clients and servers, are usually organized in a multi-tiered software architecture. Usually, clients and servers execute on different machines connected by networks. C/S systems exhibit a large variety of possibilities in terms of architecture design, capacity configuration, and scalability of applications. It is then essential to understand the tradeoffs brought by these possibilities. Performance modeling is an efficient technique to understand the behavior of client/server systems in order to choose characteristics that lead to a cost-effective client/server design

Performance models of C/S systems need to take into account the interaction of the various processes involved in processing a request, contention for software processes and data structures, as well as contention for hardware components (e.g., processors, disks, and networks). Product form queuing networks [2] cannot be used to model the type of situations that arise in C/S systems. However, approximations can be developed to handle most of the situations present in C/S systems. This chapter discusses the use of Layered Queuing Models [17,19] and the use of the SRP-MVA technique [12,14] for modeling C/S systems.

The remainder of this chapter is organized as follows. Section 2 describes client/server systems and the various aspects of client/server systems that are relevant to performance: the anatomy of client/server interactions, software server architectures, and system architecture. Section 3 presents Layered Queuing Networks and SRP-MVA as techniques that can be used to model the software architecture of servers. A complete example of an e-commerce site is presented in Section 4. Finally, Section 5 presents some concluding remarks.

2 Client/Server Systems

To analyze the performance of client/server systems we need to consider three issues: the anatomy of C/S interactions, the software architecture of a server, and the system architecture which includes hardware configuration and networking topologies.

G. Haring et al. (Eds.): Performance Evaluation, LNCS 1769, pp. 201–218, 2000.

The anatomy of C/S interactions describes the sequence of requests and replies exchanged between clients and servers including the types of communication paradigms (i.e., synchronous or asynchronous) used in these exchanges. At this level, the server is seen as a black box that just reacts to requests from clients. In the course of doing so, it may request the help of other servers. The software architecture of a server describes how the services of a server are implemented by a collection of processes and or threads. The system architecture specifies the various hardware resources (e.g., processors, disks, local area networks, and wide area networks) used to support a C/S system. It also describes how these resources are interconnected and what are their inherent performance attributes (e.g., processor speeds, disk access times, and network bandwidth).

2.1 Anatomy of Client/Server Interactions

The basic type of interaction in a C/S system is a *C/S request*. It starts when a client process makes a request to a server process, called primary server, and ends when the client process receives a reply from the primary server. The primary server may need to request assistance from other servers, called secondary servers, to execute the request from the client. In this case, the primary server acts as a client to the secondary servers. For example, in an electronic commerce transaction, a Web server, the primary server, receives a purchase request from a Web browser, the client, and sends a request to the DB server, a secondary server, to check for price and estimated shipping time for the item (see Fig. 1-(a)).

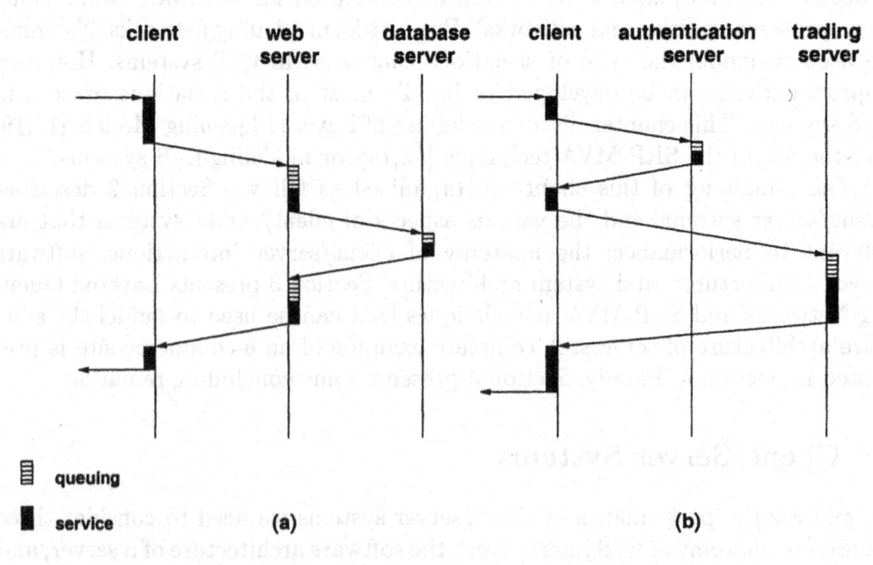

Fig. 1. (a) C/S request (b) C/S transaction

More complex C/S interactions involve a sequence of C/S requests as illustrated in Fig. 1-(b). This is called a *C/S transaction*. The individual requests of a C/S transaction may involve primary and secondary servers also. As an example of a C/S transaction, consider a Web-based financial investment system. A request to sell stocks on-line would include a request to the authentication server followed by a request to the trading server. C/S transactions are generally associated with classes in queuing network models. Similar transactions can be aggregated into a single class depending on the nature and goal of the performance study. C/S transactions are not necessarily deterministic in the sequence of client and server interactions. For example, in the case of Fig. 1-(b), a request will only be sent to the trading server if the authentication is successful. So, probabilities should be assigned to each message exchange.

A notation is needed to describe the interaction between clients and servers during C/S transactions. Several notations have been used to describe software architectures and the interaction between software components. Some notable examples include sequence diagrams in the Unified Modeling Language (UML) [15], Message Sequence Charts (MSC) [8], Chemical Abstract Machines (CHAM) [7], the Specification and Description Language (SDL) [18], and communication-processing diagrams [11]. To be useful for performance modeling, these software specification notations have to be annotated with performance related parameters.

No standards for performance annotation of software specification languages exist yet. We use our own graphical notation, called *C/S Interaction Trees (CSITs)* (see Fig. 2), which must be specified for each different C/S transaction. A CSIT is a directed tree whose nodes represent visits to clients and or servers during the execution of a transaction. For example, nodes 5 and 8 indicate visits to the trading server TS at two different points in the execution of the transaction. The root of the tree represents the client that originates the transaction. The leaves of the tree always represent the client when it receives

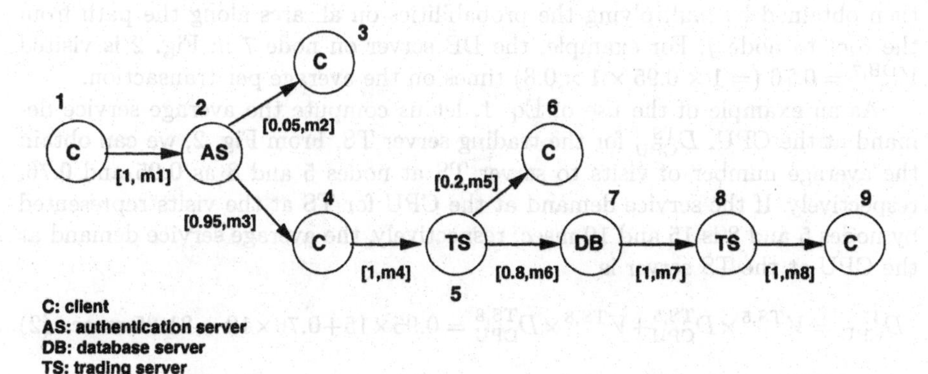

Fig. 2. Example of a C/S Interaction Tree (CSIT)

the final message of the transaction. A directed arc (i, j) in a CSIT indicates that a message is being sent from node i to node j. Each node in the CSIT has an interior label that indicates the client or server involved in the message exchange as well as an exterior label which is a unique number of the node in the tree. The exterior label is used to identify visits to a server during the execution of a transaction.

Arcs in a CSIT are labeled by pairs of the type $[p, m]$ where p is the probability that the message is sent and m is the message size, in bytes. The service demand at the various resources of a client or server represented by a node in the CSIT may be different at each visit to the same client or server. Consider a CSIT that represents the possible executions of a given class of transactions. An analysis of the CSIT provides an expression for the average service demand at a resource of a server given the average service demands per visit to the server. Let,

- $D_i^{s,j}$: average service demand at resource i of server s during the visit to server s labeled j in the CSIT of the transaction.
- $V^{s,j}$: probability that server s is visited by the transaction during visit labeled j in the CSIT.
- D_i^s: average service demand of the transaction at resource i of server s, i.e., average total service time spent by the transaction at resource i of server s.

Thus,

$$D_i^s = \sum_{j \in N_s} V^{s,j} \times D_i^{s,j} \tag{1}$$

where N_s is the set of all nodes in the CSIT that correspond to visits to server s.

A path from the root to a leaf node in the CSIT indicates a possible execution of the transaction. For example, the path $1 \rightarrow 2 \rightarrow 3$ illustrates the case when the transaction fails to be authenticated by the authentication server AS. The probability of occurrence of a path is the product of the probabilities of all arcs in the path. The probability that a node numbered j is visited, $V^{s,j}$, is then obtained by multiplying the probabilities on all arcs along the path from the root to node j. For example, the DB server on node 7 in Fig. 2 is visited $V^{\mathrm{DB},7} = 0.76$ $(= 1 \times 0.95 \times 1 \times 0.8)$ times on the average per transaction.

As an example of the use of Eq. 1, let us compute the average service demand at the CPU, $D_{\mathrm{CPU}}^{\mathrm{TS}}$ for the trading server TS. From Fig. 2, we can obtain the average number of visits to server TS at nodes 5 and 8 as 0.95 and 0.76, respectively. If the service demand at the CPU for TS at the visits represented by nodes 5 and 8 is 15 and 10 msec, respectively, the average service demand at the CPU at the TS server is

$$D_{\mathrm{CPU}}^{\mathrm{TS}} = V^{\mathrm{TS},5} \times D_{\mathrm{CPU}}^{\mathrm{TS},5} + V^{\mathrm{TS},8} \times D_{\mathrm{CPU}}^{\mathrm{TS},8} = 0.95 \times 15 + 0.76 \times 10 = 21.85 \text{ msec.} \tag{2}$$

A CSIT can also be used to compute the average service demands at the networks involved in the exchanges of messages between clients and servers and between servers. Consider an arc (i, j) with label $[p, m]$ in the CSIT and assume that a network with bandwidth B is used to send the message from i to j. The message transmission time is just m/B and the probability that the message is sent is $V^{s,j}$ where s is the server associated to node j. Thus the arc (i,j) contributes with $V^{s,j} \times (m/B)$ to the service demand of the network in question. In general, we can write the service demand, D_w at a network w as

$$D_w = \frac{1}{B_w} \sum_{(i,j) \in \mathcal{N}_w} V^{s,j} \times m_{(i,j)} \tag{3}$$

where B_w is the bandwidth of network w, $\mathcal{N}_w$ is the set of arcs in the CSIT that correspond to messages exchanged over network w, and $m_{(i,j)}$ is the average message size of arc (i,j). To illustrate the use of Eq. 3, assume that in the CSIT of Fig. 2, clients are connected to the authentication server AS and to the trading server TS through a Wide Area Network (WAN) and that the TS is connected to the database server DB through a local area network (LAN). The bandwidths of these networks are B_{WAN} and B_{LAN}, respectively. So,

$$\begin{aligned} D_{\text{WAN}} &= \frac{1}{B_{\text{WAN}}}(V^{\text{AS},2} \times m_1 + V^{\text{C},3} \times m_2 + V^{\text{C},4} \times m_3 + \\ &\quad V^{\text{TS},5} \times m_4 + V^{\text{C},9} \times m_8) \\ D_{\text{LAN}} &= \frac{1}{B_{\text{LAN}}}(V^{\text{DB},7} \times m_6 + V^{\text{TS},8} \times m_7) \end{aligned} \tag{4}$$

2.2 Server Software Architecture

A server is usually implemented by a collection of interacting concurrent processes and/or threads. The software architecture of a server may impact performance in many different ways. For the purpose of the discussion that follows, consider the multithreaded server illustrated in Fig. 3 consisting of the following types of threads:

- Dispatcher: examines the queue of requests from clients, removes the first request from the queue of incoming requests, stores the request in the Table of Request Descriptors, and starts a new thread (a Worker thread) to execute the request.
- Worker: removes its assigned request from the Table of Request Descriptors, executes the request, and places the result in the Table of Replies.
- Replier: removes replies from the Table of Replies and sends them back to the appropriate client.

The software architecture described in Fig. 3 shows contention for software resources, i.e., for the Dispatcher and Replier threads, as well as possible contention for access to shared data structures. The tables described are shared by more than one thread and mutual exclusion has to be guaranteed when accessing these tables. These two types of contention may affect performance significantly. Contention at the software level can be represented by Queuing Networks (QNs) [12,17] as described in Sec. 3.

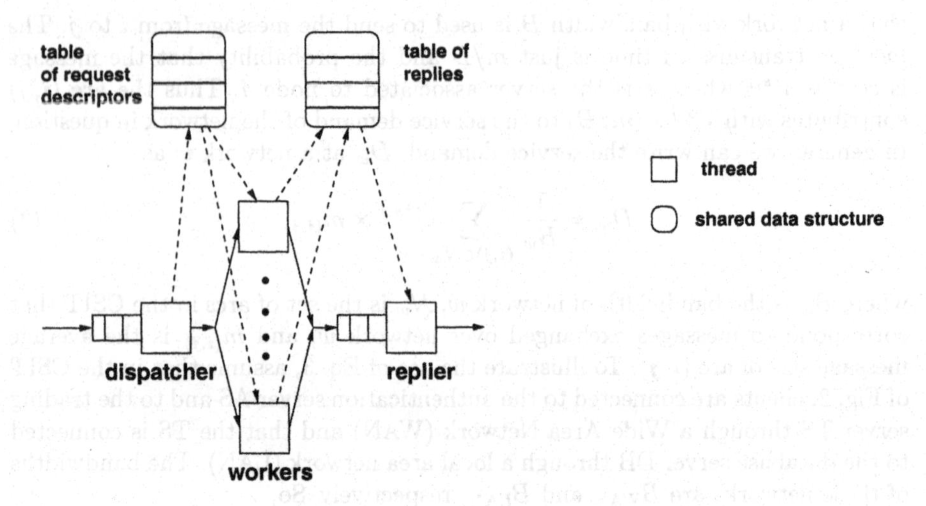

Fig. 3. Example of server software architecture

Another important aspect to consider is that software processes or threads contend for the use of hardware resources such as processors and disks. Therefore, having an unlimited number of worker threads may lead to poor performance due to high utilization of hardware resources and high operating system overhead.

In general, the software architecture of a server may have a significant impact on its performance. The following examples illustrate the point.

1. *Process-oriented vs. thread-oriented servers*. Servers built around operating system level processes tend to be less efficient than those organized around threads of a single process. Threads of the same process share a common address space. Thus, context switching between them is much faster than context switching between OS-level processes because address spaces do not need to be switched. This architectural difference results in lower processor utilization, and therefore less service demand, for multithreaded servers since less processor time is needed by the operating system to process all context switches.
2. *Threading allocation strategy.* The strategy used to allocate worker threads to incoming requests may lead to different performance levels. We discuss here three strategies: dynamic thread creation, fixed size thread pool, variable size thread pool.
   - *Dynamic thread creation.* Threads of a process may be created (and destroyed) dynamically as requests arrive at the server. Dynamically created threads can be represented in a QN model by a delay server since there is no queuing for the threads as new requests arrive. Thread creation time should be included as part of the service demand of each worker thread.

- *Fixed size thread pool.* In this case, there is a fixed size pool of threads that can be dynamically allocated to incoming requests. Under this approach, requests do not have to wait for threads as long as there is at least an idle thread in the pool. Otherwise, requests have to queue for a thread. This situation can be represented by a multiple server service center in a QN and can be modeled by a load dependent resource in a QN.
- *Variable size thread pool.* Under this strategy, the number of threads in the pool may increase or decrease according to the load in the system. If the queue length exceeds a certain threshold, more threads may be added to the pool. When the load decreases below a certain threshold, threads may be destroyed to conserve system resources. This situation is known as threshold-based multiserver queues. Some exact and approximate analysis for the single queue case may be found in [6,13]. Including threshold-based queues in a QN model poses challenges even for finding good approximate solutions. Iterative two-level models may present a solution.

Web servers are a good example to illustrate the use of different threading allocation strategies. To handle multiple HTTP requests, some servers clone a copy of the `httpd` program for each incoming request. Each request is actually processed by a new copy of the server program. However, the creation of a new process is a relatively expensive operation. Another way to handle multiple requests is to follow the thread pool strategy. The Web server is designed to have multiple threads of execution, where each thread in the main program executes a single request. In this case, it is possible to have either a fixed or a variable number of threads in the pool [21].

3. *Threading level.* The maximum number of active threads is an important consideration in the performance of a server. A higher number of threads reduces the waiting time for threads but at the same time increases contention for hardware resources. A model based on a combination of non-linear programming and analytic techniques was presented in [9] to determine optimal threading levels.
4. *Server parallelism.* Performance can be potentially improved if a server can break down the execution of its tasks into parallel tasks that execute in parallel in a fork-and-join type of model. The evaluation of the performance gains of parallel servers must consider the effects of the overhead, and the contention for underlying resources [3].

2.3 C/S System Architecture

The system architecture of a C/S system is an important element in determining the performance of a C/S system. Among the relevant issues to consider are:

1. *Server replication level.* Servers may be replicated to reduce contention for access to the server. To assess the net gain of adding more servers one has to evaluate the contention these servers pose on shared hardware resources as well as on shared data structures.

2. *Allocation of servers to server machines.* Different servers as well as different instances of a replicated server may be allocated to the same or to different server machines. If servers that interact are allocated to different machines, they need to exchange messages through the network that connects them, adding a delay to the request. However, if interacting servers are on the same machine, they interfere with one another since they share physical resources (e.g., processors, memory, and disks). The best allocation of servers to server machines depends on the anatomy of C/S transactions, the amount of inter-server communication required to execute a transaction, on the capacity of the underlying hardware resources, and on the networking topology used to interconnect various server machines.
3. *Load balancing strategies among server machines.* In many C/S systems, several server machines may be used to support the requests submitted by clients. This is true of many high performance e-commerce and Web sites. The strategy used to balance the load among the various server machines is an important consideration in determining overall performance. While most systems use pure round robin as a load balancing technique, other strategies that are based on current load levels and server machine capacity may be more appropriate.

Next section discusses how QNs can be used to build performance models of C/S systems.

3 Performance Modeling Techniques for Client/Server Systems

In this section we describe two techniques that can be used to model Client/server systems. Both techniques are based on extensions of basic Queuing Network (QN) models [10].

3.1 Layered Queuing Networks

Due to its multi-tier architecture, client/server systems are suitable to be represented by models composed of multiple layers. In this section, we first describe Layered Queuing Models [17] (LQMs), that can be used to represent the performance behavior of client/server applications. LQMs are queuing network models that combine contention for both software resources and for hardware components, such as processors, disks, and networks.

In a LQM model, processes with similar behavior form a group or a class of processes. For example, Fig. 4 shows a layered queuing model of a Web server. In the HTTP protocol [11], for each URL chosen, a client browser establishes a new TCP connection with the appropriate server, sends the requests on the connection, and receives the server's response. Let us consider that in the Web server, there is a process that listens for connections and accepts them. After accepting a connection, a Web server process reads the HTTP request, processes

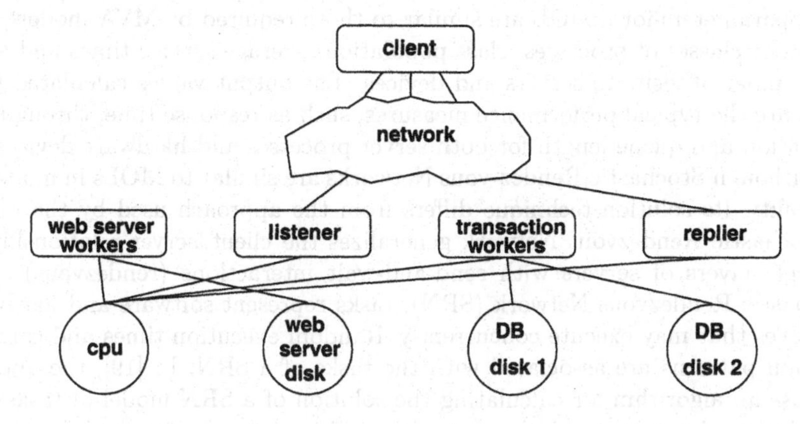

Fig. 4. LQN model of a Web server

it and passes the response to a replier process, that sends the response back to the client and closes the connection. When the requested URL implies in a query to a database, the Web server activates a transaction process (e.g., a GCI process) that executes it.

At the higher level, interactions between groups of client and groups of server processes of the Web server are explicitly represented. At the lower level, contention for the system's devices shared by the processes is directly modeled. Therefore, an LQM for a client/server system is able to account for software delays, that stem from the contention for shared processes (e.g., the Web server processes), as well as hardware delays due to contention for shared devices such as processors, disks, and networks. Approximate analytic techniques based on MVA are used to estimate performance measures of layered queuing models with L levels. Two of those techniques, the Method of Layers [17] (MOL) and Stochastic Rendez-vous Networks [19], are briefly outlined here.

The MOL is an iterative technique that decomposes an LQM into two complementary models, one for software resources and one for hardware devices. These software models consist of $L-1$ two-level models that estimate software contention delays between successive levels of queuing network models (QNM), that represent the several layers of the system being modeled. Performance estimates for each of the QNMs are calculated and used as input for subsequent QNMs. The goal of the MOL is to obtain a fixed point where mean performance measures (i.e., response time, utilization, and queue length) are consistent with respect to all of the QNMs that make up the LQM. The MOL solution method consists of an iterative algorithm, that starts assuming no device or software contention. The algorithm iterates until the response times of successive groups reach a fixed point. Groups that request service at the higher level represent customers and groups that provide service are considered servers. Thus, delays incurred by groups requesting service can be calculated as a function of activities of the serving groups. The algorithm is described in detail in [17]. Basically, the input parameters for a MOL are similar to those required by MVA models, i.e., groups or classes of processes, class population, average service times and average number of visits to servers and devices. The output values calculated by a MOL are the typical performance measures, such as response time, throughput, utilization and queue length for both server processes and hardware devices.

Although Stochastic Rendez-vous Networks are similar to MOLs in modeling capability, its solution technique differs from the approach used by the MOL. A Stochastic Rendezvous Network generalizes the client/server relationship to multiple layers of servers with send-and-wait interactions (rendezvous). In a Stochastic Rendezvous Network (SRN), tasks represent software and hardware resources that may execute concurrently. Random execution times and communication patterns are associated with the tasks of a SRN. In [19], the authors propose an algorithm for calculating the solution of a SRN model of tasks and their interactions.

3.2 SRP-MVA

Layered queueing models of client/server systems exhibit a common trait: multiple resources at different levels may be simultaneously held by a request during its execution. This characteristic, known in queuing theory as "simultaneous resource possession" requires specific techniques to solve the queuing model. We provide here an intuitive and informal description of a modified Mean Value Analysis technique to handle simultaneous resource possession. This technique, called SRP-MVA, is described in more detail in [12,14] for the multiple class case. We then show how this technique can be used to model software contention in servers.

Figure 5 shows the time axis for resources i, i_1, and i_2 in a QN. Requests arrive at resource i, queue for the resource and then receive some service. At this point, requests may need to use resource i_1 or i_2 while holding resource i. Every time simultaneous access to either i_1 or i_2 is needed, the request needs to queue for one of these resources. After using i_1 or i_2, requests may need more service from resource i. No additional queuing is necessary then. So, the total residence time at resource i is equal to the sum of the total queuing time at that resource, the total service time at resource i, the simultaneous residence times at i_1 and i_2. We call i an SRP resource and i_1 and i_2 dependent SRP resources of resource i.

The SRP-MVA technique consists of modifying the basic MVA equations [16] to reflect the effect of simultaneous resource possession. Consider the following notation:

- K: number of resources in the QN.
- n: total number of requests in the QN.
- S_i: average service per visit to resource i.
- V_i: average number of visits made by a request to resource i.
- D_i: average service demand at resource i per request, i.e., the total service time at resource i. Thus, $D_i = V_i \times S_i$. If resource i is an SRP resource, D_i only includes non simultaneous service time.

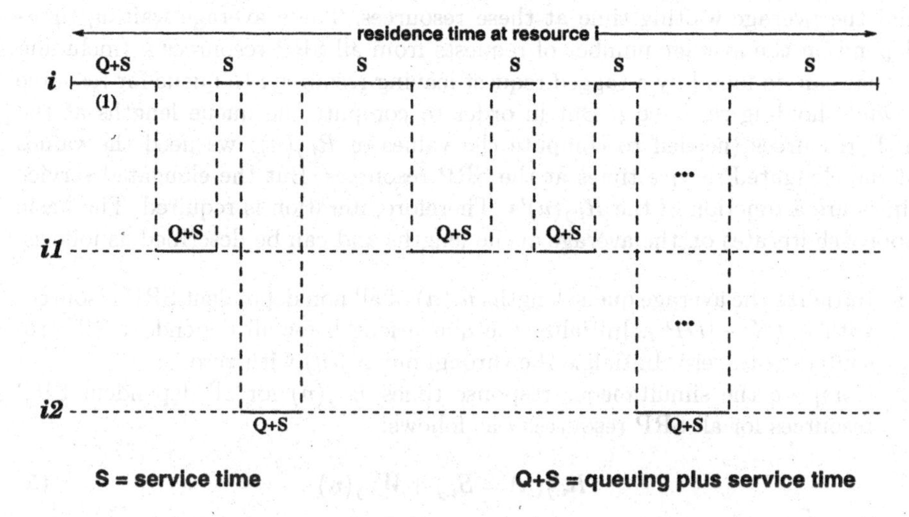

Fig. 5. Simultaneous resource possession

- $R_i(n)$: average response time at resource i per visit to the resource.
- $\bar{n}_i(n)$: average number of requests at resource i.
- $X_0(n)$: average system throughput.
- $R_0(n)$: average response time.
- SP: set of SRP resources.
- DP: set of dependent SRP resources.
- $SRP(i)$: set of dependent SRP resources associated with SRP resource i.
- $R_{i:j}(n)$: average simultaneous response time at dependent SRP resource j associated with the sojourn of a request at SRP resource i.
- $S_i^*(n)$: elongated service time at resource i, defined as service time S_i at resource i plus the sum of all simultaneous response times at all resources $j \in SRP(i)$. So, $S_i^*(n) = S_i + \sum_{j \in SRP(i)} R_{i:j}(n)$. Note that the time S_i does not include any time during which resource i is held concurrently with any other resource.
- $V_{i:j}$: average number of visits to resource j while simultaneously holding resource i.
- $S_{i:j}$: average simultaneous service time at dependent SRP resource j of SRP resource i, i.e., the service time at resource j when resource j is being held simultaneously with resource i.
- $W_{i:j}(n)$: average waiting time at resource j of a tagged request that leaves resource i to queue for resource j while still holding resource i.
- $\bar{n}^a_{k:j}(n)$: average number of requests that are simultaneously holding resource k with resource j and are found by a tagged request upon arrival at resource j.

The basic approach consists in computing the simultaneous response times $R_{i:j}(n)$ at the SRP resources as a function of the simultaneous service times and the average waiting time at these resources. These average waiting times depend on the average number of requests from all SRP resources k (including i) that can be found by a tagged request leaving resource i to queue for resource j while holding resource i. But in order to compute the queue lengths at the SRP resources (needed to compute the values of $R_{i:j}(n)$) we need the values of the elongated service times at the SRP resources. But the elongated service times are a function of the $R_{i:j}(n)$'s. Therefore, iteration is required. The basic approach iterates on the average queue lengths and can be described as follows:

1. Initialize the average queue lengths $\bar{n}_i(n)$ of all non dependent SRP resources with $n/(K - |DP|)$. Initialize the queue length for all dependent SRP resources with zero. Initialize the throughput $X_0(n)$ with zero.
2. Compute the simultaneous response times $R_{i:j}(n)$ for all dependent SRP resources for all SRP resources i as follows:

$$R_{i:j}(n) = S_{i:j} + W_{i:j}(n) \; . \tag{5}$$

The value of $W_{i:j}(n)$ can be computed as

$$W_{i:j}(n) = \sum_{k \mid j \in SRP(k)} \bar{n}^a_{k:j}(n) \; S_{k:j} \; . \tag{6}$$

The computation of $\bar{n}^a_{k:j}(n)$ depends on whether $k = i$ or $k \neq i$ and on the type of resource (i.e., delay or queuing resource). For example, if $k = i$ and resource i is of the single server queuing type, the tagged transaction cannot find any other request also holding i at resource j. So, in this case, $\bar{n}^a_{i:j}(n) = 0$. If i is a delay resource, it is possible to find requests at j that are also holding i. If resource i does not have any other dependent SRP resource besides j, then all requests queued at resource i can be found at j by the tagged request. So, in this case, $\bar{n}^a_{i:j}(n) = \bar{n}_i(n)$. Suppose now that $k \neq i$ and that k is a queuing resource. If j is the only dependent SRP resource of k, then only the request being served at k, if any, can be found by the tagged request. Since the average number of requests in service at resource k is the utilization of resource k, $U_k(n)$ which is equal to $X_0(n) \times V_k \times S^*_k(n)$, we have that $\bar{n}^a_{k:j}(n) = X_0(n) \times V_k \times S^*_k(n)$.
3. Compute the response time for each SRP resource i using the regular MVA residence time equations and the elongated service times. Hence,

$$R_i(n) = S^*_i(n)[1 + \bar{n}_i(n-1)] \quad \forall \, i \in SP \; . \tag{7}$$

4. Compute the response times of all resources which are not SRP nor dependent SRP resources using the regular MVA equations.
5. Compute the response time $R_0(n)$ as the sum of the response time over all visits at all resources except for the dependent SRP ones. Thus,

$$R_0(n) = \sum_{i \notin DP} V_i \times R_i(n) \tag{8}$$

It is necessary to exclude the response times at the dependent SRP resources from the above summation since they are already accounted for in the response times at the SRP devices.
6. Compute the throughput as $X_0(n) = n/R_0(n)$.
7. Compute the average queue length $\bar{n}_i(n)$ for all resources that are non dependent SRP using the MVA equations, i.e., $\bar{n}_i(n) = X_0(n)\ V_i R_i(n)$.
8. Compute the average queue length for the dependent SRP resources as a function of the values of the queue lengths at the SRP resources of which they depend on. The argument here is very similar to the one used to compute the values of $\bar{n}^a_{i:j}(n)$ in Step 2.
9. Check for convergence by comparing the maximum absolute error in the average queue lengths with a given convergence. If it has not converged go to step 2, otherwise stop.

The SRP-MVA technique discussed above can be generalized to QNs with multiple classes (see [12,14]). The accuracy of the SRP-MVA technique was validated against detailed discrete-event simulation [12,14]. In general, when using the SRP-MVA technique to model software and hardware resources, the software resources are modeled as SRP resources and the hardware resources as dependent SRP resources of one or more software resources. The service times S_i at the SRP resources (which represent software resources) are equal to zero in this case. The SRP-MVA approximation has the characteristic of being consistently pessimistic, in the sense that it overestimates the response time and underestimates the throughput.

Other techniques have been presented to solve the simultaneous resource possession problem [4]. The technique in [4] is a two-level modeling technique restricted to single class models. Special purpose techniques to model delays due to serialization have been discussed in [1,5,20]. The model discussed in [20] is based on Markov chains and QNs and has the problem of state-space explosion.

Next section illustrates a more complete example of a client/server system in the context of an electronic commerce site.

4 An Example of a C/S System

Consider that clients access an e-commerce site through a Wide Area Network (WAN) (see Fig. 6). The top portion of the figure shows the software threads involved in the processing of a C/S request. A *listener* thread handles the incoming requests and after verifying their validity, passes them to one of the available *Web server worker* threads. With a probability p, the request may require an access to the database. In this case, the request has to be initially treated by a thread called *DBMS dispatcher* which hands the request to one of the *transaction worker* threads. The e-commerce site has the following hardware resources: one CPU, one disk dedicated to the Web server, and two disks used only by the DBMS. This example assumes a fixed size pool of threads for the Web server worker threads and for the transaction worker threads.

Using the terminology of the SRP-MVA technique, resources 3 through 7 are SRP resources and resources 8 through 11 are dependent SRP resources. Resource 8, the CPU, is a dependent SRP resource of all SRP resources (3 through 7) since all the SRP resources need the CPU. Resource 9, the Web server disk, is a dependent SRP resource of SRP resource 4, the Web server worker. Resources 10 and 11, the two DB disks, are dependent SRP resources of SRP resource 6, the transaction worker. Resources 4 and 6 in Fig. 6 are multi-server queues.

Table 1 shows the service demands for all software processes at the CPU and disks. The actual service demands for the DBMS dispatcher and for the transaction workers have to be multiplied by the probability p (chosen as 0.2 in this example) that a request from the client requires an access to the database. The service demand at the WAN was assumed to be 86 msec for this numeric example.

Figure 7 illustrates the variation of the response with the number of clients for three different situations. All of them assume one transaction processing thread. The bottom curve, shows the variation of the response time for the case of 2 Web server threads while the middle curve considers the case of a single Web server thread. For the latter case, the bottleneck is the Web server worker thread which achieved almost 100% utilization at 300 clients. The throughput at this point was equal to 9.40 requests/sec, very close to its maximum value of 9.73. Note that if only looked at the hardware resources one would find that the bottleneck

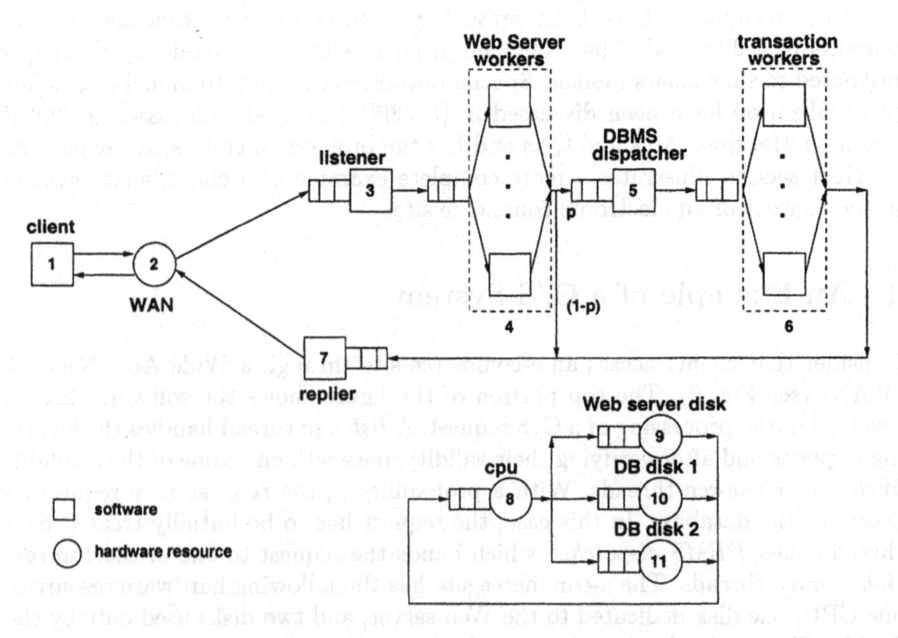

Fig. 6. Web site for e-commerce.

Table 1. Service Demands (msec)

Resource	CPU	Web server disk	DB disk 1	DB disk 2
Listener	20	0	0	0
Replier	10	0	0	0
Web server worker	60	22	0	0
DBMS dispatcher	15	0	0	0
Transaction worker	27	0	140	100

would have to be the CPU which has a service demand, D_{CPU} equal to 98 msec $(= 20+10+60+0.2\,(15+27))$. So the maximum throughput would be $1/0.098 = 10.16$ request/sec, as shown in the graph of Fig. 8. Because of contention for software resources, the maximum throughput cannot be attained. The middle curve shows that when one additional Web server thread is added, the bottleneck shifts from the software resource to the CPU. The maximum throughput of 10.16 requests/sec is achieved for 350 clients. The top curve in Fig. 7 shows a situation in for two Web server workers but with an increased database activity. In this case, the probability a request generates a DB transaction was increased from 0.2 to 0.5. The bottleneck is now shifted to the transaction processing worker thread which reaches 100% utilization at around 250 clients. The maximum throughput in this case is 6.37 requests/sec, well below the maximum throughput that would have been achieved if software contention is not taken into account. For $p = 0.5$, the service demand at the CPU is 111 msec $(= 20 + 10 + 60 + 0.5\ (15 + 27))$, which would result in a maximum throughput of $1/0.111 = 9.01$ requests/sec.

Table 2 shows the variation of the response time versus the number of Web worker threads for 350 clients. The probability of accessing the database was kept at 0.2 and the number of transaction processing threads at one. It can be seen that in this case, there is a 28.6% reduction in response time when the number of Web worker threads is increased from 1 to 2. Further increases in the number of Web worker threads bring significantly smaller reductions in the response time since the software bottleneck disappears.

5 Concluding Remarks

Performance modeling of client/server applications is a key issue to obtain cost-effective system designs. Performance models of client/server systems can be developed using simulation or analytic techniques. This paper focused on analytic techniques based on queuing networks. In this paper, we looked into three different aspects of client/server systems: the anatomy of C/S interactions, the software architecture of a server, and the system organization. We then showed that performance models should integrate these three different aspects.

Layered queuing networks are adequate representations for modeling C/S systems with their software and hardware components. Layered queuing models

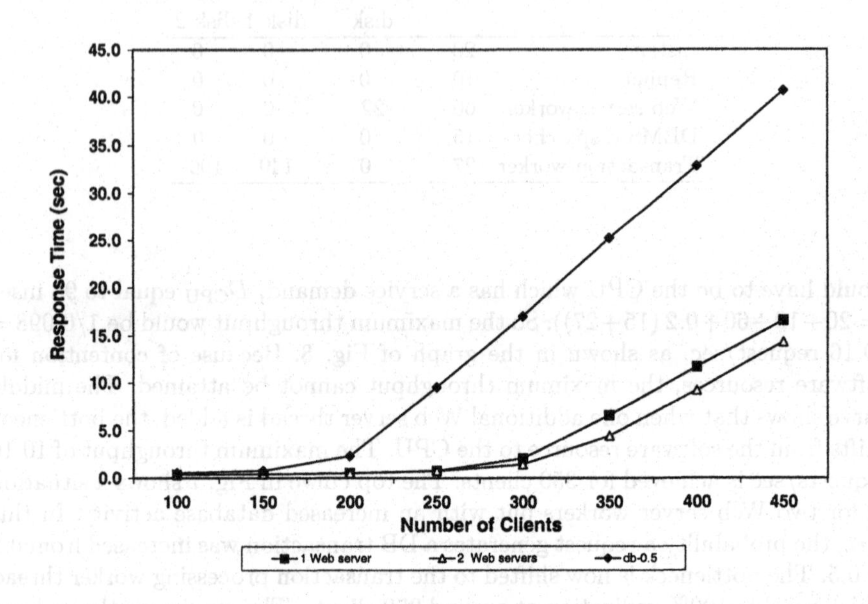

Fig. 7. Response time (sec) vs. number of clients.

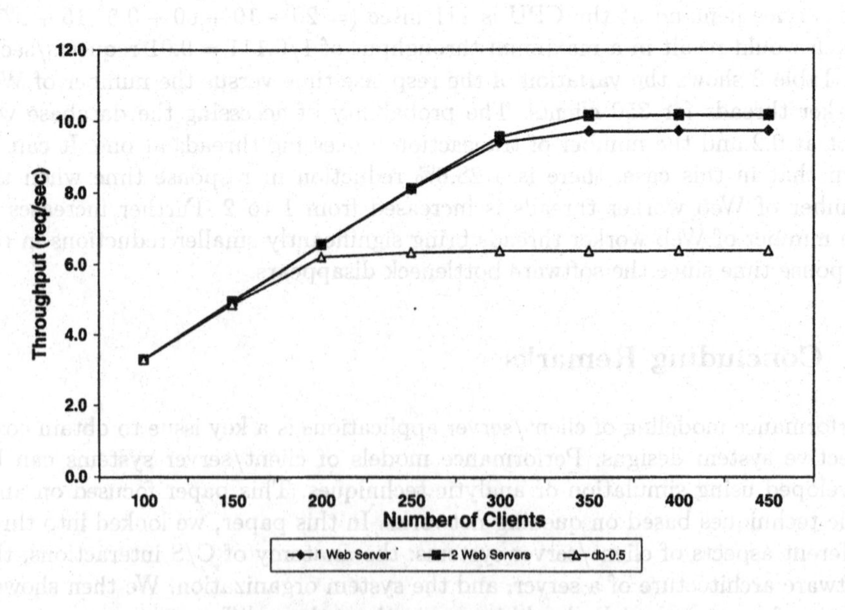

Fig. 8. Throughput (req/sec) vs. number of clients.

Table 2. Response time (sec) vs. number of worker threads for 350 clients and $p = 0.2$

No. Web Worker Threads	Response Time (sec)
1	6.58
2	4.70
3	4.62
4	4.61
5	4.55
6	4.55
7	4.46
8	4.43
9	4.42
10	4.41
11	4.41
12	4.40

of C/S systems exhibit a common trait: multiple resources at different levels may be simultaneously held by a request during its execution.

Approximate solutions based on MVA techniques have been developed for solving models with simultaneous resource possession. In this paper, we show a novel approach to solve the problem and use it to analyze the performance of a typical client/server system: a Web server.

Acknowledgements

The work of Daniel A. Menascé was partially supported by the National Science Foundation under grant CCR-9804113.

References

1. Agrawal, S., Buzen, J. P.: The Aggregate Server Method for Analyzing Serialization Delays in Computer Systems, ACM TOCS, **1**, no. 2 (1983) 116–143
2. Baskett, F., Chandy, K. M., Muntz, R. R., Palacios, F. G.: Open, Closed, and Mixed Networks of Queues with Different Classes of Customers, J. ACM, **22**, no. 2, (1975) 248–260
3. Franks, G., Woodside, M.: Performance of Multi-Level Client-Server Systems with Parallel Service Operations, Proc.First International Workshop on Software and Performance (WOSP'98), Santa Fe, NM, October 12-16, (1998) pp. 120–130
4. Jacobson, P. A., Lazowska, E. D.: Analyzing Queueing Networks with Simultaneous Resource Possession, Comm. ACM, **25**, no. 2, (1982)
5. Jacobson, P. A., Lazowska, E. D.: A Reduction Technique for Evaluating Queuing Networks with Serialization Delays, Performance'83, eds. A. K. Agrawal and S. K. Tripathi, North-Holland Publishing Company (1983) 45–59

6. Golubchik, L., Lui, J. C. S.: Bounding Performance Measures for a Threshold-based Queuing System with Hysteresis, Proc. 1997 ACM Sigmetrics Conference, Seattle, Washington, June 15-18, (1997) 147–157
7. Inverardi, P. A. L. Wolf.: Analysis of Software Architecture Using the Chemical Abstract Machine Model. IEEE Tr. Software Engineering, **21**, no. 4, April 1995 373–386
8. International Telecommunications Union: Criteria for the Use and Applicability of Formal Description Techniques, Message Sequence Charts (MSC), (1996)
9. Litoiu, M., J. Rolia, Serazzi, G,: Designing Process Replication and Threading Policies: a Quantitative Approach, Proc. 10th International Conference on Modeling Techniques and for Computer Performance Evaluation (Tools'98), Palma de Mallorca, Spain, Lectures Notes in Computer Science, Puigjaner, R., Savino, N., Sera B. (Eds.) **1469** 15–26
10. Menascé, D., V. A. F. Almeida, L. W. Dowdy: Capacity Planning and Performance Modeling: from mainframes to client-server systems, Prentice Hall, Upper Saddle River, (1994)
11. Menascé, D., Almeida, V. A. F.: Capacity Planning for Web Performance: metrics, models, and methods, Prentice Hall, Upper Saddle River, NJ, (1998)
12. Menascé, D., Pentakalos, O., Yesha, Y.: An Analytic Model of Hierarchical Mass Storage Systems with Network-Attached Storage Devices, Proc. 1996 ACM Sigmetrics Conference, Philadelphia, PA, May (1996)
13. Nelson, R., Towsley, D.: Approximating the Mean Time in System in a Multiple-server Queue that uses Threshold Scheduling, Operations Research, **35**, (1987) 419–427
14. Pentakalos, O., Menascé, D., Y. Yesha: Analytic Modeling of Distributed Hierarchical Mass Storage Systems with Network-Attached Storage Devices, to appear in the IEEE Transactions on Parallel and Distributed Systems.
15. Rational Software Corporation: Unified Modeling Language: Notation Guide, Version 1.1, Santa Clara, CA, September 1997.
16. Reiser, M., S. Lavenberg: Mean-value analysis of closed multi-chain queuing networks, J. ACM, **27**, no. 2, (1980)
17. Rolia, J. A., K. C. Sevcik: The Method of Layers, IEEE Tr. Software Eng., **21**, no. 8, (1995) 689–700
18. Olsen, A., O. Faergemand, B. Moeller-Pedersen, R. Reed, J. R. W. Smith: Systems Engineering Using SDL-92, North-Holland, (1994)
19. Woodside, C. M., J. E. Neilson, D. C. Petriu, and S. Majumdar: The Stochastic Rendezvous Network Model for Performance of Synchronous Client-Server-like Distributed Software, IEEE Tr. Computers, **44**, no. 1, (1995)
20. Thomasian, A.: Queueing Network Models to Estimate Serialization Delays in Computer Systems, Performance'83, eds. A. K. Agrawal and S. K. Tripathi, North-Holland Publishing Company (1983) 61–81
21. Yeager, N., McCrath, R.: Web Server Technology, Morgan Kauffman, San Francisco, CA (1996)

Performance Characteristics of the World Wide Web

Mark E. Crovella

Department of Computer Science
Boston University, Boston, MA 02215, USA
crovella@cs.bu.edu

1 Introduction

The Web is a distributed client-server system on a scale greater than any other. Its large scale and increasingly important role in society make it an important object of study and evaluation. In recent years a large literature on the performance of the Web has developed. At the time of writing (1999) there are workshops, conferences, journals, and books whose focus is on of performance evaluation of the Web—encompassing protocols, servers and clients [1,2,3,4,5,28].

The remarkable popularity of the Web seems to arise from a combination of its utility and its ease of use. It is useful as a means of publishing and delivering information in a wide variety of formats: raw data, formatted text, graphics, animation, audio, video, and even software. Its ease of use stems from the fact that it hides the details of contacting remote sites on the Internet, transporting data across the network, and formatting, displaying or playing the requested information regardless of the type of particular computers involved.

Information in the Web exists as files on computer systems (*hosts*); each file has a globally unique identifier called a Uniform Resource Locator (URL). It is only necessary to know a file's URL in order to transfer it from wherever it is stored (potentially, anywhere in the global Internet) and display it on the user's local computer.

The Web is organized using a client-server model. Each file is stored on a specific host, specified as part of its URL; such hosts are *servers*. When a user requests a file, it is transferred to the user's local host, the *client*. (In fact, a single host can act as both a client and a server.) The software used by the client to retrieve and display files is called a *browser*.

Surprisingly, given the near-ubiquity of the Web, its appears to exhibit some unusual performance characteristics. In particular, many of the workloads charateristics of the Web can be characterized as exhibiting *high variability*. By high variability, we mean that the workload seems to be well modeled by a distribution with *infinite variance*. This effect is defined formally in Section 2 but can be informally described as having a distribution whose upper tail follows an inverse power law with exponent less than 2. Such distributions are called *heavy-tailed*.

Heavy-tailed distributions exist in sharp contrast to distributions commonly encountered in computer and telecommunication systems modelling. Distribu-

G. Haring et al. (Eds.): Performance Evaluation, LNCS 1769, pp. 219–232, 2000.

tions like the Exponential, Normal, and Poisson all have tails that decline exponentially (or faster). For these distributions, the probability of a large observation is infinitesimally small. On the other hand, for heavy-tailed distributions, the probability of extremely large observations is non-negligible. The result is that observation sizes typically span many orders of magnitude; and that while most observations are small, it is the large observations that dominate empirical statistics.

In this chapter we examine three examples of high variability in Web workloads. First, we show that file sizes (and file transfer times) show high variability, and that this effect occurs consistently over a wide range of file sets, including sets captured at clients and at servers. Next we discuss the relationship between high variability in file sizes and the phenomenon of *self-similarity* in network traffic. Finally we discuss the presence of high variability in file popularity — that is, in the distribution of requests across sets of files in the Web.

In the next section we provide background on high variability and discuss some of its statistical implications. Then the next three sections discuss each type of high variability in turn. Finally, we conclude with some observations about the implications of high variability for Web engineering.

2 High Variability: Background

In this section we motivate and explain the notion of high variability for modeling Web workloads. First we discuss the high variability on an intuitive level; we then follow with formal definitions and implications.

2.1 Why Assume Infinite Variance?

The condition of high variability refers to the situation in which it appears that a dataset is well modeled by a distribution with *infinite variance*. Since any particular dataset cannot in practice exhibit an infinite sample variance, the decision to adopt a model with infinite variance rests on a number of considerations.

The starting point for considering infinite variance models is that for many datasets considered in this chapter, the upper tail of the dataset's empirical distribution function appears to decline like a power law. This suggests that a hyperbolically declining function can provide a good fit to the empirical tail. Since the empirically measured exponent typically appears to be less than 2, this implies a distribution with infinite variance.

The immediate difficulty with infinite variance models is that the property of infinite variance requires the distribution to have unbounded upper support. However, the timescale of interest to the analyst is often short compared to the timescale over which the effects of a dataset's finite distributional support would be noticed. For example, the distribution of file sizes on a Web server may show power law shape over five orders of magnitude; however a performance analyst may only be concerned with timescales over which only three or four orders of magnitude in file sizes are important. To take a more extreme example: the number of files available in the Web at any instant is finite, implying the existence of a largest file; however for many practical modeling questions the distribution of file sizes available in the Web may be considered to have no upper limit.

The choice to use an infinite variance model to describe any particular dataset has two strengths in particular. First, it often yields a parsimonious representation involving a small number of parameters, each of which can be assigned some intuitive significance. Second, it serves to expose and draw attention to properties of the dataset (such as slow convergence or nonconvergence of sample moments) that are important in practice.

For these reasons, the principal focus of this chapter is on the phenomenon of high variability in Web workloads. To provide a formal basis for discussion, the next subsection summarizes relevant theory regarding infinite variance distributions, based on [21,34].

2.2 Infinite Variance and Heavy Tails

A random variable X shows infinite variance when its distribution has a *heavy tail.* We say here that a random variable X follows a heavy-tailed distribution (with tail index α) if

$$P[X > x] \sim cx^{-\alpha}, \quad \text{as } x \to \infty, \ 0 < \alpha < 2,$$

where c is a positive constant, and where $\sim$ means that the ratio of the two sides tends to 1 as $x \to \infty$.

Random variables that follow heavy-tailed distributions typically show many small observations mixed with a few very large observations. The large observations tend to dominate the sample statistics; eliminating a small number of them can change sample statistics by orders of magnitude.

Smaller values of α make this effect more pronounced. The smaller the value of α, the more unstable the sample statistics, and the more pronounced the degree of difference between the typical (small) observations and the dominating (large) observations. For example, as α declines from 2 towards 1, the random variable's mean explodes, eventually becoming infinite when $\alpha = 1$. Thus heavy tailed random variables with values of α close to 1 exhibit highly unstable sample statistics.

The implication of infinite moments in practice is that sample realizations of a heavy-tailed random variable will exhibit nonconvergence of sample moments. A related implication is that subsets of the sample will not provide good estimates of the entire sample's statistics. This can be seen in Fig. 1, which shows the sample standard deviation s_n of a collection of sizes of files transferred over the Web (described in Section 3), as a function of the number of samples included (n). This figure shows how the sample statistic is dominated by a few large observations, and exhibits the generally upward trend indicating lack of convergence.

The convergence properties of sample moments can be explored quantitatively by considering central limit theorems for heavy tailed random variables.

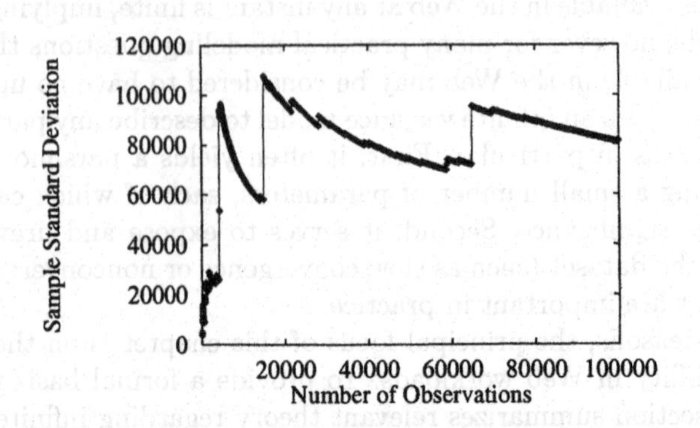

Fig. 1. Sample Standard Deviation for Web File Data

To start, consider one version of the *usual* Central Limit Theorem (CLT): For X_i i.i.d. and drawn from some distribution F with mean $\mu = 0$ and variance $\sigma^2 < \infty$, let $\Sigma_n = \sum_{i=1}^{n} X_i$. Then

$$n^{-\frac{1}{2}} \Sigma_n \xrightarrow{d} N(0, \sigma^2) \quad \text{as} \quad n \to \infty$$

where N is the Normal distribution and $A \xrightarrow{d} B$ means that random variable A converges in distribution to B.

However the usual CLT applies only to sums of random variables with finite variance. In the place of the CLT we instead have limit theorems for heavy tailed random variables first formulated by Lévy [21]. For heavy tailed random variables X_i i.i.d. with tail index $\alpha \leq 2$,

$$n^{-1/\alpha} \Sigma_n \xrightarrow{d} S_\alpha \quad \text{as} \quad n \to \infty$$

where S_α is an α-*Stable* distribution. For a detailed discussion of α-Stable distributions see [34]; the significance here is that since the term on the left converges in distribution, the variability of Σ_n is increasing like $n^{1/\alpha}$. Thus the variability of the empirical mean $M_n = \Sigma_n / n$ goes like $n^{-1+1/\alpha}$ [24,15].

The influence of α in the expression $n^{-1+1/\alpha}$ is profound. When $\alpha = 2$, the variability of M_n decreases like $n^{-1/2}$, that is, like the usual case for the CLT. However as α declines, the variability of the sample mean (for any fixed n) increases; when $\alpha = 1$ the variability of the sample mean becomes equal to that of any observation, and independent of the number of samples used! Furthermore, when $\alpha < 1$, the variability of the sample mean is greater than that of any observation, reflecting the fact that the true mean is infinite and the sample mean is a nonconvergent statistic.

One way of interpreting these properties is with respect to achieving a given accuracy in measurement, or steady state in a simulation. For example, suppose one would like to use M_n to form a estimate of a distributional mean μ that is accurate to k digits. Alternatively, one might be determine that a simulation has reached steady state when the observed mean of the input M_n agrees with μ to k digits. In either of these examples we would like

$$|M_n - \mu|/\mu \leq 10^{-k}.$$

Now, as a rough approximation:

$$|M_n - \mu| = c_1 n^{1/\alpha - 1}$$

for some positive constant c_1. Then we find that:

$$n \geq c_2 10^{\frac{k}{1-1/\alpha}}.$$

We can say that given this many samples, k digit accuracy is "highly likely."

For example, assume we would like 2-digit accuracy in M_n, and suppose $c_2 \approx 1$. Then the number of samples n necessary to achieve this accuracy is shown in Table 1. This table shows that as $\alpha \to 1$, the number of samples necessary to obtain convergence in the sample mean explodes. Thus, for conditions of α less than about 1.5, it is not feasible in any reasonable amount of time to observe an accurate measure of the distributional mean, or steady state in a simulation as we have defined it.

Table 1. Number of Samples Necessary to Achieve 2 Digit Accuracy in Mean as a Function of α

α	n
2.0	10,000
1.7	72,000
1.5	1,000,000
1.2	10^{12}
1.1	10^{22}

This discussion highlights the practical importance of the specific value of α that describes the dataset in question. A number of methods exist for estimating the value of α [25,33,16]. However, the simplest approach can often be quite effective: the value of α can be estimated by plotting the complementary distribution (CD) function $\overline{F}(x) = 1 - F(x) = P[X > x]$ on log-log axes. Plotted in this way, heavy-tailed distributions have the property that

$$\frac{d \log \overline{F}(x)}{d \log x} \sim -\alpha,$$

for large x. Linear behavior on the plot for the upper tail is evidence of a heavy-tailed distribution. If such evidence exists, one can form an estimate for α by plotting the CD plot of the dataset and selecting a minimal value x_0 of x above which the plot appears to be linear. Estimating the slope for points greater than x_0 then gives an estimate of α.

The technique, called the log-log complementary distribution (LLCD) plot, is shown in Fig. 2 for the same set of files used in Fig. 1. This figure shows that for this set of files transferred over the Web, the distribution of sizes appears to show power-law behavior over approximately 5 orders of magnitude.

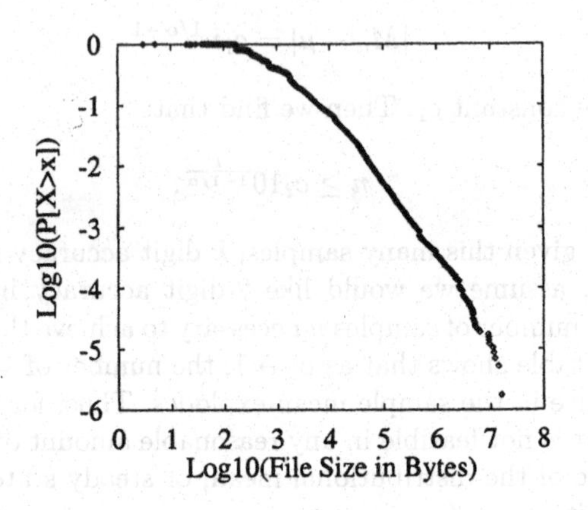

Fig. 2. LLCD of Web File Data

3 Sizes and Durations

Fig. 2 showed a single example of high variability in a Web dataset. In this section we show that high variability appears to be a common feature of file sizes and transmission times of files in the Web.

File collections may be observed at a number of points in the Web. Depending on the performance question being asked, an analyst may be concerned with one or more of the following datasets (as shown in Fig. 3):

Transmission Times: the transmission durations of Web files. This set gives insight into the nature of the network demands of Web activity.

File Transfers: the set of files actually transferred over a network.

File Requests: the set of files requested by a user or a collection of users. This set consists of all files that are either "clicked on" by users or contained by reference in files clicked on by users. This set is different from the set of file transfers because of the action of caching.

Available Files: the set of files present on a server or a set of servers. This set may be different from the set of files transferred because some files may be transferred more often than others.

Each of these datasets implies a different type of data collection process. Measurements of file requests require the ability to intercept user requests before they

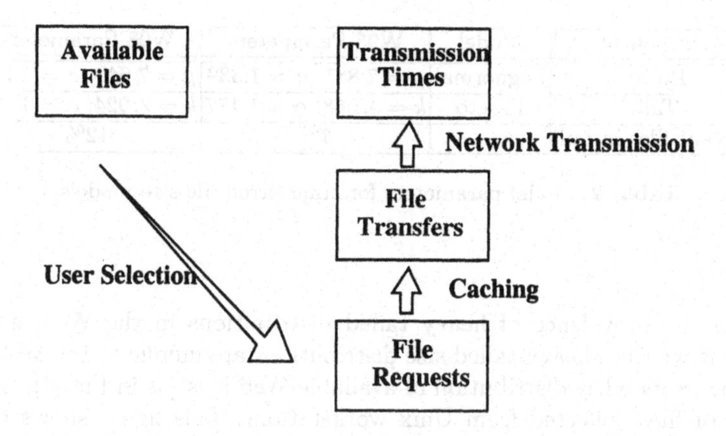

Fig. 3. Relations among Web Datasets of Interest.

are applied to the browser cache; measurements of file transfers and trasmission durations requires the ability to observe network traffic; and measurements of available files are taken from server logs or server filesystems directly.

A number of studies, taking measurements at different points, have presented evidence of high variability in Web files [8,17,14]. We show here data from [17] because it examines all four of the datasets in Fig. 3. In this study the Web browser *NCSA Mosaic* [22] was modified and installed for general use in a large general-purpose workstation laboratory. At the time of the study (November 1994 through February 1995) Mosaic was the browser preferred by nearly all users at the site. By instrumenting only this program it was possible to capture a log of the transmission times, file transfers, and file requests taking place in the laboratory. In addition, the complete contents of 32 Web servers were collected and analyzed.

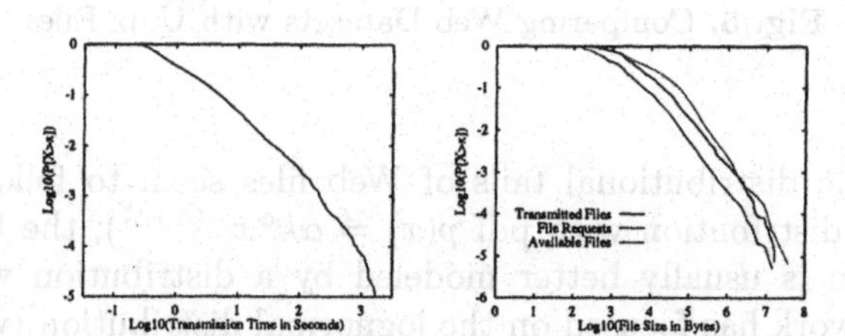

Fig. 4. High Variability in Web Datasets: Transfer Durations (left); File Sizes (right).

The results are shown in Fig. 4; on the left of the figure is a plot of the LLCD of transmission times; on the right of the figure is the LLCDs of the three file size sets. Each of the datasets shows approximate power-law scaling of the upper distributional tail over at least four orders of magnitude. These figures show how prevalent heavy-tailed distributions are in these samples of Web files.

Component	Model	W95 Parameters	W98 Parameters
Body	Lognormal	$\mu = 7.881$; $\sigma = 1.339$	$\mu = 7.640$; $\sigma = 1.705$
Tail	Pareto	$k = 3,558$; $\alpha = 1.177$	$k = 2,924$; $\alpha = 1.383$
Percent files in tail		7%	12%

Table 2. Model parameters for transferred file size models.

Given the prevalence of heavy tailed distributions in the Web, a natural question is whether heavy-tailed size distributions are unique to the Web. Fig. 5 shows the probability distribution of available Web files (as in Fig. 4) compared to a set of files collected from Unix workstations. This figure shows that the Unix files also show a heavy-tailed distribution and suggest that the heavy-tailed phenomenon may not be restricted to the Web in general.

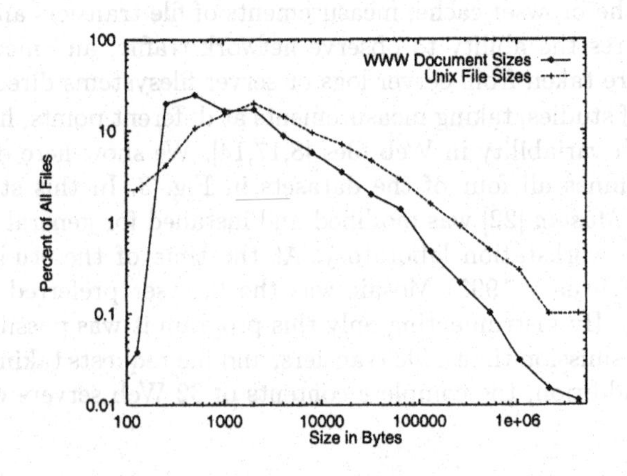

Fig. 5. Comparing Web Datasets with Unix Files

Although the distributional tails of Web files seem to follow a power-law (*e.g.*, a Pareto distribution with pdf $p(x) = \alpha k^{\alpha} x^{-(\alpha+1)}$), the body of the file size distribution is usually better modeled by a distribution with a different shape. Recent work has focused on the lognormal distribution (with pdf $p(x) = \frac{1}{x\sigma\sqrt{2\pi}} e^{-(\ln x - \mu)^2/2\sigma^2}$) as a good model for the body of file size distributions in the Web [10].

For example, in [9] models are presented for the sizes of files transferred via the Web. Two datasets are analyzed; one (W95) is the same as used for Figs. 4 and 5; the other was collected more recently, in 1998 (W98). Table 2 shows the complete models developed for those two datasets. In each case the cutoff between the two distributions is specified implicitly in terms of the number of files contained in the Pareto upper tail.

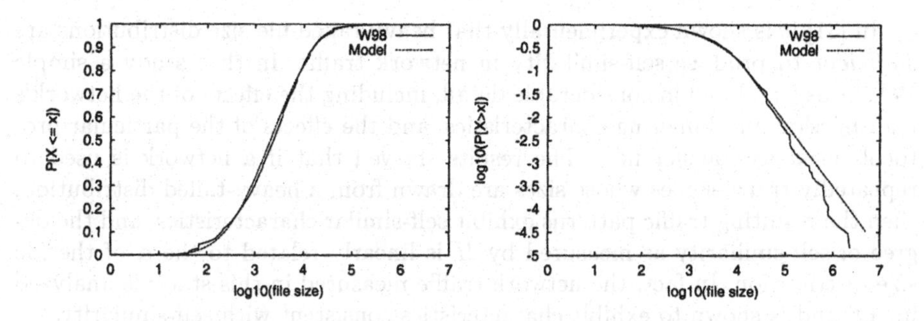

Fig. 6. CDF and LLCD of log-transformed transferred file sizes for W98 and corresponding hybrid lognormal-Pareto model.

The fit of these models against empirical data is shown in Fig. 6 for the W98 dataset. On the left is the CDF of the log-transformed dataset; this shows the characteristic shape of the Normal distribution, indicating that body is well modeled with a lognormal distribution. On the right is the LLCD plot of the data along with the fitted model. The model fits closely except in the extreme tail where there are very few data points.

4 Self-Similarity

One of the important implications of heavy-tailed file size distributions for network engineering lies in their connection to traffic self-similarity. Research has shown that network traffic, considered as a time series representing bytes or packets per unit time, typically shows self-similar characteristics with a scaling parameter $H > 1/2$ [26,36]. Intuitively, this means that traffic shows noticeable "bursts" (sustained periods above or below the mean) at a wide range of time scales — perhaps at all scales of interests to network engineers.

Heavy-tailed distributions have been suggested as a cause of self-similarity in network trafic. The authors in [37] show that if traffic is constructed as the sum of many ON/OFF processes, in which individual ON or OFF periods are independently drawn from a heavy-tailed distribution, then the resulting traffic series will be asymptotically self-similar. If the distribution of ON or OFF times is heavy tailed with parameter α, then the resulting series will be self-similar with $H = (3 - \alpha)/2$. If both ON and OFF times are heavy-tailed, the resulting H is determined by whichever distribution is heavier-tailed, *i.e.*, has the lower α; see [36] for further details.

In the context of the World Wide Web, we can consider individual ON/OFF processes to be analogous to Mosaic sessions. Each Mosaic session can be considered to be either silent, or receiving transmitted data at some regular rate. This is a simplification of a real Web environment, but it indicates that if transmission durations are heavy-tailed, then it is likely that the resulting traffic will be self-similar in nature.

In [31] it is shown experimentally that heavy-tailed file size distributions are *sufficient* to produce self-similarity in network traffic. In that study a simple WAN was simulated in considerable detail, including the effects of the network's transmission and buffering characteristics, and the effects of the particular protocols used to transfer files. The results showed that if a network is used to repeatedly transfer files whose sizes are drawn from a heavy-tailed distribution, then the resulting traffic patterns exhibit self-similar characteristics, and the degree of self-similarity as measured by H is linearly related to the α of the file size distribution. In fact, the network traffic measured in this study is analyzed in [14] and is shown to exhibit characteristics consistent with self-similarity.

While transmission times correspond to ON times, the size distribution of OFF times (corresponding to times when the browser is not actively transferring a file) is also important. [13] contains further analyses showing that silent times appear to exhibit heavy-tailed characteristics with α approximately in the range of 1.5. Thus, since the transmission time distribution appears to be heavier tailed than the silent time distribution, it seems more likely to be the primary determinant of Web traffic self-similarity.

Since Web traffic is currently responsible for more than half the traffic on the global Internet, the presence of strong self-similarity in Web traffic has implications for the performance of the Internet as a whole. In [20,32] it is shown that the presence of self-similarity with large values of H in network traffic can have severe performance effects when the network has significant buffering. Buffering refers to the use of storage in the network to temporarily hold packets while they wait for transmission. Buffer use is related to the burstiness of traffic, because when a burst occurs, transmission channels can become overloaded, and packets need to be buffered (queued) while waiting for transmission channels to become available.

When traffic is strongly self-similar in nature, bursts can occur at a wide range of timescales. When very long bursts occur, many packets may require buffering. There are two negative effects that can result. First, packets stored in a large buffer will wait for long periods before they can be transmitted. This is the problem of *packet delay.* Second, since buffers are finite, the demand placed on them by a large burst may exceed their capacity. In this case, networks discard these packets leading to the problem of *decreased throughput* (because network bandwidth must be used to retransmit packets). Both problems lead to delays in transmitting files; in the Web, this is perceived by the user as an unresponsive browser. That is, because of long bursts in network traffic, users experience long delays in transfers, and the network appears to perform in an unresponsive manner.

5 Popularity of Documents

A final, important form high variability in the Web occurs in the form of document popularity. *Popularity* refers to how requests are distributed over the set of available documents. In the Web, this distribution of requests is typically highly nonuniform.

The nonuniform popularity of Web files can be captured by *Zipf's Law* [27,38]. Zipf's Law (in a generalized form) states that the relative probability of a request for the i'th most popular page is proportional to $i^{-\beta}$ where β is typically close to or less than 1.

An example of Zipf's Law for the set of file requests from [18] is shown in Fig. 7. In this figure the number of references to a file is plotted against the file's rank in order of popularity, on log-log axes. The distinctive straight line, indicative of a power-law relationship, has a slope (found using least-squares fitting) of -0.99, meaning that in this case, $\beta = 0.99$.

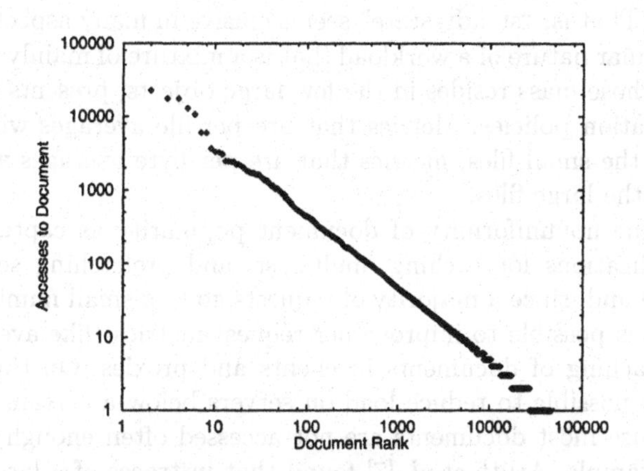

Fig. 7. Zipf's Law in Web Documents

Many other researchers have noted that Web reference sets appear to follow Zipf's Law. The first use of Zipf's Law to model the nonuniform distribution of Web requests was in [23]. The authors in [6] found that Zipf's Law applied to requests arriving at Web servers. Nahum [29] found that Zipf's Law applied to documents dowloaded from IBM's corporate web site as well as from the Kasparov-Deep Blue site. Arlitt [7] discusses the extreme nonuniformity of popularity in Web requests. Finally, Breslau *et al.* [12] examine whether Zipf's law holds in six different proxy traces and concluded that it was present in all cases, with values of β typically in the range of 0.7 to 0.8.

6 Conclusions

The presence of high variability in Web workloads has some notable implications. First, the heavy-tailed distribution of Web files means that systems that manipulate such files (like Web servers) must cope with objects whose size spans many orders of magnitude. The authors in [19] show that load imbalance in a multi-server system with heavy-tailed job sizes and no task migration (like a distributed Web server) can be particularly long-lasting.

The empirical values of α typically measured in the Web can be close to 1. In this range, the true variance is infinite; furthermore, the empirical mean is a very unstable metric, and for all practical purposes the true mean cannot be estimated accurately. Summary statistics of Web file datasets should therefore focus on distribution percentiles (like the median) rather than distributional moments like the mean and variance. The variability in file size translates to highly variable network performance, as captured by the phenomenon of self-similarity in network traffic.

In fact, since sums of heavy-tailed random variables converge in distribution so slowly, it seems that transient effects are the most likely mode of behavior for Web systems. That is, "steady-state" seems elusive in many aspects of the Web.

The particular nature of a workload that is a mixture of mainly small objects, but most of whose mass resides in the few large objects, presents challenges for resource allocation policies. Metrics that are per-file averages will be strongly influenced by the small files; metrics that are per-byte averages will be mainly influenced by the large files.

The extreme nonuniformity of document popularity as captured by Zipf's Law has implications for caching, multicast, and prefetching schemes in the Web. On one hand, since a majority of requests go to a small number of popular documents, it is possible to improve per-request metrics (like average response time) using caching of documents in clients and proxies. On the other hand, it may not be possible to reduce load on servers below a certain level through caching, because most documents are not accessed often enough to be held in caches. For example, Arlitt *et al.* [7] found that in traces of a large Web proxy, over 60% of the distinct objects requested were requested only once. This seems to be one reason that Web caching studies typically show low maximum hit rates (65% or less) [12,30,11,35].

References

1. The International World Wide Web conference. Annual, 1992-.
2. International WWW caching workshop. Yearly, 1996-.
3. USENIX symposium on internet technologies and systems. Biennial, 1997,1999-.
4. ACM/SIGMETRICS workshop on internet server performance (WISP). Annual, 1998-.
5. World Wide Web. Published by Baltzer Science Publishers, The Netherlands (ISSN 1386-145X), 1998-.
6. Virgílio Almeida, Azer Bestavros, Mark Crovella, and Adriana de Oliveira. Characterizing reference locality in the WWW. In *Proceedings of 1996 International Conference on Parallel and Distributed Information Systems (PDIS '96)*, pages 92–103, December 1996.
7. M. Arlitt, R. Friedrich, and T. Jin. Performance evaluation of Web proxy cache replacement policies. *Proceedings of Performance Tools '98. Lecture Notes in Computer Science*, 1469:193–206, 1998.

8. Martin F. Arlitt and Carey L. Williamson. Internet web servers: Workload characterization and performance implications. *IEEE/ACM Transactions on Networking*, 5(5):631–645, 1997.
9. Paul Barford, Azer Bestavros, Adam Bradley, and Mark Crovella. Changes in Web client access patterns: Characteristics and caching implications. *World Wide Web*, Special Issue on Characterization and Performance Evaluation, 1999.
10. Paul Barford and Mark E. Crovella. Generating representative Web workloads for network and server performance evaluation. In *Proceedings of Performance '98/SIGMETRICS '98*, pages 151–160, July 1998.
11. Jean-Chrysostome Bolot and Philipp Hoschka. Performance engineering of the World Wide Web: Application to dimensioning and cache design. In *Proceedings of the Fifth Interntional Conference on the WWW*, Paris, France, 1996.
12. Lee Breslau, Pei Cao, Li Fan, Graham Phillips, and Scott Shenker. Web caching and zipf-like distributions: Evidence and implications. In *Proceedings of INFOCOM '99*, 1999.
13. Mark E. Crovella and Azer Bestavros. Explaining World Wide Web traffic self-similarity. Technical Report TR-95-015 (Revised), Boston University Department of Computer Science, October 1995.
14. Mark E. Crovella and Azer Bestavros. Self-similarity in World Wide Web traffic: Evidence and possible causes. *IEEE/ACM Transactions on Networking*, 5(6):835–846, December 1997.
15. Mark E. Crovella and Lester Lipsky. Long-lasting transient conditions in simulations with heavy-tailed workloads. In *Proceedings of the 1997 Winter Simulation Conference*, pages 1005–1012, 1997.
16. Mark E. Crovella and Murad S. Taqqu. Estimating the heavy tail index from scaling properties. *Methodology and Computing in Applied Probability*, 1(1), 1999.
17. Mark E. Crovella, Murad S. Taqqu, and Azer Bestavros. Heavy-tailed probability distributions in the World Wide Web. In *A Practical Guide To Heavy Tails*, chapter 1, pages 3–26. Chapman & Hall, New York, 1998.
18. Carlos A. Cunha, Azer Bestavros, and Mark E. Crovella. Characteristics of WWW client-based traces. Technical Report TR-95-010, Boston University Department of Computer Science, April 1995.
19. N. G. Duffield and Ward Whitt. Recovery from congestion in a large multi-server system. In V. Ramaswami and P. Wirth, editors, *Teletraffic Contributions for the Information Age, Proceedings of the 15th International Teletraffic Congress (ITC-15)*, pages 371–380, 1997.
20. A. Erramilli, O. Narayan, and W. Willinger. Experimental queueing analysis with long-range dependent packet traffic. *IEEE/ACM Transactions on Networking*, 4(2):209–223, April 1996.
21. William Feller. *An Introduction to Probability Theory and Its Applications*, volume II. John Wiley and Sons, second edition, 1971.
22. National Center for Supercomputing Applications. Mosaic software. Available at `ftp://ftp.ncsa.uiuc.edu/Mosaic`.
23. Steven Glassman. A caching relay for the World Wide Web. In *Proceedings of the First International World Wide Web Conference*, pages 69–76, 1994.
24. Michael Greiner, Manfred Jobmann, and Lester Lipsky. The importance of power-tail distributions for telecommunication traffic models. Technical report, Institut für Informatik, T. U. München, August 25 1995.
25. B. M. Hill. A simple general approach to inference about the tail of a distribution. *The Annals of Statistics*, 3:1163–1174, 1975.

26. W.E. Leland, M.S. Taqqu, W. Willinger, and D.V. Wilson. On the self-similar nature of Ethernet traffic (extended version). *IEEE/ACM Transactions on Networking*, 2:1–15, 1994.
27. Benoit B. Mandelbrot. *The Fractal Geometry of Nature.* W. H. Freedman and Co., New York, 1983.
28. Daniel A. Menascé and Virgílio A. F. Almeida. *Capacity Planning for Web Performance: Metrics, Models, Methods.* Prentice Hall, PTR, 1998.
29. Erich Nahum, Tsipora Barzilai, and Dilip Kandlur. Performance issues in WWW servers. In *Proceedings of Performance '99/ACM SIGMETRICS '99*, Atlanta, GA, 1999.
30. Norifumi Nishikawa, Takafumi Hosokawa, Yasuhide Mori, Kenichi Yoshida, and Hiroshi Tsuji. Memory-based architecture for distributed WWW caching proxy. *Computer Networks and ISDN Systems*, 30:205–214, 1998.
31. Kihong Park, Gi Tae Kim, and Mark E. Crovella. On the relationship between file sizes, transport protocols, and self-similar network traffic. In *Proceedings of the Fourth International Conference on Network Protocols (ICNP'96)*, pages 171–180, October 1996.
32. Kihong Park, Gi Tae Kim, and Mark E. Crovella. On the relationship between file sizes, transport protocols, and self-similar network traffic. Technical Report TR-96-006, Boston University Computer Science Department, August 7 1996.
33. Sidney Resnick and Catalin Starica. Tail index estimation for dependent data. Technical Report 1174, School of OR&IE, Cornell University, 1996.
34. Gennady Samorodnitsky and Murad S. Taqqu. *Stable Non-Gaussian Random Processes.* Stochastic Modeling. Chapman and Hall, New York, 1994.
35. Stephen Williams, Marc Abrams, Charles R. Standridge, Ghaleb Abdulla, and Edward A. Fox. Removal policies in network caches for World-Wide Web documents. In *Proceedings of ACM SIGCOMM '96*, 1996.
36. Walter Willinger, Vern Paxson, and Murad S. Taqqu. Self-similarity and heavy tails: Structural modeling of network traffic. In *A Practical Guide To Heavy Tails.* Chapman & Hall, New York, 1998.
37. Walter Willinger, Murad S. Taqqu, Robert Sherman, and Daniel V. Wilson. Self-similarity through high-variability: Statistical analysis of Ethernet LAN traffic at the source level. In *Proceedings of ACM SIGCOMM '95*, pages 100–113, 1995.
38. G. K. Zipf. *Human Behavior and the Principle of Least-Effort.* Addison-Wesley, Cambridge, MA, 1949.

Parallel Job Scheduling: A Performance Perspective

Shikharesh Majumdar and Eric W. Parsons

Department of Systems and Computer Engineering
Carleton University, Ottawa, Canada
{majumdar,eparsons}@sce.carleton.ca

1 Introduction

When first introduced, parallel systems were dedicated systems that were intended to run a single parallel application at a time. Examples of the types of applications for which these systems were used include scientific modelling, such as computational fluid dynamics, and other grand challenge problems [44]. As the cost of multiprocessor systems continues to decrease and software support becomes increasingly available for parallel application development, a wider range of users are becoming interested in using such systems.

It is very difficult, however, for a single application to efficiently utilize all processors in the system simultaneously. In order to increase resource utilization, as well as responsiveness, it is necessary to *multiprogram* the parallel system, running multiple applications simultaneously. Although multiprogramming has a tremendous potential for improving performance in many environments, it also introduces a new problem. In particular, it is now necessary to manage the resources of the system and *schedule* the jobs that are in the current multiprogramming mix.

Parallel job scheduling involves allocating system resources (e.g., processors, memory, I/O channels) to the available set of jobs.[1] Scheduling is generally an NP-hard problem, and so heuristic strategies are often employed, as described in the literature in both computer science and operations research for project management. Considerable theory and experience exist in the area of scheduling on conventional uniprocessor systems.

Scheduling in multiprogrammed parallel systems is a significantly harder problem, requiring new strategies and solutions. Effective strategies for both partitioning the available processing resources among competing jobs as well as for determining the order in which jobs are executed can significantly improve performance. Once a job has been allocated a certain number of processors there is the additional question of how these processors are to be shared by the active threads of the job. Careful construction of scheduling strategies is required

[1] The type of scheduling discussed in this paper is different than the task-mapping problem, which involves mapping the tasks within a job to the available set of processors in order to minimize the job's completion time. In this paper, we are concerned about scheduling at the job level rather than at the task level within jobs.

G. Haring et al. (Eds.): Performance Evaluation, LNCS 1769, pp. 233–252, 2000.

for the parallel applications to effectively harness the power of the underlying parallel hardware.

Scheduling on multiprogrammed parallel systems first received attention from performance analysts. Since the late eighties a significant amount of research has been conducted in this area (see Feitelson's survey [13] for example). The results of this research have been disseminated through SIGMETRICS, Performance, and other important conferences as well as through journals that include several IEEE and ACM transactions and Performance Evaluation. Interest in parallel job scheduling continues to grow. The existence of an annual workshop in the area attests to its importance and popularity.

A significant amount of knowledge has been developed in the area of scheduling on multiprogrammed parallel systems, some of which has been applied to practice whereas some theories still need to be verified on real systems. In addition there are a number of new issues that warrant investigation. Research in parallel job scheduling started with shared memory systems and the current focus is on distributed memory systems. Existing research has been concerned primarily with the scheduling of processors. Techniques for scheduling of other resources such as memory and parallel disk systems on multiprogrammed parallel environments are also important for improving system performance and deserve attention from researchers. Although the focus of the research is on job scheduling strategies, work is required in the area of developing analytic techniques for evaluating the performance of new schedulers and in workload modelling. Overall, parallel job scheduling provides a number of interesting challenges for future research.

This paper presents parallel job scheduling from the perspectives of a performance analyst. We focus on performance issues that underlie scheduling in multiprogrammed parallel systems, demonstrate how performance analysts have influenced research in the area, and how the problem of parallel job scheduling has inspired new work in analytic and workload modelling. A significant number of papers have been written and, due to space constraints, we have limited our discussion to a subset of these papers. A more general survey of parallel job scheduling research is provided in [13]. In the following section we describe different ways of classifying parallel job scheduling policies. The role of different performance analysis methods in parallel job scheduling research is discussed next. The subsequent section summarizes a few key results in the area, whereas Section 5 presents our conclusions and directions for future research.

2 Classification of Scheduling Policies

Different criteria have been used for classifying parallel job scheduling policies, which are briefly described next. Each criterion corresponds to a particular perspective resulting from a specific type of system-application combination and gives rise to a set of classes of scheduling policies. Note that because a scheduling policy has multiple attributes, it can belong to more than one category.

2.1 Assignment of Partition Size

Job scheduling on parallel systems involves assigning each job a set of processors (partition) on which to execute. Both *static* and *dynamic* [31,61] partition allocations are possible. In the static case, the partition assigned to a job does not change during the lifetime of the job [52,30]. Three classes of static allocation policies are [20]:

Fixed The partition size is determined at system generation time and can only be changed through a reboot.

Variable The size of the partition is determined at the time a job is submitted and is specified by the user.

Adaptive The size of the partition is computed before starting job execution and both user input and current system load may be used in arriving at the partition size.

In dynamic scheduling the partition allocation may change as the job executes, based on either job characteristics [29,27] or system load [30,33]. Although dynamic scheduling offers the parallel job scheduler great flexibility, there is a cost associated with each such change in allocation. *Semi-static* disciplines can be used in systems where the scheduling cost is not negligible [30]; changes to job partition allocations are performed at a frequency such that the associated cost does not offset the performance improvement that accrues from the reassignment of processors.

2.2 Partition Sharing

Processor partitions can be shared among jobs in a variety of ways, leading to the following classes of schedulers [50,47]:

Space Sharing Strategies These strategies divide the processors into partitions with a single job running on each partition. In general, jobs retain the partition until termination.

Time Sharing Strategies A pure time sharing strategy uses a single partition comprised of the entire system, but allocates the partition to a job for a fixed time quantum at a time. Once the quantum expires, another ready job is run in the partition.

Time sharing the entire system is inefficient, as each job is allocated all processors during each of their quanta; as a result, *hybrid* [4,50,7] approaches are often used, where the system is divided into multiple partitions, and each partition is time shared.

2.3 Work-Conservation

A work-conserving scheduling policy always allocates idle processing resources to jobs that are waiting for processors. Most parallel job scheduling policies discussed in the literature are work-conserving. However using non-work-conserving scheduling policies that reserve processing resources for handling irregular system behavior and processor failures at the expense of temporarily increasing the number of waiting jobs are observed to be preferable on certain systems. For example, adaptive scheduling policies that save processors for future arrivals have been observed to perform better than work-conserving scheduling policies on systems characterized by bursty job arrivals and high variability in job execution times [47].

2.4 Application Architecture

The software architecture of the application can have a strong influence on the type of scheduling policies that can be used. Different degrees of flexibility in application architecture can give rise to the following four categories [20].

Rigid A rigid job exhibits the least flexibility in terms of processor allocation. With rigid applications, the number of processors is determined outside the scheduler and the processor allocation remains unchanged until the job completes.

Moldable The application architecture is such that it can accommodate a variable number of processors. The number of processors allocated to a job is determined by the scheduler. However the processor assignment to a job remains unaltered during the lifetime of a job. Such an architecture is also called an adaptive architecture in [7].

Evolving The number of threads in a job can increase and decrease during execution. The job is capable of accepting different number of processors during different phases of execution. Such a change in processor allocation may be made in response to a change in the execution behavior of the jobs by program behavior-based scheduling techniques described in [30].

Malleable Jobs with a malleable architecture are able to handle changes in processor allocation during program execution even when the execution behavior of the job has not changed. Such an application architecture is required by the equi-partitioning scheduling policy for example [33]. In general, malleable jobs are required when the scheduler adds/removes processors from an application depending on the system state rather than the current execution state of the job.

2.5 Type of Preemption and Level of Coordination

Preemptive scheduling policies can suspend an executing thread and reallocate the processor to another. The preempted thread is resumed at a later point in time. Although preemption can lead to a significant gain system performance also depends on the associated overhead. Depending on the level of preemption supported scheduling policies can be divided into the following classes:

Non-Preemptive Once a job starts execution it runs to completion without releasing its processing resources.

Preemptive Preemption can occur at various levels:

- *Local Preemption* A preempted thread of a job may resume execution only on the processor on which it was originally running. By restricting the thread to run on the same processor the cost of preemption is reduced. A stronger restriction used in some scheduling policies allow an executing thread to be preempted only by another thread of the same job [52,30]. Such a policy avoids the overhead associated with address space switching that accompanies the reallocation of a processor from one job to another.
- *Migratable Preemption* A preempted thread of a job can resume execution on any processor on the system.

Note that time-sharing systems belong to a special class of preemptive systems in which preemptions occur at regular intervals of time. Preemption and resumption of threads in jobs can be performed in either a coordinated or an uncoordinated fashion. The difference between the two approaches is briefly described.

Coordinated Under coordinated scheduling policies all the threads of a given job are preempted/resumed at the same time. An example is the gang scheduling strategy [14].

Uncoordinated Under uncoordinated scheduling a thread may be preempted and the processor reallocated to another thread irrespective of the status of the other threads in the job. Policies described in [29,61,27] are example of policies that perform uncoordinated processor allocations.

Although coordinated scheduling is attractive because it makes inter-process communication efficient by running the communicating threads of the same job at the same time, additional synchronization delays may be incurred for starting and stopping threads of the gang on independent processors.

2.6 Type of Job Characteristics Used in Scheduling

Scheduling policies can be divided into two classes. Policies in the first class do not use any explicit knowledge of job characteristics [29,27,33]. One example of such a policy is where the system simply executes tasks in the order in which they arrive. Policies in the second class are based on job characteristics. Parallel job characteristics such as average parallelism, knee of execution-time efficiency profile have been found to be useful in scheduling (see [52,30] for example). Three classes of job characteristics have been used in job scheduling:

- *CPU execution characteristics of jobs*
- *Memory requirement of jobs*
- *I/O requirement of jobs*

A detailed discussion of these characteristics and their relationship with parallel job scheduling is presented in Section 3.3.

3 Performance Analysis

In this section, we now present the various aspects of performance analysis as it relates to the study of parallel job schedulers. We first define the various performance metrics that are used to quantitatively assess the performance of disciplines. We then describe three approaches used to analyze disciplines in Section 3.2. Finally, we describe the various aspects of modelling workloads in Section 3.3.

3.1 Performance Metrics

In order to objectively evaluate the performance of a scheduling algorithm, a metric must be defined. One should recognize, however, that "performance" is quite often a subjective characteristic of a system, which is only approximated by a given analytic metric. Users and operators of a system seek a scheduler which offers good response times, makes efficient use of the system resources, offers some measure of predictability, offers equitable treatment of jobs of a particular class, and so on. It is difficult to capture mathematically the range of characteristics viewed as being important, especially since it will differ from one individual to the next.

The traditional metrics used to assess the performance of a scheduling discipline are:

Mean Response Time Mean response time is the average amount of time that jobs spend in the system (from arrival to departure). Low mean response times can be obtained by favouring those jobs which will complete soonest. The mean response time is considered to be a user-centered metric, as minimizing this metric means that results are returned more quickly.

Throughput Throughput is the number of jobs the system processes per unit time.[2] In unsaturated open systems, the throughput is equal to the arrival rate, so in these systems, one typically considers the maximum arrival rate that the system can sustain (or *sustainable throughput*). The sustainable throughput is considered to be a system-centered metric, as maximizing this metric means that more work is completed per unit time.

In some cases, favouring one of these two metrics can negatively affect the other. This tradeoff is captured in the *power* metric proposed by Kleinrock, which has been used in some parallel computing work [21,45].

Power Power is the ratio of the throughput to the mean response time. In an open system, the throughput is equal to the arrival rate, so maximizing the power at a given load is equivalent to minimizing the mean response time. However, it is claimed that the power metric may give an indication as to the "optimal" operating load for the system (namely where the power metric is maximized).

[2] For batch workloads, a related metric is the *makespan*, which is the total amount of time required to complete all jobs in the batch.

Some metrics very specific to parallel job scheduling have also been proposed. One example is the *efficiency preservation* metric, which captures the degree to which a scheduler degrades or improves the efficiency of the system relative to running each job on its own on the entire system [34].

3.2 Analysis Methods

Research into the scheduling of parallel jobs has been quite extensive, and a variety of approaches have been used to analyze the performance of such disciplines. This section gives an overview of how these various approaches have been applied to this domain.

Queueing Modelling

Queueing modelling has been used to study the performance of scheduling algorithms of all kinds, and parallel job scheduling is no exception. Parallel job scheduling introduces, however, some novel complexities in workload and system modelling:

- For non-rigid jobs, the execution time of a job depends on its parallelism characteristics, which is often described by a speedup (or equivalently efficiency) function. This function effectively defines the departure rate of a job for each potential processor allocation size.
- For non-fixed partitioning schedulers, the number and size of partitions may vary with every job arrival or departure based on load conditions and characteristics of the jobs in the system (queued or running). Changes made to partitions in this way is generally difficult to capture in queueing models.

As such, several queueing models assume that the system is always partitioned into equal-sized partitions in order to simplify the model. Moreover, it has been show that, for a class of jobs that are assumed to exist in practice, equal processor allocations appear to offer the best performance [45] (and a proof has since been developed supporting this observation [42]). Such models can be readily applied to systems where partition sizes are fixed for a particular workload [30,45,55] as well as to systems employing dynamic or semi-static partitioning where all partitions are the same size [30]. Some queueing models, however, have been developed for systems in which partitions are not necessarily all the same size, for both dynamic partitioning [34,30] and for fixed partitioning [10] systems.

In modelling non-rigid jobs, two approaches have been used to model the execution rate given different processor allocations. Synthetic jobs can be modelled explicitly, making simplifying assumptions that make such modelling practical. For instance, one can assume that jobs follow a fork-join structure, where the amount of computation required by each processor within a phase and across phases are statistically similar [50,34]. Alternatively, it is possible to consider a small number of job classes, and use their speedup function as input to the model [10,30].

Some significant applications of queueing models to parallel job scheduling include the following:

- A queueing model has been developed which captures the memory access pattern of an application, allowing the effects of paging on performance to be assessed [43]. This model is used to determine the best processor allocation size for a given load (assuming equal-sized partitions).
- A queueing model has been developed to study a restricted gang scheduling system, where the system rotates among a set of distinct job classes [55]. This model can be used to determine the best partition size and quantum lengths for each job class in a given workload.
- A queueing model has been developed which incorporates I/O as a job characteristics to understand its effects on scheduling disciplines [46]. It is shown that, when I/O is present, better performance can be obtained when multiple jobs are running simultaneously in a partition, assuming that I/O prefetching is not successful at hiding I/O latency.

Non-queueing Mathematical Models

Another classical approach used to analyze the performance of scheduling disciplines is to use mathematical methods which are not based on queueing modelling. Quite often, these methods are used to prove certain optimality results, like worst-case performance or competitive ratios[3]. In order to prove such results, however, numerous simplifications must often be made that may limit the applicability of the results to real systems. In addition, system performance practicians are often more interested in average case performance (as offered by queueing models) given particular statistical distributions of input parameters rather than worst-case performance across arbitrary input parameters. Nonetheless, if one is developing and analyzing new parallel scheduling disciplines, some familiarity with these results can be useful.

Some of the earlier work in this area was focussed towards proving results related to the makespan of an algorithm, which is the amount of time required to complete a given set of jobs [58,57,28], for both rigid and moldable job cases (with few restrictions on the speedup characteristics of jobs). More recently, interesting results have been developed related to the mean response time of a scheduling algorithm [36,60,59,9,12], in some cases incorporating preemption [36,9,12]. In particular, it has been shown that dynamic equi-allocation (where all jobs are given an equal number of processors), offers in the worst case a mean response time within a factor of 3.74 of an optimal "clairvoyant" scheduler for jobs whose efficiency is non-increasing with the number of processors [12]. Some of the simplifying assumptions that may limit the applicability of the results to real sys-

[3] The competitive ratio is defined as the minimum worst-case ratio that is achievable within a class of disciplines [53]

tems are either that all jobs arrive at the same time [60,59,9,12] or that jobs are perfectly parallelizable [36,9].

Another use of mathematical analysis has been to develop bounds on a particular metric, given a particular workload but independent of any scheduling disciplines. For example, methods to determine the bounds on the sustainable throughput of a system given certain characteristics of the workload have been developed [42,41] which can be used to relate the performance of a scheduling discipline against what is theoretically achievable. As well, bounds on the achievable mean response time based on the average parallelism characteristics of jobs has been developed [31].

Simulation

One of the most common approaches to assessing the performance of parallel job scheduling disciplines is discrete-event simulation (e.g, [29,27,61,21,50,8,45,34,35], [40,49,42,41,5] to list a few). Simulation provides the greatest flexibility in terms of modelling precisely those aspects of a system that are deemed relevant. The primary drawbacks with simulation, however, are the difficulty in verifying that the simulator is correct and the amount of computation required to obtain statistically valid measures. This is especially the case for parallel workloads where the variability in execution times is extremely high [8,17], requiring very long simulations for results to converge statistically.

In most cases, the simulation is driven by synthetically-generated workloads, where the arrival of jobs, their execution requirements (e.g., processing, memory), and their speedup characteristics are generated according to certain statistical distributions. A variety of different approaches can be used to model job speedups, as described in the next section, but the most common is to use a parameterized speedup function (e.g., [8,40,5]). In some cases, simulations are driven by actual applications or workload traces, which help in assessing the performance of an algorithm for specific workloads.

3.3 Workload Modelling

Whichever approach is used to evaluate the performance of parallel scheduling disciplines, some means is required to model workloads. Research on workload modelling has played an important role in the investigation of parallel job scheduling, a brief overview of which is presented next.

Arrival Process

The two basic types of arrival processes considered are batch, where all jobs under consideration present themselves to the system simultaneously, and continuous, where jobs arrive on an on-going basis. Continuous job arrival processes more accurately reflects typical computing environments, but in some cases, batch arrivals may be of interest.

To generate a synthetic workload having continuous job arrivals, one can either draw jobs from a statistical distribution or from workload traces. In queueing models, one typically uses a Poisson arrival process, for reasons of simplicity. This choice has likely influenced simulation-based research, as Poisson arrival processes are most common there too, even though recent workload studies have shown that actual production workloads do not appear to match this distribution [17,24]. It is unclear at this point how much this affects results which are based on a Poisson arrival process.

Job Execution

The next element to model is the amount of time a job will require to execute. In a uniprocessor system, this might simply be the total processing requirements of a job, but in a parallel system, the number of processors allocated to a job represents an added dimension to modelling jobs.

It is generally accepted that the processing demands of parallel jobs in production workloads typically has a high degree of variability [8,17]. This variability is often expressed in terms of the coefficient of variation (CV), which is the ratio of the standard deviation to the mean. Production workloads have demonstrated coefficient of variations of 4 to 70.[4]

In the case of variable partitioning, the processor allocation size simply represents a job resource requirement. To obtain a synthetic workload, one can readily examine workload traces from production centers, and generate a distribution that captures the correlation between processor allocation requirements and execution time [24].

In variable or adaptive scheduling, where the processor allocation given to a job is determined by the system, one must also model how a job's execution time is affected by processor allocation. To do this, one of the following approaches is typically used:

Parallelism Structure The first approach is to explicitly model the parallelism structure of an application [51]. In its most detailed form, the parallelism structure is a graph that depicts all the tasks along with their precedence relationships. An important area of research (which is outside the scope of this paper) is how the tasks of an application can be scheduled on a given set of processors to minimize the overall execution time [38]. However, a large number of applications exhibit simpler "fork-join" behaviour, where the threads of an application repeatedly perform computations in relative isolations, and then synchronize at well-defined points [50].
As such, a relatively simple approach for generating a synthetic workload is to assume that jobs have a fork-join structure where the amount of computation required by each thread in a given phase and the number of phases in the job are modelled by appropriate statistical distributions.

[4] To place this in context, a deterministic distribution has a CV of 0 and an exponential distribution a CV of 1. Distributions with $CV > 1$ are often modelled using a bi-phase hyper-exponential distribution.

Execution-Time Function In practice, many system-related factors affect the performance of the application, such as hardware contention across shared elements, software contention for synchronization structures, and software overheads. The *execution-time function* of an application is the application's execution time when allocated a given number of processors, taking into account both the application's parallelism structure as well as the system-related factors it will experience when running on a certain type of machine.

In performance analysis work, the execution-time function $T(p)$ is often approximated by a continuous function, the most popular being that proposed by Dowdy:

$$T(p) = D_1 + D_2/p$$

where D_1 and D_2 are constants which can be obtained from empirical measurements [10]. In effect, the first parameter represents the amount of work that is sequential, while the second represents the amount that is fully parallel. Dowdy's execution-time function can therefore be re-written in a form similar to Amdahl's Law [1]:

$$T(w,p) = w(s + (1-s)/p)$$

where $w = D_1 + D_2$ is the service demand (or work), and $s = D_1/(D_1 + D_2)$ is the fraction of work that is sequential.

Although widely used, this type characterization of an application can be unrealistic because it suggests that increasing the number of processors always leads to a reduction in execution time (assuming $s < 1$). In reality, parallelism-related overheads can often negate the gains obtained from increased parallelism, leading to a slowdown after a certain point. Other execution-time functions have been proposed that do not share this problem [51].

In creating synthetic workloads for analyzing the performance of scheduling algorithms, two approaches that have been taken are (1) to use parameters derived from a small set of applications [21] or (2) to draw the parameters from some distribution [8]. Unfortunately, there is as yet very little empirical data regarding the speedup characteristics of production workloads to help guide the choice of distributions, and some of the choices that have been made may possess unexpected (and likely invalid) properties [5].

The execution-time function also gives rise to the execution-time-efficiency profile, which is a curve depicting the efficiency of a job as a function of its execution time. This profile is closely related to the power metric, and like the latter, suggests an "optimal" processor allocation size at the knee of the curve [11], and has been used as the basis of some disciplines [21].

Memory and I/O Requirements

The majority of work in parallel job scheduling has concentrated on processing as the primary resource of interest. However, parallel applications typically also have intensive memory and I/O requirements, which may also affect scheduling decisions.

In distributed-memory systems, the memory requirements of jobs essentially places a lower bound on the number of processors to allocate a job as there is a fixed amount of memory available per processors. Most performance studies considering memory have used simple distributions (namely uniform) to determine these lower bounds, which are unlikely to be representative of real workloads [49,42]. There have been recent workload studies, however, that provide the necessary empirical data to develop more realistic distributions [15]. In shared-memory systems, the processor allocation size is less constrained to the memory requirements of a job (albeit may be to some degree for locality reasons). It is still an open question, however, how the memory requirements of a particular job varies in relation to the number of processors it is allocated.

I/O requirements of parallel jobs may arise either from implicit demand paging (due to insufficient memory) [43,49] or from explicit I/O operations [32,46]. The implications of I/O on parallel job scheduling is discussed in greater detail in the next section.

4 Key Results

The previous section presented the variety of approaches that have been used in studying the performance of parallel job scheduling algorithms. In this section, we present some of the significant results that have been developed in this area.

4.1 Co-scheduling

One of the first major results in parallel job scheduling was based on the observation that an important class of applications that is run on parallel systems is highly compute intensive, and that these applications communicate or synchronize frequently during their execution. In order to effectively make use of the processing resources, software designers strive to structure their applications to minimize any delays in communication and synchronization. For example, for application that have a fork-join structure, a key objective is to balance as much as possible the amount of computation on each processor within each phase, so as to avoid having processors be idle waiting for other processors to reach the synchronization point.

Some of the early timesharing scheduling systems for parallel systems, however, were designed so that scheduling decisions made on different processors were performed independently. That is, if two or more jobs were running on a given set of nodes, each node would schedule the threads of those jobs independently from other nodes. This type of scheduling adversely affects the ability of the threads of a parallel application from communicating or synchronizing without blocking, and the context-switching overheads begin to overwhelm the system.

Thus, in order to make efficient use of processing resources, parallel job schedulers for these types of jobs must ensure that all threads of a job are allocated simultaneously [39,22,19,16]. This is known as co-scheduling [39] or gang scheduling [18,19]. In many production centers, this is achieved by allowing jobs to run until completion once they start execution, but, as will be discussed shortly, some greater degree of co-scheduled timesharing is required to achieve low mean response times.

4.2 Use of System Load and Job Characteristics

Both system load and characteristics of jobs can be useful for making effective scheduling decisions. The range of job characteristics that are used vary from attributes of individual jobs in the multiprogramming mix (such as a job's current parallelism) to general characteristics of the workload (such as properties of speedup functions) (see [29,52,27,21,41] for example).

One key characteristic of workloads is that, in general, compute-intensive parallel jobs make less efficient use of processing resources as the number of processors increases [52]; in the limit, a system is most efficiently utilized when jobs are allocated a single processor (ignoring constraints due to memory). Such an inefficient use of processing resources can give rise to premature saturation of the system.

This observation led to the deduction that the system scheduler should determine suitable processor allocation sizes for jobs rather than the user, since the system can monitor and respond to the current load conditions. In particular, as the load increases, the average number of processors allocated to jobs can be decreased to increase the overall efficiency of the system. There has been a significant amount of research that focuses on determining processor allocation sizes, using information regarding both the load and characteristics of jobs [52,27,21,30,48,37,8,45,2]. One significant observation for many workloads is that, if applications support dynamic repartitioning, then allocating each job the same number of processors is a good strategy to pursue (assuming memory is abundant) [33,8,34,42,5,12]. This approach does not require any explicit knowledge of job characteristics, which are still, practically speaking, difficult to obtain.

4.3 Job Preemption

As mentioned in the previous sections, an important characteristic that is repeatedly observed in production computing center workloads is the high variability in execution time of jobs [8,17,23]. This means that a large fraction of jobs are relatively short in duration, but a significant amount of total computation is embodied in a small fraction of very long-running jobs. Despite this, many high-performance computing centers employ run-to-completion disciplines, which lead to high mean response times and highly variable response times for short jobs. (Highly variable response times manifests itself as unpredictability from a user's perspective.)

Recent research in parallel job scheduling has been to illustrate the need for job preemption[5] given the types of workloads found in practice [8,40,16]. This need was predicted in earlier synthetic workload based studies [29,27], before workload characteristics of production centers became available. In fact, significant improvements in response time characteristics can be achieved with a small amount of preemption (i.e., limited gang scheduling), so as to minimize the overheads associated with swapping running jobs in and out of secondary storage [8].

4.4 Implications of Memory

Recently, attention in parallel job scheduling has turned towards the need to consider the memory requirements of jobs in scheduling disciplines [49,35,42,41]. First, it should be noted that generation of page faults can significantly deteriorate the performance of a wide range of parallel compute-intensive scientific applications [6,43]. The basic reason is that paging causes processors to become blocked for I/O (in absence of effective I/O prefetching), causing the processor to either delay or switch to a different thread. As described above with respect to co-scheduling, this disrupts the ability for parallel applications to synchronize or communicate without blocking, and causes the system to become overwhelmed by context switch overheads. Thus, these types of parallel applications typically require as much physical memory as their total memory requirements, and given their nature, these memory requirements continue to be constrained by existing memory capacities [3].

An important way in which memory requirements of jobs affect parallel job scheduling is devising strategies to maximize memory usage and in effectively allocating processors taking into account memory demand [42,41]. In fact, when memory is limited, it becomes increasingly important to collect speedup information of jobs to make more efficient usage of this memory [41]. This is less of an issue if memory is abundant, because processor allocations can be reduced to whatever level is needed to sustain the current load.

Another implication of memory in parallel job scheduling relates to the memory hierarchy of parallel systems. In particular, it is important to take into account the cache context of processors in scheduling threads by avoiding the frequent migration of threads from one processor to another [54,56]. In NUMA architectures, it is also important to take into account the interconnect topology in selecting processor allocation sizes [62].

[5] Job preemption is not needed if applications support dynamic repartitioning, since in this case, new jobs can always start executing as soon as they arrive in the system.

4.5 Implications of I/O

Finally, research in parallel job scheduling has started to consider jobs that perform significant amounts of explicit disk I/O [32,46]. These types of applications break many of the traditional assumptions made about parallel job scheduling. In particular, it may not be the case that decreasing processor allocation necessarily improves system performance at higher system load and co-scheduling is no longer an effective use of processing resources [26,46]. In purely space-sharing systems, the degree of overlap between computation and I/O operations within an applications as well as the relative overall computation and I/O demand of jobs have a strong influence on the choice of processor partition size [32].

5 Summary and Conclusions

Processor management on parallel systems has addressed both processor allocation and job scheduling. Earlier work in the area has been concerned primarily with heuristic techniques for processor allocation: the mapping of the threads in a parallel application to the processors in the system. As the popularity of parallel processing is increasing many types of users are getting interested in running a variety of different applications on the system. When parallel programs with widely varying characteristics use the parallel hardware it is better to multiprogram the system and run multiple applications at the same time for achieving good mean response times for users at acceptable levels of resource utilization. Since the late eighties a great deal of work that concerns the performance of job scheduling on multiprogrammed parallel systems has been reported. For providing a better understanding of the existing research on parallel job scheduling we have classified the proposed scheduling techniques in different ways. One such classification for example, divides the scheduling policies into two categories: work conserving and non-work conserving. Other classifications are done on the basis of whether the assignment of partition size to jobs is fixed or can change with time, of what type of partition sharing can occur among jobs, and of the type of application architectures that is supported by the scheduler. Scheduling strategies can also be classified based on the type of preemption and the level of coordination used in scheduling, and the type of job characteristics used by the scheduler.

Researchers have used different techniques for evaluating the performance of their scheduling strategies. We have presented a discussion of how the different methods of performance evaluation: analytical model-based, simulation-based, and experiment-based, have influenced the research in the area and the valuable results they have produced. Two interesting spin-offs from the scheduling research are the development of new analytic techniques for investigating the performance of parallel job scheduling, and research on workload modelling required in the performance evaluation of the proposed scheduling strategies.

We have compiled a number of key results from the literature. These include the importance of balancing the load on processors and co-scheduling of threads that belong to the same computation as well as of adapting the number of processors allocated to jobs to the variation in system and job states. The ability to preempt an executing job and reallocate its resources is observed to be crucial for achieving high performance on many environments. The importance of considering the memory and I/O requirements of jobs in processor scheduling have also been noted.

A number of researchers have contributed to research on parallel job scheduling. For limitations of space we have not been able to discuss more of the existing contributions. We refer the interested reader to two other surveys in the area [13,20]. In spite of the existence of substantial work, research on parallel job scheduling still remains quite active and vibrant: an annual workshop on the topic demonstrates the existing interest and enthusiasm of the researchers. A number of challenging problems remain. Adapting the existing knowledge to job scheduling on a network of workstations is important and has started receiving attention (see [2] for example). Scheduling of other resources such as memory and I/O can also have a strong impact on performance. The availability of parallel file systems and inexpensive disks provide a strong motivation for using parallel I/O on multiprogrammed systems. Management of data and scheduling of I/O requests will influence system performance in a significant way when programs with high demand for both CPU and I/O run on the system [25]. Investigation of such I/O management strategies and the co-ordination among the different resource managers form an important direction for future research.

Acknowledgements

We acknowledge the help from Sivarama Dandamudi who read the manuscript and provided valuable comments. We would also like thank all the researchers who have contributed to the area making the challenging problem of parallel job scheduling such an exciting topic for research.

References

1. G. M. Amdahl. Validity of the single processor approach to achieving large scale computing capabilities. In *Proceedings of the AFIPS Spring Joint Computer Conference*, pages 483–485, April 1967.
2. Stergios V. Anastasiadis and Kenneth C. Sevcik. Parallel application scheduling on networks of workstations. *Journal of Parallel and Distributed Computing*, June 1997. To appear.
3. Greg Astfalk. Fundamentals and practicalities of MPP. *The Leading Edge*, 12:839–843, 907–911, 992–998, 1993.
4. Samir Ayaachi and Sivarama P. Dandamudi. A hierarchical processor scheduling strategy for multiprocessoe systems. In *IEEE Symposium on Parallel and Distributed Processing*, pages 100–109, 1996.
5. Timothy B. Brecht and Kaushik Guha. Using parallel program characteristics in dynamic processor allocation policies. *Performance Evaluation*, 27&28:519–539, 1996.

6. Douglas C. Burger, Rahmat S. Hyder, Barton P. Miller, and David A. Wood. Paging tradeoffs in distributed-shared-memory multiprocessors. In *Proceedings Supercomputing '94*, pages 590–599, November 1994.
7. Yuet-Ning Chan, Sivarama P. Dandamudi, and Shikharesh Majumdar. Performance comparison of processor scheduling strategies in a distributed-memory multicomputer system. In *Proceedings of the 11th International Parallel Procesing Symposium*, pages 139–145, 1997.
8. Su-Hui Chiang, Rajesh K. Mansharamani, and Mary K. Vernon. Use of application characteristics and limited preemption for run-to-completion parallel processor scheduling policies. In *Proceedings of the 1994 ACM SIGMETRICS Conference on Measurement and Modelling of Computer Systems*, pages 33–44, 1994.
9. Xiaotie Deng, Nian Gu, Tim Brecht, and KaiCheng Lu. Preemptive scheduling of parallel jobs on multiprocessors. In *Proceedings of the Seventh Annual ACM-SIAM Symposium on Discrete Algorithms*, pages 159–167, January 1996.
10. Lawrence W. Dowdy. On the partitioning of multiprocessor systems. In *Performance 1990: An International Conference on Computers and Computer Networks*, pages 99–129, March 1990.
11. Derek L. Eager, John Zahorjan, and Edward D. Lazowska. Speedup versus efficiency in parallel systems. *IEEE Transactions on Computers*, 38(3):408–423, March 1989.
12. Jeff Edmonds, Donald D. Chinn, Tim Brecht, and Xiaotie Deng. Non-clairvoyant multiprocessor scheduling of jobs with changing execution characteristcs. In *Proceedings of the Twenty-Ninth Annual ACM Symposium on the Theory of Computing*, pages 120–129, 1997.
13. Dror Feitelson. A survey of scheduling in multiprogrammed parallel systems. Technical Report RC19790 (87657), IBM T.J. Watson Research Center, 1994.
14. Dror G. Feitelson. Packing schemes for gang scheduling. In *Job Scheduling Strategies for Parallel Procesing*, pages 89–110. Springer Verlag, Lecture Notes in Computer Science, 1996.
15. Dror G. Feitelson. Memory usage in the LANL CM-5 workload. In Dror G. Feitelson and Larry Rudolph, editors, *Job Scheduling Strategies for Parallel Processing*, Lecture Notes in Computer Science Vol. 1291, pages 78–94. Springer-Verlag, 1997.
16. Dror G. Feitelson and Morris A. Jette. Improved utilization and responsiveness with gang scheduling. In Dror G. Feitelson and Larry Rudolph, editors, *Job Scheduling Strategies for Parallel Processing*, Lecture Notes in Computer Science Vol. 1291, pages 238–261. Springer-Verlag, 1997.
17. Dror G. Feitelson and Bill Nitzberg. Job characteristics of a production parallel scientific workload on the NASA Ames iPSC/860. In Dror G. Feitelson and Larry Rudolph, editors, *Job Scheduling Strategies for Parallel Processing*, Lecture Notes in Computer Science Vol. 949, pages 337–360. Springer-Verlag, 1995.
18. Dror G. Feitelson and Larry Rudolph. Distributed hierarchical control for parallel processing. *Computer*, 23(5):65–77, May 1990.
19. Dror G. Feitelson and Larry Rudolph. Gang scheduling performance benefits for fine-grain synchronization. *Journal of Parallel and Distributed Computing*, 16:306–318, 1992.
20. Dror G. Feitelson, Larry Rudolph, Uwe Schwiegelshohn, Kenneth C Sevcik, and Parkson Wong. Theory and practice in parallel job scheduling. In *1997 IPPS Workshop on Job Scheduling Strategies for Parallel Procesing*, pages –, 1997.
21. Dipak Ghosal, Guiseppe Serazzi, and Satish K. Tripathi. The processor working set and its use in scheduling multiprocessor systems. *IEEE Transactions on Software Engineering*, 17(5):443–453, May 1991.

22. Anoop Gupta, Andrew Tucker, and Shigeru Urushibara. The impact of operating system scheduling policies and synchronization methods on the performance of parallel applications. In *Proceedings of the 1991 ACM SIGMETRICS Conference on Measurement and Modeling of Computer Systems*, pages 120–132, 1991.
23. Steven Hotovy. Workload evolution on the Cornell Theory Center IBM SP-2. In Dror G. Feitelson and Larry Rudolph, editors, *Job Scheduling Strategies for Parallel Processing*, Lecture Notes in Computer Science Vol. 1162, pages 27–40. Springer-Verlag, 1996.
24. Joefon Jann, Pratap Pattnaik, Hubertus Franke, Fang Wang, Joseph Skovira, and Joseph Riordan. Modeling of workload in MPPs. In Dror G. Feitelson and Larry Rudolph, editors, *Job Scheduling Strategies for Parallel Processing*, Lecture Notes in Computer Science Vol. 1291, pages 95–116. Springer-Verlag, 1997.
25. P. Kwong and S. Majumdar. Study of data distribution strategies in parallel I/O management. In *Third International Conference of the Austrian Committee on Parallel Computing (ACPC'96)*, September 1996.
26. Walter Lee, Matthew Frank, Victor Lee, Kenneth Mackenzie, and Larry Rudolph. Implications of I/O for gang scheduled workloads. In Dror G. Feitelson and Larry Rudolph, editors, *Job Scheduling Strategies for Parallel Processing*, Lecture Notes in Computer Science Vol. 1291, pages 215–237. Springer-Verlag, 1997.
27. Scott T. Leutenegger and Mary K. Vernon. The performance of multiprogrammed multiprocessor scheduling policies. In *Proceedings of the 1990 ACM SIGMETRICS Conference on Measurement and Modelling of Computer Systems*, pages 226–236, 1990.
28. Walter Ludwig and Prasoon Tiwari. Scheduling malleable and nonmalleable parallel tasks. In *Proceedings of the Fifth Annual ACM-SIAM Symposium on Discrete Algorithms (SODA)*, pages 167–176, 1994.
29. S. Majumdar, D. L. Eager, and R. B. Bunt. Scheduling in multiprogrammed parallel systems. In *Proceedings of the 1988 ACM SIGMETRICS Conference on Measurement and Modelling of Computer Systems*, pages 104–113, May 1988.
30. S. Majumdar, D. L. Eager, and R. B. Bunt. Characterization of programs for scheduling in multiprogrammed parallel systems. *Performance Evaluation*, 13(2):109–130, October 1991.
31. Shikharesh Majumdar. *Processor Scheduling in Multiprogrammed Parallel Systems*. PhD thesis, University of Saskatchewan, April 1988.
32. Shikharesh Majumdar and Yiu Ming Leung. Characterization and management of I/O in multiprogrammed parallel systems. In *Proceedings of the Sixth IEEE Symposium on Parallel and Distributed Processing*, pages 298–307, October 1994.
33. Cathy McCann, Raj Vaswani, and John Zahorjan. A dynamic processor allocation policy for multiprogrammed shared-memory multiprocessors. *ACM Transactions on Computer Systems*, 11(2):146–178, May 1993.
34. Cathy McCann and John Zahorjan. Processor allocation policies for message-passing parallel computers. In *Proceedings of the 1994 ACM SIGMETRICS Conference on Measurement and Modeling of Computer Systems*, pages 19–32, 1994.
35. Cathy McCann and John Zahorjan. Scheduling memory constrained jobs on distributed memory parallel computers. In *Proceedings of the 1995 ACM SIGMETRICS Joint International Conference on Measurement and Modelling of Computer Systems*, pages 208–219, 1995.
36. Rajeev Motwani, Steven Phillips, and Eric Torng. Non-clairvoyant scheduling. In *Proceedings of the Fourth Annual ACM-SIAM Symposium on Discrete Algorithms*, pages 422–431, 1993.

37. Vijay K. Naik, Sanjeev K. Setia, and Mark S. Squillante. Performance analysis of job scheduling policies in parallel supercomputing environments. In *Supercomputing '93*, pages 824–833, 1993.
38. Michael G. Norman and Peter Thanisch. Models of machines and computation for mapping in multicomputers. *ACM Computing Surveys*, 25(3):263–302, September 1993.
39. John K. Ousterhout. Scheduling techniques for concurrent systems. In *Proceedings of the 3rd International Conference on Distributed Computing (ICDCS)*, pages 22–30, October 1982.
40. Eric W. Parsons and Kenneth C. Sevcik. Multiprocessor scheduling for high-variability service time distributions. In Dror G. Feitelson and Larry Rudolph, editors, *Job Scheduling Strategies for Parallel Processing*, Lecture Notes in Computer Science Vol. 949, pages 127–145. Springer-Verlag, 1995.
41. Eric W. Parsons and Kenneth C. Sevcik. Benefits of speedup knowledge in memory-constrained multiprocessor scheduling. In *Proceedings of the 1996 International Conference on Performance Theory, Measurement and Evaluation of Computer and Communication Systems (PERFORMANCE '96)*, pages 253–272, 1996. Proceedings published in *Performance Evaluation*, vol. 27&28.
42. Eric W. Parsons and Kenneth C. Sevcik. Coordinated allocation of memory and processors in multiprocessors. In *Proceedings of the 1996 ACM SIGMETRICS Conference on Measurement and Modelling of Computer Systems*, pages 57–67, 1996.
43. Vinod G. J. Peris, Mark S. Squillante, and Vijay K. Naik. Analysis of the impact of memory in distributed parallel processing systems. In *Proceedings of the 1994 ACM SIGMETRICS Conference on Measurement and Modeling of Computer Systems*, pages 5–18, 1994.
44. Yale N. Pratt. The i/o subsystem: A candidate for improvement. *Computer*, 27(3):15–16, March 1994.
45. E. Rosti, E. Smirni, L. W. Dowdy, G. Serazzi, and B. M. Carlson. Robust partitioning policies of multiprocessor systems. *Performance Evaluation*, 19:141–165, 1994.
46. Emilia Rosti, Giuseppe Serazzi, Evgenia Smirni, and Mark S. Squillante. The impact of i/o on program behaviour and parallel scheduling. In *Joint International Conference on Measurement and Modeling of Computer Systems*, pages 56–65, 1998.
47. Emilia Rosti, Evgenia Smirni, Lawrence W. Dowdy, Guiseppe Serazzi, and Kenneth C. Sevcik. Processor saving scheduling policies for multiprcessor systems. *IEEE Transactions on Computers*, 47(3):178–189, February 1998.
48. Sanjeev Setia and Satish Tripathi. A comparative analysis of static processor partitioning policies for parallel computers. In *Proceedings of the International Workshop on Modeling and Simulation of Computer and Telecommunication Systems (MASCOTS)*, pages 283–286, January 1993.
49. Sanjeev K. Setia. The interaction between memory allocations and adaptive partitioning in message-passing multiprocessors. In Dror G. Feitelson and Larry Rudolph, editors, *Job Scheduling Strategies for Parallel Processing*, Lecture Notes in Computer Science Vol. 949, pages 146–164. Springer-Verlag, 1995.
50. Sanjeev K. Setia, Mark S. Squillante, and Satish K. Tripathi. Processor scheduling on multiprogrammed, distributed memory parallel computers. In *Proceedings of the 1993 ACM SIGMETRICS Conference on Measurement and Modeling of Computer Systems*, pages 158–170, 1993.

51. K. C. Sevcik. Application scheduling and processor allocation in multiprogrammed parallel processing systems. *Performance Evaluation*, 19:107–140, 1994.
52. Kenneth C. Sevcik. Characterizations of parallelism in applications and their use in scheduling. In *Proceedings of the 1989 ACM SIGMETRICS International Conference on Measurement and Modeling of Computer Systems*, pages 171–180, May 1989.
53. D. Sleator and R. Tarjan. Amortized efficiency of list update and paging rules. *Communications of the ACM*, 28(2):202–208, February 1985.
54. Mark S. Squillante and Edward D. Lazowska. Using processor-cache affinity information in shared-memory multiprocessor scheduling. *IEEE Transactions on Parallel and Distributed Systems*, 4(2):131–143, February 1993.
55. Mark S. Squillante, Fang Wang, and Marios Papaefthymiou. Stochastic analysis of gang scheduling in parallel and distributed systems. *Performance Evaluation*, 27&28:273–296, 1996.
56. Josep Torrellas, Andrew Tucker, and Anoop Gupta. Benefits of cache-affinity scheduling in shared-memory multiprocessors: A summary. In *Proceedings of the 1993 ACM SIGMETRICS Conference on Measurement and Modeling of Computer Systems*, pages 272–274, 1993.
57. J. Turek, J. Wolf, K. Pattipati, and P. Yu. Scheduling parallelizable tasks: Putting it all on the shelf. In *Proceedings of the 1992 ACM SIGMETRICS and PERFORMANCE '92 International Conference on Measurement and Modeling of Computer Systems*, pages 225–236, 1992.
58. J. Turek, J. Wolf, and P. Yu. Approximate algorithms for scheduling parallelizable tasks. In *4th Annual ACM Symposium on Parallel Algorithms and Architectures (SPAA '92)*, pages 323–332, 1992.
59. John Turek, Walter Ludwig, Joel L. Wolf, Lisa Fleischer, Prasoon Tiwari, Jason Glasgow, Uwe Schwiegelshohn, and Philip S. Yu. Scheduling parallelizable tasks to minimize average response time. In *6th Annual ACM Symposium on Parallel Algorithms and Architectures*, pages 200–209, 1994.
60. John Turek, Uwe Schwiegelshohn, Joel L. Wolf, and Philip S. Yu. Scheduling parallel tasks to minimize average response time. In *Proceedings of the Fifth Annual ACM-SIAM Symposium on Discrete Algorithms (SODA)*, pages 112–121, 1994.
61. John Zahorjan and Cathy McCann. Processor scheduling in shared memory multiprocessors. In *Proceedings of the 1990 ACM SIGMETRICS Conference on Measurement and Modelling of Computer Systems*, pages 214–225, 1990.
62. Songnian Zhou and Timothy Brecht. Processor pool-based scheduling for large-scale NUMA multiprocessors. In *Proceedings of the 1991 ACM SIGMETRICS Conference on Measurement and Modeling of Computer Systems*, pages 133–142, 1991.

Scheduling of Real-Time Tasks with Complex Constraints

Seonho Choi[1] and Ashok K. Agrawala[2]

[1] Department of Computer Science
Bowie State University, Bowie, MD 20715, USA
seonho@cs.umd.edu

[2] Institute for Advanced Computer Studies, Department of Computer Science
University of Maryland, College Park, MD 20742, USA
agrawala@cs.umd.edu

1 Introduction

Real-time computer systems are characterized by the existence of timing constraints as well as logical correctness requirements on computations they carry out. The timing constraints are statically determined prior to system operation time from the characteristics of physical systems they interact with. In *hard real-time systems*, a timing failure is considered catastrophic and a guarantee should be given prior to runtime that every timing constraint will be satisfied throughout the system operation time. Examples are found in application domains such as avionics, process control, automated manufacturing, robotics, etc. In this paper, the issues and approaches on real-time system design will be addressed in uni-processor environment.

In addition to the timing constraints, the characteristics and arrival patterns of real-time tasks should be known ahead of system operation time. These information have to be used in system design time to derive a guarantee that all the timing constraints will be satisfied. First, the execution time information of each task should be made available including the upper and lower bounds of task execution times. Second, real-time tasks may be classified into one of the following three categories according to the arrival patterns of their instances.

- Periodic Task: task instances arrive to the system periodically.
- Sporadic Task: task instances arrive to the system with a minimum inter-arrival time requirement.
- Aperiodic Task: no restriction on the arrival times of task instances.

Sporadic tasks may be transformed into periodic tasks as in [29]. Hence, in this paper, we consider only two types of tasks as follows:

- Static Tasks: Tasks whose invocation times are known at design time. Usually, these are periodic tasks, or those that have been converted to periodic tasks as in [29].
- Dynamic Tasks: Tasks whose executions are dynamically requested at runtime. Aperiodic tasks belong to this class.

G. Haring et al. (Eds.): Performance Evaluation, LNCS 1769, pp. 253–282, 2000.

The types of temporal constraints that can be found in most real-time systems can also be classified as follows:

- Absolute Timing Constraints: a valid time interval is given in an absolute time line in which a single event can occur.
  - Ready Time Constraint: a start time of a task instance execution should be greater than or equal to a given ready time (absolute time).
  - Deadline Constraint: a finish time of a task instance execution should be less than or equal to a given deadline (absolute time).
- Relative Timing Constraints: constrains the inter-event-occurrence-time, i.e., the time difference between two event occurrence times.
  - Relative Deadline Constraint: inter-event-occurrence-time should be less than or equal to a given value.
  - Separation Constraint: inter-event-occurrence-time should be greater than or equal to a given value.

Some real-time systems often possess *relative timing constraints*, in which operations are temporally dependent on each other. These constraints are usually described in the system specification [14,20], which contains clauses such as [16]:

1. Move the robot arm within $10\mu s$ of an object being detected.
2. Wait at least $50\mu s$ between sending two messages.

As another example, control output events in two consecutive task instances of a periodic task may have to occur with jitter requirements satisfied [3,5]. That is, a difference of two event occurrence times, called a *jitter*, should lie between a lower and an upper bound given from the specification. Other application systems which have this type of constraints are process control systems [19] and flight control systems [3]. In these systems, it has been shown that relative timing constraints sometimes have more influence on control systems performance than the frequency constraints.

Fig. 1 shows an example task set consisting of two periodic tasks that have both absolute and relative (jitter) timing constraints. In this figure, f_i^j denotes an actual finish time of a task instance τ_i^j.

In addition to the aforementioned timing constraints, synchronization constraints may exist in real-time systems. *Precedence* constraints may exist among task instances. If two task instances are constrained with precedence relationship, the first task instance should be completed before the second one is started. For example, producer/consumer relationship between task instances may be imposed using this type of constraints since a consumer task instance may start its execution only after its producer task instance produces its output data to be fed into the consumer task instance. *Mutual exclusion* constraints may also exist if multiple tasks share resources that permit only mutually exclusive accesses, such as critical sections.

Given all the information on task characteristics, constraints, and the resource characteristics[1], the fundamental issue is how to execute the tasks on a

[1] The CPU speed, memory amount, etc.

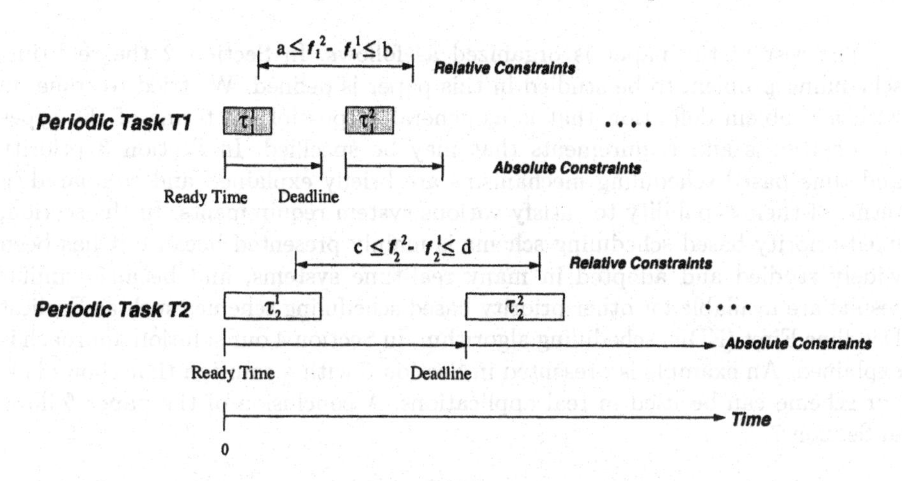

Fig. 1. Example periodic tasks with absolute and relative timing constraints

given hardware platform at system operation time such that all those constraints are satisfied in any system operation scenario. The process of making decisions on which task instance is executed at each time instant is called a *scheduling*. If a set of given tasks can be successfully executed by a given scheduling algorithm with the constraints satisfied, we say that the task set is *schedulable* by the scheduling algorithm. Scheduling can be classified according to various criteria. In terms of preemptibility, they can be classified into preemptive scheduling vs. non-preemptive scheduling. According to the mechanisms utilized, they can be classified into time based scheduling or priority based scheduling. In time based scheduling algorithms, the time line is explicitly managed and task executions are mapped into time intervals in a time line. In priority based scheduling algorithms, tasks are assigned priorities and those priorities are used to decide which task instance is to be executed next. At any time instant, the task instance whose priority is the highest is chosen to be executed among the ready task instances. Priorities may be statically assigned at pre-runtime or they can be dynamically decided according to a given discipline. In this regard, the priority based scheduling algorithms are further classified into *static priority* and *dynamic priority* scheduling algorithms.

A great amount of research has been carried out on priority based and time based scheduling algorithms [37,27,1,25,17,2,36,26,28,6,8,7,18,34,21,10,32]. In this paper these two approaches for designing real-time systems are explained and compared in terms of their capability to accommodate various system requirements or constraints, and a new time-based scheduling scheme is presented, which is called *dynamic time based scheduling*, in which a wider class of timing constraints can be incorporated and a more flexible and dynamic resource management is possible compared to the traditional static time based scheduling scheme.

The rest of the paper is organized as follows. In Section 2 the real-time scheduling problem to be studied in this paper is defined. We tried to come up with a problem definition that is as general as possible in terms of the types of constraints and requirements that may be specified. In Section 3 priority and time based scheduling mechanisms are briefly explained and compared in terms of their capability to satisfy various system requirements. In the section, fixed-priority based scheduling scheme is mainly presented because it has been widely studied and adopted in many real-time systems, and because similar results are available for other priority based scheduling schemes such as Earliest Deadline First (EDF) scheduling algorithm. In Section 4 our solution approach is explained. An example is presented in Section 5 with a solution that shows how our scheme can be used in real applications. A conclusion of the paper follows in Section 7.

2 Problem

It is assumed that a set of periodic tasks $\mathcal{T} = \{T_1, T_2, \ldots, T_q\}$ is given with the following:

- Lower and upper bounds of the execution time of T_i, which are denoted as l_i and u_i, respectively[2]
- Period P_i.
- Offset Φ_i which denotes a ready time of the first instance of T_i. Otherwise stated, this is assumed to be equal to 0. The ready time of kth instance of T_i is equal to $\Phi + (k-1)P_i$.
- Relative deadline D_i from the ready time of each instance. That is, the execution of each instance of T_i should be completed within D_i time units from its ready time. $D_i \leq P_i$ is assumed in this paper.

Since we are restricting ourselves only to periodic tasks, we can find out the Least Common Multiple (LCM) of the periods of all tasks in $\mathcal{T}$, and also we can obtain a set, Θ, of task instances of all T_i, $1 \leq i \leq q$, that should be completed in a time interval $[0, LCM]$. Θ has LCM/P_i number of task instances from T_i for each $1 \leq i \leq q$. Let Θ^j denote a set of task instances in a jth scheduling window $[(j-1) \cdot j \cdot LCM]$ where $1 \leq j$.

In addition to the above-mentioned constraints, the following constraints can be specified between task instances in one scheduling window, Θ^j, or in two consecutive scheduling windows, Θ^j and Θ^{j+1}, where $j \geq 1$.

- Precedence constraints may be specified between any task instances.
- Relative timing constraints may be specified between start/finish times of any two task instances.

According to this description, any two task instances may be relatively constrained even if they belong to different scheduling windows (Θ^j and Θ^{j+1}).

[2] C_i is also used to denote a worst case execution time in this paper.

Fig. 1 shows two periodic tasks, T_1 and T_2, whose periods satisfy $2 \cdot P_1 = P_2$. Note that the LCM of the periods is equal to P_2 and there exist 3 task instances in one scheduling window $[0, LCM]$, τ_1^1, τ_1^2, and τ_2^1. Jitter constraints exist between consecutive finish times of task instances of T_1 and T_2, and the offsets of the two tasks are equal to 0.

Note that, even though we are assuming that relative timing constraints may be specified only between start/finish times, this model can also be used, in cases where the events in the middle of task instances are relatively constrained, by decomposing the task into multiple sub-tasks with their boundaries put just before (or after) each event. This approach is actually employed in *Maruti* system design, and each sub-task obtained in this procedure is called an *elemental unit* [33].

The justification of allowing arbitrary types of precedence constraints is that, in some real-time systems, there exist precedence constraints between tasks with different periods or cyclic dependency constraints [5], which makes the scheduling problem more complicated. This point will be discussed in more detail in the next section.

3 Fixed Priority Based Scheduling vs. Time Based Scheduling

In this section, a fixed-priority based scheduling scheme and a time based scheduling scheme is briefly explained with their schedulability analysis results, and their strengths and limitations are compared in the presence of various constraints. Again, the reasons why fixed-priority based scheduling scheme is chosen in this paper are that it is well-studied and that similar arguments can still be applied to other (dynamic) priority based scheduling schemes.

In priority based scheduling schemes, among all ready task instances, the task instance whose priority is the highest is chosen to be executed at any time instant. In fixed-priority scheduling scheme, each periodic task is assigned a fixed priority prior to system operation time and all task instances of the task inherit the priority of the task at run-time. The execution of task instances in priority based systems is *work conserving*, i.e., if there exists one or more ready task instances to be executed some of them is executed without letting CPU idle. Also, this scheduling algorithm is fully preemptive in a sense that, at any time instant, currently executing task instance may be preempted when a higher priority task instance arrives to the system. Fig. 2 shows how the task instances in Fig. 1 can be executed if a fixed priority based scheduling algorithm is used. Note that the actual execution times of task instances are non-deterministic and may vary between their best and worst case execution times.

In time based scheduling scheme, a total ordering among all task instances and their static start times are found at pre-runtime in a scheduling window, and that static schedule is cyclically re-used at runtime by wrapping around the end point to the start point. Usually, during obtaining the static schedule,

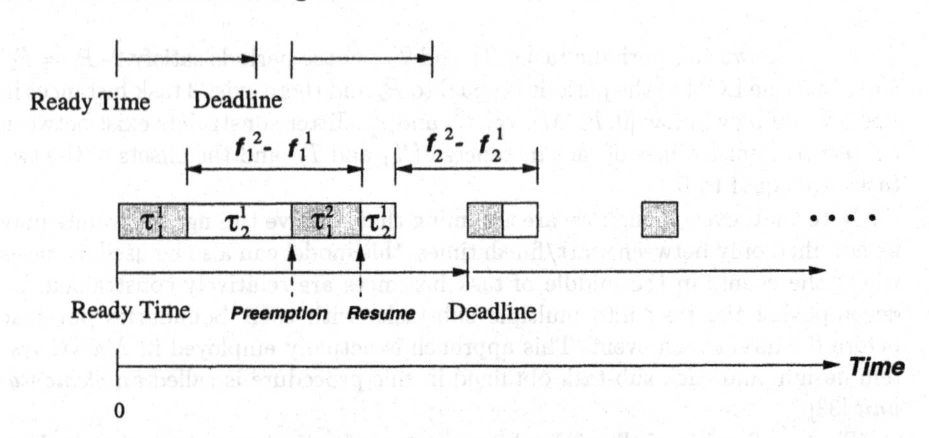

Fig. 2. Fixed priority scheduling

each task instance is assumed to be non-preemptible, or preemptible at predetermined preemption points. The execution of task instances may be either work-conserving or non-work-conserving depending on the implementations. If a non-work-conserving policy is used, the CPU may sit idle even though there is some ready task instance. Fig. 3 shows how the task instances in Fig. 1 are executed when a non-work-conserving time based scheduling scheme is used. Note that the static start times are used to dispatch task instances, and the CPU is idle until the start time of the next task instance is reached.

In Section 3.1, the schedulability analysis results are briefly explained in the presence of various constraints. In Section 3.2, main results on scheduling in time based scheduling scheme is presented. Finally, two scheduling schemes are compared in Section 3.3

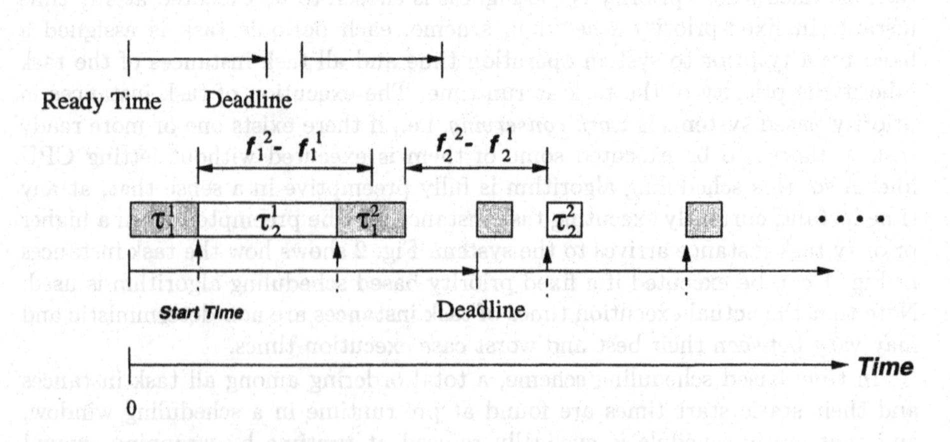

Fig. 3. Time based scheduling

3.1 Main Results from Fixed-Priority Scheduling Theory

In fixed priority based scheduling scheme, a natural question is how to assign priorities to tasks so that all task instances can be executed satisfying all timing constraints. Among all fixed-priority assignment policies, a *deadline-monotonic* scheduling algorithm is shown to be optimal in the presence of deadline constraints, which assigns a higher priority to a task with shorter D_i. An *optimal* priority assignment is the one satisfying the following property:

- If there exists any fixed priority assignment by which all task instances can be executed satisfying the deadline constraints, then an optimal priority assignment will do that, too.

The schedulability analysis results are summarized in the following in the presence of different constraints. The basic schedulability analysis technique is to find out worst case response time of each task by analyzing the interference from higher priority tasks at a *critical instant.* A response time of a task instance is defined to be a time difference between the task ready time and its completion time. Critical instant is when all tasks are released at the same time with 0 offsets, and it has been shown that worst case response times can be found in such scenario [22,36]. Fig. 4 shows how the worst case response time can be found at critical time instant.

1. Basic schedulability analysis technique in fixed-priority scheduling.
   (a) Obtain the worst case response time for each task at the critical instant when all tasks are released at the same time, i.e., $\Phi_i = 0$ for all $1 \leq i \leq q$.
   (b) Usually, a recursive equation is solved to find it.
   (c) The worst case response time for a task is compared to its relative deadline.
   (d) If each task has a smaller worst-case response time than its deadline, then the entire task set is schedulable.

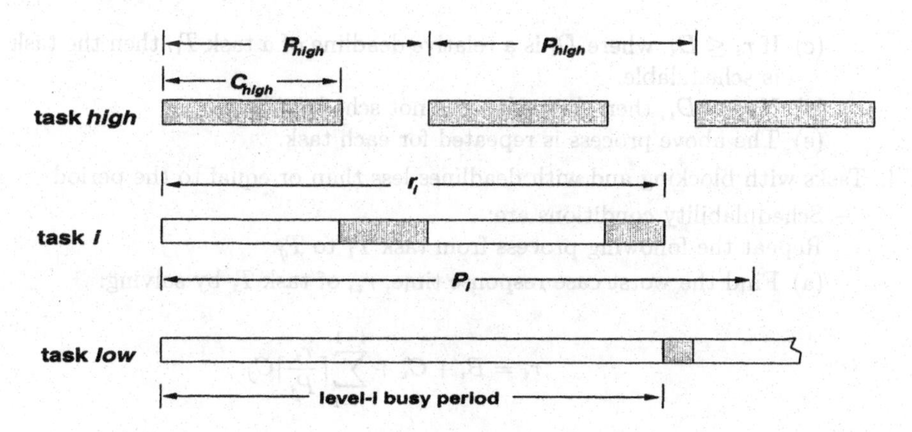

Fig. 4. Critical instant and worst case response time r_i for task i.

2. Tasks with deadlines equal to the end of the period.
   - Rate-monotonic priority assignment is optimal among fixed priority scheduling schemes. A task with a shorter period will be assigned a higher priority.
   - One utilization bound can be used to check the schedulability for the entire situations[27].
     •
     $$\sum_{i=1}^{q} C_i/P_i \leq q(2^{1/q} - 1)$$
     • C_i and P_i are the maximum execution time and the period of a task T_i.
     • This is a sufficiency test.
3. Tasks with deadlines less than or equal to the period
   - Deadline-monotonic priority assignment is optimal among fixed priority scheduling schemes[1].
   - Schedulability conditions are:
     Repeat the following process from task 1 to q:
     (a) Find the worst case response time, r_i, of task T_i by solving:
     $$r_i = C_i + \sum_{j=1}^{i-1} \lceil \frac{r_i}{P_j} \rceil C_j$$
     where a task T_i has a higher priority than a task T_{i+1}.
     (b) The first approximation to r_i is set to
     $$\sum_{j=1}^{i} C_j$$
     (c) If $r_i \leq D_i$, where D_i is a relative deadline of a task T_i, then the task is schedulable.
     (d) If $r_i > D_i$, then the task set is not schedulable.
     (e) The above process is repeated for each task.
4. Tasks with blocking and with deadlines less than or equal to the period
   - Schedulability conditions are:
     Repeat the following process from task T_1 to T_q:
     (a) Find the worst case response time, r_i, of task T_i by solving:
     $$r_i = B_i + C_i + \sum_{j=1}^{i-1} \lceil \frac{r_i}{P_j} \rceil C_j$$
     where a task T_i has a higher priority than a task T_{i+1}.

(b) The first approximation to r_i is set to

$$B_i + \sum_{j=1}^{i} C_j$$

where B_i is the maximum blocking delay that can be caused by a lower priority task(e.g., by a priority ceiling protocol[35]).

(c) If $r_i \leq D_i$, where D_i is a relative deadline of a task T_i, then the task is schedulable.

(d) If $r_i > D_i$, then the task set is not schedulable.

5. Tasks with arbitrary deadlines and blocking
   - Optimal priority assignment is found from a pseudo-polynomial time algorithm. Deadline-monotonic priority assignment is no more optimal.
   - In addition to the interference from higher priority tasks, the task instance is delayed from the late completion of the previous task instance of the same task. This is possible since the deadlines can be greater than the period.
   - The worst case response time should be found at critical instant by examining consecutive scheduling windows for each task T_i until a level-i idle time is encountered.
   - Fig. 5 explains the schedulability analysis.
   - Schedulability conditions are:
     The following process is repeated from task T_1 to task T_q:
     (a) Initialize the scheduling window counter,m, for task T_i as 1.

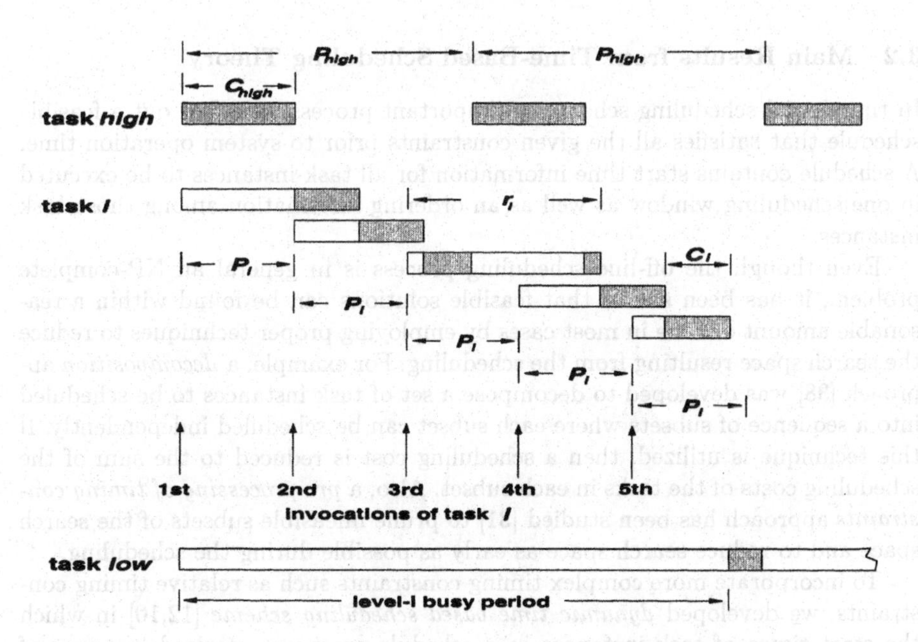

Fig. 5. Worst case response time analysis with arbitrary deadlines

(b) The first approximation to a_i^m is set to

$$B_i + \sum_{j=1}^{i} C_j$$

(c) Find the worst case completion time, a_i^m, of the m-th task instance of a task T_i by recursively solving:

$$a_i^m = B_i + mC_i + \sum_{j=1}^{i-1} \lceil \frac{a_i^m}{P_j} \rceil C_j$$

(d) Check if $a_i^m \leq (m-1)P_i + D_i$ where P_i is a period of task T_i. If not, the task set is not schedulable.
(e) The worst case response time of the m-th task instance is:

$$W_i^m = a_i^m - (m-1)P_i$$

(f) Determine if the level-i busy period is over. If it is over, proceed to step (g). Otherwise, add 1 to m and goto step (b).
(g) The worst case response time of task i is:

$$r_i = \max_{1 \leq j \leq m} W_i^j$$

– If $r_i > D_i$, then the task set is not schedulable. Otherwise, continue.

3.2 Main Results from Time-Based Scheduling Theory

In time based scheduling scheme, an important process is to find out a feasible schedule that satisfies all the given constraints prior to system operation time. A schedule contains start time information for all task instances to be executed in one scheduling window as well as an ordering information among those task instances.

Even though the off-line scheduling process is in general an NP-complete problem, it has been shown that feasible solutions can be found within a reasonable amount of time in most cases by employing proper techniques to reduce the search space resulting from the scheduling. For example, a *decomposition* approach [38] was developed to decompose a set of task instances to be scheduled into a sequence of subsets where each subset can be scheduled independently. If this technique is utilized, then a scheduling cost is reduced to the sum of the scheduling costs of the tasks in each subset. Also, a *pre-processing of timing constraints* approach has been studied [31] to prune infeasible subsets of the search space and to reduce search space as early as possible during the scheduling.

To incorporate more complex timing constraints such as relative timing constraints, we developed *dynamic time based scheduling scheme* [12,10] in which the start times of task instances in a schedule are parameterized in terms of start/finish times of prior task instances. Employing this new scheme, the schedulability of a task set can be checked even in the presence of the relative timing constraints, and slack times can be flexibly managed at system operation time while the real-time guarantees not sacrificed. This new scheme will be explained in more detail in Section 4.

3.3 Comparison Between Priority-Based and Time-Based Systems

In this section, the fixed-priority based scheduling and time based scheduling schemes are compared from various points of view[3].

The priority based scheduling schemes are usually implemented by employing tick-based implementation technique [36]. That is, every clock tick interrupt, the kernel decides which task will be assigned a CPU until the next clock tick occurs. The ready tasks are ordered in a ready queue by their priorities, and a task at the head of the queue is dispatched. If a different higher priority task is going to be assigned a CPU, a context switch has to be performed by the kernel. If a task which is assigned a CPU until the next clock tick finishes its execution before the next tick interrupt, the kernel suspends the task until the next ready time (if it has not been reached) and selects the next task to be executed in the ready queue. Note that, even though the formal definition of priority based scheduling scheme assumes that tasks may be preempted at any time instant when a higher priority task arrives, in real implementations this is no longer true. In the worst case, a higher priority task has to wait until the next tick interrupt occurs.

In time-based scheduling scheme, a schedule is referred to by a dispatcher whenever the kernel gets the CPU to decide a next task instance to be executed. If task instances are non-preemptive, then the kernel structure becomes simpler compared to the priority based one since the CPU will be voluntarily released by the currently executing task instance when it finishes its execution.

In the following, we compare two scheduling schemes in terms of their capabilities to satisfy various constraints that may exist in real-time systems such as deadline constraints, precedence constraints, synchronization constraints, relative timing constraints, etc.

[3] The mechanisms and approaches for fixed-priority based scheduling scheme provided in this section are mainly based on the contents of [23]

1. Deadline Constraints

Issue	Fixed Priority Scheduling	Time-based Scheduling
Guaranteeing Mechanism	– Guaranteed by assuring the worst case response time of a task is less than or equal to the deadline. – Worst case response time is found by analyzing the interference from higher priority tasks at critical instant.	– Guaranteed by pre-runtime scheduling. – Worst case condition may be avoided through scheduling.

One limitation of fixed-priority based scheduling is that CPU can't be fully utilized in performing schedulability tests. In the worst case, only 69.99% of the CPU utilization can be used in schedulability analysis. The actual CPU utilization that can be used to provide real-time guarantees can vary depending on the actual periods, deadlines, and offsets of the tasks. The statistical analysis of the available utilizations is presented in [24].

2. Precedence Constraints

Issues	Fixed Priority Scheduling	Time-based Scheduling
Mechanism	– No general solution exists when the precedence constraints are given between two different tasks. – Two possible solutions for tasks with the same period: • By introducing offsets. • By imposing partial ordering on the priorities of the tasks.	– Any precedence constraints may be allowed between any two tasks and may be satisfied through pre-runtime scheduling.

In the presence of complex precedence constraints as in [3], applying fixed-priority based scheduling may become difficult. For example, precedence constraints may be imposed between tasks with different periods, or they may be cyclically imposed between task instances of two tasks[3]. Basically, precedence constraints are ordering based constraints among different task instances. Time based scheduling scheme is quite a suitable mechanism for imposing such constraints.

3. Synchronization Constraints

– For accessing shared-resources such as critical section.

Issue	Fixed Priority Scheduling	Time-based Scheduling
Mechanism	– Enforced through priority ceiling protocol. – Tasks are required to change their priorities dynamically to bound priority inversion.	– Resolved through scheduling.

Mutual exclusion constraints may be interpreted as *non-overlapping* constraints between critical sections of tasks on a time line. That is, only one task is allowed to access a critical section at a time, and the others that want to access the critical section should wait until the current task finishes its access. Resolving this time-line-based constraints by using priorities introduces the requirement of dynamic priority changes. Using pure fixed-priority based scheduling in these situations may result in unbound indefinite priority inversion, and a high priority task instance may be indefinitely delayed by lower priority task instances. To resolve this limitation, a *priority inheritance protocol* was developed [35]. This dynamic change of priorities introduces more runtime overhead such as managing semaphore queues.

4. Relative Timing Constraints

From the definition of relative timing constraints, we should be able to explicitly control the elapsed times between events. A mechanism exists in fixed priority based scheduling scheme that can be used to impose some relative timing constraints such as jitter constraints.

Issue	Fixed Priority Scheduling	Time-based Scheduling
Mechanism	– Extract events as separate tasks and assign highest priorities them so that their execution times become predictable(with little jitter). – Usually it is assumed that such event routines are short.	– Satisfied through constructing a schedule.

However, the limitation of assigning high priorities to the event-tasks is that, if the number of such jitter-constrained events becomes large, then jitter control may not be feasible using this approach. Another limitation is that schedulability may be affected from such priority assignment since it doesn't conform to the optimal priority assignment such as deadline-monotonic pri-

ority assignment. Furthermore, not all the relative timing constraints defined in Section 2 can be supported in this approach.
As you will see in Section 4, our new dynamic time based scheduling scheme doesn't suffer from these limitations and it allows flexible management of slack times at runtime unlike priority based schemes.

5. Issues in Multi-processor and Distributed Systems In distributed real-time systems, various timing constraints may be given between tasks located at different processors. End-to-end deadline and end-to-end jitter constraints are examples of such constraints. The problems to enforce such constraints across different resources are more difficult and the solution approaches depend on the characteristics of the communication protocols used. Because we are focusing on real-time systems in uni-processor environment in this paper, we will not go over this topic in detail. However, interested readers are referred to [15,9].

We have separately examined and compared priority based and time based scheduling schemes for each constraint. However, when different constraints coexist, which is true in many applications, the issue of priority assignment becomes more complicated if a priority based scheduling scheme is used. No simple way exist to assign priorities without affecting the schedulability.

In time based scheduling scheme, those various constraints may be satisfied by constructing schedules at pre-runtime by directly controlling time line. Hence, if the characteristics of the physical environment can be figured out at system design time, time based scheduling scheme can be a more suitable platform than priority based scheduling scheme.

4 Dynamic Time Based Scheduling

If task instances have only ready time and deadline constraints, it is possible to statically assign start times of task instances in $[0, LCM]$ under the assumption that each task instance consumes its maximum execution time. And, the static schedule can be cyclically repeated at system operation time. However, the following example shows the limitation of static scheduling in the presence of relative timing constraints among task instances [30].

Consider a simple example shown in Fig. 6 which consists of two jobs, τ_1 and τ_2. Suppose that $l_1 = 2$, $u_1 = 6$, and there exists a constraint $s_2 - f_1 \leq 3$. In this example, it is not possible to statically assign start times for two jobs due to large variability of first job's execution time and due to the existence of relative deadline constraint between first job's finish time and second job's start time. However, if we allow the start time s_2 for τ_2 be parameterized with f_1, then the relative deadline constraint is satisfied under all execution scenarios.

In our task model every task instance is assumed to be non-preemptive, and our objective is to find out a mechanism by which we can find out a feasible schedule, if there is any, prior to system operation time, and by which we can

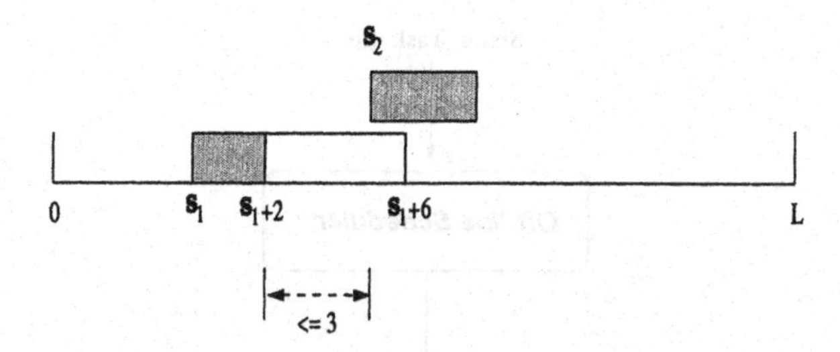

Fig. 6. Limitation of static scheduling scheme

flexibly manage task executions at system operation time such that dynamically arriving aperiodic tasks can be executed as early as possible while all the timing constraints of real-time tasks not violated. For this objective we have developed a new time based scheduling scheme, which is named as *dynamic time based scheduling scheme*, for *Maruti* hard real-time operating system that has been developed since 1989 [33].

Dynamic time based scheduling scheme has been developed to overcome the limitation of static time based scheduling scheme, and consists of two components, an off-line scheduler that generates a *dynamic calendar* for static tasks, and a dynamic dispatcher that is responsible for dispatching both static and dynamic tasks while maintaining the total order among static task instances found by an off-line scheduler. The architecture of this scheduling system is shown in Fig. 7.

A *dynamic calendar* is constructed from a totally ordered static task instance set found by an off-line scheduler. Each task instance in a dynamic calendar may have *attribute functions* denoting any of its attributes, such as the task's valid start time range, its execution mode denoting which version of the task will be executed, etc. The functions may be parameterized with any information available to the system at task instance dispatching time such as any attribute values of previously executed tasks, or current physical system state, etc. At system operation time, the dynamic dispatcher makes use of such information to dynamically evaluate the attribute functions for the next task instance in the dynamic calendar, and it decides the attributes of the next task instance, such as actual task instance start time, actual execution mode of the task instance if multiple task versions exist, etc. Then, it records selected attributes of the next task instance for future usage.

The dynamic attribute evaluation nature of our scheme allows more flexible and efficient resource management at system operation time compared to traditional time-based schemes. To show its applicability and advantages we present a solution approach, based on this scheme, for dispatching task instances in Θ^j, $1 \leq j$, defined in the previous section.

As is shown in Fig. 7, the total ordering of the task instances in Θ should be obtained first before the dynamic calendar can be constructed. In a previous paper [4], several heuristic algorithms were presented and their performances

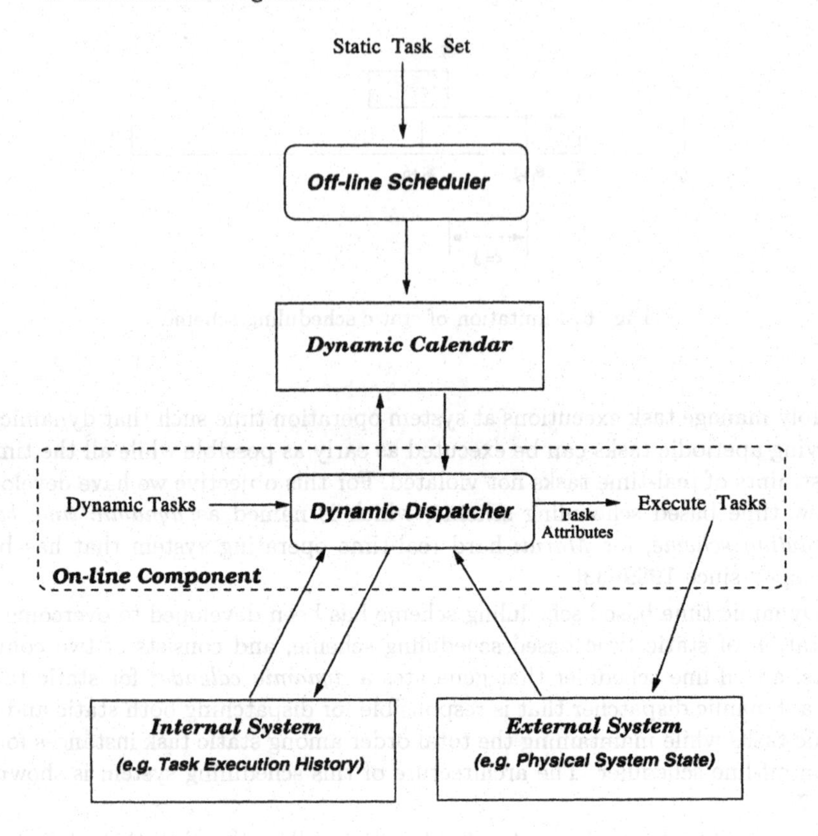

Fig. 7. Overview of dynamic time-based scheduling scheme

were compared for task instance sets similar to the one presented in this paper. Hence, in this paper, we will concentrate on describing the issues of

- How to check if a given total ordering on Θ is dispatchable?
- How to create dynamic calendars if the total ordering is dispatchable?
- How to evaluate attribute functions of each task instance at system operation time?

In our solution approach relative timing constraints may be defined across the boundary of two consecutive scheduling windows as well as within one scheduling window. We present the solution approach with which we are not only able to test the dispatchability of a task instance set, but also able to obtain maximum slack time by postponing static task executions at run-time. This slack time can be used to accommodate the execution of dynamic tasks without compromising the guarantees given to the tasks already accepted.

4.1 Refined Problem Description

Because we are assuming that a total ordering among task instances in Θ is already obtained from the off-line scheduler, we will denote a totally ordered set of task instances in Θ as Γ. Also, Γ^j denote an ordered set of task instances in Θ^j according to the total ordering.

Let $\Gamma^j = \{\tau_i^j \mid i = 1, \ldots, N\}$ denote an ordered set of N task instances to be dispatched sequentially in a j-th scheduling window $[(j-1)L, jL]$ where L denotes an LCM of periods. The task instances are executed non-preemptively in this order. At runtime, this task instance set will be cyclically scheduled in consecutive scheduling windows. In other words, τ_i^j and τ_i^k are task instances of the same task.

Then, let $\Gamma^{1,k} = \Gamma^1 \cup \Gamma^2 \cup \ldots \cup \Gamma^k$ denote a set of task instances to be executed in a time interval $[0, kL]$. Each task instance τ_i^j ($j \geq 1$, $1 \leq i \leq N$) has the following set of parameters that may have integer values:

- A runtime variable s_i^j denoting the actual start time of τ_i^j
- A runtime variable e_i^j representing the actual execution time spent for τ_i^j
- A runtime variable $f_i^j = s_i^j + e_i^j$ denoting the actual finish time of τ_i^j
- A constant l_i^j corresponding to the minimum execution time of τ_i^j
- A constant u_i^j denoting the maximum execution time of τ_i^j.

Note that it is simply assumed that execution times of task instances are non-deterministic and bounded from above and below, which is a realistic assumption in many real-time systems.

Standard constraints are defined next that may be imposed on $\{s_i^j, e_i^j \mid 1 \leq j \leq k,\ 1 \leq i \leq N\}$ for $\Gamma^{1,k}$.

Definition 1 (Standard Constraints) *A standard constraint involves the variables of at most two task instances, τ_a^j and $\tau_b^l (1 \leq a \leq b \leq N, \mid j-l \mid \leq 1)$, where s_a^j(or $s_a^j + e_a^j$) appears on one side of "$\leq$," and s_b^l(or $s_b^l + e_b^l$) appears on the other side of the "$\leq$." For two task instances, τ_a^j, τ_b^l, the following constraints are permitted(where c_i is an arbitrary constant) and called* relative *standard constraints:*

$$\begin{array}{rr}
s_a^j - s_b^l \leq c_1 & s_b^l - s_a^j \leq c_5 \\
s_a^j - (s_b^l + e_b^l) \leq c_2 & s_b^l - (s_a^j + e_a^j) \leq c_6 \\
s_a^j + e_a^j - s_b^l \leq c_3 & s_b^l + e_b^l - s_a^j \leq c_7 \\
s_a^j + e_a^j - (s_b^l + e_b^l) \leq c_4 & s_b^l + e_b^l - (s_a^j + e_a^j) \leq c_8
\end{array} \tag{1}$$

In addition, each task instance has release time and deadline constraints. These constraints are called absolute *standard constraints. A task instance τ_a^j has the following absolute constraints:*

$$c_9 \leq s_a^j \qquad s_a^j + e_a^j \leq c_{10} \tag{2}$$

We also include as standard any constraint that can be rewritten in one of the above forms; e.g., $s_a^j \geq s_b^l + e_b^l - e_a^j + c$ falls into this category.

Next, the *k-fold cyclically constrained task instance set* is formally defined.[4] Any $\Gamma^{1,k}$ considered in this paper belongs to this class.

Definition 2 (k-fold Cyclically Constrained Task Instance Set) *A task instance set $\Gamma^{1,k} = \Gamma^1 \cup \Gamma^2 \cup \ldots \cup \Gamma^k$ $(k = 1, 2, \ldots, \infty)$ is classified as a k-fold* cyclically constrained task instance set *if it has the following linear constraints:*

1. *The set of standard* relative *constraints:*

$$\forall j \in [1, k) :: A_1\mathbf{x}^j + A_2\mathbf{x}^{j+1} \leq \mathbf{a} \tag{3}$$

where $\mathbf{x}^j$ is a $2N$-dimensional column vector $[s_1^j, e_1^j, s_2^j, e_2^j, \ldots, s_N^j, e_N^j]^T$. A_1, A_2 are $m_1 \times 2N (m_1 \geq 0)$ matrices of 0, 1, or -1, and $\mathbf{a}$ is an m_1-dimensional column vector whose elements are integers. Included in the m_1 constraints are those denoting the total ordering on task instances:

$$\forall j \in [1, k] :: \forall i \in [1, N) :: s_i^j + e_i^j \leq s_{i+1}^j$$

$$\forall j \in [1, k) :: s_N^j + e_N^j \leq s_1^{j+1}$$

2. *The set of release time and deadline constraints:*

$$\forall j \in [1, k] :: B\mathbf{x}^j \leq \mathbf{b}^j \tag{4}$$

$$\forall j \in [1, k] :: D\mathbf{x}^j \leq \mathbf{d}^j \tag{5}$$

where $\mathbf{b}^j$ is an m_2-dimensional column vector of non-positive integers satisfying:

$$\mathbf{b}^j = \mathbf{b}^1 + (1 - j)L$$

and $\mathbf{d}^j$ is an m_3-dimensional column vector of non-negative integers satisfying:

$$\mathbf{d}^j = \mathbf{d}^1 + (j - 1)L$$

We define $C^{1,k}$ to represent the logical conjunction of the constraints induced by each row of (3), (4), and (5).

In the above definition, the same matrices A_1, A_2, B, D are cyclically used to represent the standard constraints on consecutive task instance sets.

Fig. 8 shows an example ∞-fold cyclically constrained task instance set which has two task instances in one scheduling window.

One traditional approach for scheduling with complex timing constraints is a time-based scheduling scheme that assigns static start times to the task instances in the scheduling window such that the relative constraints are satisfied if the static schedule is cyclically repeated at runtime. However, this approach can't be used in the presence of arbitrary relative constraints between start or finish times of task instances [16]. Also, this approach suffers from the loss of

[4] Note that k may be equal to ∞.

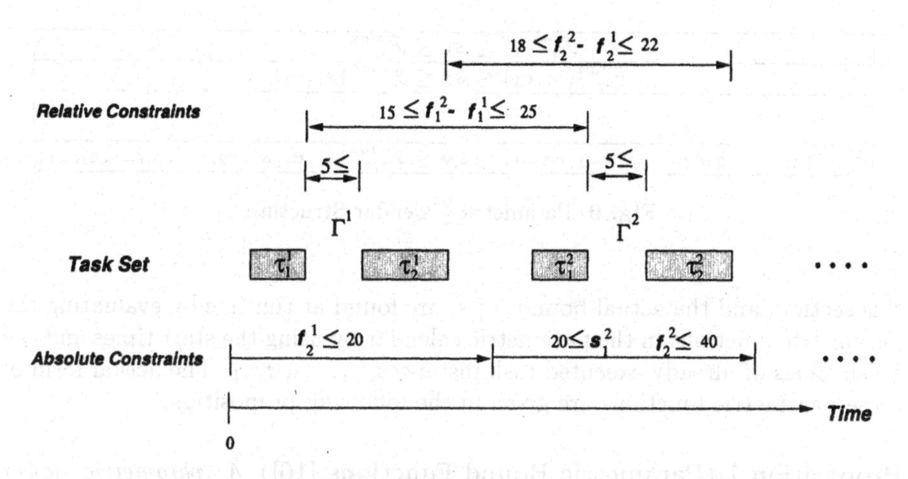

Fig. 8. Example ∞-fold cyclically constrained task instance set.

schedulability problem. Some task sets are not schedulable in this approach, even though they are schedulable if our approach is employed. This will be explained through an example later. To cope with some of the above limitations the parametric scheduling scheme was developed in scope of real-time transaction scheduling [16]. However, as far as we know, the solution approach has not been found for general periodic task models where task instances in different scheduling windows may have relative constraints. The objective of this paper is to develop a schedulability test for $\Gamma^{1,\infty}$, and to develop a flexible task instance dispatching mechanism for schedulable task instance sets, $\Gamma^{1,\infty}$.

4.2 Background – Parametric Scheduling

Gerber *et al.* [16] proposes a parametric scheduling scheme in the scope of transaction scheduling, in which any standard constraints may be given between task instances in one transaction. Let $\Pi =< \tau_1, \ldots, \tau_N >$ denote a sequence of task instances constituting one transaction with a set of standard constraints, $\mathcal{C}$. Then, Π is said to be *dispatchable* if there exists any way that the task instances can be dispatched satisfying all the timing constraints in any execution time scenario. Then, a dispatchability of Π is defined as follows:

$$Disp \equiv \exists s_1 :: \forall e_1 \in [l_1, u_1] :: \ldots :: \exists s_N :: \forall e_N \in [l_N, u_N] :: \mathcal{C} \quad (6)$$

From this *Disp* predicate, parametric lower and upper bound functions for each start time s_i are obtained by eliminating the variables in an order e_N, s_N, ..., e_i. The parametric lower and upper bound functions, denoted as $\mathcal{F}^{min}_{s_i}$ and $\mathcal{F}^{max}_{s_i}$, are parameterized in terms of the runtime variables, s_1, e_1, ..., s_{i-1}, e_{i-1} of already executed task instances. The parametric calendar structure is shown in Fig. 9.

This parametric calendar is obtained from an off-line component of the algorithm by applying variable elimination techniques that will be given later in

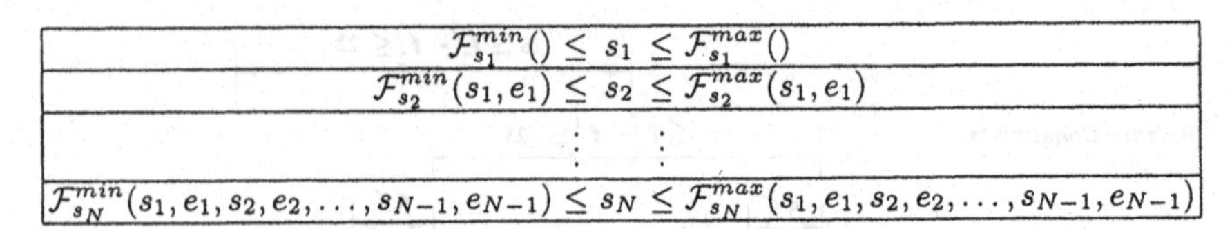

$\mathcal{F}_{s_1}^{min}() \leq s_1 \leq \mathcal{F}_{s_1}^{max}()$
$\mathcal{F}_{s_2}^{min}(s_1, e_1) \leq s_2 \leq \mathcal{F}_{s_2}^{max}(s_1, e_1)$
$\vdots \quad \vdots$
$\mathcal{F}_{s_N}^{min}(s_1, e_1, s_2, e_2, \ldots, s_{N-1}, e_{N-1}) \leq s_N \leq \mathcal{F}_{s_N}^{max}(s_1, e_1, s_2, e_2, \ldots, s_{N-1}, e_{N-1})$

Fig. 9. Parametric Calendar Structure

this section, and the actual bounds of s_i are found at runtime by evaluating the parametric functions in the parametric calendar by using the start times and the finish times of already executed task instances, $\tau_1, \ldots, \tau_{i-1}$. The actual form of these parametric functions are given in the following proposition.

Proposition 1 (Parametric Bound Functions [16]) *A parametric lower bound function for s_j is of the following form:*

$$\mathcal{F}_{s_j}^{min}(s_1, f_1, \ldots, s_{j-1}, f_{j-1}) \\ = \max(p_1 + c_1, p_2 + c_2, \ldots, p_a + c_a, \alpha_j^{min}) \quad (7)$$

where each p_i, $1 \leq i \leq a$, belongs to $\{s_1, f_1, \ldots, s_{j-1}, f_{j-1}\}$, and c_i is an arbitrary constant.[5] *And, α_j^{min} is a non-negative integer.*

Similarly, a parametric upper bound function for s_j is of the following form:

$$\mathcal{F}_{s_j}^{max}(s_1, f_1, \ldots, s_{j-1}, f_{j-1}) \\ = \min(q_1 + d_1, q_2 + d_2, \ldots, q_b + d_b, \alpha_j^{max}) \quad (8)$$

where each q_i, $1 \leq i \leq b$, belongs to $\{s_1, f_1, \ldots, s_{j-1}, f_{j-1}\}$, and d_i is an arbitrary constant..

The main result obtained by the paper is that, for an arbitrary set of standard constraints on $\Pi = \{\tau_1, \ldots, \tau_N\}$, we can find the parametric calendar in $O(N^3)$ time and the run-time evaluation of each bound function can be carried out in $O(N)$ time.

By applying this parametric scheduling scheme, we are not only able to schedule any sequence of task instances with standard constraints, but also able to take advantage of the flexibility offered by the scheme. That is, the task instance start times may be decided dynamically at runtime to incorporate other dynamic activities in the system. Even though this scheme is directly applicable to our k-fold cyclically constrained task instance sets, if the number of task instances in $\Gamma^{1,k}$ becomes large, the bounds need to be found on the size of parametric functions and for the memory requirements for them.

In the rest of this section, the parametric scheduling scheme in the paper is presented with an example.

[5] Note that $f_i = s_i + e_i$.

Elimination of Quantified Variables Consider a set of linear constraints $\mathcal{C}$ in n variables $(x_1, x_2, \ldots, x_n)$,

$$\mathcal{C} \equiv H\mathbf{x} \leq \mathbf{h}$$

which must be satisfied with respect to some defined existential and universal quantification over the variables. In this section we show how an innermost universally quantified variable x_n, with associated lower (l_n) and upper (u_n) bounds can be eliminated to obtain a new set of equivalent constraints. The set of constraints $\mathcal{C}$ may be partitioned into three subsets, depending on whether the coefficient of x_n is positive, negative or zero. Thus,

$$\mathcal{C} \equiv \mathcal{C}_P \wedge \mathcal{C}_N \wedge \mathcal{C}_Z$$

where

$$\begin{aligned} \mathcal{C}_P &\equiv \{x_n \geq D_i(\mathbf{x}'),\ 1 \leq i \leq p\} \\ \mathcal{C}_N &\equiv \{x_n \leq E_j(\mathbf{x}'),\ 1 \leq j \leq q\} \\ \mathcal{C}_Z &\equiv \{0 \leq F_k(\mathbf{x}'),\ 1 \leq k \leq r\} \end{aligned}$$

$D_i(\mathbf{x}'), E_j(\mathbf{x}'), F_k(\mathbf{x}')$ are linear functions of $\mathbf{x}' = [x_1, \cdots, x_{n-1}]^T$. The elimination of variable x_n leads to a new system of constraints $\mathcal{C}'$ obtained from $\mathcal{C}$ by substituting x_n with l_n or u_n, depending on its coefficient:

$$\mathcal{C}' \equiv (\mathcal{C}_P)_{l_n}^{x_n} \wedge (\mathcal{C}_N)_{u_n}^{x_n} \wedge (\mathcal{C}_Z)$$

Lemma 1 ([16]) *Let $\mathcal{C}$ be a system of linear constraints and let $\mathcal{C}'$ be the resulting set of constraints after eliminating a universally quantified variable x_n with lower bound l_n and upper bound u_n. Then the sentence $\forall x_n \in [l_n, u_n] :: \mathcal{C}$ holds if and only if $\mathcal{C}'$ holds.*

The existential quantifier can be eliminated by using Fourier-Motzkin variable elimination technique [13].

Fourier-Motzkin Elimination. Consider a system of linear constraints $\mathcal{C}$ in n variables $(x_1, x_2, \ldots, x_n)$. We wish to find a system of linear constraints $\mathcal{C}'$ over $\mathbf{x}' = [x_1, \ldots, x_{n-1}]^T$, such that $\mathbf{x}'$ is a solution to $\mathcal{C}'$ if and only if $\mathbf{x}'$ is a solution to $\exists x_n :: \mathcal{C}$. As before, the constraints in $\mathcal{C}$ may be partitioned into three subsets.

$$\mathcal{C} \equiv \begin{cases} x_n \geq D_i(\mathbf{x}'), 1 \leq i \leq p \\ x_n \leq E_j(\mathbf{x}'), 1 \leq j \leq q \\ 0 \leq F_k(\mathbf{x}'), 1 \leq k \leq r \end{cases}$$

The elimination of variable x_n leads to a new system of constraints:

$$\mathcal{C}' \equiv \exists x_n :: \mathcal{C} \equiv \begin{cases} D_i(\mathbf{x}') \leq E_j(\mathbf{x}'), 1 \leq i \leq p, 1 \leq j \leq q \\ 0 \leq F_k(\mathbf{x}'), 1 \leq k \leq r \end{cases}$$

The correctness of this procedure is stated in the following lemma.

Lemma 2 ([16]) *Let C be a set of linear constraints. Let C' represent the set of constraints as a result of eliminating x_n using Fourier Motzkin elimination as described above. Then,*

$$\exists x_n :: C$$

holds if and only if C' holds.

4.3 Generation of a Dynamic Calendar for $\Gamma^{1,\infty}$

As in the parametric scheduling approach developed for transaction scheduling [16], we want to devise a dispatchability test and an efficient dispatching mechanism when the totally ordered ∞-fold cyclically constrained task instance set, $\Gamma^{1,\infty}$, is given with its constraint matrices and vectors. We say $\Gamma^{1,k}$, is *dispatchable* if there exists any method which can successfully dispatch the task instances in $\Gamma^{1,k}$.

Definition 3 (Dispatchability of $\Gamma^{1,k}$) *The k-fold cyclically constrained task instance set $\Gamma^{1,k}$ $(1 \leq k)$ is dispatchable if the following predicate holds:*

$$disp^{1,k} \equiv \exists s_1^1 :: \forall e_1^1 \in [l_1^1, u_1^1] :: \exists s_2^1 :: \forall e_2^1 \in [l_2^1, u_2^1] :: \ldots$$
$$\exists s_{N-1}^k :: \forall e_{N-1}^k \in [l_{N-1}^k, u_{N-1}^k] :: \exists s_N^k :: \forall e_N^k \in [l_N^k, u_N^k] :: C^{1,k} \quad (9)$$

where $C^{1,k}$ is a set of standard constraints defined on $\{s_1^1, e_1^1, \ldots, s_N^k, e_N^k\}$.

Then, the following proposition holds for all $k \geq 1$.

Proposition 2

$$\forall k \geq 1 :: disp^{1,k+1} \Longrightarrow disp^{1,k}$$

Proof: Obvious from the definition of $disp^{1,k}$ in (9).

Hence, once $disp^{1,k}$ turns out to be **False**, then all $disp^{1,j}$, $k \leq j$, are **False**, too. By this proposition, the dispatchability of $\Gamma^{1,\infty}$ is defined.

Definition 4 (Dispatchability of $\Gamma^{1,\infty}$) *$\Gamma^{1,\infty}$ is dispatchable if and only if*

$$\lim_{k \to \infty} disp^{1,k} = \textbf{True}$$

In [16], it is shown that checking Predicate (6) is not trivial because of the nondeterministic task instance execution times and because of the existence of standard relative constraints among the task instances. This is also true for the above $disp^{1,k}$ predicate. The variable elimination techniques are used in [16] to eliminate variables from Predicate (6). At the end of the variable elimination process parametric bound functions for s_i, that are parameterized in terms of the variables in $\{s_1, e_1, \ldots, e_{i-1}\}$, are found as well as the predicate value.

However, if we want to apply the variable elimination techniques to $disp^{1,k}$, the following problems have to be addressed first:

1. On which subset of $\{s_1^1, e_1^1, \ldots, s_{i-1}^j, e_{i-1}^j\}$ does the parametric bound functions for s_i^j depend?
2. Is it required to store parametric bound functions for every task instance in $\Gamma^{1,k}$?
3. What parametric bound functions have to be used if k is not known at pre-runtime and dynamically decided at runtime?

Let $\mathcal{F}_{s_i^j}^{min,k}$ and $\mathcal{F}_{s_i^j}^{max,k}$ denote parametric lower and upper bound functions for s_i^j, respectively, that are found after the variable elimination algorithms are applied to $disp^{1,k}$. If the number of variables is unbounded with which $\mathcal{F}_{s_i^j}^{min,k}$ or $\mathcal{F}_{s_i^j}^{max,k}$ is parameterized, then it is not possible to evaluate them at run-time within bounded computation times. Also, if it is required that parametric bound functions for every task instance in $\Gamma^{1,k}$ be stored at runtime, the scheme is not implementable for large k because of memory requirements. Finally, if the value of k is not known at pre-runtime and is decided dynamically at runtime, which is true in most real-time applications, parametric bound functions to be used have to be selected.

In this section, the answers to the above questions are presented from our previous paper [11] without proof due to the space limitation. In that paper we found out the answers by first transforming $disp^{1,k}$ into a *constraint graph* and by investigating the properties of such graphs. The following properties can be found in our previous paper [11] with proofs.

Lemma 3 *Parametric bound functions for s_i^j found from $\Gamma^{1,k}$ depend only upon $\{s_1^{j-1}, e_1^{j-1}, s_2^{j-1}, e_2^{j-1}, \ldots, s_{i-1}^j, e_{i-1}^j\}$ where $2 \leq j \leq k$.*

This lemma answers the first question raised before. Before answering the second and third questions above, we need to define the concept of homogeneity between parametric bound functions for corresponding task instances in consecutive scheduling windows. Two task instances, τ_i^j and τ_i^{j+1}, are said to be *corresponding* task instances in j-th and $(j+1)$-th scheduling windows for $j \geq 1$.

Next, the homogeneity between parametric bound functions of corresponding task instances are defined. Let $\mathcal{F}_{s_i^j}^{min,k}$ and $\mathcal{F}_{s_i^{j+1}}^{min,k}$, $2 \leq j \leq k$, denote two parametric lower bound functions that are obtained from $\Gamma^{1,k}$ after applying variable elimination algorithms. From Proposition 1 and Lemma 3, we can represent them as follows:

$$\mathcal{F}_{s_i^j}^{min,k}(s_1^{j-1}, e_1^{j-1}, \ldots, s_{i-1}^j, e_{i-1}^j)$$
$$= \max(p_1 + c_1, p_2 + c_2, \ldots, p_a + c_a, \alpha_j^{min}) \quad (10)$$

where each p_l, $1 \leq l \leq a$, belongs to $\{s_1^{j-1}, s_1^{j-1} + e_1^{j-1}, s_2^{j-1}, s_2^{j-1} + e_2^{j-1}, \ldots, s_{i-1}^j, s_{i-1}^j + e_{i-1}^j\}$, and c_l is a constant. And, α_j^{min} is a non-negative integer.

$$\mathcal{F}_{s_i^{j+1}}^{min,k}(s_1^j, e_1^j, \ldots, s_{i-1}^{j+1}, e_{i-1}^{j+1})$$
$$= \max(q_1 + d_1, q_2 + d_2, \ldots, q_b + c_b, \alpha_{j+1}^{min}) \quad (11)$$

where each q_m, $1 \le m \le b$, belongs to $\{s_1^j,\ s_1^j + e_1^j,\ s_2^j,\ s_2^j + e_2^j, \ldots, s_{i-1}^{j+1},$ $s_{i-1}^{j+1} + e_{i-1}^{j+1}\}$, and d_m is a constant. And, α_{j+1}^{min} is a non-negative integer.

Definition 5 *$\mathcal{F}_{s_i^j}^{min,k}$ and $\mathcal{F}_{s_i^{j+1}}^{min,k}$ are defined to be* homogeneous *to each other if the following is satisfied:*

1. $a = b$
2. $\alpha_{j+1}^{min} = \alpha_j^{min} + L$
3. *For all $1 \le l \le a$, there exists an m such that*

$$g_{(1)}(p_l) + c_l = q_m + d_m$$

where $g_{(1)}(s_y^x) = s_y^{x+1}$ and $g_{(1)}(f_y^x) = f_y^{x+1} = s_y^{x+1} + e_y^{x+1}$ for any x, y.

If $\mathcal{F}_{s_i^j}^{min,k}$ and $\mathcal{F}_{s_i^{j+1}}^{min,k}$ are homogeneous, then it is denoted as

$$\mathcal{F}_{s_i^j}^{min,k} \sim \mathcal{F}_{s_i^{j+1}}^{min,k}$$

The homogeneity between two corresponding upper bound functions are defined similarly. Note that, according to this definition, it is easy to derive $\mathcal{F}_{s_i^j}^{min,k}$ from $\mathcal{F}_{s_i^{j+1}}^{min,k}$ if we know they are homogeneous. Also, if $\mathcal{F}_{s_i^j}^{min,k} \sim \mathcal{F}_{s_i^{j+1}}^{min,k}$, then $\mathcal{F}_{s_i^{j+1}}^{min,k}$ may be viewed as a function of variables that are isomorphically shifted from Γ^j, Γ^{j+1} into Γ^j, Γ^{j+1} except that absolute standard constraints are adjusted by adding scheduling window size L.

The following theorem presents the main result we obtained in our paper [11] which gives an answer to the second and third questions raised before.

Theorem 1 *Let n be the number of task instances in a scheduling window that have relative constraints with task instances in the next scheduling window. $disp^{1,\infty}$ is* **True** *if and only if the following is satisfied:*

- *During the elimination of variables from $disp^{1,n^2-n+4}$, a scheduling window index j is found ($1 \le j \le n^2 - n + 3$) such that*

$$\mathcal{F}_{s_i^j}^{min,k} \sim \mathcal{F}_{s_i^{j+1}}^{min,k}$$

$$\mathcal{F}_{s_i^j}^{max,k} \sim \mathcal{F}_{s_i^{j+1}}^{max,k}$$

for all $1 \le i \le N$

One property proved in our previous paper is that, even if k is increased in $disp^{1,k}$, after eliminating variables in the last $n^2 - n + 2$ scheduling windows, *asymptotic*[6] convergent parametric bound functions will be obtained. In other words, if $disp^{1,\infty}$ is **True**, then we can find asymptotic homogeneous parametric

[6] Asymptotic in terms of homogeneity.

bound functions that may be used to dispatch task instances in $\Gamma^{1,k}$ for any $1 \leq k$. Once we figure out homogeneous functions in Theorem 1, we can easily obtain the asymptotic parametric bound functions for an i-th task instance in each scheduling window by incorporating a scheduling window index into them. This means that all i-th task instances in all scheduling windows(except the first scheduling window) have the same asymptotic parametric functions if we also parameterize the scheduling window index into the functions. This is shown in the following example section.

Even though variable elimination algorithms need to be applied to $disp^{1,n^2-n+4}$, the actual off-line algorithm can be implemented on $disp^{1,2}$ by utilizing the cyclic nature of constraints in the predicate. The constraint set in $disp^{1,2}$ will be cyclically changed after each loop in our algorithm. The following steps are performed by the *cyclic* off-line algorithm. The correctness of the algorithm can be found in our previous paper [11].

1. Construct $disp^{1,2}$ from given total ordering and timing constraints among task instances in $\Gamma^{1,2}$.
2. Repeat the following steps $n^2 - n + 2$ times.
   (a) Eliminate variables in Γ^2. (That is, e_N^2, s_N^2, e_{N-1}^2, s_{N-1}^2, $\ldots$, e_1^2, s_1^2)
   (b) Check if asymptotic parametric functions are found.
      i. If true, then return(**True**).
   (c) Cyclically reflect newly created constraints between variables in Γ^1 by creating homogeneous(corresponding) constraints in Γ^2.
   (d) Remove newly created constraints in Γ^1.
3. Return(**False**)

The complexity is $O(n^2N^3)$ since eliminating variables for one scheduling window takes $O(N^3)$ time and the upper bound on the number of scheduling windows to be examined is $O(n^2)$. It is shown in our previous paper that step 2-(b) will take $O(n^2)$ time. Also, from Lemma 3, it is clear that each parametric bound functions will contain $O(N)$ number of variables, which implies that the on-line algorithm to evaluate each parametric bound functions will take $O(N)$ time. It is further proved that, if only jitter type relative constraints are allowed[7], then the off-line complexity is $O(n^4N)$ and the on-line complexity is $O(n)$.

Finally, the overview of our scheme is shown in Fig. 10.

5 Example

The asymptotic parametric bound functions are found for the task instance set, $\Gamma^{1,\infty}$, in Fig. 8. Fig. 11 shows the parametric bound functions found from $\Gamma^{1,4}$, and Fig. 12 shows asymptotic parametric bound functions for $disp^{1,\infty}$.

It is clear from this figure that the following hold:

$$\mathcal{F}^{min,4}_{s_1^2} \sim \mathcal{F}^{min,4}_{s_1^3}$$

[7] More precisely, if the number of task instances with which a task instance may have relative standard constraints is less than or equal to 1.

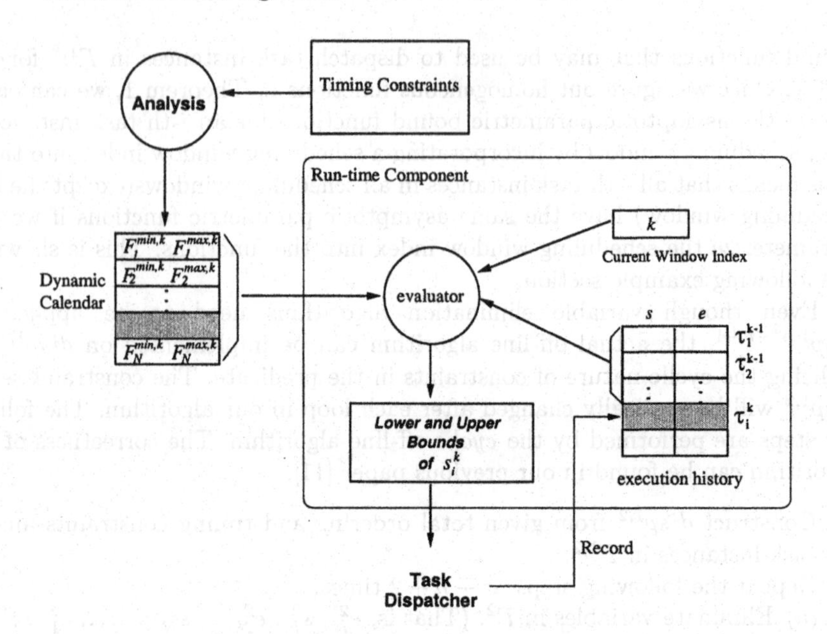

Fig. 10. Overview of dynamic time-based scheduling scheme

$0 \le s_1^1 \le 2$
$\max(8, s_1^1 + e_1^1) \le s_2^1 \le \min(10, s_1^1 + e_1^1 + 5)$
$\max(20, s_2^1 + e_2^1, s_1^1 + e_1^1 + 10) \le s_1^2 \le \min(22, s_1^1 + e_1^1 + 17, s_2^1 + e_2^1 + 4)$
$\max(28, s_1^2 + e_1^2, s_2^1 + e_2^1 + 10) \le s_2^2 \le \min(30, s_2^1 + e_2^1 + 12, s_1^2 + e_1^2 + 5)$
$\max(40, s_2^2 + e_2^2, s_1^2 + e_1^2 + 10) \le s_1^3 \le \min(42, s_1^2 + e_1^2 + 17, s_2^2 + e_2^2 + 4)$
$\max(48, s_1^3 + e_1^3, s_2^2 + e_2^2 + 10) \le s_2^3 \le \min(50, s_2^2 + e_2^2 + 12, s_1^3 + e_1^3 + 5)$
$\max(60, s_2^3 + e_2^3, s_1^3 + e_1^3 + 10) \le s_1^4 \le \min(62, s_1^3 + e_1^3 + 17, s_2^3 + e_2^3 + 4)$
$\max(s_1^4 + e_1^4, s_2^3 + e_2^3 + 10) \le s_2^4 \le \min(70, s_2^3 + e_2^3 + 12, s_1^4 + e_1^4 + 5)$

Fig. 11. Parametric bound functions found from $disp^{1,4}$

$$\mathcal{F}^{max,4}_{s_1^2} \sim \mathcal{F}^{max,4}_{s_1^3}$$

$$\mathcal{F}^{min,4}_{s_2^2} \sim \mathcal{F}^{min,4}_{s_2^3}$$

$$\mathcal{F}^{max,4}_{s_2^2} \sim \mathcal{F}^{max,4}_{s_2^3}$$

Note that $n = 3$, and $n^2 - n + 2 = 8$ is the upper bound given in Theorem 1 on the number of scheduling windows to be eliminated before obtaining asymptotic parametric bound functions. But, we found homogeneous parametric bound functions after eliminating variables in the last 3 scheduling windows of $\Gamma^{1,4}$. This shows that the upper bound on the number of scheduling windows given in Theorem 1 is not tight in general, and the dispatchability may be checked within less amount of time.

$$
\begin{aligned}
\mathcal{F}_{s_1^1}^{min} &= 0\\
\mathcal{F}_{s_1^1}^{max} &= 2\\
\mathcal{F}_{s_2^1}^{min} &= \max(8, s_1^1 + e_1^1)\\
\mathcal{F}_{s_2^1}^{max} &= \min(10, s_1^1 + e_1^1 + 5)\\
\mathcal{F}_{s_1^j}^{min} &= \max(20 + (j-2)20, s_2^{j-1} + e_2^{j-1}, s_1^{j-1} + e_1^{j-1} + 10)\\
\mathcal{F}_{s_1^j}^{max} &= \min(22 + (j-2)20, s_1^{j-1} + e_1^{j-1} + 17, s_2^{j-1} + e_2^{j-1} + 4)\\
\mathcal{F}_{s_2^j}^{min} &= \max(28 + (j-2)20, s_1^j + e_1^j, s_2^{j-1} + e_2^{j-1} + 10)\\
\mathcal{F}_{s_2^j}^{max} &= \min(30 + (j-2)20, s_2^{j-1} + e_2^{j-1} + 12, s_1^2 + e_1^2 + 5)
\end{aligned}
$$

Fig. 12. Asymptotic parametric bound functions for $disp^{1,\infty}$

6 On-Line Dispatcher

The structure of an on-line dispatcher is shown in Fig. 10. As is explained in the previous section, the parametric lower and upper bound functions for each task instance can be evaluated within $O(N)$ time, where N denotes the number of task instances in one scheduling window. Especially, if only jitter type relative constraints are allowed, then the run-time dispatcher will take at most $O(n)$ time.

The run-time dispatcher only need to keep track of the start and execution times of task instances that belong to a current scheduling window or previous scheduling window. In other words, the start and execution times of at most $2N$ task instances need to be stored at run-time. Hence, the number of variables to be stored at run-time is $4N$. This is true since the memory for $2N$ variables can be cyclically reused as in double buffering technique. And, it is very straightforward to keep track of the scheduling window index by the run-time dispatcher.

7 Conclusion

In this paper, a new scheme was presented for dynamic real-time systems and it was applied to find a solution approach for dispatching tasks with complex constraints. By allowing some of the task attributes to be represented as functions and to be evaluated dynamically at run-time, we could obtain more flexibility in managing resources at run-time. As a result, dynamic tasks can be incorporated into the schedule at run-time without compromising real-time guarantees given to static tasks. This is a unique feature compared to prior works including those on priority-based scheduling as well as those on time-based scheduling. For example, in priority-based scheduling schemes, it is very difficult to incorporate relative timing constraints.

We believe that our scheme has an advantage over traditional schemes and can be applied to a wide range of complex real-time systems that require more dynamic resource management at system operation time. Clearly, we may allow other attributes to be expressed as functions as well as start time ranges, and the implication is enhanced flexibility in resource management in various class of applications. We are currently working on extending the scheme to distributed hard real-time systems with complex timing constraints and fault-tolerance requirements.

Acknowledgements

This work is supported in part by Mississippi State University (MSU) under contract 96144601 to the Computer Science Department at the University of Maryland. Under their contract with the U.S. Air Force Grant No. F30602-96-1-0329, the views, opinions, and/or findings contained in this report are those of the author(s) and should not be interpreted as representing the official policies, either expressed or implied, of MSU, the Advanced Research Projects Agency, USAF or the U.S. Government.

References

1. N. C. Audsley. Deadline monotonic scheduling. YCS 146, University of York, Department of Computer Science, October 1990.
2. A. Burns. Fixed Priority Scheduling with Deadlines Prior to Completion. Technical Report YCS 212 (1993), Department of Computer Science, University of York, England, 1993.
3. T. Carpenter, K. Driscoll, K. Hoyme, and J. Carciofini. Arinc 659 scheduling: Problem definition. In *Proc., IEEE Real-time Systems Symposium*, San Juan, PR, December 1994.
4. S. Cheng and A. K. Agrawala. Scheduling of periodic tasks with relative timing constraints. Technical report, CS-TR-3392, UMIACS-TR-94-135, Department of Computer Science, University of Maryland, December 1994.
5. S. Cheng and Ashok K. Agrawala. Allocation and scheduling of real-time periodic tasks with relative timing constraints. Technical Report CS-TR-3402, UMIACS-TR-95-6, Department of Computer Science, University of Maryland, January 1995.
6. H. Chetto and M. Chetto. Scheduling Periodic and Sporadic Task in a Real-Time System. *Information Processing Letters*, 30(4):177–184, 1989.
7. H. Chetto and M. Chetto. Some Results of the Earliest Deadline First Algorithm. *IEEE Transactions on Software Engineering*, SE-15(10):1261–1269, October 1989.
8. H. Chetto, M. Silly, and T. Bouchentouf. Dynamic Scheduling of Real-Time Tasks under Precedence Constraints. *Real-Time Systems*, 2:181–194, 1990.
9. S. Choi. End-to-end optimization in heterogeneous distributed real-time systems. In *ACM/SIGPLAN Workshop on Languages, Compilers, and Tools for Embedded Systems*, June 1998.
10. Seonho Choi. *Dynamic Time-Based Scheduling for Hard Real-Time Systems*. PhD thesis, University of Maryland at College Park, 1997.
11. Seonho Choi and A. K. Agrawala. Dynamic dispatching of cyclic real-time tasks with relative constraints. Technical report, CS-TR-3770, UMIACS-TR-97-30, Department of Computer Science, University of Maryland, March 1997. Submitted to Journal of Real-Time System.

12. Seonho Choi and Ashok K. Agrawala. Dynamic dispatching of cyclic real-time tasks with relative constraints. Technical Report CS-TR-3770, UMIACS-TR-97-30, Department of Computer Science, University of Maryland, March 1997.
13. G. Dantzig and B. Eaves. Fourier-Motzkin Elimination and its Dual. *Journal of Combinatorial Theory(A)*, 14:288–297, 1973.
14. B. Dasarathy. Timing constraints for real-time systems: Constructs for expressing them, methods of validating them. *IEEE Transactions on Software Engineering*, SE-11(1):80–86, January 1985.
15. R. Gerber, S. Hong, and M. Saksena. Guaranteeing End-to-End Timing Constraints by Calibrating Intermediate Processes. In *Proceedings IEEE Real-Time Systems Symposium*, 1994. Also available as University of Maryland CS-TR-3274, UMIACS-TR-94-58.
16. R. Gerber, W. Pugh, and M. Saksena. Parametric Dispatching of Hard Real-Time Tasks. *IEEE Transactions on Computers*, 44(3), Mar. 1995.
17. M. G. Harbour, M. H. Klein, and J. P. Lehoczky. Fixed Priority Scheduling of Periodic Tasks with Varying Execution Priority. In *Proceedings, IEEE Real-Time Systems Symposium*, pages 116–128, December 1991.
18. X. Homayoun and P. Ramanathan. Dynamic priority scheduling of periodic and aperiodic tasks in hard real-time systems. *Real-Time Systems*, 6(2), March 1994.
19. Seung H. Hong. Scheduling Algorithm of Data Sampling Times in the Integrated Communication and Control Systems. *IEEE Transactions on Control Systems Technology*, 3(2):225–230, June 1995.
20. F. Jahanian and A. K. Mok. Safety analysis of timing properties in real-time systems. *IEEE Transactions on Software Engineering*, SE-12(9):890–904, September 1986.
21. E. D. Jensen, C. D. Locke, and H. Tokuda. A Time-Driven Scheduling Model for Real-Time Operating Systems. In *Proceedings, IEEE Real-Time Systems Symposium*, pages 112–122, Dec. 1985.
22. M. Joseph and P. Pandya. Finding Response Times in a Real-Time System. *The Computer Journal*, 29(5):390–395, October 1986.
23. M. Klein, T. Ralya, B. Pollak, R. Obenza, and M. Harbour. *A Practitioner's Handbook for Real-Time Analysis*. Kluwer Academic Publishers, 1993.
24. J. P. Lehoczky, L. Sha, and Y. Ding. The Rate Monotonic Scheduling Algorithm: Exact Characterization and Average Case Behavior. In *Proceedings, IEEE Real-Time Systems Symposium*, pages 166–171, Dec. 1989.
25. J. P. Lehoczky, J. Strosnider, L. Sha, and H. Tokuda. Fixed priority scheduling theory for hard real-time systems. In *Proc. of the Third Annual Workshop on Foundations of Real-Time Computing*, pages 49–71, Oct. 1990.
26. J.Y. Leung and J. Whitehead. On the Complexity of Fixed-Priority Scheduling of Periodic, Real-Time Tasks. *Performance Evaluation*, 2(4):237–250, 1982.
27. C. L. Liu and J. Layland. Scheduling Algorithm for Multiprogramming in a Hard Real-Time Environment. *Journal of the ACM.*, 20(1):46–61, Jan. 1973.
28. C. D. Locke. Software architecture for hard real-time applications: Cyclic executives vs. fixed priority executives. *Real-Time Systems*, 4(1):37–53, March 1992.
29. A. K. Mok. *Fundamental Design Problems for the Hard Real-time Environments*. PhD thesis, MIT, May 1983.
30. M. Saksena. *Parametric Scheduling for Hard Real-Time Systems*. PhD thesis, University of Maryland, College Park, MD 20742, 1994.
31. M. Saksena and A. K. Agrawala. Temporal Analysis for Hard-Real Time Scheduling. In *Proceedings 12th International Phoenix Conference on Computers and Communications*, pages 538–544, March 1993.

32. Manas Saksena. *Parametric Scheduling for Hard Real-Time Systems.* PhD thesis, University of Maryland at College Park, 1994.
33. Manas Saksena, James da Silva, and Ashok K. Agrawala. *"Design and implementation of Maruti-II"*, chapter 4. Prentice Hall, 1995. In *Advances in Real-Time Systems*, edited by Sang H. Son.
34. K. Schwan and H. Zhou. Dynamic Scheduling of Hard Real-Time Tasks and Real-Time Threads. *IEEE Transactions on Software Engineering*, 18(8):736–748, August 1992.
35. L. Sha, R. Rajkumar, and J. P. Lehoczky. Priority Inheritance Protocols: An Approach to Real-Time Synchronization. *IEEE Transactions on Computers*, 39(9):1175–1185, September 1990.
36. K. Tindell, A. Burns, and A. Willings. An extendible approach for analyzing fixed priority hard real-time tasks. *Real-Time Systems*, 6(2), March 1994.
37. J. Xu and D. L. Parnas. On Satisfying Timing Constraints in Hard-Real-Time Systems. In *Proceedings of the ACM SIGSOFT'91 Conference on Software for Critical Systems*, pages 132–146, December 1991.
38. X. Yuan, M. Saksena, and A. Agrawala. A Decomposition Approach to Real-Time Scheduling. *Real-Time Systems*, 6(1), 1994.

Software Performance Evaluation by Models

Murray Woodside

Department of Systems and Computer Engineering
Carleton University, Ottawa, Canada
cmw@sce.carleton.ca

1 What Software Performance Evaluation Is About

To assess the performance of a software design or product on a particular platform, performance measures such as response time and throughput are determined, and compared to required values. If they miss the mark some changes may be made in the design while it is still being shaped. Early analysis and corrections save time and money and reduce the risk of project failure through performance failure, as has been argued eloquently by Smith [1] and Hesselgrave [2]. Fig. 1 shows how different performance information is connected to different aspects of software development.

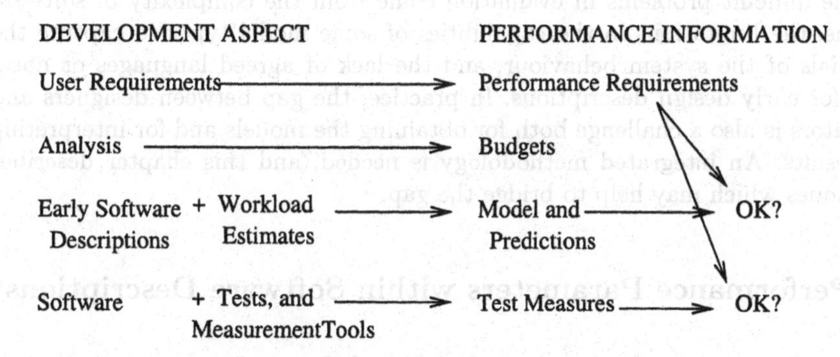

Fig. 1. Performance Information During Software Development

To manage the performance aspects of a new product, evaluation extends all through the process of development:

1. It begins with a sound and testable statement of *requirements*.
2. This may be broken down during analysis into *budgets* for subsystem responses.
3. For early analysis of a new product or new feature, some *estimates of workload demands* are made based on experience, and attached to the early design description.
4. Measured demands are used once they are available.

G. Haring et al. (Eds.): Performance Evaluation, LNCS 1769, pp. 283–304, 2000.

5. A *model* is created and validated and used to make early predictions, which may be used to recognize problems and improve the design.
6. As code is produced, *tests* are run to give better demand estimates, and finally performance measures from system performance tests, to compare to requirements.

This chapter focuses on building models for performance prediction based on information attached to the early high-level design descriptions. This is the bridge linking the expertise of the designer to that of the modeler. The design descriptions may be custom made for performance analysis, as in the execution graphs in Smith's SPE method [1], or may be created as part of the software design, as in the software CAD tools CAEDE [3] and SARA [4] and their successors such as the tools based on SDL that are described in [5].

The early design descriptions divide into two broad categories or viewpoints, which have characteristic performance parameters and steps for extracting performance models from them. A broad integrating framework connects the two designer viewpoints with the model viewpoint.

This discussion focuses on abstract simplified models. Simulation models are an alternative approach, explored for instance in MIDAS [6]. Material may be found elsewhere on performance requirements [7], measurements [8], testing [9] and on methodology for improving designs [1].

The difficult problems in evaluation come from the complexity of software designs, the limitations in the capabilities of some model types to capture the essentials of the system behaviour, and the lack of agreed languages or notations for early design descriptions. In practice, the gap between designers and evaluators is also a challenge both for obtaining the models and for interpreting the results. An integrated methodology is needed, and this chapter describes techniques which may help to bridge the gap.

2 Performance Parameters within Software Descriptions

Designers use a variety of more or less formal descriptions and notations to represent the requirements, the intended behaviour, and the design of a software system. Although these descriptions have many forms they fall into two broad categories or viewpoints, one describing structure and one describing behaviour, with a few cases that combine the two.

- A behaviour description (called a *path model* here) captures the sequence of operations of the program in response to a particular stimulus. It tends to be used more at the beginning of a project, to capture requirements and functionality.
- A description of structure (called a *module model* here) captures the design as a set of modules and relationships. It is used to define the architecture, design and deployment of the system.

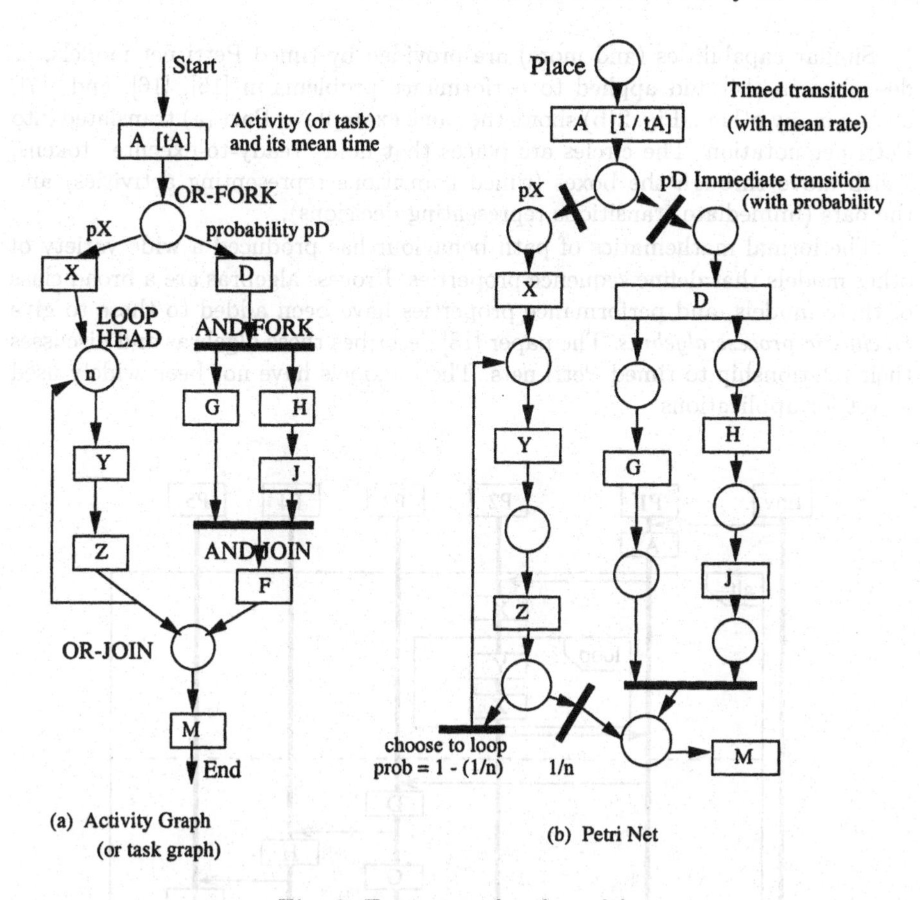

Fig. 2. Two types of path models

2.1 Typical Path Models

A path model defines the processing to be done in response to a particular class of requests, as a sequence of activities (which are the operations of the program). It can be shown directly as a task graph or activity graph, as illustrated in Fig. 2(a), and described in many works (e.g. [10]). Events and activities are defined by nodes, and predecessor-successor relationships are given by directed arcs. An activity may be "refined" by a further description by another graph. There are nodes for AND-FORK/AND-JOIN, and for OR-FORK/OR-JOIN (with the relative frequency of each branch), and for a loop (with a mean loop count). These graphs are based on activity graphs in scheduling theory, and have been widely used in performance modeling (e.g. in [11], [12], [10], [13])

Some simple requirements models define an end-to-end operation as just a single activity, with just two events, start and end, and a specified maximum delay between them. The requirements analysis process then adds detail to the path, and breaks down the overall delay into delay budgets for sub-paths.

Similar capabilities (and more) are provided by timed Petri net models, as described in [14] and applied to performance problems in [15], [16], and [17], among many others. Fig. 2(b) shows the same example as Part (a) translated into Petri net notation. The circles are places that hold "ready-to-execute" tokens, which move through the boxes (timed transitions representing activities) and the bars (immediate transitions representing decisions).

The formal mathematics of path behaviour has produced a wide variety of other models that define sequence properties. Process algebras are a broad class of these models, and performance properties have been added to these to give *stochastic process algebras.* The paper [18] describes these algebras and discusses their relationship to timed Petri nets. These models have not been widely used as yet for applications.

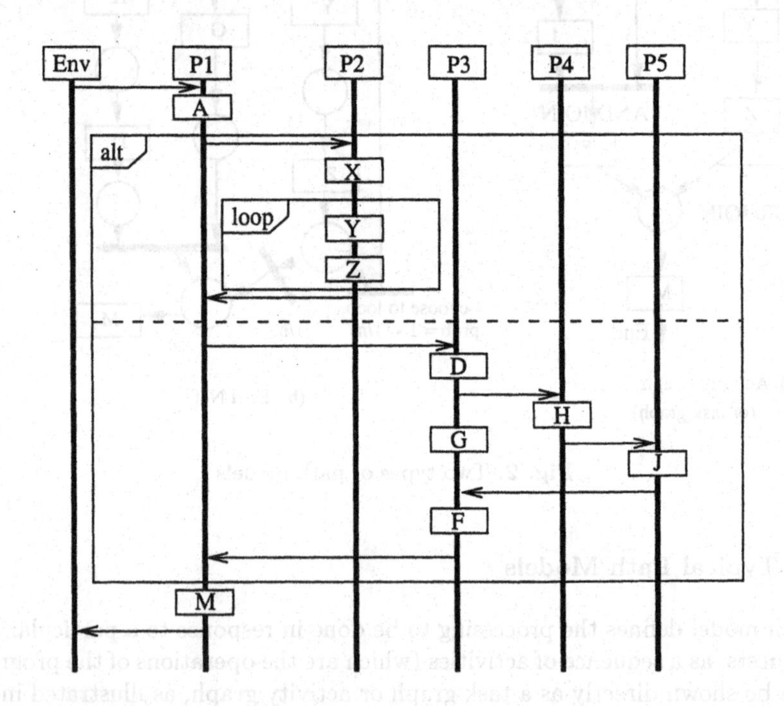

Fig. 3. A Message Sequence Chart for the Same Example, with Five Processes

From the telecommunications field another notation has emerged called Message Sequence Charts (MSCs), a standard of the International Telecommunications Union (see for instance [19] for references and an explanation of their use). A MSC defines the execution path as a sequence of messages between objects or processes. To create a MSC, each activity must be located in a process, so this is a hybrid model with some structural aspects. Fig. 3 shows the example of Fig. 2, as a MSC with processes P1 to P5 and with activities added. Horizontal arrows are messages between processes which are shown as vertical bars, with time progressing downwards. The boxes used to denote alternatives and loops are recent extensions to MSCs; the boxes for activities are not part of the standard but are convenient here. There are also arrowhead styles for different kinds of messages. MSCs have been adopted for path descriptions in the new UML (Universal Modeling Language) standard for object-oriented design descriptions [20]. MSCs have been used to identify performance requirements for responses but not (so far) for performance modeling.

2.2 Performance Properties of Execution-Path Descriptions

All the path models are sufficiently similar, from our point of view, to be considered together. They may incorporate both performance and workload measures. The performance measures may include required and predicted values for:

- delays of activities,
- end-to-end delays or response times,
- sub-path delays including synchronization delays,
- frequency of requests for the entire response or for individual activities.

and workload parameters (which will be used for model-building), such as:

- demand parameters for individual activities, including
  - the demands of an activity for operations by system devices,
  - the demands for operations by other system resources,
  - requests for logical resources such as critical sections

These quantities may be given by deterministic values, maximum or minimum values, mean values (perhaps with variances), percentiles or distributions.

The path model provides the information needed for specifying and computing end-to-end delays, for breaking an end-to-end delay into budgets for activities or sub-graphs, for calculating the holding time of a critical section, and for calculating the delay for a parallel execution between a fork and a join.

Total delay through a graph or subgraph: It is straightforward to compute the total delay for an activity graph or subgraph (see for instance [1], chapter 5). Suppose the mean delay for activity i is t_i, then:

- for activities in series, $t_{TOTAL} = \sum_i t_i$,
- for activities in a loop with count n, $t_{TOTAL}=n. \sum_i t_i$,
- for a set of alternatives with probability p_i for the ith choice, $t_{TOTAL} = \sum_i p_i t_i$,

Delay variances satisfy the same relationships as the means, provided the values of activity delays may be assumed to be independent. For a fork-join parallel section, there is a special calculation considered next. Budget calculations are just the converse process, in which a total delay is broken into parts.

Parallel sections of a program: The total delay from a fork to a join is determined by the distribution $F_i(t)$ for the total delay on each parallel sub-path $i = 1, ..., K$, which can be found from the activity delay distributions along the path. Then the total delay τ is the maximum of the sub-path delays, with the distribution $F(t) = \prod_i F_i(t)$. From the distribution the mean and variance are easily found.

Since it is often difficult to find complete information for distributions, one may prefer to use an approximation based on the mean, or the mean and variance. If one has only the means for the sub-paths, and one assumes that the *ith* delay is exponentially distributed with mean τ_i, the mean total delay is (see for example [11]):

$$\tau = \sum_{i=1}^{K} \tau_i - \sum_{i<j} [1/(\tau_i^{-1} + \tau_j^{-1}] + \sum_{i<j<k} [1/(\tau_i^{-1} + \tau_j^{-1} + \tau_k^{-1})]...$$

$$+(-1)^{K-1} \sum_{i<j<k...<z} [1/(\tau_i^{-1} + \tau_j^{-1} + \tau_k^{-1}\tau_z^{-1})] \quad (1)$$

or if the K paths all have equal mean delay τ^*, $\tau = \tau^*(1 + 1/2 + 1/3 + ... + 1/K)$. If one has means and variances for the paths, an approximation for τ and its variance is given in [13].

Resource holding times. For a logical resource like a lock, the points at which it is obtained and released are indicated in the activity graph. This specifies a sub-graph of the activities executed while holding the lock. The delay through the subgraph is the lock holding time, which is needed for estimating lock contention delays.

2.3 Module Models

Module models capture the organization of the system into subsystems and objects, and their relationships such as control, style of communications (e.g. blocking, asynchronous, data-sharing), inheritance, lists and collections, etc. Early architectural design defines a large-scale module model with just the major subsystems and how they partition the functionality among them, and later design breaks this down further to the point where the software can be programmed.

Classical structured design produces structure graphs such as Fig. 4(a), which may simply represent calls between procedures [21]. This program reads data from a file, processes it and writes an output file. Call graphs like this have been parameterized and used to build performance models, for instance by Opdahl [22].

Object-oriented designers use various forms of diagram similar to the Object Interaction Diagram ([23]) shown in Fig. 4(b), for a system with a similar purpose to part (a). The collaboration diagrams of UML are an example (described for example in [24]). In the figure, the large rectangles are objects, the small ones

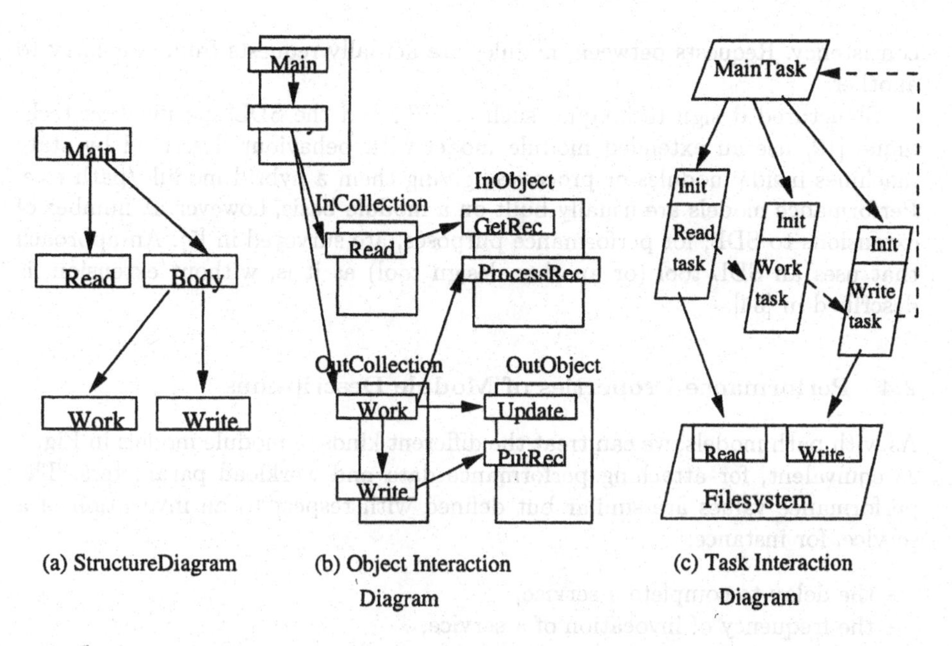

(a) StructureDiagram (b) Object Interaction Diagram (c) Task Interaction Diagram

Fig. 4. Different Kinds of Module Model

such as Read and GetRec are methods within the objects, which provide different services. Different methods do quite different things, and call different methods in other objects. Arrows in this diagram represent messages to methods, which are equivalent to call-return interactions.

Performance models created from object models have been described by Liu, Petriu and Corriveau [25], Hills, Rolia and Serrazzi [26] and by Smith and Williams [27], although the latter work depended also on a path analysis of the same system.

Concurrent task designers may use a model like the Task Interaction Diagram shown in Fig. 4(c), which describes a third system with the same goals, but implemented in five concurrent tasks. They have a pipelined structure, and have services offered by different entries such as Read and Init. The Main task initializes the pipeline for a new job through the Init entries, and sets it running; the completion of the Write task sends it an asynchronous "Finished" signal. Solid arrows here represent synchronous send-reply or remote procedure call interactions; the dashed arrow is an asynchronous message.

For communicating tasks the layered queueing model of Woodside et al [28] [29], Rolia and Sevcik [30], and Ramesh and Perros [31] is based directly on parameters added to the module structure shown in Fig. 4(c). Menasce has described an equivalent language model for client-server systems, and used it to build queueing network models [32].

An important observation is that modules in each design style may have multiple methods or entries or services; we use the term *entry* for these for consistency. Requests between modules are actually requests from one entry to another.

Structured design techniques such as [33], and the SDL specification technique [19] use an extended module model with behaviour described by state machines inside modules or processes, giving them a hybrid module/path role. Performance models are usually built on a module basis, however. A number of extensions to SDL, for performance purposes, are surveyed in [5]. An approach that uses an SDL tool (or another design tool) as it is, without extension, is described in [34].

2.4 Performance Properties of Module Descriptions

As with path models, we can treat the different kinds of module models in Fig. 4 as equivalent, for attaching performance data and workload parameters. The performance values are similar but defined with respect to an invocation of a service, for instance:

- the delay to complete a service,
- the frequency of invocation of a service,
- the CPU utilization (as a percentage) by each service and by each module as a whole,
- the request rate by the services and by entire modules, for other system services.

We can also attach workload parameters for a performance model, including:

- the CPU demand of each service, per invocation,
- overhead costs of invoking a module's services, and of the invocations it makes, per invocation of the module.
- the demands by each service for other system services,

Module parameters gain in importance as the project continues, because many measurements are made on a module basis.

The workload parameters in a module model are given for each entry, and can be expressed by a set of values $Y_i(entry)$ giving the number of operations by entity i demanded by $entry$. i can denote a device in the set DEV or another module entry in the set $ENTRIES$. The demands of the system can be reduced to just the device demands, eliminating the effect of the software structure, by recursively applying

$$Y_i(entry) = \sum_{e \in ENTRIES} Y_e(entry) Y_i(e) \qquad i \in DEV \tag{2}$$

We may call the result of applying this recursively to a given entry as $Y_i^*(entry)$. For layered systems those modules which are also operating system tasks with task resources can be kept separate by moving them out of the set $ENTRIES$ into a set $TASKS$, and treating $TASKS$ like DEV in the above elimination.

For devices with a known operation time t_i the total demand, per invocation of a top-level entry *topentry*, is $D_i(topentry)$ given by

$$D_i(topentry) = Y_i^*(topentry)t_i$$

Where there is a state machine defined for a module (as in SDL), demand parameters are defined for activities which are triggered by state changes. To obtain the entry parameters $Y_i(entry)$ the activity demands are summed, weighted by the frequency of each activity per module entry invocation.

This section has assumed that demands have some fixed value, however various factors including the choice and size of data structures will affect the demands. This was addressed early by Sholl and Booth [35]. A general approach to this question is to introduce load parameters describing how the system is to be used, which can include data size parameters, and study the dependence of the demand parameters and performance results on these load parameters. Vetland and his co-workers call this dependence "complexity functions" [36].

3 Describing the Platform and the Workload Intensity

Even when the principal goal is to evaluate a software design it must be done with reference to a platform and a workload. The platform which includes the processor, hardware details such as the bus structure, cache and peripherals, networks linking remote computers, and the supporting software (operating system, communications protocols, middleware). The hardware devices and connections become the foundation of the performance model; the supporting software creates overhead workload that must be combined with the application software. However, the platform description should be kept separate from the application, so when the application is targeted to multiple platforms it can be evaluated separately on each one.

For modeling, the operations of each device need to be specified with their characteristic service times, and the topology of the system in terms of device connectivity. Service disciplines for devices (FIFO, priority, etc) must be specified, as well as the task scheduling discipline of the operating system.

The operating system and communications software may impose some additional performance constraints, apart from their overhead of execution, through software resources such as buffer limits, flow control limits or file locking. This may require describing such software by sub-models showing the resource usage, that can be combined with the application software model. For instance a file system sub-model might be given as a module model, and a communications protocol might be described by a path model.

The platform may have a complex structure and may contribute a significantly complicated component to the overall performance model. Further, detailed modeling of the platform places more demands on the description of the software. For instance a good model of the cache needs a model of locality in the data references, which may be difficult to produce in advance of detailed design!

The workload intensity describes the intensity of user demands on the system, including the arrival rates of types of requests from users, or the numbers of users of different types.

4 Building Performance Models with Flat Resources

The term *flat resources* is used here to describe a model in which the program uses just one resource at a time (this is rarely precisely correct, but it is assumed because it gives quick simple calculations). The resources in this case are just the devices that execute the operations in the program, and the model only requires the average total time demands $D_{i,r}$ required from each resource i, during a response of a given class r.

We have already seen how these demands can be found from either a path model or a module model. In fact, over the life of the project both models are needed. At the start we often have only a path model; then (as the architecture is defined) we use a module model to give the module interface overhead, and finally we may have a module model alone based on workload measurements (which tend to be on a module basis).

Very quick back-of-envelope calculations from the demands $D_{i,r}$ can give average capacity constraints and response time bounds, sometimes called bottleneck calculations. For example, with a single response class, throughput cannot exceed the smallest value (over i) of $1/D_i$.

4.1 Product Form Queueing Models

If product-form queueing is assumed, then the same demand values are enough to also give contention results by well-known, economical calculations. Smith develops queueing models from path descriptions in the methodology she calls SPE [1]. SPE puts special emphasis on early analysis for capacity planning based on "execution graphs" (which are similar to the present activity graphs) and on usability. In its simplest form, the approach is to estimate the demands of each activity for operations either by devices, or by software services (such as a file operation). Operations by demands are summed to give the total demand for one response. If there are several execution graphs the total demands for each one are found separately. A separable queueing model is constructed with a class for each execution graph, and the model is evaluated for average performance.

Several features are included to assist in building complex models. Demands for software services are estimated first (e.g., how many file operations of a certain size are needed), and then the demands made by each file operation for CPU cycles, messages to a file server, right down to disk operations, can be found separately and substituted later. Libraries of demands can be maintained for different subsystems and servers. A complex portion of an execution graph can be represented by a single high-level activity, which references a separate graph for the details, and this can be extended to any number of levels of refinement. Parallel operations and logical resources like locks can be included in the execution graph and queueing approximations for locks are suggested.

Pure module-based modeling has also been used to develop queueing models. Opdahl, in [22], uses them to study the sensitivity of system performance to certain parameters of the modules, such as the request demands for a subsidiary module. Menasce, in [32], defines the modules of a client-server system with a language called CLISSPE, that includes performance parameters, and derives a separable queueing model from them.

Path and module information were combined to capture inter-object overheads in [27], which describes an object-oriented extension of SPE and also builds separable queueing models.

4.2 More Complex Cases of Flat Resources

Product-form queueing assumptions are usually violated in some degree. If service time distributions are important, or there are priority disciplines, or routing between resources is not random, then extended queueing models may be helpful. When there are deadlines to be met a completely different line of attack is appropriate. For flat resource systems, a schedulability analysis can be performed to show that a response can, or cannot meet its deadline, provided the demands for each request for service are deterministic or can be bounded [37].

4.3 Parallel Activities

An example described by Heidelberger and Trivedi in [11] shows how a path model may define a flat extended queueing model. N programs loop endlessly as shown in Fig. 5(a). The acitivities all share a set of M processors (which share memory and are scheduled together) and four disks. Fig. 5(b) shows the

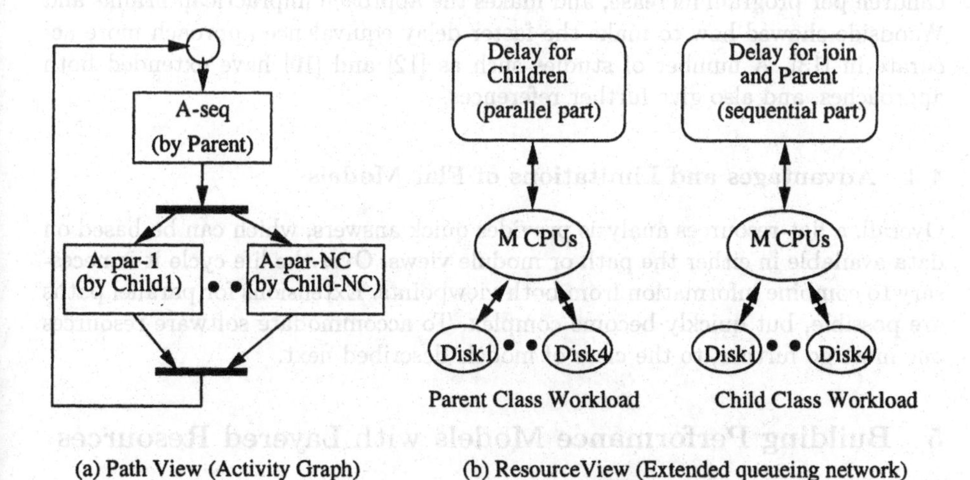

Fig. 5. Program with Alternating Sequential and Parallel Sections

queueing model with the devices and the classes of processes which run on them. The "Parent" processes execute activity A_{seq} with demand $D_{CPU,seq}$ at the CPU, and demand $D_{d,seq,i}$ at Disk i, and then enter a delay for the parallel part for that one group of children. The "Child" processes have demand $D_{CPU,par,n}$ at the CPU and $D_{d,i,par,n}$ at Disk i, and then wait for the synchronization delay, and the delay for the sequential part.

Two extended queueing models were compared, using product- form queueing networks and either delay equivalence or a kind of state decomposition. The delay equivalence approach is based on Fig. 5(b). There is a single queueing network model with a Parent class and NC Child classes, with N Parent customers and $N * NC$ Child customers. The behaviour of each class is shown in a separate diagram. For the Child class, the "Delay for Parent" was estimated as the mean time for a parent process between joining and forking again, (i.e. between leaving the Child surrogate delay and re-entering it), found from the solution for the Parent class. For the Parent class, the "Delay for Children" was estimated as the mean delay between the fork and the join, calculated from the Path model on the left in the Fig., and the equation (1). The parallel sub-path delays are assumed to be exponentially distributed.

In the decomposition approach the same model, without the delay blocks shown in the figure, was solved with different numbers $NPar$ of active parent tasks and $NChild(i)$ of type-i active child tasks, representing all the possible states of the two classes. From the class throughputs the mean rate of occurrence of events that give a change of the state $(NPar, NCh(1), ..NCh(NC))$ was found, giving the rate parameters of a a Markov Chain model over the states.

In [11] it was found that both methods give useful results, but the decomposition was more accurate. On the other hand, the number of states ($NPar$, $NCh(1), ...$) in the decomposition explodes as the number of programs and the children per program increase, and makes the approach impractical. Franks and Woodside showed how to make the faster delay equivalence approach more accurate in [13]. A number of studies such as [12] and [10] have extended both approaches, and also give further references.

4.4 Advantages and Limitations of Flat Models

Overall, a flat-resources analysis provides quick answers, which can be based on data available in either the path or module views. Over the life cycle it is necessary to combine information from both viewpoints. Extensions for parallel paths are possible, but quickly become complex. To accommodate software resources one must go further, to the class of models described next.

5 Building Performance Models with Layered Resources

When the software contains logical resources then a program may possess several of them at once, and this gives rise to resource layering. We can see how a layered resource enters a design by considering a critical section. Fig. 6 shows a series

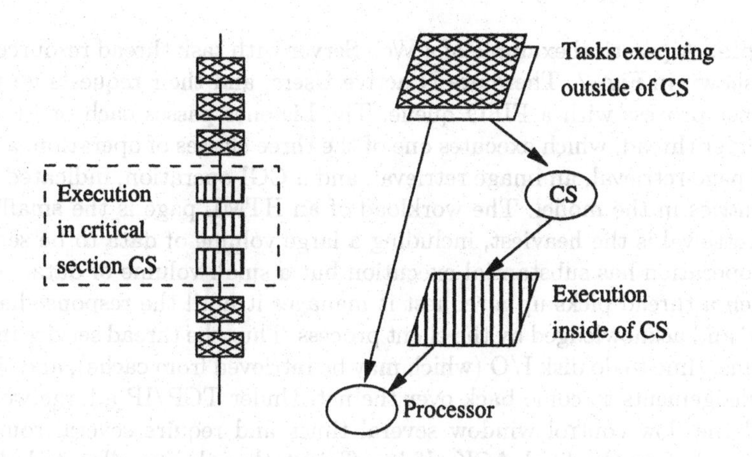

Fig. 6. A Critical Section Leading to Layered Resources

of activities, with the central three activities being in a critical section named "CS". On the right side, the Fig. shows the program divided into two pseudo-tasks, one for the execution outside CS and one for the execution inside. When it reaches the point of needing CS, the program stops and goes through a resource request. The resource partitions the task workload into two parts.

Software resources include critical sections, locks on data, buffer pools, window flow control tokens, and task thread resources. There are many examples of extended queueing models for software resources, beginning with a model of a critical section in [38] and including locks in [1], multi-level window flow control tokens in [39], and task thread resources in [40], [41], [13], and in chapter 7 of [42].

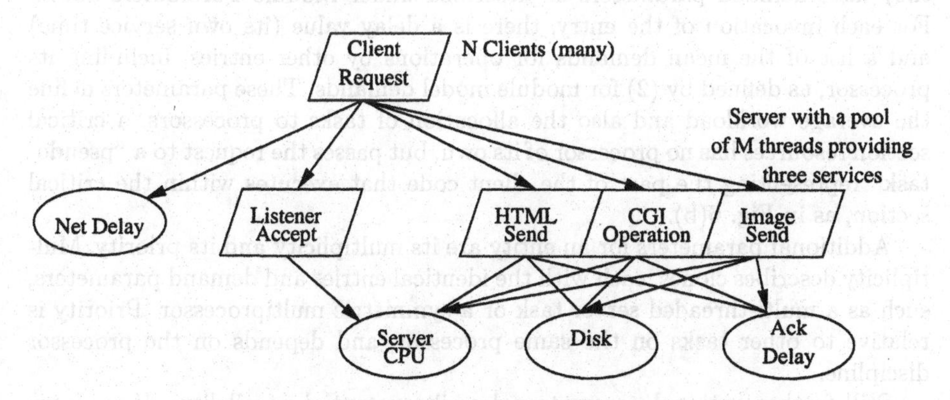

Fig. 7. Layered Queueing Model for a Web Server [41]

Example. A practical example of a Web Server with task thread resources from [41] is shown in Fig. 7. There are N active Users, and their requests go first to a Listener process with a FIFO queue. The Listener passes each one to a free Web Server thread, which executes one of the three classes of operation: a simple HTML page retrieval, an image retrieval, and a CGI operation, indicated by the three entries in the model. The workload of an HTML page is the smallest; an image retrieval is the heaviest, including a large volume of data to be sent, and a CGI operation has substantial execution but a small volume of data.

When a thread picks up a request it manages it until the response has been received and acknowledged by the client process. Thus the thread service includes CPU time, time to do disk I/O (which may be retrieved from cache), and time for acknowledgements to come back over the net. Under TCP/IP a large web-page may fill the flow control window several times and require several round-trip net delays before the final ACK. If insufficient threads are allocated then all the threads may become busy waiting for the time to transfer data back to the clients. In these cases the CPU and Disk have low utilization yet the server pool is saturated.

5.1 Layered Queueing Formalism

A layered queueing model uses a single kind of entity called a "task" to represent devices, servers, customers and software resources. The web server in Fig. 7 plays a server role to entities that request it (the Users), and a client role to entities it uses itself (the CPU, Disk and Net). Client entities can make three kinds of requests to their servers: blocking (as shown in Fig. 7 – the client waits for a reply), asynchronous (there is no reply) and forwarding (the request is being passed on and the reply should be sent to the original requester). The Listener could have been modeled as forwarding the service request to the Server.

An entity ("task") has one or more entries which provide its services and they have demand parameters as described under Module Parameters above. For each invocation of the entry, there is a delay value (its own service time) and a list of the mean demands for operations by other entries, including its processor, as defined by (2) for module model demands. These parameters define the average workload and also the allocation of tasks to processors. a critical section resources has no processor of its own, but passes the request to a "pseudo-task" representing the part of the client code that executes within the critical section, as in Fig. 6(b).

Additional parameters for an entity are its multiplicity and its priority. Multiplicity describes clones, each with the identical entries and demand parameters, such as a multi-threaded server task or a symmetric multiprocessor. Priority is relative to other tasks on the same processor, and depends on the processor discipline.

Still further optional parameters describe potential parallelism. If an entry can send a reply before completing all the execution, its demands are divided into a first phase (with the sender blocked) and a second phase (in parallel with the sender, after the reply) in [28]. Parallelism within a task has been introduced by Franks and Woodside in [13] by embedding an activity graph in a task. The graph can define forking to parallel sub-threads which make requests in parallel. Using similar ideas, a class of Petri nets was modeled by layered queues by Rolia and Sevcik in [43] and asynchronous requests with joins were modeled by Sheikh et. al. in [44].

A model of a complex concurrent industrial application which demonstrates the ability of the approach to scale up to many object classes, and to represent critical sections and shared memory, is given by Shousha, Petriu, Jalnapurkar and Kennedy in [45].

Tools. Computational approximations for layered queueing models have been based on standard methods for extended queueing networks with simultaneous resource possession, and mean value analysis. They have been described by Woodside and others in [28], [29], by Rolia and Sevcik in [30], by Petriu and Woodside in [46] and by Ramesh and Perros in [31].

The Layered Queueing Network Solver described in [28], [13] includes approximations for parallel activities and several kinds of task interactions, an environment for multi-run experiments over parameters, graphical display of models and tools for automated model-building [47], which can be integrated with design tools ([48], [34]).

5.2 Web Server Example

In [41], Dilley, Freidrich, Jin, and Rolia analyzed a large web server with the model shown in Fig. 7, that gave unexpected response times. At night the number of users would drop but the server response times would increase. This work was done after the system was implemented and was based on measurements on the modules, there was no path analysis. The model was validated against two months of operating data from a web server, and predicted mean response times seen at the server (between receiving the request and finishing dealing with it) within about 20%, and with the correct relative magnitudes of delays for HTML, CGI and image responses.

The thread holding time in this system is dominated by waiting for acknowledgements from the Clients, whenever the net delays are long. Then the client response time becomes large and unstable and increases rapidly with larger net delays, or numbers of clients. For example, if there are 10 ACK delays of 300 ms each, the thread service time is at least 3 sec. What was happening at night is that there were fewer requests, but they were coming from further away, from the other side of the planet, and the increase in net delay more than offset the decrease in numbers.

Notice that very large numbers of threads may be demanded in this case. If there were 100 requests per second, even if the processor and disk can handle them comfortably it will take at least 300 threads to handle the requests at 100% thread utilization, and considerably more than this (perhaps a thousand) for good service.

5.3 Value of Layered Resource Models

The advantages of layered models are:

- they handle any depth of layering without having to create customized extended queueing approximations,
- they are scalable. Models of hundreds of tasks can be solved with little effort, with existing tools, and for simple enough structures it can be thousands of tasks,
- they have a small semantic gap for software engineering. that is, they are understandable, since they so closely resemble module models of concurrent systems. They take a module model with parameters, and solve it.
- they are almost always applicable, since it seems that most software designs are actually layered, for safety and understandability.

5.4 General (Unlayered) Resource Systems

For general resource systems with no layered structure an appropriate approach would be to use timed Petri nets or perhaps stochastic process algebras. For these approaches a Markov chain model is created automatically from the description, and solved. The good aspect of this is that the model building is automatic (as is also true of layered queueing models), and the full power of a very general descriptive language is available. The bad aspect is that the Markov chain models do not scale up well. They quickly explode, and this has severely limited this approach, and the analysis of general resource systems, so far.

Nonetheless there are numerous applications of Petri nets to performance. Cherkasova, Kotov and Rokicki [17] used high-level Petri Nets to describe a complex industrial Transaction Processing (TP) system. Their model is too large to reproduce here, but it consisted of a top-level sub-model for the flow of a transaction class representing a standard TP benchmark, a sub-model for data access operations (including locking and storage operations) that is parameterized for the different kinds of operations, a page cleaning sub-model, two sub-models describing the disk interface and devices, and two sub-models for communications in multiprocessor systems, that introduce network access and a model of the interconnection substrate. The tool they used could include code segments and data to represent program logic, and simulated the final model for performance results. They also validated their model against data on a real system, with excellent agreement. The model predicted the delay at a near-capacity throughput within 5%.

5.5 Model-Based Design Analysis

Once one has a model that can be solved quickly, one can carry out higher-level analyses of sensitivity, optimization, etc. This is a large topic that is just beginning to bear fruit, but a few examples are sensitivity analysis by Opdahl [22] and Sheikh and Woodside [49], scalability analysis by Jogalekar and Woodside [50], and threading policy analysis by Litoiu et al. [51].

6 Combining and Navigating Between Viewpoints

Integration of designer information and performance information requires some kind of framework. An example was described in [52], which helps to understand what is needed. It gives support for navigating between the path and module viewpoints, which are familiar to designers and which were described in earlier sections, and the performance model, which is familiar to the performance analyst. It was called MPR, for Maps, Paths and Resources, corresponding to the present viewpoints of modules (the maps describing locations in the system), paths, and performance models (describing contention for resources). It defines the viewpoints as different *perspectives* on a central reality, represented by the triangle in the center of Fig. 8. From this is identifies relationships which can be used to translate parameters and results between views. Fig. 8 shows some of the typical kinds of information exported from each viewpoint, and the information it imports from others.

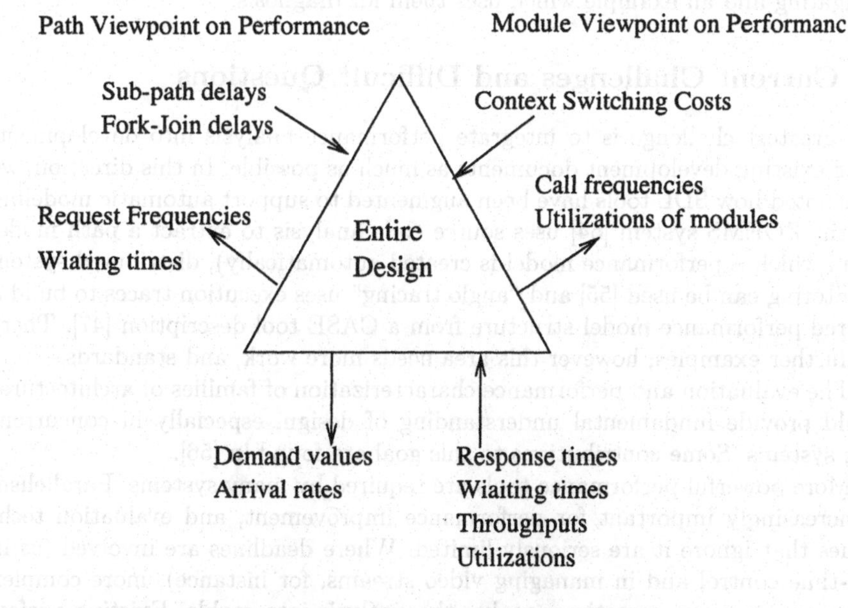

Fig. 8. The Integrating Framework, with Three Viewpoints M, P, and R, and Information Exchanges Between Them

A framework like this could have other uses. It could be extended to include reliability aspects and other software quality viewpoints, which designers must also consider.

Another similar framework was described by Kruchten for architectural design (not necessarily for performance), using "4 + 1" views [53]. His views are

(1) functional design (outside our scope), (2) concurrency and synchronization (software resources), (3) physical (hardware resources), (4) "development", the allocation of activities to modules (path/module relationships), and the fifth is Use Cases, which is effectively our path view. It is interesting that Kruchten regards the last view as additional redundant information, while for performance analysis it is central.

Operations Between Viewpoints Many design operations combine information in two viewpoints. For example dividing the functions among the modules can be seen as allocating activities to modules. Similarly modules are allocated to tasks and processors, and interactions are allocated to links between devices.

Navigating Between Viewpoints When the different viewpoints are brought together in a framework like MPR, it becomes possible to relate effects that are visible in one viewpoint to causes in another. The paper gives heuristics for navigating and an example which uses them for diagnosis.

7 Current Challenges and Difficult Questions

The greatest challenge is to integrate performance analysis into development, using existing development documents as much as possible. In this direction, we have noted how SDL tools have been augmented to support automatic modeling [5], the POEMS system [54] uses source code analysis to extract a path model (from which a performance model is created automatically), distributed system monitoring can be used [55] and "angio tracing" uses execution traces to build a layered performance model structure from a CASE tool description [47]. There are further examples, however this area needs more work, and standards.

The evaluation and performance characterization of families of architectures would provide fundamental understanding of design, especially in concurrent task systems. Some contributions to this goal are found in [56].

More powerful performance tools are required by many systems. Parallelism is increasingly important for performance improvement, and evaluation techniques that ignore it are seriously limited. Where deadlines are involved (as in real-time control and in managing video streams, for instance), more complex software structures sometimes makes the analysis intractable. Existing performance tools may be enhanced by combining them in an environment like IMSE [57] which allows flexibility in the choice of model technique. IMSE also included an "Experimenter" component which supports higher level analysis, such as searches for better parameter values or allocations.

Hardware/software co-design is a new problem which may require new tools.

We need to go beyond evaluation into "engineering", including design patterns with known properties, and design improvement principles and techniques. Some principles and techniques are reported in [1]. Others will emerge, and more use could be made of models to pinpoint the cause of a problem and suggest a cure. This leads in the direction of design optimization techniques.

8 Summary

The many different approaches to formulating models of software have been organized into two viewpoints for describing software, based around paths and modules. Within each viewpoint the differences between descriptions are relatively minor. Both viewpoints are needed; the path viewpoint does more to support early analysis, the module viewpoint is associated more with design and the final product. Parameters for many kinds of models are easily obtained from workload demands attached to activities or modules.

Combining these two viewpoints with a third one for resources and performance models gives an integrating framework which helps to understand performance methodologies. Many of them use paths as the dominant viewpoint, and insufficient attention has, perhaps, been paid to module based information. A framework like MPR is needed as a guide to structuring an integrated software and performance methodology.

Layered resource usage appears to be common in distributed systems, and layered queue modeling is a promising approach to these systems.

The biggest challenge is to create an integrated methodology between software developers and performance evaluators. In this sense the integrating framework may be more important than the details of which model is used. In practice another difficulty is found in obtaining good quality estimates of exeuction-time costs of operations. The best information available must be used, including estimates from experience and measurements as they become available.

References

1. C.U. Smith, *Performance Engineering of Software Systems.* Addison-Wesley, 1990.
2. M. Hesselgrave, "Avoiding the software performance crisis," in *Proc. 1st Int. Workshop on Software and Performance (WOSP98)*, pp. 78–79, Oct 1998. ACM order no. 448983.
3. R.J.A. Buhr, G.M. Karam, C.J. Hayes, and C.M. Woodside, "Software CAD: A revolutionary approach," *Trans. on Software Engineering*, vol. 15, pp. 235–249, March 1989.
4. G. Estrin et. al., "SARA (system ARchitects' Apprentice): Modeling, analysis and simulation support for design of concurrent systems," *IEEE Trans. on Software Engineering*, vol. SE-12, pp. 293–311, Feb 1986.
5. A. Mitschele-Thiel and B. Muller-Clostermann, "Performance engineering of SDL/MSC systems," *Computer Networks and ISDN Systems*, 1998. (to appear).
6. R.L. Bagrodia and C.-C. Shen, "MIDAS: integrated design and simulation of distributed systems," *IEEE Trans. on Software Engineering*, vol. 17, pp. 1042–1058, October 1991.
7. B.A. Nixon, "Managing performance requirements for information systems," in *Proc. 1st Int. Workshop on Software and Performance (WOSP98)*, pp. 131–144, Oct 1998. ACM order no. 448983.
8. R. Jain, *The Art of Computer Systems Performance Analysis.* John Wiley & Sons Inc., 1991.

9. F.I. Vokolos and E.J. Weyuker, "Performance testing of software systems," in *Proc. 1st Int. Workshop on Software and Performance (WOSP98)*, pp. 80–87, Oct 1998. ACM order no. 448983.
10. W.W. Chu, C-M. Sit, and K.K. Leung, "Task response time for real-time distributed systems with resource contentions," *IEEE Trans. on Software Engineering*, vol. 17, pp. 1076–1092, October 1991.
11. P. Heidelberger and K.S. Trivedi, "Analytic queueing models for programs with internal concurrency," *IEEE Transactions on Computers*, vol. C-32, pp. 73–82, January 1983.
12. A. Thomasian and P. Bay, "Analytic queuing network models for parallel processing of task systems," *IEEE Transactions on Computers*, vol. C-35, December 1986.
13. R. Franks and C. Woodside, "Performance of multi-level client-server systems with parallel service operations," in *Proc. 1st Int. Workshop on Software and Performance (WOSP98)*, (Santa Fe, NM, USA), October 1998. ACM order no. 448983.
14. K. Jensen and G. Rozenberg, *High-Level Petri Nets*. Springer for Science, 1980.
15. D. Peng and K.G. Shin, "Modeling of concurrent task execution in a distributed system for real-time control," *IEEE Trans. on Computers*, vol. C-36, pp. 500–516, April 1987.
16. H. Beilner, J. Mater, and N. Weissenberg, "Towards a performance modelling environment: News on HIT," in *Modeling Techniques and Tools for Computer Performance Evaluation*, pp. 57–75, 233 Spring Street, New York, N.Y. 10013: Plenum Press, 1989.
17. L. Cherkasova, V. Kotov, and T. Rokicki, "On scalable net modeling of OLTP," in *Proc. 5th Int. Wkshp. on Petri Nets and Performance Models*, (Toulouse, France), pp. 270–279, October 1993.
18. N. Gotz, U. Herzog, and M. Rettelbach, "Multiprocessor and distributed system design: The integration of functional specification and performance analysis using stochastic process algebras," in *Performance Evaluation of Computer and Communication Systems*, Springer Verlag, 1993.
19. A. Olsen et al., *Systems Engineering Using SDL-92*. North-Holland, 1998.
20. Rational Software Inc. et al., *Unified Modeling Language Notation Guide*. 1998. (Web document available at http://www.rational.com/uml/html/notation).
21. R.S. Pressman, *Software Engineering, A Practitioner's Approach*. McGraw-Hill, 1996. fourth edition.
22. A.L. Opdahl, "Sensitivity analysis of combined software and hardware performance models: Open queueing networks," in *Computer Performance Evaluation - Modeling Techniques and Tools*, pp. 257–271, Springer-Verlag, Sept 1992. (Proc. 6th Int. Conf on Modeling Techniques and Tools).
23. G. Booch, *Object Oriented Design, with Applications*. The Benjamin/Cummings Publishing Co. Inc., 1991.
24. M. F. with K. Scott, *UML Distilled - Applying the Standard Object Modelling Language*. Addison-Wesley Longman, 1997.
25. D. Jennifer Liu and J.P. Corriveau, "Performance modelling of concurrent oo systems," in *Proceedings of 17th International Conference on Technology of Object-Oriented Languages and Systems (TOOLS USA '95)*, (Santa Barbara), pp. 241–253, Aug 1995.
26. G. Hills, J. Rolia, and G. Serrazzi, "Performance engineering of distributed software process architectures," in *Computer Performance Evaluation - Modeling Techniques and Tools*, pp. 357–371, Springer-Verlag, LNCS, 1995. (Proc. 8th Int. Conf on Modeling Techniques and Tools).

27. C.U. Smith and L.G. Williams, "Performance engineering evaluation of object-oriented systems with SPEED," in *Computer Performance Evaluation - Modeling Techniques and Tools*, pp. 135–154, Springer-Verlag, LNCS 1245, June 1997. (Proc. 9th Int. Conf on Modeling Techniques and Tools).
28. C.M. Woodside, J.E. Neilson, D.C. Petriu, and S. Majumdar, "The stochastic rendezvous network model for performance of synchronous client-server-like distributed software," *IEEE Transactions on Computer*, vol. 44, pp. 20–34, January 1995.
29. R. Franks, A. Hubbard, S. Majumdar, J. Neilson, D. Petriu, J. Rolia, and C. Woodside, "A Toolset for performance engineering and software design of client-server systems," *Performance Evaluation*, vol. 24, pp. 117–135, November 1995. Also as technical report SCE-94-14, June 1994.
30. J.A. Rolia and K.C. Sevcik, "The method of layers," *IEEE Trans. on Software Engineering*, vol. 21, pp. 689–700, August 1995.
31. S. Ramesh and H.G. Perros, "A multi-layer client-server queueing network model with synchronous and asynchronous messages," in *Proc. 1st Int. Workshop on Software and Performance (WOSP98)*, pp. 107–119, Oct 1998. ACM order no. 448983.
32. D.A. Menasce and H. Gomaa, "On a language based method for software performance engineering of client/server systems," in *Proc. 1st Int. Workshop on Software and Performance (WOSP98)*, pp. 63–69, Oct 1998. ACM order no. 448983.
33. D.J. Hatley and I.A. Pirbhai, *Strategies for Real-Time System Specification*. New York, NY 10014: Dorset House Publishing Co., Inc., 1987.
34. Hesham El-Sayed, D. Cameron, M. Woodside, "Automated performance modeling from scenarios and SDL designs of Telecom systems," in *Proc. of Int. Symposium on Software Engineering for Proc. Parallel and Distributed Systems (PDSE98)*, (Kyoto), April 1998.
35. H.A. Sholl and T.L. Booth, "Software performance modeling using computation structures," *IEEE Transactions on Software Engineering*, vol. 1, December 1975.
36. V. Vetland, P. Hughes, and A. Solvberg, "Improved parameter capture for simulation based on composite work models of software," in *Proceedings of the 1993 Summer Computer Simulation Conference*, July 1993.
37. S.T. Levy and A.K. Agrawala, *Real-Time System Design*. New York: McGraw-Hill, 1990.
38. S.C. Agrawal and J.P. Buzen, "The aggregate server method for analyzing serialization delays in computer systems," *ACM Trans. on Computer Systems*, vol. 1, pp. 116–143, May 1983.
39. H. S. Fdida and A. Wilk, "Semaphore queues: Modeling multilayered window flow control mechanisms," *IEEE Trans. on Communications*, vol. COM-38, pp. 929–937, July 1990.
40. J.E. Neilson, C.M. Woodside, D.C. Petriu, and S. Majumdar, "Software bottlenecking in client-server systems and rendezvous networks," *IEEE Transactions on Software Engineering*, vol. 21, pp. 776–782, September 1995.
41. J. Dilley, R. Friedrich, T. Jin, and J.A. Rolia, "Measurement tools and modeling techniques for evaluating web server performance," in *Proc. 9th Int. Conf. on Modelling Techniques and Tools*, (St. Malo, France), pp. 155–168, June 1997.
42. D.A. Menasce, V.A.F. Almeida, and L.W. Dowdy, *Capacity Planning and Performance Modeling*. Englewood Cliffs, New Jersey 07632: Prentice Hall PTR, 1994.
43. J.A. Rolia and K.C. Sevcik, "Fast performance estimates for a class of generalized stochastic Petri Nets," in *Proc. 6th Int. Conf. on Modelling Techniques and Tools for Performance Evaluation*, (Edinburgh, Scotland), pp. 31–47, September 1992.

44. F. Sheikh, J. Rolia, P. Garg, S. Frolund, and A. Shepherd, "Layered modelling of large scale distributed applications," in *Proc. 1st World Congress on Systems Simulation, Workshop on Quality of Service Modeling*, (Singapore), Sept. 1997.
45. C. Shousha, D.C. Petriu, A. Jalnapurkar, and K. Ngo, "Applying performance modeling to a telecommunication system," in *Proc. 1st Int. Workshop on Software and Performance (WOSP98)*, pp. 1–6, Oct 1998. ACM order no. 448983.
46. D.C. Petriu and C.M. Woodside, "Approximate mean value analysis for Markov model of software client/server systems," in *Proc. Third IEEE Symposium on Parallel and Distributed Processing*, (Dallas, Texas), pp. 322–329, December 1991.
47. C. Hrischuk, J.A. Rolia, and C.M. Woodside, "Automatic generation of a software performance model using an object-oriented prototype," in *Proc. of Third Int. Workshop on Modeling, Analysis and Simulation of Computer and Telecommunication Systems (MASCOTS '95)*, (Durham, NC), pp. 399–409, January 1995.
48. B. M. Woodside, C. Hrishuk and S. Bayarov, "A wideband approach to integrating performance prediction into a software design environment," in *Proc. Int. Workshop on Software and Performance (WOSP98)*, (Santa Fe, NM, USA), pp. 31–41, October 1998. ACM order no. 448983.
49. C. W. F. Sheikh, "Sensitivity analysis of performance predictions of distributed application models," in *Proc. of Second Int. Symposium on Sensitivity Analysis of Model Output*, (Venice), April 1998.
50. P.P. Jogalekar and C.M. Woodside, "Evaluating the scalability of distributed systems," in *Proc. 31st Hawaii Int. Conf. on System Sciences*, vol. 7, (Hawaii, USA), pp. 7–524 to 7–531, January 1998.
51. M. Litoiu, J. Rolia, and G. Serazzi, "Designing process replication and threading policies: a quantitative approach," in *Proc. 10th International Conference on Modelling Techniques and Tools for Computer Performance Evaluation (Tools '98)*, (Palma de Mallorca, Spain), Sept. 1998.
52. C.M. Woodside, "A three-view model for performance engineering of concurrent software," *IEEE Transactions on Software Engineering*, vol. 21, pp. 754–767, September 1995.
53. P.B. Kruchten, "The 4+1 view model of architecture," *IEEE Software*, vol. 12, no. 6, pp. 42–50, 1995.
54. Ewa Deelman et. al., "Poems: End-to-end performance design of large parallel adaptive computational systems," in *Proc. Int. Workshop on Software and Performance (WOSP98)*, (Santa Fe, NM, USA), pp. 18 – 30, October 1998. ACM order no. 448983.
55. F. ElRayes, J. Rolia, and R. Friedrich, "The performance impact of workload characterization for distributed applications using arm," in *Proc. Computer Measurement Group (CMG '98)*, (Anaheim, California, USA), Dec. 1998.
56. *Proc. 1st Int. Workshop on Software and Performance (WOSP98)*. Santa Fe, N.M., USA, Oct. 1998. ACM order no. 448983.
57. R. Pooley, "The integrated modeling support environment," in *Proc. 5th Int. Conf on Modeling Techniques and Tools*, Feb 1991.

Performance Analysis of Database Systems

Alexander Thomasian

Dept. of Computer Science and Eng.
University of Connecticut, 191 Auditorium Rd.,
Storrs, CT 06269
athomas@uconnvm.uconn.edu

1 Introduction

Database management systems (DBMSs) handle data for commercial applications, as well as scientific and engineering data, geographical information systems, images and videos, etc. We are mainly concerned with relational databases, since it is the prevalent database technology which in some cases underlies object-oriented databases [92].

A subset of the external world, which is of interest, may be represented by the *entity-relationship -ER* model [92], e.g., where the entities are students, courses, professors and an example of a relationship is student enrollments, i.e., a student taking a course taught by a professor at a given time and classroom. An ER model can be directly mapped onto a relational database, which consists of *tables* comprising rows and columns [92]. The table for students has multiple rows, one row per student. Each row consists of multiple columns, which correspond to student attributes, such as name, student social security number (SSN), etc. Student names may not be unique, while student SSNs are unique and serve as the *primary key* for the table. The table for student enrollments may consist of student SSN, course number, classroom, grade, etc. The student SSN is a *foreign key*, which links the enrollments table with the students table.

Operations on relational databases can be specified via a *relational algebra* [92], whose major operators are: *select*, which selects a subset of the rows of a table meeting a certain criterion, e.g., select students whose GPA is greater than 3.5; *project*, which picks out a subset of columns in a table; and *join*.

The simplest form of join is the *equijoin*, which concatenates rows of two tables with equal values in the join columns, e.g., joining the aforementioned tables based on student SSNs to determine the names of students taking various courses. Basic relational algebraic operations result in tables, i.e., relational operators can be applied recursively.

Operations on relational databases are mainly specified by the SQL set-oriented query language, which is first translated to directed graphs with relational algebra operations as its nodes. *Query optimization* is then applied to find a low-cost method to evaluate the query, which is then converted to executable code.

DBMS performance is especially important for *online transaction processing -OLTP* applications with stringent response time requirements at high throughputs, e.g., airline reservation systems. The relational database model is especially

G. Haring et al. (Eds.): Performance Evaluation, LNCS 1769, pp. 305–327, 2000.

attractive for decision support applications. Ad hoc queries tend to access large volumes of data, since by their nature they are not adequately supported by indexes (see Section 7). This has led to highly parallel database machines to make the processing of such queries feasible [89], [29].

Database performance is affected by hardware resources, the workload, database design, how well the database is tuned, the query optimizer (in relational databases), the buffer management policy, etc. For given hardware resources performance can be improved via balanced allocation of data on disks, appropriate sharing of buffer space, transaction scheduling, etc. The mean response time of the disk subsystem can be minimized by balancing disk utilization via *striping*, i.e., allocating successive chunks of a file on successive disks. Parity blocks are used in RAID5 disk arrays to prevent data loss when a single disk fails [14]. Analytic solutions to evaluate disk array performance are reviewed in [118].

Databases utilize complex data structures and algorithms, which makes their performance evaluation quite complex. Simplifying assumptions are usually made in most performance studies and more importantly by query optimizers (see Section 8), e.g., all values in a column occur equally frequently, rows in a table are accessed uniformly, etc. *Majorization theory* [79] is used in [20] to investigate "the effect of nonrandom placement, nonuniformity, and dependencies of database values on database design and database performance evaluation".

There are several database benchmarks, most of which are intended for relational databases [46]. Unfortunately these benchmarks reflect the speed of hardware, the efficiency of systems software, and the proficiency of the benchmarking team in tuning the system. The key performance measure in database benchmarks is the maximum system throughput at which a certain percentile of transaction response time does not exceed a prespecified value. More detailed performance measures are required to compare the performance of DBMS products. For example, the number of page references required to access an object, the hit ratio of the database buffer, and the probability of lock conflict, which reflect the efficiency of *access path*, the buffer manager, and the locking protocol, respectively.

A comprehensive methodology to evaluate database performance is proposed in [102], which classifies performance models as follows: (i) evaluation models: as parameters for a specific design are varied; (ii) selection models: select a design with best performance; (iii) optimization models: select the set of parameters which optimize performance. Obviously, type (ii) models can be based on type (i) models and type (iii) models on type (ii) models. A more detailed discussion of the application of this methodology appears in Section 9.

The literature on database performance is vast and includes performance studies of file systems, network databases, and hierarchical databases [126]. Relational database performance is emphasized in this study. The performance of concurrency control methods is covered in [116] (see also the accompanying article by the author).

This chapter is organized as follows. In Section 2 we consider performance issues in file structures. In Sections 3 and 4 we discuss models for evaluating

OLTP and query processing performance. This is followed by performance issues related to the database buffer, logging and checkpointing, database design, and query optimization in Sections 5-8. Analysis of the overall performance of database systems appears in Section 9. Data sharing, client-server and shared-nothing multicomputer systems are discussed in Sections 10-12. Data mining and multidimensional indexing are discussed in Sections 13-14. Conclusions appear in Section 15.

2 Data Storage Representation and File Structures

Network and hierarchical databases can be considered to be linked lists on disk [126]. A generalized model for such database organizations and cost equations for database access are presented in [131]. Relational databases tend to have a much simpler implementation (even at the physical level) than network and hierarchical databases, e.g., tables, possibly indexed by one or more B+ trees [69].

The performance of list structures is determined by the number of comparisons required to find a list item. Since list items are usually not accessed uniformly, the number of comparisons required can be reduced significantly by ordering them according to their frequency of access. Since these frequencies are not known a priori, a "move-to-front" policy provides a self-organizing list structure. The mean number of comparisons required is $0.5 + \sum_{i,j}(p_i p_j)/(p_i + p_j)$, where p_i denotes the frequency of access to the ith item [69], [54]. In fact this method at worst makes four times the number of comparisons of the best possible algorithms, e.g., an algorithm that takes advantage of future references [69], [104]. This is an instance of *competitive analysis* [37].

Index structures are introduced to improve the efficiency of data access, e.g., for equality and range searches. B-trees are high-degree multiway trees with few levels for reasonably sized tables [69], [92]. The dynamic structure of B-trees adjusts according to additions and insertions. The mean node occupancy is ln(2)=0.693 [129].

Hashing is an efficient method for equality searches. For example, the K records in the students table can be mapped into $K \times F$ (with $F > 1$) slots by using the remainder of the 9 digit social security number and a prime number slightly larger than $K \times F$ (hash functions are described in [69]). Collisions are possible even when the load factor $1/F$ is small. This is ascribed to the *birthday paradox* in [69], that it takes only 23 people for a 50% probability that two people share the same birthday. Numerous methods have been proposed to handle collisions, e.g., store a record in a neighboring empty slot. Collision resolution by chaining uses linked lists of records hashed to the same slot. The mean and standard deviation of the number of required probes is given in [69].

Hashing is usually to buckets which can hold b records. *Chaining with separate lists* is one method to handle overflows. It is used in IBM's index sequential files, which designate a few extra tracks on each cylinder as overflow buckets to obviate extra seeks to access overflow records. A pointer from the original bucket points to the overflow bucket in which the record resides. *Collision resolution by open addressing* is another method, where a predetermined sequence of buckets is checked before the record is found or it is determined that the record does not exist. These two methods lend themselves to combinatorial analysis [69]. The relative performance of methods for handling collisions in hashing methods is determined by the mean number of probes for successful and unsuccessful searches versus the load factor [69].

There have been numerous analyses of hashing methods. Random-walk and diffusion process models have been used to determine the number of bucket overflows as a function of time in [53]. An analysis to determine the first time to bucket overflow with additions and deletions of records is given in [24]. *Extendible* and *linear hashing* are two elegant methods to deal with the problem of increasing and decreasing load factors [92]. *Coalesced hashing* which is an efficient method to maintain overflow lists is analyzed in [123]. There are numerous analytical studies of dynamic hashing methods, see e.g., [72].

Sorting is frequently used in batch processing applications and in evaluating relational algebra operators, such as merge-join and eliminating duplicates after applying projection [92]. There are numerous sorting methods with the better methods requiring $O(N log_2(N))$ comparisons [69]. The reader is referred to [54] and [69] for the analysis of the performance of sorting methods.

External sorting involving disk I/O is of interest in database applications, because of the usually high volumes of data to be sorted. It is implemented by successive merging, after an initial step creates K sorted subfiles. Given that m subfiles are merged in each pass, the number of passes $log_m(k)$ tends to be small, since k is small due to the availability of very large main memories. External sorting methods are discussed in great detail in [69]

Parallel sorting methods are surveyed in [8]. One of the difficulties associated with parallel sorting is balancing processor loads. One method is to split each run into range-disjoint partitions and assign separate partitions to processors [122]. This is an instance of *skew avoidance*, where quantiles are estimated through sampling.

Periodic database reorganization saves space, e.g., eliminating records marked as deleted, and more importantly improves performance, e.g., reloading the data reduces search time in hashing by eliminating overflow chains. An algorithm which uses the increased database search cost to initiate reorganization is described in [130]. Performance degradation over time for hashed and index-sequential files is analyzed in [5]. Online database reorganization, i.e., reorganization while the database is processing its normal workload, is desirable due to high availability considerations [135]. User requests are given a higher priority than background processing, but might be delayed by locks held by the reorganization process.

3 Transaction Processing Model

Transactions in OLTP systems belong to different classes, which are characterized by their pathlength, the database access pattern, I/O requirements, and their frequency in the arrival stream. CPU time is determined by CPU speed and software pathlengths. The number of disk accesses is determined by the hit ratio of the *database buffer*. Given that disk access time tends to be several orders of magnitude higher than CPU time, the buffer hit ratio determines transaction response time. A disk access may not be required in the case of a buffer miss, because of hits in the disk controller cache or the cache local to the disk [14].

Transactions in different classes are processed with different priority levels depending on their urgency. Approximate solutions for queueing network models with "population size constraints" are described and compared against simulation results in [112]. The queueing network model of a transaction processing system with multiprogramming level constraints and priority queueing is analyzed approximately in [101]. Methods to analyze queueing network models for transaction processing systems are described in [116].

While numerous queueing disciplines have been proposed and analyzed successfully [21], the synthesis of schedulers to meet prespecified performance goals has received limited attention [43]. Dynamic goal-oriented schedulers provide a robust solution to this problem [6], [2].

4 Query Processing Model

A relational query after query optimization can be represented by a *task system* [21], whose nodes correspond to relational algebra operators. Queueing network models of task systems are not product-form and cannot be solved directly because of parallelism. The decomposition based analytic solution in [113] determines the mean completion time of a single query, which may be processed concurrently with other jobs in the system. At the higher level we have a Markov chain with states representing the composition of tasks in execution. The transition rates among the states of the Markov chain are determined by analyzing the lower level model, i.e., solving the closed queueing network models for all feasible compositions of tasks to obtain their throughputs.

In the central-server queueing network model jobs are alternatively serviced by the CPU (the central server) and disks (peripheral servers). A job completing its service at the CPU is finished with its execution with probability p or accesses disks with probability $1-p$. The number of visits to the CPU is thus geometrically distributed. This distribution does not affect the usual performance measures of interest, such as system throughput, mean queue lengths at various nodes, etc., since only the mean number of cycles is required for the analysis. This distribution affects the response time distribution, which matters when dealing with parallelism.

In *hybrid simulation* jobs in a multiprogrammed computer system are specified by the mean number of remaining cycles and the mean time per cycle for the current multiprogramming mix [98]. When a job completes, the remaining number of cycles of other jobs is recomputed based on elapsed time and their mean cycle time. Hybrid simulation reduces simulation cost [98], because the lower level computer system model is not simulated and is analyzed to yield the mean time per cycle for each job. A decomposition based approach to evaluate the "transient" solution for queueing networks with a nongeometric distribution for the number of job cycles appears in [114], which is applicable to modeling task parallelism.

Overlap in CPU and disk processing due to *prefetching* complicates the determination of query processing time, which equals disk time when the system is I/O bound, but some CPU bursts may exceed the associated I/O time. An analysis based on the decomposition method to evaluate the effect of this overlap appears in [120].

Disk processing time is determined by the number of disk pages accessed, which is affected by the query processing strategy, e.g., the join method, the blocking factor for I/O accesses, the amount of buffer space allocated and buffer allocation policy, disk characteristics, data allocation on disks, etc. The mean latency required to read two randomly placed records on the same cylinder is the expected value of the maximum of two uniformly distributed random variables, i.e., 2/3 of disk rotation time. The completion time for multipage disk accesses is analyzed in [99].

Pipelining is a performance enhancement technique, which bypasses the storing of intermediate results from one relational algebra operator to another, e.g., when multiple joins are involved, the table resulting from one join operation is joined directly with another table. This effect is difficult to analyze and is investigated via simulation in [55].

5 The Database Buffer

The database buffer is controlled by the DBMS rather than the operating system. This is because general-purpose page replacement policies, such as LRU (least-recently used), are not suited for the database environment. For example, a query which sequentially scans the pages of a large table will fill the database buffer with pages which are of no further use. The buffer allocation method in [95] allocates and reuses a small number of pages for this purpose (referred to as the query hot-set) once a sequential data access pattern is detected. In this case insight into application behavior, rather than detailed performance analysis, was adequate for resolving the performance problem.

Embedding the database buffer in a virtual storage may lead to double-paging, i.e., a page in the database buffer may not be main memory resident. Database buffer paging in virtual storage systems is investigated in [71].

The performance measure of interest in buffer management is the *long run expected page fault rate* or the hit ratio [21]. Some of the early analyses of page replacement policies and models of program paging behavior appear in [21], [107].

The analysis of FIFO (first-in, first out) and LRU using a Markov chain model appears in [68]. This analysis, like many others that followed it, is based on the *independent reference model (IRM)*, i.e., each page is accessed with a fixed nonuniform probability [21]. Other models of paging behavior are reviewed in [107]. A state-space explosion problem arises in the analysis of the CLOCK page replacement algorithm, which is dealt with via state aggregation [88]. It is verified that this state aggregation introduces little error. A simplified analysis of the LRU policy, which considers the warmup transient is described in [7]. The analysis of a more realistic model with "stack depth processes" considers whether to share or split the buffer [73]. A comprehensive trace-driven simulation study for evaluating the performance of buffer management policies appears in [33].

Specialized paging policies are required for relational databases and their indexes and this is facilitated by maintaining separate buffers. Buffer management strategies for relational databases are described in [19], while IBM's DB2 buffer manager is described in [110]. A performance comparison of two page replacement methods for B-trees is given in [108]. A validated I/O model for index scans in a system with a finite buffer with the LRU policy is given in [77]. This model which leads to a closed-form approximate equation takes into account the limited size of the index buffer and that multiple records may be associated with each index value. A more recent investigation of this topic is reported in [109].

The database buffer is usually shared among several processes. A sharing technique based on the *marginal gains* paradigm is proposed in [86]. A study characterizing workloads for managing database buffers appears in [27]. Pages are grouped according to their access frequencies to reflect *access skew.* The issue of sharing the database buffer is also addressed in [128], which is discussed below.

The optimum number of blocks to prefetch is determined using a dynamic programming formulation in [105]. Prefetching relies on sequentiality of access, but the following costs are to be taken into account: (i) buffer misses; (ii) fetching additional blocks at fault time; (iii) fetching blocks that are never referenced.

A method complementary to prefetching is clustering. An algorithm for optimal clustering in a hierarchical database (i.e., IMS) is presented in [97]. A trivial example of anticipated access behavior in hierarchic database is that child nodes are referenced after parent nodes (a singly or doubly linked list is provided to facilitate this). Clustering is also applicable to object-oriented databases, i.e., for prefetching objects from disk or from servers in a client-server environment.

Data compression reduces the size of the database, which improves buffering efficiency in addition to preserving disk space. Lossless data compression based on a variant of Lempel-Ziv methods, which compresses individual records is implemented in DB2 [63]. The data is decompressed on demand (with or without hardware assistance) before it is processed. The effect of data compression on improving database performance is studied in [93].

6 Logging and Checkpointing

Transaction *durability* ensures that transaction updates will not be lost if the system crashes after the transaction is completed. Durability is achievable by forcing database blocks modified by the transaction in the database buffer onto disk at its completion. However, the *force policy* is inefficient and is seldom used in practice [94]. Transaction durability can be attained at less cost by *logging* database modifications or log records to a disk file called the database log. A transaction is considered *committed* once this is done. If the system crashes and the contents of the database buffer are lost, the log records can be used to update the disk.

The commonly used *steal* policy allows the writing to disk of database buffer pages modified by uncommitted transactions to make space when database buffer space is exhausted. The log is used to undo the modifications to disk pages by uncommitted transactions when the system crashes [92]. This require the logging "before values" of database contents, before the modified disk page is written out [92]. If the transaction is aborted, the before values can be used to rollback updates by aborted transactions.

Write-ahead logging allows the writing of disk pages to be deferred, since the transaction is made durable by writing log records which reflect the modifications. The *no-force policy* improves performance by reducing disk access requirements since: (i) it is more efficient to write log records, since they tend to be smaller than disk pages and because they are written sequentially; (ii) deferring the writing of a disk page has the advantage that a page might be modified several times before it is written to disk; (iii) the deferred writing of dirty pages can be carried out more efficiently by sorting them according to their disk address to minimize seek and latency time.

The evaluation of recovery techniques based on the maximum transaction throughput is reported in [94]. A transaction recovery method supporting fine-granularity locking and partial rollbacks using write-ahead logging is described in [82]. A logging protocol which batches updates and uses timeouts to balance transaction response time versus disk bandwidth requirements is described in [51]. The analysis of recovery time for the write-ahead logging protocol is described in [66].

Checkpointing saves the state of the database to minimize recovery time after system crashes. Checkpoints are taken periodically at fixed intervals, after a specified number of transactions are completed, although some other criterion can be used for this purpose. There have been numerous performance studies of checkpointing and recovery, see e.g., [87], [70].

Checkpointing at the transaction level can be used to minimize the processing required to complete the execution of transactions whose processing is interrupted. Data conflicts leading to transaction abort are a possibility with the optimistic kill concurrency control method (see accompanying article by the author). An analytical solution to determine the optimum number of checkpoints and their position with respect to database accesses appears in [115].

7 Design of Relational Databases

Relational database design consists of two steps: *logical* and *physical* design. The former is preceded by the aforementioned ER (entity-relationship) modeling step, which leads to the definition of relational tables. *Normalization* is used to eliminate redundancies in tables, usually by decomposing larger tables into smaller ones [92].

Physical database design involves the selection of indexes for individual tables, including the clustering index, which determines the ordering of records. Since the workload varies over time this selection has to be reevaluated as part of *database tuning* [92]. There are 2^n indexing possibilities with n columns, even when composite indexes comprising multiple attributes are not considered. Indexes incur overhead in space, to the extent that the combined size of indexes for a table may exceed its size. There is also updating of the index with its overhead for concurrency control. The viability of an index can determined by using appropriate cost functions (as provided by the query optimizer) for a given workload. Index selection tools are described in [38], [17].

Performance may be improved by utilizing unnormalized tables, since it obviates certain joins. Conversely, *vertical partitioning* splits "wide" records to frequently and infrequently accessed columns. The frequently accessed data can then be accessed more efficiently, but there is a penalty if both tables have to be accessed together. The choice of the columns has been formulated as an optimization problem, which lends itself to heuristic and rigorous solutions [84].

8 Query Optimizer

One advantage of the relational data model is that the user need be aware of the logical database structure, but not the physical database structure. The query optimizer selects the least costly access path, usually in terms of number of database page accesses.

Given an SQL query, a query execution graph whose nodes correspond to relational algebra operations (with several extensions, e.g., aggregation operators such as max and min) is generated. Query optimization is first performed top-down, where the query execution graph is modified via valid transformations to attain a lower execution cost, regardless of physical database design. For example, it may be advantageous to carry out selections on two relations involved in a join, rather than computing their Cartesian product first, since this will significantly reduce the volume of data to be processed.

There are usually several choices for evaluating a relational operator [92]. The three major methods to evaluate the join operator are: (i) *Sort-merge join*, which is only applicable to equijoins. After possible selection and projection steps on the two tables, they are sorted according to the join attributes before they are merged. Duplicates can be eliminated as part of the sorting. (ii) *Nested loop join*, which maintains the smaller of two tables in main memory (if possible), while scanning the larger table to check whether the join condition is being met. If the smaller table is n times the size of available memory space, it is partitioned n-ways and n passes over the larger table are required. (iii) A *hash-based join* method can be alternatively used for equijoins [92]. The cost of the first two methods, plus two other variations were evaluated using cost equations based on the number of disk accesses in [9]. The performance of several hash-join methods are compared with merge-join methods using appropriate cost equations in [103]. A hybrid join method combining (i) and (ii) is proposed in [16]. This method requires one index or multiple join indexes covering all join columns of the "inner table" index. Index "ANDing" and "ORing" is performed to achieve the effect of a single composite index in the latter case [81].

When there are multiple joins, the ordering of the joins has a significant effect on the evaluation cost, regardless of the join method being used (note similarity to matrix multiplications). This problem becomes more complicated due to the presence of intervening operators in SQL queries. The number of alternatives to be evaluated increases rapidly with the number of tables involved and usually a subset of these alternatives is considered by query optimizers [92]. Query optimizers use *dynamic programming* and the *branch and bound method* to minimize CPU processing and the number of disk accesses, while favoring execution plans that will yield results in the desired order [100] The *simulated annealing* method can be also used for this purpose [60]. Other papers dealing with query optimization are [45], [3], [49], [62]. Query optimization techniques are reviewed in [61].

Optimizers are guided by the statistical profile of the database [92], such as the number of distinct attributes in a column and their histogram. The latter allows a more accurate estimation of selectivity, but this is at the cost of higher overhead (in space and in time). Statistical methods used for estimating the database profile are surveyed in [78]. Methods to determine "optimum histograms" are discussed in [4], [64].

It is difficult to estimate selectivities for intermediate tables, hence *dynamic query optimizers* reevaluate the execution plan during query execution [23]. In case the processing of components of a query has been scheduled on multiple nodes, there is also the issue of allocating the processing to less heavily utilized notes, which as an instance of the load balancing problem [75].

The cost of processing aggregate queries in very large databases can be reduced significantly by *online query processing*, which utilizes statistical sampling to evaluate a query [52]. Consider the estimation of the average student GPA. The user specifies the stopping rule for the sampling process via the confidence interval and its level.

The allocation of buffer space for processing queries is an important function of the query optimizer. Consider the processing of *block nested loop* joins [92]. This can be formulated as a *resource allocation problem* via *marginal allocation* [59], but the solution cost is of the order of the product of the number of relations and buffer size. Solutions to this problem based on *dynamic programming* and *branch and bound* methods are offered in [128].

9 Analysis of Overall Performance of Database Systems

While there are numerous performance analyses of database components, there have been very few studies to evaluate overall performance. Notable are a set of studies [101], [12], [57], and [58], which follow the performance evaluation methodology in [102].

The seven layers of modeling required for the performance evaluation of relational databases are as follows [57], [58]: semantic model, schema database, query optimizer, internal database, physical I/O, resource allocation, and concurrency. The model is used for evaluating a design rather than optimization.

The semantic and database schema layer correspond to the entity relationship model and logical database design through normalization.

Given optimizer strategies, database indexes, and database statistics, the query optimizer determines the access path and record selectivities and hence the number of pages to be accessed by different transaction classes.

The internal database layer estimates block accesses per transaction and CPU usage. Given the buffer policy and its size, the physical I/O layer estimates the buffer hit ratio and hence the number of actual disk I/Os per transaction.

Given the characteristics of the underlying computer system, the resource allocation layer determines the service demands for queueing network modeling. Finally given transaction arrival rates and scheduling policies, the concurrency layer computes device utilizations and transaction response times.

The performance analysis is facilitated by considering only dominant transaction classes, which are the main contributors to resource consumption. An important aspect of this work is validation against measurement results for the two hardware platforms: mainframes with the MVS operating system and the Teradata database machine.

There are also commercially available software products such as BEST/1 [10] and an accompanying tool (Crystal) to evaluate the performance of DB2 applications from BGS Systems (now part of BMC Software).

10 Data Sharing and Client-Server Systems

In data sharing several computers access data on shared disks to attain a higher processing capacity than possible with a single computer system [91]. Transactions executing at one system require the most up-to-date copies of disk pages for their execution. These pages may reside in the buffer of another system, rather than on disk, since a no-force policy is assumed to be in effect. When a transaction commits, stale copies of database blocks modified by it are invalidated or updated at other systems. Performance can be improved by integrating cache coherence and concurrency control [31]. A methodology based on trace-driven simulation for evaluating the performance of data sharing systems is described in [91], while an analytic approach is developed in [26]. The analysis required for modeling buffer coherence is similar to the analysis of cache coherence paradigms in multiprocessors [96].

Client-server systems similarly to data sharing systems use *data shipping* as opposed to *query shipping*, which is the paradigm used in distributed relational databases. In object-oriented DMBSs it is the objects rather than disk blocks that are transmitted to the clients. A comprehensive simulation study of the implications of various design alternatives on the performance of client-server systems is reported in [40]. An experimental study of offloading database functions to a backend processor in the context of the Ingres DBMS appears in [48].

11 Data Allocation and Transaction Routing

In distributed databases we are concerned with data allocation at a course granularity, e.g., vertical and/or horizontal partitions of tables. The *file assignment problem* in distributed databases is to attain an "optimal allocation" in terms of cost or performance. There have been numerous studies in this area, which are surveyed in [32].

In a system with multiple nodes transactions arrive at a router which assigns transactions to nodes to balance their load at their bottleneck resource, which tends to be the CPU. With the data shipping paradigm the processing associated with data objects is carried out at the node to which the transaction is routed, as opposed to function shipping where the processing is at the node where the data resides (see accompanying article by the author on concurrency control).

An additional goal in allocating data to nodes is to minimize communication costs (number of disk pages transmitted). Thus it is preferable to collocate database objects which are referenced by the same transactions. Transaction assignments and data allocations can be formulated as a quadratic 0/1 integer programming problem, which is converted to a linear 0/1 integer programming problem by an appropriate change in variables [25].

Further improvement in mean transaction response time can be attained through *optimal static* transaction routing, which follows the data allocation obtained by the integer programming formulation. The optimality is in the sense of minimizing the overall mean response time, but other measures of optimality may be considered, such as equalizing the mean response time at heterogeneous nodes [44]. Transaction assignments obtained by the integer programming method are used as a starting point to determine fractions of transaction classes to be routed to different nodes [133]. A simplex method for function minimization is used in this work [85].

Dynamic transaction routing with a centralized transaction router can be used to further improve transaction response times [124]. In the case of a single resource *join the shortest queue -JSQ* is a popular paradigm, i.e., the router sends the transaction to the node with the fewest jobs [124]. This execution model is simplistic, since transactions require processing at multiple resources, e.g., active resources such as CPU and disks, and passive resources such as the main memory. The activation of a new transaction causes the response time of previously active transactions to be degraded.

The improvement in transaction response time at a node may be due to the optimized mix of processed transactions. Consider two nodes where one node is processing an I/O bound transaction, while the other node is processing a CPU bound transaction. It is preferable to route a CPU-bound transaction to the former node, unless it is known that the processing at the latter node is nearing completion.

To estimate the mean transaction response time at various nodes each node is represented by a closed queueing network model. The transaction router keeps track of transaction completions, so it knows which transactions are still in progress at each node. It determines the mean response time that would be attained by a newly arrived transaction at each node. The service demands of various transaction classes are known, so that the corresponding queueing network model can be solved easily. The transaction is routed to the node providing the minimum mean response time thus estimated [132].

The queueing network models for the nodes to which the target transaction can be routed are solved using estimates of the remaining CPU/IO cycles in [114], which is an improvement to considering a closed model. However, further transactions routed to a node invalidate the mean response time estimates for transactions in progress at that node. This is because activated transactions alternate in CPU and I/O processing. This would not be the case if the activation of further transactions is delayed due to multiprogramming level constraints.

12 Parallel Databases and Database Machines

The first successful commercial database machine to allow highly parallel processing of relational algebra operators was the Teradata DBC/1012 with the *shared nothing* paradigm. Tandem's NonStop SQL system similarly uses this paradigm. Both systems were demonstrations of the scalability in computing power achievable with this paradigm as opposed to the shared everything paradigm or shared memory multiprocessing. This may be attributed to the data filtering effect by associating more processing power with each disk, which has recently led to a proposal for "intelligent disks" with each disk equipped with its own microprocessor [67].

Data allocation for relational databases in multicomputer systems and database machines may be based on range partitioning, hashing on a certain key, or a round-robin allocation [80]. The latter methods tend to result in a uniform distribution and a negligible degree of load imbalance or skew. Range-partitioning is amenable to skew, even if an equal number of records are assigned to each node, e.g., a range of product numbers may correspond to highly referenced items. Secondary skew may arise due to the application of relational operators. For example, the rows of two tables which are hashed on the join attribute may result in load imbalance or skew, if one attribute is much more popular than others and its rows are sent to the same node. The interaction of hashing and parallelism is explored in [83].

A collection of papers dealing with the performance analysis of database machines appears on [13]. More detailed performance studies of database machines are mainly based on simulation. For example, it is shown through simulation how repartitioning can be used to resolve the skew problem due to hashing [30]. A large number of simulation studies have concerned themselves with parallel query processing, see e.g., [56], [76].

Shared nothing architectures can also be used for OLTP applications. A performance comparison of OLTP performance via a queueing model of shared everything and nothing systems appears in [50]. This study was conducted at a time when mainframe processors using bipolar technology were faster than available microprocessors.

There are some unique scheduling problems in this area. Queries in a parallel environment may be processed with higher degrees of parallelism to take less time, i.e., the query execution time is a nonincreasing function of the number of allotted processors. The scheduling of such *"malleable tasks"* is reported in [121], based on results in multiprocessor scheduling theory [22]. Scheduling of queries in a parallel database machines is treated as a multidimensional resource scheduling problem in [42].

13 Data Mining

Data mining as applied to databases can be considered as a subarea of exploratory data analysis in statistics and knowledge discovery and machine learning in artificial intelligence.

The finding of *association rules* in data mining is usually illustrated in conjunction with "market basket transactions" [1]. The goal is to determine whether the purchase of a certain itemset implies the purchase of another one (referred to LHS and RHS itemsets). The measures for association rules are *support* and *confidence*. The former is the fraction of purchases of LHS itemsets (among all purchases) and the latter the fraction of times that RHS itemsets were bought together with LHS itemsets. The determination of frequent itemsets is expensive and requires multiple scans of very large tables. Numerous algorithms have been proposed to minimize the number of scans to reach a certain goal.

Clustering (see e.g., [65]) can be applied to the *classification rules* problem, where the values of certain variables are used to predict the value of others. The cost of clustering when applied to large volumes of data is determined by the I/O cost, i.e., the number of scans required to determine the clusters. The BIRCH method incrementally and dynamically clusters multidimensional data in a single pass [134], although further passes can be used to improve quality. Clustering methods applicable to high volumes of data and generating high quality clusters at a reasonable cost is a challenging problem.

Data mining is done on a data warehouses (defined below), which holds ever-increasing data volumes, e.g., due to the need for more detailed information or mining data over longer time intervals. The high volumes of "raw" data to be sent on I/O buses to processors is one of the motivations for intelligent disks as noted earlier.

A data warehouse is a data repository which integrates data from multiple information sources. It is in fact a materialized view [92] so that queries can be processed on it directly. The data warehouse configuration problem is that of "selecting a set of views to materialize in the data warehouse that answers all the queries of interest, while minimizing the total query evaluation and view maintenance cost" [111]. An exhaustive incremental and a heuristic algorithm are developed in [111] to solve this state space optimization problem.

14 Multidimensional Indexing

High-dimensional indexes are useful in many applications and numerous indexing structures have been proposed for this purpose [41]. R-trees, which are the generalization of B-trees to higher dimensions, form the basis for many other indexing structures. R-trees dynamically partition space into high-dimensional hyperrectangles, which may overlap and are embedded in hyperrectangles forming the higher level of the index. The overlapping of hyperrectangles is one source of inefficiency, since it entails the following of multiple paths in traversing the index. For point data the efficiency of nearest neighbor search (discussed below) can be improved by presorting the data according to the Hilbert curve [36].

There are several analytic studies of R-tree performance, e.g., to determine the mean number of disk accesses to retrieve an object or estimate the selectivity of spatial joins, assuming that objects are distributed uniformly in space. It has been shown that the *fractal dimension* is a good measure of nonuniformity [36]. The estimation of the selectivity of window queries is carried out in [90].

A popular query is nearest-neighbor search based on Euclidean distance. It is used for similarity search, where the coordinates correspond to object attributes, e.g., color, texture, etc. There have been numerous performance studies in this area, which with few exceptions are experimental in nature [125]. The effectiveness of indexes for nearest neighbor search drops rapidly with increasing dimensionality, to the extent that such a search amounts to a scan of all index pages [125]. Dimensionality reduction via singular-value decomposition can be used to cope with the "curse of dimensionality", but this results in a loss of accuracy [119]. The accuracy level can be maintained by retrieving more nearest neighbor points than required. The decrease in efficiency is quantified experimentally in [119].

Lossy data compression is applicable to numerical data obtained from scientific experiments, etc. [4]. This approaches are especially appropriate for reducing the volume of high dimensional data [36], [4].

15 Conclusions

Database performance is important since it affects the performance of applications which rely on it. Factors affecting database performance are not well understood, which is because of the complexity of disk resident databases.

With the ever-increasing capacity of random access memories, main storage database systems for transaction processing are becoming viable. Data structures and algorithms for main memory resident data are then applicable [28], [127], leading to CPU pathlengths which are an order of magnitude smaller than ordinary databases.

DBMSs have builtin measurement tools to monitor their performance [15]. Parameters for analyzing database performance are either not readily available or measurements for various subsystems are not related to each other to make this task possible. For example, lock conflict rates are not related to transaction classes making the lock request or database tables being accessed. The situation is similar to that of estimating the parameters of queueing network models, which was resolved two decades ago by providing appropriate instrumentation and data reduction tools [10].

One very promising approach for improving database performance, which obviates the need for human intervention and the associated costs is that of self-tuning databases. For example, [18] describes how self-tuning technology has been incorporated into Microsoft's SQL Server product.

There are numerous emerging database areas, many of which have been mentioned earlier in the text, which pose new problems with concomitant performance issues. One such area is efficiently finding relevant information from a wide variety of sources on the world wide web. The need is then for specialized retrieval methods from imperfect and semi-structured data on the web, techniques to merge the results from such searches [35], caching paradigms for this environment [11], [34], alternative mapping schemes for storing XML data in relational databases [39], and many other topics.

It should be finally mentioned that the vastness of the database area makes it impossible to cover it with sufficient depth, but hopefully there is enough detail to stimulate interest in database performance analysis, especially in areas which have received less attention.

References

1. R. Agrawal, T. Imielinski, and A. Swami. "Mining association rules between sets of items in large databases," *Proc. ACM SIGMOD Int'l Conf. on Management of Data,* 1993, 207-216.
2. J. Aman, C. K. Eilert, D. Emmens, P. Yacom, and D. N. Dillenberger. "Adaptive algorithms for managing a distributed data processing workload," *IBM Systems Journal 36*,2 (1997), 242-283.
3. G. Antoshenkov and M. Ziauddin. "Query processing and optimization in Oracle Rdb," *The Very Large Data Base Journal 5,* (1996), 229-237.

4. D. Barbara et al. "The New Jersey data reduction report," *Bulletin Technical Committee on Data Engineering 20*,4 (1997), 3-45.
5. D. S. Batory. "Optimal file designs and reorganization points," *ACM Trans. on Database Systems 7*,1 (1982), 60-81.
6. P. P. Bhattacharya, I. Viniotis, L. Georgiadis, and P. Tsoucas. "Ergodicity and optimality of an adaptive multi-objective scheduling algorithms," *IBM Research Report RC 15547*, Hawthorne, NY, 1990.
7. A. Bhide, A. Dan, and D. M. Dias. "A simple analysis of the LRU buffer policy and its relationship to buffer warmup transient," *Proc. 9th IEEE Int'l Conf. on Data Engineering* 1993, pp. 125-133.
8. D. Bitton, D. J. DeWitt, D. K. Hsiao, and J. Menon. "A taxonomy of parallel sorting," *ACM Computing Surveys 16*,3 (1984), 287-318.
9. M. W. Blasgen and K. P. Eswaran. "Storage and access in relational databases," *IBM Systems J. 16*,4 (1977), 362-377.
10. J. P. Buzen. "A queueing network model of MVS," *ACM Computing Surveys 10*,3 (1978), 319-331.
11. P. Cao and C. Liu. "Maintaining strong cache consistency in the world wide web," *IEEE Trans. on Computers 47*,4 (April 1998), 445-457.
12. I. R. Casas and K. C. Sevcik. "Structure and validation of an analytic performance predictor for System 2000 databases," *INFOR 27*,2 (May 1989), 129-144.
13. F. Cesarini and S. Silvio. *Database Machine Performance: Modeling Methodology and Evaluation Strategies*, in *Lecture Notes in Computer Science Vol. 257*, Springer-Verlag, 1987.
14. P. M. Chen, E. K. Lee, G. A. Gibson, R. H. Katz, and D. A. Patterson. "RAID: High-performance, reliable secondary storage," *ACM Computing Surveys 26*,2 (June 1994), 145-185.
15. J. M. Cheng, C. R. Loosley, A. Shibamiya, and P. S. Worthington. "IBM database 2 performance: Design, implementation, and tuning," *IBM Systems J. 23*,2 (1984), 189-210.
16. J. Cheng, D. Haderle, R. Hedges, B. R. Iyer, T. Messinger, C. Mohan, and Y. Wang. "An efficient hybrid join algorithm: A DB2 prototype," *Proc. 7th IEEE Int'l Conf. on Data Engineering*, 1991, pp. 171-180.
17. S. Chaudhuri and V. Narasayya. "AutoAdmin what-if index analysis utility," *Proc. ACM SIGMOD Int'l Conf. on Management of Data*, 1998, pp. 367-378.
18. S. Chaudhuri, E. Christensen, G. Graefe, V. Narasayya, and M. Zwilling. "Self-tuning technology in Microsoft SQL Server," *IEEE Data Engineering Bulletin 22*,2 (June 1999), pp. 20-26.
19. H. T. Chou and D. J. DeWitt. "An evaluation of buffer management strategies for relational database systems," *Algorithmica 1*,3 (1986), 311-336.
20. S. Christodoulakis. "Implications on certain assumptions in database performance evaluation," *ACM Trans. on Database Systems 9*,2 (June 1984), 163-186.
21. E. G. Coffman Jr. and P. J. Denning. *Operating Systems Theory*, Prentice-Hall, 1973.
22. E. G. Coffman Jr., M. R. Garey, and D. S. Johnson. "Approximations algorithms for bin packing- An updated survey," in *Algorithm Design for Computer System Design*, G. Ausiello abd P. Serafini (eds.), 1984, pp. 51-106.
23. R. Cole and G. Graefe. "Optimization of dynamic query evaluation plans," *Proc. ACM SIGMOD Int'l Conf. on Management of Data*, 1994, pp. 150-160.
24. R. B. Cooper and M. K. Solomon. "The average time until bucket overflow," *ACM Trans. on Database Systems 9*,3 (1984), 392-408.

25. D. W. Cornell, D. M. Dias, and P. S. Yu. "On multisystem coupling through function request shipping," *IEEE Trans. Software Engineering 12*,10 (Oct. 1990), 1006-1017.
26. A. Dan. *Performance Analysis of Data Sharing Environments,* MIT Press, 1992.
27. A. Dan, P. S. Yu, and J. Y. Chung. "Characterizing of database access pattern for analytic prediction of buffer hit ratio," *The Very Large Data Base Journal 4,* (1995), 127-154.
28. D. J. DeWitt, R. H. Katz, D. Olken, L. D. Shapiro, M. Stonebraker, and D. Wood. "Implementation techniques for main storage database systems," *Proc. ACM SIGMOD Conf. on Management of Data,* 1984, pp. 1-8.
29. D. J. DeWitt and J. Gray. "Parallel database systems: The future of high performance database systems," *Commun. of the ACM 35*,6 (June 1992), 85-98.
30. D. J. DeWitt, J. F. Naughton, D. A. Schneider, and S. Seshadri. "Practical skew handling in parallel joins," *Proc. 18th Int'l Conf. on Very Large Data Bases,* 1992, pp. 27-40.
31. D. M. Dias, B. R. Iyer, J. T. Robinson, and P. S. Yu. "Integrated concurrency-coherency control for multisystem data sharing," *IEEE Trans. on Software Engineering 15*,4 (1989), pp. 437-448.
32. L. W. Dowdy and D. V. Foster. "Comparative models of the file assignment problem," *ACM Computing Surveys 14*,2 (1984), 287-313.
33. W. Effelsberg and T. Haerder. "Principles of database buffer management," *ACM Trans. on Database Systems 9*,4 (1984), 560-595.
34. L. Fan, P. Cao, W. Lin, and Q. Jacobson. ""Web prefetching between low-bandwidth clients and proxies: Potentials and performance," *Proc. ACM SIGMETRICS Conf. on Measurement and Modeling of Computer Systems,* 1999, pp. 178-187.
35. R. Fagin. "Combining fuzzy information from multiple sources," *Journal of Computer and System Sciences 58*,1 (1999), 83-99.
36. C. Faloutsos. *Searching Multimedia Databases by Content,* Kluwer Academic Publishers, 1997.
37. A. Fiat and G. J. Woeginger. "Competitive analysis of algorithms," in *Online Algorithms 1996, Lecture Notes in Computer Science Vol. 1442,* Springer-Verlag, pp. 1-12.
38. S. Finkelstein, M. Schkolnick, and P. Tiberio. "Physical database design for relational databases," *ACM Trans. on Database Systems 9*,4 (Dec. 1988), 526-559.
39. D. Florescu and D. Kossmann. "A performance evaluation of alternative mapping schemes for storing XML data in a relational database," *INRIA Research Report No. 3680,* May 1999.
40. M. J. Franklin, M. J. Carey, and M. Livny. "Transactional client-server cache consistency: Alternatives and performance," *ACM Trans. on Database Systems 22*,3 (Sept. 1997), 315-363.
41. V, Gaede and O. Guenther. "Multidimensional access methods," *ACM Computing Surveys 30*,2 (June 1998), 170-231.
42. M. N. Garofalakis and Y. E. Ioannidis. "Parallel query scheduling and optimization with time- and space-shared resources," *Proc. 23rd Int'l Conf. on Very Large Data Bases,* 1997, pp. 296-305.
43. E. Gelenbe and I. Mitrani. *Analysis and Synthesis of Computer Systems.* Academic Press, 1980.
44. L. Georgiadis, C. Nikolaou, and A. Thomasian. "A fair load balancing policy for heterogeneous systems." *IBM Research Report RC 14323,* Hawthorne, NY, Nov. 1989.

45. G. Graefe. "Query evaluation techniques for large databases," *ACM computing Surveys 25*,2 (June 1993), 73-120.
46. J. Gray (ed.) *The Benchmark Handbook for Database and Transaction Processing Systems, 2nd ed.* Morgan Kaufmann, 1993.
47. L. M. Haas, M. J. Carey, M. Livny, and A, Shukla. "Seeking the truth about *ad hoc* join costs," *The Very Large Data Base Journal 6*, (1997), 241-256.
48. R. B. Hagmann and D. Ferrari. "Performance analysis of several back-end database architectures," *ACM Trans. on Database Systems 11*,1 (March 1986), 1-26.
49. E. P. Harris and K. Ramamohanarao. "Join algorithm cost revisited," *The Very Large Data Base Journal 5*, (1996), 64-84.
50. P. Heidelberger and M. Seetha Lakshmi. "A performance comparison of multimicro and mainframe database architectures," *IEEE Trans. Software Engineering 14*,4 (April 1988), 522-531.
51. P. Helland, H. Sammer, J. Lyon, R. Carr, P.Garret, and A. Reuter. "Group commit times and high volume transaction processing," in *High Volume Transaction Systems*, D. Gawlick, M. N. Hayne, and A. Reuter (eds.), Springer-Verlag, 1987, pp. 301-327.
52. J. M. Hellerstein, P. J. Haas, and H. Wong. "Online aggregation," *Proc. ACM SIGMOD Int'l Conf. on Management of Data*, 1997, pp. 171-182.
53. D. P. Heyman. "Mathematical models of database reorganization," *ACM Trans. on Database Systems 7*,4 (1982), 615-631.
54. M. Hofri. *Analysis of Algorithms: Computational Methods and Mathematical Tools.* Oxford University Press, 1995.
55. H.-I. Hsiao, M.-S. Chen, and P. S. Yu. "Parallel execution of hash joins in parallel databases," *IEEE Trans. Parallel and Distributed Systems 8*,8 (Aug. 1997), 872-883.
56. K. A. Hua, C. Lee, and C. M. Hua. "Dynamic load balancing in multicomputer database systems using partition tuning," *IEEE Trans. on Knowledge and Data Engineering 7*,6 (Dec. 1995), 968-983.
57. W. Hyslop. *Performance Prediction of Relational Database Management Systems*, Ph.D. Thesis, Computer Science Dept., University of Toronto, 1991.
58. W. F. Hyslop and K. C. Sevcik. "Performance prediction of relational database systems," *Proc. Canadian Computer Measurement Group (CMG) Conf.*, pp. 298-312.
59. T. Ibaraki and N. Katoh. *Resource Allocation Problems*, MIT Press, 1984.
60. Y. E. Ioannidis and E. Wong. "Query optimization by simulated annealing," *Proc. ACM SIGMOD Int'l Conf. on Management of Data*, 1987, pp. 9-22.
61. Y. E. Ioannidis. "Query Optimization," in *The Computer Science and Engineering Handbook*, 1997, pp. 1038-1057.
62. Y. E. Ioannidis, R. T. Ng, K. Shim, and T. K. Sellis. "Parametric query optimization," *The Very Large Data Base Journal 6*, (1997), 132-151.
63. B. R. Iyer and D. Wilhite. "Data compression support in databases," *Proc. 20th Int'l Conf. on Very Large Data Bases*, 1994, 695-704.
64. H. V. Jagadish, N, Koudas, S. Muthukrishna, V. Poosala, K. Sevcik, and T. Suel. "Optimal histograms with quality guarantees," *Proc. 24th Int'l Conf. on Very Large Data Bases*, 1998, 275-286.
65. A. Jain and R. Dubes. *Algorithms for Clustering Data*, Prentice-Hall, 1988.
66. A. Jhingran and P. Khedkar. "Analysis of recovery in a database system using a write-ahead logging protocol," *Proc. ACM SIGMOD Int'l Conf. on Management of Data*, 1992, 175-184.

67. K. Keeton, D. A. Patterson, and J. M. Hellerstein. "A case for intelligent disks (IDISKS)," *Proc. ACM SIGMOD Int'l Conf. on Management of Data,* 1998, pp. 24-32.
68. W. F. King III. "Analysis of demand paging algorithms," *Information Processing 71,* North-Holland, 1972, pp. 485-490.
69. D. E. Knuth. *The Art of Computer Programming Vol. 3: Sorting and Searching, 2nd Ed.* Addison-Wesley, 1998.
70. V. Kumar and M. Hsu (eds.) *Recovery Mechanisms in Database Systems,* Prentice-Hall, 1998.
71. T. Lang, C. Wood, and E. B. Fernandez. "Database buffer paging in virtual storage systems," *ACM Trans. on Database Systems 2,*4 (Dec. 1977), 339-351.
72. P. A. Larson. "Dynamic hash tables," *Commun. of the ACM 31,*4 (April 1988), 446-457.
73. H. Levy and R. J. T. Morris. "Should caches be split or shared? Analysis using the superposition of bursty stack depth processes," *Performance Evaluation 27/28* (1996), 175-188.
74. R. J. Lipton, J. F. Naughton, and D. A. Schneider. "Practical selectivity estimation through adaptive sampling," *Proc. ACM SIGMOD Int'l Conf. on Management of Data,* 1990, pp. 1-11.
75. H. Lu and M. J. Carey. "Some experimental results on distributed join algorithms," *Proc. 11th Int'l Conf. on Very Large Data Bases,* 1985, pp. 292-304.
76. H. Lu, B.-C. Ooi, and K.-L. Tan. *Query Processing in Parallel Relational Database Systems,* IEEE Computer Society Press, 1994.
77. L. F. Mackert and G. M. Lohman. "Index scans using a finite LRU buffer: A validated I/O model," *ACM Trans. on Database Systems 14,*3 (Sept. 1989), 401-424.
78. M. Mannino, P. Chu, and T. Sager. "Statistical profile estimation in database systems," *ACM Computing Surveys 20,*3 (Sept. 1988), 191-221.
79. A. Marshall and I. Olken. *Inequalities: Theory of Majorization and Its Applications,* Academic Press, 1979.
80. M. Mehta and D. J. DeWitt. "Data placement in shared-nothing parallel database systems," *The Very Large Data Base Journal 6,*1 (1997), 53-72.
81. C. Mohan, D. Haderle, Y. Wang, and J. Cheng. "Single table access using multiple indexes: Optimization, execution, and concurrency control techniques," *Proc. Int'l Conf. on Extending Data Base Technology,* 1990, pp. 29-43.
82. C. Mohan, D. Haderle, B. Lindsey, H. Pirahesh, and P. Schwartz. "ARIES: A transaction recovery method supporting fine-granularity locking and partial rollbacks using write-ahead logging," *ACM Trans. on Database Systems 17,*1 (March 1992), 94-162.
83. A. N. Mourad, R. J. T. Morris, A. N. Swami, and H. C. Young. "Limits of parallelism in hash-join algorithms," *Performance Evaluation 20,*(1-3), (1994), 301-316.
84. S. B. Navathe, S. Ceri, G. Wiederhold, and J. Dou. "Vertical partitioning algorithms for database design," *ACM Trans. on Database Systems 9,*4 (Dec. 1984), 680-710.
85. J. A. Nelder and R. Mead. "A simplex method for function minimization," *Computer Journal 7,* (1965), 308-314.
86. R. T. Ng, C. Faloutsos, and T. K. Selis. "Flexible buffer allocation based on marginal gains," *Proc. ACM SIGMOD Int'l Conf. on Management of Data,* 1991, pp. 387-396.

87. V. F. Nicola and J. M. van Spanje. "Comparative analysis of different models of checkpointing and recovery," *IEEE Trans. on Software Engineering 16*,8 (Aug. 1990), 807-821.
88. V. F. Nicola, A. Dan, and D. M. Dias. "Performance analysis of the clock page replacement policy," *Proc. ACM SIGMETRICS/PERFORMANCE '92 Joint Conf.*, pp. 35-46.
89. H. Pirahesh, C. Mohan, J. M. Cheng, T. S. Liu, and P. G. Selinger. "Parallelism in relational data base systems: Architectural issues in design approaches," *Proc. Int'l Symp. on Databases in Parallel and Distr. Systems,* 1990, pp. 4-29.
90. G. Proietti and C. Faloutsos. "Selectivity estimation of window queries," *Proc. Conf. on Information and Knowledge Management (CIKM),* 1998, pp. 340-347.
91. E. Rahm. "Empirical performance evaluation of concurrency and coherency controls for database sharing systems," *ACM Trans. on Database Systems 18*,2 (June 1993), 333-377.
92. R. Ramakrishnan. *An Introduction to Database Systems, 2nd ed.*, McGraw-Hill, 1999.
93. G. Ray, J. R. Haritsa, and S. Seshadri. "Database compression: A performance enhancement tool," *Proc. 7th Int'l Conf. on Management of Data (COMAD),* 1995.
94. A. Reuter. "Performance analysis of recovery techniques," *ACM Trans. on Database Systems 9*,4 (Dec. 1984), 526-559.
95. G. M. Sacco and M. Schkolnick. "Buffer management in relational database systems," *ACM Trans. on Database Systems 11*,4 (Dec. 1986), 473-496.
96. H. S. Sandhu and K. C. Sevcik. "An analytic study of dynamic hardware and software cache coherence strategies," *Proc. ACM SIGMETRICS Conf. on Measurement and Modeling of Computer Systems,* 1995, pp. 167-177.
97. M. Schkolnick. "A clustering algorithm for hierarchical structures," *ACM Trans. on Database Systems 2*,1 (March 1988), 27-44.
98. H. Schwetman. "Hybrid simulation models of computer systems," *Commun. of the ACM 21*,9 (1978), 718-723.
99. B. Seeger. "An analysis of schedules for performing mult-page requests," *Information Systems 21*,5 (July, 1996), 387-407.
100. P. G. Selinger, M. M. Astrahan, D. D. Chamberlin, R. A. Lorie, and T. G. Price. "Access path selection in a relational database management system," *Proc. ACM SIGMOD Int'l Conf. on Management of Data,* 1979, pp. 23-34.
101. A. Serry. *An Analytical Approach to Modelling IMS Systems,* Ph.D. Thesis, Computer Science Dept., University of Toronto, 1984.
102. K. C. Sevcik. "Data base system performance prediction using an analytic model," *Proc. 7th Int'l Conf. on Very Large Data Bases,* 1981, pp. 182-196.
103. L. D. Shapiro. "Join processing in database systems with large main memories," *ACM Trans. on Database Systems 11*,3 (Sept. 1986), 239-264.
104. D. Sleator and R. E. Tarjan. "Amortized efficiency of list update and paging rules," *Commun. of the ACM 28*,2 (Feb. 1985), 202-208.
105. A. J. Smith. "Sequentiality and prefetching in database systems," *ACM Trans. on Database Systems 3*,3 (March 1978), 223-247.
106. A. J. Smith. "Disk cache: Miss ratio analysis and design considerations," *ACM Trans. on Computer Systems 3*,3 (1985), 161-203.
107. J. T. Spirn. *Program Behavior: Models and Measurements,* Elsevier, 1977.
108. J. T. Spirn and S. Tsur. "Memory management for B-trees," *Performance Evaluation 4,* (1985), 159-174.

109. A. Swami and K. B. Shiefer. "Estimating page fetches for index scans with finite LRU buffers," *The Very Large Data Base Journal 4,* (1995), 675-701.
110. J. Z. Teng and R. A. Gumaer. "Managing IBM Database 2 buffers to maximize performance," *IBM Systems J. 23*,2 (1984), 211-218.
111. D. Theodoratos and T. Sellis. "Data warehouse configuration," *Proc. 23rs Int'l Conf. on Very Large Data Bases,* 1997, pp. 126-135.
112. A. Thomasian and P. Bay. "Analysis of queueing network models with population size constraints and delayed blocked customers," *Proc. ACM SIGMETRICS Conf. on Measurement and Modeling of Computer Systems,* 1984, pp. 202-216.
113. A. Thomasian and P. Bay. "Analytic queueing network models for parallel processing of task systems," *IEEE Trans. on Computers 35*,12 (Dec. 1986), 1045-1054.
114. A. Thomasian. "A performance study of dynamic load balancing in distributed systems," *Proc. 7th IEEE Int'l Conf. on Distributed Computing Systems,* 1987, pp. 178-185.
115. A. Thomasian. "Checkpointing for optimistic concurrency control methods," *IEEE Trans. Knowledge and Data Engineering 7*,2 (April 1995), 322-329.
116. A. Thomasian. *Database Concurrency Control: Methods, Performance, and Analysis,* Kluwer Academic Publishers, 1996.
117. A. Thomasian and J. Menon. "RAID5 performance with distributed sparing," *IEEE Trans. on Parallel and Distributed Systems 8*,6 (June 1997), 640-657.
118. A. Thomasian. "RAID5 Disk Arrays and Their Performance Analysis," Chapter 37 in *Recovery in Database Management Systems* V. Kumar and M. Hsu (Eds.), Prentice-Hall, 1998.
119. A. Thomasian, V. Castelli, and C. S. Li. "Clustering and singular value decomposition for approximate indexing in high-dimensional spaces," *Proc. Conf. on Information and Knowledge Management (CIKM),* 1998, pp. 267-272.
120. D. F. Towsley, K. M. Chandy, and J. C. Browne. "Models for parallel processing within programs: Application to CPU:O/O and I/O:I/O overlap," *Commun. of the ACM 21*,10 (Oct. 1978), 821-831.
121. J. Turek, J. L. Wolf, K. R. Pattipati, and P. S. Yu. "Scheduling parallelizable tasks: Putting it all on the shelf," *Proc. Joint PERFORMANCE '92/AXM SIGMETRICS Conf.* pp. 225-236.
122. P. J. Varman, S. D. Sheuffler, B. R. Iyer, and G. R. Ricard. "Merging multiple lists on hierarchical memory multiprocessors," *Journal of Parallel and Distributed Computing 12,* (1991), 171-177.
123. J. S. Vitter and W. C. Chen. *Design and Analysis of Coalesced Hashing,* Oxford University Press, 1987.
124. Y. T. Wang and R.J.T. Morris. "Load sharing in distributed systems," *IEEE Trans. on Computers 43*,3 (March 1985), 204-217.
125. R. Weber, H. J. Scheck, and S. Blott. "A quantitative analysis and performance study for similarity-search methods in high-dimensional spaces," *Proc. 24th Int'l Conf. on Very Large Data Bases,* 1998, pp. 194-205.
126. G. Wiederhold. *Database Design,* McGraw-Hill, 1983.
127. K. Y. Whang and R. Krishnamurthy. "Query optimization in a memory resident domain relational calculus database systems," *ACM Trans. on Database Systems 15*,1 (March 1990), 67-95.
128. J. L. Wolf. B. R. Iyer, K. R. Pattipati, and J. Turek. "Optimal buffer partitioning for the nested block join algorithm," *Proc. IEEE Int'l Conf. on Data Engineering,* 1991, pp. 510-519.
129. A. C. Yao. "On random 2-3 trees," *Acta Informatica 9,* (1978), 159-170.

130. S. B. Yao, K. S. Das, and T. J. Teorey. "A dynamic database reorganization algorithm," *ACM Trans. on Database Systems 1*,2 (1976), 159-174.
131. S. B. Yao. "An attribute based model for database access cost analysis," *ACM Trans. on Database Systems 2*,1 (March 1977), 45-67.
132. P. S. Yu, S. Balsamo, and Y. H. Lee. "Dynamic transaction routing in distributed database systems," *IEEE Trans. on Software Engineering 14*,9 (Sept. 1988), 1307-1318.
133. P. S. Yu, D. W. Cornell, D. M. Dias, and A. Thomasian. "Performance comparison of the IO shipping and database call shipping schemes in multisystem partitioned database systems," *Performance Evaluation 10,* (1989), 15-33.
134. T. Zhang, R. Ramakrishnan, and M. Livny. "Birch: A new data clustering algorithm and its applications," *Data Mining and Knowledge Discovery 1*,2 (1997), 141-182.
135. C. Zou and B. Salzberg. "Towards efficient database reorganization," *IEEE Data Engineering Bulletin 19*,2 (1996), 33-40.

Performance Analysis of Concurrency Control Methods

Alexander Thomasian

Dept. of Computer Science and Eng.
University of Connecticut, 191 Auditorium Rd.,
Storrs, CT 06269
athomas@uconnvm.uconn.edu

1 Introduction

Since the appearance of the first papers in mid-70's formalizing *two-phase locking* as a means of Concurrency Control (CC) [23], there have been numerous proposals based on *locking, time-stamp ordering, and optimistic CC* [6], [52], [77]. CC is required to ensure correctness and database integrity when it is updated by several transactions concurrently [23].

Standard locking, i.e., strict two-phase locking with on demand lock requests and blocking on lock conflict, is almost exclusively used by current database management systems. Transaction blocking may lead to a *thrashing* behavior, where the majority of transactions in the system are blocked. Techniques to reduce the number of blocked transactions are based on *restart-oriented locking methods* and *two-phase processing methods* [18].

Restart-oriented locking methods allow some transactions encountering lock conflicts to be blocked, but reduce the level of lock contention by restarting transactions encountering or causing lock conflicts. Two-phase processing methods execute transactions in two (or multiple) phases taking advantage of the fact that transaction re-execution may not require disk I/O provided a database buffer is available and *access invariance* prevails [17]. *Optimistic CC* is a special case [33].

We provide an overview of developments in the area of performance evaluation of CC methods with emphasis on analytic solutions. Thorough reviews of these topics also appear in [65] (Chapter 4) and [77], [81].

A single lock is used in some systems, such that the processing of transactions is tantamount to the readers and writers problem. Readers can be processed concurrently, while writers are processed one at a time. A matrix-geometric approach to the analysis of readers and writers with a FCFS discipline and a restriction on the maximum number of concurrent readers appears in [44]. The maximum throughput attainable in processing readers and writers can be increased considerably by means of a threshold scheduling policy, i.e., the processing of readers is interrupted and writers are processed exhaustively when the number of writers initially exceeds a certain threshold. The analysis of this system using a vacationing-server model (see e.g., [61]) and a Markov chain model appears in [74].

G. Haring et al. (Eds.): Performance Evaluation, LNCS 1769, pp. 329–354, 2000.

This paper is organized as follows. Section 2 describes the transaction execution model, the database access model, and the computer system model. In Section 3 we review the analyses of locking methods and outline the analysis in [71]. In Section 4 (resp. Section 5) we review analytic studies of the performance of restart-oriented locking methods (resp. optimistic CC). Section 6 summarizes the performance analyses of distributed databases. Conclusions and areas of further investigation are discussed in Section 7.

2 Models of Transaction Processing Systems

We consider an abstract model for evaluating the performance of transaction processing systems as affected by hardware and data resource contention, since we are interested in evaluating the relative performance of CC methods. This model which has been used in numerous performance evaluation studies of CC methods is not detailed enough for predicting the performance of real transaction processing systems. In operational systems hardware resource contention has the primary effect on performance and data contention has a secondary effect. The performance comparison of CC methods is carried out by postulating "infinite" hardware resources, which allow high multiprogramming levels resulting in high lock contention levels.

We consider short update transactions accessing k database objects. Each transaction consists of $k + 1$ steps involving CPU processing and disk accesses. The mean time per step is determined by the analysis of the underlying queueing network model of the computer system [77], [81]. The last k steps start with an access to a *single* database object, after an appropriate lock on the object has been acquired. The completion of the last step leads to transaction *commit,* which requires the writing of a log record to non-volatile storage, usually a disk, after which the locks held by the transaction are released [6], [23].

A system may process multiple transaction classes, where transaction class k (denoted by C_k) is determined by its size (the number of objects accessed by the transaction) or other transaction attributes, such as update versus read-only queries.

We consider a closed system, such that a completed transaction is immediately replaced by a new transaction and the degree of transaction concurrency in the system is always M. This seemingly unrealistic model is quite useful in comparing the performance of CC methods, since it is easier to estimate the peak throughput of a closed rather than an open system using simulation. The performance of a closed system with M transactions is specifiable by its *effective throughput characteristic* $T(M)$, $M \geq 1$, i.e., its throughput taking data and hardware resource contention into account. The mean transaction residence time is $R(M) = M/T(M)$. The performance of an *open* system can be obtained from the *closed* system using the hierarchical decomposition method for queueing network models, see e.g., [56].

In the case of a system with multiple transaction classes we may specify the degree of transaction concurrency M_k of transactions in C_k. Alternatively, with a *frequency-based model* we specify transaction frequencies, i.e., a completed transaction is immediately replaced by a new transaction in C_k with probability f_k (see e.g., [55], [56]). Restarted transactions are replaced by transactions in the same class and the throughput for transactions in C_k is $T_k(M) = f_k T(M)$, $1 \leq k \leq K$. The performance comparison of CC methods with a frequency-based closed system simply requires the comparison of their effective throughput characteristics [55], [71], while an open model requires the comparison of the mean response time characteristics, which are more difficult to obtain (see e.g., [68]).

2.1 Database Access Model

The *granule* is the unit of data at which CC is applied to the database. A granule may be associated with a single object, e.g., a record, or multiple database objects, e.g., a page containing multiple records or even a whole table [23]. A finer granularity of locking introduces more overhead, but potentially reduces the level of lock contention [23]. The effect of granularity of locking on performance has been considered in several studies [63], [65]. Coarse granularity of locking is required to ensure that the locking overhead for queries accessing high data volumes is acceptable.

Database access patterns (or granule placements) are reviewed in [34]. Sequential database access has been considered in some early simulation studies of static locking (see Chapter 4 in [65]). In most studies all lock requests are uniformly distributed over the D database objects. Objects may be replaced after selection and sampled again or with the more realistic no replacement policy all selected objects are distinct. The simpler analysis with the replacement assumption leads to numerical results which are indistinguishable from results with the without replacement assumption when D is large.

We are mainly concerned with a database with D objects, which are locked in *exclusive* or *shared* mode. Objects are accessed uniformly and replacement is allowed.

Nonuniformity of database accesses is captured by the hot-spot model and the $b - c$ rule [63], [65], i.e., a fraction b (resp. $1 - b$) of transaction accesses are to a fraction c (resp. $1 - c$) of the database. A ***homogeneous database access model*** postulates that all granules are accessed from a single database region. A more realistic database access model for transaction processing with multiple transaction classes and multiple database regions is based on the ***heterogeneous database access model*** [78], which is discussed in Section 3.5.

2.2 Computer System Model

The *infinite resource* model, while unrealistic, is useful in comparing the performance limits of CC methods [16], [55], [63]. [64], [65], [71]. According to this model each transaction has its own virtual processor and its execution time is independent from the number of transactions being executed concurrently.

A *finite resource* model allows the level of hardware resource contention to be varied to determine its effect on overall performance [2], [18], [71]. This model can be represented by a finite number of virtual processors [79]. The *throughput characteristic* $t(M), M \geq 1$ of a computer system is determined by analyzing its queueing network model.

The performance degradation due to CC methods is in the form of transaction blocking, restarts, or both. There is also performance degradation due to overhead associated with transaction blocking and aborts.

1. *Performance degradation due to blocking.* Standard locking with dynamic lock requests meets this criterion, since transaction aborts to resolve deadlocks are rare and transaction blocking due to lock conflicts incurs a negligible overhead [63], [65], [56], [77], [78]. Given that the mean number of *active* transactions is $\overline{M}_a$ and the mean number of blocked transactions is $\overline{M}_b = M - \overline{M}_a$, we have $T(M) \approx t(\overline{M}_a)$.
2. *Performance degradation due to restarts.* The optimistic CC method [33], and the no-waiting locking method [64] fall into this category. The system efficiency is the fraction of useful processing in the system and can be expressed as $T(M)/t(M)$.
3. *Performance degradation due to blocking and restarts.* The running priority method and WDL belong to this category [16], [18]. Since the wasted processing is due to active transactions, the system efficiency is defined as $T(\overline{M}_a)/t(\overline{M}_a)$.

Separation of hardware and data resource contention is desirable, since the system throughput characteristic need be computed once, after which it can be used in an iterative solution for data contention. This separation is possible if the data contention overhead, e.g., due to transaction blocking or aborts, is insignificant or it is independent of the level of lock contention [65], [77]. Otherwise, the iterative solution requires recomputing the effect of hardware resource contention.

3 Standard Locking

The identities of all required locks are assumed to be known a priori in *static locking*, which in practice is only possible with coarse granularity locking, e.g., for batch processing [68]. The execution of a transaction with static locking is started only when all locks have been acquired. In *dynamic locking* locks are requested on demand during transaction execution.

This section is organized as follows. We first review earlier studies on this subject, followed by a rather detailed discussion of the model in [71].

3.1 Performance Analyses of Static Locking

Static locking is more amenable to an analytic solution than dynamic locking, which is the reason why most analytic studies of static locking preceded dynamic locking [47], [21], [72], [42], [68], [63], and [65].

An analysis of static locking using the decomposition method for queueing network models appears in [47]. The probabilistic analysis is based on the assumption that all possible lock assignments are equally probable (Bose-Einstein statistic), which does not correspond to a uniform distribution of lock requests assumption made in the paper [34], [77]. This analysis makes the unrealistic assumption that a fixed number of m transactions are unblocked when a transaction completes (only the case $m = 1$ is considered).

The analysis in [47] is extended in [72],[42], which alleviate its shortcomings. *Strict FCFS* and *nonstrict FCFS* transaction scheduling policies are considered in [72]. The nonstrict FCFS scheduler activates a transaction if all of its lock requests can be satisfied, while the strict FCFS scheduler activates transactions strictly in that order. Alternatively, required locks can be requested atomically upon a transaction's arrival [21], but this is less efficient than nonstrict-FCFS scheduling, since no locks are held by blocked transactions. The number of transactions activated upon the completion of a transaction is determined based on the probability that the remaining transactions hold requested locks.

Incremental static locking is a form of dynamic locking where locks are requested in quick succession at the beginning of transaction execution [63], [65]. The analysis for dynamic locking is applicable to the analysis of this method.

The analysis in [21] is interesting in that it is shown that the iteration converges to a unique solution, but the results obtained from this analysis are not very accurate.

A simplified analysis of static locking in [63], [65] turns out to be inaccurate in a few high contention cases considered in [42]. This analysis is extended in [70].

The analysis in [68] postulates a fixed number of transaction classes with given frequencies. Each transaction class accesses a predetermined subset of the objects in the database in exclusive mode. Hence only a set of compatible transactions accessing disjoint subsets of the database can be processed concurrently. Given the service demands of the transactions, the system throughputs in processing feasible compositions of transactions is easy to compute. A higher-level Markov chain representing transaction arrivals and completions can then be used to obtain the mean response times for transaction classes. A finite number of transactions is allowed into the system to limit the number of states for solving the set of corresponding linear equations. An aggregation method with a lower computational cost is also proposed in this work. A birth-death model is analyzed where state are identified by the number of transactions in the system. The birth-rate is the total transaction arrival rate and the death-rate equals the mean throughput with FCFS scheduling of transactions based on their compatibility.

Exact analysis of static locking is carried out in the case when transactions arrive according to a Poisson process and blocked transactions are lost [39]. This analysis leads to a simple asymptotic expression as the number of database locks is increased to infinity. The analysis obtains a product-form for the stationary state probabilities. A simple analysis of the same problem is also presented in

[35], which furthermore considers shared and exclusive locks, which is also done in [40].

Also of interest are models which specify the probability of lock conflict with the pairwise lock conflict probability p. The analysis in [83] obtains bounds for the maximum arrival rate of such transactions as $1/e \leq \lambda_{max} \times p \leq 0.75$ in the limit as $p \rightarrow 0$.

3.2 Performance Analyses of Dynamic Locking

Solution methods for dynamic locking are surveyed in [63], [65], [56], and [73]. Most studies consider a single transaction in isolation, while a different approach is used in [56].

Fixed Size Transactions The mean response time of a transaction requesting k locks in a system with M transactions is expressed as $R(M) = r(\overline{M}_a) + kP_cW$, where $r(\overline{M}_a) = (k+1)s(\overline{M}_a)$ is the mean time the transaction is active and $s(\overline{M}_a)$ is the mean duration of a transaction step, which is a function of $\overline{M}_a$, since only active transactions compete for the hardware resources, P_c is the probability of lock conflict per lock request, and W is the mean waiting time per lock conflict.

The fraction of time transactions are blocked in the system (β) is the ratio of transaction blocking time and its mean response time, which is given as $\beta = kP_cW/R(M) = \overline{M}_b/M$. It follows that $R(M) = r(\overline{M}_a)/(1-\beta)$.

The probability of lock conflict when lock requests are uniformly distributed over the D locks is $P_c = (M-1)\overline{L}/D$, where $\overline{L}$ is the mean number of locks held per transaction given by the ratio of the time-space of lock holding time (per transaction) and the mean transaction residence time [73], [71]. When lock requests are uniformly distributed over its residence time $\overline{L} \approx k/2$ and $P_c \approx (M-1)k/(2D)$.

The probability that a transaction encounters a lock conflict is

$$P_w = 1 - (1-P_c)^k \approx kP_c \approx \frac{(M-1)k^2}{2D}. \quad (1)$$

The probability that two transactions are involved in a (two way) deadlock is [23]

$$P_D(2) = Pr[T_1 \rightarrow T_2]Pr[T_2 \rightarrow T_1](M-1) = \frac{P_w^2}{M-1} \approx \frac{(M-1)k^4}{4D^2}. \quad (2)$$

Similar expressions apply to multiway deadlocks, but since P_w is very small, $P_D(i)$ for $i > 2$ is negligibly small.

A more accurate expression for $P_D(2)$ is obtained by noting that a deadlock is possible only if the conflicting transaction is blocked. We obtain the mean waiting time of a transaction (W_1) with respect to an active transaction by noting that the probability of lock conflict increases with the number of locks (j) that the (active) transaction holds [73]

$$W_1 = \sum_{j=1}^{k} \frac{2j(k-j)}{k(k+1)}[s(\overline{M}_a) + u] + s'(\overline{M}_a) = \frac{k-1}{3}[s(\overline{M}_a) + u] + s'(\overline{M}_a). \quad (3)$$

The fraction of time the conflicting transaction is blocked is $A = W_1/R(M) \approx 1/3$, which leads to $P'_D(2) \approx P_D(2)/3$ [73]. The analysis in [63], [65] leads to $4/3P'_D(2)$.

The analysis in [36] considers an $M \times k$ table denoting the k lock requests by the M transactions and obtains the probability that two transactions have a deadlock. The analysis yields $2P'_D(2)$, which is an overestimate attributable to the fact that a full table is considered, i.e., transaction blockings are ignored.

Analytic solutions based on queueing network models augment the hardware resource contention model with D pseudo-servers to represent lock contention delays for the D database locks [27], [67]. The pseudo-servers are identical and can be aggregated into a single server.

The mean service time at the pseudo-servers is the mean waiting time $W = F \times R(M)$. Simulation results show that $F \approx 0.5$, which is the midpoint for $1/3 \leq F \leq 2/3$ according to the analysis in [63], [65]. An iterative solution is used in [67], since $R(M)$ is not known a priori.

The analysis of a closed system with $\Lambda = M/D$ and k lock requests per transaction leads to a cubic equation in $\overline{M}_a$, which has a solution when $k^2\Lambda/D < 1.5$ [63], [65]. Only one out of three roots is of interest. The analysis is shown to be very accurate through validation against simulation results, although it ignores the possibility of deadlocks.

The analysis in Section B in [73] allows variable transaction sizes and different processing times for transaction steps. Only two levels of transaction blocking with currently active transactions and transactions which are blocked by active transactions are considered. Simulation results show that this analysis is quite accurate up to relatively high lock contention levels. A similar analysis is presented in [86].

There is a state-space explosion problem associated with modeling locking methods. The state of a system with M transactions each requesting k locks is specifiable by M vectors, whose elements denote the identities of requested locks. An extra element specifies the position of the last lock request in a FCFS queue for the lock (zero if the lock is held). The transitions among the states of the Markov chain are deterministic in this case. A more compact state representation is possible, by specifying the number of locks held by a transaction and whether the last lock request is granted or not. The probability of a successful lock request equals the ratio of the number of locks held by other transactions and D. The probability of deadlock can be also determined by a simple calculation. There is a significant decrease in the size of the state-space, which is at the cost of increased complexity in computing state transition probabilities.

An ultimately compact state representation is considered in [56], which is based on the number of active transactions $J \leq M$. At the completion of a step a transaction requests a new lock or commits. A lock request may result in the transition $S_J \rightarrow S_J$, $S_J \rightarrow S_{J-1}$, and $S_J \rightarrow S_I$, $I \geq J$. The transition probability $S_J \rightarrow S_I$ is given by $P_t(J, I)$, which varies depending on whether the lock request is successful, unsuccessful with blocking, and unsuccessful with an abort to resolve the deadlock caused by the lock request (the locks released by an aborted transaction may activate other transactions). Deadlocks are resolved by aborting the transaction causing the deadlock, since a more sophisticated deadlock resolution method is not expected to improve performance to a significant degree. A multilevel solution method is adopted, which facilitates bottom-up validation and allows modifications to some levels of the analysis without affecting others, e.g., a different lock conflict model can be adopted.

The *equilibrium point analysis* method (see Chapter 2 in [62]) is utilized in [72], [56] to reduce the computational cost by a factor of $M/log_2(M)$. Equilibrium point analysis assumes that the system is always at an equilibrium point, such that *the probability of entering a state equals the probability of exiting a state.* This is expressed as a nonlinear equation which has one or more solutions for equilibrium states. In this case the mean number of active transactions J satisfies $\sum_{I=J-1}^{M}(I-J)P_t(J,I) = 0$. The state-equilibrium probability is symmetric about the equilibrium point.

The thrashing behavior associated with standard locking observed in [67], [63], [65], [77] is an instance of *catastrophe theory* (see e.g., [45]), i.e., a small increase in the multiprogramming level for transactions leads to a sudden decrease in throughput.

Variable Size Transactions The mean response time for transactions in C_k is $R_k(M) = (k+1)s(\overline{M}_a) + kP_cW$, from which the mean response time over all transaction classes is given as follows

$$R(M) = \sum_{k=1}^{K} R_k(M) f_k = r(\overline{M}_a) + K_1 P_c W, \tag{4}$$

where $K_i = \sum_{j=1}^{K} k^j f_j$ is the ith moment of requested locks. It follows from $\overline{M}_k = f_k R_k(M)/R(M)$ that $\overline{M}_k \approx M k f_k / K_1$. The mean number of locks held per transaction is then

$$\overline{L} = \frac{1}{M}\sum_{k=1}^{K} \overline{L}_k \overline{M}_k \approx \frac{1}{M}\sum_{k=1}^{K} \frac{k}{2}\overline{M}_k \approx \frac{1}{2K_1}\sum_{k=1}^{K} k^2 f_k = \frac{K_2}{2K_1}. \tag{5}$$

It follows that P_c (resp. $P_D(2)$) for the geometric distribution is twice (resp. an order of magnitude) higher than for fixed transaction sizes [73].

W_1 for variable size transactions can be obtained from Eq. (3). $A = W_1/R(M)$ can then be expressed as follows [73], [71]

$$A = \frac{W_1}{R(M)} \approx \frac{K_3 - K_1}{3K_1(K_2 + K_1)}. \tag{6}$$

The probability that a transaction is blocked by an active (resp. blocked) transaction is $1-\beta$ (resp. β) and the mean blocking time is W_1 (resp. $W_2 = 1.5W_1$). More generally, the probability that the *effective level of blocking* of a transaction is at level i is approximated by $P_b(i) = \beta^{i-1}$, $i > 1$ and $P_b(1) = 1-\beta-\beta^2-\beta^3....$ The mean waiting time at level $i > 1$ is approximated by $W_i = (i-0.5)W_1$. The mean overall waiting time is a weighted sum of delays incurred by transactions blocked at different levels [1]

$$W = \sum_{i \geq 1} P_b(i)W_i = W_1[1 - \sum_{i \geq 1} \beta^i + \sum_{i>1}(i-0.5)\beta^{i-1}]. \tag{7}$$

We define $n_c = K_1 P_C$ as the mean number of lock conflicts per transaction. Multiplying both sides by $K_1 P_c/R(M)$ and defining $\alpha = K_1 P_c A$ (with $A = W_1/R(M)$) and since $\beta = K_1 P_c W/R(M)$ we have

$$\beta = \alpha(1 + 0.5\beta + 1.5\beta^2 + 2.5\beta^3 + ...). \tag{8}$$

We can obtain a closed-form expression for $\beta < 1$, by assuming that the series is infinite:

$$\beta^3 - (1.5\alpha + 2)\beta^2 + (1.5\alpha + 1)\beta - \alpha = 0. \tag{9}$$

Note that α is a single metric which determines the level of lock contention for standard locking.

The cubic equation has three roots $0 \leq \beta_1 < \beta_2 \leq 1$ and $\beta_3 \geq 1$ for $\alpha \leq \alpha^* = 0.226$ and a single root $\beta_3 > 1$ for $\alpha > \alpha^*$. *α^* can be used as an indicator of whether the system is operating in the thrashing region or not.* The smallest root β_1 for $\alpha \leq \alpha^*$ determines system performance.

It follows from $d\overline{M}_a/d\alpha = 0$, that $\alpha_{max} \approx 0.21$ with a corresponding $\beta_{max} \approx 0.3$. The effective throughput characteristic $(T(M), M \geq 1)$ increases with M, reaches a peak at $\hat{\alpha}$ corresponding to M_{max} at which point $\overline{M}_a$ and hence $T(M_{max}) \approx t(0.7M_{max})$ reach their maximum value (assuming $t(m)$ is non-decreasing).

The variability of transaction size has a major effect on system performance, e.g., α for fixed size transactions is one sixth of that of geometrically distributed transactions with the same mean size.

The analysis with different per step processing times is summarized at this point. The probability of lock conflict with a blocked transaction with identical per step processing times can be approximated by β, since active and blocked transactions hold the same number of locks approximately [56]. When transaction steps have different processing times this probability is approximated by $\rho \approx \overline{L}_b/\overline{L}$, where $\overline{L} = \overline{L}_a + \overline{L}_b$ with $\overline{L}_a$ and $\overline{L}_b$ denoting the mean number of locks held by active and blocked transactions, respectively. The *conflict ratio*, which is defined as the ratio of the total number of locks held by transactions

[1] Simulation studies show that the wait depth of blocked transactions tends to be limited to a few levels for reasonable parameters, e.g., transaction sizes much smaller than database size.

and the total number of locks held by active transactions [84], is related to ρ as $conflict\ ratio = 1/(1-\rho)$ or conversely $\rho = 1 - 1/conflict\ ratio$.

The probability that a transaction is blocked at level i is approximated by $P_b(i) = \rho^{i-1}, i > 1$ with $P_b(1) = 1 - \rho/(1-\rho)$. The mean waiting time with one level of blocking can be expressed as

$$W_1 = \frac{1}{H}\sum_{k=1}^{K} f_k \sum_{i=1}^{k} i s_k^i(\overline{M_a})[\sum_{j=i}^{k} s_k^j(\overline{M_a}) + (k-i)P_c W], \tag{10}$$

where $H = \sum_{k=1}^{K} f_k \sum_{i=1}^{k} i s_k^i(\overline{M_a})$ is a normalization constant.

The mean waiting time of a transaction blocked at level i is approximated by $W_i = (i-0.5)W_1, i > 1$ as before. Similarly to Eq. (8) we have

$$W = W_1(1 + 0.5\rho + 1.5\rho^2 + 2.5\rho^3 + \ldots). \tag{11}$$

Multiplying both sides of the equation by $K_1 P_c / R(M)$ for $\rho < 1$ we have

$$\beta = \alpha[1 + \frac{0.5\rho(1+\rho)}{(1-\rho)^2}]. \tag{12}$$

An iterative solution is required in this case.

The range of values for ρ is $1.25 < conflict\ ratio < 1.43$ is consistent with [84], which is based on trace-driven simulations. Similarly to the case of transactions with identical per step processing times $\overline{M}_a$ is maximized at $\beta \approx 0.3$.

3.3 More Realistic Lock Contention Models

The *effective database size paradigm* can be used to deal with shared and exclusive lock requests and nonuniform database accesses [63], [65]. It allows uniform accesses to be considered in exclusive mode. This paradigm is applicable only to standard locking and should be used with caution in the case of restart-oriented methods [79], [82]. Shared and exclusive lock requests to a database with size D can be substituted with exclusive lock requests to a database of size $D_{eff} = D/(1-s^2)$, where s denotes the fraction of lock requests in shared mode. In the case of the nonuniform database access model, where a fraction b of database accesses are to a fraction c of the database $D_{eff} = D/[b^2/c + (1-b)^2/(1-c)]$ [63], [65].

A heterogeneous database access model is described in [78]. J transaction classes and I database regions are considered. Transactions in class j (C_j) have a frequency f_j and in their n^{th} step (denoted by $C_{j,n}$) access database region i (denoted by D_i) with probability $g_{j,n,i}$. This can be represented by a bypartite graph, where one set of nodes represent transaction steps and the other set the database regions, i.e., with probability $g_{j,n,i}$ $C_{j,n} \rightarrow D_i$. The analytic solution method in [71] is extended in [78] to analyze this model.

Relational models provide locking at multiple granularity levels, intent locks, and cursor locks [23]. A better characterization of the locking behavior of transaction processing systems is required for specifying realistic locking models.

Valuable insights about locking behavior are provided by the analysis of several locking traces in [59].

Locking methods for index structures with provisions for recovery are rather complex [23]. There here have been numerous proposals for more efficient locking methods with accompanying simulation results to justify the superiority of the proposed method. Two analytic and simulation studies compare the performance of a set of representative methods [30], [60]. The analysis in [30] obtains the response time and maximum throughput for several locking methods. Two-phase locking, which involves the locking of all nodes, is unnecessary in this case, since only one node is affected by an insertion if the node is not full. The results of this analysis, which are validated against simulation results, indicates that the best performance is attained by a method that minimizes the lock holding time for higher level nodes. One weakness of this analysis is that it does not handle hot spots.

Multidimensional indexes [20] have many applications, including content based search in image databases. There have been few proposals for CC methods for such indexes, see e.g., [31], but no analytic studies of CC performance have been reported.

4 Restart-Oriented Locking Methods

A large number of restart-oriented locking methods have been proposed, some for the sake of being amenable to an analytic solution and others to cope with the performance limitations of standard locking.

This section is organized as follows. After describing restart-oriented methods, we review the performance analyses of such methods. This is followed by a detailed discussion of the analysis in [82].

4.1 Description of Restart-Oriented Methods

A concise specification of restart-oriented locking methods is as follows:

- According to the *no waiting* or the *immediate restart* method a transaction T_A which has a lock conflict with a transaction T_B is aborted.
- The *asymmetric running priority* method [16] aborts T_B in the waits-for graph $T_A \rightarrow T_B \rightarrow T_C$. This action improves performance by increasing the degree of transaction concurrency [18]. The *symmetric running priority* method aborts the originally active transaction T_B when it becomes blocked by T_C.
- The *asymmetric cautious waiting* method [26] aborts T_A when it is blocked by T_B which is itself blocked by T_C as in $T_A \rightarrow T_B \rightarrow T_C$. The *symmetric cautious waiting* method first checks if T_A is blocking other transactions as in $(T_X, T_Y, ..., T_Z) \rightarrow T_A \rightarrow T_B$ and aborts them when T_A becomes blocked. The wait depth is maintained at $d = 1$ with symmetric cautious waiting.
  The symmetric and asymmetric running priority and cautious waiting methods are deadlock-free [16], [26].

- The WDL and MWDL methods limit the wait depth of blocked transactions to one, while taking into account transaction progress in deciding which transaction to abort [18]. Consider a lock request by T_A which results in $[(T_X, T_Y, ..., T_Z) \rightarrow] T_A \rightarrow T_B [\rightarrow T_C]$. The following rules are applied when a lock conflict occurs with the MWDL method:
  1. If T_A, which is blocking some other transactions, has a lock conflict with T_B, then if $L(T_A) < L(T_B)$ then abort T_A, else abort T_B.
     WDL makes the comparison $L(T_A) < max(L(T_B), L(T_X), ..., L(T_Z))$ when T_A is blocking transactions $T_X, T_Y, ..., T_Z$ [18].
  2. If T_A, which is not blocking any other transactions, has a lock conflict with T_B, which is itself blocked by an active transaction (T_C), if $L(T_B) \leq L(T_C)$ then abort T_B, else abort T_C.
     WDL makes the comparison $L(T_B) \leq max(L(T_A), L(T_C))$ [18].
- The *wound-wait* method blocks transaction T_A requesting a lock held by T_B if T_A is not older than T_B, otherwise T_B is aborted [54].
- The *wait-die* method allows a younger transaction to wait if it is blocked by an older transaction, otherwise the transaction encountering a lock conflict is aborted [54].

Aborted transactions are automatically restarted by the system. *Cyclic restarts* or *livelocks* need to be prevented: (i) to reduce the wasted processing incurred in this manner; (ii) to ensure transaction completion within a finite time interval. Cyclic restarts can be prevented by *restart waiting*, i.e., delaying the restart of an aborted transaction until *all* conflicting transactions are completed [18]. *Random delays* or *conflict avoidance delays* are a less certain method to prevent cyclic restarts [2], [64], [65]. *Immediate restarts* are possible in a system with a backlog of transactions, such that an aborted transaction is set aside and is replaced by a new transaction with a different *script* [64], [65], [2], which is, as if, the locks requested by a transaction are resampled. The restart waiting-no lock resampling combination of options is pertinent to simulation studies.

Lock resampling is an inherent shortcoming of analytic solutions of restart-oriented methods, which results in overestimating system performance. This effect is quantified via simulation in the case of the no waiting method in [2]. Resampling also applies to transaction classes and results in overly optimistic results, since shorter transactions are less susceptible to restarts.

4.2 Performance Analysis

There have been numerous simulation studies of restart-oriented locking methods, most notably [3], [18], and [79]. These results are summarized in [77], [79], [81] and will not be repeated here. A brief review of analytic studies is as follows.

A method according to which a transaction encountering a lock conflict repeats its request L times before it is aborted is described in [14]. A Markov chain model representing the progress of a single transaction is used to analyze system performance. Numerical results with the immediate restart/lock resampling option and the infinite resource assumption lead to the conclusion that the best performance is attained at $L = 0$, i.e., the no waiting method.

The analysis of the no waiting and general waiting methods using flow diagrams presented in [63], [64], and [65] is discussed below. This method is applied to the analysis of the asymmetric cautious waiting method in [26].

We first consider the analysis of the the symmetric running priority method via a Markov chain with $2k+1$ states. Active (resp. blocked) states correspond to $S_{2j}, 0 \leq j \leq k$ (resp. $S_{2j+1}, 0 \leq j \leq k-1$).

The state equilibrium equations for the Markov chain can be solved easily to obtain the steady-state probabilities $\pi_i, 0 \leq i \leq 2K$. The mean number of visits to S_i (v_i) can be similarly obtained by noting that $v_{2K} = 1$. Given that h_i denotes the mean holding time at S_i then $\pi_i = v_i h_i / \sum_{j=0}^{2K} v_j h_j, 0 \leq i \leq 2K$. Note that $v_0 - 1$ denotes the mean number of transaction aborts.

The transition rates of the Markov chain for the symmetric running priority method are as follows.

1. $S_{2j} \rightarrow S_{2j+2}$ with rate a_{2j}, $0 \leq j \leq K-1$ designate successful lock requests, while $S_{2K} \rightarrow S_0$ with rate $a_{2K} = \mu_K$ corresponds to the completion of a transaction. The probability that a transaction T encountering a lock conflict at S_{2j} is blocking another transaction is given by Q_j. Let P_a (resp. P_b) denote the probability of lock conflict with an active (resp. blocked) transaction, with $P_c = P_a + P_b$. We have $a_{2j} = [(1 - P_c) + P_b(1 - Q_j)]\mu_j = (1 - P_a - P_b Q_j)\mu_j$, $0 \leq j \leq K-1$.
2. $S_{2j} \rightarrow S_{2j+1}$ with rate b_{2j}, $1 \leq j \leq K-1$ designate unsuccessful lock requests leading to transaction blocking. T is blocked only if it is not blocking any other transactions, hence $b_{2j} = P_a(1 - Q_j)\mu_j$, $0 \leq j \leq K-1$.
3. $S_{2j} \rightarrow S_0$ with rate $c_{2j} = P_c Q_j \mu_j$, $1 \leq j \leq K-1$ correspond to transaction aborts.
4. $S_{2j+1} \rightarrow S_{2j+2}$ with rate d_{2j+1}, $0 \leq j \leq K-1$. The waiting time for the acquisition of a lock is approximated by an exponential distribution $W(t) = 1 - e^{-\nu t}$, $t \geq 0$, with $\nu = 1/W$.
5. $S_{2j+1} \rightarrow S_0$ with rate e_{2j+1}, $0 \leq j \leq K$ designate the abort of T, which occurs when T', which is not blocking other transactions, requests a lock held by T. We assume that the process according to which T is aborted at S_{2j+1} is Poisson with parameter ω_j.

The probability of lock conflict with active (resp. blocked) transaction is $P_a \approx (M-1)\overline{L}_a/D$ (resp. $P_b \approx (M-1)L_b/D$), where $\overline{L}_a = \sum_{j=1}^{K} j\pi_{2j}$ (resp. $\overline{L}_b = \sum_{j=1}^{K-1} j\pi_{2j+1}$) is the mean number of locks held by active (resp. blocked) transactions. Also $\overline{L} = \overline{L}_a + \overline{L}_b$ and hence $P_c \approx (M-1)\overline{L}/D$. The fraction of blocked transactions in the system is given by $\beta (= \sum_{j=1}^{K} \pi_{2j-1})$. The mean number of active and blocked transactions is given by $\overline{M}_a = M(1-\beta)$ and $\overline{M}_b = M\beta$, respectively. The probability that an active transaction T at S_{2j} is blocking at least one of the $\overline{M}_b$ blocked transactions in the system is approximated by

$$Q_j = 1 - [1 - j/(M\overline{L}_a)]^{\overline{M}_b}, \quad 1 \leq j \leq K, \tag{13}$$

$j/(M\overline{L}_a)$ is the probability that another transaction is blocked by the target transaction at S_{2j}.

The mean waiting time W_j due to a lock conflict with an active transaction at S_{2j} is $W_j = \sum_{l \geq 2j}^{2K} v'_l h_l$. Visit ratios with respect to S_{2j} are obtained as follows $v'_{2j} = 1$, $v'_{2i+1} = b_{2i} v'_{2i}$ and $v'_{2i+2} = (a_{2i} + b_{2i} d_{2i+1}) v'_{2i}, j \leq i \leq K$. The mean holding time at S_l is $h_l = s_i = 1/\mu_i$ when $l = 2i$, $j \leq i \leq K$. The residual processing time at S_{2j} equals the processing time in that step, since the per step processing times are exponentially distributed. The mean delay at the blocked state S_l is the expected value of the minimum of two exponential distributions $h_l = 1/(\omega_i + \nu)$ with $l = 2i+1$, $j \leq i \leq K-1$. The mean waiting time is given by

$$W = \sum_{j=1}^{K} q_j W_j, \tag{14}$$

q_j is the probability of lock conflict with an *active* transaction at S_{2j}, which equals $q_j = j\pi_{2j}/H$, where $H = \sum_{j=1}^{K} j\pi_{2j}$ is a normalization constant. The rate of lock requests by the other transactions in the system is

$$\lambda = (1 - \frac{1}{M}) T(M) \sum_{l=0}^{K-1} v_{2l}(1 - Q_l). \tag{15}$$

The summation takes into account the increase in the rate of requested locks due to transaction restarts and the fact that lock conflicts due to transactions which are blocking other transactions do not have an effect, since these transactions are aborted upon lock conflict.

The rate at which a transaction at S_{2j+1} is aborted is proportional to the number of locks that it holds

$$\omega_j = j\lambda/D, \quad 0 \leq j \leq K-1. \tag{16}$$

The mean transaction response time is

$$R(M) = \sum_{j=0}^{K} v_{2j} s_j + \sum_{j=0}^{K-1} v_{2j+1}/(\nu + \omega_j). \tag{17}$$

Transaction throughput is given by $T(M) = M/R(M)$ or alternatively by $T(M) = M\mu_K \pi_{2K}$. Since some of the variables required for the analysis are not known a priori, an iterative solution is required, which tends to converge in a few cycles. Validation of the infinite resource model against simulation shows that the analysis of the symmetric running priority method to be quite accurate up to very high lock contention levels. The main difficulty with the analysis is the accurate estimation of Q_j [82].

For the no waiting method there are only two transition types: $a_{2j} = \mu_j(1 - P_a)$, $0 \leq j \leq K-1$ and $c_{2j-1} = \mu_j P_a$, $0 \leq j \leq K$. It can be easily shown that

$\pi_{2j} = \pi_0(1 - P_a)^j$, $1 \leq j \leq K$. Multiplying both sides of this equation by M yields the mean number of transactions in different states, as obtained by the analysis of flow diagrams. The analysis in this case is tantamount to solving a polynomial equation in $q = 1 - P_a$, which can be derived from the last equation noting that $P_a \approx M \sum_{j=1}^{K} j\pi_j/D$, where the numerator is the mean number of locks held in the system. The polynomial has a unique root in the range $(0, 1)$ [64], [65].

For the general waiting method there are three transition types, provided that the effect of deadlocks is ignored [63], [65]: : $a_{2j} = \mu_j(1 - P_c)$, $0 \leq j \leq K - 1$ and $b_{2j} = \mu_j P_c$, $0 \leq j \leq K$, and $d_{2j-1} = \nu = 1/W, 1 \leq j \leq K$. The state equilibrium equations are given by $\pi_{2j-1} = (\mu P_c/\nu)\pi_{2j-2}, 1 \leq j \leq K$ and $\pi_{2j} = \pi_0 = [1 + K(1 + \mu P_c/\nu)]^{-1}$, $1 \leq j \leq K$. Active states and blocked states have equal probabilities, which is due to the fact that the probability of a transaction encountering a lock conflict is independent of its step and the possibility of abort to resolve deadlocks is ignored. System performance in this case depends on P_c and $\nu = 1/W$ [73], [71].

The analyses in [63], [64], and [65] are based on flow-diagrams, which are equivalent to semi-Markov chains. The holding times of the states of a semi-Markov chain have a general distribution, while this holding time is exponential for Markov chains. The disadvantage of a semi-Markov chain model is that asynchronous transitions from certain states cannot be readily specified, e.g., the abort and restart of a blocked transaction [82]. Dynamic locking, the no-waiting policy [65], and the cautious waiting method [26] only allow transaction restarts when a transaction makes a lock request. W is estimated by a detailed analysis of the forest of blocked transactions [63], [65].

The analysis of the frequency based model of the no waiting method in [64], [65] uses different transition points from a single flow-diagram to denote transaction completions. A similar method is used in [58] to analyze the timestamp-ordering method. These analyses do not ensure the *conservation of transaction class frequencies*, i.e., the fraction of transactions completed by the system differs from the original frequencies in a manner favoring shorter transactions, which have a higher probability of success than longer transactions. The analysis for a single transaction class can be extended to multiple classes with the frequency-based model, by using a separate Markov chain per class in the analysis, as is done in [82]. A system with a given number of transactions in two classes is analyzed by a simple extension of the analysis for a single transaction class in [64], [65].

5 Two-Phase Processing Methods

Transaction execution takes one, but sometimes two or multiple phases. The first phase of transaction execution may lead to its commit, but even if it is not successful, the automatically restarted transaction will execute efficiently with data prefetched from disk as a result of its first execution phase. Two-phase processing methods increase the chances of successful transaction re-execution, if necessary, by allowing a shorter processing time for transactions in the second phase and a lower *effective degree of transaction concurrency* in this and further phases, provided that the database buffer is large enough to retain pages accessed by transactions and *access invariance* prevails [18].

Access invariance can be at the *logical* or *physical* level. In the first case a transaction accesses the same logical objects (records), while in the second case the same physical objects (blocks) are accessed upon re-execution [18]. Optimistic CC methods are an instance of two-phase processing, although multi-phase processing is possible with optimistic CC, since transaction completion is not guaranteed in the second execution phase.

Section 5.1 is a brief introduction to optimistic CC. Mechanisms for two-phase transaction processing are described in Section 5.2, followed in Section 5.3 by a description of transaction scheduling methods and their relative performance with respect to each other and other methods. In Section 5.4 we outline analytic solution methods for optimistic CC.

5.1 Optimistic Concurrency Control

Optimistic CC is a major alternative to locking [33], but is considered to be less suitable than locking for implementing high performance transaction processing systems. The execution of a transaction with optimistic CC comprises three phases [37],[55]:

1. During the *read phase* transactions access database objects. A clean or committed copy of requested objects is made available to transactions, while dirty copies of the same objects may exist in the *private workspace* of other transactions. Reciprocally, a transaction's updates only affect its private workspace.
2. The *validation phase* ensures serializability by checking for data conflicts, which are resolved by aborting the transaction which failed its validation. There is a data conflict where the version of the data read earlier by a transaction is not up-to-date anymore.
3. A read-only transaction is considered completed after a successful validation, while otherwise a transaction initiates commit processing by writing the log records onto disk and then externalizes updated objects to the database buffer.

Aborted transactions can be restarted right away, since the conflicting transactions have committed and left the system, i.e., no further conflicts will occur. A transaction may run in optimistic *die* or *kill* modes. The former was explained above, while in optimistic kill mode a conflicted transaction is immediately restarted. To take advantage of the two-phase processing paradigm a transaction should be run in the die mode in the first phase and the kill mode in latter phases.

Optimistic methods are susceptible to repeated restarts. This problem can be fixed by using a locking method in the second phase. In fact the possibility of restart can be alleviated by preclaiming lock requests as in static locking, since their identity is known. Such a policy in the context of a distributed system is described in [81].

Two-phase processing methods can be implemented via a restart-oriented locking method, such as the running priority method. An aborted transaction is not restarted, but continues its processing in *virtual execution* mode [18], which is similar to optimistic mode except that there is no validation phase.

5.2 Performance of Two-Phase Processing Methods

Simulation results comparing the performance of two-phase processing methods are reported in [18] and summarized in [77], [81]. Analytic solutions of the optimistic CC method have appeared in [37], [42], [55], and [76].

The analysis in [37] considers the die method with static data access. We simplify the discussion by considering a closed system with M transactions, rather than an open system with multiprogramming level constraints.

The probability of a data conflict in a database with size D when the committing (resp. conflicting) transaction is updating m (resp. accessing n) data objects, which are accessed with uniform probabilities, is given by: $\phi(n,m) = 1-\binom{D-n}{m}/\binom{D}{m} \approx 1-(1-n/D)^m \approx nm/D$. In the case of fixed size transactions with size k, where all k accessed objects are updated is $\psi = \phi(k,k) \approx k^2/D$ [18]. Thus the probability of transaction abort increases with the square of its size, which is referred to as the *quadratic effect* [18]. Thus when transactions steps have equal processing times, the probability of conflict with an optimistic die (resp. kill) method increases proportionally to k^2/D (resp. $k^2/(2D)$). Numerical results show that in a system with variable transaction sizes the wasted processing is dominated by the largest transaction sizes [55], since they restart with higher probability due to the quadratic effect.

The system in [37] is represented by a Markov chain model, whose states (S_j) specify the number of transactions (j) which can complete successfully. The transition rates of the Markov chain are obtained by solving the queueing network model of the underlying computer system to obtain the system throughput characteristic $t(M), M \geq 1$. The probability that a committing transaction at S_j conflicts with l transactions from the remaining $j-1$ transactions is given by $\binom{j-1}{l}\psi^l(1-\psi)^{j-1-l}$.

The analysis in [37] underestimates the mean response times attained by optimistic CC [42], because optimistic CC favors the successful validation of transactions with shorter processing times. The processing times of restarted transactions, which are assumed to be exponentially distributed in the Markov chain analysis, are resampled when a transaction is restarted. Thus the mean execution time of completed transactions is shorter than the intended average.

We next outline the analysis in [42], which fixes the deficiency in the analysis in [37]. Transaction processing times are postulated to be exponentially distributed (with mean $1/\mu$) and the effect of hardware resource contention is specified by the processing rate $s(M)$, such that transactions proceed with rate $\mu s(M)$. Let u denote the system efficiency or the fraction of time the system does useful work. Then the transaction completion rate is $T(M) = u\mu s(M)$. A key assumption used in the analysis (as well as in [37]) is that *running transactions observe the commits of other transactions as a Poisson process* with rate $\lambda = (1 - 1/M)u\mu s(M)$. The rate at which a transaction is conflicted is then $\gamma = \lambda\psi$. The probability of a data conflict for a transaction with processing time x is $q = 1 - e^{-\gamma x M/s(M)}$. Provided that the execution time of a transaction is not resampled (it remains equal to x), the number of its executions in the system follows a geometric distribution $P_j = q(1-q)^{j-1}, j \geq 1$ with a mean $\overline{J}(x) = 1/q = e^{\gamma x M/s(M)}$. The analysis in [37] assumes that the number of transaction executions ($\tilde{J}$) is independent from transaction execution time ($\tilde{X}$) and hence $E[\tilde{J}\tilde{X}] = \overline{J} \times \overline{X}$.

The system efficiency u is specified as the ratio of the mean execution time of a transaction and its residence time in the system

$$u = \frac{E[xM/s(M)]}{E[xMe^{\gamma x M/s(M)}/s(M)]} = \frac{\int_0^\infty xe^{-\mu x}dx}{\int_0^\infty xe^{-(\mu - \gamma M/s(M))x}dx} \quad (18) \quad \gamma M/s(M) < \mu$$
$$= [1 - (M-1)\psi u)]^2,$$

for the denominator to converge. The equation yields one acceptable root: $u = (1 + 2a - \sqrt{1+4a})/4a^2 \approx 1 - 2a$, where $a = (M-1)\psi$ is small and the higher terms in expanding $(1+4a)^{1/2}$ can be ignored.

Similarly to [37], [42] considers the relative performance of static locking and the optimistic die method. Static locking outperforms the optimistic die method, while the more efficient optimistic kill method (with static data access) has a performance indistinguishable from static locking in a system with infinite resources, where the wasted processing time due to transaction restarts does not affect the processing time of other transactions.

These analyses are extended in several directions in [55]. Numerical results show that the transaction processing time distribution affects performance with the optimistic die method. The analysis of the kill method with exponential processing times yields $u = (1+a)^{-1} \approx 1 - a$, which indicates that *the die method is twice as inefficient as the kill method.* The analysis of optimistic CC with dynamic object accesses takes into account the fact that the conflict rate varies according to the number of data objects that have been accessed. The analysis of a system with multiple transaction classes, where class is determined by transaction size, considers each class separately to ensure that the fraction of transactions in the stream of completed transactions is the same as in the arrival stream. The analysis can be extended to take into account the variability in transaction processing times across executions, e.g., due to the prefetching effect. Also different methods can be modeled for different phases, e.g., optimistic die in the first phase and optimistic kill or locking in the second phase.

The effect of checkpoints or volatile savepoints by individual transactions [23] on overall performance is investigated in [76]. Checkpointing is appropriate for optimistic CC, since: (i) it solely uses aborts to resolve data conflicts; (ii) checkpointing is facilitated by the private workspace paradigm. There is a tradeoff between checkpointing overhead and the saved processing due to *partial rollbacks,* which allows a transaction to resume execution from the checkpoint preceding access to the data item to be released.

6 Distributed Databases

The literature on CC in distributed databases and their performance is vast [12], [6], [11], [23]. In what follows we first discuss CC methods for distributed databases, followed by studies for their performance evaluation.

6.1 Concurrency Control Methods

Standard locking is the prevalent CC method in distributed databases. Numerous algorithms have been proposed to detect deadlocks in this environment [12].

The wound-wait method and the wait-die locking method (described in Section 3.1) rely on timestamps to resolve lock conflicts [54]. They are suited for a system with a low lock contention level and high message costs. The WDL method [18] (see Section 3.1) also prevents deadlocks, but incurs more messages than these methods [19].

The *two-phase commit* protocol required to guarantee atomicity [12], [23] requires additional messages. This increases lock holding times.

The timestamp ordering method obviates additional messages for data conflict resolution in distributed databases, by resolving them locally [12], [6], [11]. A transaction can successfully read (respectively update) an object if transaction's timestamp precedes object's update timestamp (respectively read and update timestamp) and otherwise the transaction is aborted and restarted with a new timestamp. The basic timestamp ordering method may result in *cascading aborts,* because the updates of uncommitted transactions are exposed to others [58]. Other variants of timestamp ordering methods are described in [12], [11]. The reader is referred to [11], [58] for performance analyses of this method.

A large number of distributed optimistic CC methods have been proposed [81]. A key problem in correctly implementing a distributed optimistic CC method is to ensure that transaction validation is carried out in the same order at all relevant nodes, e.g., by using global timestamps. The hybrid optimistic method with the optimistic die mode in the first phase and lock preclaiming in the second phase, is extended to a distributed hybrid optimistic CC method in [81]. A key feature of the hybrid optimistic CC method is the combination of validation and two-phase commit messages. Commit duration locking ensures that the second phase of transaction execution, which is necessary if the transaction fails validation, is always successful because data blocks accessed by the transaction cannot be invalidated by others.

Data replication is a desirable feature in distributed databases from the viewpoint of increased data availability and reduced communication cost by accessing the most convenient site. The correctness criterion in replicated databases is *one copy serializability,* i.e., the interleaved execution of concurrent transactions is equivalent to serializability on a single copy of the database [6]. Improved performance in such databases can be achieved at the cost of reduced consistency [13]. An alternative to data replication is the *fractional data allocation* method, which allocates *tokens*, e.g., airline seats, to nodes based on anticipated demand [75]. Tokens can be disposed off without external coordination. A background process is required to redistribute tokens among nodes and to deliver new tokens. A preliminary study of methods for this purpose appears in [22].

6.2 Performance Evaluation Studies

The performance of a distributed database is affected by the transaction processing paradigm:

- *Data request shipping* or database call shipping involves making remote database calls, when the referenced data is not locally available [85].
- A node requiring access to remote data invokes an appropriate procedure at the remote node [12], which is referred to as *distributed transaction processing*. The performance gains are high, but this is at the cost of loss of *location transparency*, i.e., the location of data need to be exposed to the programmer.
- Request data pages from other nodes for local processing, referred to as *I/O request shipping* [85]. This approach off-loads the node holding the data from the associated processing. This method is used in *data sharing systems* discussed below.

Transaction parallelism in distributed and especially parallel databases, i.e., shared nothing database machines, is important from the viewpoint of reducing lock holding time and hence lock contention [9].

The relative performance of distributed CC methods is not as well understood as centralized CC methods, but some of the insights gained from performance studies of centralized systems are applicable to distributed systems. A survey of earlier simulation and analytic studies appears in [57], which also provides formulas applicable to analyzing the performance of distributed database systems. The number of such studies is relatively small because of the complexity of distributed systems. Simplifying assumptions are usually used, e.g., a fully replicated database, fully interconnected network, network delays computed based on *M/M/1* queues, etc. [49].

The optimal number of sites (or copies of the database) to maximize query processing throughput in a replicated database is determined in [15]. Transactions update all sites preempting active queries at the sites. The communication time is a function of the number of sites, so that the optimal number of sites varies according to this function.

The *resequencing problem* is relevant to the timestamp ordering method [4]. Transactions numbered according to the order of their generation encounter a communication delay with a given distribution, which results in their out-of-order "arrival" for processing. Since transactions should be processed in their original order, they are held in a queue which results in a resequencing delay. Three resequencing policies are considered and analyzed. (i) each transaction should respect the ordering with all previous transactions with some fixed probability. (ii) the ordering is with respect to transactions in some time interval with a given distribution; (iii) the ordering is with respect to a given number of geometrically distributed preceding transactions.

Simulation is the main performance evaluation tool for distributed databases. Two comprehensive simulation studies of CC methods appear in [9], [10]. A simulation study of the distributed WDL method is reported in [19], where it is shown to outperform the standard locking and the wound-wait methods. Several alternative distributed WDL methods are proposed for improved performance.

Shared nothing and *shared disk* systems are of current interest for transaction processing. In shared nothing systems the data is partitioned to balance the load, e.g., by using hashing on primary keys in a relational database. From the viewpoint of CC, these systems behave as distributed databases, although some optimizations are possible, e.g., broadcast capability to all processors for two-phase commit. The simulation of a preliminary version of the TPC-C benchmark on a shared nothing system appears in [29].

In shared disk or data sharing systems multiple computers have access to a set of shared disks. Transactions are routed to computers to achieve a balanced load and to attain a higher database buffer hit ratio [50]. In addition to CC, there is the issue of coherency control for the contents of database buffers across systems [50]. A similar problem arises in client-server systems.

7 Conclusions

An abstract model of a standard locking system is analyzed in this paper to provide an understanding of factors leading to its performance degradation. Restart-oriented locking methods relieve lock contention by selectively aborting transactions, while two-phase processing methods reduce the data contention level in systems with access invariance by shortening the holding time of locks or access entries by prefetching the data required for transaction execution in the second phase, if it is required. We summarize the conclusions of previous simulation and analytic studies regarding the relative performance of CC methods and survey methods applicable to the analysis of standard locking, restart-oriented locking methods, and optimistic CC.

There has been little effort in evaluating the performance of transaction processing systems taking into account lock contention effects. This is due to the difficulty of characterizing transaction processing systems from the lock contention viewpoint, rather than the inability to develop appropriate methods for performance evaluation. Analytic results need be validated against measurement results rather than just simulations.

Statistics of lock contention levels are provided by most database management systems, but the measurement data is not sufficiently detailed and cannot be easily correlated with other events in the system. Furthermore, additional information is required about the database, transactions processed by the system, and transaction scheduling to develop a realistic lock contention model. Some of this information is proprietary in nature and not available externally.

Some additional topics related to CC are as follows.

Specialized methods are required to handle the interaction between read-only queries and transactions which update the database Numerous versioning methods have been proposed for this purpose, see e.g., [41]. A performance analysis of a versioning method is reported in [38].

The "random batch" method allows database access by other transactions, while a batch update is in progress [5]. The basic idea behind this method is to update records out-of-order to make the updated record available to transactions which need to access it (it is assumed that batch transaction releases locks on updated records). A moving pointer which separates updated records from not updated records by a batch transaction is considered in [48]. A transaction does not encounter a conflict if it only accesses updated or not updated records. An on-demand versioning method is proposed in [69] for the reverse problem of a query scanning a table, which is being updated by transactions. A record is versioned if its access is anticipated by the query.

Real-time transactions or *databases* is another area of current research. Transaction *deadline* is defined as arrival time plus resource time expanded by slack. *Soft* rather than *hard* real-time systems are of interest. Different performance measures are used in this case, such as the fraction of transactions that missed the deadline and mean lateness. One of the earliest works in this area is [1]. The *priority inheritance* paradigm [53], which is used in this study raises the priority of lower priority tasks blocking higher priority tasks.

Numerous CC methods have been evaluated to determine their suitability for real-time transaction processing and many new CC methods have been proposed [51]. These include methods based on access invariance, because it provides an opportunity to preanalyze the objects required by the transaction for its second phase execution [46] and hybrid methods [25]. Transaction spawning for improving performance in real-time systems has been considered in [7]. There have been few performance analyses of real-time database systems [24].

Active databases provide timely responses to time-critical events and this is accomplished by providing *event-condition-action rules* to be specified for the database management system. A performance evaluation of active databases, which takes into account locking effects and distinguishes between external and rule management tasks, is reported in [8].

References

1. R. K. Abbott and H. Garcia-Molina. "Scheduling real-time transactions: A performance evaluation," *ACM Trans. on Database Systems 17*,3 (Sept. 1992), 513-560.
2. R. Agrawal, M. J. Carey, and M. Livny. "Concurrency control performance modeling: Alternatives and implications," *ACM Trans. on Database Systems 12*,4 (Dec. 1987), 609-654.

3. R. Agrawal, M. J. Carey, and L. W. McVoy. "The performance of alternative strategies for dealing with deadlocks in database management systems." *IEEE Trans. on Software Engineering 13*,12 (Dec. 1987), 1348-1363.
4. F. Baccelli, and E. Gelenbe and B. Plateau. "An end-to-end approach to resequencing problem," *Journal of the ACM 31*,3 (July 1984), 474-485.
5. R. Bayer. "Consistency of transactions and random batch," *ACM Trans. on Database Systems 11*,4 (Dec. 1986), 397-404.
6. P. A. Bernstein, V. Hadzilacos, and N. Goodman. *Concurrency Control and Recovery in Database Systems,* Addison-Wesley, 1987 (free download from http://www.research.microsoft.com/ philbe/).
7. A. Bestavros and S. Braoudakis. "Value cognizant speculative concurrency control," *Proc. 21st Int'l Conf. on Very Large Data Bases,* 1995, pp. 122-133.
8. M. J. Carey, R. Jauhari, and M. Livny. "On transaction boundaries in active databases: A performance perspective," *IEEE Trans. on Knowledge and Data Engineering 3*,3 (Sept. 1991), 320-336.
9. M. J. Carey and M. Livny. "Parallelism and concurrency control performance in distributed database machines," *Proc. ACM SIGMOD Int'l Conf. on Management of Data,* 1989, pp. 122-133.
10. M. J. Carey and M. Livny. "Conflict detection tradeoffs for replicated data," *ACM Trans. Database Systems 16*,4 (Dec. 1991), 703-746.
11. W. Cellary, E. Gelenbe, and T. Morzy. *Concurrency Control in Distributed Databases,* North-Holland, 1988.
12. S. Ceri and G. Pelagatti. *Distributed Databases-Principles and Systems,* McGraw-Hill, 1984.
13. S. Ceri, M. A. W. Houtsma, A. M. Keller, and P. Samarati. "Independent updates and incremental agreement in replicated databases," *Distributed and Parallel Databases 3*,3 (July 1995), 225-246.
14. A. Chesnais, E. Gelenbe, and I. Mitrani. "On the modeling of parallel access to shared data," *Commun. of the ACM 26*,3 (March 1983), 198-202.
15. E. G. Coffman, E. Gelenbe, and B. Plateau. "Optimization of the number of copies in a distributed data base," *IEEE Trans. on Software Engineering 7*,1 (Jan. 1981), 78-84.
16. P. Franaszek and J. T. Robinson. "Limitations of concurrency in transaction processing," *ACM Trans. on Database Systems 10*,1 (March 1985), 1-28.
17. P. Franaszek, J. T. Robinson, and A. Thomasian. "Access invariance and its use in high contention environments," *Proc. 6th IEEE Int'l Conf. on Data Engineering,* 1990, pp. 47-55.
18. P. Franaszek, J. T. Robinson, and A. Thomasian. "Concurrency control for high contention environments," *ACM Trans. Database Systems 17*,2 (June 1992), 304-345.
19. P. A. Franaszek, J. R. Haritsa, J. T. Robinson, and A. Thomasian. "Distributed concurrency control based on limited wait depth," *IEEE Trans. Parallel and Distributed Systems 4*,11 (Nov. 1993), 1246-1264.
20. V. Gaede and O. Guenther. "Multidimensional access methods," *ACM Computing Surveys 30*,2 (June 1998), 170-231.
21. B. I. Galler and L. Bos. "A model of transaction blocking in databases," *Performance Evaluation 3* (1983), 95-122.
22. L. Golubchik and A. Thomasian. "Token allocation in distributed systems," *Proc. 12th IEEE Int'l Conference on Distributed Computing Systems,* 1992, pp. 64-71.
23. J. N. Gray and A. Reuter. *Transaction Processing: Concepts and Facilities,* Morgan Kauffman, 1992.

24. J. Haritsa. "Approximate analysis of real-time database systems," *Proc. 10th IEEE Int'l Conf. on Data Engineering,* 1994, pp. 10-19.
25. J. Huang, J. A. Stankovic, K. Ramamritham, and D. S. Towsley. "Experimental evaluation of real-time concurrency control methods," *Proc. 17th Int'l Conf. on Very Large Data Bases,* 1991, pp. 35-46.
26. M. Hsu and B. Zhang. "Performance evaluation of cautious waiting," *ACM Trans. Database Systems 17,*3 (Sept. 1992), 477-512.
27. K. B. Irani and H. L. Lin. "Queueing network models for concurrent transaction processing in database systems," *Proc. 1979 ACM Int'l SIGMOD Conf. on Management of Data,* 1979, pp. 134-142.
28. B. C. Jenq, W. H. Kohler, and D. Towsley. "A queueing network model for a distributed database testbed," *IEEE Trans. Software Engineering 14,*7 (July 1988), 908-921.
29. B. C. Jenq, B. C. Twichell, and T. W. Keller. "Locking performance in a shared nothing parallel database machine," *IEEE Trans. on Knowledge and Data Engineering 1,*4 (Dec. 1989), 530-543.
30. T. Johnson and D. Shasha. "The performance of concurrent B-tree algorithms," *ACM Trans. on Database Systems 18,*1 (March 1993), 51-101.
31. M. Kornacker and D. Banks. "High concurrency locking for R-trees," *Proc. 21st Int'l Conf. on Very Large Data Bases,* 1995, pp. 134-145.
32. V. Kumar (Editor). *Performance of Concurrency Control Mechanisms in Centralized Database Systems,* Prentice-Hall, 1995.
33. H. T. Kung and J. T. Robinson. "On optimistic concurrency control methods," *ACM Trans. on Database Systems 6,*2 (June 1981), 213-226.
34. A. M. Langer and A. W. Shum. "The distribution of granule accesses made by database transactions," *Commun. of the ACM 25,*11 (Nov. 1982), 831-832.
35. S. S. Lavenberg. "A simple analysis of exclusive and shared lock contention in a database system," *Proc. ACM SIGMETRICS Conf. on Measurement and Modeling of Computer Systems,* 1984, pp. 143-148.
36. W. Massey. "A probabilistic analysis of database system," *Proc. Joint Performance and ACM SIGMETRICS Conf. on Measurement and Modeling of Computer Systems,* 1986, pp. 141-146.
37. D. A. Menasce and T. Nakanishi. "Optimistic versus pessimistic concurrency control mechanisms in database management systems," *Information Systems 7,*1 (Jan. 1982), 13-27.
38. A. Merchant, K. L. Wu, P. S. Yu, and M. S. Chen. "Performance analysis of dynamic versioning schemes: Storage cost vs. obsolescence," *IEEE Trans. on Knowledge and Data Engineering 8,*6 (Dec. 1996), 985-1001.
39. D. Mitra and P. J. Weinberger. "Some results on database locking: Solution, computational algorithms, and asymptotics," *Mathematical Computer Performance Evaluation and Reliability,* G. Iazeolla, P. J. Courtois, and A. Hordjik (editors), North-Holland, 1984, pp. 372-386.
40. D. Mitra. "Probabilistic models and asymptotic results for concurrent processing with exclusive and non-exclusive locks," *SIAM Journal of Computing 14,*4 (Nov. 1985), 1030-1051.
41. C. Mohan, H. Pirahesh, and R. A. Lorie. "Efficient and flexible methods for transient versioning of records to avoid locking by read-only transactions," *Proc. ACM SIGMOD Int'l Conf. on Management of Data,* 1992, pp. 124-133.
42. R. J. T. Morris and W. S. Wong. "Performance analysis of locking and optimistic concurrency control algorithms," *Performance Evaluation 5,*2 (1985), 105-118.

43. T. Nakanishi and D. M. Menasce. "Correctness and performance evaluation of two-phase commit-based protocol for DDBs," *Computer Performance 5*,1 (March 1984), IPC Press, UK, 38-54.
44. R. D. Nelson and B. R. Iyer. "Analysis of replicated databases," *Performance Evaluation 5*,3 (1985), 133-148.
45. R. D. Nelson. "Stochastic catastrophe theory in computer performance modeling," *Journal of the ACM 34*,3 (July 1987), 661-685.
46. P. E. O'Neil, K. Ramamritham, and C. Pu. "A two-phase approach to predictably scheduling real-time transactions," Chapter 18 in *Performance of Concurrency Control Methods in Centralized Databases,* V. Kumar (ed.), Prentice-Hall, 1995, pp. 494-522.
47. D. Potier and Ph. LeBlanc. "Analysis of locking policies in database management systems," *Commun. of the ACM 23*,10 (Oct. 1980), 584-593.
48. C. Pu. "Incremental, consistent reading of entire databases," *Algorithmica 1*,3 369-375.
49. A. Raghuram, R. W. Morgan, B. Rajaraman, and Y. Ronen. "Approximation for the mean value performance of locking algorithms for distributed database systems: A partitioned database," *Annals of Operations Research 36* (1992), 299-346.
50. E. Rahm. "Empirical performance evaluation of concurrency and coherency controls for database sharing systems," *ACM Trans. on Database Systems 18*,2 (1993), 333-377.
51. K. Ramamritham. "Real-time databases," *Distributed and Parallel Databases 1*,2 (April 1993), 199-226.
52. K. Ramamritham and P. K. Chrisanthis. *Advances in Concurrency Control and Transaction Processing,* IEEE Computer Society Press, 1996.
53. R. Rajkumar. *Synchronization in Real-Time Systems: A Priority Inheritance Approach,* Kluwer Academic Publishers, 1991.
54. D. J. Rosenkrantz, R. E. Stearns, and P. M. Lewis II. "System level concurrency control for distributed database systems." *ACM Trans. on Database Systems 3*,2 (June 1978), 178-198.
55. I. K. Ryu and A. Thomasian. "Performance evaluation of centralized databases with optimistic concurrency control," *Performance Evaluation 7*,3 (1987), 195-211.
56. I. K. Ryu and A. Thomasian. "Analysis of database performance with dynamic locking," *Journal of the ACM 37*,3 (July 1990), 491-523.
57. K. C. Sevcik. "Comparison of concurrency control methods using analytic models," in *Information Processing 83,* pp. 847-858.
58. M. Singhal. "Performance analysis of the basic timestamp ordering algorithm via Markov modeling," *Performance Evaluation 12* (1991), 17-41.
59. V. Singhal and A. J. Smith. "Analysis of locking behavior in three real database systems," *Very Large Data Base Journal 6*,1 (Jan. 1997), 40-52.
60. V. Srinivasan and M. J. Carey. "Performance of B+ tree concurrency control algorithms," *Very Large Data Base Journal 2*,4 (Oct. 1993), 361-406.
61. H. Takagi. *Queueing Analysis, Vol. 1: Vacation and Priority Systems, Part 1,* North-Holland, 1991.
62. S. Tasaka. *Performance Analysis of Multiple Access Protocols,* MIT Press, 1986.
63. Y. C. Tay, N. Goodman, and R. Suri. "Locking performance in centralized databases," *ACM Trans. on Database Systems 10*,4 (Dec. 1985), 415-462.
64. Y. C. Tay, R. Suri, and N. Goodman. "A mean value performance model for locking in databases," *Journal of the ACM 32*,3 (July 1985), 618-651.
65. Y. C. Tay. *Locking Performance in Centralized Databases,* Academic Press, 1987.

66. Y. C. Tay. "Some performance issues for transactions with firm deadlines," *Proc. 16th IEEE Real-Time Systems Symp.*, 1995, pp. 322-331.
67. A. Thomasian. "An iterative solution to the queueing network model of a DBMS with dynamic locking," *Proc. 13th Computer Measurement Group Conf.* pp. 252-261.
68. A. Thomasian. "Performance evaluation of centralized databases with static locking," *IEEE Trans. Software Engineering 11*,2 (April 1985), 346-355.
69. A. Thomasian. "Concurrency control schemes to support the concurrent processing of update transactions and read-only queries," *IBM Research Report RC 12420*, Yorktown Heights, NY, Dec. 1986.
70. A. Thomasian and I. K. Ryu. "A recursive solution to analyze the performance of static locking," *IEEE Trans. Software Engineering 15*,10 (Oct. 1989), 1147-1156.
71. A. Thomasian. "Two-phase locking and its thrashing behavior," *ACM Trans. on Database Systems 18*,4 (Dec. 1993), 579-625.
72. A. Thomasian and I. K. Ryu. "A decomposition solution to the queueing network model of the centralized DBMS with static locking," *Proc ACM SIGMETRICS Conf. on Measurement and Modeling of Computer Systems,* 1983, pp. 82-92.
73. A. Thomasian and I. K. Ryu. "Performance analysis of two-phase locking," *IEEE Trans. on Software Engineering 17*,5 (May 1991), 386-402.
74. A. Thomasian and V. Nicola. "Performance evaluation of a threshold policy for scheduling readers and writers." *IEEE Trans. on Computers 42*,1 (Jan. 1993), pp. 83-98.
75. A. Thomasian. "A fractional data allocation method for distributed databases," *Proc. 3rd Int'l Conf. on Parallel and Distributed Information Systems,* 1994, pp. 168-175.
76. A. Thomasian. "Checkpointing for optimistic concurrency control methods." *IEEE Trans. on Knowledge and Data Engineering* 7,2 (April 1995), 332-339.
77. A. Thomasian. *Database Concurrency Control: Performance, Analysis, and Methods,* Kluwer Academic Publishers, 1996.
78. A. Thomasian. "Realistic modeling of lock contention and its analysis," *Information Systems 21*,5 (July 1996), 409-430.
79. A. Thomasian. "A performance comparison of locking policies with limited wait-depth," *IEEE Trans. Knowledge and Data Engineering 9*,3 (May/June 1997), 421-35.
80. A. Thomasian. "Distributed optimistic concurrency control methods for high performance transaction processing," *IEEE Trans. on Knowledge and Data Engineering 10*.1 (Jan./Feb. 1998), 173-189.
81. A. Thomasian. "Concurrency control: Methods, performance, and analysis," *ACM Computing Surveys 30*,1 (March 1998), 70-119.
82. A. Thomasian. "Performance analysis of locking policies with limited wait-depth," *Performance Evaluation J. 33*,1 (June 1998), 1-21.
83. J. Tsitsiklis, C. H. Papadimitriou, and P. Humblet. "The performance of a precedence-based queueing discipline," *Journal of the ACM 33*,3 (July 1986), 593-602.
84. G. Weikum, C. Hasse, A. Moenkeberg, and P. Zabback. "The COMFORT automatic tuning project," *Information Systems 19*,5 (1994), 381-432.
85. P. S. Yu, D. Cornell, D. M. Dias, and A. Thomasian. "Performance comparison of the IO shipping and database call shipping schemes in multi-system partitioned database systems," *Performance Evaluation 10,* (1989), 15-33.
86. P. S. Yu, D. M. Dias, and S. S. Lavenberg. "On modeling database concurrency control," *Journal of the ACM 40*,4 (Sept. 1993), 831-872.

Numerical Analysis Methods

William J. Stewart

Department of Computer Science
North Carolina State University, Raleigh, NC 27695-8206
billy@csc.ncsu.edu

1 Introduction and Short History

In the context of Performance Evaluation (PE), numerical analysis methods refer to those methods which work with a Markov chain representation of the system under evaluation and use techniques from the domain of numerical analysis to compute stationary and/or transient state probabilities or other measures of interest. As is evident from reading through this book, the use of mathematical models to analyze complex systems has a long history. With the advent of high powered workstations and cheap memory, these applications have greatly expanded. More and more frequently, however, the characteristics of the system to be modeled are such that analytical solutions do not exist or are unknown so that systems engineers turn to computing numerical solutions rather than analytical solutions.

It is often possible to represent the behavior of a physical system by describing all the different states that it can occupy and by indicating how the system moves from one state to another in time. If the time spent in any state is exponentially distributed, the system may be represented by a *Markov process*. Even when the system does not possess this exponential property explicitly, it is usually possible to construct a corresponding implicit representation. When the state space is discrete, the term *Markov chain* is employed. The system being modelled by the chain is assumed to occupy one and only one of these states at any moment in time and the evolution of the system is represented by transitions of the Markov chain from one state to another. The information that is most often sought from such a model is the probability of being in a given state or subset of states at a certain time after the system becomes operational. Often this time is taken to be sufficiently long that all influence of the initial starting state has been erased. The probabilities thus obtained are referred to as the *long-run* or *stationary probabilities*. Probabilities at a particular time t are called *transient probabilities*.

It follows that the three steps involved in carrying out this type of evaluation are firstly, to describe the system to be analyzed as a Markov chain; secondly, to determine from this Markov chain description, a matrix of transition rates or probabilities; and thirdly, from this matrix representation, to numerically compute all performance measures of interest. The first involves characterizing the states of the system and formulating the manner in which it moves from one state to another; the second requires finding a manner in which to store the

G. Haring et al. (Eds.): Performance Evaluation, LNCS 1769, pp. 355–376, 2000.

transition matrix efficiently; the third requires the application of matrix equation solving techniques to compute stationary or transient probabilities.

The first application of the numerical analysis approach to PE problems was in 1966 by Wallace and Rosenberg. Their Recursive Queue Analyzer, RQA-1, [60], essentially avoided the first step by requiring a user to describe the transition matrix directly. Since the applications envisaged derived from queueing networks, the nonzero elements in the transition matrix often repeat at well defined patterns in the matrix. RQA-1 defined a data structure which attempted to capture such regularities and to store them as the trio (nonzero element, pattern, initialization point). The amount of storage used was therefore minimized. The numerical solution technique employed by RQA-1 was the *Power method.* In the literature, the authors reported some success with this approach, [61].

This was followed in the early 1970's by Stewart's *Markov Chain Analyzer, MARCA*, [59]. This provided a means of expressing a Markov chain as a system of "Balls and Buckets", essentially allowing a single state of the chain to be represented as a vector, the *state descriptor vector.* The user has to characterize the way in which the system changes states by describing the interactions among the components of the state descriptor vector. With this information MARCA automatically generates the transition rate matrix and stores it in a compact form. The original solution method used in MARCA was simultaneous iteration, a forerunner of the currently popular projection methods. In 1974, a restriction of MARCA to queueing networks was developed and incorporated into QNAP (Queueing Network Analysis Package), [47].

The 80's witnessed the popularization of the matrix-geometric approach of Neuts, [41], and the establishment of Generalized Stochastic Petri Nets (GSPN) as a valuable modelling paradigm, [1,10]. These advances were accompanied by a flurry of activity in numerical aggregation and disaggregation methods, [8,37,52] — extending the seminal work of Courtois, [13], on nearly completely decomposable systems. This period also saw advances in the computation of bounds, [20,53], in specification techniques, [3], in state-space exploration, [7,4], and so on. The most popular applications were, and still are, in the fields of computer communications and reliability modelling, [30,34,64,65]. And, of course, this period was also rich in advances led by the numerical analysis community, especially in the development of projection methods, preconditioning techniques and in sparse matrix technology in general, [50].

In this final decade of the 20th century, research continues along the same paths. Advances continue to be made in all the aforementioned areas. In addition we see an increased emphasis placed on stochastic automata networks (SANs), and other structured analysis approaches, [5,6,11,35,44,58]. These have advanced hand in hand with compositional approaches, such as the stochastic process algebra package, PEPA, [26]. Given the ease of with which GUIs (Graphical User Interaces) can now be programmed and the availability of cheap memory and fast CPUs, many more numerical analysis software packages specifically designed for PE have made their apparation. This period also witnessed international conferences devoted to the topic, the first in 1990 and the second in 1995. It is significant that the third in this series is to be held in 1999 jointly with the PNPM (Petri Nets and Performance Models) conference and the PAPM (Process Algebra and Performance Modelling) conference.

It is impossible in a single chapter to describe all the events and research that have led us to where we are today. Here we must be content with highlighting some of the major thrusts and refer the interested reader to the literature for more information. We face the same restriction in our discussion of the numerical procedures themselves. Our overviews are necessarily brief; our goal is simply to provide the reader with the basis upon which to gauge the state of the art in numerical analysis methods for performance evaluation.

2 Problem Definition

2.1 Model Definition and Matrix Generation

In developing a Markov chain model, the first step is to choose a *state descriptor vector*. This is a vector whose components describe the various parts of the system being modeled. Frequently, several components are needed to adequately represent a single part of a model. For example, if processes are forced to queue for service, it may be necessary to assign a component of the state descriptor vector to denote the priority of the process, another to specify the phase of service of the process already in service and yet a third to signal whether this particular part of the system is blocked. What is important is that the state descriptor vector be sufficiently detailed to completely describe those aspects of the system that are to be evaluated. On the other hand, it should also be as succinct as possible to keep the number of states that will be generated to the smallest possible number. This is where the skill of the modeler becomes evident.

Once the state description has been designed, it becomes necessary to characterize the ways in which the components of the descriptor vector interact with each other. This is where the dynamics of the system are modelled. Process movement within the system is specified by incrementing and decrementing components, a change of status is reflected by a corresponding change in the value of a component, and so on. The rates at which these transitions take place must also be specified. When this has been completed, it becomes possible to generate the (usually huge) matrix of transition rates. The standard approach is to begin with some well formed initial state in which all the components of the state descriptor vector are assigned values. This initial (source) state is examined and the states it can reach in a single step (the destination states) are constructed and stored. The rate at which the source state moves to each destination state is also computed at this time. It becomes the <origin,destination> value of the transition rate matrix. As new states are found they are added to a list of states. Each state in this list is taken in turn to be a source state and states that are a single step transition from this state become its destination states; thus the rows of the transition rate matrix are formed one after the other. As destination states are formed, it is necessary to check whether they have already been entered into the list of states. As this is often the most time consuming part of the matrix generation process, it is important that efficient search methods be used. Mostly hashing techniques are employed. Recent research on algorithms based on hash compaction as well as techniques specificially designed for parallel and distributed computer systems have appeared in the literature and seem very promising. Among these we cite the work of Knottenbelt, [31,32], Allmaier and Horton, [2], and Ciardo et al., [11]. It is also possible to ease the computational burden by attempting to generate only a subset of states, those that are most probable. In models that have very large numbers of states, it is possible that a considerable percentage will have a stationary probability that is close to zero. Some approaches use an exploration algorithm that attempts to localize only highly probable states. This is a direct attack on the state space explosion problem. This method works well when some insight into the performance of the system is know in advance, such as in reliability modelling.

Although the above approach is the generic method of generating the transition matrices of large-scale Markov chains, it is not the only one. Given the difficulty in constructing these models, a number of alternatives present themselves. Chief among these are the stochastic Petri net formalisms which are described elsewhere in this text. These give rise to transition rate matrices that are usually solved with the numerical techniques described in this chapter. Some software packages in which models are formulated as queueing networks also give rise to Markov chains. This is the case of XMARCA, [29], and the numerical approach that is available in QNAP, [47]. Finally, the SAN (Stochastic Automata Network) methodology leads to Markov chains whose transition matrices are described as a sum of tensor products, and which again must be solved using numerical methods.

2.2 Matrix Size and Condition Considerations

With Markov chain models, the numerical problem is not difficult to describe. The solution at any time t, $\pi(t)$, is calculated from the Chapman-Kolmogorov differential equation,

$$\frac{d\pi(t)}{dt} = \pi(t)Q. \tag{1}$$

Here Q is a square matrix of order n, the number of states in the Markov chain, and is called the infinitesimal generator. Its elements satisfy $q_{ij} \geq 0$ for $i \neq j$ and $q_{ii} = -\sum_{j=1,j\neq i}^{n} q_{ij}$, for all $i = 1, 2, \ldots, n$. The vector $\pi(t)$ is also of length n and its ith component, $\pi_i(t)$, expresses the probability that the Markov chain is in state i at time t.

When the number of state in the Markov chain is small, less than two hundred for example, then computing numerical solutions of Markov chain equations is generally easy. Equation (1) can be fed into a software package with robust solvers such as *Matlab*, and the solution found rather effortlessly. The difficulties arise when the number of states is large. These difficulties are two-fold. The first is the sheer size of the matrices involved; the second is how well-conditioned or how ill-conditioned the equations are. These difficulties exist even in the simpler setting when all that is required is the stationary solution of the Markov chain, obtained be setting the left hand side of (1) to zero and solving the linear system of equations that results.

It is not unusual for the number of states in the Markov chain to exceed one million. This size impacts both the means used to store the matrix and the number of vectors needed to compute the solution. Very large matrices cannot be stored in the usual two-dimensional array format; there is simply not enough storage space available. In addition this would be very wasteful, since most of the matrix elements are zero. In general, each state communicates directly with only a small number of states and so the number of nonzero elements in the matrix is usually equal to a small multiple of the number of states. If the states can be ordered sequentially so that each communicates only with its closest neighbors, then the nonzero elements of Q lie close to the diagonal and a banded storage technique can be used. Otherwise, it is usual to store only the nonzero elements in a double-precision one-dimensional array and use two integer one-dimensional arrays to indicate the position of each nonzero element in the matrix. In addition to storing the transition matrix, a certain number of double-precision vectors, of size equal to the number of states, is also needed. In the simplest numerical methods, two such vectors suffice. In other more sophisicated methods many more (possibly in excess of 50) may be needed. The size of the Markov chain is therefore a source of numerical difficulty to which attention must be paid.

A second difficulty in solving Markov chains numerically is the degree of ill-conditioning of Q. In certain models, the difference in the rates at which events can occur may be many orders of magnitude, as is the case when a model allows for both human interaction and electronic transactions. These differences in magnitude may lead to ill-conditioned systems, that is to say, a small change in one of the parameters, can result in a large change in the solution. We distinguish between numerical conditioning and numerical stability; the first has already been described and is a function of the problem itself; the second describes the behavior of an *algorithm* in attempting to compute solutions. A stable algorithm will not allow the error to grow out of proportion to the degree of ill-conditioning of the problem. In other words, a stable algorithm will give us as good a solution as we can expect for the particular problem to be solved. A further effect of large differences in transitions rates is that they can create convergence problems for iterative solution methods.

3 Numerical Methods for Computing Stationary Distributions

We wish to solve the matrix equation

$$\pi Q = 0. \tag{2}$$

By setting $P = Q\Delta t + I$, where $\Delta t \leq (\max_i |q_{ii}|)^{-1}$, this equation may be written as

$$\pi P = \pi. \tag{3}$$

When we perform this operation we essentially convert the continuous-time system represented by the *transition rate* matrix, Q, to a discrete-time system represented by the stochastic *transition probability* matrix, P. In the discrete-time system, transitions take place at intervals of time Δt, this parameter being chosen so that the probability of two transitions taking place in time Δt is negligible. The stationary distribution π may be computed from either of these equations. Throughout this chapter we shall assume that the state space of the Markov chain is finite, unless specified otherwise.

3.1 Direct Methods

Since equation (2) is a homogeneous system of linear equations, we may use standard linear solution methods based on Gaussian elimination. Let us assume that the Markov chain is ergodic. In this case the fact that the system of equations is homogeneous does not create any problems, since we may replace any of the n equations by the normalizing equation, $\sum_{j=1}^{n} \pi_j = 1$, and thereby convert it into a nonhomogeneous system with nonsingular coefficient matrix and nonzero right hand side. The solution in this case is well defined. It turns out that replacing an equation with the normalizing equation is not really necessary. The usual approach taken is to construct an LU decomposition of Q and replace the final zero diagonal element of U with an arbitrary value. The solution computed by backsubstitution on U must then be normalized. Furthermore, since the diagonal elements are equal to the negated sum of the off-diagonal elements (Q is, in a restricted sense, diagonally dominant), it is not necessary to perform pivoting while computing the LU decomposition. This simplifies the algorithm considerably. The problem of the size and nonzero structure (the placement of the nonzero elements within the matrix) still remain. Obviously this method will work, and work well, when the number of states is small. It will also work well when the nonzero structure of Q fits into a narrow band along the diagonal. In these cases a very stable variant, referred to as the GTH (Grassmann, Taskar and Heyman, [24]) algorithm may be used. In this variant, all subtraction is avoided by computing diagonal elements as the sum of off-diagonal elements. This is possible since the zero-row-sum property of an infinitesimal generator is invariant under the basic operation of Gaussian elimination, namely adding a multiple of one row into another. For an efficient implementation, the GTH variant requires convenient access to both the rows and the columns of the matrix. This is the case when a banded structure is used to store Q, but is generally not the case with other compact storage procedures.

When the number of states becomes large and the structure in not banded, the direct approach loses its appeal and one is obliged to turn to other methods.

3.2 Basic Iterative Methods

For iterative methods we first take the approach of solving equation (3) in which P is a matrix of transitions probabilities. Let the initial probability distribution vector be given by $\pi^{(0)}$. After the first transition, the probability vector is given by $\pi^{(1)} = \pi^{(0)}P$; after k transitions it is given by $\pi^{(k)} = \pi^{(k-1)}P = \pi^{(0)}P^k$. If the Markov chain is ergodic, then $\lim_{k\to\infty} \pi^{(k)} = \pi$. This method of determining the stationary probability vector, by successively multiplying some initial probability distribution vector by the matrix of transition probabilities, is called the *Power* method. Observe that all that is required is a vector-matrix multiplication operation. This may be conveniently performed on sparse matrices that are stored in compact form. Because of its simplicity, this method is widely used, even though it often takes a very long time to converge. Its rate of convergence is a function of how close the subdominant eigenvalue of P is to its dominant unit eigenvalue. In models in which there are large differences in the magnitudes of transition rates, the subdominant eigenvalue can be pathologically close to one, so that to all intents and purposes, the Power method fails to converge.

It is also possible to apply iterative equation solving techniques to the system of equations (2). The well-known *Jacobi* method is closely related to the Power method, and it also frequently takes very long to converge. A better iterative method is that of *Gauss-Seidel*. Unlike the previous two methods, in which the equations are only updated after each completed iteration, the Gauss-Seidel method uses the most recently computed values of the variables as soon as they become available and, as a result, almost always converges faster than Jacobi or the Power method. All three methods can be written so that the only numerical operation is that of forming the product of a sparse matrix and a probability vector so all are equal from a computation per iteration point of view.

3.3 Block Methods

In Markov chain models it is frequently the case that the state space can be meaningfully partitioned into subsets. Perhaps the states of a subset interact only infrequently with the states of other subsets, or perhaps the states possess some property that merits special consideration. In these cases it is possible to partition the transition rate matrix accordingly and to develop iterative methods based on this partition. In general such block iterative methods require more computation per iteration, but this is offset by a faster rate of convergence.

If the state space of the Markov chain is partitioned into N subsets of size $n_1, n_2, \ldots, n_N$ with $\sum_{i=1}^{N} = n$, then block iterative methods essentially involve the solution of N systems of equations of size n_i, $i = 1, 2, \ldots, N$ within a *global* iterative structure, such as Gauss-Seidel, for instance: thus the *Block Gauss-Seidel* method. Furthermore, these N systems of equations are nonhomogeneous and have nonsingular coefficient matrices and either direct or iterative methods may be used to solve them. It is not required that the same method be used to solve all the diagonal blocks. Instead, it is possible to tailor methods to the particular block structures.

If a direct method is used, then a decomposition of the diagonal block may be formed once and for all before initializing the global iteration process. In each subsequent global iteration, solving for that block then reduces to a forward and backward substitution operation. The nonzero structure of the blocks may be such that this is a particularly attractive approach. For example, if the diagonal blocks are themselves diagonal matrices, or if they are upper or lower triangular matrices or even tridiagonal matrices, then it is very easy to obtain their LU decomposition, and a block iterative method becomes very attractive.

If the diagonal blocks do not possess such a structure, and when they are of large dimension, it may be appropriate to use an iterative method to solve each of the block systems. In this case, we have many inner iterative methods (one per block) within an outer (or global) iteration. A number of tricks may be used to speed up this process. First, the solution computed for any block at global iteration k should be used as the initial approximation to the solution of this same block at iteration $k+1$. Second, it is hardly worthwhile computing a highly accurate solution in early (outer) iterations. We should require only a small number of digits of accuracy until the global process begins to converge. One convenient way to achieve this is to carry out only a fixed, small number of iterations for each inner solution.

The *IAD — Iterative Aggregation/Disaggregation* methods are related to block iterative methods. They are particularly powerful when the Markov chain is *NCD — Nearly Completely Decomposable*, as the partitions are chosen based on how strongly the states of the Markov chain interact with one another, [13,38]. The choice of good partitions for both block iterative methods and IAD methods is an active area of current research.

3.4 Projection Methods

An idea that is basic to sparse linear systems and eigenvalue problems is that of projection processes. Such processes have begun to be applied successfully to Markov chain problems, [42]. Whereas iterative methods begin with an approximate solution vector that is modified at each iteration and which (supposedly) converges to a solution, projection methods create vector subspaces and search for the best possible approximation to the solution that can be obtained from that subspace. With a given subspace, for example, it is possible to extract a vector $\hat{\pi}$ that is a linear combination of a set of basis vector for that space and which minimizes $\|\hat{\pi}Q\|$ in some vector norm. This vector $\hat{\pi}$ may then be taken as an approximation to the solution of $\pi Q = 0$. This is the basis for the *GMRES, Generalized Minimal Residual* algorithm. Another popular projection method is the method of *Arnoldi.* The subspace most often used is the Krylov subspace, $K_m = span\{v_1, v_1 Q, \ldots, v_1 Q^{m-1}\}$, constructed from a starting vector v_1 and successive iterates of the power method. The computed vectors are then orthogonalized with respect to one another. It is also possible to construct "iterative" variants of these methods. When the subspace reaches some maximum size, the best approximation is chosen from this subspace and a new subspace generated using this approximation as the initial starting point.

Preconditioning techniques are frequently used to improve the convergence rate of iterative Arnoldi and GMRES. This typically amounts to replacing the original system $\pi Q = 0$ by

$$\pi Q M^{-1} = 0,$$

where M is a matrix whose inverse is easy to compute. The objective of preconditioning is to modify the system of equations to obtain a coefficient matrix with a fast rate of convergence. It is worthwhile pointing out that preconditioning may also be used with the basic power method to improve its rate of convergence. The inverse of the matrix M is generally computed from an *Incomplete LU factorization* of the matrix Q.

3.5 Recursive Methods for Hessenberg Matrices

We now consider numerical solution methods that are only applicable when the transition matrices possess some special structure. Notice that when the balance equation of the $M/M/1$ queue with service rate μ and arrival rate λ are written in matrix form, it is immediately obvious that the solution satisfies

$$\pi_{i+1} = (\lambda/\mu)\pi_i.$$

Thus, once π_0 is known, the remaining values π_i may be determined recursively. For the $M/M/1$ queue it is easy to show that the probability that the queue is empty is given by $\pi_0 = (1 - \lambda/\mu)$. This recursive approach may be extended to upper and lower Hessenberg matrices. A matrix H is said to be upper Hessenberg if $h_{ij} = 0$ for $i > j + 1$. H is said to be lower Hessenberg if $h_{ij} = 0$ for $i < j - 1$. When the transition probability matrix P of an irreducible Markov chain is upper Hessenberg, the global balance equations may be written as

$$\pi_j = \sum_{i=0}^{j+1} \pi_i p_{ij}, \quad j = 0, 1, 2, \ldots$$

or equivalently

$$\pi_{j+1} = p_{j+1j}^{-1} \left[\pi_j(1 - p_{jj}) - \sum_{i=0}^{j-1} \pi_i p_{ij} \right], \quad j = 0, 1, 2, \ldots$$

This latter form exposes the recursive nature of these equations. If π_0 is known or may be determined, then all remaining π_i may be computed. If the matrix is finite then it is possible to assign π_0 an arbitrary value, $\pi_0 = 1$ for example, to compute the remaining π_i, and then renormalize the vector π such that $\|\pi\|_1 = 1$.

This may be viewed from a matrix approach by considering the corresponding finite homogeneous system of n equations in n unknowns

$$\pi Q = 0$$

and partitioning it as

$$(\pi_0, \pi_*) \begin{pmatrix} a^T & \gamma \\ B & d \end{pmatrix} = 0,$$

in which a, d and $\pi_* \in \Re^{(n-1)}$, $B \in \Re^{(n-1)\times(n-1)}$ and γ and π_0 are scalars. We have

$$\pi_0 a^T + \pi_* B = 0,$$

i.e.,

$$\pi_* B = -\pi_0 a^T.$$

If we assume that $\pi_0 = 1$ then this non-homogeneous system of $(n-1)$ equations in $(n-1)$ unknowns (π_*) may be solved very efficiently for π_*. Since the coefficient matrix B is triangular and has non-zero diagonal elements, it is simply a forward substitution procedure. Since forward substitution is a numerically stable procedure, recursive algorithms based on it are also stable.

Block upper (or lower) Hessenberg matrices are the obvious generalization of the upper (respectively lower) Hessenberg matrices just discussed. The diagonal blocks are square matrices of order n_i, $i = 0, 1, \ldots, K$; the off-diagonal blocks Q_{ij} $i \neq j$ have dimension $(n_i \times n_j)$. All of the elements of all of the blocks of Q are non-negative except the diagonal elements of the diagonal blocks which are all strictly negative. (As always the sum of elements across any row of Q is zero).

As for their point counterparts, it is sometimes possible to develop recursive methods to solve block Hessenberg matrices for the stationary probability vector (see, for example, [21,27,40,62,63], etc.). These recursive procedures often arise naturally from the formulation of the Chapmann-Kolmogorov equations and are easily programmed. Unfortunately, implementations based on block recursions *may* lead to inaccurate results; the recursive process may be numerically unstable. The analyst must be acutely aware of the conditions under which recursive solution methods will give accurate results. See Stewart, [57], for further details.

Let us consider the case of a block upper Hessenberg infinitesimal generator matrix. To implement a *forward* recursive procedure, we require that the subdiagonal blocks $Q_{k+1,k}$, $k = 0, 1, \ldots K-1$, be nonsingular. Among other properties, this implies that these blocks must be square. Let the stationary probability vector π be partitioned conformally with Q: i.e.,

$$\pi = (\pi_1,\ \pi_2,\ \ldots,\ \pi_K).$$

The ith block equation of $\pi Q = 0$ may be written as

$$\sum_{k=0}^{i+1} \pi_k Q_{ki} = 0 \quad \text{for } i = 0, 1, \ldots, K-1$$

$$\sum_{k=0}^{K} \pi_k Q_{kK} = 0 \quad \text{for } i = K.$$

We consider first the case when π_0 is known. Then from the first block equation we can write π_1 in terms of the known quantity π_0. We have

$$\pi_0 Q_{00} + \pi_1 Q_{10} = 0$$

and hence

$$\pi_1 = -\pi_0 Q_{00} Q_{10}^{-1}.$$

Similarly, from the second block equation, we have

$$\pi_0 Q_{01} + \pi_1 Q_{11} + \pi_2 Q_{21} = 0$$

and since by this time both π_0 and π_1 are known, we can express π_2 in terms of known quantities. We get

$$\pi_2 = -(\pi_0 Q_{01} + \pi_1 Q_{11}) Q_{21}^{-1} = -\pi_0 Q_{01} Q_{21}^{-1} + \pi_0 Q_{00} Q_{10}^{-1} Q_{11} Q_{21}^{-1}$$

Continuing in this fashion, we may determine all the subvectors π_i in terms of the known subvector π_0. The process is essentially a block forward substitution procedure. Algorithmically, the operation we perform at step k, $k = 0, 1, \ldots, K-1$, is

$$\pi_{k+1} = -\left(\sum_{i=0}^{k} \pi_i Q_{ik} \right) Q_{k+1,k}^{-1}. \quad (4)$$

This operation is not possible unless all the subdiagonal blocks are non-singular, and this is an obvious condition that must be fulfilled if this recursion is to be implemented.

It is not always necessary to know π_0 to implement a forward recursion (or π_K to implement backward recursion). Note that only the first $K-1$ block equations are needed to write all π_i in terms of π_0. The final block equation

$$\sum_{k=0}^{K} \pi_k Q_{kK} = 0 \quad (5)$$

may be used to compute the subvector, (π_0 in this case), that is used in the recursion. In other words, the procedure is to write all π_i, $i \neq 0$ in terms of the still unknown π_0 and then to use the final block equation (5) to determine π_0. Once π_0 has been computed, the previously mentioned recursions, (4), can be carried out to find the other π_i.

3.6 Matrix Geometric Solutions

The recursive procedures described in the preceding section are applicable to transition matrices that have a block Hessenberg form. Frequently, when the initial subvector π_0 can be computed independently, they may also be used to handle infinite systems. The disadvantage with this approach is the lack of stability. Much more stable is the matrix geometric approach developed by Neuts, [41]. This approach is applicable when the blocks themselves become identical after some initial point. Consider, for example, an irreducible Markov chain with transition probability matrix

$$P = \begin{pmatrix} B_0 & A_0 & 0 & 0 & \ldots \\ B_1 & A_1 & A_0 & 0 & \ldots \\ B_2 & A_2 & A_1 & A_0 & \ldots \\ \vdots & \vdots & \vdots & \vdots & \ddots \\ B_j & A_j & A_{j-1} & A_{j-2} & \ldots \\ \vdots & \vdots & \vdots & \vdots & \ddots \end{pmatrix}$$

in which all submatrices, A_j, B_j, $j = 0, 1, 2, \ldots$ are square and of order N. Since P is stochastic, $Pe = e$ and so

$$B_j e + \sum_{i=0}^{j} A_j e = e$$

for all j. We shall assume that the matrix A, defined as $A = \sum_{i=0}^{\infty} A_i$, is stochastic and irreducible. Neuts, [41], defines a sequence of matrices $\{R(l)\}$ as

$$R(0) = 0; \quad R(l+1) = \sum_{i=0}^{\infty} [R(l)]^i A_i \quad \text{for } l \geq 0,$$

and shows that $R(l) \leq R(l+1)$ for $l \geq 0$. Additionally, he proves that the sequence $\{R(l)\}$ converges to a matrix $R \geq 0$. If the Markov chain is positive recurrent, the matrices R^i , $i \geq 1$ are finite. Also R satisfies the equation

$$R = \sum_{i=0}^{\infty} R^i A_i, \tag{6}$$

and is the minimal non-negative solution to

$$X = \sum_{i=0}^{\infty} X^i A_i.$$

Our interest is in Markov chains that are irreducible and possess a stationary probability vector. As such they are positive recurrent and Neuts shows that the stationary probability vector π satisfying $\pi P = \pi$ is given by

$$\pi = (\pi_0,\ \pi_0 R,\ \pi_0 R^2,\ \ldots).$$

The matrix R is computed from equation (6) by writing it as

$$R = A_0 + RA_1 + \sum_{i=2}^{\infty} R^i A_i,$$

i.e.,

$$R = A_0 (I - A_1)^{-1} + \sum_{i=2}^{\infty} R^i A_i (I - A_1)^{-1}.$$

Therefore R may be computed by means of the iterative procedure

$$R_{l+1} = A_0 (I - A_1)^{-1} + \sum_{i=2}^{\infty} R_l^i A_i (I - A_1)^{-1}, \tag{7}$$

using $R_0 = 0$ to initiate the process. As is shown by Neuts, the sequence $\{R_l\}$ is monotone increasing and converges to R.

Since A_1 is substochastic, $(I - A_1)$ is non-singular. When implementing an algorithm based on equation (7), the inversion of $(I - A_1)$ and the matrix multiplications $A_i(I - A_1)^{-1}$ need be performed only once at the beginning of the procedure. Furthermore, in many applications $A_i = 0$ for $i \geq L$ where L is a small integer constant. In Quasi-Birth-Death (QBD) processes, for example, $A_i = 0$ for $i \geq 3$ and so equation (7) simplifies to

$$R_{l+1} = V + R_l^2 W$$

where $V = A_0(I - A_1)^{-1}$ and $W = A_2(I - A_1)^{-1}$.

Once R has been computed, it only remains to determine π_0. This vector may be computed from the first set of Chapman-Kolmogoroff equations with π_i written in terms of $\pi_0 R^i$. Neuts shows that

$$\pi_0 = \pi_0(B_0 + RB_1 + R^2 B_2 + \ldots).$$

In many applications, $B_i = 0$ for all $i > L$, where again L is a small integer constant. The $(N \times N)$ matrix $(B_0 + RB_1 + R^2 B_2 + \ldots)$ is then easy to form and the vector π_0 may be subsequently determined by direct computation. In other applications, this will not be the case and the method of computing $(B_0 + RB_1 + R^2 B_2 + \ldots)$ will be dictated by the problem itself. Numerous examples have been provided by Neuts and his colleagues. The vector π_0, once computed, should be normalized according to $\pi_0(I - R)^{-1} e = 1$.

Equation (7) is not the only iterative approach for computing the matrix R. In fact, another procedure, based directly on equation (6), is given by

$$R_0 = 0; \quad R_{l+1} = \sum_{i=0}^{\infty} R_l^i A_i, \quad \text{for } i \geq 0$$

and this may also be shown to converge monotonically to R as $i \to \infty$. However, from numerical experiments reported by Ramaswami in [48], convergence of this scheme can be excruciatingly slow. Unfortunately, the first proposed iterative procedure, (equation 7), is only marginally better. This is the major challenge of the matrix geometric approach; viz, the difficulty in computing the matrix R. It often takes many many iterations to obtain R to an acceptable accuracy. There is currently some research being conducted into applying Newton and Newton-related methods to find R more rapidly, [48].

Attempts to derive quadratic convergence procedures for the computation of the matrix R for QBD processses have concentrated on two different approaches. The first falls into the "spectral decomposition" approach of Daigle and Lucantoni, [15], and Elwalid, Mitra and Stern, [17]. The second is a logarithmic reduction process recently developed by Latouche and Ramaswami, [33]. These approaches appear to be very promising indeed. More information on the theory and application of this approach can be found in recent conference proceedings, including [9]. Among available computational tools, we cite that of Squillante, [56].

4 Numerical Methods for Computing Transient Distributions

There exists several numerical techniques for obtaining transient solutions of homogeneous, irreducible Markov chains. These techniques are based either on computing matrix exponentials or integrating the Chapman-Kolmogorov system of differential equations:

$$\begin{cases} \dfrac{d\pi(t)}{dt} = \pi(t)Q, \; t \in [0,\; T] \\ \pi(0) \quad = \pi_0 \qquad \text{an initial probability distribution.} \end{cases} \tag{8}$$

The transient distribution, $\pi(t)$ is the solution of (8) and is known to be:

$$\pi(t) = e^{Qt}\pi_0.$$

Since the matrix exponential is full even when the original matrix is sparse, the practical computation of e^{Qt} in full remains possible only when Q is relatively small, i.e., when the number of states in the Markov chain does not exceed a few hundreds. In [39], Moler and Van Loan provide an instructive review of possible methods applicable in this context. Although this review shows that none of the methods are unconditionally acceptable for all classes of problems, methods such as those of the Padé-type or matrix decompositions, with careful implementation, can be satisfactory in many contexts. These methods involve matrix-matrix operations.

To address large problems, the family of series methods, in which matrix-vector operations are paramount, appears to be a reasonable choice. Here we will consider one of this class, the *uniformization* method. The use of this method is particularly widespread for reasons that we shall see later. Also, the class of ordinary differential equations solvers is appealing because of the high availability of ready-to-use efficient library routines for solving initial value problems in ODEs. In addition to being multiple- or single-step, ODE solvers can be explicit or implicit, yielding four possible categories. Each category yields new classes of methods in their own right — depending on their derivation, their analytic and numerical properties, or on implementation aspects. For example, some of the particularities of a method can be: multistage or otherwise, order, stability region, matrix-free or otherwise, stiff or non-stiff, computational cost, etc. In general, implicit methods — which are more costly, appear suitable for stiff-problems while cheap explicit methods are satisfactory only on non-stiff problems. In the interests of space efficiency, we shall not discuss these methods further at this point. We shall however briefly discuss a Krylov projection-type method.

Systematic and extensive numerical comparisons of various methods for computing matrix exponentials in general, and transient solutions of Markov chains in particular are modest in the literature. One can mention the attempt made in Sidje, [54], where ODE solvers from the NAG library were used. However, the assessment provided is debatable because, with regard to other ODE libraries, the efficiency of the ODE chapter of NAG is questioned. In Clarotti, [14], a brief description of a customized implicit-type method is outlined. Unfortunately no experiments nor comparisons, are reported that confirm or deny the superiority of the approach. The work in Reibman and Trivedi, [49], later continued in Malhorta and Trivedi, [36], are also worth mentioning, for the ODE solution techniques used therein have been tailored specifically for the Markovian context. In [36] for instance, a comprehensive analysis of the issues (namely, largeness, stiffness and accuracy) faced when solving Markov chains numerically is presented and a comparison of four different solution techniques is undertaken. The comparison suggests that uniformization is best on non-stiff problems but is inferior to implicit ODE-solvers, such as the implicit third-order RK method, on stiff-problems.

4.1 Uniformization

The uniformization (or randomization) technique is based on the evaluation of the pth partial Taylor series expansion of the matrix exponential, [23,25]. The length p is fixed so that a prescribed tolerance on the approximation is satisfied. Since Q is essentially nonnegative (i.e., the diagonal elements of Q are negative and the off-diagonal elements are nonnegative), a naive use of the expression $\pi(t) = e^{Qt}\pi_0 \approx \sum_{k=0}^{p}(1/k!)(Qt)^k\pi_0$ is subject to severe roundoff errors due to terms of alternating signs. Uniformization uses the modified formulation $\pi(t) = e^{\alpha(P-I)t}\pi_0 = e^{-\alpha t}e^{\alpha Pt}\pi_0$ where $\alpha \equiv \max_i |q_{ii}|$ and $P \equiv \frac{1}{\alpha}Q + I$ is nonnegative with $\|P\|_1 = 1$. The resulting truncated approximation

$$\tilde{\pi}(t) = \sum_{k=0}^{p} e^{-\alpha t}\frac{(\alpha t)^k}{k!}\pi_0 P^k$$

involves only nonnegative terms and becomes numerically stable. If ϵ denotes the prescribed error tolerance, the condition $\|\pi(t) - \tilde{\pi}(t)\|_1 \leq \epsilon$ leads to a choice of p such that

$$1 - \sum_{k=0}^{p} e^{-\alpha t}\frac{(\alpha t)^k}{k!} \leq \epsilon. \tag{9}$$

The value p may be determined simply by adding-up the above series until the inequality is satisfied. The popularity of Unifomization is due to three reasons. Firstly, its handiness and malleability facilitate its implementation – only a matrix-vector product is needed per iteration. Secondly, the transformation from Q to P has a probabilistic interpretation. Thirdly and perhaps most important, it works surprizingly well in a great variety of circumstances.

4.2 The Krylov-Based Method

The Krylov-based algorithm generates an approximation to $\pi(t) = \exp(Qt)\pi_0$ and computes the matrix exponential times a vector rather than the matrix exponential in isolation. The underlying principle is to approximate

$$\pi(t) = e^{Qt}\pi_0 = \pi_0 + \frac{(Qt)}{1!}\pi_0 + \frac{(Qt)^2}{2!}\pi_0 + \cdots \tag{10}$$

by an element of the Krylov subspace

$$\mathcal{K}_m(Qt, \pi_0) = \text{Span}\{\pi_0, (Qt)\pi_0, \ldots, (Qt)^{m-1}\pi_0\}, \tag{11}$$

where m, the dimension of the Krylov subspace, is small compared to n, the order of the coefficient matrix (usually $m \leq 50$ whilst n can exceed many hundreds of thousands). The approximation used is

$$\tilde{\pi}(t) = \beta V_{m+1} \exp(\bar{H}_{m+1}\, t) e_1 \tag{12}$$

where $\beta = \|\pi_0\|_2$; $V_{m+1} = [\pi_{01}, \ldots, \pi_{0m+1}]$ and $\bar{H}_{m+1} = [h_{ij}]$ are, respectively, the orthonormal basis and the upper Hessenberg matrix resulting from the well-known Arnoldi process (see, e.g., [22,51]); e_1 is the first unit basis vector. The distinctive feature is that the original large problem (10) is converted to the small problem (12) which is more desirable. In reality however, due to stability and accuracy considerations, $\pi(t)$, is not computed in one go. On the contrary, a time-stepping strategy along with error estimation is embedded within the process. In other words, there is an integration scheme similar to that of a standard ODE solver. Typically, the algorithm evolves with the integration scheme

$$\begin{cases} \pi(0) & = \pi_0 \\ \pi(t_{k+1}) & = e^{Q(t_k+\tau_k)}\pi_0 = e^{Q\tau_k}\pi(t_k), \quad k = 0, 1, \ldots, s \end{cases} \tag{13}$$

where

$$\tau_k = t_{k+1} - t_k, \qquad 0 = t_0 < t_1 < \cdots < t_s < t_{s+1} = t.$$

It is clear from (13) that the crux of the problem remains an operation of the form $e^{Q\tau}\pi_0$, albeit with different π_0's. The selection of a specific step-size τ is made so that $e^{Q\tau}\pi_0$ is now effectively approximated by $\beta V_{m+1} \exp(\bar{H}_{m+1}\,\tau)e_1$. Following the procedures of ODEs solvers, an *a posteriori* error control is carried out to ensure that the intermediate approximation is acceptable with respect to expectations on the global error. More information may be obtained from [55].

Within the framework of Markov chains, relevant studies are those of Philippe and Sidje, [43], and Sidje, [54,55]. The Markovian context brings other considerations. We need to compute $\pi(t) = \exp(Qt)\pi_0$ subject to the constraint that the resulting vector is a probability vector and thus with components in the range [0, 1] and with sum equal to 1. Since the analytic solution of the Chapman-Kolmogorov system of differential equations is $\pi(t)$, its computation can be addressed totally in the perspective of ODEs.

Some results of interest are presented in [43,54], by exploiting the fact that the matrix Q satisfies certain inherent properties when it originates from a Markov chain model. Firstly it was established that the computed Krylov approximation is mathematically guaranteed to be a probability vector for small enough step-sizes and secondly, the global error in the approximation grows at most linearly. Additionally, it is possible to detect and cope with excessive roundoff errors. The ensuing code referred to as *EXPOKIT/DMEXPV*(m) implementing this customization is a component of the EXPOKIT package, a full description of which may be found in [55].

5 Stochastic Automata Networks

Stochastic Automata Networks (SANs), which have been discussed in the literature, for over a decade, [5,16,19,28,44,45,46], provide a means of performing Markov chain modelling without the problem of having to store huge transition matrices. A SAN consists of a number of individual stochastic automata that operate more or less independently of each other. Each individual automaton is represented by a number of states and rules that govern the manner in which it moves from one state to the next. The state of an automaton at any time t is just the state it occupies at time t and the state of the SAN at time t is given by the state of each of its constituent automata. An automaton may be thought of as a component in a Markov chain state descriptor. It has been observed that SANs provide a natural means of describing parallel and distributed systems since such systems are often viewed as collections of components that operate more or less independently, requiring only infrequent interaction such as synchronizing their actions, or operating at different rates depending on the state of parts of the overall system. This is exactly the viewpoint adopted by SANs.

The compact form in which the transition matrix that characterizes the model is kept (called the SAN *Descriptor*) helps keep memory requirements within manageable limits and avoids the state space explosion associated with other state based approaches. This descriptor is written as

$$\sum_{j=1}^{(N+2E)} \bigotimes_{i=1}^{N} Q_j^{(i)}, \tag{14}$$

where N is the number of automata in the SAN, E is the number of synchronizing events and $Q_j^{(i)}$ is a square matrix of low dimension. This may also be written as

$$= \bigoplus_{i=1}^{N} Q_l^{(i)} + \sum_{e \in \epsilon} \left(\bigotimes_{i=1}^{N} Q_{e^+}^{(i)} + \bigotimes_{i=1}^{N} Q_{e^-}^{(i)} \right),$$

where matrices corresponding to local transitions, $Q_l^{(i)}$, have been separated from those corresponding to synchronizing events; ϵ, being the set of synchronizing events. Therefore, the state space explosion problem associated with Markov chain models is mitigated by the fact that the state transition matrix is not stored, nor even generated. Instead, it is represented by a number of much smaller matrices and from these all relevant information may be determined without explicitly forming the global matrix. The implication is that a considerable saving in memory is effected by keeping the infinitesimal generator in this fashion. A potential source of memory waste with the SAN approach is due to the fact that the tensor product state space can become much larger than the actual model state space. While this is not a problem for storing the transition matrix itself (since it is not stored) it can pose a problem for storing the vectors needed to compute numerical solutions. Research by Ciardo, [12], and others have produced techniques that go a long way towards eliminating this problem.

In order to benefit from this compact form, the descriptor is never expanded into a single large matrix. Consequently, all subsequent operations must necessarily work with the model in its descriptor form and hence numerical operations on the underlying Markov chain infinitesimal generator become more costly. Previously, this cost was sufficiently high to discourage the application of SAN technologies. Recent results will most likely change this situation. These show how the application of successive modelling strategems and numerical savoir-faire reduce the time needed to compute stationary distributions by several orders of magnitude, thereby reducing considerably this perceived disadvantage. In particular, the essential role that funtional transitions play in this scenario needs to be emphasized. Functional transitions allow a system to be modeled as a SAN using fewer automata and fewer synchronizing transitions. In other words, if functional transitions cannot be handled by the modelling techniques used, then a given system can be modeled as a SAN only if additional automata are included and these automata linked to others by means of synchronizing transitions. Furthermore, as shown in [18], to effectively include functional transitions into a SAN, the concept of a generalized tensor product must be employed. The generalized tensor algebra developed in [18] permits functional transitions to be handled at the same low costs as constant transitions, Other ongoing research efforts directed at reducing these costs include the design of algorithms to reduce the amount of computation involved in forming the product of a vector and a SAN descriptor, and efforts into finding suitable preconditioners with which to speed up iterative methods.

6 Status and Directions

It could be argued that numerical analysts were the first computer scientists. Certainly, computing solutions to systems of linear, nonlinear and differential equations were among the very first computer applications. Today, there are still many many researchers who work in the numerical analysis field, possibly many times more than those who research interests lie in performance evaluation. The performance evaluation community has been slow to venture into the numerical analysis arena, possibly because of ignorance but more probably because there has not been a great need to. The success that has accompanied queueing modelling has largely eliminated the need to set up and solve global balance equations numerically. However, as models become more complex, it is becoming increasing evident that there is place for numerical analysis methods in the modelers toolbox. The challenges for the future will be for performance analysts to keep abreast of the research conducted by numerical analysts in the areas of aerospace, civil engineering, and so on and to successfully apply these novel approaches to the special structures that arise in performance evaluation.

As well as keeping abreast of developments in the numerical analysis field there needs be better efforts directed at incorporating the numerical approach into other performance evaluation techniques. Some work has already begun in this direction.

References

1. M. Ajmone Marsan, G. Balba and G. Conte. A class of generalized stochastic Petri nets for the performance evaluation of multiprocessor systems. *ACM Trans. Comput. Systems*, Vol. 2, No. 2, pp 93–122, 1994.
2. S.C. Allmaier and G. Horton. Parallel shared-memory state-space exploration in stochastic modelling. Lecture Notes in Compuer Science, #1253. Springer 1997.
3. S. Berson, E. de Souza e Silva and R.R. Muntz. A methodology for the specification and generation of Markov models. *Numerical Solution of Markov Chains*, William J. Stewart, Ed., Marcel Dekker Inc., New York, pp. 11–36, 1991.
4. S. Berson and R.R. Muntz. Detecting block GI/M/1 and block M/G/1 matrices from model specifications. *Computations with Markov Chains*, W.J. Stewart, Ed., Kluwer International Publishers, Boston, pp. 1–19, 1995.
5. P. Buchholz. Equivalence relations for stochastic automata networks. *Computations with Markov Chains*, W.J. Stewart, Ed., Kluwer International Publishers, Boston, pp. 197–215, 1995.
6. P. Buchholz. An aggregation-disaggregation algorithm for stochastic automata networks. *Prob. in the Eng and Inf. Sci.*, Vol. 11, pp. 229–254, 1997.
7. S. Caselli, G. Conte and P. Marenzoni. Parallel state space exploration for GSPN models. Lecture Notes in Computer Science # 935. Proceedings of the 16th International Conference on the Application and Theory of Petri Nets. Springer Verlag, Turin, Italy, June 1995.
8. W-L. Cao and W.J. Stewart. Iterative aggregation/disaggregation techniques for nearly uncoupled Markov chains. *Journal of the ACM*, Vol 32, pp. 702–719, 1985.
9. *Advances in matrix-analytic methods for stochastic models,* S.R. Chakravarthy and A.S. Alfa, Ed. Lecture Notes in Pure and Applied Mathematics, 1998.
10. G. Ciardo, J. Muppala and K.S. Trivedi. SPNP: stochastic Petri net package. In *Proceedings of the Third International Workshop on Petri Nets and Performance Models,* (PNPM89), Kyoto, Japan, 1989.
11. G. Ciardo and M. Tilgner. On the use of Kronecker operators for the solution of generalized stochastic Petri nets. ICASE Report 96–35, Hampton, VA, may 1996.
12. G. Ciardo and A.S. Miner. Storage alternatives for large structured state spaces. *IEEE International Computer Performance and Dependability Symposium,* R. Marie et al., eds., Springer Verlag, LNCS 1245, pp. 44–57, 1997.
13. P.J. Courtois. *Decomposability.* Academic Press, New York, 1977.
14. C. A. Clarotti. The Markov approach to calculating system reliability : Computational Problems. In A. Serra and R. E. Barlow, editors, *International School of Physics "Enrico Fermi", Varenna, Italy,* pp. 54–66, Amsterdam, 1984. North-Holland Physics Publishing.
15. J.N. Daigle and D.M. Lucantoni. Queueing systems having phase-dependent arrival and service rates. *Numerical Solution of Markov Chains,* William J. Stewart, Ed., Marcel Dekker Inc., New York, pp. 161–202, 1991.
16. S. Donatelli. Superposed stochastic automata: A class of stochastic Petri nets with parallel solution and distributed state space. *Performance Evaluation,* Vol. 18, pp. 21–36, 1993.
17. A.I. Elwalid, D. Mitra and T.E. Stern. Theory of statistical multiplexing of Markovian sources: Spectral expansions and algorithms. *Numerical Solution of Markov Chains,* William J. Stewart, Ed., Marcel Dekker Inc., New York, pp. 223–238, 1991.
18. P. Fernandes, B. Plateau and W.J. Stewart. Efficient descriptor-vector multiplication in stochastic automata networks. *Journal of the ACM,* Vol. 45, No. 3, May 1998.

19. J-M. Fourneau and F. Quessette. Graphs and stochastic automata networks. *Computations with Markov Chains.* W.J. Stewart, Ed., Kluwer International Publishers, Boston, 1995.
20. G. Franceschinis and R. Muntz. Computing bounds for the performance indices of quasi-lumpable stochastic well-formed nets. *Proceedings of the 5th International Workshop on Petri Nets and Performance Models*, Toulouse, France, IEEE Press, pp. 148–157, October 1993.
21. S.B. Gershwin, I.C. and Schick. Modelling and analysis of three-stage transfer lines with unreliable machines and finite buffers. *Operations Research*, 31, 2, pp. 354–380, 1983.
22. G. H. Golub and C. F. Van Loan. *Matrix Computations.* The Johns Hopkins University Press, Baltimore, second edition, 1989.
23. W. Grassmann. Transient solutions in Markovian queueing systems. *Comput. Opns. Res.*, 4:47–56, 1977.
24. W. Grassmann, M.I. Taksar and D.P. Heyman. Regenerative analysis and steady state distributions, *Operations Research*, Vol. 33, pp 1107–1116, 1985.
25. D. Gross and D. R. Miller. The randomization technique as modelling tool and solution procedure for transient Markov processes. *Operations Research*, 32(2):343–361, 1984.
26. J. Hillston. Computational Markovian modelling using a process algebra. *Computations with Markov Chains*, W.J. Stewart, Ed., Kluwer International Publishers, Boston, 1995.
27. M.A. Jafari and J.G. Shanthikumar. Finite state spacially non-homogeneous quasi birth-death processes. Working Paper #85-009, Dept. of Industrial Engineering and Operations Research, Syracuse University, Syracuse, New York 13210.
28. P. Kemper. Closing the gap between classical and tensor based iteration techniques. *Computations with Markov Chains*, W.J. Stewart, Ed., Kluwer International Publishers, Boston, 1995.
29. R. Klevans and W.J. Stewart. From queueing networks to Markov chains: The XMarca interface. *Performance Evaluation*, Vol. 24, pp. 23–45, 1995.
30. U. Krieger, B. Muller-Clostermann and M. Sczittnick. Modeling and analysis of communication systems based on computational methods for Markov chains. *IEEE Journ. on Selec. Ar. in Comm*, Vol. 8, pp. 1630–1648, 1990.
31. W.J. Knottenbelt. *Generalized Markovian analysis of timed transition systems.* Master's thesis, University of Capetown, 1995.
32. W.J. Knottenbelt, M. Mestern, P. Harrison and P. Kritzinger. Probability, parallelism and the state space exploration problem. Lecture Notes in Computer Science, #1469. R. Puigjaner, N.N. Savino and B. Serra, Eds. Springer Publishers, 1998.
33. G. Latouche and Y. Ramaswami. A logarithmic reduction algorithm for quasi birth and death processes. Technical Report, Bellcore TM-TSV-021374 and Université Libre de Bruxelles, Sémin. Théor. Prob., Rapp. Tech. 92/3, 1992.
34. S.Q. Li and J.W. Mark. Performance of voice/data integration on a TDM system. *IEEE Trans. Communications*, Vol. COM-33, No. 12, Dec. 1985, pp. 1265–1273.
35. C. Lindemann. Exploiting isomorphisms and special structures in the analysis of Markov regenerative stochastic Petri nets. *Computations with Markov Chains*, W.J. Stewart, Ed., Kluwer International Publishers, Boston, pp. 383–402, 1995.
36. M. Malhotra and K. S. Trivedi. Higher-order methods for transient analysis of stiff Markov chains. Duke University Technical Report DUKE-CCSR-91, Center for Computer Systems Research, Durham, USA, 1991.

37. D.F. McAllister, G.W. Stewart and W.J. Stewart. On a Rayleigh-Ritz refinement technique for nearly uncoupled stochastic matrices. *Journal of Linear Algebra and Its Applications,* Vol. 60, pp. 1–25, August 1984.
38. C.D. Meyer. Stochastic complementation, uncoupling Markov chains and the theory of nearly reducible systems. *SIAM Rev.*, Vol. 31, pp. 240–272, 1989.
39. C. B. Moler and C. F. Van Loan. Nineteen dubious ways to compute the exponential of a matrix. *SIAM Review.*, Vol. 20, No. 4, pp. 801–836, October 1978.
40. E.J. Muth and S. Yeralan. Effect of buffer size on productivity of work stations that are subject to breakdowns. The 20-th IEEE Conference on Decision and Control, pp. 643–648, 1981.
41. M.F. Neuts. *Matrix geometric solutions in stochastic models – An algorithmic approach.* Johns Hopkins University Press, Baltimore, (1981).
42. B. Philippe, Y. Saad, and W. J. Stewart. Numerical methods in Markov chains modeling. *Operations Research*, Vol. 40, No. 6, 1992.
43. B. Philippe and R. B. Sidje. Transient solutions of Markov processes by Krylov subspaces. *Computations with Markov Chains*, W.J. Stewart, Ed., Kluwer International Publishers, Boston, pp. 95–119, 1995.
44. B. Plateau. On the stochastic structure of parallelism and synchronization models for distributed algorithms. *Proc. ACM Sigmetrics Conference on Measurement and Modelling of Computer Systems*, Austin, Texas, August 1985.
45. B. Plateau and K. Atif. Stochastic automata network for modelling parallel systems. *IEEE Trans. on Software Engineering*, Vol. 17, No. 10, pp. 1093–1108, 1991.
46. B. Plateau, J.M. Fourneau and K.H. Lee. PEPS: A package for solving complex Markov models of parallel systems. In R. Puigjaner, D. Potier, Eds., *Modelling Techniques and Tools for Computer Performance Evaluation*, Spain, September 1988.
47. M. Veran and D. Potier. QNAP2: A portable environment for queueing systems modelling. In D. Potier, ed. *Modelling and Tools for Performance Analysis*, pp. 25–63. Elsevier Science Publishers, 1985.
48. V. Ramaswami. Nonlinear matrix equations in applied probability — Solution techniques and open problems. *SIAM Review*, Vol.30, No. 2, pp. 256–263, June 1988.
49. A. Reibman and K. Trivedi. Transient analysis of cumulative measures of Markov model behavior. *Commu. Statist.-Stochastic Models*, 5(4):683–710, 1989.
50. Y. Saad. *Iterative solution of sparse linear systems.* PWS Publishing, New York, 1996.
51. Y. Saad. *Numerical methods for large eigenvalue problems.* John Wiley & Sons, Manchester Univ. Press, 1992.
52. P.J. Schweitzer. Aggregation methods for large Markov chains. In *Mathematical Computer Performance and Reliability*, G. Iazeolla, P.J. Courtois and A. Hordijk, Eds. North-Holland, Amsterdam, pp 275–286, 1984.
53. P. Semal. Two bounding schemes for the steady state solution of Markov chains. *Computations with Markov Chains*, W.J. Stewart, Ed., Kluwer International Publishers, Boston, pp. 307–320, 1995.
54. R. B. Sidje. *Parallel algorithms for large sparse matrix exponentials: Application to numerical transient analysis of Markov processes.* PhD thesis, University of Rennes 1, July 1994.
55. R. B. Sidje. EXPOKIT. A software package for computing matrix exponentials. Accepted for publication in ACM-Transactions of Mathematical Software, 1997.

56. M. Squillante. MAGIC: A computer performance modeling tool based on matrix geometric techniques. *Computer Performance Evaluation: Modeling Techniques and Tools*, G. Balbo and G. Serazzi, Eds. North-Holland Publishers, pp. 411–425, 1992.
57. W.J. Stewart. *An Introduction to the Numerical Solution of Markov Chains*, Princeton University Press, New Jersey, 1994.
58. W.J. Stewart, K. Atif and B. Plateau. The numerical solution of stochastic automata networks. *European Journal of Operations Research*, Vol. 86, No. 3, pp. 503–525, 1995.
59. W.J. Stewart. MARCA: Markov chain analyzer. *IEEE Computer Repository* No. R76 232, 1976. (See the URL: *http://www.csc.ncsu.edu/faculty/WStewart/*)
60. V.I. Wallace and R.S. Rosenberg. RQA-1, The recursive queue analyzer. Technical report No.2, Systems Engineering Laboratory, University of Michigan, Ann Arbor, Feb. 1966.
61. V. Wallace. The solution of quasi birth and death processes arising from multiple access computer systems. Ph.D. Dissertation, Systems Engineering Laboratory, University of Michigan, Tech. Report No. 07742-6-T, 1969.
62. Wong, Giffin, and Disney, Two finite M/M/1 queues in tandem: A matrix solution for the steady state. *OPSEARCH* 14, 1, pp 1–18, 1977.
63. T. Yang, M.J.M. Posner and J.G.C. Templeton. A generalized recursive technique for finite Markov processes. *Numerical Solution of Markov Chains*, William J. Stewart, Ed., Marcel Dekker Inc., New York, pp. 203–221, 1991.
64. J. Ye and S.Q. Li. Analysis of multi-media traffic queues with finite buffer and overload control — Part I: Algorithms. *Proc. of INFOCOM '91*, pp. 1464–1474.
65. J. Ye and S.Q. Li. Analysis of multi-media traffic queues with finite buffer and overload control — Part II: Applications. *Proc. of INFOCOM '92*, pp. 848–859.

Product Form Queueing Networks

Simonetta Balsamo

Department of Mathematics and Computer Science
University of Udine, Italy
balsamo@dimi.uniud.it

1 Introduction and Short History

System performance evaluation is often based on the development and analysis of appropriate models. Queueing network models have been extensively applied to represent and analyze resource sharing systems, such as production, communication and computer systems. They have proved to be a powerful and versatile tool for system performance evaluation and prediction.

A queueing network model is a collection of service centers representing the system resources that provide service to a collection of customers that represent the users. The customers' competition for the resource service corresponds to queueing into the service centers. The analysis of the queueing network models consists of evaluating a set of performance measures, such as resource utilization and throughput and customer response time. The popularity of queueing network models for system performance evaluation is due to a good balance between a relative high accuracy in the performance results and the efficiency in model analysis and evaluation. In this framework the class of product form networks has played a fundamental role. Product form queueing networks have a simple closed form expression of the stationary state distribution that allows to define efficient algorithms to evaluate average performance measures. We introduce product form queueing networks and their properties.

Queueing network models extend the basic queueing systems that are stochastic models first introduced to represent the entire system by one service center. The basic queueing systems have been applied to analyze congestion in telephonic systems and then they have been applied to study congestion in computer and communication systems [38,43,27,61,45,24,35].

Queueing network models represent such systems as a network of interacting service centers whose analysis often provides quite accurate prediction of their performance. Despite of several assumptions of the class of queueing networks, they have been observed to be very robust models [59].

Queueing network models can be analyzed by analytical methods or by simulation. Simulation is a general technique of wide application, but its main drawback is the potential high development and computational cost to obtain accurate results. Analytical methods require that the model satisfies a set of assumptions and constraints and are based on a set of mathematical relationships that characterize the system behavior.

G. Haring et al. (Eds.): Performance Evaluation, LNCS 1769, pp. 377–401, 2000.

We consider analytical methods to analyze queueing network models and specifically product form queueing networks that have a simple closed form of the stationary state probability distribution, which allow the definition of efficient algorithms to evaluate their performance.

Jackson [34] introduced product form queueing network models for open exponential networks and Gordon and Newell [28] for closed exponential networks. They introduce several assumptions on the model characteristics and provide a simple closed form expression of the stationary state distribution and some average performance indices. This class of models was then extended to include various interesting and useful characteristics to represent more complex system. These features include different types of customers of the networks, various queueing disciplines (i. e., the scheduling algorithms of the waiting queues), state-dependent service rate, state-dependent routing of customers between the service centers and some constraints on the population of subnetworks.

The most famous result concerning product form queueing networks was presented by Baskett, Chandy, Muntz and Palacios in 1975 [6] known as BCMP theorem. It defines the well-known class of BCMP queueing networks with product form solution for open, closed or mixed models with multiple classes of customers and various service disciplines and service time distributions. The stationary state distribution is expressed as the product of the distributions of the single queues with appropriate parameters and, for closed networks, with a normalization constant.

An important property of product form queueing networks is the arrival theorem. It states that the distribution at arrival times at a service center is identical to the distribution at arbitrary times of the same network, for open networks, and of a network with one less customer for closed networks [44,57].

This led to the definition of a set of recurrence equations between average performance measure for closed networks from which it was derived a recursive computational algorithm, the Mean Value Analysis (MVA) [53], that avoids the direct evaluation of the normalization constant.

We can analyze product form networks with various computational algorithms to evaluate the performance indices. These algorithms provide a powerful tool in the efficient analysis of large queueing network models. The most important ones are the Convolution Algorithm [13] and the Mean Value Analysis [53,52] for closed networks. They provide the evaluation of average performance indices with a polynomial space and time computational complexity in the network dimension, that is the number of service centers and the network population.

Product form networks with multiple classes of customers are more difficult to analyze. Various types of customers define the customers' classes in the network that are gathered in chains. Both Convolution and MVA algorithms have been extended to multiple classes networks [53,52,54,41], but their cost grows exponentially with the number of customer classes or chains. Other algorithms for multiclass queueing networks have been proposed. The tree Convolution and tree MVA algorithms for multichain networks are based on a tree data structure to optimize the algorithm computation [42,62,31]. Multichain networks with several types of customers can be analyzed by the algorithms named Recursion by Chain Algorithm (Recal) [20,21], Mean Value Analysis by Chain [19] and Distribution Analysis by Chain (DAC) [23]. Their computational complexity is polynomial with the number of classes of customers, but exponential in the number of service centers.

The computational algorithms have been integrated in various software tools for performance modelling and analysis that include user friendly interfaces based on different languages to take into account the particular field of application, e.g. computer networks, computer systems. This allows not expert users to apply efficient performance modelling techniques. More recently some tools provide a combined functional and quantitative system analysis, by integrating the solution performance algorithms with model specification techniques.

Product form networks yield various interesting properties. The insensitivity property states that the analytical results, i. e. the stationary state distribution and the average performance indices, depend on the service time requirements only through their average. Similarly, the performance indices depend on the customers routing only through the average visit ratio to each service center [6,15,16,55,66].

Another important property of product form queueing network models is that aggregation methods yield exact results. Chandy, Herzog and Woo [14] first introduced the aggregation theorem. It allows substituting a subnetwork with a single service center, so that the new aggregated network has the same behavior in terms of a set of performance indices. From the performance viewpoint exact aggregation allows us to apply the hierarchical system design process by relating the performance indices of the models at different levels in the hierarchy [45]. In a bottom-up analysis of systems represented by a succession of queueing network models exact aggregation defines the next model. Similarly, in a hierarchical top-down design of system with given performance requirements, the inverse process of disaggregation or development of the network can be applied to define a more detailed model with the same performance indices [4].

Aggregation is an efficient technique when applied to the analysis of nearly complete decomposable systems. Informally, such a system can be decomposed into subsystems whose internal interactions are much higher than the interactions among the subsystems [22]. Exact aggregation for product form queueing networks provides a basis for approximate solution methods of more general non-product form network models [46].

More recently further research has devoted to the extension of the class of product form network models and to its characterization. Some interesting new features have been defined such as networks with positive and negative customers proposed by Gelenbe [26] that can be used to represent special dynamic of actual systems. Some other more complex models include various functions of state-dependent routing and several special cases of queueing networks with finite capacity queues, finite population constraints and blocking [1,5,2,8,64,40,60,63]. Nelson in [49] has discussed the mathematics leading to the product form results and the properties of the stochastic process underlying the network model. Product form solution has been extended to queueing networks with batch arrivals and batch services [29,30] that are also related to discrete time queueing network models.

We shall now provide an introduction to product form network models, their properties and applications to system performance evaluation. We will present the basic results, the key ideas and we discuss why this class of models is important in system performance evaluation, whereas we refer to the literature for the mathematical details of the properties. In the next section we introduce queueing networks to represent and evaluate system performance. Section 3 deals with the key ideas of product form network models and their basic properties. The main algorithms and tools for product form network analysis are introduced in Section 4. Current and future directions of research and application of this class of models are discussed in Section 5.

2 Queueing Network Models for System Performance Evaluation

Queueing network models have been extensively applied as performance evaluation models of congestion systems, such as production, communication and computer systems. They provide a simple model at a high level of abstraction, intuitively understandable and that can clearly represent resource contention. System performance evaluation with queueing network models consists in the definition and parameterization of the model to evaluate of a set of figures of merit that are performance indices, such as resource utilization, system throughput and customers' response time.

First simple queueing systems have been proposed to model a system as a unique service center. These stochastic models were originally proposed for the congestion analysis in telephonic systems and then they have been applied to study congestion in various systems including computer and communication systems [38,27,43,61].

2.1 Queueing Systems with a Single Service Center

A single resource model is described by an arrival process of incoming customers, a service process, a buffer space for holding the waiting customers, a scheduling algorithm of the queue and a set of servers that provide the service to customers. Fig. 1 illustrates a single service center. The Kendall's notation $A/B/c$ denotes a queueing system with arrival process A, service process B and c service centers, by assuming infinite buffer and First Come First Server scheduling. For example $M/M/1$ denotes the system with Poisson (Markov) arrival process, exponential (Markov) service process and a single server and $M/G/1$ the same system except for the service time that has a general or arbitrary distribution. The single resource queueing systems are analyzed by defining an associated discrete-space continuous-time stochastic process, whose state include the system population.

Under independent and exponential assumptions the associated Markov process has a simple stationary solution in terms of state probability [38]. Some queueing systems, such as the $M/M/1$ and $M/M/m$ systems have an associated Markov process with special structure, that is a birth-death Markov process, which yield a simple closed-form solution of the stationary state probabilities. Hence such queueing systems can be easily analyzed and the average performance indices show simple analytical expressions.

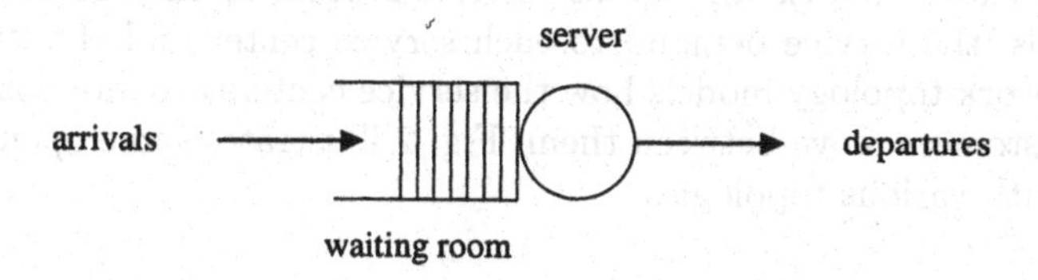

Fig. 1. A single service center queueing system

For example an $M/M/1$ system with exponential arrival rate λ and service rate μ has an associated birth and death Markov process whose state is given by $k = 0, 1, \ldots$ with constant birth rate λ from any state k to state $k+1$ and constant death rate μ from any state $k+1$ to state k. If the system is stable, i.e. if the arrival rate is less than the service rate ($\lambda < \mu$), then the queue length distribution is geometric with parameter $\rho = \lambda/\mu$, that is the stationary probability $\pi(k)$ of k customers in the system is

$$\pi(k) = \rho^k(1-\rho) \qquad k \geq 0 \tag{1}$$

The average queue length is $E[n] = \rho/(1-\rho)$ and the average response time is $R = 1/(\mu - \lambda)$. Similarly the $M/M/m$ system with exponential arrival rate λ, m servers with service rate μ has an associated birth-death Markov process whose state is given by $k = 0, 1, \ldots$ with constant birth rate λ from any state k to state $k+1$ and state-dependent death rate $\min\{k+1, m\}\mu$ from any state $k+1$ to state k. The system is stable when $\lambda < m\mu$ and then the stationary queue length probability $\pi(k)$ of k customers in the system is given by

$$\pi(k) = \pi(0)(m\rho)^k/k! \qquad 1 \leq k \leq m \tag{2}$$

$$\pi(k) = \pi(0)(m^m\rho^k)/m! \qquad k > m \tag{3}$$

where $\rho = \lambda/m\mu$ and $\pi(0)$ is determined by the normalizing condition $\sum_{k=0}^{\infty} \pi(k) = 1$. The average queue length is $E[k] = [m\rho + \pi(m)\rho/(1-\rho)^2]$ and the average response time is $R = [1/\mu + \pi(m)/(m\mu(1-\rho)^2)]$.

Hence we can immediately apply these simple performance model to evaluate several performance indices of a system that can be represented by $M/M/1$ or $M/M/m$ models. For a detailed discussion of these and other single service center models see [38].

2.2 Queueing Networks

With more details we can represent a system as a network of resources. A queueing network model is a collection of interconnected single service center queueing systems that provide service to a set of customers. Informally, a queueing network is defined by the service centers, the customers and network topology. Service center characteristics include the service time, the buffer space with its queueing scheduling and the number of servers. Customers are described by their number for closed models and by the arrival process to each service center for open models, the service demand to each service center and the types of customer. Network topology models how the service centers are interconnected and how the customers move between them. Fig. 2 illustrates some open and closed networks with various topologies.

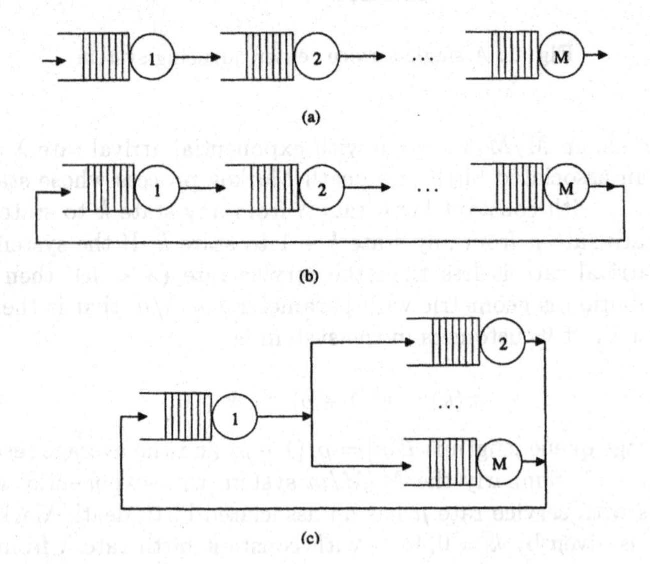

Fig. 2. Example of queueing network topologies: (a) tandem, (b) cyclic, (c) central server

Different types of customer in the queueing network model can model different behaviors of the customers. This allows representing various types of external arrival process, different service demands and different types of network routing. A chain gathers the customers of the same type. A chain consists of a set of classes that represent different phases of processing in the system for a given type of customer. Classes are partitioned on the service centers and each customer in a chain moves between the classes. A chain can be used to represent a customer routing behavior dependent on the past history. For example two classes of the same chain in a service centers can represent the customer requirement of two successive services (e.g. a customer representing a job in a computer system that requires two services: program loading and execution). Each chain can be open or closed depending on whether external arrivals and departures are allowed. Multiclass or multichain networks may be open or closed if all the chains are open or closed, respectively. A mixed network has both open and closed chains. A simple example of a multiclass network with two chains and four classes is illustrated in Fig. 3. The service time requirement for each class can be different. Chain 1 is open and describes the type 1 customer routing behavior of two successive visits to the same service center first in class a and then in class b. Chain 2 is closed and there is a constant number of type 2 customers circulating between the service centers in class c and d. Multiclass models can be used for a more precise representation of system behavior and to obtain more detailed performance indices.

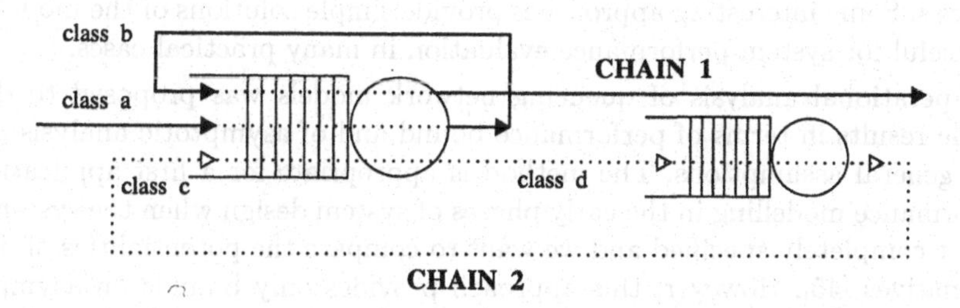

Fig. 3. Example of a mixed network with two service centers, an open chain with two classes (a and b) and a closed chain with two classes (c and d)

The analysis of a queueing network model provides information on the performance of each system component modeled by a service center, and on the overall system performance. Performance indices are obtained by the model analysis.

Queueing network analysis is based on the definition and analysis of an underlying stochastic process that is usually a discrete space continuous time homogeneous Markov process. The process state definition typically includes the number of customers in each queue. The behavior of the queueing network models is represented by the evolution of the associated process. Consider a network with M service centers. Let n_i denote the customer population at node i, $\mathbf{n} = (n_1, \ldots, n_M)$ the network joint queue length and $\pi(\mathbf{n}) = \pi(n_1, \ldots, n_M)$ the stationary joint queue length distribution. Let $\boldsymbol{\pi}$ denote the stationary state probability vector of the Markov process and Q its transition rate matrix. If the queueing network is stable, then the stationary state probability $\boldsymbol{\pi}$ is defined by the normalized solution of the following linear system:

$$\boldsymbol{\pi}\, Q = 0 \tag{4}$$

also called system of *global balance equations*. Performance indices of the queueing network are derived by the stationary state distribution of the process.

Unfortunately the generality of this approach is limited by its computational complexity. One can easily observe that the process state space cardinality, that is the number of global balance equations, often makes the solution of the system of global balance equation intractable. More precisely, for an open network the process state space is infinite and we can obtain an exact solution only in some special cases, when the matrix Q shows a particular regular structure. For a closed network the process state space grows exponentially with the network parameters that are the number of service centers, customers and customers types. For example, for a single class exponential queueing networks with M service centers and K customers the state space cardinality is $\binom{M+K-1}{K}$.

So why queueing networks became so popular as performance models? The answer is that in some cases, such as for product form networks, we can obtain a simple and efficient solution of the network model analysis.

There is a trade-off between the accuracy and the efficiency of the model analysis. Some interesting approaches provide simple solutions of the model that are useful for system performance evaluation in many practical cases.

Operational analysis of queueing network models was proposed to derive simple results in terms of performance bound and of asymptotic analysis under very general assumptions. The method is appropriate for a first application of performance modelling in the early phases of system design when the system can be not completely specified and we want to compare the potentialities of design alternatives [45]. However, this approach provides only bounds on asymptotic performance measures.

Product form queueing networks provide more precise and detailed results than operational analysis, in terms of performance indices such as queue length distribution, average response time, resource utilization and throughput. These performance indices are evaluated for each component and for the overall network. Product form network analysis is based on a set of assumptions on the system parameters that lead to a closed form expression of the stationary state distribution. The stationary joint queue length probability π defined by the solution of the associated Markov process, given by the linear system (4) has a *product form solution*, as follows:

$$\pi(\mathbf{n}) = \frac{1}{G} V(n) \prod_{i=1}^{M} g_i(n_i) \tag{5}$$

where G is a normalizing constant, n is the total network population, function V is defined in terms of network parameters and g_i is a function of state n_i and depends on the type of service center i, $1 \leq i \leq M$. For open networks $G = 1$, whereas for closed networks $V(n) = 1$. For open network function g_i is the stationary queue length distribution of node i in isolation with appropriate parameters.

Similarly, for networks with multiple types of customers let R denote the number of chains and $\mathbf{S}$ the network state that include the customer population at each service center. For a multiclass product form network we can express the stationary state probability π as follows:

$$\pi(\mathbf{S}) = \frac{1}{G} \prod_{r=1}^{R} V_r(K_r) \prod_{i=1}^{M} g_i(n_i) \qquad (6)$$

where G is a normalizing constant, K_r is the total network population in chain r, function V_r, $1 \leq r \leq R$ is defined in terms of network parameters and function g_i depends on the state and the type of service center i, $1 \leq i \leq M$.

Product form networks can be analyzed by efficient algorithms with a polynomial time computational complexity in the number of network components. This class of models allows a good balance between a relative high accuracy in the performance results and the efficiency in model analysis and evaluation. Moreover product form networks yield several interesting properties such as insensitivity and exact aggregation that greatly influenced the application of this class of models as a powerful tool for performance evaluation.

Various degrees of details can be used to define the performance model at the appropriate level of abstraction, depending on the goal of the system performance analysis. System components are represented by the model components that are the service centers, the classes of customers and the customer routing according to the objective of the performance evaluation study and depend on the performance measures of interest. This concerns the model definition.

Product form networks are simple and intuitive models that can be solved by efficient algorithms and tools that we shall introduce in Section 4. But first, in order to apply this class of models a question is: how can we characterize product form queueing networks?

3 Product Form Queueing Network Models: Basic Ideas

Product form solution of queueing networks holds under special assumptions. The precise characterization of the class of product form network is not easy. The product form solution is related to some properties of the queueing network model that are defined on the Markov process underlying the queueing model. Some sufficient conditions for product form solution based on these properties has been derived. Important properties are *quasireversibility* and partial balance. Informally, quasireversibility of a service center states that the current state, the past departures and the future arrivals are mutually independent. This property refers to the relation between the arrival and departure process. The so called $M \Rightarrow M$ property was first proved by Burke [12] and states that in an $M/M/1$ system a Poisson arrival process produces a Poisson departure process, independent of the queue state. Examples of *quasireversible* queues are:

I Multiclass service center with First Come First Served (FCFS) queueing discipline and exponential service time distribution, identical for each customer class.

II Multiclass service center with Processor Sharing (PS) scheduling and arbitrary phase type service time distribution, i. e. formed by a network of exponential stages [38].

III Multiclass service center with infinite number of servers, that is with IS scheduling and arbitrary phase type service time distribution.
IV Multiclass service center with Last Come First Served with preemption (LCFS-Pr) scheduling and arbitrary phase type service time distribution.

Other examples of quasireversible queues are defined in terms of the particular class of symmetric queueing discipline. A service discipline is called *symmetric* [36] if the probability that an arrival enters the queue in the i-th position when there are n customer is equal to the fraction of the service capacity destined to the customer in the i-th queue position when there are $n+1$ customer in the queue. Examples of symmetric disciplines are LCFS-Pr and PS. However, this is only a sufficient condition for product form solution. A similar condition was defined as station balancing [16] to characterize the queueing disciplines that yield product form queues. In this case, by assuming a special form of the product form expression one can define a necessary and sufficient condition for product form solution that requires station balance discipline for non-exponential queues.

Given a single queue with product form solution a problem is how to combine a set of queues into a network in order to maintain the product form solution.

3.1 Preliminary Results

First we can simply connect the queues so that the $M \Rightarrow M$ property holds. Tandem exponential networks with Poisson arrivals where the service times are mutually independent satisfy this condition. Similarly, acyclic exponential networks with Poisson external arrivals and routing with Bernoulli splitting can be analyzed as a set of independent $M/M/1$ queueing system with appropriate arrival rates. This immediately derives from the decomposition and superposition of Markov independent processes. However, when we consider networks with feedback, for example a tandem network with feedback, even if the external arrival is a Poisson process the total arrival process is not Poisson. Nevertheless under exponential and independence assumptions one can still derive a product form solution for the associated Markov process.

The first important result concerning product form queueing networks was proved by Jackson [34] for open exponential networks with FCFS queues and arbitrary Markovian routing. For this network let λ denote the overall arrival rate to the network, p_{0i} the probability that an external arrival enters queue i and μ_i the exponential service rate of center i, $1 \leq i \leq M$. Customers' behavior between service centers of the network is described by routing matrix $P = [p_{ij}]$ where p_{ij} denotes the probability that a customer leaving center i immediately goes to center j, whereas p_{i0} is the probability that it leaves the network, $1 \leq i, j \leq M$. Hence $\sum_{1 \leq j \leq M} p_{ij} + p_{i0} = 1$. The routing matrix defines the set of *traffic equations* that determine the visit ratio x_i for each service center i as follows:

$$x_i = \lambda p_{0i} + \sum_{1 \leq j \leq M} x_j p_{ji} \tag{7}$$

The visit ratio x_i is the stationary average arrival rate of customers at center i from outside and inside the network. For stationary and stable open networks x_i is equal to node i throughput. So the traffic equations immediately provide this performance measure for each network component. Jackson proved that for a stable network the stationary joint queue length distribution $\pi(\mathbf{n}) = \pi(n1, \dots, n_M)$ is given by formula (5) where $G = 1$, $V(n) = \lambda^n$, $n = \sum_{1 \le i \le M} n_i$ and function $g_i(n_i)$ is the stationary state distribution of center i analyzed as an isolated $M/M/\mu_i$ queue where m_i is the number of center i servers, with arrival rate x_i and service rate μ_i. In particular let $\rho_i = x_i/m_i\mu_i$. The stationary queue length probability of service center i is given by formulas (2) and (3). When service center i has a single server ($m_i = 1$) the queue length distribution reduces to the solution of the $M/M/1$ system given by formula (1).

The stability condition requires that each queue is stable, i. e. $\rho_i < 1$ for each center i.

Note that a surprising property of Jackson networks is that the service centers *behaves as* independent $M/M/m$ type queueing systems, although in general they *are not* independent.

Closed exponential queueing networks with FCFS discipline and arbitrary Markovian routing has been studied by Gordon and Newell [28] that proved that product form solution (5) holds where G is a normalizing constant and $V(n) = 1$. Similarly to the Jackson open networks, the routing matrix P defines the customers' behavior. Since in closed networks customers cannot enter or leave the network, P is a stochastic matrix, i. e. $\sum_{1 \le j \le M} p_{ij} = 1$ and $p_{0i} = p_{i0} = 0$ for each i. Hence the system of traffic equations (7) has $M - 1$ linear dependent equations and has infinite solutions. In other words the visit ratio x_i is defined up to an arbitrary constant and it represents the *relative* throughput of node i.

Function $g_i(n_i)$ in formula (5) is proportional to the stationary distribution of center i analyzed as an isolated M/M/m_i with arrival rate x_i, service rate μ_i and m_i servers, i. e. it is defined by formulas (2)-(3) without factor $\pi(0)$ for multiple servers ($m_i > 1$) and by formula (1) without factor $(1 - \rho)$ for single server ($m_i = 1$) where $\rho_i = x_i/m_i\mu_i$. Like Jackson networks in such a closed network the service centers *behaves as* independent $M/M/m$ type queueing systems, although this is not the case.

Note that in closed networks the queue length distribution of any center i does not correspond to function g_i as for open networks, but is derived from the joint queue length distribution $\pi(\mathbf{n})$ given by formula (5). This requires the computation of functions g_j for each node j and of the normalization constant G that guarantees that $\sum_{\mathbf{n}} \pi(\mathbf{n}) = 1$. Hence the computation of the performance indices in closed queueing networks is a non trivial problem. In Section 4 we shall deal with this problem.

3.2 Main Result

The quasireversibility of the queues in network models was discussed and studied by Kelly [36]. A sufficient condition for product form solution network is that it consists of quasireversible queues interconnected by a Markovian routing. Such a routing is defined when the customer routing decision only depends on the state of the current customer's class and service center and is independent of the state of the rest of the network. The characterization of product form solution related to quasireversibility of queueing network is discussed in [36,65,49].

If this sufficient condition for product form holds then the stationary state distribution π has the closed form expression given by formulas (5) and (6) for single class and multiclass queueing networks, respectively.

The well-known BCMP theorem proved by Baskett, Chandy, Muntz and Palacios in [6] defines the so-called BCMP queueing networks with product form solution for open, closed or mixed models with multiple classes of customers, various service disciplines and service time distributions. In particular they defined the four types I-II-III-IV of service centers introduced above that are quasireversible queues. The stationary state distribution is expressed as the product of the distributions of the single queues with appropriate parameters and, for closed networks, with the normalization constant.

External arrivals in BCMP networks are Poisson process and the average arrival rate may depend on the total network population or on the population of a chain. Let $\lambda(n)$ and $\lambda_r(K_r)$ denote the overall arrival rate to the network dependent on the total number of customers in the network (n) and in chain r (K_r), respectively. The routing for each chain r is described by a routing matrix $P^{(r)} = [p_{ic;jd}^{(r)}]$ where $p_{ic;jd}$ denotes the probability that a customer leaving center i from class c immediately goes to center j in class d, whereas $p_{ic;0}$ is the probability that it leaves the network. Then the traffic equations (7) are defined for each chain r and provide the visit ratio $x_{ic}^{(r)}$ for each class c in service center i. Let C_{ir} the set of the classes in service center i that belong to chain r. Hence $x_{ir} = \sum_{c \in C_{ir}} x_{ic}^{(r)}$ is the visit ratio for node i and chain r. Let μ_{ir} denote the service rate of service center i and chain r and let $\rho_{ir} = x_{ir}/\mu_{ir}$. Then the BCMP product form solution is given by formulas (5) and (6) with $V(n) = \prod_{k=0}^{n-1} \lambda(k)$, $V_r(K_r) = \prod_{r=1}^{R} \prod_{k=0}^{K^{(r)}-1} \lambda_r(k)$, $g_i(n_i) = \prod_{r=1}^{R} \frac{\rho_{ir}^{n_{ir}}}{n_{ir}!}$ for type I-II-IV queues and $g_i(n_i) = n_i! \prod_{r=1}^{R} \frac{\rho_{ir}^{n_{ir}}}{n_{ir}!}$ for type III queue, $G = 1$ for open networks and the normalizing constant for mixed and closed networks.

The service rate of each node i can be dependent on the service center load, i. e. the number of customers in node i and chain r. For type I node (with exponential service and FCFS scheduling) it can depend only on node i population.

Note that as observed for FCFS-exponential networks, in a BCMP network the service centers *behaves as* a set of independent queueing systems ($M/M/m$ for type I queue and $M/G/m$ with PS discipline for type II queue, IS for type III queue and LCFS-Pr for type IV queue) although this is *not true*.

Quasireversible queues and Markovian routing provide a sufficient condition for product form solution of queuing networks. As discussed above, queues with symmetric queueing discipline are quasireversible [36,65]. Another similar sufficient condition for product form solution is station balance, a property of queueing discipline similar to symmetric queues, that characterizes the scheduling for non-exponential queues that yield product form solution by assuming a special closed form solution [16].

Partial balance is a necessary condition for quasireversibility. It is defined on the Markov process associated to the queueing network and states that the probability flux, i. e. the time average transition rate, out of a state S due to arrivals of type r customers is equal to the probability flux in state S due to departures of type r customers. An extensive discussion of partial balance, quasireversibility, product form and other properties was presented in [49].

The partial balance condition as a characterization of product form networks is given on the underlying process and it allows identifying more general cases of product form networks. However, it cannot be always easily translated in terms of a simple characterization of queueing network components, i. e. types of service centers, queueing scheduling, number of servers and routing.

3.3 Extensions

Various extensions of the class of BCMP product form networks have been derived.

They include state dependent routing [8,40,60], i. e. the definition of routing probabilities are special functions that may depend on the state of the entire network or of subnetworks and/or single service centers. This allows representing systems with more complex features such as dynamic load balancing algorithms or adaptive routing strategies.

Such models usually assume some additional constraints on the network parameters and a special structure of the routing state dependent functions. For example Towsley [60] considered closed queueing networks where the routing for some service centers may be a rational function of the queue length of the service centers belonging to a downstream subnetwork with a particular topology, called parallel subnetwork.

Example 1. A simple example is the central server network illustrated in Fig. 2c with BCMP type service centers and where the routing probability from the central node 1 to the other nodes may depend on the state of the downstream node and the state of subnetwork $2, \ldots, M$, i. e. the routing probability from service center 1 to i, $2 \le i \le M$, can be defined as the following state dependent function: $p_{1i}(\mathbf{n}) = h_i(n_i)h(n_2 + \ldots + n_M)$ where h_i and h are arbitrary nonnegative functions. The network has a product form solution (5) where $V(n) = \prod_{k=0}^{n-1} h(k)$ and g_i is defined as for BCMP networks time a factor $\prod_{k=0}^{n_i-1} h_i(k)$ for each node i, $2 \le i \le M$.

Boucherie and VanDijk have proposed an extension to more complex state dependent routing by considering a more detailed definition of routing functions dependent on the state of subnetworks called clusters and the state of service centers [8]. The model assumes that the service centers are partitioned into a set of subnetworks that are linked by a state dependent routing. Then the routing function between two service centers i and j that respectively belong to two disjoint subnetworks I and J has the following expression: $p_{i0}^{(I)}\ p'_{IJ}\ p_{0j}^{(J)}$, where $p_{i0}^{(I)}$ and $p_{0j}^{(J)}$ are routing functions internal to subnetworks I and J, respectively, and p'_{IJ} denotes the routing between subnetworks. This model can be useful to represent hierarchical and decomposable systems.

Queueing networks with finite capacity queues, subnetwork population constraints and blocking have product form solution in some special cases [1,5,2,64]. Various blocking types that describe different behaviors of customer arrivals at full capacity service centers and the servers' activity in the network have been defined. For several special combinations of network topology, types of service centers and blocking mechanisms one can derive a product form solution for the stationary state distribution. Moreover, one can derive various equivalence properties between product form networks with and without blocking and between networks with different blocking type, as discussed in [5].

Example 2. For example consider an exponential cyclic network illustrated in Fig. 2b where each queue i has a finite capacity B_i. When a queue becomes full the upstream service center is blocked until there is a free buffer position in the destination node. This is called the Blocking Before Service (BBS). If the number of customers in the network K is such that any node can never be empty, i. e. $K > \sum_{1\leq i\leq M} B_i - \min_{1\leq i\leq M} B_i$ [64] then product form solution given by formula (5) holds with $V(n) = 1$, G the normalizing constant, $g_1(n_1) = (\mu_M)^{n_1}$, $g_i(n_i) = (\mu_{i-1})^{n_i}, 2 \leq i \leq M$.

Example 3. Consider a network with BCMP type service centers and finite capacity queues. When a job attempts to enter a destination node with full capacity, it goes back to the sending node where it receives a new service according to the service discipline. This is called Repetitive Service Blocking (RS). If the network has reversible routing, i. e. if matrix P is such that $x_i p_{ij} = x_j p_{ji}$ and $\lambda p_{0i} = x_i p_{i0}$ for each i and j, then the network has the same product form solution (5) as the BCMP network with infinite capacity queues, but normalized on the restricted state space. The central server network shown in Fig. 2c is an example of reversible routing network.

Another extension of queueing networks with product form is the class of networks proposed by Gelenbe [26] with positive and negative customers that can be used to represent special system behaviors. For example negative customers may represent commands to delete some transactions in databases or in a distributed computer system due to inconsistency or data locking. A negative customer arriving to a service center reduces the total queue length by one if the queue length is positive and it has no effect otherwise. Negative customers do not receive service. A customer moving between service centers can become either negative or remain positive. Such a queueing network has product form solution under exponential and independence assumptions and with a Markovian routing and the solution is based on a set of non linear traffic equations of the customers.

Extension of BCMP networks to different service discipline has been derived. Le Boudec proved product form solution for queueing networks with multiserver nodes with concurrent class of customers that allow to represent special systems [10].

Product form solution has been extended to queueing networks with batch arrivals and batch services [29,30] that are also related to discrete time queueing network models. The model evolution is described by a discrete time Markov chain and assumes special expressions for the probability of batch arrivals and departures and correlated batch routing. The product form solution is based on a generalized expression of the traffic equations and the quasireversibility property of the network. The product form solution holds for continuous time and discrete time queueing networks.

3.4 Properties

Product form networks yield various properties.

Insensitivity is an interesting property that states that some performance indices are insensitive to certain network parameters [6,15,16,55,66]. The stationary queue length distribution and the average performance indices (throughput, resource utilization, average waiting time and response time) depend on the service time distributions only through the average. Hence in BCMP networks different service time distributions with the same mean value for a given node of type II, III or IV do not affect the queue length distribution and average performance indices. Insensitivity is related to the station balance property as discussed in [15].

A practical consequence of insensitivity is that when a system is represented by a product form network one has to estimate only the first moment of the service time distribution for each resource to define the model parameter.

Insensitivity of product form networks holds also for the customers routing. Indeed, the product form solution definition depends on the customers routing only through the average visit ratio to each service center. They are obtained by the linear system of traffic equations (7). Hence product form networks with different routing matrix P but with the same visit ratios x_i's, for each service center i, provide the same queue length distribution and average performance indices. Moreover in multiclass networks if we want to evaluate performance indices for each chain and not for each class it is sufficient to estimate the visit ratios at each service center for each customer chain. In the example of Fig. 3, one can simply estimate the visit ratios for chain 1 and 2 to each service center to derive the queue length distribution for each queue and chain.

As a consequence in order to define the network parameters for a system represented by a product form network it is not necessary to describe the routing matrix but it is sufficient to estimate the visit ratios at each service center for each customer chain.

Another property of product form queueing network models is *exact aggregation.* The aggregation theorem or Norton's theorem for queueing networks proved by Chandy, Herzog and Woo [14] allows substituting a subnetwork with a single service center, so that the new aggregated network has the same behavior in terms of a set of performance indices. The aggregated or flow-equivalent service center is usually defined as a FCFS service center with exponential service time and load dependent service rate. This service rate when there are n customers represents the throughput of the subnetwork analyzed in isolation with n customers circulating. A simple example of aggregation is shown in Fig. 4 where subnetwork $\{2, \ldots, M\}$ is aggregated into the flow equivalent node C. The service rate $\mu_C(n)$ is set equal to the throughput $X(n)$ of the subnetwork analyzed in isolation when there are n customers, for each n. The aggregated network in Fig. 4c is obtained by substituting the subnetwork with the aggregated node C. The aggregated network and the original one have the same marginal queue length distribution and average performance indices.

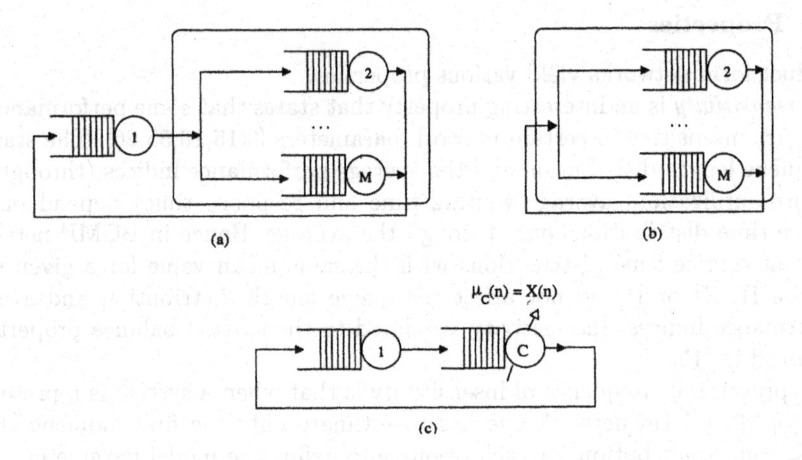

Fig. 4. Aggregation theorem: (a) original network, (b) isolated subnetwork, (c) aggregated network.

Exact aggregation in queueing networks holds for any subnetwork, i. e. for subnetworks with multiple entry and exit points and for which we have also to define a new routing matrix for the aggregated network [3], and for multichain networks [39].

Exact aggregation can be used in hierarchical system analysis. In a bottom-up system design process we can relate the performance indices of the network models at different levels in the hierarchy [45]. Exact aggregation provides a tool to define an equivalent aggregated model at the higher level. Similarly, in a hierarchical top-down system design with predefined performance requirements, we can apply the inverse process called disaggregation or synthesis of the network to define a more detailed model with the same performance indices [4]. The disaggregation process answer the question of what the system topology and parameter should be in order to achieve the given performance goal.

An important application of exact aggregation for product form queueing networks is the definition of various *approximate methods for non product form networks* [46]. These algorithms are usually based on an iterative scheme and they basically apply the aggregation theorem to non product form networks, although in this case it provides only approximate results. At each iteration step several subnetworks are analyzed and aggregated in the flow-equivalent service centers. This principle has been applied for the approximate analysis of various types of non product-form networks, such as for example networks with simultaneous resource possession and finite capacity queues.

Another interesting property of product form queueing networks is the *arrival theorem*. It states that the stationary queue length distribution at arrival times at a service center is identical to the stationary distribution at arbitrary times of the same networks, for open networks, and of a network with one less customer for closed networks [44,57]. A practical important consequence of this theorem is the definition of a set of recurrence equations between the performance indices of closed networks with K customers and those of the same network with $K-1$ customers. This led to the definition of Mean Value Analysis (MVA) [53], a recursive algorithm to evaluate performance indices of closed product form networks, without the direct evaluation of the normalization constant. This was a significant contribution in the research area of algorithms and tools for the efficient evaluation of product form queueing networks.

We shall now discuss the computational algorithms to analyze product form queueing networks.

4 Product Form Queueing Networks: Computational Algorithms and Tools

The main advantage of product form queueing networks is that several efficient algorithms have been developed for their performance analysis. As a consequence efficient and powerful performance evaluation tools based on product form network models have been developed and applied to obtain performance indices for large networks with many service centers and customers.

We shall now introduce the most used algorithm for product form BCMP networks. Two well-known algorithms for closed networks are Convolution Algorithm [13] and the Mean Value Analysis [53,52]. They provide the evaluation of a set of performance indices with a polynomial space and time computational complexity in the number of service centers and the network population.

4.1 Convolution Algorithm

For closed networks the computation of the stationary state distribution $\boldsymbol{\pi}$ requires the evaluation of the normalizing constant G in formula (5). Since $V(n) = 1$, constant G is defined as $G = \sum_{\mathbf{n}} \prod_{i=1}^{M} g_i(n_i)$. Direct computation of G as a summation over all the feasible states $\mathbf{n}$ of the network would take an exponential time in the number of service centers and customers of the network, i. e. proportional to the number of states of the network. The Convolution Algorithm avoids this direct computation and evaluates G recursively. For a network with M service centers and K customers let $G_j(k)$ denote the normalizing constant of the network with k customers and the first j service centers, $1 \le j \le M$ and $0 \le k \le K$. Then $G = G_M(K)$ and we can write the recursive relation that is the convolution

$$G_j(k) = \sum_{n=0}^{k} g_j(n) G_{j-1}(k-n) \tag{8}$$

where $G_j(0) = 1$. This basic scheme can be further simplified in some cases. If the first j service centers have infinite server discipline (type III BCMP node) then we can immediately write $G_j(k) = \left(\sum_{i=0}^{j} \rho_i\right)^k / k!$, with $\rho_i = x_i/\mu_i$. If service center j has a single server then we simply have $g_j(k) = \rho_j^k$. Hence convolution (8) reduces to

$$G_j(k) = G_{j-1}(k) + \rho_j^k G_{j-1}(k-1)$$

for $0 \le k \le K$. Therefore the time computational complexity of evaluating $G = G_M(K)$ is O(MK) operations. It is worthwhile noticing that several performance measures can be directly evaluated by function G_M. For a single server node j with load independent service rate we can write:

queue length distribution	$\pi_j(k) = \rho_j^k \frac{G_M(K-k) - \rho_j G_M(K-k-1)}{G_M(K)}, 0 \le k \le K$
average queue length	$N_j = \sum_{k=1}^{K} \rho_j^k G_M(K-k)/G_M(K)$
throughput	$X_j = [x_j G_M(K-1)]/G_M(K)$
utilization	$U_j = X_j/\mu_j$

However, for a service center j with load dependent service rate the queue length distribution can be written as follows $\pi_j(k) = g_j(k) G_{M-\{j\}}(K-k)/G_M(K)$, where $G_{M-\{j\}}$ is the normalizing constant of the entire network except for node j. This requires the solution of another network. Hence, the Convolution Algorithm efficiency is reduced when the network has several load dependent service centers.

A limitation of this algorithm is its potential numerical instability, i. e. possible overflow or underflow in the computation of constant G. Some scaling techniques to overcome this problem have been proposed [41].

4.2 MVA Algorithm

MVA Algorithm avoids the direct evaluation of the normalization constant. Consider a closed networks with M load independent service centers and K customers. Let $R_j(K)$, $X_j(K)$ and $N_j(K)$ denote respectively the average response time, the throughput and the average queue length of service center j. The algorithm is based on the following recursive scheme:

$$R_j(K) = [1/\mu_j](1 + N_j(K-1)) \quad (9)$$

$$X_j(K) = K / \left[\sum_{i=1}^{M} x_i R_i(K)/x_j \right] \quad (10)$$

$$N_j(K) = X_j(K) R_j(K) \quad (11)$$

for $1 \leq j \leq M$, and $N_j(0) = 0$. Formula (9) derives from the arrival theorem for product form closed networks while formulas (10) and (11) are Little's law applied to the entire network and node j, respectively. For infinite server queueing discipline the first relation simplifies in $R_j(K) = 1/\mu_j$. For load dependent service centers it is necessary to compute the queue length distribution of node j when there are K customers in the network, denoted by $\pi_j(k|K)$, $0 \leq k \leq K$. Then the first recursive relation of the algorithm becomes:

$$R_j(K) = \sum_{k=1}^{K} k \; \pi_j(k-1|K-1)/\mu_j(k)$$

and probability π_j is recursively evaluated as follows:

$$\pi_j(k|K) = \pi_j(k-1|K-1)X_j(K)/\mu_j(k), 1 \leq k \leq K, \pi_j(0|K) = 1 - \sum_{k=1}^{K} \pi_j(k|K)$$

Such a computation of the queue length distribution can lead to numerical instability. A modified MVA algorithm was proposed to overcome this drawback at the expenses of increased computational complexity. The empty node probability is recursively computed as follows: $\pi_j(0|K) = \pi_j(0|K-1)\left(X_i(K)/X_i^{M-\{j\}}(K)\right)$ where $X_i^{M-\{j\}}(K)$ is the throughput of a service center i in the network obtained by the original one without node j. Hence for a network with J load dependent service center this modified version of the MVA algorithm requires the solution of 2^{J-1} additional networks to evaluate the throughput [43].

Another interesting result of recursive relations for product form networks is the set of recursive expressions for the derivatives of higher moments of the queue length derived by McKenna and Mitrani [47] that with the asymptotic expansion method allows obtained bounds for the higher moments of the queue length.

4.3 Multichain Models

Convolution and MVA algorithms apply also to multiclass and multichain networks [53,52,43,54,41]. However, their computational complexity for a network with M load independent service center, R closed chains and K_r customers in chain $r = 1, \ldots, R$ is of $O(MR\prod_{1 \leq r \leq R} K_r)$ operations, i. e. it is exponential with the number of closed chains. This limitation led to the definition of special exact and approximate algorithms for multichain networks.

Exact methods are the tree Convolution and tree MVA algorithms that are efficient when customers of any given chain visit only a small number of service centers. This feature has been observed in models of computer and communication systems and in communication networks [42]. Tree Convolution and tree MVA algorithms extend respectively Convolution and MVA and are based on a tree data structure to optimize the algorithm computation [42,62,31].

Recursion by Chain Algorithm (Recal) [20,21] has a computational cost polynomial in the number of closed chains but exponential in the number of service centers. Recal recursively computes the normalization constant G of the product form solution and then one can observe overflow and underflow instability. The analogue extension of MVA to multichain is the Mean Value Analysis by Chain algorithm [19] that avoids the computation of the normalizing constant. If we want to evaluate the joint queue length distribution we can use the Distribution Analysis by Chain (DAC) [23] that also provides the average performance indices. The three algorithms Recal, MVA by Chain and DAC are efficient for a small number of service centers and many closed chains. Details on the algorithms can be found in literature [18,43,21,35].

Exact solution of multichain product form networks with a large number of customers, classes, chains and service centers is possible only if they have few closed chains by using tree structured algorithms or few service centers with Recal, MVA by Chain and DAC algorithms.

Approximate algorithms for product form networks can be non-iterative or iterative.

Simple non-iterative methods provide bounds on the performance measures. Various bounding methods such as Balanced Job Bounds, Proportional Bound and Performance Bound Hierarchies (PBH) techniques [67,25,32,33] provide bounds on the average performance measures. Some techniques are based on the MVA equations, such that the PBH method that provides increasingly tighter bounds at the expense of increasing computation cost.

A different approach is the asymptotic expansion method [48] where the normalization constant G can be rewritten as a linear combination of terms that can be interpreted as normalizing constants of simple networks, with few chains and a small population. Hence G is approximated by these simpler computations. Moreover the method provides error bounds on the average performance measures.

Most iterative approximate methods are based on the MVA algorithm. The Bard-Schweitzer Proportional Estimation [56] is a popular and widely applied approximate algorithm [50]. The average queue length $N_j(K-1)$ of a service center j for a network with $K-1$ customers is approximated as follows:

$$N_j(K-1) = N_j(K)\, K - 1/K$$

Then by substituting this equation in formula (9) MVA becomes an approximate iterative algorithm. An improved algorithm called Linearizer [17] defines the difference between the fractional queue length of each service center at population K and $K-1$ as $D_j(K) = [N_j(K-1)/(K-1)] - [N_j(K)/K]$. While Schweitzer's approximation assumes that $D_j(K) = 0$ for each service center j, Linearizer assumes that $D_j(K)$ is independent of K and approximates its value by iterations starting with $D_j(K) = 0$. Linearizer is a quite accurate algorithm and further improvements have been developed [50]. Special extensions of these algorithms have been defined for networks with load dependent service centers.

Remark. The computational algorithms surveyed in this section solve BCMP product form networks. Note that, as discussed in the previous section, various extensions of this class of product form networks have been defined. However, the solution algorithms do not always immediately apply to non-BCMP product form networks. We have pointed out how load dependent service centers often lead to special recursive formulas, like in Convolution and MVA algorithms. Similarly, solving product form networks with special features, such as state dependent routing, finite capacity queues and blocking, special queueing disciplines, negative customers and batch arrivals and services is in general a non trivial problem. Some algorithms have been defined for some classes of product form networks. For example special algorithms have been defined for some product form networks with a particular queueing discipline that models multiserver centers with concurrent classes of customers [11] or for networks with finite capacity queues and blocking [2].

4.4 Queueing Networks Tools

Beside performance measurement tool, performance modelling tools based on queueing networks have been developed. The workload characterization tools provide the quantitative characterization of the system resource demands of workload that is used to define the performance models. Software tools for performance modelling and analysis integrate the computational algorithms to solve queueing network models with a model specification language. Such tools usually have user friendly interfaces based on different languages to take into account the particular field of application, e.g. computer networks, communication networks, distributed computer systems. This allows not expert users to apply efficient performance modelling techniques.

Some tools include hierarchical modelling techniques and allow the definition of various system performance models at various levels. Two models at different level are related by the aggregation and disaggregation technique.

Most performance evaluation packages include exact BCMP product form solution methods, e.g. at least Convolution and/or MVA algorithms and possibly other algorithms. Some tools provide approximate solution methods usually based on an approximate product form solution. Many packages give the user the choice between analytical methods and simulation. Examples of performance evaluation packages are Best-1, RESQ/IBM, QNAP2, HIT [43,45,7,51] just to mention a few.

More recently the solution performance algorithms have been integrated with model specification techniques to provide tools for the combined functional and quantitative system analysis [58].

5 Status and Future Directions

The class of product form queueing network models has proved to be very useful for system performance evaluation. This is due to a good balance between the relative high accuracy and robustness of performance results and the efficiency in model solution. The precise characterization of product form networks is not trivial in terms of model characteristics, as discussed in Section 3, since the properties are basically related to the associated Markov process.

Several special extensions of the class of BCMP product form networks have been obtained to include various interesting system features, such as state dependent routing, blocking, negative customers and batch customer movements. However, most of these models have product form solution under several constraints on the system structure and parameters. An open problem is the definition of efficient algorithms for the computation of performance indices of non-BCMP queueing networks, such as for example the models with batch arrivals and departures. Efficient analysis of discrete-time queueing networks is a related open problem.

Today the product form class seems to be well defined and it is difficult to expect that further wide extensions will be discovered or defined.

Product form networks provide the basis for many approximate algorithms to solve more general non product form models. Hierarchical modelling and decomposition-aggregation techniques are the main tools in this area. Hence exploiting the robustness of the properties of product form networks can still be useful to solve more general networks. Interesting and useful properties are insensitivity, exact aggregation and the arrival theorem. A research issue is how to efficiently combine subnetwork solution in a decomposition aggregation framework to obtain an approximate possibly error bounded solution. This potentially leads to develop simple and efficient performance modelling tools.

Another research issue is the integration and/or the relation between queueing networks and other classes of models with different characteristics, such as for example stochastic Petri nets or stochastic process algebra. A challenge could be to develop efficient and integrated tools that combine qualitative and quantitative system analysis, such as software architecture specification and system performance.

References

1. I. F. Akyildiz. Exact product form solution for queueing networks with blocking. *IEEE Trans. on Computer*, C-36(1):122–125, 1987.
2. S. Balsamo and M. C. Clò. A convolution algorithm for product-form queueing networks with blocking. *Annals of Operations Research*, 79:97–117, 1998.

3. S. Balsamo and G. Iazeolla. An extension of Norton theorem for queueing networks. *IEEE Trans. on Software Engineering*, SE-8, 1982.
4. S. Balsamo and G. Iazeolla. Product-form synthesis of queueing networks. *IEEE Trans. on Software Engineering*, SE-11(2):194–199, 1985.
5. S. Balsamo and V. De Nitto. A survey of product-form queueing networks with blocking and their equivalences. *Annals of Operations Research*, 48:31–61, 1994.
6. F. Baskett, K. M. Chandy, R. R. Muntz, and G. Palacios. Open, closed, and mixed networks of queues with different classes of customers. *Journal of the ACM*, 22(2):248–260, 1975.
7. H. Beilner, J. Mäter, and C. Wysocki. The hierarchical evaluation tool HIT. Report 581/1995, University of Dortmund, Dortmund, Germany, 6-9, 1995.
8. R. Boucherie and N. M. van Dijk. Product-form queueing networks with state dependent multiple job transitions. *Adv. in Applied Prob.*, 23:152–187, 1991.
9. R. Boucherie and N. M. van Dijk. On the arrival theorem for product-form queueing networks with blocking. *Performance Evaluation*, 29:155–176, 1997.
10. J. Y. Le Boudec. A BCMP extension to multiserver stations with concurrent classes of customers. *Proc. Performance '86 and 1986 ACM Sigmetrics Conf.*, pages 79–81, 1986.
11. J. Y. Le Boudec. The multibus algorithm. *Performance Evaluation*, 8:1–18, 1988.
12. P. J. Burke. The output of a queueing system. *Oper. Res.*, 4:699–704, 1956.
13. J. P. Buzen. Computational algorithms for closed queueing networks with exponential servers. *Comm. of the ACM*, 16(9):527–531, 1973.
14. K. M. Chandy, U. Herzog, and L. Woo. Parametric analysis of queueing networks. *IBM Journal of Res. and Dev.*, 1(1):36–42, 1975.
15. K. M. Chandy, J. H. Howard, and D. Towsley. Product form and local balance in queueing networks. *Journal of the ACM*, 24(2):250–263, 1977.
16. K. M. Chandy and A. J. Martin. A characterization of product-form queueing networks. *Journal of the ACM*, 30(2):286–299, 1983.
17. K. M. Chandy and D. Neuse. Linearizer: a heuristic algorithm for queueing network models of computer systems. *Comm. of the ACM*, 25:126–134, 1982.
18. K. M. Chandy and C. H. Sauer. Computational algorithms for product form queueing networks. *Comm. of the ACM*, 23(10):573–583, 1980.
19. A. E. Conway, E. de Souza e Silva, and S. S. Lavenberg. Mean value analysis by chain of product-form queueing networks. *IEEE Trans. on Computers*, C-38(10):573–583, 1989.
20. A. E. Conway and N. D. Georganas. RECAL - a new efficient algorithm for the exact analysis of multiple-chain closed queueing networks. *Journal of the ACM*, 33:768–791, 1986.
21. A. E. Conway and N. D. Georganas. *Queueing Networks - Exact Computational Algorithms*. MIT Press, Cambridge, Massachusetts, 1989.
22. P. J. Courtois. *Decomposability*. Academic Press, New York, 1977.
23. E. de Souza e Silva and S. S. Lavenberg. Calculating the joint queue length distribution in product-form queueing networks. *Journal of the ACM*, 36:194–207, 1989.
24. E. de Souza e Silva and R. R. Muntz. Queueing networks: Solutions and applications. In H. Takagy, editor, *Stochastic Analysis of Computer and Communication Systems*, pages 319–399. Elsevier, North Holland, 1990.
25. D.L. Eager and K. C. Sevick. Bound hierarchies for multiple-class queueing networks. *Journal of the ACM*, 33:179–206, 1986.
26. E. Gelenbe. Product form networks with negative and positive customers. *Journal of Applied Prob.*, 28(3):656–663, 1991.

27. E. Gelenbe and I. Mitrani. *Analysis and Synthesis of Computer Systems.* Academic Press, New York, 1980.
28. W. J. Gordon and G. F. Newell. Cyclic queueing networks with exponential servers. *Operations Research*, 15(2):254–265, 1967.
29. W. Henderson and P. Taylor. Product form in networks of queues with batch arrivals and batch services. *Queueing Systems*, 6:71–88, 1990.
30. W. Henderson and P. Taylor. Some new results on queueing networks with batch movements. *J. of Applied Prob.*, 28:409–421, 1990.
31. K. P. Hoyme, S. C. Bruell, P. V. Afshari, and R. Y. Jain. A tree structured mean value analysis algorithm. *ACM Trans. on Computer Systems*, 4:178–185, 1986.
32. C. T. Hsieh and S. S. Lam. Two classes of performance bounds for closed queueing networks. *Performance Evaluation*, 7:3–30, 1987.
33. C. T. Hsieh and S. S. Lam. PAM - a noniterative approximate solution method for closed multichain queueing networks. *Performance Evaluation*, 9:119–133, 1989.
34. J. R. Jackson. Jobshop-like queueing systems. *Management Science*, 10:131–142, 1963.
35. K. Kant. *Introduction to Computer System Performance Evaluation.* MacGraw-Hill, 1992.
36. F. P. Kelly. *Reversibility and Stochastic Networks.* Wiley, New York, 1979.
37. P. J. B. King. *Computer and Communication System Performance Modelling.* Prentice-Hall, Englewood Cliffs, 1990.
38. L. Kleinrock. *Queueing Systems*, volume 1: Theory. John Wiley, New York, 1975.
39. P. Kritzinger, S. van Wyk, and A. Krezesinski. A generalization of Norton's theorem for multiclass queueing networks. *Performance Evaluation*, 2:98–107, 1982.
40. S. S. Lam. Queueing networks with capacity constraints. *IBM Journal of Res. and Dev.*, 21(4):370–378, 1977.
41. S. S. Lam. Dynamic scaling and grow behavior of queueing networks normalization constant. *Journal of the ACM*, 29(2):492–513, 1982.
42. S. S. Lam and Y. L. Lien. A tree convolution algorithm for the solution of queueing networks. *Comm. of the ACM*, 26(3):203–215, 1983.
43. S. S. Lavenberg. *Computer Performance Modeling Handbook.* Academic Press, New York, 1983.
44. S. S. Lavenberg and M. Reiser. Stationary state probabilities at arrival instants for closed queueing networks with multiple types of customers. *Journal of Applied Prob.*, 17:1048–1061, 1980.
45. E. D. Lazowska, J. L.Zahorjan, G. S. Graham, and K. C. Sevcick. *Quantitative System Performance: Computer System Analysis Using Queueing Network Models.* Prentice Hall, Englewood Cliffs, 1984.
46. R. Marie. An approximate analytical method for general queueing networks. *IEEE Trans. on Software Eng.*, 5(5):530–538, 1979.
47. J. McKenna and I. Mitrani. Asymptotic expansions and integral representations of moments of queue lengths in closed Markovian networks. *Journal of the ACM*, 31:346–360, 1984.
48. D. Mitra and J. McKenna. Asymptotic expansions for closed Markovian networks with state dependent service rates. *Journal of the ACM*, 33:568–592, 1986.
49. R. Nelson. The mathematics of product-form queueing networks. *ACM Computing Survey*, 25(3):339–369, 1993.
50. K. R. Pattipati, M. M. Kostreva, and J. L. Teele. Approximate mean value analysis algorithms for queueing networks: Existence, uniqueness and convergence results. *Journal of the ACM*, 37:643–673, 1990.

51. D. Potier. The modelling package QNAP2 and applications to computer networks simulation. In *Computer Networks and Simulation*. North Holland, 1986.
52. M. Reiser. Mean value analysis and convolution method for queue-dependent servers in closed queueing networks. *Performance Evaluation*, 1(1):7–18, 1981.
53. M. Reiser and S. S. Lavenberg. Mean value analysis of closed multichain queueing networks. *Journal of the ACM*, 27(2):313–320, 1980.
54. C. H. Sauer. Computational algorithms for state-dependent queueing networks. *ACM Trans. on Computer Systems*, 1(1):67–92, 1983.
55. R. Schassberger. The insensitivity of stationary probabilities in networks of queues. *Journal of Applied Prob.*, 10:85–93, 1978.
56. P. J. Schweitzer. Approximate analysis of multiclass closed networks of queues. In *Proc. of Int. Conference on Stochastic Control and Optimization*, pages 25–29, Amsterdam, The Netherlands, 1979.
57. K. S. Sevcik and I. Mitrani. The distribution of queueing network states at input and output instants. *Journal of the ACM*, 28(2):358–371, 1981.
58. C. Smith. *Performance Engineering of Software Systems*. Addison-Wesley, Reading, MA, US, 1990.
59. R. Suri. Robustness of queueing network formulas. *Journal of the ACM*, 30(3):564–594, 1983.
60. D. Towsley. Queueing network with state dependent routing. *Journal of the ACM*, 27(2):323–337, 1980.
61. K. S. Trivedi. *Probability and Statistics with Reliability, Queueing and Computer Science Applications*. Prentice Hall, Englewood Cliffs, 1982.
62. S. Tucci and C. H. Sauer. The tree MVA algorithm. *Performance Evaluation*, 5:187–196, 1985.
63. N. van Dijk. *Queueing networks and product forms*. John Wiley, 1993.
64. G. F. Newell W. J. Gordon. Cyclic queueing networks with restricted length queues. *Operations Research*, 15(2):266–277, 1967.
65. J. Walrand. *An Introduction to Queueing Networks*. Prentice-Hall, 1988.
66. P. Whittle. Partial balance and insensitivity. *J. of Applied Prob.*, 22:168–175, 1985.
67. J. L. Zahorjan, K. C. Sevcik, D. L. Eager, and B. Galler. Balanced job bound analysis of queueing networks. *Comm. of the ACM*, 25:134–141, 1981.

Stochastic Modeling Formalisms for Dependability, Performance and Performability

Katerina Goševa-Popstojanova and Kishor Trivedi

Center for Advanced Computing and Communication
Department of Electrical and Computer Engineering
Duke University, Durham, NC 27708 – 0291, USA
{katerina,kst}@ee.duke.edu

1 Introduction

Rapid advances in technology resulted in the proliferation of complex computer and communication systems that are used in different applications ranging from spacecraft flight-control to information and financial services. Dependability, performance, and performability evaluation techniques provide a useful method for examining the behavior of a computer or communication system right from the design stage to implementation and final deployment. The relative importance of performance and dependability requirements will differ depending on the system requirements and typical usage. Sometimes performance and dependability issues can be addresses separately, but sometimes their interactions and corresponding tradeoffs demand a measure that combines aspects of both.

Suppose that a multiprocessor system has to be designed. Some of the questions that need to be answered are the following. How much better will performance get by adding a processor? How would adding a processor affect the reliability of the system? Would this make system go down more often? If so, would an increase in performance outweigh the decrease in reliability?

The system designer has several options for predicting values: make an educated guess based on experience with previous similar systems; build prototypes and take measurements; use discrete event simulation to model the system; and construct analytic models of the system.

The actual measurement is the most direct method for assessing an existing system or a prototype, but it is not a feasible option during system design and implementation phases. It is also sometimes impossible to assure by measurement that a system meets the design criteria. For example, in the case of highly reliable systems waiting for the system to fail enough times to obtain statistically significant sample would take years.

Discrete-event simulation (DES) is commonly used modeling technique in practice. It can capture system characteristics to the desired degree, and many software packages are available that facilitate the construction and execution of DES models. However, DES tends to be relatively expensive since it takes quite long time to run such models, particularly when results with high accuracy are required. Also, it is a non-trivial problem to simulate with high confidence

G. Haring et al. (Eds.): Performance Evaluation, LNCS 1769, pp. 403–422, 2000.

scenarios entailing relatively rare events while others are occurring much more often.

Analytical modeling has proven to be an attractive cost-effective alternative in these cases. A model is an abstraction of a system that includes sufficient detail to facilitate an understanding of system behavior. To be useful, the model of current day complex computer and communication systems should reflect important system characteristics such as fault-tolerance, automatic reconfiguration and repair, contention for resources, concurrency and synchronization, deadlines imposed on tasks, and graceful degradation. Due the recent development in model generation and solution techniques, and the availability of software tools, large and realistic models can be developed and studied. A system designer has a wide range of different types of analytical models to choose from. Each type has its strengths and weaknesses in terms of accessibility, easy of construction, efficiency and accuracy of solution algorithms, and availability of software tools. The most appropriate type of model depends upon the complexity of the system, the questions to be studied, the accuracy required, and the resources available for the study.

Analytical models can be broadly classified into non-state space models and state space models. Reliability block diagrams, fault trees and reliability graphs are non-state space models commonly used to study dependability of systems. They are concise, easy to understand, and have efficient solution methods. However, realistic features such as non-independent behavior of components, imperfect coverage, non-zero reconfiguration delays, and combination with performance can not be captured by these models.

In the performance modeling, the examples of non-state space models are directed acyclic task precedence graphs and product form queueing networks. Directed acyclic task precedence graphs can be used to model concurrency for the case of unlimited resources. On the other hand, contention for resources can be represented by a class of queueing networks known as product form queueing networks (PFQN) for which efficient solution methods to derive steady state performance measures exist. However, they cannot model concurrency, synchronization, or server failures, since these violate the product form assumptions.

State space models enable us to overcome the limitations of the non-state space models in modeling complicated interactions between components and tradeoffs between different measures of interest. Although in this chapter we concentrate on state space models, whenever it is possible we consider an alternative non-state space model.

Most commonly used state space models are Markov chains. They provide great flexibility for modeling dependability, performance, and combined dependability and performance measures. But the size of their state space grows much faster then the number of system components, making model specification and analysis difficult and error-prone process. One way to deal with large models is largeness-tolerance. A number of concise descriptions have evolved, and software tools that automatically generate the underlying Markov chain and provide effective methods for solution are now available. Many such high level specification techniques, queueing networks and stochastic Petri nets being the most prominent representatives, have been suggested in literature. Another way to deal with large models is to use techniques that avoid largeness, such as state truncation, state lamping, and model composition.

This chapter is organized as follows. First, we define Markov chains, and then introduce Markov reward models. Next, we demonstrate how a number of different pure dependability and pure performability measures can be derived by choosing the appropriate reward structure. We illustrate the combined performance and dependability analysis, and then examine two major difficulties that are encountered in the use of monolithic Markov models, namely, largeness and stiffness. Both problems of largeness and stiffness can be avoided by composing the overall model from a set of smaller non-stiff submodels. The overall solution is obtained by composing submodels solutions. Reward based performability analysis is an example of model composition approach; the performance submodel is solved and its results are passed as reward rates to the dependability submodel. Although in the chapter we use Markov reward models, the general concept of reward based modeling is not limited to a specific model type. Thus, we show how the Markovian constraints can be relaxed, and other paradigms such as semi Markov reward models or Markov regenerative reward models can be used as well. Finally, techniques for high level specification of the underlying computational model type are briefly reviewed.

Through the chapter we demonstrate the use of different model types and the derivation of a number of measures that may be of interest on the example of a multiprocessor system with n processors with a limited number of buffers m, in the presence of failure, reconfiguration, and repair.

2 Markov Reward Models: Definition and Measures

In this section we present a brief introduction to the concepts and notation of Markov chains and Markov reward models. Let $\{X(t), t \geq 0\}$ be a homogeneous finite state continuous time Markov chain (CTMC) with state space S and infinitesimal generator matrix $\boldsymbol{Q} = [q_{ij}]$. Let $P_i(t) = P\{X(t) = i\}$ denote the unconditional probability of the CTMC being in state i at time t, and the row vector $\boldsymbol{P}(t) = [P_1(t), P_2(t), \ldots, P_n(t)]$ represent the transient state probability vector of the CTMC. The transient behavior of the CTMC can be described by the Kolmogorov differential equation:

$$\frac{d\boldsymbol{P}(t)}{dt} = \boldsymbol{P}(t)\,\boldsymbol{Q}, \qquad \text{given } \boldsymbol{P}(0) \tag{1}$$

where $\boldsymbol{P}(0)$ represents the initial probability vector (at time $t = 0$). The steady-state probability vector $\boldsymbol{\pi} = \lim_{t\to\infty} \boldsymbol{P}(t)$ satisfies:

$$\boldsymbol{\pi}\boldsymbol{Q} = 0, \qquad \textstyle\sum_{i\in S} \pi_i = 1. \tag{2}$$

In addition to transient state probabilities, sometimes cumulative probabilities are of interest. Define $\boldsymbol{L}(t) = \int_0^t \boldsymbol{P}(u)\,du$; then $L_i(t)$ denotes the expected total time the CTMC spends in state i during the interval $[0,t)$. $L(t)$ satisfies the differential equation:

$$\frac{d\boldsymbol{L}(t)}{dt} = \boldsymbol{L}(t)\,\boldsymbol{Q} + \boldsymbol{P}(0), \qquad \boldsymbol{L}(0) = 0. \tag{3}$$

With these definitions, most of the interesting measures can be defined. CTMC with absorbing states deserves additional attention. Here, the measures of interest are based on the time a CTMC spends in non-absorbing states before an absorbing state is ultimately reached. For that purpose the state space $S = A \cup T$ is partitioned into the set A of absorbing states and the set T of non-absorbing (transient) states. Let $\boldsymbol{Q}_T$ be the submatrix of $\boldsymbol{Q}$ corresponding to the transitions between transient states. Then the time spent in transient states before absorption can be calculated by $\boldsymbol{L}_T(\infty) = \lim_{t\to\infty} \boldsymbol{L}_T(t)$ restricted to the states of the set T. The mean time to absorption (MTTA) can be written as $MTTA = \sum_{i \in T} L_i(\infty)$.

Assigning rewards to states or to transitions between states of CTMC defines Markov reward model (MRM). In the former case rewards are referred to as reward rates and in the letter as impulse rewards. In this chapter we consider state-based rewards only. Let the reward rate r_i be assigned to state i. Then, the random variable $Z(t) = r_{X(t)}$ refers to the instantaneous reward rate of the MRM at time t. The accumulated reward over the interval $[0,t)$ is given by

$$Y(t) = \int_0^t Z(u)\,du = \int_0^t r_{X(u)}du. \tag{4}$$

Based on the definitions of $X(t)$, $Z(t)$, and $Y(t)$, which are non-independent random variables, various measures can be defined. The most general is the distribution of the accumulated reward over time $[0,t)$, that is, $P\{Y(t) \le y\}$ which is difficult to compute for unrestricted models and reward structures [5]. The problem is considerably simplified if we restrict to the expectations and other moments of random variables. Thus, the expected instantaneous reward rate can be computed from

$$E[Z(t)] = \sum_{i \in S} r_i\, P_i(t) \tag{5}$$

and the expected reward rate in steady-state (when the underlying CTMC is ergodic)

$$E[Z] = \sum_{i \in S} r_i\, \pi_i. \tag{6}$$

To compute the expected accumulated reward we use

$$E[Y(t)] = \sum_{i \in S} r_i\, L_i(t). \tag{7}$$

For models with absorbing states, the limit as $t \to \infty$ of the expected accumulated reward is called the expected accumulated reward until absorption

$$E[Y(\infty)] = \sum_{i \in T} r_i\, L_i(\infty). \tag{8}$$

Given the MRM framework, the next question that arises is "What are the appropriate reward rate assignments?". The reward structure clearly depends on whether we are interested in dependability, performance or composite dependability and performance measures. In the next section we will illustrate the use of this general framework for deriving a number of different measures.

3 Separate Analysis of Dependability and Performance

We begin by introducing a dependability model of multiprocessor system that considers failure/repair behavior and derive a number of dependability related measures by choosing appropriate reward structures. Next, the performance model of the multiprocessor system that describes the arrival and service completion of the jobs is presented and we demonstrate that the concept can also be used to derive performance measures of interest.

3.1 Dependability Model

Reliability, availability, safety and related measures are collectively known as dependability. Thus, dependability modeling encompasses failure, reconfiguration, and repair related aspects of system behavior. We present dependability model of a multiprocessor system with two processors, adapted from [5]. Each processor is subject to failures so that its MTTF is $1/\gamma$. A processor failure is covered with probability c, that is, not covered with probability $1-c$. A covered failure is followed by a brief reconfiguration period, the average reconfiguration time being $1/\delta$. An uncovered failure is followed by a reboot, which requires a longer time to take place; the average reboot time being $1/\beta$, $(1/\beta > 1/\delta)$. In either case the failed processor needs to be repaired, with mean time to repair being $1/\tau$. The other processor continues to run and provides service normally, that is, the system comes up in a degraded mode. Should the other processor fail before the first one is repaired, the system becomes out of service until the repair of the one of the processors is completed. Only one processor can be repaired at a time. Neither reboot nor reconfiguration is performed when the last processor fails. It is assumed that no other event can take place during a reconfiguration or reboot. The justification for this assumption lies in the fact that in practice the reconfiguration and reboot times are extremely small compared to the time between failures and repair times. If all the times are assumed to be independent exponentially distributed random variables, then the multiprocessor system can be modeled by the CTMC shown in Fig. 1.

System Availability Measures. System availability measures show the likelihood that the system is delivering adequate service, or equivalently, the proportion of potential service actually delivered. These measures fit best with the system where brief interruptions in system operation can be tolerated, but no significant annual outage. For example, commercial telephone switching systems

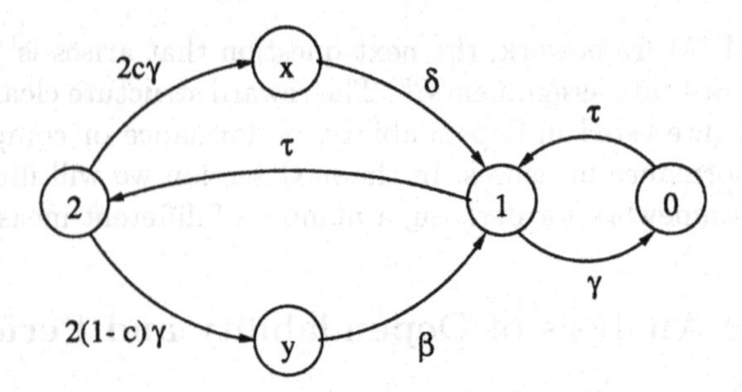

Fig. 1. Dependability model of multiprocessor system

and database systems are designed to provide high system availability over a long periods of time.

The most simplest availability measures are based on a binary reward structure. Assuming for the model in Fig. 1 that one processor is sufficient for the system to be up, the state space S can be partitioned into a set of up states $U = \{2, 1\}$ and set of down states $D = \{x, y, 0\}$, that is, $S = U \cup D$. A reward rate 1 is attached to the up states and a reward rate 0 to down states. It follows that the probability that the system is up at a specific time t, that is, instantaneous availability is given by

$$A(t) = E[Z(t)] = \sum_{i \in S} r_i P_i(t) = \sum_{i \in U} P_i(t) = P_1(t) + P_2(t). \tag{9}$$

Steady-state availability, on the other hand, is given by

$$A = E[Z] = \sum_{i \in S} r_i \pi_i = \sum_{i \in U} \pi_i = \pi_1 + \pi_2. \tag{10}$$

The interval availability provides a time average value

$$\bar{A}(t) = \frac{1}{t} E[Y(t)] = \frac{1}{t} \sum_{i \in S} r_i L_i(t) = \frac{1}{t} \sum_{i \in U} L_i(t) = \frac{1}{t} [L_1(t) + L_2(t)], \tag{11}$$

that is, the expected fraction of time from the system start until time t that the system is up. Note that unavailability can be calculated with a reverse reward assignment to that for availability.

Instantaneous, interval, and steady-state availabilities are the fundamental measures to be applied in this context, but there are other availability related measures that do not rely on the binary reward structure [5].

System Reliability Measures. System reliability measures emphasize the occurrence of undesirable events in the system. These measures are useful for systems where no down time can be tolerated, such as flight control systems. System reliability represents the probability of uninterrupted service exceeding a certain length of time, that is, $R(t) = P\{T > t\}$. What kind of event is to be considered as an interruption depends on the application requirements. In computing reliability for our example, we consider three different variants. In the most restrictive application context (variant 1) any processor failure is considered a system failure, that is, both reconfiguration and reboot are considered as interruption. In variant 2 uncovered processor failure and a failure of the last remaining functional processor is considered to be a system failure, that is, reconfiguration may be tolerated. As a variant 3 we assume that both reconfiguration and reboot can be tolerated, that is, only the failure of the last remaining functional processor is considered as a system failure. The three possible variants are captured in Fig. 2. Note that for the purpose of reliability modeling the CTMC in Fig. 1 has been adopted by making all system down states absorbing that reflect the fact that they are considered as representing interruptions. Again, a binary reward structure is defined that assigns reward rates 1 to up states and reward rates 0 to (absorbing) down states. It follows that reliability can be computed by

$$R(t) = E[Z(t)] = \sum_{i \in S} r_i P_i(t) = \sum_{i \in U_j} P_i(t) \tag{12}$$

where U_j represents the set of corresponding up states of the variant j. The three different reliability functions give the probabilities that in time interval $[0, t)$ there is:

- no outage $R_1(t) = P_2(t)$,
- no outage due to uncovered failure or lack of processors $R_2(t) = P_2(t) + P_x(t) + P_1(t)$,
- no outage due to lack of processors $R_3(t) = P_2(t) + P_x(t) + P_y(t) + P_1(t)$.

In the case of binary reward structure the system mean time to failure (MTTF) is just an MTTA for the CTMC with absorbing states, that is,

$$MTTF = MTTA = E[Y(\infty)] = \sum_{i \in U_j} L_i(\infty). \tag{13}$$

3.2 Performance Model

The MRM framework can also be used in pure (failure-free) performance models to conveniently describe performance measures of interest. In many computer performance studies, expected throughput, mean response time, or utilization are the most important measures. These measures can easily be specified by means of appropriate reward functions. To illustrate the reward assignment for these measures we consider $M/M/1/m$ queue as a performance model of a single processor system. Imagine jobs (tasks, customers) are arriving at the system with exponentially distributed interarrival times with mean $1/\lambda$. In the system they compete for the service from a single server station. Since service is exclusively received by each job, if more then one job is in the system at the same time, the

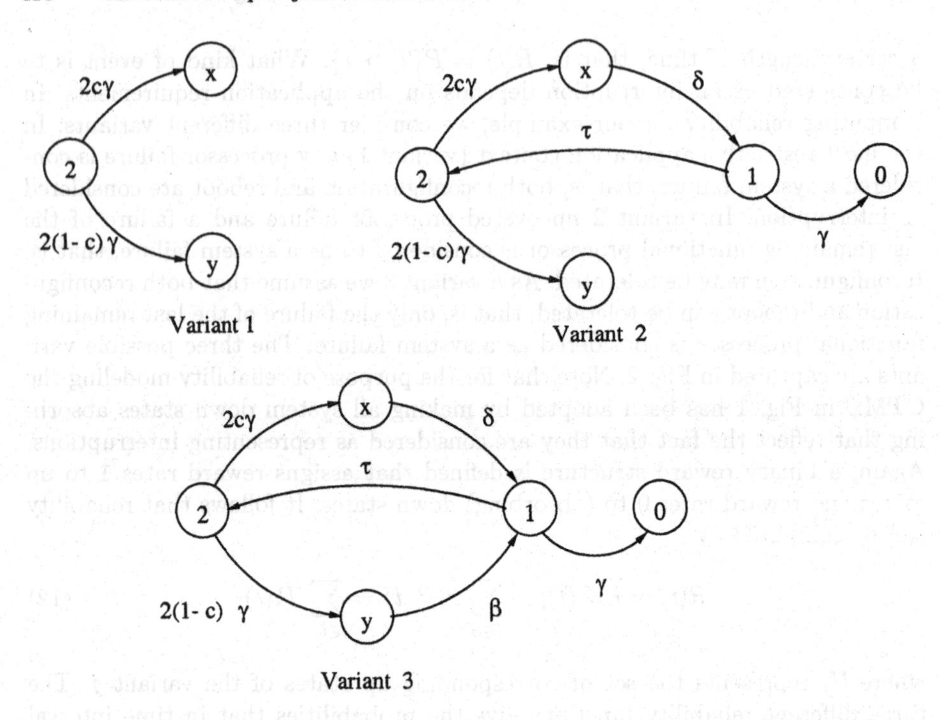

Fig. 2. Model variants with absorbing states capturing reliability requirements

others have to wait in queue until their turn comes. Service times are independent exponentially distributed with mean $1/\mu$. To keep the example simple, we limit the maximum number of customers in system to three. The system is described by the CTMC shown in Fig. 3. Every state in $S = \{0, 1, 2, 3\}$ represents the number of customers in the system. A state transition occurs if a new job arrives or if a job being served completes the service.

The throughput characterization can be achieved by assigning the state transition rate corresponding to departure from a queue (service completion) as a reward rate to the state where the transition originates. It follows that the reward assignment for our example is $r_i = \mu$ for $i = 1, 2, 3$ and $r_0 = 0$. With this

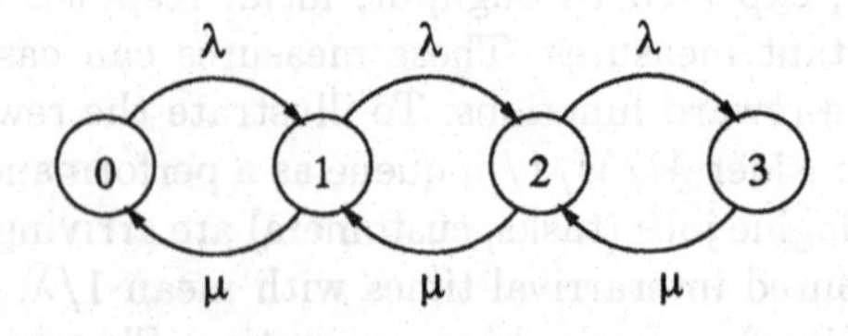

Fig. 3. Performance model (CTMC of M/M/1/3 queue)

reward structure we can compute the steady-state throughput

$$\lambda = E[Z] = \sum_{i \in S} r_i \, \pi_i = \mu[\pi_1 + \pi_2 + \pi_3]. \tag{14}$$

The mean number of jobs in the system can be computed by assigning to each state the reward rate equal to the number of jobs in the system in that state, that is, $r_i = i$. It follows that the mean number of jobs in steady-state is

$$\bar{K} = E[Z] = \sum_{i \in S} r_i \, \pi_i = \pi_1 + 2\pi_2 + 3\pi_3. \tag{15}$$

Mean response time measures of queueing system can be calculated from the mean number of jobs with the help of Little's theorem [12] as

$$\bar{T} = \frac{1}{\lambda} \bar{K}. \tag{16}$$

Finally, the utilization measures can be computed based on a binary reward assignment. Thus, if the particular resource is occupied in a given state, reward rate 1 is assigned, otherwise reward rate 0 indicates the idleness of the resources. With reward structure $r_i = 1$ for $i = 1, 2, 3$ and $r_0 = 0$ the utilization becomes

$$\rho = E[Z] = \sum_{i \in S} r_i \, \pi_i = \pi_1 + \pi_2 + \pi_3. \tag{17}$$

4 Composite Performance and Dependability Analysis

In the previous section, we saw that the goal of an availability model is to determine the fraction of time spend in up states and that the reliability measures answer the question "Assuming that the system is working initially, how long will it continue to work without interruptions?". We also saw that the performance model is developed when we are interested in the level of productivity of a system, or in answering the question "How well is the system working, given that it does not fail?".

Modeling any system with either a pure performance model or a pure dependability model can lead to incomplete or even misleading results. Analysis from pure performance viewpoint tends to be optimistic since it ignores the failure/repair behavior of the system. On the other hand, pure dependability analysis is carried out in the presence of component failures, disregarding the different performance levels in different configurations, that is, tend to be too conservative. Complex systems are designed to continue working even in the presence of failures, guaranteeing a minimum level of performance. These systems are gracefully degradable and have redundant components that are all used at the same time to increase the system processing power. If a component in a degradable system fails, the system itself detects the failure and reconfigures, reaching a degraded state of operation in which it continues to provide service, but at a reduced capacity. A degradable system can have several degraded operational states between being fully operational and having completely failed. Each state provides different performance level. In such cases, pure performance or pure dependability models do not capture the entire system behavior. The measures of interest for a degradable system aim to answer the following question "What is the expected performance of the system at time t including the effects of failure, repair, contention for resources and so on ?".

Several different types of interactions and corresponding tradeoffs have prompted the researchers to develop methods for combined evaluation of performance and dependability. The first approach is to combine the performance and dependability behavior into an exact monolithic model. Let us consider our example of a single processor system. So far we have presented separate dependability and performance models for this example. Now we will generalize the $M/M/1/m$ queueing model presented in Fig. 3 by allowing for the possibility that a server could fail, and that a failed server could be repaired. Again, let the job arrival rate be λ and the job service rate be μ. Let the processor failure rate be γ and the processor repair rate be τ. This system can be modeled using an irreducible CTMC shown in Fig. 4 with the state space $S = \{(i,j), 0 \le i \le m, j = 0,1\}$, where i denotes the number of jobs in the system and j the number of functioning servers.

Two distinct problems arise from this monolithic approach: largeness and stiffness. The largeness problem can be tolerated to some extent by using high level specification techniques, such as generalized stochastic Petri nets (GSPN), and automated methods for generating the Markov chain. GSPN model that is equivalent to the Markov model in Fig. 4, adopted from [14], is shown in Fig. 5. The cycle in the upper part of the figure is a representation of an $M/M/1/m$ queue. The lower cycle models a server that can fail and be repaired. The in-

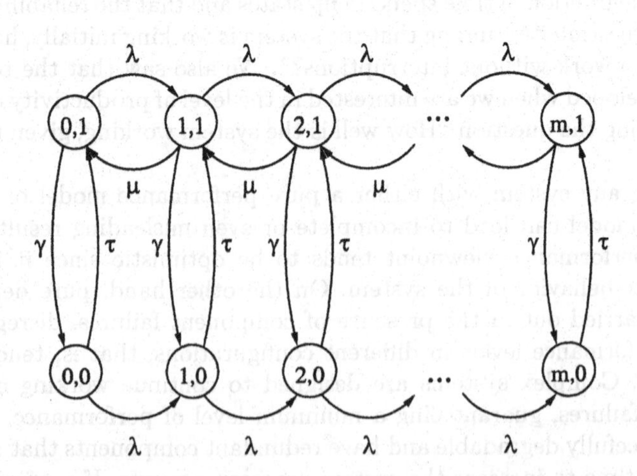

Fig. 4. CTMC model of a $M/M/1/m$ queueing system subject to server failure and repair (Monolithic model)

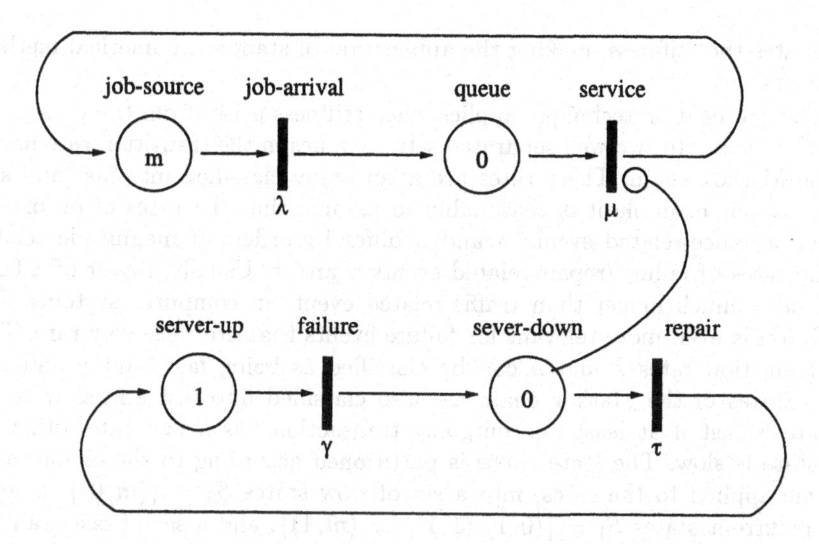

Fig. 5. GSPN model for queue with server failure and repair

hibitor arc from place *server-down* to the transition *service* reflects the fact that jobs cannot be served while the server is not functioning. The number in each place is the initial number of tokens in the place. All of the transitions are timed, and each transition's rate is shown below the transition.

The GSPN description of the model is concise and allows us to vary the values of m without changing the models structure. However, since no model reduction is employed the underlying CTMC is very large. Therefore, large model tolerance must also apply to storage and solution of the model, that is, the appropriate data structures for sparse matrix storage and sparsity preserving solution methods must be used.

Stiffness is another undesirable characteristic of monolithic models. It is due to the different orders of magnitude (sometimes 10^6 times) between the rates of occurrence of performance-related events and the rates of the rare, failure-related events. Stiffness leads to difficulty in the solution of the model and numerical instability. Current research in the transient solution of stiff Markov models follows two main lines: stiffness-tolerance and stiffness-avoidance. The first one is aimed at employing solution methods that remain stable for stiff models (see for extensive survey [5] and references therein). In the second approach, stiffness is eliminated from a model by solving a set of non-stiff submodels. One such technique based on aggregation proceeds by decomposing the original model into smaller submodels [3]. An approximate solution can be obtained by first solving the submodels in isolation (the aggregation step) and then combining the submodel solutions into the solution of the original model (the disaggregation step). A notable property of the decomposition technique is that besides reducing the size of the submodels on which transient analysis is carried out, it also eliminates the stiffness, making the application of standard numerical methods more efficient.

The aggregation technique applies when stiffness arises from the presence of rates belonging to two well separated sets of values in the transition rate matrix of the Markov chain. These rates are accordingly classified into fast and slow rates. In our example it is reasonably to assume that the rates of occurrence of performance-related events λ and μ differ by orders of magnitude relative to the rates of failure/repair-related events γ and τ. Usually, repair of a failed unit takes much longer than traffic-related events in computer systems. This condition is even more relevant for failure events that are relatively rare. Thus the transition rates λ and μ can be classified as being fast, and γ and τ as slow. States of the Markov chain are also classified into fast and slow states; a state is fast if at least one outgoing transaction has a fast rate, otherwise the state is slow. The state space is partitioned according to the classification scheme applied to the rates, into a set of slow states $S_0 = \{(m,0)\}$, a set of fast recurrent states $S_1 = \{(0,1),(1,1),\ldots,(m,1)\}$, and a set of fast transient states $S_2 = \{(0,0),(1,0),\ldots,(m-1,0)\}$. An appropriate aggregation algorithm is separately applied to each subset of fast states. The model of Fig. 4 after aggregation of fast recurrent subset into macro-state 1 is shown in Fig. 6a, while the final aggregated macro-state chain after elimination of the fast transient states is presented in Fig. 6b. Thus, transient approximate solution is obtained by integrating a smaller, non-stiff set of linear differential equations. Next, the disaggregation must be performed to provide an approximation to the transient probability vector $P(t)$. Then, all measures of interest can be calculated from the transient state probabilities. For the detailed algorithm the reader is referred to [5]. The empirical results presented there support the assumption of the approximation being better for stiffer models.

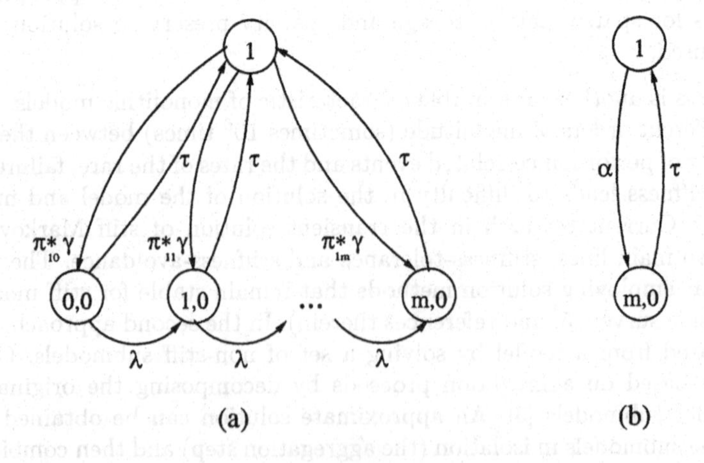

Fig. 6. (a) The model of Fig. 4 after the aggregation of the fast recurrent subset into macro-state 1. (b) Final aggregated macro-state chain after elimination of the fast transient subset

Both the problems of largeness and stiffness can be avoided by using hierarchical model composition. Occurrence rates of failure/repair events are several orders of magnitude smaller than the job arrival/service rates. Consequently, we can assume that the system attains a (quasi-) steady state with respect to performance related events between successive occurrences of failure/repair events, that is, the performance measures would reach a stationary condition between changes in the system structure. This leads to a natural hierarchy of models. The structure state model is the higher level dependability model representing the failure/repair processes. For each state in the dependability model, there is a reward model, which is a performance model for the system with a given, stationary structural state. Several authors have used the letter concept in developing techniques for combined performance and dependability analysis. Early and defining work in this field was done by Beaudry [2] who computed the computational availability until failure. Meyer [11] proposed a conceptual framework of performability, that enable us to characterize degradable systems in terms of their ability to provide a given amount of useful work in a given period of time. Most of the proposed approaches for performability modeling can be brought under the broad framework of Markov reward processes [8] summarized in Sect.2.

In the next section we present the case study (adapted from [13]) which illustrates the use of hierarchical model composition on the example of a multiprocessor system.

5 Case Study of a Multiprocessor System

For the case study we consider a multiprocessor system with n processors (subject to failure and repair) with a limiting number of buffers m. First, we determine the optimal number of processors based on either pure performance or pure dependability measures. Then, we consider the total loss probability which combines performance and availability measures as the most appropriate measure of system effectiveness. The optimal configuration in terms of number of processors is shown to be a function of the chosen measure of system effectiveness.

5.1 Sizing Based on Performance

The performance model is an $M/M/n/m$ queue which can be modeled using a birth and death type Markov chain, as shown in Fig. 7 for the case where $n = 5$ and $m = 100$.

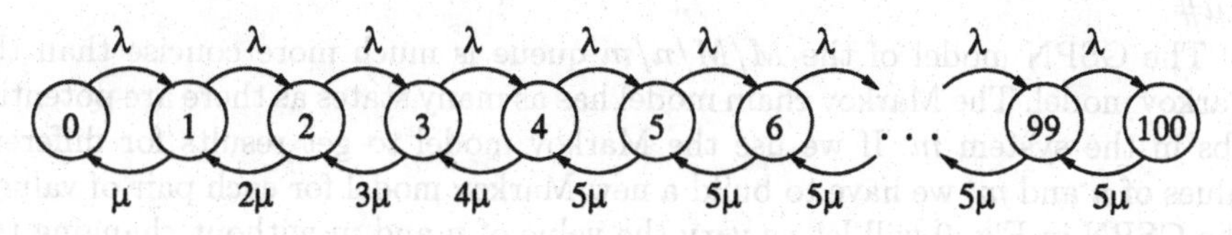

Fig. 7. Birth and death type Markov chain for the $M/M/n/m$ queueing system

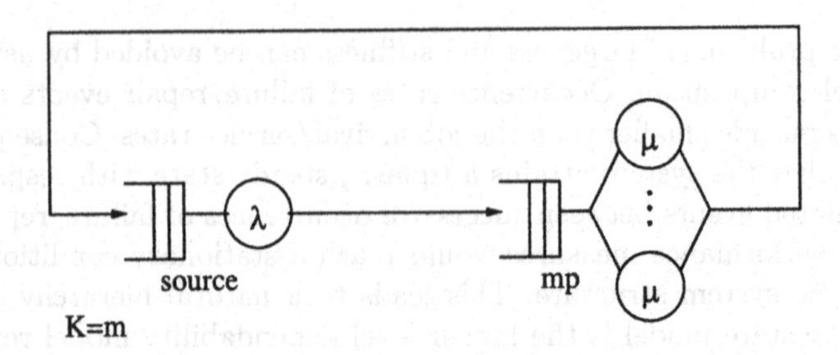

Fig. 8. Closed PFQN model of the $M/M/n/m$ queueing system

The state space of the associated Markov chain grows fast as the size of a queueing network increases. As discussed in Sect.4, high level specification techniques, such as queuing networks or stochastic Petri nets can be used to describe the CTMC in Fig. 7. Thus, it is possible to convert this open queueing model into a closed product-form queueing network, which is shown in Fig. 8. This model contains two stations. Station *mp* is the processor station with n processors, each having service rate μ. The other station is *source*, which represents the job source with rate λ. Because there is a limited number of buffers available for queueing the jobs, the closed product-form network with a fixed number m of jobs is chosen.

PFQN is a useful class of queueing networks that can be analyzed without generating the underlying state space for the whole network. In other words, they belong to the class of non-state space models. PFQN can be used as efficient method for the large model tolerance since many algorithms for exact and approximate solutions for steady-state performance measures exist. However, PFQN cannot be used to model concurrency, synchronization, or server failures, since these violate the product form assumptions.

It is also possible to model the $M/M/n/m$ queue using the GSPN in Fig. 9. The initial number *nproc* of tokens in place *proc* means that there are *nproc* processors available. When a new job arrives in place *buffer*, a token is removed from place *proc*. Jobs arrive at the system when transition *arr* fires. There is a limitation for new jobs entering the system caused by the inhibitor arc from place *buffer* to transition *arr*. Thus *arr* can only fire when the system is not already full. There can be only m jobs in the system altogether, *nproc* being served (in place *serving*) and m – *nproc* in place *buffer*. The firing rates are λ for transition *arr* and $k\mu$ for transition *service*. Here k is the number of tokens in place *serving* and the notation for this marking dependent firing rate in Fig. 9 is $\mu\#$.

The GSPN model of the $M/M/n/m$ queue is much more concise than the Markov model. The Markov chain model has as many states as there are potential jobs in the system m. If we use the Markov model to get results for different values of n and m, we have to build a new Markov model for each pair of values. The GSPN in Fig. 9 will let us vary the value of n and m without changing the model structure. We just need to change the initial marking in place *proc* and

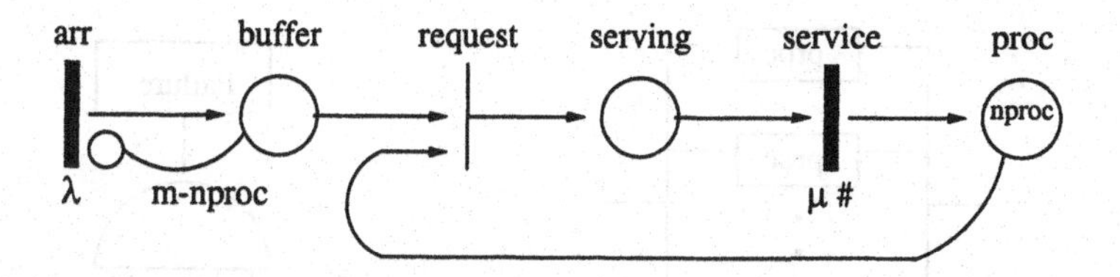

Fig. 9. GSPN model of the $M/M/n/m$ queueing system

the multiplicity of the inhibitor arc. It is important to note that the smaller size of the GSPN model does not mean that the model analysis is correspondingly easier. While increasing n and m does not change the size of GSPN model, it does make the underlying CTMC bigger as already discussed in Sect.4.

Returning to our example of sizing of multiprocessor system based on performance, as an appropriate performance measure we use the job loss probability due to a system being full or too slow. The closed form solutions are available to calculate the probability of a job being rejected because the buffers are full $q_m(n)$ [7]. For an accepted job, define the response time random variable to be $R_n(m)$. The closed form formula for the response time distribution can be derived based on the formula for waiting time given in [7]. If there is a deadline d imposed on the job response times then we can find the probability of system being too slow, that is, a late completion of a job due to deadline violations as $P\{R_n(m) > d\}$.

The job loss probability reflects the effect of job rejection due to buffer full as well a deadline violation of accepted job (system slow)

$$lp(n) = q_m(n) + [1 - q_m(n)]\, P\{R_n(m) > d\}. \tag{18}$$

The equations for $q_m(n)$ and $P\{R_n(m) > d\}$, and the numerical results for the loss probability could be found in [13]. Since the loss probability of a task is monotonically decreasing in the number of processors, the conclusion from the model in this subsection is that the performance of fault free system improves as we increase the number of processors in the multiprocessor system.

5.2 Sizing Based on Availability

For dependability analysis we consider a multiprocessor system with n processors subject to failure and repair. Reliability block diagram and fault tree model of this system are shown in Fig. 10a and Fig. 10b respectively. These models belong to the class of non-state space models specialized for dependability analysis. They are concise, easy to understand, and have efficient solution methods under the assumption that components failure and repair times are independently distributed, and there are enough repair resources to repair all components at the same time, if necessary. However, non-state space models do not allow us to model realistic features such as shared repair facilities, imperfect coverage, and non-zero reconfiguration delays.

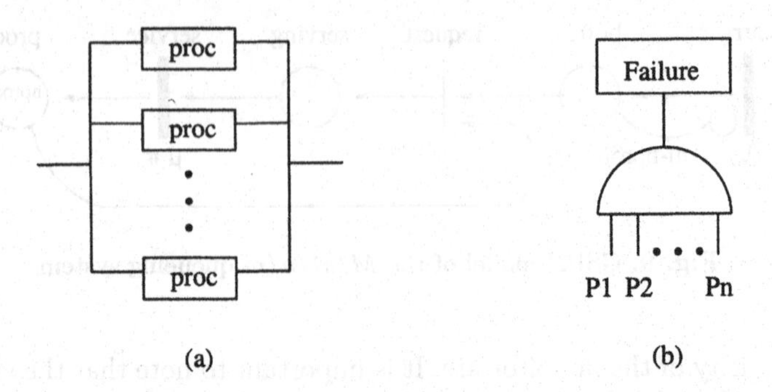

Fig. 10. Non-state space dependability models of a multiprocessor system (a) Reliability block diagram model (b) Fault tree model

By contrast, state space models enable us to account for such details easily, as we have shown in Sect.3. Thus, for the availability model we consider the CTMC presented in Fig. 1 for the general case with n processors. The Markov chain for this system is shown in Fig. 11. In state i, $1 \leq i \leq n$, the system is up with i processors functioning, and $n-i$ processors waiting for on-line repair. The processors share the repairing facility and only one processor can be repaired at a time. Following a covered failure the system is undergoing a reconfiguration in states x_{n-i}, $i = 0, \ldots, n-2$, while an uncovered failure is followed by a reboot in states y_{n-i}, $i = 0, \ldots, n-2$. In state 0, the system is down waiting for off-line repair. If we assume that the system is down while a reconfiguration, reboot or an off-line repair is in progress, the steady-state availability $A(n)$ defined as a function of n is given by

$$A(n) = \sum_{i=0}^{n-1} \pi_{n-i}. \tag{19}$$

The equations for steady-state probabilities π_{n-i}, $\pi_{x_{n-i}}$ and $\pi_{y_{n-i}}$ could be found in [13]. Under the assumptions that the coverage is not perfect and there is non-zero reconfiguration delay, the unavailability $1 - A(n)$ is minimized at a small number (two) of processors [13].

5.3 Sizing Based on Performability

The goal of an availability model is to determine the fraction of time spent in up states. If we use only the result of previous subsection, we could come to the conclusion that the best system configuration is one with two processors. However, increasing the number of processors improves system performance. It is clear that measures such as availability and reliability do not reflect the increased performance due to the increasing number of processors. The most appropriate measure of system effectiveness that reflects both fault-free behavior and behavior in the presence of failures is the total loss probability due to a system being full or too slow or system being down.

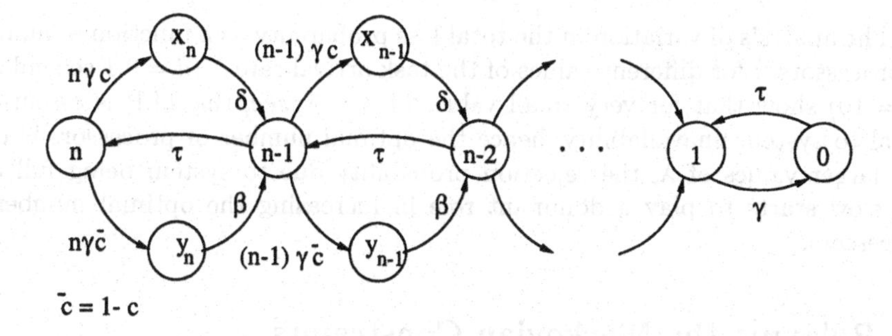

Fig. 11. CTMC for computing availability of a multiprocessor system

For the purpose of deriving the combined performance and availability measure we use hierarchical model composition, that is, a Markov reward model, which avoids both problems of largeness and stiffness. The higher level model (the structure state model), is the Markov chain in Fig. 11 which represents the state of the system with regard to failures and repairs. The total loss probability is obtained by assigning a reward rate to each state, equal to the probability that a task is rejected in that state. In other words, the rewards are assigned to the structural states as follows:

- For all up states with i $(1 \leq i \leq n)$ processors functioning the lower level model which captures the performance of the system is an $M/M/i/m$ queue. Thus, for up states we set the reward rate $r_i = lp(i)$ which is the probability of job rejection due to the buffer full or to deadline violation of accepted job (system slow).
- For all down states x_{n-i}, y_{n-i} $(0 \leq i \leq n-2)$ and state 0 the reward rate assigned is 1, since an arriving job is always rejected when the system is unavailable.

It follows that the total loss probability is the expected steady-state reward rate given by

$$TLP(n) = E[Z] = \sum_{i=0}^{n-1} lp(n-i)\,\pi_{n-i} + \sum_{i=0}^{n-2} (\pi_{x_{n-i}} + \pi_{y_{n-i}}) + \pi_0. \qquad (20)$$

Note that the first term in (20) is the loss probability due to the system full or too slow. The last two terms give the loss probability due to the system being down which is equal to unavailability $1 - A(n)$.

Using the reward structure just discussed and (20), [13] compute the optimal number of processors. For example, it is shown that if $m = 10$ and $\lambda = 80$ per second the optimal number of processors is 3 for one second deadline on task response time, 4 for 0.1 second deadline on task response time, and greater then 8 for 0.01 second deadline on task response time. There is an obvious tradeoff with availability criteria which imposes optimal number of two processors.

The analysis of variation in the total loss probability as a function of number of processors n for different values of the task arrival rate λ ($d = 0.1$ second and $m = 10$) show that for very small values of $\lambda = 1/sec$, the TLP is essentially equal to system unavailability, hence the optimal number of processors is two. For larger values of λ, the rejection probability due to system being full and too slow starts to play a dominant role in increasing the optimal number of processors.

6 Relaxing the Markovian Constraints

A major objection to the use of Markov models in the evaluation of performance and dependability behavior of systems is the assumption that sojourn (holding) time in any state is exponentially distributed. Exponential distribution has many useful properties which lead to analytic tractability, but does not always realistically represent the observed distribution functions. One way to deal with non-exponential distributions is the phase approximation, that is, modeling a distribution by a set of states and transitions between those states such that the holding time in each state is exponentially distributed. The simplest examples of phase approximation are the hyperexponential distribution with a coefficient of variation larger than one, and hypoexponential distribution with a coefficient of variation less than one. Although the method of phase approximation enable us to use the CTMC model, its major drawback is that it usually results in a large state space.

If transition rates in CTMC are allowed to be time dependent, where time is measured from the beginning of system operation, the model becomes non-homogeneous CTMC. Such models are used in software reliability modeling and in hardware reliability models of non-repairable systems.

Due to the assumptions that holding times in the state are exponentially distributed and that past behavior of the process is completely summarized by the current state of the process, every state transition in a homogeneous CTMC acts as a regeneration point for the process. The first assumption can be generalized by allowing the holding time to have any distribution, thus resulting in the semi Markov process (SMP). The seconds assumption can also be generalized by allowing not all state transitions to be regeneration points, thereby resulting in the Markov regenerative process (MRGP). For the mathematical definitions of these stochastic processes the reader is referred to [9].

7 Generation Techniques for State Space Models

We have already pointed out the importance of high level specification and automated generation of large Markov chains. The approach of separation of higher level model description and lower level computational model has many advantages. Besides reducing the size of the description, such models provide visual and conceptual clarity, and are closer to a designer's intuition. They allow the designer to focus more on the system being modeled rather than on error-prone and tedious creation of lower level models manually.

In this section we will briefly review the stochastic Petri net models and their extensions, whose popularity is partially due to the number of software tools available for their specification and analysis; these include SHARPE [14] and SPNP [6].

As originally introduced by C.A.Petri in 1962, Petri nets did not have a time element. A stochastic Petri nets (SPN) is a Petri net with timed transitions where the firing time distributions are assumed to be exponential. A generalized stochastic Petri nets (GSPN), first proposed in [1], is a Petri net where both immediate and timed transitions are allowed. The underlying stochastic process of the SPNs and GSPNs is a Markov chain.

In the last decade many extensions to the basic Petri net model have been proposed. Some of these extensions have enhanced the flexibility of use and allowed even more concise description of performance and dependability models. Some other extensions have enhanced the modeling power by allowing for a reward rate functions or non-exponential distributions. Specifically, besides several structural extensions, Stochastic Reward Nets (SRN) allow a reward rate to be associated with each reachable marking. SRNs have been shown to be isomorphic to Markov reward processes. The Extended Stochastic Petri net (ESPN), in which general firing time distributions are allowed, under suitable conditions has as the underlying stochastic process a semi Markov process. Deterministic Stochastic Petri nets (DSPN) allow the definition of immediate, exponential and deterministic transitions. The stochastic process underlying a DSPN is a Markov regenerative process. The Markov regenerative Stochastic Petri nets (MRSPN) generalize DSPNs and still have MRGP as an underlying stochastic process. The Concurrent Generalized Petri nets (CGPN) allow simultaneous enabling of any number of immediate, exponentially distributed and generally distributed timed transitions, provided that the latter are all enabled at the same instant. Stochastic process underlying a CGPN is also MRGP.

To summarize, the use of SPNs and their extensions for a high level specification of stochastic models has received a lot attention in current research. An excellent survey could be found in [10], [4].

8 Conclusion

Analytical modeling is a cost effective method for examining the behavior of current day complex computer systems. To be useful, the model should be realistic and reflect important system characteristics such as failure behavior, reconfiguration and repair, fault tolerance, graceful degradation, contention for resources, concurrency and synchronization, and deadlines imposed on tasks. The recent advances in the development of different model types, exact and approximate solution techniques, and tools that help in automatic model generation and solution from a high level description enable large and realistic models to be developed and studied effectively.

In this chapter we have discussed the use of analytical models for performance, dependability and performability analysis of computer systems. The choice of an appropriate model type and measures of interest clearly depends on the system requirements. For some systems performance and dependability can be addressed separately, while for others such an analysis can lead to incomplete or even misleading results thus making it essential to combine them in a single framework. A modeler who is familiar with many different types of models, can easily choose the models and measures that best suit a particular system.

At the end we would like to emphasize that analytical modeling is not an exclusive technique for computer system evaluation. Model composition approaches, such as Markov reward models, are particularly suitable for combining different types of models, as well as analytical modeling with measurement or discrete event simulation.

References

1. Ajmone Marsan, M., Balbo,G., Conte, G.: A Class of Generalized Stochastic Petri Nets for the Performance Analysis of Multiprocessor Systems. ACM Trans. on Computer Systems. **2** (1984) 93–122
2. Beaudry, M.D.: Performance – related Reliability Measures for Computing Systems. IEEE Trans. on Computers. **27** (1978) 540–547
3. Bobbio, A., Trivedi, K.: An Aggregation Technique for the Transient Analysis of Stiff Markov Chains. IEEE Trans. on Computers. **35** (1986) 803–814
4. Bobbio, A., Puliafito, A., Telek, M., Trivedi, K.: Recent Developments in Stochastic Petri Nets. Journal of Circuits, Systems, and Computers. **8** (1998) 119–158
5. Bolch, G., Greiner, S., de Meer, H.. Trivedi, K.: Queueing Networks and Markov Chains, John Wiley & Sons, (1998)
6. Ciardo, G., Blakemore, A., Chimento, P.F., Muppala, J.K., Trivedi, K.S.: Automated Generation and Analysis of Markov Reward Models using Stochastic Reward Nets. In Mayer, C., Plemmons, R.J. (eds.): Linear Algebra, Markov Chains and Queueing Models. IMA Volumes in Mathematics and Its Applications. Vol.48. Springer-Verlag (1993) 145–191
7. Gross, D., Harris, C.M.: Fundamentals of Queueing Theory. John Wiley & Sons, (1985)
8. Howard, R.A.: Dynamic Probabilistic Systems, Vol.II: Semi–Markov and Decision Processes. John Wiley & Sons, (1971)
9. Kulkarni, V.G.: Modeling and Analysis of Stochastic Systems. Chapman Hall (1995)
10. Lindemann, C.: Performance Modelling with Deterministic and Stochastic Petri Nets. John Wiley & Sons, (1998)
11. Meyer, J.F.: On Evaluating the Performability of Degradable Computing Systems. IEEE Trans. on Computers. **29** (1980) 720–731
12. Trivedi, K.S.: Probability and Statistics with Reliability, Queuing and Computer Science Applications. Prentice–Hall, (1982)
13. Trivedi, K.S., Sathaye, A.S., Ibe, O.C., Howe, R.C., Aggarwal, A.: Availability and Performance – Based Sizing of Multiprocessor Systems, Communications in Reliability, Maintainability and Serviceability. (1996)
14. Sahner, R.A., Trivedi, K.S., Puliafito, A.: Performance and Reliability Analysis of Computer Systems. Kluwer Academic Publishers, (1996)

Analysis and Application of Polling Models

Hideaki Takagi

Institute of Policy and Planning Sciences, University of Tsukuba
1-1-1 Tennoudai, Tsukuba-shi, Ibaraki 305-8573, Japan
takagi@shako.sk.tsukuba.ac.jp

1 Origin and Short History

Let me begin this essay by quoting a few passages from a nontechnical article by Dr. Martin A. Leibowitz (1968) entitled "Queues" in an old issue of *Scientific American* that refer to a polling model [11].

> Queuing theory was founded by the work of A. K. Erlang, who began in 1908 to study problems of congestion in telephone service for the Copenhagen Telephone Company. Since then workers in the field have tended to concentrate on describing fairly uncomplicated situations, involving at most a few queues. It seems likely that the pressures of a rapidly advancing technology will direct the attention of queuing theorists increasingly toward the analysis of systems containing many interacting queues. Such systems include the national and international telephone networks; large computers dealing with a variety of users or problems, and traffic-control systems covering wide areas.
>
> ...I should like to discuss what is called in queuing theory "the polling problem." Consider a large number of queues, each with its own input, served cyclically by a single server. The server goes from one queue to the next, taking a certain amount of travel time in the process, and serves everyone in a queue before proceeding to the next queue. A commonplace example would be a bus that stops at various places to load and unload passengers while it plies a circular route.
>
> My interest was stimulated by a different application, in which the server is a computer. It cyclically polls a number of remote terminals to ascertain what demands have arrived since its last visit. This is the mode of operation in many time-shared systems.

As clearly described in the above quotation, a *polling model* in its most naive form is a system of multiple queues attended by a single server in cyclic order (Fig. 1). The term *polling* originated with the *polling* data link control scheme in which the central computer interrogates each terminal on a multidrop communication line to determine whether or not it has data to transmit. The addressed terminal transmits data, and the computer then examines the next terminal. Here, the server represents the computer and a queue corresponds to a terminal. This was an application of a polling model studied in the early 1970s. Situations

G. Haring et al. (Eds.): Performance Evaluation, LNCS 1769, pp. 423–442, 2000.

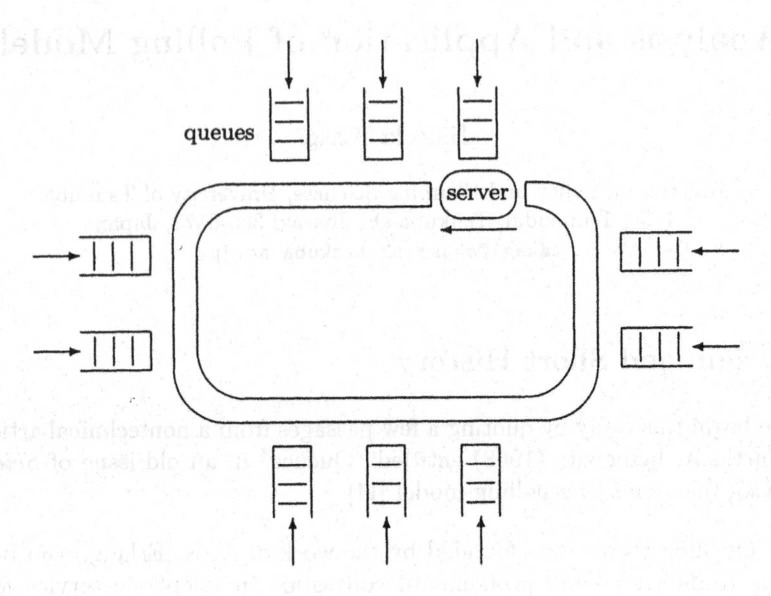

Fig. 1. A polling system

represented by polling models and their variations appear not only in computers and communications but also in other fields of engineering such as manufacturing and transportation systems. The ubiquitous application is not surprising because the cyclic allocation of the server (resource) is a natural and simple way for fair arbitration to multiple queues (requesters). Therefore, polling models in various settings have been studied by many researchers since the late 1950s, focusing on the applications to technologies emerging at each period.

In the late 1950s, a polling model with a single buffer for each queue was used in an investigation of a problem in the British cotton industry involving a patrolling machine repairman. In the 1960s, polling models with two queues were considered for the analysis of vehicle-actuated road traffic signal control. There are some early studies by queueing theoreticians, apparently independent of traffic analysis. In the 1970s, with the advent of computer communication networks, an extensive study was carried out on a polling scheme for data transfer from terminals on multidrop lines to a central computer. Around the early 1980s, the same model was revived for token passing protocols (e.g., token ring and token bus) in local area networks (LANs). More recently, polling models with additional control features (priority, time limit, etc.) have been applied to channel access protocols in metropolitan area networks (MANs), high-speed LANs, ISDN, and land mobile and satellite radio communication networks. In the application to computer systems, the polling model was used for the scheduling of moving arms in secondary storage devices, and for load sharing in multiprocessor computers. Numerous applications exist in manufacturing systems, such as assembly work on a carousel, an automated guided vehicle (AGV) system, and multiproduct economic lot scheduling. Applications to transportation systems include the public bus service on a circular route, an elevator on an up-and-down route, internal mail delivery, and shipyard loading for multiple destinations.

Regarding the mathematical analysis of polling systems, Dr. Leibowitz stated that "the complexity of such systems defies exact mathematical analysis," and proposed approximate modeling. Fortunately, however, subsequent progress in queueing theory has made it possible to handle the polling model in a much more tractable way than he envisaged somewhat pessimistically.

In this short essay, I would like to present an introductory overview of the analysis results of the polling model and its applications to the performance evaluation of several communication protocols. Besides hundreds of original research papers, polling models have been referred to in many books and survey papers on general communication networks as well as described in several dedicated surveys. Thus I will also include a brief discusion of these surveys and books for the convenience of those readers who want to proceed with further study. I conclude by suggesting some possible future directions.

2 Models and Performance Measures

Let me mainly describe the very basic system for the sake of conciseness, and refer to its variations only briefly. My description shall be given in terms of queueing theory, with which the reader is assumed to have some familiarity. The generic queueing theoretic terms should correspond to the specific technical terminologies in each application context.

A *basic polling system* consists of several, say N, queues served by a single server in cyclic order. Assume that the characteristics of all queues are identical. Customers arrive at each queue according to an independent Poisson process at rate λ. Let b and $b^{(2)}$ be the mean and the second moment, respectively, of the service time. The total load offered to the system is then given by

$$\rho = N\lambda b.$$

The server walks through all the queues in cyclic order. Let r and δ^2 be the mean and the variance, respectively, for the time needed by the server to switch from one queue to the next. These switchover times are assumed to be independent of the arrival and service processes. The total mean switchover time per polling cycle is then given by

$$R = Nr.$$

Two important performance measures of the polling system are the *mean polling cycle time* C that it takes the server to complete a cycle of visiting all the queues in the system, and the *mean customer waiting time* W that it takes a customer from arrival to service start. Analytical results are available in closed form for C and W in the two extreme cases, i.e., a single-buffer system and an infinite-buffer system when all the queues are statistically identical.

2.1 Single-Buffer Systems

A system in which each queue can accommodate at most one customer at a time is called a *single-buffer system.* Those customers that arrive to find the buffer occupied are lost. This system can model a *patrolling machine repairman problem* (in which the breakdown of a machine corresponds to the customer arrival and the patrolling repairman to the roving server) and an interactive transaction processing system on a computer shared by multiple users. If both service times and switchover times are constant ($b^{(2)} = b^2, \delta^2 = 0$) in a single-buffer system, the mean cycle time and the mean waiting time are given by

$$C = R + Qb$$

and

$$W = (N-1)b - \frac{1}{\lambda} + \frac{NR}{Q},$$

where

$$Q = \frac{N \sum_{n=0}^{N-1} \binom{N-1}{n} \prod_{j=0}^{n} \left[e^{\lambda(R+jb)} - 1 \right]}{1 + \sum_{n=1}^{N} \binom{N}{n} \prod_{j=0}^{n-1} \left[e^{\lambda(R+jb)} - 1 \right]}$$

is the mean number of customers served in a polling cycle. The *throughput* γ of the system, or the mean number of customers served per unit time, is given by

$$\gamma = \frac{Q}{C} = \frac{N}{W + b + 1/\lambda}.$$

Fig. 2 plots W against ρ when $b = R = 1$ for $N = 5$, 20, 100, and ∞. For N finite, $W \approx R + (N-1)b$ when $\rho \to \infty$ as all the queues are occupied most of the time. The throughput then approaches its maximum, the *capacity* of the system $\gamma_{\max} = N/(R + Nb)$. On the other hand, $W \approx R/2$ when $\rho \to 0$.

Taking the limit $N \to \infty$ with ρ and R fixed at finite values, one obtains the *continuous polling model* in which the server travels at constant speed around a circular route on which customers arrive at points uniformly distributed over the circle. In this case we get

$$C = \frac{R}{1-\rho} \quad ; \quad W = \frac{R + \rho b}{2(1-\rho)}.$$

2.2 Infinite-Buffer Systems

At the other extreme, a system in which any number of customers can wait without loss upon arrival at each queue is called an *infinite-buffer system.* It is natural to assume that if the server finds at least one customer at a queue it visits, service is immediately started there. However, several rules can be

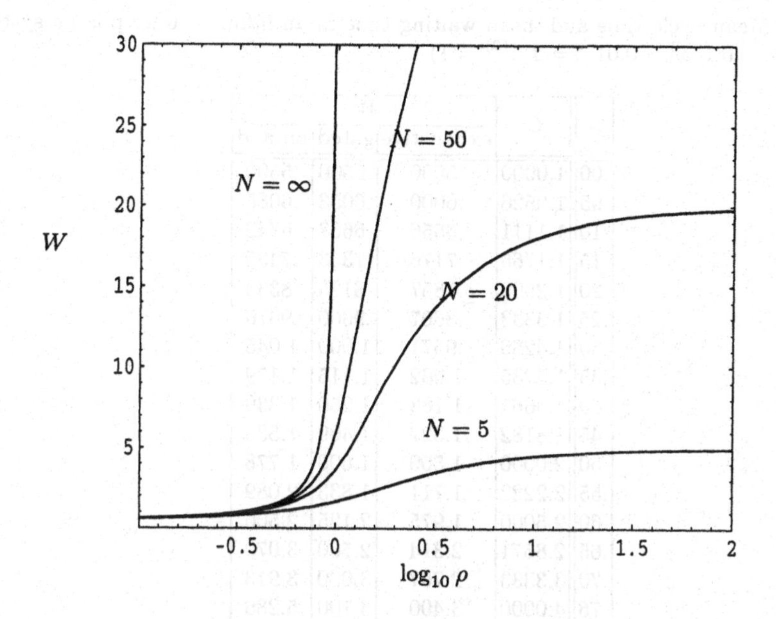

Fig. 2. Mean waiting time in a single-buffer polling system ($b = R = 1$)

considered with respect to the instant at which the server leaves the queue. The following three rules are typical among others. In an *exhaustive service* system, the server continues to serve each queue until it empties. Customers that arrive at the queue being served are also served in the current service period. In a *gated service* system, the server serves only those customers that were found waiting when it visited the queue. Those that arrive at the queue during its service period are set aside to be served in the next round of polling. In a *limited service* system, at most one customer is served at each visit to a queue.

For a broad class of infinite-buffer systems, including those with the three typical service rules mentioned above, the mean cycle time is simply given by

$$C = \frac{R}{1-\rho}$$

if $\rho < 1$, which is the condition for the stability of the system. The mean waiting times are given as follows:

$$W_{\text{exhaustive}} = \frac{\delta^2}{2r} + \frac{N\lambda b^{(2)} + r(N-\rho)}{2(1-\rho)},$$

$$W_{\text{gated}} = \frac{\delta^2}{2r} + \frac{N\lambda b^{(2)} + r(N+\rho)}{2(1-\rho)},$$

$$W_{\text{limited}} = \frac{\delta^2}{2r} + \frac{N\lambda b^{(2)} + r(N+\rho) + N\lambda\delta^2}{2(1-\rho-N\lambda r)}.$$

Table 1. Mean cycle time and mean waiting time in an infinite-buffer polling system ($N = 10, r = 0.1, \delta^2 = 0.01, b = 1, b^{(2)} = 1$)

ρ	C	W		
		exhaustive	gated	limited
.00	1.0000	.5500	.5500	.5500
.05	1.0526	.6000	.6053	.6085
.10	1.1111	.6556	.6667	.6742
.15	1.1765	.7176	.7353	.7485
.20	1.2500	.7857	.8125	.8333
.25	1.3333	.8667	.9000	.9310
.30	1.4286	.9571	1.000	1.045
.35	1.5385	1.062	1.115	1.179
.40	1.6667	1.183	1.250	1.339
.45	1.8182	1.327	1.409	1.535
.50	2.0000	1.500	1.600	1.778
.55	2.2222	1.711	1.833	2.089
.60	2.5000	1.975	2.125	2.500
.65	2.8571	2.314	2.500	3.070
.70	3.3333	2.767	3.000	3.913
.75	4.0000	3.400	3.700	5.286
.80	5.0000	4.350	4.750	7.917
.85	6.6667	5.933	6.500	15.00
.90	10.000	9.100	10.00	100.0
.95	20.000	18.60	20.50	-

Table 1 shows the numerical values of the mean cycle time and the mean waiting times for the three rules. The mean waiting times are ordered as

$$W_{\text{exhaustive}} \leq W_{\text{gated}} \leq W_{\text{limited}}.$$

In fact it has been proven mathematically that the exhaustive service rule stochastically minimizes the unfinished work and the number of customers in the system at all times. However, an operational advantage of the limited service rule is the *fairness* in service opportunity in the sense that it prevents heavily loaded queues from monopolizing the server.

2.3 Variations

Numerous variations and extensions to the above-mentioned basic systems have been proposed and analyzed. Some have been introduced to model the operation of practical systems more precisely, while others seem to have been made up as academic exercises. Let me focus on major variations briefly here. Readers who are interested in the numerous variations of the basic system and their detailed analysis may search the literature by first consulting the survey papers mentioned in Section 4.

Asymmetric Systems. Each queue may have different stochastic characteristics such as different arrival rate, service time distribution, and switchover time distribution. In this case, the mean waiting time can be obtained through the numerical solution to the set of linear equations for the single-buffer system and for the infinite-buffer systems with exhaustive and gated service rules.
A theoretically important and practically useful relationship valid for asymmetric infinite-buffer systems with mixed service rules is the *pseudoconservation law*

$$\sum_{i\in E,G} \rho_i W_i + \sum_{i\in L} \rho_i \left(1 - \frac{\lambda_i R}{1-\rho}\right) W_i$$

$$= \frac{\sum_{i=1}^{N} \rho_i b_i^{(2)}}{2(1-\rho)} + \frac{\rho \Delta^2}{2R} + \frac{R\left(\rho - \sum_{i=1}^{N} \rho_i^2 + 2 \sum_{i\in G,L} \rho_i^2\right)}{2(1-\rho)}$$

where $\rho_i = \lambda_i b_i$, and subscript i refers to the quantity associated with queue i. Δ^2 is the variance of the total switchover time. E, G, and L stand for the index sets of the queues with exhaustive, gated, and limited service rules, respectively. While it does not yield individual W_i's, the merits of the pseudoconservation law include a measure of overall performance, a demonstration of the effects of various parameters on W_i's, a basis for approximations and bounds, and a validity check of simulation results. When there are no switchover times, the pseudoconservation law reduces to *Kleinrock's conservation law* for nonpreemptive work-conserving queueing systems:

$$\sum_{i=1}^{N} \rho_i W_i = \frac{1}{2(1-\rho)} \sum_{i=1}^{N} \rho_i b_i^{(2)}.$$

Discrete-Time and/or Batch Arrival Systems. A motivation for discrete-time system models comes from clock-synchronized operation in digital computers and communications, where time is slotted and the service times are multiples of the slot size. The batch arrival of customers models the transmission unit consisting of several messages, packets, frames, cells, etc. These features can be incorporated in the analysis of basic systems without many additional difficulties.

Noncyclic Polling Order and Optimization. There are many systems in which the server does not visit all the queues exactly in cyclic order. For example, the physical structure of the system may require the server to visit queues first in one direction and then in the reverse direction. Such cases apply to the elevator in a building and to the scanning policy in the moving-arm disk device of a computer. Systems may be designed so as to visit some queues more often than others in a cycle to establish priority service; the polling order table was implemented in the multidrop data link controller. A system with Markovian server

movement (the server visits queue j after queue i with given probability p_{ij}) has also been proposed; a special case is random polling in which the server chooses the next queue to serve completely at random. For those systems in which the server movement does not depend on the system state such as the queue lengths, one can again extend the analysis of the basic system rather easily.
In other systems, the server's movement/action may be controlled based on the local or global system state. For example, service may not start unless a large enough number of customers are found upon a visit, as sometimes is seen in manufacturing and transportation systems. As another example, the server may visit the longest queue in the system after each service. If there are no customers in the system, what should the server do? Options include to keep cycling, staying at the last visited queue, going back to some home base queue, and waiting at the queue with the highest static load. Many optimization problems with respect to the server movement remain unsolved theoretically.

Network of Queues. In usual queueing networks, each queue has it own dedicated server(s). In a polling system for a network of queues, there is a single server visiting all the queues one at a time, while the customers served at a queue may move to other queues or depart from the network. Analytical work has been done for both open and closed networks, but useful applications seem to remain unidentified.

K-Limited and Time-Limited Service. Under a limited service rule, at most one customer is served at each visit of the server to the queue. This has been extended to the *K-limited service* rule in which the service continues until K customers are served or the queue is empty, whichever occurs first. The pipeline polling scheme in satellite communication is such an example. Another extension is the *time-limited service* rule in which the duration of server attendance to each queue (instead of the number of customers served) is limited. This is important from the application viewpoint because several communication protocols implement timed-token operation. Unfortunately, the exact analysis of a polling system with time-limited service rule is very difficult, and the results do not seem to be readily usable for practitioners yet. Alternatively, simple approximations have been proposed.

3 Application to Communication Networks

In this section, I will highlight three successful applications of the polling model to the performance evaluation of communication networks. They are rather classical, but simple and therefore instructive. Again, those who want to know more about application examples are referred to the survey papers mentioned in Section 4.

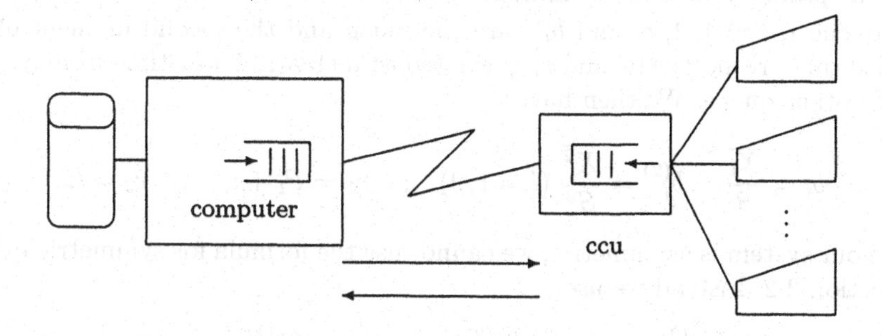

Fig. 3. Half-duplex transmission for an inquiry system

3.1 Half Duplex Transmission

Half duplex transmission is a mode of transmitting data between two parties on a shared communication line. Transmission is possible in either direction but not in both directions simultaneously. (A similar situation can be observed in everyday life, e.g., a traffic light at the intersection of two one-way streets, a narrow bridge or passage, conversation with Walkie-Talkie.) Suppose that a central computer and a communication control unit (ccu) connected to several data terminals exchange messages over a half duplex line (Fig. 3). When the transmission from the ccu is complete, a finite time is needed to reverse the direction of transmission on the line. Output messages are sent from the computer to the ccu, which delivers them to the terminals. After receiving a polling message from the computer and again reversing the direction of transmission, the ccu can start sending input messages to the computer, and this cycle is repeated.

In the queueing model of this system, customers correspond to the input and output messages, and the server represents the communication line between the computer and the ccu that allows the alternating transmission of messages. Let us call the computer queue 1 and the ccu queue 2. The service time at queue 1 is the transmission time of an output message, and that at queue 2 is the transmission time of an input message. The switchover time from queue 1 to queue 2 consists of the time for sending the polling message and the facility reversal time. The switchover time from queue 2 to queue 1 consists only of the facility reversal time.

Let us introduce parameters for the above quantities. Let λ_1 and λ_2 (messages/sec) be the arrival rates of the output and input messages, respectively. Let $\overline{X_1}$ and $\overline{X_1^2}$ be the mean and the second moment of the length (in characters) of an output message. Similarly, we use $\overline{X_2}$ and $\overline{X_2^2}$ as the mean and the second moment of the length of an input message. The transmission speed of the line is denoted by S (characters/sec). The transmission time of a polling message is given by a constant P_1 (sec). Finally, the constant facility reversal time is denoted by t_r (sec). We can neglect the signal propagation time in this system, as the line speed is usually very low. These parameters of the system are converted into the parameters of an asymmetric polling model with two queues as follows. For queue i, $i = 1, 2$, b_i and $b_i^{(2)}$ are the mean and the second moment of the service time, respectively, and r_i is the (constant) switchover time from queue i to the other queue. We then have

$$b_i = \frac{\overline{X_i}}{S}, \quad b_i^{(2)} = \frac{\overline{X_i^2}}{S^2} \ (i = 1, 2) \quad ; \quad r_1 = P_1 + t_r \quad ; \quad r_2 = t_r.$$

Since our system is asymmetric, we cannot use the formula for symmetric queues in Section 2.2. Instead we use

$$W_1 = \frac{\lambda_1 b_1^{(2)}}{2(1-\rho_1)} + \frac{\lambda_1 \rho_2^2 b_1^{(2)} + \lambda_2 (1-\rho_1)^2 b_2^{(2)}}{2(1-\rho_1)(1-\rho)(1-\rho+2\rho_1\rho_2)} + \frac{(1-\rho_1)R}{2(1-\rho)}$$

and a similar formula for W_2 obtained by exchanging subscripts 1 and 2, where

$$\rho_i = \lambda_i b_i \ (i = 1, 2) \quad ; \quad \rho = \rho_1 + \rho_2 \quad ; \quad R = r_1 + r_2.$$

Sykes [16] applies this model to the calculation of the *mean retrieval time* T_r in an inquiry-response system, which is given by

$$T_r = W_2 + b_2 + C_p + W_1 + b_1,$$

where C_p is the mean time for processing an inquiry at the computer. He uses the values

$$S = 120 \text{ characters/sec} \quad ; \quad \overline{X_2} = 15 \text{ characters}$$

$$c_1^2 = \mathrm{Var}[X_1]/\overline{X_1}^2 = 0.1 \quad ; \quad c_2^2 = \mathrm{Var}[X_2]/\overline{X_2}^2 = 0.5$$

$$t_r = 0.2 \text{ sec} \quad ; \quad P_1 = 0.2 \text{ sec} \quad ; \quad C_p = 2.0 \text{ sec}$$

and assumes that $\lambda_1 = \lambda_2$, because each inquiry is assumed to generate a response. In Fig. 4, we plot the mean retrieval time T_r against the line utilization ρ for $\overline{X_1} = 75$, 150, and 300 characters.

3.2 Polling Data Link Control

Polling control has often been employed in network configurations in which geographically dispersed terminals are connected to a central computer in a tree topology or a loop topology (Fig. 5). There are two types of polling control. In *roll-call polling*, the computer has a polling sequence table according to which it interrogates each terminal. The addressed terminal then transmits all waiting messages to the computer. When the transmission from one terminal is complete, the computer starts polling the next terminal. In the polling sequence table, the network designer can order terminals in exact cyclic order, or in any sequence and frequency to prioritize terminals. Roll-call polling is suitable for a tree topology. In a loop topology, on the other hand, *hub polling* is often used. In this case, a natural polling sequence is determined by the position of terminals

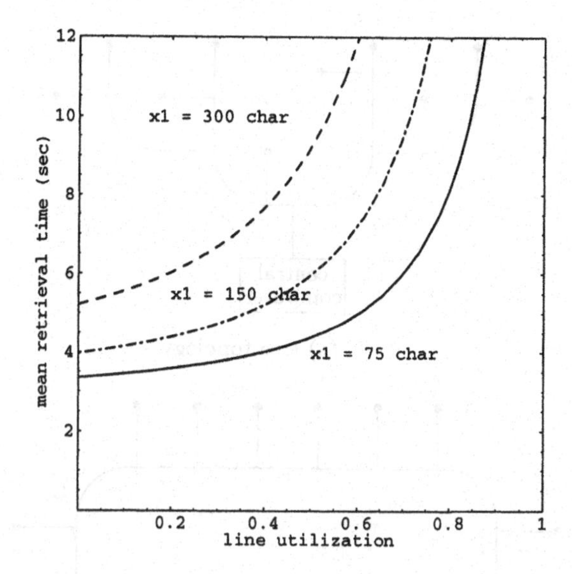

Fig. 4. Mean retrieval time in an inquiry-response system with a half-duplex transmission

on the loop. The central computer initiates polling by interrogating the terminal at the end of the loop. This terminal transmits its waiting messages, to which it appends a polling message for the next downstream (in the direction of transmission) terminal. The latter terminal similarly adds its own messages followed by another polling message, and so on. At the completion of a polling cycle, the central computer collects all the messages and assumes control.

Polling was implemented in byte-oriented protocols, such as the early IBM Programmed Airlines Reservation System (PARS) and IBM's Binary Synchronous Communication (BSC). Polling has also been implemented in bit-oriented protocols such as IBM's Synchronous Data Link Control (SDLC), ANSI's Advanced Data Communication Control Procedure (ADCCP), and CCITT's High-level Data Link Control (HDLC). SDLC provides hub polling under the name *SDLC loop*.

The operation in normal response mode (NRM) of HDLC is as follows. A single station (usually the central computer) designated the *primary station* is responsible for control of the link, issuing commands to terminals called *secondary stations*, and receiving responses from them. The fifth bit of the control (C) field in the HDLC frame is the polling/final (P/F) bit. The primary station initiates a polling cycle by transmitting a receive-ready (RR) frame with P=1 to the first secondary station in the polling sequence table. The addressed secondary station transmits waiting messages in information (I) frames. A station can only transmit up to seven I frames per poll without waiting for an acknowledgment. If there are no errors and the primary station is ready to accept further frames, a positive acknowledgment is sent from the primary station. The secondary station

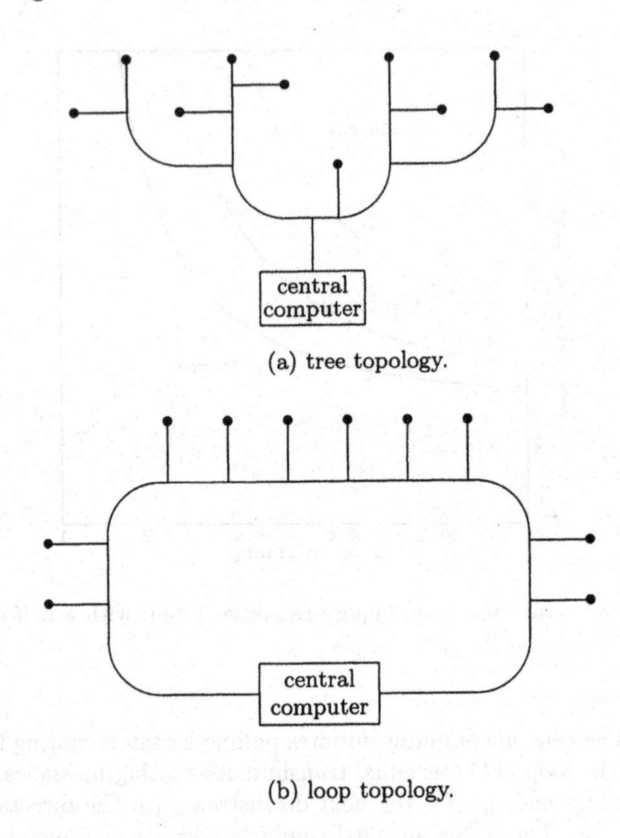

Fig. 5. Typical topologies for polling networks

starts to transmit messages again, and continues in this way until it transmits the last frame with F=1, indicating the completion of its reply to this poll. The primary station acknowledges this transmission, and polls the next secondary station.

For simplicity of analysis, let us employ a symmetric model so that the formulas in Section 2.2 can be used. The assumptions for this model include the following. N terminals are connected to a computer. The arrival processes at each terminal are independent Poisson processes with equal arrival rates of λ messages/sec. The switchover time between adjacent terminals, which depends on the network topology and whether roll-call or hub polling is used, is the same for every adjacent pair, and is further assumed to be constant ($\delta^2 = 0$), so that the round-trip switchover time is R sec. The message length distributions are the same for each station; if $\overline{X}$ and $\overline{X^2}$ are the mean and the second moment of the message length in bits, and S (bits/sec) is the line speed, we have

$$b = \frac{\overline{X}}{S} \quad ; \quad b^{(2)} = \frac{\overline{X^2}}{S^2} .$$

Finally, the polled terminal continues to transmit queued messages until it empties (exhaustive service). Under these assumptions, we get

$$W = \frac{N\lambda b^{(2)} + R(1 - \rho/N)}{2(1 - \rho)}.$$

The switchover time R consists of the following components. In roll-call polling, it includes the time t_P taken to transmit a polling message to each terminal (if an RR frame of 48 bits long is used in HDLC, $t_P = 48/S$ sec), the synchronization time t_S for a terminal to recognize its address and take action to begin transmitting, and the propagation time required for polling messages and data messages to physically propagate on the transmission line. If $\tau_{\text{roll-call}}$ denotes the total propagation time for the entire system, the total switchover time for roll-call polling is given by

$$R_{\text{roll-call}} = Nt_P + Nt_S + \tau_{\text{roll-call}}.$$

Note that $\tau_{\text{roll-call}}$ depends on the topology and the line length of the network. The total switchover time is reduced through the use of hub polling (even for the same topology and line length) for two reasons. First, the propagation time is reduced, since there is no back-and-forth transmission of polling and response messages for each terminal. Thus, the propagation time is just one round-trip delay, denoted by τ_{hub}. Second, the polling message is transmitted by the computer only once to the first terminal, and then propagated downstream in cyclic polling. If we denote this contribution by t'_P, the total switchover time for hub polling is

$$R_{\text{hub}} = t'_P + Nt_S + \tau_{\text{hub}}.$$

Hence, hub polling usually has higher performance than roll-call polling, particularly for large-scale networks.

As a numerical example, Schwartz [14, sec. 8.1] considers the network topology shown in Fig. 6, where the length of the line from the central computer to the Nth terminal is denoted by l (miles). Let τ be the round-trip propagation time (milliseconds) between the computer and the Nth terminal. The signal propagation time is assumed to be 2 milliseconds per 100 miles. Thus

$$\tau = l\text{ (miles)} \times 2 \times \frac{2\text{ milliseconds}}{100\text{ miles}}.$$

For the topology of Fig. 6, we obviously have

$$\tau_{\text{roll-call}} = \frac{\tau}{2}(1 + N) \quad ; \quad \tau_{\text{hub}} = \tau.$$

Schwartz uses the values

$$S = 4,800\text{ (bits/sec)} \quad ; \quad N = 10 \quad ; \quad t_P = t'_P = t_S = 10\text{ millisec}$$

$$\overline{X} = 1,200\text{ bits} \quad ; \quad \overline{X^2} = 2\overline{X}^2 = 2,880,000\text{ (bits)}^2 \quad \text{(exponential distribution)}.$$

Using these values and $l = 2,000$ miles or 100 miles, we plot the mean message waiting times W for both roll-call and hub polling in Fig. 7. This figure illustrates that the difference in the two polling schemes becomes evident for a long network.

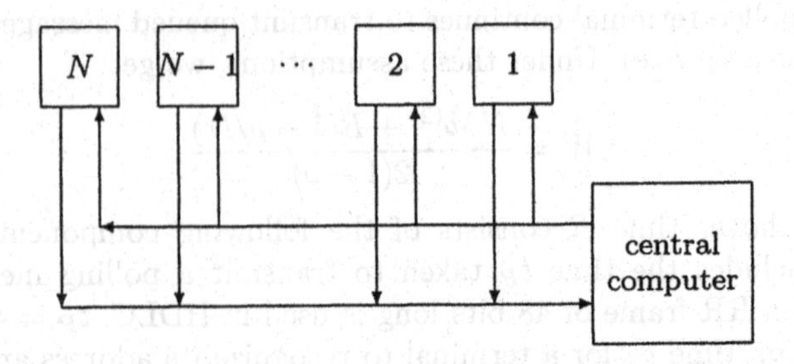

Fig. 6. Model of a polling network

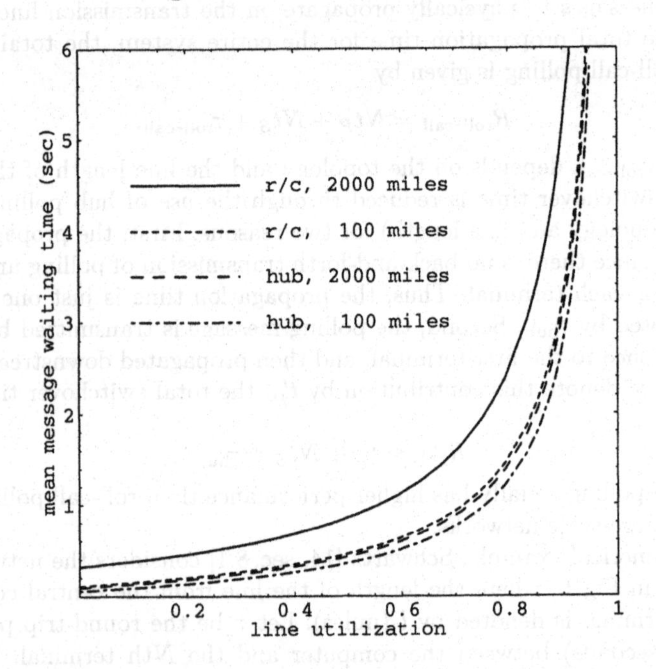

Fig. 7. Mean message waiting times under two polling schemes

3.3 Token Ring Network

Two major types of access schemes for local area computer networks developed in the early 1980s were the *random access* scheme represented by Carrier Sense Multiple Access/Collision Detection (CSMA/CD) implemented in Xerox Ethernet, and the *controlled access* scheme represented by the *token ring* protocol developed at IBM Zürich Research Laboratory. They were later included in IEEE 802 standards as 802.3 for a CSMA/CD bus, 802.4 for a token-passing bus, and 802.5 for a token-passing ring. Token-ring and token-bus are examples of networks in which *explicit token* messages are used to control the transmission rights.

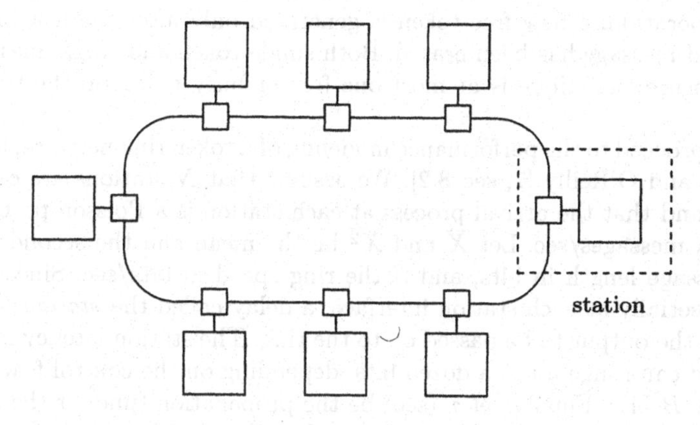

Fig. 8. Configuration of a ring network

A ring network is a group of *stations* (terminals or computers) that are interconnected via a communication line in the form of a loop (Fig. 8). (The words *ring* and *loop* are used interchangeably). Each station is attached to the ring by an interface unit. Traffic on the communication line is usually unidirectional, so that each station receives messages from one of its neighbors and passes them to its other neighbor. Messages sent from a source station to a destination station are relayed by intermediate stations. A ring supervisor may be present (for initialization, access control, congestion monitoring, statistics gathering, error recovery, etc.), or stations may control themselves in a distributed manner.

In a token ring network, a number of stations are connected to the ring network through an adapter, and all information goes through each station when it circulates. A permit to transmit is controlled through the use of a *token*, which is passed from station to station according to a given rule. In the IEEE 802.5 token ring, the fourth bit of the access control (AC) field in a frame specifies whether the token is free or busy. A station that receives a free token modifies the bit to busy, and inserts the destination address (DA), its own address (SA), and messages (INFO) when it sends out the frame. The transmitting station is responsible for removing its frame from the ring and for generating a new free token when its transmission is over.

With respect to the time at which a new free token is generated by the transmitting station, distinction is made for the *multiple-token*, *single-token*, and *single-message* operations. For multiple-token operation, the transmitting station generates a new free token and places it immediately after the last bit of a transmitted message. Therefore, for a long ring, the chances are that there are several message frames and a free token frame on the ring at one time. For single-token operation, a new free token is generated by erasing the busy token bit in the header of a transmitted message when it returns. If a message is long, the transmitting station will receive the busy token before it has finished transmitting. In this case, a free token is generated only after the last bit of a message has been transmitted, as in the multiple-token operation. For single-message operation, a new free token is generated only after the last bit of the transmitted message has been erased. Both single-token and single-message operations ensure that there is at most one free or busy token on the ring at all times.

Let us proceed to the performance modeling of a token ring network, following Hammond and O'Reilly [7, sec. 8.2]. We assume that N stations are connected to a ring, and that the arrival process at each station is a Poisson process with a rate of λ messages/sec. Let $\overline{X}$ and $\overline{X^2}$ be the mean and the second moment of the message length in bits, and S the ring speed in bits/sec. Since bits are processed serially at each station interface, a delay called the *station latency* is needed for the output to be passed on to the ring. The station latency is at least one bit and can range up to a dozen bits, depending on the control feature; it is denoted by B bits. Finally, let τ (sec) be the propagation time for the ring. If l (kilometers) is the length of the ring, a good estimate of τ is given by

$$\tau = l \times 5 \times 10^{-6} \text{ sec}$$

on the assumption that the signal propagates at two-thirds of the speed of light. The time for the circulation of a token is then given by

$$R = \tau + \frac{NB}{S}.$$

As a performance measure, let us consider the mean time T_f from the instant at which a message arrives at a transmitting station to the instant that it is received at a destination station. If we assume that destination stations are uniformly distributed over the ring, the mean propagation time from a transmitting station to a destination station is given by $R/2$. Since there are no simple results available for a polling model with a time-limited service rule as in the ANSI/IEEE 802.5 Standard, we will instead use W for the exhaustive service polling system given in Section 2.2 to compute the mean time from the arrival to the transmission start of a message. Hence the mean message transfer time is given by

$$T_f = \frac{\overline{X}}{S} + \frac{R}{2} + \frac{N\lambda b^{(2)}}{2(1-\rho)} + \frac{R(1-\rho/N)}{2(1-\rho)},$$

where $\rho = N\lambda b$, and b and $b^{(2)}$ are determined according to the free-token generation policies discussed above. When this formula is applied to multiple-token operation we use

$$b = \frac{\overline{X}}{S} \quad ; \quad b^{(2)} = \frac{\overline{X^2}}{S^2}.$$

For single-token operation, we have

$$b = R + \frac{1}{S}\int_{SR}^{\infty} [1 - B(x)]dx \quad ; \quad b^{(2)} = R^2 + \frac{2}{S^2}\int_{SR}^{\infty} x[1 - B(x)]dx,$$

where $B(x)$ is the probability distribution function of the message length X. For single-message operation, we have

$$b = \frac{\overline{X}}{S} + R \quad ; \quad b^{(2)} = \frac{\overline{X^2}}{S^2} + \frac{2\overline{X}R}{S} + R^2.$$

Substituting these into T_f, we get

$$T_f(\text{single-message}) > T_f(\text{multiple-token}),$$
$$T_f(\text{single-message}) > T_f(\text{single-token}).$$

For numerical comparison of the mean transfer times for the three operations, we assume a constant message length and consider the normalized mean transfer time given by

$$\frac{T_f}{\overline{X}/S} = 1 + \frac{a}{2} + \frac{\rho b}{2(1-\rho)(\overline{X}/S)} + \frac{a(1-\rho/N)}{2(1-\rho)},$$

where $a := RS/\overline{X}$ and

$$\frac{b}{\overline{X}/S} = \begin{cases} 1 & \text{multiple-token} \\ \max[a,1] & \text{single-token} \\ 1+a & \text{single-message} \end{cases}$$

In Fig. 9, we plot the normalized mean transfer time $T_f/(\overline{X}/S)$ against the throughput $\gamma = N\lambda\overline{X}/S$ of the system for the three operations; therefore $\rho = N\lambda b = \gamma \times b/(\overline{X}/S)$. Here we assume that

$N = 50$ stations ; $S = 4$ megabits/sec ; $B = 1$ bit latency per station.

In the first case, we assume that $l = 1$ kilometer and $X = 1{,}000$ bits, which results in $\tau = 5$ microsec, $R = 17.5$ microsec, and $a = 0.07$. In the second case, we assume that $l = 10$ kilometers and $X = 100$ bits, which results in $\tau = 50$ microsec, $R = 62.5$ microsec, and $a = 2.5$. The difference in performance of the three operations is clearly shown in Fig. 9.

4 A Survey of Surveys

Until a few years ago I maintained a fairly complete (neither classified nor annotated) bibliography on polling models; it can be found at http://www.sk.tsukuba.ac.jp/~takagi/polling.html. (This does not mean that I have the hardcopy of all the publications in the list. So please do not order copies from me. But I welcome the correcting and updating of the information.) The bibliography contained over 700 publications, including journal and conference papers, books, theses, and technical reports. Since publications on polling continue to appear (although not at as high a pace as in the years around 1990), the number by now may total nearly 1,000.

When I began searching the literature on the analysis of polling models because I needed it for the performance evaluation of the token ring network in the early 1980s, I found that such models had been studied seemingly independently by researchers in different fields. I was fortunate in organizing all the results available at that time in a unified framework into a research monograph

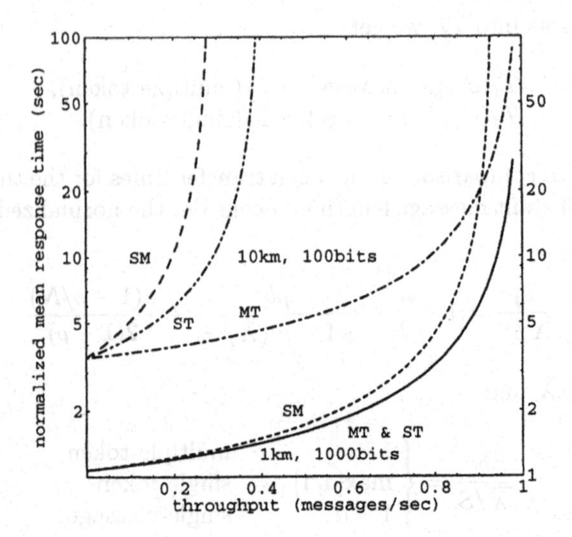

Fig. 9. Normalized mean transfer time in token ring networks

Analysis of Polling Systems published by the MIT Press in 1986 [17] and a survey paper "Queuing analysis of polling models" in the *ACM Computing Surveys* in 1988 [18]. Since then I have twice updated my survey to include subsequent developments: [19] covers the period until 1989 and [21] for 1990–1994. I also surveyed the applications to computer networks in [20].

Other researchers have also contributed surveys of polling models based on their own views. Let me mention some of them that have appeared after 1990. Grillo (1990) presents a classification of various polling models with an emphasis on communications [6]. Levy and Sidi (1990) summarize the analysis of polling models with variations, and describe the capabilities and limitations in their applications [12]. Rubin and Baker (1990) refer to both single and infinite buffer polling systems in their comprehensive review of media access control protocols for high-speed local area and metropolitan area communication networks [13]. Conti et al. (1993) show how single and infinite buffer polling systems with limited service rule have been used to model the Fiber Distributed Data Interface (FDDI) [4]. Boxma (1991) addresses static optimization problems with respect to server movement in polling systems [2]. Campbell (1991) demonstrates the difference between two "cyclical" queueing systems; one is the cycling server model (i.e., a polling system) and the other is the cycling customer model (i.e., a closed queueing network) [3]. Gupta and Günalay (1997) review the recent advances in the analysis of polling models in which the server uses system-state information to affect its behavior [5].

Polling models have been a part of many survey papers and books on the performance evaluation of communication networks. One such early survey is by Kobayashi and Konheim (1977) [10], and a more recent one is Kleinrock (1988)

[9]. Relevant books are Akimaru and Kawashima [1], Hammond and O'Reilly [7], Hayes [8], Schwartz [14], and Stuck and Arthurs [15].

5 Future Directions

Let me conclude this essay with some personal views on possible future research directions. The analysis of polling models gained momentum as queueing systems that are easy to understand, analyze, and extend. The study has been accelerated largely by applications to the modeling of communication, manufacturing and transportation systems. I believe that it is one of the few successful theoretical performance evaluation models developed in the last decades.

There still remain many unsolved mathematical problems in basic polling systems, such as stability conditions for multiple queues and the exact analysis of systems with limited service rules. Recent theoretical developments can be found in a special issue (Vol. 11, No. 1–2, 1992) of the *Queueing Systems* journal and in Volume 35 of *Annals of Operations Research* (1992). From the application viewpoint, one of the major directions of interest is the dynamic control and optimization of the server movement/action. Channel access protocols with polling schemes continue to appear; e.g., IEEE 802.12 100VG-Any LAN (demand priority) and IEEE 1394 arbitration. Approximate analysis of polling systems with multiple servers would also be of interest.

Acknowledgements

The author would like to thank Professor Robert B. Cooper of Florida Atlantic University, Dr. H. Richard Gail of IBM Thomas J. Watson Research Center, and Dr. Robert D. van der Mei of AT&T Labs for valuable comments on the draft of this article.

References

1. Akimaru, H., and Kawashima, K. *Teletraffic: Theory and Applications*, Springer-Verlag, Heidelberg, 1993.
2. Boxma, O. J., Analysis and optimization of polling systems. In: *Queueing, Performance and Control in ATM (ITC-13)*, J. W. Cohen and C. D. Pack (editors), pp.173–183, Elsevier Science Publishers B.V. (North-Holland), Amsterdam, 1991.
3. Campbell, G. M., Cyclic queueing systems. *European Journal of Operational Research*, Vol.51, No.2, pp.155–167, March 1991.
4. Conti, M., Gregori, E., and Lenzini, L., Metropolitan area networks (MANs): protocols, modeling and performance evaluation. In: *Performance Evaluation of Computer and Communication Systems, Joint Tutorial Papers of Performance '93 and Sigmetrics '93*, L. Donatiello and R. Nelson (editors), pp.81–120, Lecture Notes in Computer Science 729, Springer-Verlag, Berlin, 1993.
5. Gupta, D., and Günalay, Y., Recent advances in the analysis of polling systems. In: *Advances in Combinatorial Methods and Applications to Probability and Statistics*, N. Balakrishnan (editor), pp.339–360, Birkhäuser Boston, 1997.

6. Grillo, D., Polling mechanism models in communication systems – some application examples. In: *Stochastic Analysis of Computer and Communication Systems*, H. Takagi (editor), pp.659–698, Elsevier Science Publishers B. V. (North-Holland), Amsterdam, 1990.
7. Hammond, J. L., and O'Reilly, P. J. P., *Performance Analysis of Local Computer Networks.* Addison-Wesley Publishing Company, Reading, Massachusetts, 1986.
8. Hayes, J. F., *Modeling and Analysis of Computer Communications Networks.* Plenum Press, New York, 1984.
9. Kleinrock, L., Performance evaluation of distributed computer-communication systems. In: *Queueing Theory and Its Applications – Liber Amicorum for J. W. Cohen*, O. J. Boxma and R. Syski (editors), pp.1–57, Elsevier Science Publishers B.V. (North-Holland), Amsterdam, 1988.
10. Kobayashi, H., and Konheim, A. G., Queueing models for computer communications system analysis. *IEEE Transactions on Communications*, Vol.COM-25, No.1, pp.2–29, January 1977.
11. Leibowitz, M. A., Queues. *Scientific American*, Vol.219, No.2, pp.96–103, August 1968.
12. Levy, H., and Sidi, M., Polling systems: applications, modeling, and optimization. *IEEE Transactions on Communications*, Vol.38, No.10, pp.1750–1760, October 1990.
13. Rubin, I., and Baker, J. E., Media access control for high-speed local area and metropolitan area communication networks. *Proceedings of the IEEE*, Vol.78, No.1, pp.168–203, January 1990.
14. Schwartz, M., *Telecommunication Networks: Protocols, Modeling and Analysis.* Addison-Wesley Publishing Company, Reading, Massachusetts, 1987.
15. Stuck, B. W., and Arthurs, E., *A Computer and Communications Network Performance Analysis Primer.* Prentice-Hall, Englewood Cliffs, New Jersey, 1985.
16. Sykes, J. S., Analysis of the communications aspects of an inquiry-response system. *AFIPS Conference Proceedings, 1969 Fall Joint Computer Conference*, Vol.35, pp.655–667, Las Vegas, Nevada, November 18–20, 1969.
17. Takagi, H., *Analysis of Polling Systems.* The MIT Press, Cambridge, Massachusetts, 1986.
18. Takagi, H., Queuing analysis of polling models. *ACM Computing Surveys*, Vol.20, No.1, pp.5–28, March 1988.
19. Takagi, H., Queueing analysis of polling models: an update. In: *Stochastic Analysis of Computer and Communication Systems*, H. Takagi (editor), pp.267-318, Elsevier Science Publishers B. V. (North-Holland), Amsterdam, 1990.
20. Takagi, H., Application of polling models to computer networks. *Computer Networks and ISDN Systems*, Vol.22, No.3, pp.193–211, October 1991.
21. Takagi, H., Queueing analysis of polling models: progress in 1990–1994. In: *Frontiers in Queueing: Models and Applications in Science and Technology*, J. H. Dshalalow (editor), pp.119–146 (Chapter 5), CRC Press, Boca Raton, Florida, 1997.

Discrete-Event Simulation in Performance Evaluation

David M. Nicol

Dartmouth College
Hanover NH 03755, USA,
nicol@cs.dartmouth.edu

1 Introduction

Simulation is a computational paradigm used to enable a computer program to emulate the behavior of certain types of physical models. Simulation and computation go hand-in-hand to the earliest days of digital computers. A principle war-time motivation for developing digital computers in the 1940's was to make possible the simulation of fired projectiles, to aid in the publication of aiming tables on U.S. Navy vessels. Simulations like these are now called *continuous* simulations, because the essential state of the model changes continuously in time, e.g., the position, direction, and velocity of a projectile. Time-dependent differential equations are used to describe the rules for model state-evolution, and the simulation is essentially the numerical solution of those equations. Numerical solution means that time is discretized, the rules for state evolution are similarly discretized in time, and the entire state of the model is computed at each discretized time as a function of the model state at the previous time-step and the state-evolution rules.

Shortly after digital computers came into use, another type type of simulation emerged, for *discrete* models. Here the essential model state does not change continuously, but instead at irregular epochs. Furthermore, when the state changes, only small pieces of it typically change. In a network of queues for example, the essential queue state is the number of jobs present (including any in service). A queue state changes with an arrival or departure, at times that may be driven by pseudo-random number generation. The model state is a vector of queue states; when this vector changes, only one or two of its components change. The state evolution rules for a discrete-event model are not usually tied to differential equations, and in principle can be anything at all.

Simulation of discrete models can be organized to focus all of the computational effort on where the model state changes, at only those epochs where it changes. An "event" is a description of a point in time where the model state changes, hence the term discrete-event simulation, or DES. A discrete-event simulation can be conducted using a priority data structure called an event list. The simulation executes a loop whose body removes the event with least time-stamp from the event list and performs the model state modification computation the event describes. Execution of the event may cause generation of other events in

G. Haring et al. (Eds.): Performance Evaluation, LNCS 1769, pp. 443–457, 2000.

the future; part of the job of executing the event is inserting newly generated events into the event list. After executing the last event with time-stamp t (it is possible there may be multiple such), the data structures encoding the model reflect the state at time t.

Instances of discrete-event simulation are known to have been developed in the late 1950's. A survey on programming languages for discrete-event simulation [8] reports that Tocher's General Simulation Program (GSP) was used to analyze steel mill operations, that discrete-event simulation was used to study job-shop scheduling at General Electric, and was used at UCLA in the late 50's by Jackson.

Since the early days, DES methodology has become widely used in academic research, in government planning, and in commercial enterprises. The key areas of development have been in simulation language design, in statistical analysis of simulation output, in pseudo-random number generation, and in various means of reducing simulation time. We'll talk more about this later.

2 Problem Definition

Performance analysis of a system usually involves construction of a model which shapes stochastic input (e.g., arrival processes and service times) into stochastic output (e.g., response time, distribution of buffer lengths). When the model is mathematically tractable, the stochastic output of interest can be expressed symbolically, either in closed form or in a form suitable for numerical computation.

Simulation is most useful in stochastic performance analysis when the model of interest is not mathematically tractable. Instead of using mathematics to express how stochastic input is molded into stochastic output, we (i) *generate* samples of that stochastic input using pseudo-random number generators, (ii) execute program fragments to *compute* how the model molds input, and (iii) *estimate* the stochastic output of interest, using statistical techniques. These three functions identify the core problems associated with using DES. We consider each of them in turn.

2.1 Random Number Generation

Imagine a simulation model of a queue, where the arrivals to the queue are to form a Poisson process. Operationally this means that if we were to observe a long sequence of inter-arrival times, that sequence should have two properties. First, we require that the samples be consistent with the exponential distribution, as might be established by plotting the samples on a histogram. Second, we require that the sequence show no signs of statistical correlation, we want the samples to be be statistically independent.

The first requirement turns out to be easier than the second. With just a little bit of computation one can transform a random number sampled uniformly from [0, 1] into a random sample from any other distribution (at least in principle, sometimes computational issues interfere). If random variable X has cumulative distribution function F, with inverse function F^{-1}, one generates a sample of X by generating a uniform sample $u \in [0, 1]$, and computing $F^{-1}(u)$. This is called the *inverse transform method.* Therefore, to generate a sequence of independent identically distributed samples from distribution F, we need only generate a sequence of independent samples of the uniform $[0, 1]$ distribution U.

It's not hard to generate a sequence of samples from U. The usual approach is to construct a sequence generator, that given an integer "seed" value x_n, produces the next sequence value x_{n+1}. The x_i's typically range from 1 to $2^p - 1$ (with p as large as possible); in the most useful sequences each value x_i appears exactly as often as any other, and the sequence does not repeat itself for a very long time. To get the next random number, one just generates the next element in the sequence, and divides it by $2^p - 1$.

We're left now with the hard bit—constructing that sequence so that the random numbers derived from it appear to be statistically independent. This is where deep number theory gets involved, and where the effort of research in random number generation is focused. Another related hard bit is constructing sets of sequences where, not only are individual samples from within the sequence statistically independent, but the sequences themselves are statistically independent. A good place to start to learn about this type of work is the ACM TOMACS special issue on random number generation [4].

2.2 Model Expression

The most basic way of expressing a model is in terms of actions to take when events occur. The actions react to the events that cause them and the model state at the time they execute; the actions modify the model state and may schedule future events. While every discrete event simulator works this way at some level or other, we'll see that it is a primitive way of asking a modeler to describe behavior.

The data structure describing an event includes an event "type", some location information, a time-stamp, and possibly other information. There is usually an action subroutine associated with each event type. That subroutine modifies the model state, and may schedule a future event. Consider the mechanics of simulating a queue. We'll need an arrival process, so one event type will be **arrival**. We'll need a departure process, so another type will be **departure**. To start the simulation we'll sample an inter-arrival time, and schedule an **arrival** event at that time. The code handling an **arrival** event first increments the queue length variable, and then determines whether the server is busy. If not, it samples a service time, adds that to the time-stamp of the arrival to create a departure time, and schedules a **departure** event at the departure time. Then, regardless of whether the server was busy, it samples an inter-arrival time, adds that to the time of the **arrival** event and re-schedules the **arrival** to occur again in the future. The action associated with a **departure** event decrements the queue length variable, and tests its new value. If non-zero, then another job is awaiting service and so a service time is sampled, added to the current event's time, and another **departure** event is scheduled in the future.

The description above should convince you that breaking down a model's behavior into events has the potential for complexity even in the simplest case; the complexity grows as one considers larger models (e.g. a network of queues) and more complex interactions between model elements. The problem areas related to model expression are in controlling the complexity, and making the model behavior understandable from the code that expresses it.

2.3 Analysis of Output

Statistical methods are needed to analyze the output of stochastically driven simulations, but they must be applied carefully. This can be illustrated by example. Imagine that the objective of a simulation is to estimate the steady-state probability of a buffer overflowing when a packet arrives. This immediately raises an issue: how long should the simulation be run to bring the the model behavior into the equilibrium state? If the simulation is started in a state where the buffer is empty, but under normal operating conditions has 4-6 packets buffered, then clearly the simulation needs to be run for a while to get it into the equilibrium state before beginning to measure. This is called "burning off the transient".

Another problem is that traditional statistical analysis assumes that the samples analyzed are statistically independent. In simulations that is frequently not the case. For instance, if one wishes to estimate the mean queue length at a server, one could divide simulation time into periods of length Δ, and define sample X_i to be the time-averaged queue length over $i\Delta$ to $(i+1)\Delta$. It is clearly possible for X_i and X_{i+1} to be correlated—if the average queue length is large over one time period, there is increased likelihood that the average queue length is large in an adjacent time period. This can be insidious, because if the correlation is positive, then statistical measures of variation which assume independence will be lower than they should be, giving overly tight confidence intervals.

In discrete-event simulation, particular ways of approaching statistical analysis are called for.

2.4 Model Execution

Problems with model execution occur if the results are not computed in a timely fashion, or if the memory available for the simulation is insufficient.

Problems with solution speed can arise in a number of ways. One way is when independent replications are used to estimate the probability of a rare event. This is easy to see from the equation for a confidence interval. If $\hat{p}$ is the statistical estimate of the probability taken from N samples and $\hat{\sigma}$ is the measured standard deviation, then the width of the confidence interval is proportional to $\hat{\sigma}/\sqrt{N}$. If the estimated quantity is of order 10^{-s}, then $\hat{\sigma}$ works out to be of the order $10^{-s/2}$. If N is order 10^n, then the ratio $\hat{\sigma}/\hat{p}$ is of the order $10^{(s-n)/2}$. This ratio gives the number of digits of precision in the estimate $\hat{p}$. That is, if the confidence interval around $\hat{p}$ is one-tenth the magnitude of $\hat{p}$, then we take the first non-zero digit of $\hat{p}$ as significant. Observe then that to get just one digit of precision we need $n \geq s+2$. Concretely, to estimate a quantity of the order 10^{-5}

with one digit of precision requires on the order of 10^7 independent replications. Each decrease in the order of magnitude of $\hat{p}$ or increase in the desired number of digits of accuracy adds *two* orders of magnitude to the needed number of replications. It is easy to get into a performance corner when using simulation to estimate small probabilities.

Another way solution speed can be too slow is if the model requires a very long time to burn off its transient. Still another is if the model needs to run in real time, or faster than real time, e.g., when using in a real-time planning environment.

Sheer model size can cause problems. For example, in one of my research projects we're simulating very large network models. State information needs to be stored for each of tens or hundreds of thousands of routers, hosts, links. Once all this state becomes too large to be retained in a computer's memory, it starts to be swapped in and out on demand through the virtual memory system. But this is disastrous to performance because simulations don't have the locality of reference needed to amortize the cost of disk activity.

There clearly are issues to be considered when performance of model execution is of concern.

3 Key Solution Ideas

3.1 Model Expression

To use DES one must choose how to express the model. Options range from expressing it in an ordinary programming language with no built-in support, to expressing it in an ordinary programming language that uses a pre-built library and run-time system, to expressing it in a unique simulation language. To use an ordinary programming language is to gain flexibility of expression and execution speed, but it also requires the modeler to build up all infrastructure (e.g., event-list code, output statistics) from scratch. To use a simulation language is to gain access to a great deal of pre-defined structure, but usually at the expense of flexibility in model expression. Simulation languages provide their own conceptual framework, their own definitions of modeling elements, their own notions of model control flow. One language might target Petri nets, another might target job-shop scheduling, another might target computer systems. It is not unusual to find that a simulation language cannot easily deal with some unique aspect of a desired model. Nor is it unusual to find that features of a simulation language considerably affect the execution speed of the simulation. Two cases in point bear consideration. Many commercial network simulators allow models to be built on a screen, graphically, connecting pre-defined model elements (some sort of box) with lines or arrows. If the model structure is not compiled before run-time then it has to be interpreted at run-time, and that can be slow. Another source of performance degradation is so-called "process-orientation". Process oriented simulation languages allow one to describe a model in terms of the interactions of independent threads of control. A classic example is the process-oriented expression of a queue. The code is written from the point of view of a job—the process. See the C++ code fragment below.

```
void job() {
  srvr->acquire();          // acquire server
  hold(Erlang(5,2);         // service distribution is Erlang
  srvr->release();          // let go of server
}
```

Execution starts with the arrival of the job at some queue. The server object (`srvr`) has a method, `acquire`, that the job calls to express its intent to acquire service. The implementation of `acquire` checks to see if service can be immediately granted. If not, the thread running this code is suspended, and resumes only when the server is allocated to this job. When execution returns to the line following the acquire attempt, the job has the server; the effects of suspension are not detectable source code text. The job then models the service time by calling another library routine, `hold`, to explicitly suspend the process for the sampled service time. When control is returned from that call, the job releases the server and exits.

A process-oriented view raises the level of abstraction in model expression. To accomplish the same functionality in an event oriented simulation requires code something like that shown below.

```
void arrive() {
  srvr->inQueue++;
  if(srvr->inQueue > 1)
    return;

  double service = Erlang(5,2);
  schedule(serveEnd,service);
}
```

```
void serveEnd() {
  srvr->inQueue--;
  if(srvr->inQueue) {
   double service =
     Erlang(5,2);
   schedule(serveEnd,service);
  }}
```

Here `schedule` is a library routine that schedules the execution of a named code body, after `service` units of simulation time have passed. The mechanism that schedules job arrives is not shown here (it would be an arrival handling routine that calls `arrive` and schedules another arrival). Ultimately, a process-oriented simulator will execute something like the code above to implement the process-oriented view, the payoff is that the modeler does not have to provide the entire mechanism. The trade-off is that process-orientation exacts a performance cost, due to inescapable overhead in performing context switches. The smaller the "grain" of computation is per process activation, the larger the impact that overhead will have. It is not uncommon to see factors of 2-10 difference between process oriented models, and event-oriented models. As process orientation takes pretty delicate programming to implement, models done entirely in a native programming language are usually event-oriented.

One of areas that has a great deal of impact on simulation model expression is object-oriented programming. The first simulation language, SIMULA (developed in the 1960s) was object oriented before anyone knew what that would come to mean. Simulations are natural targets for object oriented programming, because physical systems are full of objects! The object orientation of C++ has been exploited in many simulation systems.

Another way in which the complexity of building simulation models is reduced, is to build simulation systems for specific modeling classes. A good example of this is Petri-nets. Petri net semantics are well-understood to the degree that they can reasonably be embedded in a specialized simulation framework. A modeler's job is reduced considerably, perhaps to the point of only needing to specify the model structure. In addition, where the formal system being simulated has structure, that structure can sometimes be exploited to accelerate the simulation in ways that a naive modeler would not know to do, or expend the effort to do. For instance, when a transition fires and deposits tokens in output places, a naive implementation will check the firability of all transitions for which the affected places are inplaces. In doing so it may end up checking the same transition multiple times, it may end up checking transitions that cannot possibly be firable as a result. Sophisticated pre-analysis of Petri net structure and properties can be used to minimize the computational effort associated with checking the effects of firing a transition. This sort of tailoring a simulation system to model class specifics abounds, in no small part because it is effective in reducing modeling effort.

3.2 Analysis of Output

Entire books have been written on how to analyze simulation output; good sources of a full explanation are [2,7,3]. All we can hope to do here is sketch a key approach to estimation that arises in the steady-state analysis that so permeates performance analysis.

The simulation will make observations $Y_1, Y_2, ...Y_n$ of some random value of interest; we're interested in estimating the mean of that value, with a confidence interval. As noted before, there are two difficulties to deal with. First, the simulation state at the beginning of the run is unlikely to reflect its steady-state behavior. Second, the values Y_i are correlated with each other, a fact that confounds ordinary ways of estimating variance.

Consider first the context where we replicate the simulation, independently, r times. We can then refer to an observation $Y_{i,j}$ in terms of its replication number i and its position j within the sequence of observations defining replication i. To help identify startup bias, we compute the mean $\hat{Y}_{\cdot,j}$ of the jth observation, across replications. The set of observations $Y_{1,j}, \cdots, Y_{r,j}$ are all independent, so it is meaningful to compute a confidence interval around $\hat{Y}_{\cdot,j}$ to assess its accuracy. We can then plot $\hat{Y}_{\cdot,j}$ (and its interval) as a function of j. Graphical examination will generally reveal how values early in the plot differ from later values; after some point in the sequence, the plots tend to hover around some common mean, whereas early in the sequence they do not. To eliminate the startup bias analysts then find the earliest sequence number k after which behavior seems to have settled, and discard the first $k-1$ observations. A rule of thumb is to be sure that you have at least 10 times as many replications left as those you discard. Of course, this should be viewed as a constraint on the total number of observations gathered, not a constraint on the number of observations that are discarded.

We are left still with the problem of correlation between successive observations in a replication, but this turns out to be a non-issue when we have independent replications. If we have indeed eliminated the startup bias, then within a replication the average of the last $n-k$ observations, $\hat{Y}_i$ is an unbiased estimator of the sought mean. This follows immediately from the additive property of means: no matter how hopelessly correlated, the mean of the sum of two random variables is the sum of their means. Thus ordinary statistical analysis can applied to the data set $\hat{Y}_1, \hat{Y}_2, \ldots, \hat{Y}_r$.

One of the drawbacks of independent replications is that computational effort is needed to push the model into steady-state, for every replication. There are frequently other model startup costs that are suffered on each replication, e.g., just loading a large model. For these reasons analysts may run a single replication, for a long time, and make estimates based on observations from that single replication. The basic technique is to group observations into "batchs" of some size N. That is, the first N observations are lumped into one batch, the next N observations are lumped into one batch, and so on. The mean value of each batch is computed; that mean, say B_i for the ith batch, is an "observation". The intuition is that if N is large, then the observations B_i will be approximately independent of each other. We can check this by computing the lag-1 autocorrelation coefficient of the batch means; if nearly zero then it is safe to assume independence.

Two rules of thumb have been offered concerning batch means. One rule is that the number of batches should be at least 10, and no more than 30. On a very long run, the initialization bias is presumed to be burned off within the first batch, so much so that its contribution to the batch mean is negligible. However, 30 values are really too few to accurately compute the lag-1 autocorrelations. *That* calculation should be done on data sets of size 100-400. This can be accomplished by partitioning each batch into sub-batches. If no correlation is observed on the smaller batch means, no correlation will be present on the larger batch means.

3.3 Model Execution

We earlier identified two specific problems that can arise hindering model execution, and now consider approaches that have been considered.

Importance Sampling The problem of estimating small quantities is that the variance of the estimation procedure is so much larger than the quantity itself. There is a whole field of study into ways of reducing this variance, *importance sampling* is one that can, in certain cases, offer remarkable reductions in variance and in computational effort needed to compute a desired degree of accuracy.

The fundamental idea behind importance sampling is to simulate a different system than the one of interest, one in which the low probability event has considerably higher probability. A mathematical link exists between the simulated system and the system of interest that allows one to transform measurements in one system into statements about the other.

The mechanics of importance sampling are best expressed in terms of a simple equation. Let X be a continuous random variable, whose mean we wish to estimate through sampling. Let $f(x)$ be the density function for X, and let $g(x)$ be some other density function with the property that for any x_0 such that $f(x_0) \neq 0$, then $g(x_0) \neq 0$. We can write

$$E[X] = \int_{-\infty}^{+\infty} x\ f(x)\ dx = \int_{-\infty}^{+\infty} x\ L(x)\ g(x)\ dx$$

where the likelihood function $L(x) = f(x)/g(x)$. The normal way of estimating $E[X]$ through sampling is to generate samples $x_1, x_2, \ldots, x_n$ using probability law $f(x)$, and estimate $E[X] \approx \hat{\mu} = (1/n)\sum_{i=1}^{n} x_i$. Using the equation above we see that it is equally valid to estimate $E[X]$ by sampling n times in accordance with probability law $g(x)$, and for each sample x_i, compute $x_i L(x_i)$. $E[X]$ is then estimated as $E[X] \approx \hat{\mu} = (1/n)\sum_{i=1}^{n}(x_i L(x_i))$.

Now to see at least the *potential* for variance reduction, imagine sampling using the probability law $g(x) = (xf(x))/E[X]$. This yields likelihood function $L(x) = E[X]/x$, so that every sample of $x_i L(x_i)$ is the constant $E[X]$, a perfect estimator with no variance! Of course, there is no point in sampling if $E[X]$ is already known, but the example does highlight the general strategy one adopts in selecting the sampling law $g(x)$. Go fishing where the fish are found. To wit, $g(x)$ should focus most of its probability on x's where $xf(x)$ tends to be largest, for this is where $E[X]$ gets most of its value.

Having said all that, even if we don't presume to know $E[X]$, we're likely to be doing the simulation because we don't know $f(x)$ either, at least not explicitly. But the intuition is clear, focus sampling on system states where the events of interest happen frequently enough.

While importance sampling can yield truly remarkable reduction in the computational effort required for accurate estimation, it has the serious disadvantage that if you don't do it properly, you can get very bad estimates, with no hints at all from the sampling data that something is amiss. The only safe way to perform importance sampling is in a context where the model of interest has sufficient structure so that one can prove theorems about the effectiveness of sampling strategies. To date only relatively simple systems have yielded to this sort of analysis.

Importance sampling is a fascinating blend of mathematics and practical results; the interested reader can learn more about this in [6].

Parallel Simulation An orthogonal way of accelerating model execution is by using multiple computers, concurrently. The most obvious way to do this is to run independent replications concurrently. When it works, there is no substitute for this approach. Nevertheless, there are limitations. The stopping criteria has to be absolutely independent of the behavior of the simulation. For instance, it would not do to launch 100 independent replications, and then build an estimate using the first 25 of these to finish. Execution behavior correlates with stochastic behavior; the estimator constructed in this way would be biased. A second limitation is that the accuracy of the estimator increases only in the square root of the number of replications used, this is a law of rapidly diminishing returns in variance reduction. If one has available 100 processors, it may not be an efficient use of those resources to run 100 replications when only 10 replications gives only one digit less of significance. Finally, as we saw earlier, sampling taken from a single long run can be more efficient than sampling from multiple independent runs, because the effort of burning off the transient is suffered only once.

Things get interesting when one looks to use multiple computers simultaneously on the same replication. Early on it was recognized that synchronization between processors would be a key problem. Here's why. Think of a parallel simulation as one where a number of different serial simulations are working together on different pieces of the same overall model. For example, a large queueing network can be decomposed into subnetworks, and different subnetworks be run on different processors. On occasion a job will move from the subnet managed by one processor into a subnet managed by another. Ordinary simulators execute their events in monotone non-decreasing time-stamp order, and there's the rub: if one processor can generate an event for another processor's event-list, then we need to be concerned that when it does so, the targeted processor has not already advanced in simulation time past the time-stamp on the arriving job.

Two fundamentally different types of approaches have been explored to deal with synchronization. Optimistic approaches work by having simulators save trails of state-information as they execute, to support rolling the computation back to a prior point in simulation time. One processor may give another processor an event, at any point. If that event happens to have a time-stamp placing it in the simulation past of the targeted processor, that processor is able to rollback to the time of the late message and compute forward again. It needs also to undo interactions it has had in the false future where it speculatively executed. It can do this by the simple mechanism of sending an "anti-message" chasing every ordinary message it sent in the speculative future. Not only does the anti-message cancel the original message, it can serve to rollback the recipient (if the recipient has not already been rolled back through other means). This in turn can trigger other rollbacks, with more anti-messages, and so on.

Optimistic approaches offer the attraction of finding parallelism automatically. The flip side is that they require the extra effort of saving state information, doing garbage collection, and undoing falsely executed interactions. They require a lot of delicate programming to get right, both in the simulation system and the model. They are harder to debug than normal parallel programs because you can never tell whether execution of a routine is speculative and may be undone, or will actually "take". Current optimistic simulators are principally event-oriented, as the additional difficulties of implementing process-orientation in a state-saving environment are significant. One is more likely to use an optimistically synchronizing *system*, than write an optimistically synchronizing one-shot simulation from scratch (although I've done this a couple of times for limited variants of optimistism).

The "conservative" approach to synchronization works to prevent a processor from receiving a event in its simulation past. In other words, every processor executes its events in monotone non-decreasing time-stamp order. To ensure this it may be required to prevent a processor from executing at all, for a time. The key to success in a conservative protocol is finding *lookahead* in the model. This means partitioning the model into submodels such that there is a predictable lag between when an event is executed on one submodel, and when it can cause an event in another submodel. Lookahead is very model-specific, as can be seen in the example of a queueing network. Let $Q1$ be a FCFS queue with service times that are stochastically sampled independent of anything else in the model (e.g. just sampling from any probability distribution), and suppose jobs leaving $Q1$ are routed to $Q2$. With a little bit of effort, at any time t it is possible for $Q1$ to predict a lower bound on the time when next it routes a job to $Q2$. For example, $Q1$ can pre-sample service times for jobs before they ever arrive. Even if $Q1$ is empty at time t, it knows that if the next service requirement is s, then it will not direct a job to $Q2$ before time $t+s$. Lookahead of this type gives $Q2$ leave to simulate as far as $t+s$ without being concerned about receiving jobs in its past from $Q1$.

The attraction of conservative synchronization is that it avoids the complexity and overhead of optimistic synchronization. However, the key drawbacks are that lookahead is model specific, and if insufficient, can lead to onerous overheads of its own. Returning to the queueing network example, imagine that a job's service requirement at $Q1$ is carried along with the job, negating the lookahead achieved by pre-sampling service times. Lookahead might still be extractable, but it will be more costly to do so, and will be intimately tied to the model structure. Likewise, if $Q1$ is not FCFS but is shortest-job-first-preemptive-resume, the power of pre-sampling is somewhat lessened. No matter if $Q1$ has presampled N service times and identified the least one of these among them, without further coordination among queues it has to assume that $N+1$ jobs could arrive in an arbitrarily short period of time and the last of these would have the least service time. Lookahead could still be possible if every sample from the service time distribution can always be bounded from below by some $\epsilon > 0$, but aside from this, lookahead is problematic.

Both optimistic and conservative techniques have proven their mettle in substantive applications. A good survey of basic techniques in parallel simulation is [5].

It happens that in a broad class of performance models it is possible to find lookahead by appealing to the mathematical structure of the model. We explore this aspect next.

A number of performance models can be viewed as continuous-time Markov chains that arise from some topological model, like a queuing network or a Petri net. In a parallel context the usual approach is to partition the topological domain—create subnets—and distribute those among processors. When the overall model is a continuous-time Markov chain, then this partitioning creates a number of interacting continuous-time Markov chains (CTMC). Each submodel is a CTMC in its own right, with the additional property that a transition can be triggered from outside of it, e.g., the movement of a job from one submodel to another. One can view the stochastic process of actions taken by one submodel affecting another mathematically. The periods in time when one submodel affects another is a *non-homogeneous* Poisson process. In an ordinary Poisson process, events are emitted with constant rate, say λ, which means that the spacing between successive events is exponentially distributed with mean $1/\lambda$. Mathematically it means that the instantaneous rate of generating an event, at any time t, is λ. A non-homogeneous Poisson process is a generalization which makes the rate parameter dependent on time; the instantaneous rate of generating an event at time t is $\lambda(t)$. To see how this factors into the discussion at hand, let's return to the $Q1-Q2$ framework. If $Q1$'s service distribution is exponential with rate μ, then if at time t there is a job in service, the rate at which $Q1$ sends jobs to $Q2$ is μ. However, if $Q1$ is idle at time t, then the rate at which it sends jobs to $Q2$ is zero. Thus we see that $\lambda(t)$ varies between μ and 0, depending on the state of $Q1$ at time t. This is a non-homogeneous Poisson process whose rate function depends on the simulation state.

It is possible to capitalize on this structure, by taking advantage of a particular way of sampling non-homogeneous Poisson processes. For, suppose we can find an upper bound $\lambda_{\max}$ so that $\lambda(t) \le \lambda_{\max}$ for all t. One can sample events from the stochastic process by a technique called uniformization. Sampling is done in two steps. First, events are sampled from a homogeneous Poisson process with rate $\lambda_{\max}$. For a given event, at time t, we compute the instantaneous rate $\lambda(t)$, and accept the event with probability $\lambda(t)/\lambda_{\max}$, rejecting it otherwise. The accept/reject decision is accomplished by generating a uniform $[0, 1]$ random variable u; the event is accepted the event if $u < \lambda(t)/\lambda_{\max}$.

We can employ this technique for parallel simulation, recognizing that the homogeneous "uniformizing" process gives us the lookahead that is needed. In the $Q1$-$Q2$ case, $Q1$ can (conceptually) generate a schedule of times $t_1, t_2, ..., t_k$ from the homogeneous process, and pass those times to $Q2$. For its part it remembers those times, and when it reaches t_i it computes $\lambda(t_i)$ and decides whether to accept or reject the event. If it accepts the event it undergoes a state-transition consistent with accepting the event (in this case, removing a job from service and sending it to $Q2$). If not, no state-change is incurred, but still $Q2$ is notified of this fact. For, $Q2$ retains the list of presampled times $Q1$ sent, and never advances past t_i until being notified by $Q1$ that it must either accept a new job, or that it is safe to proceed.

This sort of logic can be applied to interactions between all submodels, provided that between each submodel a maximum transition rate $\lambda_{\max}$ can be identified from the problem structure. Further obvious generalizations are needed when a transition in one submodel can affect multiple submodels. In short, the lookahead we exploit is just as model-specific as any other form of lookahead; in performance models of computer systems there are some notable problem areas. For instance, if an infinite server queue can route jobs to other clusters, then one cannot bound its aggregate transmission rate from a description of the server.

It can be possible to do so with knowledge about job distribution, but that raises the complexity of lookahead calculations considerably. Another problem area is when typically $\lambda(t) \ll \lambda_{max}$. This means that most events sampled from the uniformized process are rejected; the overhead of generating them and testing them can then contribute significantly to the run-time, and degrade parallel performance relative to serial performance.

A solution to this approach has been explored that sets λ_{max} adaptively in an effort to close the gap between the fastest possible transition ever, and the typical transition rate. By needs the approach is optimistic, but is much less sophisticated than typical optimistic simulations. It has mechanisms for guessing what the maximum transition rate between clusters will be, and infrequently does deep global checkpoints. The actual transition rate between clusters is monitored, and if ever a "rate fault" is experienced, the location of the fault is noted and a message to halt is broadcast to all. The processors determine the earliest fault time among themselves, then all processors revert to the state at the last checkpoint. The one processor that observed a fault rate keeps precisely the same schedule of uniformization rate on the faulting interface up to the time of the fault, and then increases it sufficiently to get past the fault. This increase becomes part of the uniformization rate schedule for that interface. This method was shown to provide significant performance improvements in situations where the standard method was severely degraded.

Further discussion and analysis of these uniformization based methods is found in [9].

As pretty as parallel simulation of Markov chains is mathematically, the pointed truth is that most Markov chains that are simulated do not have either the real-time requirements or model size requirements that forces a modeler to consider parallelism. There is however a critical application area that does.

Discrete-event simulation is an indispensable tool in the study of communication networks. The importance of simulating very large networks is increasingly recognized, as is it becomes understood that long-range dependencies in traffic characteristics cause deleterious behavior in network protocols, behavior whose effects are observed at the edge of the network, but whose causes within the network cannot. Simulation offers the hope of "cracking open the box" and observing behavior—albeit simulated behavior—in the interior. Large wired networks have characteristics that make the synchronization of parallel processors simple, with low overheads. Large networks typically decompose into local networks, where latencies between machines in a local network are significantly smaller than those between larger networks. A model partitioned so that submodels are connected only by relatively high latency connections has good lookahead. In the simplest approach one identifies the least latency between any two submodels, say Δ. All processors synchronize every Δ units of simulation time, with the assurance that no event executed by one processor within a time window can affect another processor within that same window. Events that are generated in the last window can, at the end of the window, be directed to their recipients and inserted into the appropriate event lists.

Δ can actually be quite small, and still have good performance. It is all a matter of how much simulation workload can be done in parallel within that window of time. For instance, in a recent large network we simulated, there were upwards of 100,000 hosts. On average a host inserted a packet into the network every 50 milliseconds. Each packet visited about 5 routers enroute to its destination, which amounts to .1 event per host per millisecond. The network was partitioned along high-bandwidth communication channels with 10 millisecond latency, so $\Delta = 10$ milliseconds. Thus on average 100,000 events are executed each window. On a medium-scale parallel processor, that gives ample workload against which the overheads of synchronization at the window's edge can be amortized.

Another area in performance analysis where parallel simulation is important is in the evaluation of computer architectures, particularly parallel architectures. The parallelism is obvious, and ample. The computations involved are substantive. Lookahead can be more problematic though; those parallel architectural simulators that have achieve the highest performance typically make simplifying assumptions about interconnections (e.g. no contention or a very simple model of contention).

In summary, performance evaluation contains a number of subfields where high performance simulation is needed. Parallel techniques have been successful at addressing many of these needs.

4 Impact in Academia and Industry

It is not possible to underestimate the impact that simulation has had in the way research is conducted, or the way industry has developed. In academia simulations are routinely used to explore research issues of all types; the results of these simulations are routinely reported in the best journals. Likewise in industry, no complex electronic device is built today without its design first being extensively tested, using simulation. Indeed the VHDL standard of system design [1] was developed to combine system design, and simulation of that design.

The computer can and is being used to construct "virtual worlds", to explore what might be possible in the real world.

5 Status and Directions

Discrete-event simulation is a pervasive and respected field of research and activity. People involved in simulation are found in many different academic departments, in many different types of companies. Research papers on mathematical aspects of simulation are frequently published in leading operations research journals. The Association for Computing Machine publishes the ACM Transactions on Modeling and Computer Simulation, which quarterly publishes the best computer science oriented research in simulation. There is a thriving and active group of conferences dedicated to simulation, notable ones including the Winter

Simulation Conference and the Annual Workshop on Parallel and Distributed Simulation.

There are many directions in which simulation is being pursued. As Moore's Law continues to deliver astounding increases in computing power, simulations can enjoy corresponding increases in fidelity. Increasingly more detailed models can be explored. Higher computing power makes feasible better (but more computationally expensive) random number generators, and more sophisticated statistical analysis. It offers the possibility of exploring modes of model expression that formerly were too computationally expensive to consider on sizable models, e.g., rule-based expression.

Techniques like importance sampling that can dramatically reduce variance are being developed for increasingly complex systems. Parallel simulation is coming into its own, as it is developed and applied to pressing real-world problems. The field of distributed simulation—linking separate autonomous simulators through some network glue—is a huge effort in the US DoD community, who eyes integrated simulations as the key to reducing training costs.

This is indeed an exciting time to be working in the field of simulation.

References

1. P. Ashenden: The Designer's Guide to VHDL. Morgan Kaufmann, 1996.
2. J. Banks, J. Carson II, and B. Nelson: Discrete-Event System Simulation. Prentice-Hall, 1996.
3. P. Bratley and B. Fox and L. Schrage: A Guide to Simulation, second edition. Springer-Verlag, 1987.
4. R. Couture and P. L'Ecuyer (Editors): Special issue on random number generation. ACM Transactions on Modeling and Computer Simulation, 8(1), January 1998.
5. R. Fujimoto: Parallel Discrete Event Simulation. Communications of the ACM, 33(10):30-53, October 1990.
6. P. Heidelberger: Fast simulation of rare events in queueing and reliability models. ACM Transactions on Modeling and Computer Simulation, 5(1):43–85, January 1995.
7. A. Law and D. Kelton: Simulation Modeling and Analysis, second edition. McGraw-Hill, 1991.
8. D. Nance: A history of programming languages, volume 2. Addison-Wesley, 1996.
9. D. Nicol and P. Heidelberger: A comparative study of parallel algorithms for simulating continuous time markov chains. ACM Transactions on Modeling and Computer Simulation, 5(4):326–354, October 1995.

Workload Characterization Issues and Methodologies

Maria Calzarossa, Luisa Massari, and Daniele Tessera

Dipartimento di Informatica e Sistemistica, Università di Pavia,
via Ferrata, 1, I-27100 Pavia, Italy
{mcc,massari,tessera}@alice.unipv.it

1 Introduction

The performance of any type of system cannot be determined without knowing the workload, that is, the requests being processed. Workload characterization consists of a description of the workload by means of quantitative parameters and functions; the objective is to derive a model able to show, capture, and reproduce the behavior of the workload and its most important features.

A survey of workload characterization (i. e. the parameters and the techniques used for characterizing batch, interactive, database, network–based and parallel workloads) were presented in [11].

Workload characterization dates back to early 70's. Since then this discipline has evolved following the evolution of computer architectures. In the early days, computers were mainframes and their workloads were basically composed of batch jobs and transactions. The advent of time sharing systems and computer networks has changed the approach of the users toward the systems. This advent, which has been coupled with an increased processing power of the systems and with the introduction of graphical user interfaces, has opened the systems to new processing requirements. All this has also led to the development of distributed systems and of client/server applications.

The new services provided on top of Internet, such as the World Wide Web, have introduced the concept of multimedia workloads. These workloads consist of a mix of different types of application (e.g., file transfers, real time audio applications) characterized by different performance requirements on the resources of servers and clients as well as of the networks.

Vector processors, multiprocessors, and parallel systems deserve their own attention. Their workload consists of compute–intensive and I/O–intensive scientific applications which take advantage in a variety of ways of the various processing units of the system in order to reduce their overall execution time.

In these years, workload characterization has been addressing all the new application domains. The techniques applied for this purpose have evolved accordingly to cope with the nature of the workloads which have become more complex. There are many performance studies that have to be addressed by means of workload characterization. Examples are competitive procurement, system sizing, capacity planning, performance comparisons for marketing purposes.

G. Haring et al. (Eds.): Performance Evaluation, LNCS 1769, pp. 459–481, 2000.

Another key example is represented by benchmarking. The definition of benchmark suites to be used to test both the systems currently available and new emerging systems has to rely on an accurate characterization of the workload of these systems. Moreover, the design and evaluation of resource management policies, such as caching policies for World Wide Web servers, require the knowledge of the characteristics and behavior of the requests to be processed by the servers. The design of efficient parallelizing compilers has to rely on models able to predict the behavior and the performance of parallel applications.

The paper is organized as follows. Section 2 describes the approaches commonly adopted for workload characterization. We focus on the issues to be addressed in this framework and on the various techniques used to build models which resemble either the static and dynamic properties of the workload. Sections 3 and 4 present case studies where the workloads processed in client/server environments and by parallel systems are analyzed. Future directions in the field of workload characterization are outlined in Section 5.

2 Approach

The term "workload characteristics" refers to the demands placed by the requests on the various system resources. Each request, that is, each workload component, is described by a set of parameters which explain these demands. There are static parameters related to hardware and software resource consumptions and dynamic parameters related to the behavior of the requests. The magnitudes of these parameters depend on the nature of the single request and can be conveniently used to quantify the workload.

The approach commonly adopted for workload characterization is experimental, that is, based on the analysis of measurements collected on the system while the workload is being processed. Due to the complexity of the systems and of their workloads, such an experimental approach becomes quite challenging. Appropriate instrumentation has to be developed in order to ensure the quality of the measurements which have to adjust to the characteristics of the systems and of their workloads. To capture detailed information about the behavior of the workload, it might be necessary to insert into the system probes, such as event counters. Another issue to be addressed deals with the large amount of collected measurements. A good tradeoff between what has to be measured and the amount of collected data has to be achieved. Moreover, the degree of intrusiveness and the overhead introduced by the instrumentation system have to be as low as possible in order not to perturb the behavior of the system and of its workload. Once the measurements are available, appropriate techniques have to be applied for their analysis in order to ensure the accuracy and the representativeness of the workload model which will be derived.

Several issues have to be addressed when building a workload model. Representativeness is a measure of fit between the model and the actual workload. The characteristics of a representative workload model must resemble those of the actual workload with reasonable fidelity while satisfying several practical constraints. Modeling tends to smooth out details of the workload which might be desirable to investigate. Hence, the concepts of model abstraction and how much loss of information is acceptable have to be addressed. Another crucial point is to assess the most "important" features to be included in a model. There are many advantages in building and using workload models. A model is typically artificial and generative, that is, it parametrically generates the workload. Hence, performance studies can be carried out without requiring actual measurements which might be either not easily manageable or not available. Moreover, portability and reproducibility requirements are fully met by workload models.

There is a large variety of techniques used for workload characterization. Exploratory data analysis techniques are fundamental to uncover the essential characteristics of the measured quantities and their relationships. Numerical analysis techniques and stochastic processes are useful for reproducing the dynamic behavior of the workload.

Descriptive statistics of workload parameters (e.g., basic statistics, correlations, distributions) provide preliminary insights into the behavior of the workload. Emphasis has also to be put on visual examination of the data. Even though the number of parameters describing the workload, that is, the data set dimensionality, and the number of data points, that is, the number of workload components, may be quite large, data visualization suggests patterns which might be not obvious from statistical summaries only. This is often the case of the workloads processed by parallel systems.

Clustering is a numerical pattern recognition technique commonly adopted in the framework of workload characterization. The goal is to find structures in large volumes of data. The workload components are represented as points in a multi dimensional space, whose dimension is equal to the number of parameters used to describe the components. Clustering partitions the data space into groups characterized by their centroids, that is, their geometric centers. The choice of the quantitative parameters to be used for clustering has to be such that a common description of the composition of each group can be easily obtained. Moreover, the choice of these parameters has to be driven by the intended use of the clustering outcomes. This is the case, for example, of the specification of the input of system models. The groups provided by clustering specify the classes for these models. The parameters corresponding to the centroid of each group are used as input parameters of system models.

It is also important to provide a description of the composition of each group from a functional view point. In such a case, qualitative parameters, such as request type, which are not advisable to use for clustering purposes, can be profitably used to describe the workload components belonging to each group. This information will drive, for example, the choice of representative workload components to be used in benchmarking experiments.

Descriptive statistics and clustering have always been widely applied to workload characterization. Early papers (see e.g., [18], [46], [2], [41]) focus on these techniques in order to find a set of representative programs to be used for benchmarking and for system modeling. The target of these studies is batch and interactive systems, whose workload components are described by parameters, such as CPU time, number of I/O accesses, number of lines printed, amount of central memory used. Qualitative parameters, such as programming language and types of activity performed (e.g., editing, compilation, execution), are also used to combine a functional description of the workload models with their quantitative counterpart. General descriptive statistics are also used to characterize the workload of personal computers and to derive the behavior of the users (see e.g., [50]).

In most of these studies, only the static characteristics of the workload are taken into account. When the dynamic behavior of the workload has to be analyzed, descriptive approaches based on the application of graphical and mathematical methods are used. The objective is to derive workload models to be incorporated into system models, such as simulation models, or into the description of operating system policies.
There is a variety of phenomena which have to be described from a dynamic view point. In [30], statistical analysis of series of events is applied to the sequences of transactions initiated in a database system. The arrival rate of the transactions is represented by means of a non homogeneous Poisson process obtained as a superposition of a large number of non stationary point processes. Numerical fitting techniques are applied in [10] to model the fluctuations characterizing the patterns of the jobs arriving at a system. The combined application of clustering and fitting techniques leads to the identification of representative arrival patterns. In [1], sequences of job steps in a job are modeled by means of a Markov chain whose states represent the calls to the various programs (e.g., compilers, utilities). Stochastic models, based on Markov chains, are used in [23] to represent the workload of interactive systems at the task level.

Graph–based models are a common representation of the sequences of commands issued by interactive users. User behavior graphs, introduced in [19], are the most popular example of these types of model. The nodes of a user behavior graph correspond to the various types of command. The arcs, with their associated probabilities, represent the sequences of commands as issued by the users. Fig. 1 shows an example of a user behavior graph consisting of eight nodes.

The introduction of graphical user interfaces based on multiple windows has led to the development of models which have to take into account the characteristics of these operating environments (see e.g., [38]). A sort of parallelism is introduced in the user behavior, in that a user can issue many commands from different windows, without having to wait for the completion of the current one. All these commands are then simultaneously "active" in the system. Hence, workload models have to generate these sequences of commands and reproduce the parallelism characterizing their executions.

Moreover, with the advent of client/server environments, the hierarchical nature of the workload, earlier recognized for interactive workloads ([23]), has become more evident and more relevant (see e.g., [8]). Various systems are involved in processing a single request. For example, a command issued by a user

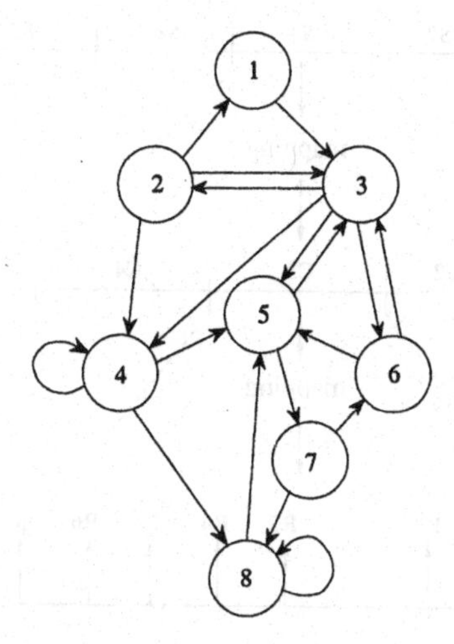

Fig. 1. User behavior graph consisting of eight nodes.

from a workstation could be processed by the local workstation only or might require, as in the case of distributed file servers, processing from remote systems, after having accessed the network. Hence, a single request is broken down into a number of sub–requests which invoke services by different systems. This means that each system "sees" different types of request, that is, a different workload. A number of layers, corresponding to the various systems which contribute to process a request, can then be identified for the characterization of the workload. Different parameters are used to describe the workload of each of these layers.

In this framework, the concept of networkload has been introduced ([39]). The networkload is a collection of user generated inputs or client generated events. Fig. 2 shows the layers (i.e., session, command, request) of the hierarchy as identified in the networkload approach. A Probabilistic Context Free Grammar is used to describe and generate these sequences. A generative model, characterized by variable levels of hierarchy, is then obtained.

Recently, notions, such as self–similarity, have been shown to apply in the framework of workload characterization ([29]). The various types of network traffic are characterized by a bursty nature and exhibit long–range dependence, which can be represented by heavy–tailed distributions. The same applies to the requests, e.g., read, write, open, close, processed by a file system ([21]). Self–similarity is able to capture and explain these phenomena.

More details about this approach and other techniques used to characterize the workload will be described on the case studies presented in the following sections.

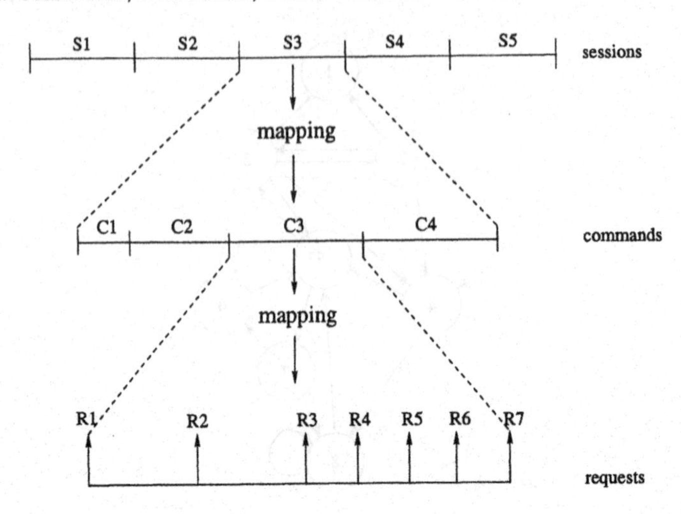

Fig. 2. Three layer hierarchy typical of the networkload.

3 Workload of Client/Server Environments

A client/server environment is typically composed of clients connected to servers through a network. Examples of these environments are distributed file systems, distributed databases, World Wide Web and distributed multimedia systems. The increasing complexity of the architectures of these systems makes their design and management quite challenging. The introduction of a large variety of advanced services, such as integrated services for mobile users, makes these issues even more crucial. In this framework, performance evaluation and, in particular, workload characterization, are very helpful. Studies related to capacity planning, load balancing, resource allocation and scheduling, and congestion control policies, rely on an accurate characterization of the workload of client/server environments. This characterization is also the basis for the definition of the input parameters of models, aimed, for example, at performance prediction.

In a client/server environment, a client generates requests, which are transmitted through a network, and received by a server. The server processes these requests and sends back the replies to the client. Hence, client/server environments can be seen as hierarchically structured into three layers, namely client, network, and server. Depending on the considered layer, workload consists of the requests, as seen at the client or server layers, or of the packets flowing on the network.

Workload characterization in client/server environments typically relies on the analysis of measurements collected at each layer. The choice of what has to be measured depends on the objective of the study, the workload characteristics to be evaluated, and the availability of tools able to collect the appropriate measures.
At the network layer, measurements, which can span hours and days (see e.g., [22], [37]), or time periods of weeks and months (see e.g., [36]), have been often

collected. Software monitors, such as `tcpdump`, capture the packets flowing on the network, and provide user level control of measurement collection. This control includes filtering on a per host, protocol, or port basis. Information, such as packet arrival times, packet lengths, as well as source and destination host, and port number, are captured. Measurements can also be collected by means of hardware monitors. Tools, such as `sniffers`, capture the packets flowing on the network, and perform some preliminary analyses on them. Timing of the packet arrivals, packet lengths, together with events, such as packet retransmissions, are gathered.
At the client and server layers, the use of accounting routines provides measurements about the processed requests. These measurements may not be enough to fully characterize the behavior of the requests. In order to obtain more detailed information, the availability of ad–hoc tools able to gather the events of interest is required. A simple way to capture these events consists of modifying the source codes of client or server applications by adding custom instrumentation. In the case of Web clients, browsers have been instrumented ([14]). In such a way, the arrival time of each request, the size of the requested file, together with the URL, session, user, and client identifiers, are captured. At the server layer, the instrumentation of the `httpd` daemon provides the CPU and disk demands of each request ([16]). In distributed file systems, kernel instrumentation is used to extract from each remote file system information, such as file lengths, access/modification times ([5]). It should be noted that all these measurement approaches require the availability of source codes.
From the analysis of the measurements collected at the client, network, and server layers, a model of the overall workload of the client/server environment can be obtained. Nevertheless, most of the studies characterize the workload of each layer separately, by using the corresponding measurements.

Early studies at the network layer are based on measurements collected on an Ethernet network (see e.g., [44], [22]). The workload consists of sequences of packets. The parameters typically considered for their characterization are packet interarrival times, packet lengths, error rates, and network utilization. For these parameters, basic statistics, together with their distributions, are computed. Figs. 3 and 4 show the distributions of packet lengths and interarrival times, respectively. As can be seen, the packet lengths are characterized by a bimodal distribution, whereas interarrival time distribution is heavy–tailed. Interarrival times are not statistically independent, that is, with a high probability a packet is followed by a second packet within a deterministic time which depends on the protocol, packet length, and traffic intensity. Hence, Poisson models, historically used for modeling network traffic, are inappropriate to represent packet arrival process.

The network traffic can also be analyzed from a functional view point. In [22], the composition of the traffic has been studied on a per protocol basis. It has been shown that three protocols, namely TCP, NFS, and ND (Network Disk), carry most of the traffic. For each of these protocols, parameters, such as packet interarrival times, are analyzed. From the interarrival time distributions, it has

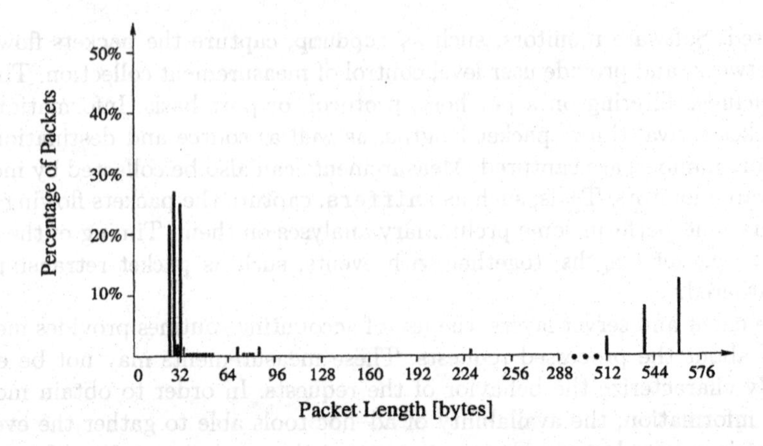

Fig. 3. Distribution of the length of the packets transmitted over the Ethernet [44].

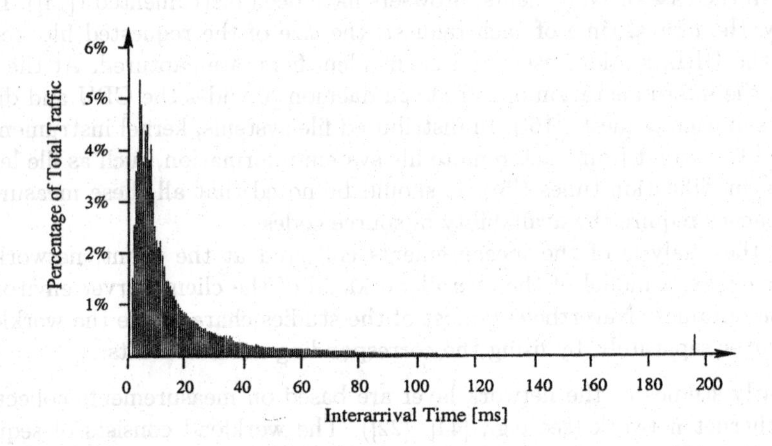

Fig. 4. Distribution of the interarrival times of the packets transmitted over the Ethernet [44].

been discovered, for example, that TCP is "slow" compared to NFS and ND. The 90th percentile of the interarrival time distribution of TCP packets is equal to 52 ms. For ND packets, this percentile is equal to 18 ms.
A functional description of the traffic can also be obtained by recognizing intranetwork and internetwork traffic. From the analysis of source/destination patterns, the distribution of the traffic among servers can be studied. The traffic is typically unevenly distributed and concentrated to and from specialized servers, like gateways, information servers, file servers, print servers.

Recent studies (see e.g., [29], [37]) have introduced the concept of "self-similarity" as a fundamental characteristic of network traffic. This concept applies to both local and wide area networks. Packet arrivals are characterized by a bursty nature. The traffic measured on the network is seen as the aggregation of bursty traffic generated by independent sources; as the number of traffic sources increases, burstiness of the total traffic increases. The burstiness of the arrivals, already discovered in earlier studies ([44]), is the most evident characteristic of self–similarity. By plotting the packet arrival counts, i.e., the number of packet arrivals per time unit, and changing the time unit, the arrival pattern maintains the same bursty structure on different time scales. Poisson arrivals, on the contrary, become smoother at coarser time scales. This bursty arrival process has been discovered as characterizing the overall and the per protocol traffic. For example, both `telnet` and `ftp` packet arrivals are characterized by a self–similar behavior. Fig. 5 shows the typical behavior of a bursty arrival process. Figs. 5(a) and 5(b) show the count of Ethernet packet arrivals for time units equal to 2.5 and 0.25 seconds, respectively.

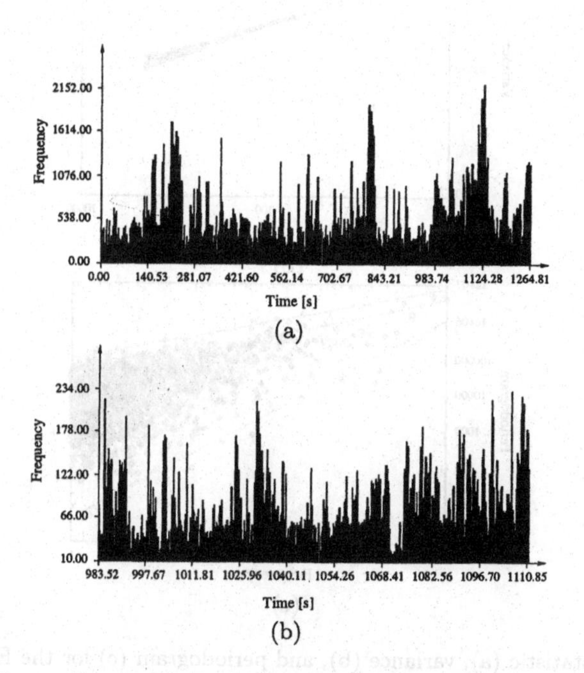

Fig. 5. Frequency of packets for two different time units.

Statistical methods for estimating the degree of self–similarity are the time–domain analysis based on R/S statistic, the variance–time analysis, and the spectral–domain method using periodograms ([29]). Fig. 6 shows the plots of these three statistics for traffic measured during one day on an Ethernet network. All the three methods provide an estimate of the Hurst parameter, which is used for quantifying the degree of self–similarity. In our example, the slopes of the R/S statistic (Fig. 6(a)) and variance curve (Fig. 6(b)) give a value of the Hurst parameter equal to 0.9, which means high degree of self–similarity. The spectral–domain method (Fig. 6(c)) is less accurate, and it only confirms what provided by the other two methods.

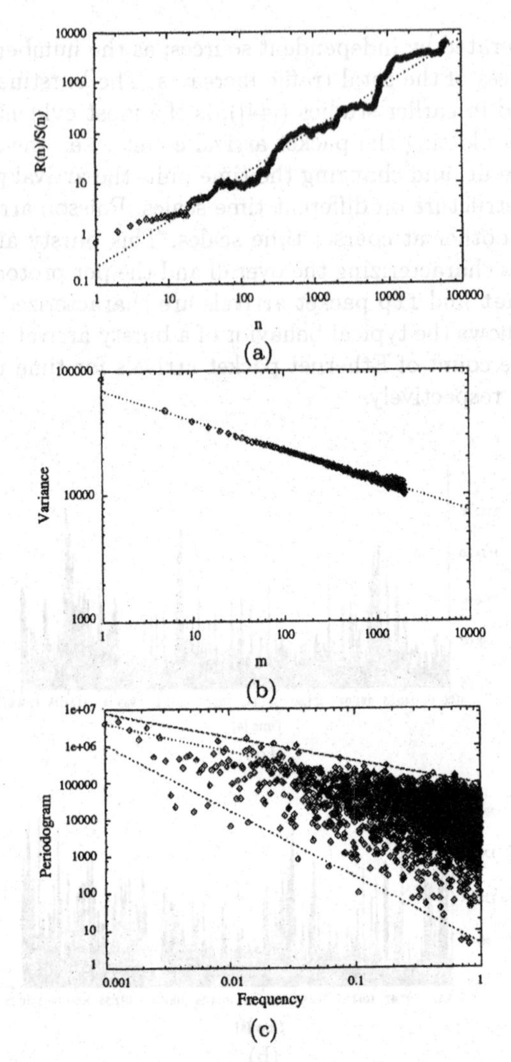

Fig. 6. R/S statistic (a), variance (b), and periodogram (c) for the Ethernet traffic.

The phenomenon of self-similarity has also been discovered as characterizing the network traffic associated with the requests issued by Web clients and with replies of Web servers ([31]). In particular, the distribution of the length of the replies is heavy tailed, i.e., the replies are large with non negligible probability, whereas the length of the requests has a bimodal distribution.

At the client and the server layers, the workload consists of the sequences of the requests generated by clients and processed by servers. At the client layer, requests are described by means of parameters, such as the arrival time, and the size of the requested file. In Web environments, these parameters are characterized by heavy–tailed distributions (see e.g., [15], [14]). In the case of file sizes, the tail of their distribution is due to multimedia applications. Even though the distribution of text files is itself heavy–tailed, the combined use of files carrying text, image, audio, and video, has the effect to increase the length of the tail. The analysis of the size of a file and of the number of times it is accessed provides a characterization of the user behavior. An inverse correlation has been discovered between these parameters, that is, users tend to access small files.

Workload invariants are identified from measurements on Web servers. These invariants refer to characteristics that apply across different servers ([4]). Invariants are the percentage of accesses to valid files, file types, mean transfer size, percentage of requests to different files, file size distribution, and parameters related to file referencing behavior, e.g., frequency of reference, inter-reference times, percentage of remote requests. A non–uniform referencing behavior characterizes the servers. Fig. 7 shows the cumulative frequency of file accesses for six Web servers. As can be seen, there are very few files responsible for most of the requests received by each server.

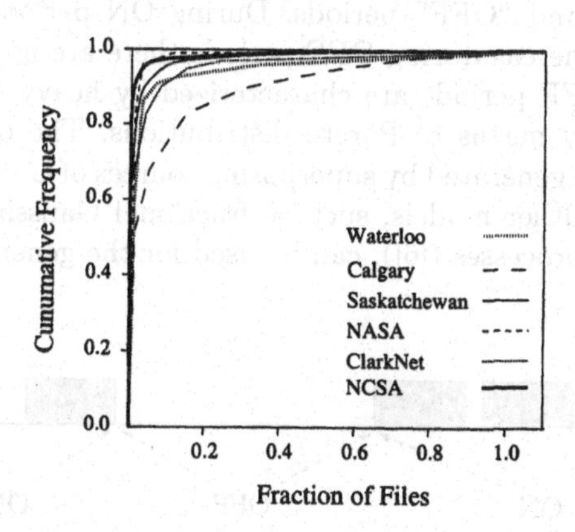

Fig. 7. Cumulative frequency of file accesses for six Web servers [4].

As already pointed out, a model of the overall workload of a client/server environment has to be based on the analysis of measurements collected at network, client, and server layers. These models are typically used as input for analytic and simulation models aimed at predicting the performance of the systems.
In [39], a generative model, which reflects the hierarchical nature of the client/server workload, is built. The data collected at different layers (i.e., session, command, request) is analyzed independently to estimate its characterizing parameters and to reduce it by means of clustering. Further analyses provide estimates of the mapping between layers. A networkload model is then obtained and used as input to simulation model of a single server multiple client network. In [16], the workload of internet and intranet Web servers is characterized with the aim of deriving the input parameters of a capacity planning model of the Web server. The requests issued by the clients are subdivided into three classes,

according to the types of file accessed on the server (i.e., text, image, CGI). Each class of requests is described by its service demands, e.g., CPU time and disk demand at the server, and network delay. A layered queueing network model of the Web server is built for predicting the client and server response times.
In [13], measurements collected at the client and server layers are used in combination to drive the scheduling policies of a distributed Web server. A number of workload parameters are derived from these measurements in order to balance the load among servers.
A generative workload model of a distributed file server is presented in [7]. The workload is described by the frequency distribution of file server requests, the request interarrival time distribution, the file referencing behavior, and the distribution of sizes of read and write requests. The workload model generates requests to the server by sampling these distributions.

Train models, first introduced in [26] to model packet arrivals in a token ring local area network, have been recently used to reproduce self-similarity of ATM, Ethernet, and Web traffic (see e.g., [27], [49], [14]). A train is seen as a sequence of "ON" and "OFF" periods. During ON periods, packets arrive at regular intervals, whereas during OFF periods there are no packet arrivals (see Fig. 8). ON and OFF periods are characterized by heavy-tailed distributions, and are modeled by means of Pareto distributions. The overall traffic of the network can then be generated by superposing sources of traffic, each represented by a train model. Other models, such as fractional Gaussian noises ([33]) and fractional ARIMA processes ([6]), can be used for the generation of self-similar traffic.

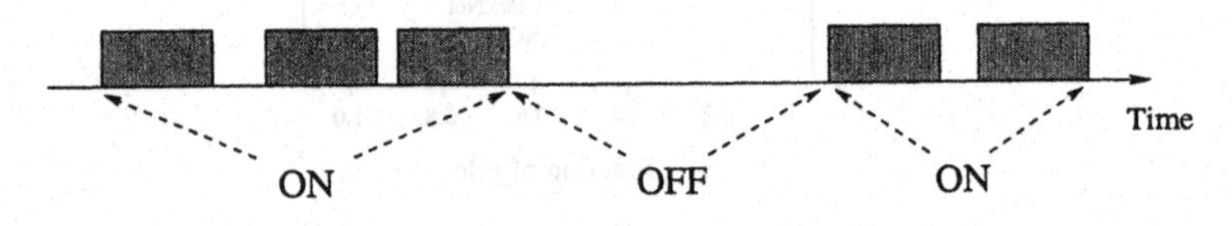

Fig. 8. ON/OFF model.

It should be noted that all these case studies enforce the importance of an accurate characterization of the workload of client/server environments, whose requests are characterized by different performance and quality of service requirements. Indeed, the more detailed the workload description is, the better will be the performance predictions.

4 Workload of Parallel Systems

The workload of parallel systems is represented by the applications being processed. The driving factor in developing parallel applications is to get better performance, i.e., to solve a given problem in a shorter time or to be able to solve bigger problems. Workload characterization focuses on the performance issues which have to be addressed to meet such objectives. Tuning, performance debugging and diagnosis require an accurate characterization of parallel applications. A detailed description of parallel applications is also required by performance prediction studies aimed, for example, at the design and evaluation of scheduling policies.

A parallel application is a collection of interrelated tasks that interact through a predetermined flow of control. Each task consists of a functional block (i.e., a sequence of statements) which is executed on a given processor; in turn, different tasks can be allocated to different processors. Data and functional dependencies existing among the various tasks are translated into communications and synchronizations activities, which can be based on explicit message passing or on shared memory. A typical representation of parallel applications is based on task graphs whose nodes correspond to the functional blocks and whose arcs correspond to the dependencies existing among them. Fig. 9 shows an example of a task graph.

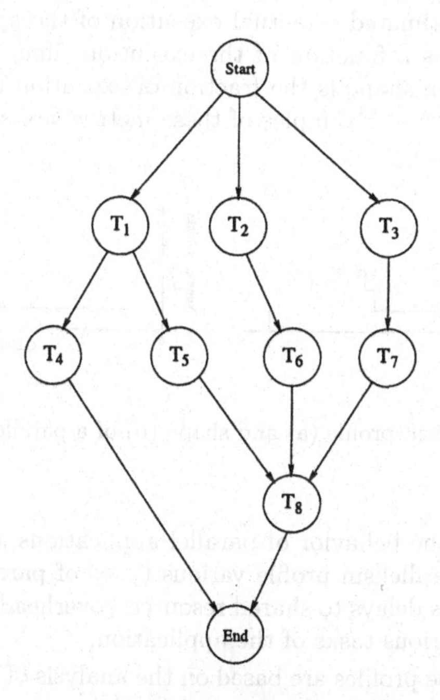

Fig. 9. Example of a task graph.

From the task graph, parameters and metrics are derived in order to obtain qualitative and quantitative descriptions of the behavior of parallel applications. Early studies (see e.g., [42], [32]) focus on the analysis of these graphs with the aim of describing the inherent parallelism of the applications.
Parameters, like the maximum cut, the depth, the average parallelism, and the sequential fraction, can be directly derived from the task graph. The maximum

cut, that is, the maximum number of arcs taken over all possible cuts from the initial to the final node, provides the maximum theoretical degree of parallelism. The depth, that is, the longest path between the initial and final node, is directly related to the overall execution time. The average parallelism is defined as the average number of "active" tasks during the execution of the application. The sequential fraction is the fraction of the overall execution time which cannot benefit from parallel execution ([3]).
From the task graph, the overall execution time of an application has to be estimated by computing the execution time of each task and considering the data and functional dependencies existing among tasks. The execution time of each task is itself estimated by considering the number of instructions executed, the number of clock cycles per instruction, and the processor clock cycle time.
All these parameters provide preliminary insights into the parallelism that can be exploited by an application. The dynamic aspects of the application are not captured. Metrics, like the parallelism profile and the application shape, have to be used to investigate such aspects. The parallelism profiles and the application shape can refer to estimated or actual execution of the application. The parallelism profile plots, as a function of the execution time, the number of active tasks. The application shape is the fraction of execution time in which a given number of tasks is active. Examples of these metrics are shown in Fig. 10.

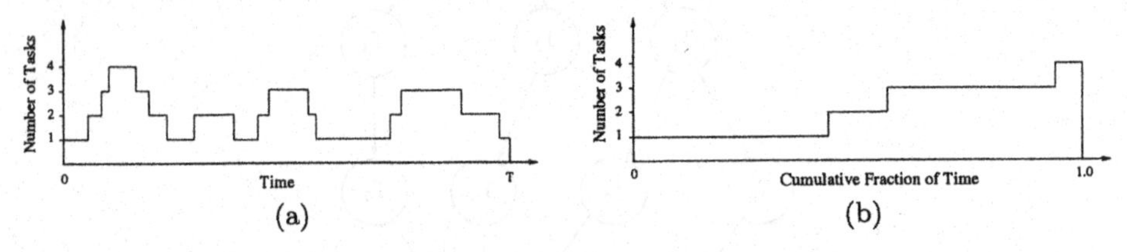

Fig. 10. Parallelism profile (a) and shape (b) of a parallel application [42].

More details about the behavior of parallel applications are obtained by incorporating into the parallelism profile various types of parallelism delay, such as contention and access delays to shared resources, overhead delays of transferring and initiating the various tasks of the application.

Even though these profiles are based on the analysis of the task graph and on estimates of the achievable performance only, they represent a first attempt to take into account the interactions of the application with the underlying parallel system. However, for most scientific parallel applications building a task graph is infeasible. Moreover, the actual performance is influenced by a large number of aspects related to the algorithms used and to their interactions with the parallel system. It is then important to gather information from the execution of the applications. Measurement based approaches work for this purpose. Depending on the objective of the study, measurements are collected at various levels of details. The selection of what has to be measured is critical. Indeed, there is a tradeoff between the amount of details to be measured and the perturbations introduced in the behavior of the application being measured.

Measurements are obtained by monitoring the applications. Instrumentation has to be statically or dynamically added to operating system schedulers, communication libraries, or source code of the applications ([25]). Events, associated, for example, with the begin or end of portions of application source code (e.g., subroutines, loops, arbitrary sequences of statements) or with communication statements, are monitored. During the execution of an application, when an event occurs, a time stamp, and the identifiers of the event itself and of the processor where the event occurred, are captured.
Flexible techniques have to be applied for selecting and presenting the most relevant characteristics of the application from the overwhelming amount of details contained into the measurements. In this framework, visualization techniques are important in that they highlight the behavior of the application by means of various types of graphical representation (see e.g., [24]).

A parallel application can be analyzed under different perspectives and at different levels of abstraction. Parameters and metrics describing its static and dynamic behavior are extracted from the measurements. Preliminary information about the behavior of the whole application can be provided by timing parameters, such as execution, computation, communication, and I/O times, and volume parameters, such as number of floating point operations, communications, and I/O operations. These parameters summarize the behavior of the application by showing the tradeoff between actual computation, communication and synchronization activities, and I/O requirements.

The dynamic behavior of an application is described by means of profiles, which express, as a function of the execution time, the number of processors involved simultaneously in a specific activity. Execution profiles describe the overall behavior of the applications.
In the case of applications which rely on communication libraries, such as MPI and PVM, the characterization of communication activities is particularly critical because of the large variety of available protocols and buffering policies. Communication profiles reflect the overall behavior of the communications. Moreover, the profiles can be specialized on a per protocol basis. Fig. 11(a) shows an example of a communication profile for an application executed with 32 processors. The profile corresponding to the MPI Allreduce protocol is shown in Fig. 11(b).

The analysis of the parallel applications as a function of the number of allocated processors, that is, the scalability of the applications, can be addressed by performance metrics, derived from timing parameters. The speedup is a figure of merit of the exploitation of available parallelism, in that, it is a measure of how much the execution time decreases with an increase in the number of allocated processors. Fig. 12 shows a speedup curve of an application executed with a number of processors ranging from 1 up to 64.

Note that the increase of the number of allocated processors does not always lead to performance improvements. As can be seen, there is a degradation of the performance when the number of processors is increased from 32 to 64. The

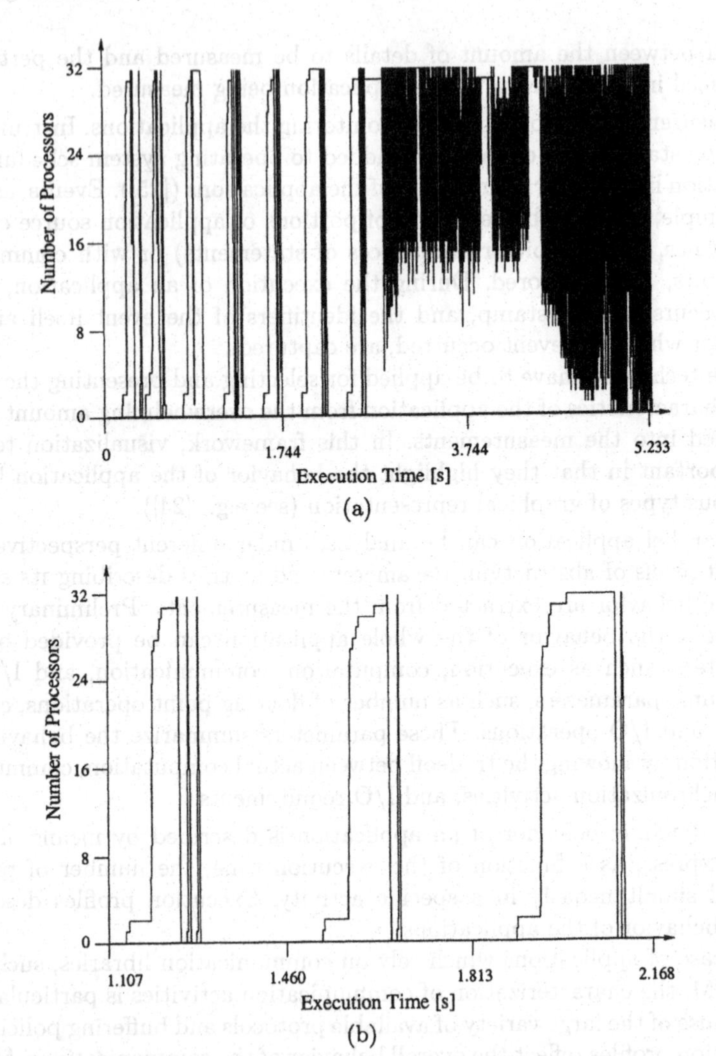

Fig. 11. Communication profile (a) and MPI Allreduce profile (b).

benefit from allocating additional processors does not compensate the costs due to the increased synchronization and communication activities.
The effective exploitation of the allocated processors can also be assessed by performance metrics, like efficiency and efficacy.

There is a number of studies, e.g., design of scheduling policies, performance prediction, tuning, performance debugging and diagnosis, which rely on a detailed characterization of parallel applications. For example, when dealing with the design and the evaluation of scheduling policies, a parallel application is described in terms of number of processors it requires and the time it takes to be executed (see e.g., [20], [43]). Moreover, the arrival process of the applications has to be specified by appropriate distributions, such as Poisson distributions and experimental distributions derived by fitting actual arrivals ([17]).

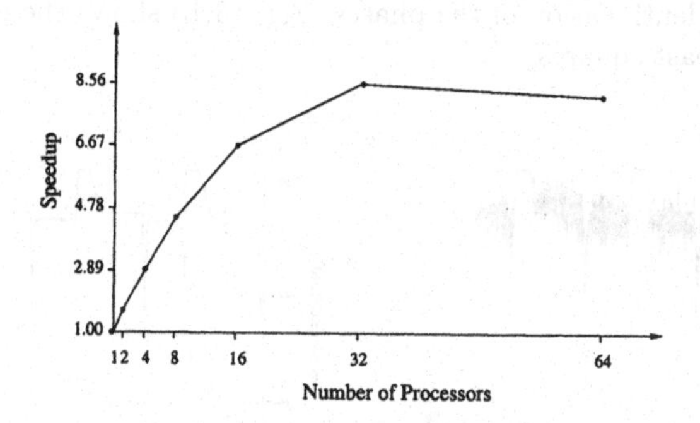

Fig. 12. Speedup curve as a function of the number of allocated processors.

Other performance studies, dealing with performance debugging and diagnosis, focus on the analysis of the various portions of application source code, e.g., loops, subroutines, arbitrary code segments. Profiling techniques provide for each portion of the code the execution time together with the number of times it has been executed. In such a way, as in the case of sequential applications, the "heaviest" portions of the code, where the application spends its time, are identified.

Moreover, the behavior of an application can be described under a multiplicity of views, each addressing a specific aspect of its execution ([28]). For example, processor and data parallelism views can be obtained. These views describe the behavior of the individual processors, with respect to the data it has to process, and the interactions among the processors, with respect to their communication and synchronization activities.

The analysis of the behavior of the individual processors is particularly useful for data parallel applications where the parallelism is basically exploited by distributing the data among the allocated processors. For example, processor views identify the presence of unevenly distributed data. In such a case, the processors are characterized by "irregular" behavior, that is, the load of the various processors becomes unbalanced and synchronization delays arise.

Another approach toward a detailed description of a parallel application is based on the identification of phases, used to represent the execution behavior of the application. The phases refer to the algorithms used or to specific activities, such as computation, communication, and I/O. An application is then seen as a sequence of phases.

In [12], the execution profile of an application is analyzed with the aim of identifying the phases it consists of. The profile is seen as a sequence of alternating periods of roughly uniform processor utilization separated by periods of sudden transition in processor utilization. These phases are analyzed with respect to their speedup behavior in order to gain insights into the performance and the scalability of the application. Fig. 13(a) shows an example of an execution profile. As can be seen, there are periods characterized by high variance in the number of utilized processors. The use of smoothing techniques reduces this variance and eases the identification of the phases. Fig. 13(b) shows the execution profile smoothed by least squares.

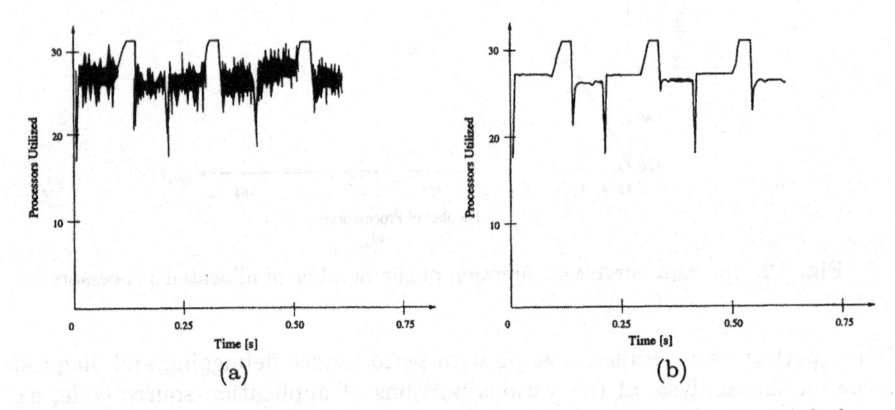

Fig. 13. Execution profile (a) and profile smoothed by least squares (b) [12].

In [48], the characterization of the phases of computational fluid dynamics applications, which solve partial differential equations, yields the identification of tuning methodologies based on resource utilization profiles as well as the evaluation of the performance of heterogeneous metacomputing environments. This characterization relies on a top–down approach. Measurements collected at the system level, together with a domain specific knowledge of this class of applications, are used to characterize the phases. The application is seen as alternating computation and communication phases. This alternation is described by means of interarrival times between successive communication phases, length of computation and communication phases. Each of these parameters is specified by an appropriate probability distribution.

The phases identified in this study are typical of explicit message passing applications, whose parallelism is expressed by means of communication statements. In the case of parallel applications which use high level languages, such as High Performance Fortran (HPF), the parallelism is expressed by means of directives provided by the language itself. The compiler will take advantage of these directives to parallelize the applications. The performance of these applications is influenced by the parallelization strategies adopted by the compiler, whereas the performance of explicit message passing applications is mainly influenced by communication mechanisms.

Explicit message passing applications require a detailed characterization of the communication activities (see e.g., [34], [47]). The characterization of HPF applications has to focus on the costs of the parallelization strategies (see e.g., [9]). These costs are seen as overhead, which results into an increase of the execution time of the application. The execution time can be broken down according to the various activities required by the parallelization. The evaluation of these costs is useful for both application and compiler developers. The impact of HPF directives on the performance of the application and the efficiency of the parallelization strategies adopted by the compiler are assessed. Fig. 14 shows the profiling of the INDEPENDENT loops of an HPF application. For each loop, the figure also presents the breakdown of the execution time with respect to the costs associated with the distribution of work and data among the allocated processors.

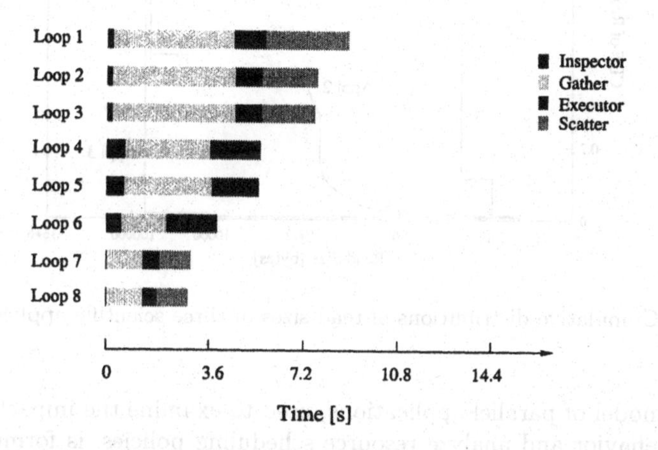

Fig. 14. Breakdown of the execution time of HPF INDEPENDENT loops.

Parallel scientific applications, typically described as computation intensive, are becoming more I/O intensive, due to the large volume of data to be manipulated. The efficiency and the scalability of an application are influenced by its I/O requirements. Moreover, these requirements influence the design of high performance I/O systems.
Recent studies (see e.g., [35], [45]), have addressed the characterization of I/O requirements of parallel applications. These studies analyze a set of applications, whose access patterns are representative of the behavior of most scientific applications. The characterization focuses on the behavior of I/O requests, such as seeks, reads, and writes. Each of these I/O requests is described by its count and its duration. The analysis of the temporal and spatial patterns of I/O requests shows the burstiness of the accesses and their non sequential behavior, as well as the presence of interleaved and strided patterns. These patterns help in identifying phases in the I/O activities of an application. An application typically starts by reading its data set, then, it might use temporary files, as in the case of out of core computations. Finally, the application writes back the results of its execution.
The distributions of the size of various types of request describe the variability

of the volume of the data being accessed. Fig. 15 shows the cumulative distributions of the read sizes for three scientific applications. As can be seen, these distributions are very different.

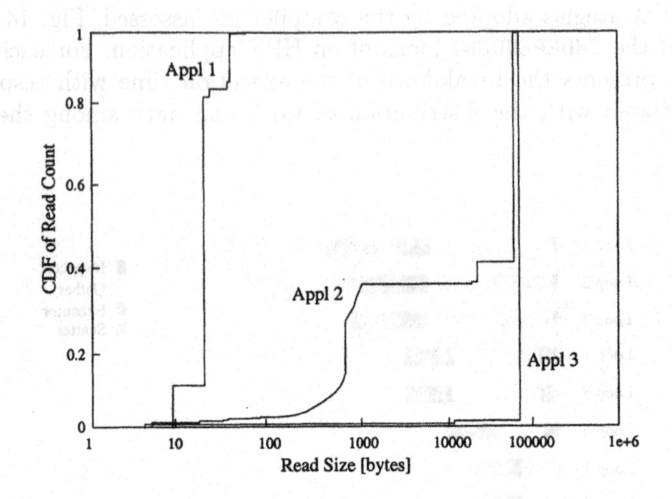

Fig. 15. Cumulative distributions of read sizes of three scientific applications [45].

In [40], a model of parallel applications, used to examine the impact of the I/O on their behavior and analyze resource scheduling policies, is formulated. The model captures the I/O and computation characteristics of the applications. An application is seen as a sequence of phases, consisting of a single burst of computation followed by a single burst of I/O. A generalization of the speedup with respect to both processor and disk resources is also derived.

5 Future Directions

The increased complexity of computer architectures and of their operating environments and the advent of new frontiers of computing enforce the use of workload characterization as the basis for performance studies. Design and tuning of new emerging systems, such as mail servers, name servers, Java virtual machines, mobile systems, require accurate studies of their workloads. The same applies to the design of software components, such as graphical user interfaces, teleconferencing applications, parallelizing compilers. For example, the performance of applications with graphical user interfaces is the reflection of user perception. Hence, the characterization of these applications has to rely on low-level measurements of the user generated events, such as keystrokes and mouse clicks, which represent the load of the systems.

New measurement and methodological approaches have to be introduced in order to cope with all these performance requirements which have also to be coupled with quality of service requirements. Moreover, since workload characterization, like performance evaluation, is still considered more as an art than as a science, the availability of integrated environments and tools able to address the performance issues encountered in the various application domains will help in mastering this art. For example, the design of efficient policies for managing the hardware and software resources of the systems will benefit from an automated process for collecting, analyzing, and modeling workload measurements. The development of tools able to automatically identify the bottlenecks and the sources of performance degradation, and to provide hints about possible solutions will also be very useful.

Acknowledgements

This work was supported in part by the European Commission under the ESPRIT IV Working Group APART, the Italian Space Agency (ASI) and the University of Pavia under the FAR program.

References

1. A.K. Agrawala and J.M. Mohr. A Markovian Model of a Job. In *Proc. CPEUG*, pages 119–126, 1978.
2. A.K. Agrawala, J.M. Mohr, and R.M. Bryant. An Approach to the Workload Characterization Problem. *Computer*, pages 18–32, 1976.
3. G.M. Amdahl. Validity of the Single–processor Approach to Achieving Large Scale Computing Capabilities. In *Proc. AFIPS Conf.*, volume 30, pages 483–485, 1967.
4. M.F. Arlitt and C.L. Williamson. Web Server Workload Characterization: The Search for Invariants. In *Proc. ACM SIGMETRICS Conf.*, pages 126–137, 1996.
5. M. Baker, J. Hartman, M. Kupfer, K. Shirriff, and J. Ousterhout. Measurements of a Distributed File System. In *Proc. ACM Symposium on Operating Systems Principles*, pages 198–212, 1991.
6. J. Beran. Statistical Methods for Data with Long–range Dependence. *Statistical Science*, 7(4):404–427, 1992.
7. R.R. Bodnarchuk and R.B. Bunt. A Synthetic Workload Model for a Distributed System File Server. In *Proc. ACM SIGMETRICS Conf.*, pages 50–59, 1991.
8. M. Calzarossa, G. Haring, and G. Serazzi. Workload Modeling for Computer Networks. In U. Kastens and F.J. Ramming, editors, *Architekture und Betrieb von Rechensystemen*, pages 324–339. Springer–Verlag, 1988.
9. M. Calzarossa, L. Massari, and D. Tessera. Performance Issues of an HPF–like compiler. *Future Generation Computer Systems*, 1999.
10. M. Calzarossa and G. Serazzi. A Characterization of the Variation in Time of Workload Arrival Patterns. *IEEE Trans. on Computers*, C-34(2):156–162, 1985.
11. M. Calzarossa and G. Serazzi. Workload Characterization: a Survey. *Proc. of the IEEE*, 8(81):1136–1150, 1993.
12. B.M. Carlson, T.D. Wagner, L.W. Dowdy, and P.H. Worley. Speedup Properties of Phases in the Execution Profile of Distributed Parallel Programs. In R. Pooley and J. Hillston, editors, *Modelling Techniques and Tools for Computer Performance Evaluation*, pages 83–95. Antony Rowe, 1992.

13. M. Colajanni, P.S. Yu, and D.M. Dias. Analysis of Task Assignment Policies in Scalable Distributed Web-server System. *IEEE Trans. on Parallel and Distributed Systems*, 9(6), 1998.
14. M.E. Crovella and A. Bestavros. Self-similarity in World Wide Web Traffic: Evidence and Possible Causes. In *Proc. ACM SIGMETRICS Conf.*, pages 160–169, 1996.
15. C.R. Cunha, A. Bestavros, and M.E. Crovella. Characteristics of WWW Client-based Traces. Technical Report BU-CS-95-010, Computer Science Dept., Boston University, 1995.
16. J. Dilley, R. Friedrich, T. Jin, and J. Rolia. Web Server Performance Measurement and Modeling Techniques. *Performance Evaluation*, 33(1):5–26, 1998.
17. D.G. Feitelson and L. Rudolph. Metrics and Benchmarking for Parallel Job Scheduling. In D.G. Feitelson and L. Rudolph, editors, *Job Scheduling Strategies for Parallel Processing*, volume 1459 of *Lecture Notes in Computer Science*, pages 1–24. Springer, 1998.
18. D. Ferrari. Workload Characterization and Selection in Computer Performance Measurement. *Computer*, 5(4):18–24, 1972.
19. D. Ferrari. On the Foundations of Artificial Workload Design. In *Proc. ACM SIGMETRICS Conf.*, pages 8–14, 1984.
20. D. Ghosal, G. Serazzi, and S.K. Tripathi. The Processor Working Set and its Use in Scheduling Multiprocessor Systems. *IEEE Trans. on Software Engineering*, SE-17(5):443–453, 1991.
21. S.D. Gribble, G.S. Manku, D. Rosselli, E.A. Brewer, T.J. Gibson, and E.L. Miller. Self–similarity in File Systems. In *Proc. ACM SIGMETRICS Conf.*, pages 141–150, 1998.
22. R. Gusella. A Measurement Study of Diskless Workstation Traffic on an Ethernet. *IEEE Trans. on Communications*, COM-38(9):1557–1568, 1990.
23. G. Haring. On Stochastic Models of Interactive Workloads. In A.K. Agrawala and S.K. Tripathi, editors, *PERFORMANCE '83*, pages 133–152. North–Holland, 1983.
24. M.T. Heath, A.D. Malony, and D.T. Rover. Parallel Performance Visualization: from Practice to Theory. *IEEE Parallel and Distributed Technology*, 3(4):44–60, 1995.
25. R. Hofmann, R. Klar, B. Mohr, A. Quick, and M. Siegle. Distributed Performance Monitoring: Methods, Tools, and Applications. *IEEE Trans. on Parallel and Distributed Systems*, 5(6):585–598, 1994.
26. R. Jain and S.A. Routhier. Packet Trains - Measurements and a New Model for Computer Network Traffic. *IEEE Journal on Selected Areas in Communications*, SAC-4(6):986–995, 1986.
27. J.L. Jerkins and J.L. Wang. Cell–level Measurement Analysis of Individual ATM Connections. *Workshop on Workload Characterization in High–Performance Computing Environments*, 1998. http://sokrates.ani.univie.ac.at/~gabi/wlc.mascots.
28. T. Le Blanc, J. Mellor-Crummey, and R. Fowler. Analyzing Parallel Program Executions Using Multiple Views. *Journal of Parallel and Distributed Computing*, 9(2):203–217, 1990.
29. W.E. Leland, M.S. Taqqu, W. Willinger, and D.V. Wilson. On the Self–similar Nature of Ethernet Traffic (Extended Version). *IEEE/ACM Trans. on Networking*, 2(1):1–15, 1994.
30. P.A. Lewis and G.S. Shedler. Statistical Analysis of Non–stationary Series of Events in a Data Base System. *IBM Journal on Research and Development*, 20:465–482, 1976.

31. B.A. Mah. An Empirical Model of HTTP Network Traffic. In *Proc. IEEE InfoCom '97*, 1997.
32. S. Majumdar, D. Eager, and R. Bunt. Characterization of Programs for Scheduling in Multiprogrammed Parallel Systems. *Performance Evaluation*, 13(2):109–130, 1991.
33. B.B. Mandelbrot and J.W. Van Ness. Fractional Brownian Motions, Fractional Noises and Applications. *SIAM Review*, 10:422–437, 1968.
34. A. Merlo and P.H. Worley. Analyzing PICL trace data with MEDEA. In G. Haring and G. Kotsis, editors, *Computer Performance Evaluation*, volume 794 of *Lecture Notes in Computer Science*, pages 445–464. Springer–Verlag, 1994.
35. N. Nieuwejaar, D. Kotz, A. Purakayastha, C. Ellis, and M. Best. File–access Characteristics of Parallel Scientific Workloads. *IEEE Trans. on Parallel and Distributed Systems*, 7(10):1075–1088, 1996.
36. V. Paxson. Growth Trends in Wide–area TCP Connections. *IEEE Network*, 8(4):8–17, 1994.
37. V. Paxson and S. Floyd. Wide–area Traffic: The Failure of Poisson Modeling. *IEEE/ACM Trans. on Networking*, 3(3):226–244, 1995.
38. S.V. Raghavan, P.J. Joseph, and G. Haring. Workload Models for Multiwindow Distributed Environments. In H. Beilner and F. Bause, editors, *Quantitative Evaluation of Computing and Communication Systems*, pages 314–326. Springer, 1995.
39. S.V. Raghavan, D. Vasukiammaiyar, and G. Haring. Generative Networkload Models for a Single Server Environment. In *Proc. ACM SIGMETRICS Conf.*, pages 118–127, 1994.
40. E. Rosti, G. Serazzi, E. Smirni, and M. Squillante. The Impact of I/O on Program Behavior and Parallel Scheduling. In *Proc. ACM SIGMETRICS Conf.*, pages 56–65, 1998.
41. G. Serazzi. A Functional and Resource–oriented Procedure for Workload Modeling. In F.J. Kylstra, editor, *PERFORMANCE '81*, pages 345–361. North–Holland, 1981.
42. K. Sevcik. Characterization of Parallelism in Applications and Their Use in Scheduling. In *Proc. ACM SIGMETRICS Conf.*, pages 171–180, 1989.
43. K.C. Sevcik. Application Scheduling and Processor Allocation in Multiprogrammed Parallel Processing Systems. *Performance Evaluation*, 19:107–140, 1994.
44. J.F. Shoch and J.A. Hupp. Measured Performance of an Ethernet Local Network. *Communications of the ACM*, 23(12):711–721, 1980.
45. E. Smirni and D. Reed. Lessons from characterizing the input/output behavior of parallel scientific applications. *Performance Evaluation*, 33(1):27–44, 1998.
46. K. Sreenivasan and A.J. Kleinman. On the Construction of a Representative Synthetic Workload. *Communications of the ACM*, 17(3):127–133, 1974.
47. D. Tessera, M. Calzarossa, and A. Malagoli. Performance Analysis of a Parallel Hydrodynamic Application. In A. Tentner, editor, *High Performance Computing*, pages 33–38. SCS Press, 1998.
48. A. Waheed and J. Yan. Workload Characterization of CFD Applications Using Partial Differential Equation Solvers. *Workshop on Workload Characterization in High–Performance Computing Environments*, 1998. http://sokrates.ani.univie.ac.at/~gabi/wlc.mascots.
49. W. Willinger, M.S. Taqqu, R. Sherman, and D.V. Wilson. Self–similarity Through High–variability: Statistical Analysis of Ethernet LAN Traffic at the Source Level. In *Proc. ACM SIGCOMM Conf.*, pages 100–113, 1995.
50. M. Zhou and A.J. Smith. Tracing Windows95. Technical Report, Computer Science Division, UC Berkeley, November 1998.

Part II

Personal Accounts of Key Contributors

From the Central Server Model to BEST/1©

Jeffrey P. Buzen
BMC Software, Inc.
880 Winter Street, Waltham, MA 02454-9111, USA
jeff_buzen@bmc.com

1 Central Server Model

The central server model [3] represented a major advance in computer performance analysis when it was first introduced. Earlier mathematical models had investigated the performance of individual system components such as central processors, disks and drums. Because they analyzed these components in isolation, early models had no way to represent the powerful interactions that take place among components and ultimately determine overall system performance.

The central server model provided the first integrated treatment of central processors, I/O devices and main memory. It enabled analysts to examine the effect that changes in any one of these components would have on a system's throughput or response time. It also enabled analysts to evaluate optimization strategies for balancing loads across I/O devices, assigning multiprogramming levels in demand paging systems, and dealing with bottlenecks that constrained overall performance.

BEST/1 is a performance modeling package that is based on the central server queuing network. It has been used for capacity planning and performance analysis in many of the world's largest data centers, and has maintained a dominant position in its market niche for more than twenty years. This article examines some of the factors that were most influential in shaping BEST/1's transition from a research project to a commercially successful software product.

2 Convolution Algorithm

The equations for the solution of the central server model involved the summation of an exceptionally large number of terms. I was concerned that a direct evaluation of these equations would be numerically unstable, and would limit the model's value as a research tool.

These concerns were the motivation for the development of the convolution algorithm [4]. This algorithm provided a highly efficient and numerically stable computational procedure for evaluating a general class of queuing networks. The central server model was included in this class, but the algorithm has since been used to evaluate models from other disciplines as well [9].

Both the central server model and the convolution algorithm were described in my doctoral dissertation, which was completed in May 1971 [3]. At the time,

G. Haring et al. (Eds.): Performance Evaluation, LNCS 1769, pp. 485–489, 2000.

I was most interested in mathematical modeling principles and computational algorithms. I believed that the central server model could be a valuable research tool for analyzing tradeoffs, interactions and relative changes in performance. However, I was not sure how accurate the model would be in absolute terms, and I had no plans to develop a commercial modeling package based on my work.

3 Initial Application

The first real world application I came across was a study carried out by A.C. Williams of Mobil Oil Corporation. A.C. Williams attended a lecture on the central server model and the convolution algorithm that I presented to corporate sponsors of Computer Science at Harvard in 1972. After my talk, he and his colleague, R. A. Bhandiwad, decided to compare the model's predictions with the results of a benchmark study being conducted at Mobil.

The benchmarks were designed to assess the performance of IBM's newly released virtual storage operating system (OS/VS1) and an older operating system that did not use virtual storage (OS/MFT). IBM had just reduced the cost of real storage to make OS/VS1 economically attractive. Williams and Bhandiwad showed that the best strategy for optimizing cost/performance was to take advantage of the price reduction to buy more memory, but to then run the older operating system (OS/MFT) and use the extra storage capacity to increase the level of multiprogramming.

Williams and Bhandiwad decided to compare their benchmark results with the predictions provided by a central server model. They began with a benchmark that required approximately 30 minutes to complete. Using measurements collected during the benchmark, they constructed a singl workload central server model, which they evaluated using the convolution algorithm. The model predicted a benchmark completion time of approximately 31 minutes.

A. C. Williams then phoned me to see if I had an explanation for the one minute error in predicted completion time. I was curious about the error, but I was much more interested in the fact that the predictions were accurate to 98%. At that point, I realized how valuable the central server model could be in a commercial setting.

4 Operational Analysis

Although I was delighted to learn of Williams and Bhandiwad's success, the observed accuracy of the central server model presented me with a new set of problems. In order to formulate and solve the original modeling problem, I had used all the standard assumptions of traditional queuing theory including independent, identically distributed exponential service times, Markovian branching probabilities, and ergodic, steady state operating conditions. It seemed highly unlikely to me that all these assumptions could be satisfied in practice. Why then did the models work so well?

To deal with this problem, I carefully reconsidered each step that an analyst would follow when applying a mathematical model to a real world problem. I ultimately concluded that the equations that were being used in these circumstances could, in fact, be derived using an alternative conceptual framework that did not depend on the stochastic assumptions of traditional queuing theory. The alternative conceptual framework, which came to be known as operational analysis, provided a much clearer understanding of the conditions that had to be satisfied for a model to provide accurate results [5], [7]. Based on this understanding, I became convinced that the central server model could be used to solve a wide range of practical problems.

5 BEST/1

By this time, I was ready to resign my faculty appointment at Harvard and my engineering position at Honeywell to join Robert Goldberg and Harold Schwenk in the founding of BGS Systems, Inc. We started the company in 1975. We had no external funding, and thus did not have the resources to begin developing a software product immediately. Instead, we supported ourselves with a variety of consulting assignments that ranged from the analysis of computer performance to the implementation of a real time system for analyzing radio-immuno assay data in a hospital laboratory.

The performance analysis assignments were obviously the most interesting to me. They not only provided funding for the incremental development of our BEST/1 modeling product, but they also helped ensure that BEST/1 would be able to address the specific analysis problems that customers cared enough about to pay us to solve. After being used internally in a number of consulting projects, BEST/1 finally emerged as an independent software product in the fall of 1977.

6 Success Factors

Our development of BEST/1 was helped enormously by the explosion of research interest in queuing networks that took place in the 1970's. The results that were most important to the success of BEST/1 were the multi-class extensions to queuing network theory developed by Baskett, Chandy, Muntz and Palacios [1], the extensions to the convolution algorithm developed by Reiser and Kobayashi [8] to evaluate the multi-class models, and the decomposition approach developed by Brandwajn [2] and Courtois [6] to represent delays for main memory and other passive resources

In addition to these theoretical advances, BEST/1 also benefited considerably from the availability of enhanced measurement facilities (SMF and RMF) that IBM provided with its new MVS operating system. Although the measurement facilities were not developed specifically to support performance modeling, the fact that they were installed in virtually all MVS data centers provided us with a reliable source of performance measurements that could always be used to build baseline models.

The advances in modeling theory and measurement technology were exceedingly helpful, but one additional factor still had to be considered to make BEST/1 a commercial success. We needed to develop a thorough understanding of the types of problems our prospective customers wanted to solve, and we had to design BEST/1 so that these problems could be solved as easily and efficiently as possible.

By and large, our prospective customers were not specialists in modeling. Instead, they were performance analysts and capacity planners responsible for ensuring that computer systems operating in large organizations provided adequate levels of service. These individuals were most interested in using models as tools that could help them do their job.

To meet their needs, we had to design a user interface for BEST/1 that expressed our mathematical modeling concepts in terms that were familiar and understandable to our customers. Instead of forcing our customers to learn our language, we had to make the effort to learn theirs.

This required us to develop a detailed understanding of the hardware components and operating systems that our customers were using. Originally, we expected to create versions of BEST/1 for a number of different hardware environments and operating systems. This proved far more difficult than we imagined, given the limited resources we had available at the time.

We decided instead to focus on the two most important operating systems used with large scale, IBM compatible mainframes: MVS and VM. This enabled us to tailor versions of BEST/1 for these two operating systems, and to develop automated tools for generating models based on the measurement data available in each environment.

The idea of developing specialized modeling tools that are tailored for specific environments and applications differs substantially from the idealized goal of developing a universal, general purpose modeling tool that can handle a very broad range of applications. Even if such an idealized tool could be built, it would probably not be a commercial success unless it was packaged in a form that made it easily accessible to paying customers with specific problems to solve. Designing well focused modeling tools with the end user's specific needs in mind is far more important to the success of these tools than any internal modeling algorithm or external data source. This is perhaps the most important lesson to be learned from the BEST/1 initiative.

7 Epilog

In March 1998, BGS Systems was merged into BMC Software, Inc. By that time, BEST/1 had been extended beyond its original mainframe orientation to include versions for several other platforms, most notably UNIX, AS/400 and VMS. A BEST/1 version for Windows NT was also under development.

BMC Software, which is the world's 12th largest independent software vendor, is continuing to provide full support for the BEST/1 modeling products. The existing BGS Systems organization retains its identity, and is now referred to as the BEST/1 division of BMC. I remain affiliated with BMC Software as a consulting scientist, and continue to pursue my original research interests in mathematical modeling and computational algorithms.

References

1. Baskett, F., Chandy, K. M., Muntz, R. R., and Palacios, J.: Open,closed, and mixed networks with different classes of customers. J. ACM 22,2 (April 1975), 248-260.
2. Brandwajn, A.: A model of a time sharing system solved using equivalence and decomposition methods. Acta Informatica 4, 1 (1974), 11-47.
3. Buzen, J. P.: Queuing network models of multiprogramming. Ph.D. Dissertation, Harvard University, Cambridge, Massachusetts, 1971.
4. Buzen, J. P.: Computational algorithms for closed queuing networks with exponential servers. C. ACM 15, 9 (September 1973), 527-531.
5. Buzen J. P.: Fundamental operational laws of computer system performance. Acta Informatica 7, 2 (1976), 167-182.
6. Courtois, P. J.: Decomposability: queuing and computer system applications. Academic Press, New York, 1977.
7. Denning, P. J., and Buzen, J. P.: The operational analysis of queuing network models. ACM Computing Surveys 10, 3 (September 1978), 225-261.
8. Reiser, M., and Kobayshi, H.: Queuing networks with multiple closed chains: theory and computation algorithms. IBM J. Res. Dev. 19 (May 1975),283-294.
9. Suri, R., Diehl, G. W. W., de Treville, S., Tomsicek, M. J.: From CAN-Q to MPX: Evolution of Queuing Software for Manufacturing. OR/MS Interfaces 25, 9 (September 1995), 128-150.

Mean Value Analysis: A Personal Account

M. Reiser

GMD, German National Research Center for Information Technology
Schloß Birlinghoven, D-53754 Sankt Augustin, Germany
martin.reiser@gmd.de

1 The Evolution of SNA in the Mid 70s

In 1977, I was manager of a small group "Distributed System Studies" in the Thomas J. Watson Research Center. At that time, ARPANET had already grown into a big US-wide meshed network using innovative technology such as adaptive routing and datagrams. By this comparison, IBM's System Network Architecture (SNA) was quite backward. It grew out of so called "Telecommunication Access Methods" and was basically a feeding network for a single mainframe complex with tree topology (Fig. 1).

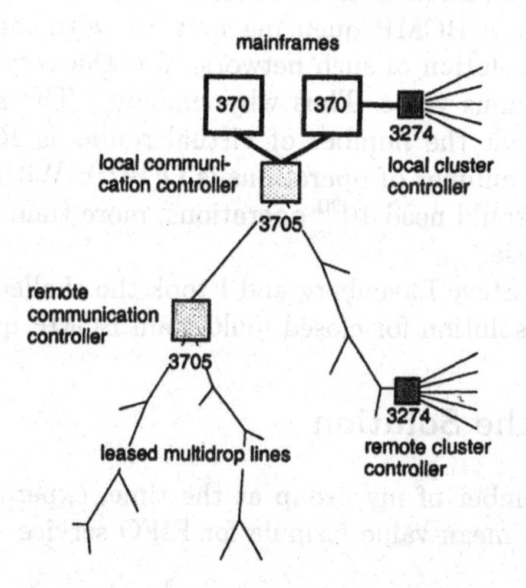

Fig. 1. SNA network in the early 70s. Tree topology feeding a host cluster.

In the mid 70s, release 3 of SNA allowed such tree subnetworks to be linked into a mesh. However, nondisruptive routing and flow-control protocols had yet to be added. This looked like a good opportunity for us at Research.

My group worked out a detailed routing architecture, based on static virtual circuits (termed virtual routes by IBM) and window flow-control protocols. To validate our approach, I wrote a SIMPL/I simulator. With a comprehensive set

G. Haring et al. (Eds.): Performance Evaluation, LNCS 1769, pp. 491–504, 2000.

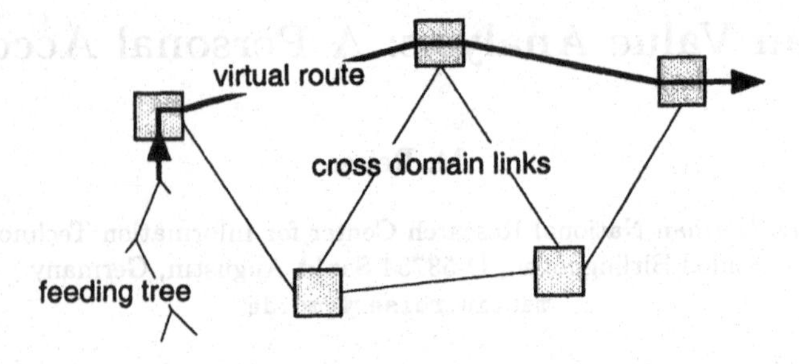

Fig. 2. SNA version 4.2: meshed network of "feeding trees." Connection oriented "Virtual Routes" provide pipes for sessions across the network.

of scenarios I could show the robustness of our proposal which eventually made its way into the major release 4.2 of SNA (Fig. 2.)

To make the simulation fast, I modeled the SNA network on the high abstraction level of a queueing network. Since window flow-control limits the number of frames in transit, each virtual route translates into a closed routing chain such as the one depicted in Fig. 3.

With the additional message independence and exponential service assumptions, my model was a BCMP queueing network with multiple closed chains [4] . The numerical solution of such networks was the very problem that I was studying in the previous years. Thus why simulate? The answer, of course, is complexity. Given that the number of virtual routes is R and the maximum window size W, the number of operations is $O(W^R)$. With only 20 routes and a window of 10 we would need 10^{20} operations, more than there are seconds in the age of the universe.

Paul Schweitzer, Steve Lavenberg and I took the challenge to find a computationally tractable solution for closed multichain BCMP queueing networks.

2 Genesis of the Solution

Paul who was a member of my group at the time, experimented with Little's law and the M/M/1 mean-value formula for FIFO service

$$t = (1 + n^{\text{arrival}})s \tag{1}$$

In (1), t is the mean waiting time of a job, s is the mean service time and n^{arrival} represents the mean backlog "seen" upon arrival instants. Equation (1) states that an arriving job has to wait for all jobs ahead of it before it spends its own service time. Since Poisson arrivals have the random observer property [14] , we can replace n^{arrival} by n, the stationary mean queue, and obtain the formula

$$t = (1 + n)s \tag{2}$$

from which the well known M/M/1 solution for the mean waiting time, $t = s/(1 - \lambda s)$, is easily obtained using Little's law $n = \lambda t$.

But what backlog does an arriving job "see" in a closed tandem network? In summer of 1977, we did not know. All we could state was that the number of jobs the arrival "sees" amounts to $N - 1$. Thus, if the arriving job "looks" at all the other queues it "sees" $N - 1$ other jobs somehow distributed over the queues. The arriving job itself is missing from the count.

Our starting point was the M station tandem system of Fig. 3.

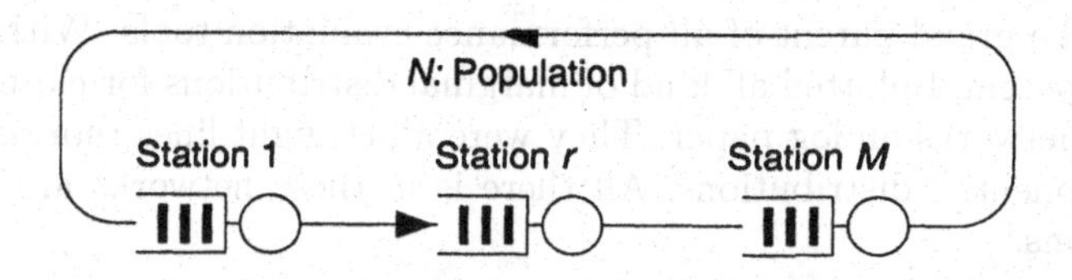

Fig. 3. Tandem queueing network, representative of a virtual route

In the remainder of the paper, I adopt the following notation:

M	:	number of queueing stations
N	:	number of jobs in the closed network (population)
γ	:	throughput
t	:	mean end-to-end time (service beginning at 1 to completion at M)
n_i	:	mean number of jobs at station i
t_i	:	mean waiting time at station i (sojourn time)
s_i	:	mean service time at station i
$\mu_i(k)$	:	queue-dependent rate of station i with queue k

Where appropriate, I will indicate with an argument notation to which population size a given performance measure relates, for example, $\gamma(N)$ is the throughput and $n_i(N)$ the mean queue size for a closed chain with population N.

The first important step towards a solution was the idea, that the "missing job" might distribute over the M stations *in proportion to the sojourn times*, in other words

$$\varepsilon_i = \frac{t_i}{\sum_{j=1}^{M} t_i} = \frac{t_i}{t} = \frac{t_i \gamma}{t \gamma} = \frac{n_i}{N} \tag{3}$$

where ε_i measures the average fraction of the "missing job" at station i.

At that point, we could write down three self consistent equations as follows:

1. Meanvalue equation: $t_i = (1 + n_i - \varepsilon_i)s = \left(1 + \frac{N-1}{N} n_i\right) s$ (4)
2. Little's law for chain: $N = \gamma t = \gamma \sum_{i=1}^{M} t_i$ (5)
3. Little's law for station: $n_i = \gamma t_i$ (6)

A fixed point of the nonlinear system (4)-(6) promises to be an approximate solution for the tandem queueing network, if indeed the missing job distributes according to (3). But does it?

For many months, this question had a strong grip on me. I was thinking incessantly about it–day and night. I still remember vividly how I was drawing sketches in a notebook while touring the fall colored Southwest of the United States in my camp mobile. But even in those beautiful surroundings, I could not find the philosopher's stone.

It was November and I was back at Watson. In my cubicle, I worked on QNET4, the grand parent of all performance evaluation tools. With the help of my APL system, I plotted all kind of marginal distributions for closed two-chain queueing networks on log paper. They were all straight lines representing truncated exponential distributions. All there is in these networks are exponential distributions.

Heureka!

If all there is are exponentials, then the arrival distribution must also be exponential, so I reasoned. Since it normalizes over $N-1$ jobs, my thought continued, it must be the stationary solution of the network with one job less. With this flash of insight, the mean backlog upon arrival is

$$n_i^{\text{arrival}} = n_i(N-1) \tag{7}$$

and the true meanvalue equation can be written as follows:

$$t_i(N) = (1 + \ n_i(N-1))\ s_i \tag{8}$$

If I use (8) instead of (4), the fixed-point problem is changed into a recurrence that allows the computation of all performance measures of interest from obvious initial conditions.

I was very excited and wrote immediately the following APL function (in obvious pseudocode notation):

$$\begin{aligned}
&n_i(0) \leftarrow 0,\ i = 1 \cdots M \\
&\text{for } k = 1\ \cdots\ N \text{ do} \\
&\quad 1.\ t_i(k) \leftarrow [1 + n_i(k-1)]\, s_i, \quad i = 1 \cdots M \\
&\quad 2.\ \gamma(k) \leftarrow k \Big/ \textstyle\sum_{i=1}^{N} t_i(k) \\
&\quad 3.\ n_i(k) \leftarrow \gamma(k)\, t_i(k), \quad i = 1 \cdots M
\end{aligned} \tag{9}$$

In less than one hour, I had numerical results, they were up to 10 decimal places identical to those of QNET4 which were based on the exact convolution algorithm [6]. Empirically I knew that I had found the solution. But empirical evidence is one thing, a proof quite another one.

3 Working out the Details

At the time, waiting times in queueing networks were considered a hard problem. I went to my colleague Steve Lavenberg for help. He is an engineer like myself, but he excels in mathematical rigor and sophistication. We explored several ideas and parted with the resolution to write two joint papers, he would prove the "Arrival Theorem" and I would try to prove (8) using the product-form solution and algebraic methods. Since I had been juggling with product-terms since 1972, I was quite confident that I would succeed.

Knowing where to look is often 90% of the solution. I wanted to relate $p_i(k|N)$, the probability of k jobs in station i, given a population of N to the related probability $p_i(k|N-1)$. It didn't take me very long to find the key result

$$p_i(k|N) = \frac{\gamma(N)}{\mu_i(k)} p_i(k-1|N-1) \tag{10}$$

By means of (10) we can compute the marginal distribution of station i for a population of size N given that the same distribution is known for a network with one job less. The recurrence is depicted in Fig. 4.

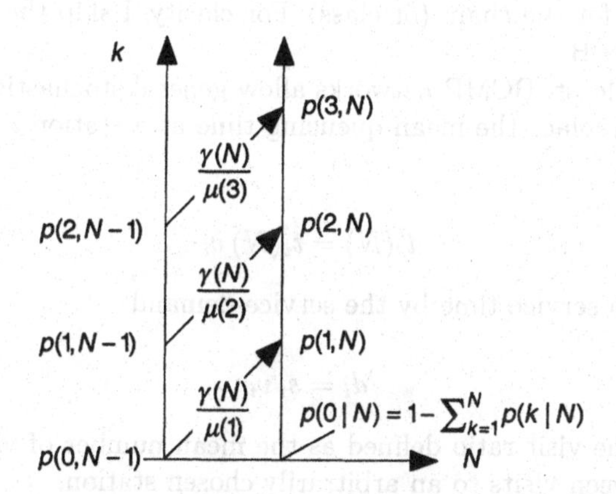

Fig. 4. Recurrence relation (10). p, γ, μ and s implicitly refer to station i.

For the important case of a server with constant rate μ_i, the mean service time is $s_i = 1/\mu_i$ and the meanvalue equation (8) follows easily from the marginal distribution (10) and the definition of the mean. I give the proof that I found in 1977 in Appendix A.

We were brought on the right track by the flow-control problem that translates into a tandem system such as the one of Fig. 3. I think it would have been unlikely, that the proper way to use Little's law in equations (5) and (6) could have been found by looking at more general systems. However, my product-term proof revealed the solution for that whole class of BCMP networks.

First, the case of queue-dependent servers is a byproduct of the proof. Knowing the marginal distribution for population $N-1$, we can compute the mean waiting times by means of Little's law as follows:

$$\begin{aligned} t_i(N) &= \frac{n_i(N)}{\gamma(N)} = \frac{1}{\gamma(N)} \sum_{k=0}^{N} k\, p(k|N) \\ &= \sum_{k=1}^{N} k\, p(k-1|N-1)/\mu_i(k) \end{aligned} \tag{11}$$

Once the throughput is known (step 2 of MVA), the new marginal distribution for population N is obtained from (10).

Second, the meanvalue equation for IS stations is trivial since jobs wait on average s_i time units regardless of other jobs at the station. Hence

$$t_i(N) = s_i \tag{12}$$

Third, PS and LCFS-PR stations have the same solution as FIFO stations, hence meanvalue equation (8) applies to this case too.

Fourth, we are of course not primarily interested in the simple tandem of Fig. 3, but in a multichain model for the SNA network. In this case, we have a throughput equation (5) for each chain and the quantities t and n have an additional index for the chain (or class). For clarity, I skip the details here and refer to Appendix B.

Last but not least, BCMP networks allow general stochastic routing. In this case, we simply replace the mean queueing time at a station i by the residency time

$$t'_i(N) = t_i(N)\, v_i \tag{13}$$

and the mean service time by the service-demand

$$d_i = s_i\, v_i \tag{14}$$

where v_i is the visit ratio defined as the mean number of visits a job makes to station i between visits to an arbitrarily chosen station.

By the summer of 1978, I had carefully worked out the proof and derived all the details of this section. The first publication of the new results was at the IFIP International Conference on Modeling and Performance Evaluation of Computer Systems in Vienna and had the immodest title "Mean Value Analysis of Queueing Networks, a New Look at an Old Problem" [23] . The "crown jewel", however, is the JACM article, co-authored with Steve, that was finished and submitted in June 1978 and appeared in April 1980 [26].

The queue-dependent solution, depicted in Fig. 4, was part of our original papers. Later scrutiny by Charly Sauer revealed a defect of the original algorithm [27] . If the probability for the empty queue is very small, the numerical difference may cause cancellation of digits up to the point of a meaningless solution. I discussed this topic comprehensively and showed an interesting connection between MVA and the convolution algorithm [24].

4 And What About the Arrival Theorem?

While, after completion of the JACM paper, my interest returned to the SNA problem, Steve Lavenberg chewed on the proof of the arrival theorem. He had to proove rigorously that the average state "seen" by arriving jobs in closed multichain networks is the time-average steady-state distribution with one job less in the arrival's chain.

For Steve, it was not "a picnic." The outline of the proof was clear, but the mathematical rigor caused delays. We submitted our paper in April 1979, it appeared a year later in the Journal of Applied Probability [15] . In the meantime, Ken Sevcik and Isi Mitrani portrayed their version of a proof at the IFIP Conference in Toronto [30] . However, they too had to overcome obstacles until the final JACM publication [31].

The arrival theorem can be proved in either of two ways: (i) by constructing and solving the embedded Markov chain for the state "seen" upon arrival and (ii) by a rate argument that expresses the arrival distribution as follows

$$p_i^{arrival}(k) = \frac{\text{Expected number of arrivals that "see" } k \text{ jobs ahead}}{\text{Expected total number of arrivals at station } i} \tag{15}$$

The arrival theorem is trivial for IS stations and proved for the FIFO case by us [15] and Sevcik and Mitrani. But what about PS and LIFO-PR service centers? To my knowledge, the corresponding theorems are yet unproved.

What is going on in a PS station? We know, that the MVA equation is the same as in the FIFO case [equation (8)]. The term $(1+n_i(N-1))$ is the average PS expansion factor, that is the fraction of the server allocated to the other jobs executing during this job's service. Thus, in the PS case, we are not looking at certain time instants, but at certain time intervals–the successive times to serve jobs. The average number of jobs observed in a sequence of such intervals is again $n_i(N-1)$, the long term time-average of the same system with one job less.

Since I don't know the proof, I leave it as an exercise for the reader.

5 Impact

When MVA came out in 1979, it was a new method that could solve general BCMP networks. Its time-complexity in the case of constant rate servers is the same as the one for the earlier convolution algorithm [25]. Hence, MVA does not solve the many chain problem of SNA either.

So is it just another academic exercise?

I think not. First, MVA works directly with the performance measures of interest: mean queue size, throughput and utilization. No normalization constants need to be computed (with their well known tendency to producing overflow).

The arrival theorem gives an intuitive explanation of the queueing behavior that can be taught at an introductory level without referring to difficult concepts of stochastic processes. And the MVA formulae are so simple that every programmable pocket calculator can solve them. Aesthetics plays a big role in my life and I admit that I was quite enamored of the MVA result.

Second, at the roots of MVA was the question of many closed chains. Now that we know the exact theory, we can take a new approach to estimating the missing customer and transform the multidimensional recurrence relation into a self-consistent set of nonlinear equations with the hope to solve the multichain problem at last.

Paul Schweitzer's suggestion that the missing customer distributes according to the mean sojourn times leads to the simplest MVA approximation, today known as Bard-Schweitzer algorithm [3,28] which is listed in Appendix C. Back in 1977, collaborating with Paul, I made first quick and dirty numerical experiments with my favorite interactive APL system. On all my flow-control samples, the iterative scheme converged quite well and the results were in reasonable agreement with my simulations. To date, the Bard-Schweitzer scheme was independently validated by several authors using many systematic and random networks and can be recommended if a fast but not very accurate solution of the multichain problem is needed.

In 1978, after I concluded the algebraic proofs of MVA, my interest returned to the flow-control problem that I wanted to study with our new MVA methodology. My goal was to get a better handle on the missing customer and to adjust MVA for nonexponential service times. I observed that Paul Schweitzer's approximation (3) underestimates the strength of the bottleneck. In the hope to do better, I constructed a representative single queueing chain to estimate the distribution of the missing job. In order to account for the nonexponential service times in communication networks, I added a term for the residual service time RST to the MVA equation as follows:

$$(N) = (1 + n(N-1) - \rho)\, s + \rho\, RST \tag{16}$$

where $\rho = \gamma(N)\, s$ is the utilization of the server. My new heuristic compared favorably with simulation results. At last, I had the desired tool to estimate the effect of flow-control windows on the throughput of SNA networks [22].

For me, the work on SNA flow-control had a special charm that made it quite different from my earlier performance evaluation work. Here, the focus of the modeling effort was on the *systems problem*, not on the complexity of mathematical concepts and solutions. The flow-control protocol was in the center and MVA provided simple building blocks to construct the solution. The heuristic inclusion for nonexponential service-times in (16) is a natural afterthought of the MVA principle.

Almost half a decade later, these ideas were picked up (or perhaps rediscovered) by various authors from the computer architecture community, most notably Mary Vernon from Wisconsin who called it AMVA (Approximate Mean Value Analysis). In AMVA, in addition to the *RST* term in (16), mean waiting times often depend on other quantities in a self-consistent manner, leading to nonlinear equations that can be solved by means of a simple iteration scheme. Hardware and software cache coherence, interconnection networks, memory and bus interference, performance of parallel algorithms and load balancing problems all were addressed using the new technique with excellent results [1,2,5,17,20,21,32,33,35,34,36,37]. Being a powerful tool in the hands of computer architects is perhaps the biggest impact that Mean Value Analysis had in the engineering community.

6 Retrospective

Since 1963, we have known the product-form solution for a general class of exponential queueing networks with a single routing chain [11]. Apparently, nobody used the model until Jeff Buzen gave the first computationally tractable algorithm almost a decade later [6]. Hisashi Kobayashi and I generalized Buzen's algorithm for BCMP networks [25]. We also found an intuitive interpretation: the off-line distributions of the stations are convoluted together. Thus, the convolution algorithm *iterates over the stations.* The convolution algorithm computes a normalization constant and performance measures have to be obtained in separate steps.

MVA that came out half a decade later, is completely different, *it iterates over jobs.* While it does so, performance measures are computed in parallel for all intermediate populations. A parametric analysis on jobs is therefore dealt with at once. But to my amazement, this was not the end. In 1986, Adrian Conway and Nicolas Georganas found yet another way to shape the computation: their algorithm, RECAL, *iterates over chains* [8]. They were able to interpret all three methods in the framework of decomposition [9].

In the two decades from 1970 to 1990, many paper appeared on all three major methods. Variations were discovered and the algorithms tuned for storage and computational efficiency. A good bibliography is found in [9] and in [13].

The Bard-Schweitzer scheme (24) was starting point for improved approximations to the multichain problem. Chandy and Neuse introduced a linear correction term in step 1 of (24), hence they called their method Linearizer [7]. Linearizer is more accurate than Bard-Schweitzer at about twice the computational cost. Serazzi and Schweitzer generalized Linearizer lately [29]. They used perturbation techniques to find a family of approximations with higher order correction terms.

No further breakthroughs were made in the 90s–the dust settled. Today MVA is the method of choice covered in many textbooks [16,13,12,10,19,18]. In 1987, the IEEE elected me as fellow and Steve Lavenberg and I received the IEEE Koij Kobayashi Computers and Communications Award "For Fundamental Contributions to the Theory and Practice of Computer and Communication Systems Performance Modeling" in 1991.

In my opinion, MVA made its mark in three areas. First, it is a great way to understand and teach queueing networks. I believe it is fair to say, that MVA brings the tool of queueing network models to engineers and programmers who would not care otherwise. Second, in the MVA framework, the multichain problem found a very satisfactory solution. The user can make a tradeoff between accuracy and speed using several well tested approximation methods. Last and most important, the MVA paradigm meshes well with the way computer architects and communication engineers think. "MVA thinking" not only solved the SNA flow-control problem but led to AMVA. In this, still virulent research endeavor, MVA principles blend with engineering insights. Since, despite the exponential increase in computing power, trace-driven simulation is "running out of gas," MVA based analytical techniques might yet prove to be, in the words of Sarita Adve "a gold mine."

Acknowledgements

I am grateful to my earlier employer, the IBM Corporation, for the great opportunity to do this research. The discovery of MVA would not have been possible without the stimulation from real problems of a real business.

I could not have discovered MVA without the work of Paul Schweitzer, who was almost there himself. Steve Lavenberg was a good discussion partner and made many contributions on the way. His mathematical care and rigor was instrumental in gaining MVA the respect of the technical community. I thank both of them for their contributions to the birth of MVA.

References

1. V. S. Adve, M. D. Hill, and M. K. Vernon. Comparison of hardware and software cache coherence schemes. *Proc. 18th Int'l. Symp. on Computer Architecture, Toronto, May 27-30*, 1991.
2. V. S. Adve and M. K. Vernon. Performance analysis of multiprocessor mesh interconnection networks with deterministic routing. *IEEE Trans. on Parallel and Distributed Systems*, 5(3):225–246, March 1994.
3. Y. Bard. Some extensions to multiclass queueing network analysis. In A. Btrimenko M. Arato and E. Gelenbe, editors, *Performance of Computer Systems*. North-Holland, 1979.
4. F. Baskett, K. M. Chandy, R. R. Muntz, and F. G. Palacios. Open, closed and mixed networks of queues with different classes of customers. *J. ACM*, 22(3):248–260, April 1975.
5. G. E. Bier and M. K. Vernon. Measurement and prediction of contention in multiprocessor operating systems with scientific application workloads. In *Proc. 1988 Int'l. Conf. on Supercomputing*, pages 9–15, St. Malo, France, July 4-8 1988.
6. J. P. Buzen. Computational algorithms for closed queueing networks with exponential servers. *Communications of the ACM*, 16(9):527–531, September 1973.
7. K. M. Chandy and D. Neuse. Linearizer: a heuristic algorithm for queueing network models of computing systems. *Communications of the ACM*, 25(2):126–134, February 1982.
8. A. E. Conway and N. D. Georganas. Recal: A new efficient algorithm for the exact analysis of multiple-chain closed queueing networks. *J. ACM*, 33(4):768–791, 1986.

9. A. E. Conway and N. D. Georganas. *Queueing Networks-Exact Computational Algorithms: A Unified Theory Based on Decomposition and Aggregation.* The MIT Press, Cambridge, Mass., 1989.
10. P. G. Harrison and N. M. Patel. *Performance Modeling of Communication Networks and Computer Architectures.* Addison-Wesley, 1992.
11. J. R. Jackson. Jobshop-like queueing systems. *Management Science*, 10(1):131–142, 1963.
12. R. Jain. *The Art of Computer Systems Performance Analysis.* John Wiley and Sons, 1991.
13. P. J. B. King. *Computer and Communication Systems Performance Modeling.* Prentice Hall, 1990.
14. L. Kleinrock. *Queueing Systems*, volume 1. J. Wiley & Sons, 1975.
15. S. S. Lavenberg and M. Reiser. Stationary state probabilities of arrival instants for closed queueing networks with multiple types of customers. *J. Applied Probability*, 17:1048–1061, 1980.
16. E. D. Lazowska, J. Zahorjan, G. S. Graham, and K. C. Sevcik. *Quantitative System Performance.* Prentice Hall, 1984.
17. S. T. Leutenegger and M. K. Vernon. A mean value performance analysis of a new multiprocessor architecture. In *Proc. 1988 ACM SIGMETRICS Conf. on Measurement and Modeling of Computer Systems*, pages 167–176, Santa Fe, New Mexico, May 24-27 1988.
18. D. A. Menasce and V. A. F. Almeida. *Capacity Planning for Web Performance, Metrics, Models and Methods.* Prentice Hall, 1998.
19. D. A. Menasce, V. A. F. Almeida, and L. W. Dowdy. *Capacity Planning and Performance Modeling, from Mainframes to Client-Server Systems.* Prentice Hall, 1994.
20. S. Owicki and A. Agarwal. Evaluating the performance of software cache coherence. In *Proc. 3rd Int'l. Conf. on Architectural Support for Prog. Lang. and Systems*, pages 230–242, Boston, April 1989.
21. J. Patel, M. J. Carey, and M. K. Vernon. Accurate modeling of the hybrid hash join algorithm. In *ACM Sigmetrics Conference on Measurement and Modeling of Computer Systems*, pages 56–66, Nashville, TN, June 1994.
22. M. Reiser. Mean value analysis of queueing networks, a new look at an old problem. In *Proc. 4th Intl. Symp. on Modeling and Performance Evaluation of Computer Systems*, Vienna, 1979. North Holland.
23. M. Reiser. A queueing network analysis of computer communication networks with window flow control. *IEEE Transactions on Communications*, COM-27(8):1199–1209, August 1979.
24. M. Reiser. Mean value analysis and convolution method for queue-dependent servers in closed queueing networks. *Performance Evaluation*, 1(1):7–18, 1981.
25. M. Reiser and H. Kobayashi. Queueing networks with multiple closed chains: Theory and computational algorithms. *IBM J. of Research and Development*, 19(3):282–294, May 1975.
26. M. Reiser and S. S. Lavenberg. Mean-value analysis of closed multichain queueing networks. *J. ACM*, 27(2):313–322, April 1980.
27. C. H. Sauer. Computational algorithms for state-dependent queueing networks. *ACM Transactions on Computer Systems*, 1(1):67–92, February 1983.
28. P. J. Schweitzer. Approximate analysis of multiclass closed networks of queues. In *Proc. International Conf. on Stochastic Control and Optimization*, 1979.

29. P. J. Schweitzer, G. Serazzi, and M. Broglia. A queue-shift approximation technique for product-form queueing networks. In *Proc. of Int.l Conf. on Computer Performance Evaluation, Modelling Techniques and Tools, LNCS 1469*, pages 267–279, 1998.
30. K. C. Sevcik and I. Mitrani. The distribution of queueing network states at input and output instants. In *Proc. 4th Internat. Symp. Modeling and Performance Evaluation of Computer Systems.* North Holland, 1979.
31. K. C. Sevcik and I. Mitrani. The distribution of queueing network states at input and output instants. *J. ACM*, 28(2):358–371, April 1981.
32. D. J. Sorin, V. S. Pai, S. V. Adve, M. K. Vernon, and D. A. Wood. Analytic evaluation of shared-memory parallel systems with ILP processors. In *Proc. 25th Int'l. Symp. on Computer Architecture (ISCA '98)*, pages 380–391, 712–727, Barcelona, Spain, July 1998.
33. T. Tsuei and M. K. Vernon. A model of multiprocessor memory and bus interference validated by system measurement. *IEEE Trans. on Parallel and Distributed Systems, Special Issue on Measurement and Evaluation of Parallel and Distributed Systems*, November 1992.
34. M. K. Vernon, R. Jog, and G. Sohi. Analysis of hierarchical cache-coherent multiprocessors. *Performance Evaluation*, 9(4), 1989.
35. M. K. Vernon, E. D. Lazowskanw, and J. Zahorjan. An accurate and efficient performance analysis technique for multiprocessor snooping cache-consistency protocols. In *Proc. 15th Int'l. Symp. on Computer Architecture*, pages 308–315, Honolulu, Hawaii, May 30 - June 2 1988.
36. G. M. Voelker, H. A. Jamrozik, M. K. Vernon, H. M. Levy, and E. D. Lazowska. Managing server load in global memory systems. In *Proc. 1997 ACM Sigmetrics Conference on Measurement and Modeling of Computer Systems*, pages 127–138, Seattle, WA, June 1997.
37. D. L. Willick and D. L. Eager. An analytical model of multistage interconnection networks. In *Proc. 1990 ACM SIGMETRICS Conf. on Measurement and Modeling of Computer Systems*, pages 192–199, Boulder, Colorado, May 1990.

Appendix

A The Product-Term Proof of 1977

I assume familiarity with Buzen's formula for the marginal

$$p_i(k|N) = \frac{1}{\mu_i(1)\mu_i(2)\cdots\mu_i(k)} \frac{G_i(N-k)}{G(N)} \tag{17}$$

and the Kobayashi-Reiser throughput equation

$$\gamma(N) = \frac{G(N-1)}{G(N)} \tag{18}$$

In (17) and (18), denotes the normalizing constant for population N, $G_i(N)$ is the normalizing constant of a related network with station i removed.

Theorem 1

Consider a closed product-form queueing network comprised of PS, LCFS-PR or FIFO servers with queue-dependent rate $\mu_i(k)$. There holds:

$$p_i(k|N) = \frac{\gamma(N)}{\mu_i(k)} p_i(k-1|N-1) \tag{19}$$

Proof: Rewrite (17) as follows:

$$p_i(k|N) = \frac{1}{\mu_i(k)} \frac{G(N-1)}{G(N)} \frac{1}{\mu_i(1)\cdots\mu_i(k-1)} \frac{G_i((N-1)-(k-1))}{G(N-1)} \tag{20}$$

On the right-hand side we recognize $p_i(k-1|N-1)$. Equation (19) follows by means of (18). q.e.d.

Corollary 1

For a station i with constant rate $\mu_i = 1/s_i$ the mean-value equation is

$$t_i(N) = (1 \;+\; n_i(N-1))\; s_i \tag{21}$$

Proof: Equation (19) simplifies to $p_i(k-1|N-1)$. Using the definition of the mean-value, we obtain:

$$\begin{aligned} n_i(N) &= \textstyle\sum_{k=1}^{N} k\, p_i(k|N) \\ &= \textstyle\sum_{k=1}^{N} p_i(k|N) \;+\; \sum_{k=1}^{N} (k-1)\, p_i(k|N) \\ &= \gamma(n)\, s_i \textstyle\sum_{k=0}^{N-1} p_i(k|N-1) \;+\; \gamma(n)\, s_i \sum_{k=0}^{N-1} k\, p_i(k|N-1) \\ &= \gamma(n)\, s_i\; (1 \;+\; n(N-1)) \end{aligned} \tag{22}$$

The mean value equation (21) follows from Little's law $t_i(N) = n_i(N)/\gamma(N)$ q.e.d.

B MVA for Multiple Routing Chains

Define

R	:	number of closed chains
$N = (N_1, N_2, \ldots, N_R)$	:	R-dimensional chain population vector
$n_{i,r}$	:	mean number of class r jobs at station i
$t_{i,r}$	:	mean waiting time of class r jobs at station i
γ_r	:	throughput of chain r

For notational convenience, we introduce the index vector $\mathbf{k} = (k_1, k_2, \ldots, k_R)$ and $\vec{1}_r = (0, 0 \underbrace{\cdots 1 \cdots}_{r\text{-th position}})$

With this notation, the MVA algorithm for multiple closed chains can be written as follows:

$$
\begin{aligned}
& n_{i,r}(\vec{0}) \leftarrow 0, \quad i = 1 \cdots M, \; r = 1 \cdots R \\
& \text{for} \quad \vec{0} \leq \mathbf{k} \leq N, \;\; r = 0 \cdots R \text{ do} \\
& \quad 1.\; t_{i,r}(\mathbf{k}) \leftarrow \left[1 \; + \; \textstyle\sum_{s=1}^{R} n_{i,s}(\mathbf{k} - \; \vec{1}_r)\right] \times s_{i,r}, \quad i = 1 \cdots M \\
& \quad 2.\; \gamma_r(\mathbf{k}) \leftarrow k_r \Big/ \textstyle\sum_{i=1}^{N} t_{i,r}(\mathbf{k}) \\
& \quad 3.\; n_{i,r}(\mathbf{k}) \leftarrow \gamma_r(\mathbf{k}) \times t_{i,r}(\mathbf{k}), \quad i = 1 \cdots M
\end{aligned}
\tag{23}
$$

The storage requirement is $O(MR\Pi_r N_r)$. It can easily be reduced to $O(M\Pi_r N_r)$ if the sum in step 1 is moved to step 3.

C Bard-Schweitzer Algorithm

$$
\begin{aligned}
& n_{i,r} \leftarrow 0, \; i = 1 \cdots M, \; r = 1 \cdots R \\
& \text{repeat until convergence:} \\
& \text{for } r = 0 \cdots R \text{ do} \\
& \quad 0.\; n_{i,r,s} \leftarrow \left\{ \begin{matrix} n_{i,r} & i \neq r \\ \frac{N_r - 1}{N_r} n_{i,r} & i = r \end{matrix} \right\} \qquad s = 1 \cdots R, \quad i = 1 \cdots M \\
& \quad 1.\; t_{i,r} \leftarrow \left(1 + \textstyle\sum_s n_{i,r,s}\right) s_i, \quad i = 1 \cdots M \\
& \quad 2.\; \gamma_r \leftarrow N_r \Big/ \textstyle\sum_{i=1}^{N} t_{i,r} \\
& \quad 3.\; n_{i,r} \leftarrow \gamma_r \, t_{i,r}, \quad i = 1 \cdots M
\end{aligned}
\tag{24}
$$

The variables $n_{i,r,s}$ stand for $n_{i,s}(k, \vec{1}_r)$ in (23).

The Early Days of GSPNs

Marco Ajmone Marsan[1], Gianfranco Balbo[2], and Gianni Conte[3]

[1] Dipartimento di Elettronica, Politecnico di Torino – Italy
ajmone@polito.it
[2] Dipartimento di Informatica, Università di Torino – Italy
balbo@di.unito.it
[3] Dipartimento di Ingegneria dell'Informazione, Università di Parma – Italy
conte@ce.unipr.it

1 B.G. (Before GSPNs)

It was 1979, when the Italian National Research Council launched the first nationwide cooperative research program in Computer Science. The research program was named "Progetto Finalizzato Informatica" (PFI for short), and comprised a number of research lines, including one devoted to multiprocessor systems, aiming at the achievement of both experimental and theoretical results. In the initial phases of the activities of PFI, much time was spent in contacts among researchers of different universities and research centers to form working groups with specific objectives. For this reason, one day in late 1979, four people met at the Electronics Department of Politecnico di Torino, in the office of Gianni Conte.

Gianni Conte had a background in the field of microelectronics, but his research interests at that time were shifting toward computer science in general, and more precisely toward microprocessor system architectures. Together with some other professors of microelectronics of Politecnico di Torino (most notably Dante Del Corso and Francesco Gregoretti) he had been involved in the research line of PFI devoted to multiprocessor systems, and was setting up a team for implementing a multiprocessor prototype (named TOMP, for TOrino MultiProcessor), and for obtaining theoretical results in the field of multiprocessor architectures. While for the prototype development the group had sufficient internal competence, the investigation of the relative merits of different multiprocessor architectures required some additional expertise, that he was seeking from his three guests.

Gianfranco Balbo was at the Computer Science Department of the Università di Torino. He had recently obtained a PhD from Purdue University under the supervision of Peter Denning, with a dissertation on queuing network models of computer systems. He was thus expert in the field of performance evaluation, and possibly quite interested in the application of his theoretical background to the performance-oriented design of multiprocessor architectures.

Gian Maria Secco Suardo was with Centro Ricerche FIAT (the research center of the Italian car manufacturer whose headquarters are located in Torino). He had just returned from MIT where he had spent a period as a visiting researcher,

G. Haring et al. (Eds.): Performance Evaluation, LNCS 1769, pp. 505–512, 2000.

working on the use of performance analytical techniques for the design of flexible manufacturing systems. As such, he too was one of the researchers in Torino with the most experience in the utilization of advanced performance analysis techniques.

Marco Ajmone Marsan was with the same Department as Gianni Conte, but he had quite a different background, since both his studies and his research experiences had been in the field of telecommunications. He had just returned from UCLA, where he had obtained a MSEE with a specialization in telecommunication networks. Since at that time among the professors teaching courses on networks and protocols at UCLA were L.Kleinrock, I.Rubin, R.Muntz, and M.Gerla, he had been exposed to quite a substantial amount of theoretical results in the field of performance analysis, with applications to the design of networks.

The meeting resulted in an agreement for the cooperation in the performance analysis of the different multiprocessor architectures that would be considered for TOMP, so as to guarantee that the prototype would be able to meet some predefined efficiency criteria. Unfortunately, the very busy schedule of a private applied research center did not allow the actual participation of Gian Maria Secco Suardo in the research activities that developed from that meeting.

The time to actually sit down and work didn't come immediately, because the selection of the candidate architectures for TOMP took almost one year to complete. However, the preliminary phases of the project were useful to understand what could be the main points on which a performance study should focus and what were the requirements for the analysis tools that could be used to face problems in which congestion and synchronization delays were the main causes of performance loss.

In the Summer of 1980, Marco Ajmone Marsan returned to UCLA for a three-month cooperation with the "Research in Distributed Processing" group, led by Algirdas Avizienis and Mario Gerla. Among the PhD students in that group was Mike Molloy, who was completing his dissertation on the definition of Stochastic Petri Nets (SPNs) and their application to the performance analysis of some simple protocols and distributed systems.

The fact that SPNs could be quite appealing for the performance investigation of multiprocessor architectures was immediately evident, so that the work of Mike Molloy was carefully studied by the group in Torino in late 1980 and early 1981. In the framework of this starting research activity, two theses were offered, one at the Electronics Department of Politecnico di Torino, the other at the Computer Science Department of Università di Torino, with the objective of writing software for the automated analysis of SPN models, and for developing models of simple multiprocessor architectures. Two exceptionally good students accepted to participate in this research with their theses: Giovanni Chiola and Gianfranco Ciardo.

In December 1981, just few days before Christmas, Mike Molloy visited Torino, and had long discussions with all the members of the team actively doing research on SPNs. The legendary moment of this visit was the first meeting between Mike Molloy and Giovanni Chiola: Giovanni entered the office that

Mike was using, said "Hallo", sat down, and continued: "Lemma five in your dissertation is wrong!" The moment of panic of all of us can be easily imagined.

2 The Birth of a Generalization

In the construction of the first models of multiprocessor systems, it became immediately clear that the SPN definition used by Molloy had some drawbacks as it forced the association of exponentially distributed random firing delays with transitions that had essentially a logical meaning, being used to implement complex changes in the marking of the Petri net. The introduction of transitions with null firing time was thus proposed.

Two options were considered for the addition of immediate transitions (this is how we decided to call transitions with null firing delay) into SPN models. On the one hand it would have been possible to allow exponential firing delays with infinite rates. On the other hand we could choose to abandon the Markovian framework for a semi-Markovian one in which markings would be of two types, depending on the distribution of their sojourn time: either exponential or deterministic (equal to zero).

The semi-Markov option allowed a simpler interpretation, and it could even be reconducted to a Markovian framework by short-circuiting the behavior in zero time and adequately accounting for firing probabilities of immediate transitions. For these reasons this was the preferred approach.

Long discussions were devoted to the choice of the names to be used for the new class of Petri nets and their elements: Generalized Stochastic Petri Nets (GSPNs) was the final choice for this new Petri net based formalism; transitions were said to be either timed or immediate, markings were called either tangible or vanishing. The names *Extended Stochastic Petri Nets* (ESPNs) and *ghost markings* were discarded in order to avoid giving the impression of a modeling paradigm based on some sort of "magic" or "Extra-Sensorial Perception".

Whereas the selection of the timed transition to be fired in a tangible marking could be easily based on firing rates, the selection of the immediate transition to be fired next when a vanishing marking was entered had to be based on some additional probability mass function (pmf). In the original definition of GSPNs, one such pmf was associated with each vanishing marking. These pmfs were called "switching distributions" and vanishing markings with several enabled immediate transitions were called "random switches". The use of random switches was a weakness of the original approach, that was later corrected in the second definition of the GSPN modeling paradigm, since the specification of random switches required information on the reachable vanishing markings of the net. The model developer thus was not able to completely define a GSPN model and all of its parameters before generating the Petri net reachability graph.

The description of the original GSPN definition, together with some preliminary examples of its application to modeling simple multiprocessor architectures went into a paper submitted to the 1982 European Workshop on Applications and Theory of Petri Nets, to be held in the beautiful village of Varenna, on Lake

Como in Italy. The paper was rejected with a 13-page review explaining in great detail how wrong and naive the approach was, and how useless the modeling paradigm would be for any sort of conceivable application.

In spite of the frustration produced by such negative comments, the research on GSPNs was continued, seeking the advice of some of the "gurus" of performance analysis in the USA. Herbert Schwetman of Purdue University was particularly helpful in this stage, and he encouraged us to continue our work, and to submit a paper with our results to SIGMETRICS'83. So we did, and, to our great surprise, the paper was selected as one of the three best papers of the conference, and thus an extended version was later published on the ACM Transactions on Computer Systems.

3 Three Keys to Success

The unexpected success of GSPNs is probably due to three quite different reasons: the simplicity of the formalism, the presence of immediate transitions, and the availability of design and analysis tools.

A low-level formalism

GSPNs are based on very few (and simple) primitive constructs that with their precise semantics make the formalism easy to learn and to apply to the analysis of many interesting practical problems. After the proposal of GSPNs, researchers from all over the world and with considerably different backgrounds, found GSPNs easy to grasp and useful for quickly obtaining and analyzing complex probabilistic models that would have been otherwise difficult to construct in a reliable manner.

In some cases, GSPN models of complex systems are cluttered with many details that are related with peculiar features of the system, but that are also due to the need of "encoding" them with low-level primitives; the need for more powerful constructs was felt since the early application of GSPNs to the analysis of multiprocessor architectures. However, instead of revising the formalism with further extensions and with the introduction of higher-level primitives that could make complex models simple to implement, but also simple models cumbersome, we decided to keep the basic definition unchanged and to leave to the proposal of a separate (but quite compatible) higher-level extension (namely, Stochastic Well formed Nets: SWNs) on which Giovanni Chiola was working in those days, the burden of fulfilling these expectations. This choice turned out to be of great advantage for the diffusion of GSPNs.

Avoiding to add complexity in the basic formalism allowed many newcomers to become quickly acquainted with GSPNs without scaring them away with cumbersome definitions. On the other hand, researchers already familiar with the features of the basic formalism found quite interesting the possibility of using with little additional effort the more complex high-level extensions, as they realized that this additional complexity pays off when it is actually required by the difficulty of the problems at hand.

The role of immediate transitions

As we already pointed out, immediate transitions were originally included in GSPNs with the purpose of allowing a simple representation of extremely short activities and logical choices. During the development of the formalism and the first years of its use, we employed GSPNs mainly as a convenient and fast vehicle for the construction of complex Markov chains. In most cases we thought that we had a clear understanding of the structure of the models, so that GSPNs were used only as a graphical description language for the specification of probabilistic representations. This was the reason for including the so-called "random switches" in the original definition of GSPNs that required the knowledge of (parts) of the state space of the model.

Only the extensive use of the formalism made us understand the role that the structure of the underlying untimed net could play in allowing many more results to be derived from the model. Time scale differences captured with timed and immediate transitions were related with the concepts of visible and invisible transitions classical in Petri net theory. The priority of immediate over timed transitions led to the study of untimed Petri net with different levels of priority. Drawing on these results, we got a clear understanding of the danger of specifying "confused" models and thus of the difficulty of constructing "correct" models including sequences of immediate transitions.

To help the analysts specify "well behaving" nets, we revised the first definition of GSPNs. The concept of *extended conflict set*, originally developed by Giovanni Chiola, was formalized and methods were developed for the identification of this structure at the net level. The new definition allowed the complete specification of a GSPN model and of its parameters with no need for a preliminary knowledge of the model reachability graph.

This early experience helped us build a first bridge between qualitative and quantitative modelling and to discover that structural results had a fundamental role for simplifying model specification and improving analysis techniques, thus allowing us to cope with larger and more complex models. Symmetry detection and exploitation, modular construction and solution, development of reduction and approximation techniques are among the many results that have been derived within the framework of GSPNs and that explicitly or implicitly rely on structural results and on immediate transitions.

Design and analysis tools

Even the simplest GSPN models that one can conceive are difficult to describe and analyze without the use of proper software tools. Immediately after we started using GSPN models for the analysis of multiprocessor architectures, we realized that developing such software was a must.

As we originally used GSPNs only as a tool for the description of complex Markov chains, we first implemented some simple solution algorithms and a textual interface. At that time we worked with computer, pencil and paper as we were first drawing our models on (huge) sheets of paper that were later-on input to the program. Since many errors were made during this input phase, we quickly upgraded the textual interface with syntax-directed ad-hoc commands that simplified the task of modifying and testing the syntactical correctness of our descriptions before starting the analysis. This software, written mostly by Gianfranco Ciardo during the preparation of his thesis in Torino, was made public in 1984, when it was presented in Paris during one of the first editions of the "Conference on Modelling Techniques and Tools for the Performance Evaluation of Computer/Communication Systems".

At the same time, Giovanni Chiola, using the first SUN workstation available at Politecnico di Torino, started the development of a graphical interface that was originally inspired by a similar work of Mike Molloy and that subsequently became the core of the software tool "GreatSPN". GreatSPN had the merit of joining a powerful graphical interface with a large variety of (both qualitative and quantitative) analysis algorithms. Models developed with GreatSPN had the important advantage of making practical the possibility for a performance analyst to first study qualitative properties with methods he was little familiar with, and for formal method experts to complete their correctness and validation analysis with efficiency considerations. The animation and (discrete event) simulation facilities of GreatSPN contributed in making GSPNs acceptable also in management-oriented environments where their intuitive representations of real problems were more important than the powerful analysis methods that could be used for their evaluation.

The free distribution of this software to academic researchers helped in widespreading the use of GSPNs and in building a deep knowledge of the formalism within the Performance Evaluation community.

4 Spreading the Word

The incredible success of the SIGMETRICS'83 paper (made even more unexpected by the failure of previous year), coupled with the discovery that beyond Mike Molloy and our group, several other researchers were conducting similar studies on stochastic Petri nets, suggested the idea of organizing a meeting devoted to the discussion of the researches conducted in this field.

The actual plans for the workshop were finalized after meeting Stephane Natkin and Gerard Florin from Paris, France, Jean-Claude Laprie from Toulouse, France, John Meyer from the University of Michigan, USA, and Kishor Trivedi from Duke University, USA, at the "International Workshop on Applied Mathematics and Performance/Reliability Models of Computer/Communication Systems" organized in Pisa by Giuseppe Iazeolla in the Fall of 1983, where their most recent results on performance/reliability analysis techniques based on Petri net-like paradigms were presented.

The title of the meeting that we originally chose: "International Workshop on Stochastic Petri Nets", was later changed to "International Workshop on Timed Petri Nets" because we feared that choosing too narrow a topic would result in limited interest and participation. Kishor Trivedi accepted to be the Workshop Chairman, and Gianfranco Balbo took the responsibility of the organization of the technical program as Program Chairman.

The international response to the call for papers was extremely good, and the participation in the Workshop, held in Torino on July 1-3, 1985, was more than we had hoped for. Thirty-four papers were presented, and among their authors were leading researchers, such as J. Billington, G. Florin, C. Girault, J. F. Meyer, M. K. Molloy, T. Murata, S. Natkin, G. S. Shedler, K. S. Trivedi, M. K. Vernon.

The success of the workshop was such that it was unanimously decided to organize a second version two years later in the USA. Mary Vernon volunteered to host it at the University of Wisconsin; Tadao Murata accepted to be the General Chairman; Mary Vernon and Mike Molloy acted as Program Co-chairs. For better reflecting the focus of the meeting, the name was changed to "International Workshop on Petri Nets and Performance Models" (PNPM for short).

The renewed success of the meeting in the USA convinced us that it would be useful to continue the series of workshops, and the following editions were held in Kyoto (Japan) in 1989, in Melbourne (Australia) in 1991, in Toulouse (France) in 1993, in Durham (USA) in 1995, in Saint Malo (France) in 1997, and the next edition will be held in Zaragoza (Spain) in 1999.

Acknowledgements

The development of GSPN theory, of the software tools for the automated solution of GSPN models, and of the numerous models that were successfully used in over fifteen years of activity in such diverse fields as computer science, telecommunications, manufacturing, and reliability, are due to a number of researchers and students that is too large to explicitly mention all of their names. We wish however to gratefully acknowledge their contributions; the success of GSPNs would not have been possible without their dedicated work.

A few individual thanks are however necessary. Extraordinary contributions to GSPN theory, software, and applications came from G. Chiola and G. Ciardo. Important results were obtained by A. Bobbio, S. Donatelli, and G. Franceschinis.

A bibliography collecting the references to the most important papers on GSPNs is not available, and in any case it would be too long to be included here. The proceedings of the PNPM workshops are probably the best source of references for most of the papers that have been published on the subject. Here we only explicitly mention the paper containing the first definition of GSPNs and the two books that we have written on the subject summarizing much of the work done in Torino about GSPNs, with many pointers to the most important results obtained within our group as well as by the many researchers that are using GSPNs throughout the world.

References

1. M. Ajmone Marsan, G. Balbo, and G. Conte. A class of generalized stochastic Petri nets for the performance analysis of multiprocessor systems. *ACM Transactions on Computer Systems*, 2(1), May 1984.
2. M. Ajmone Marsan, G. Balbo, and G. Conte. *Performance Models of Multiprocessor Systems.* MIT Press, Cambridge, USA, 1986.
3. M. Ajmone Marsan, G. Balbo, G. Conte, S. Donatelli, and G. Franceschinis. *Modelling with Generalized Stochastic Petri Nets.* John Wiley, 1995.

The Discovery of Self-Similar Traffic

Walter Willinger

AT&T Labs - Research
Florham Park, NJ 07932
walter@research.att.com

1 Background

With the proliferation of packet-switched networks in the 1980s and a strong preference in parts of the engineering and communications research communities to work on ATM (asynchronous transfer mode) related problems, teletraffic theory, that is, the application of queueing theory to the performance analysis and evaluation of communication networks, faced a new set of challenges, some of which questioned its very foundations. Originally developed to supply engineers with adequate quantitative methods and techniques for designing, managing and controlling circuit switched networks providing plain old telephone service (POTS), teletraffic theory had become arguably one of the most successful applications of mathematical modeling in industry. However, in view of the widespread and rapid deployment of packet switching based technologies and new services, and especially because of the explosive growth of the Internet, traditional teletraffic theory found itself under intense scrutiny. In particular, as some of the arguments went, performance models are only as good as their underlying assumptions – although teletraffic theory had produced a steady supply of new and ever more complex models for packet traffic, the models' foundations had generally been based on POTS-based tradition, on good faith, or on the modelers' own (mis)conceptions about the presumed dynamics of traffic in a packet-switched networking environment. Put differently, since traffic modeling is considered to be an essential ingredient of teletraffic theory and since describing packet traffic had become largely a theoretical exercise that was essentially disconnected from reality during the emergence of packet-switched networks, the question of whether or not all these theoretical models had anything in common with measured traffic as observed on links within "live" packet networks could be heard more and more frequently. Particularly vocal in this respect were members of the Internet research community who "knew" their network and had a good qualitative understanding of the traffic patterns that they observed first-hand and on a daily basis. Around 1990, there was almost unanimous agreement among the various communities involved in one way or the other in network performance modeling and evaluation, that it would be interesting or, at least worthwhile, to find out and to check how the most commonly used models of packet traffic compared against measured traffic traces collected from "real" (in contrast to "experimental") packet networks. This is the setting in which my work on analyzing measured high-time resolution traffic traces at Bellcore

G. Haring et al. (Eds.): Performance Evaluation, LNCS 1769, pp. 513–527, 2000.

should be viewed – work that ultimately led to the discovery of the self-similar nature of data traffic in the early 1990s.

2 Being in the Right Place

One of the results of the U.S. government-mandated divestiture of AT&T in 1983 was the establishment of Bell Communications Research (subsequently known as Bellcore), a company that was to provide engineering, administrative and other services to the then seven Regional Bell Operating Companies who jointly owned Bellcore. The Applied Research Area within Bellcore provided applied research in a wide range of different areas related to telecommunications (e.g., networking, computer science, mathematics, statistics, optimization) to the owners and was core-funded. This funding model has been widely cherished in the industrial research community because it does not tie individual researchers to particular projects over short time frames but instead offers greater flexibility for researchers to pursue broader multi-year research agendas focused on key problems.[1]

One such problem that intrigued a number of researchers at Bellcore (the names of Will E. Leland, a computer scientist interested in networking and systems research, and Teunis J. Ott, a mathematician working in queueing theory come to mind) in the mid-1980s was the apparent discrepancy between the blind faith with which the various theoretical models of packet traffic were used to predict or evaluate performance in the emerging packet-switched network environments, and a general lack of basic understanding of what these models had or didn't have in common with actual packet traffic that was transmitted over real networks.[2] The discussions at Bellcore gathered enough momentum that Will Leland teamed up with his colleague Daniel V. Wilson to provide the right mixture of exceptional software and hardware expertise and build from scratch a first-of-its-kind piece of equipment that enabled them to collect complete (i.e., no losses), high-time resolution (i.e., a time stamp accuracy of about 100 microseconds), and high-volume (i.e., time stamp, status, length and 60 bytes of header information for every packet seen on the network were recorded) packet traces from Ethernet LANs running at 10 Mbps. The monitor was built and stress-tested in 1987-89, and complete week-long traces started to be collected from different Ethernet LANs at Bellcore and were recorded on 8 mm tapes (about one tape a day) from 1989 onwards. The resulting tapes quickly started to fill up shoe box after shoe box (literally!), while Leland and Wilson feverishly advertized the existence of "real" traffic measurements to the research community

[1] I believe that the work at Bellcore leading to the discovery of self-similar traffic would not have been possible after 1993/94, when core-funded research was largely replaced by project-funded research.

[2] This same problem also intrigued numerous other research groups and researchers outside of Bellcore; e.g., R. Jain, S.R. Routhier and D. Feldmeier at MIT; R. Caceres and R. Gusella who worked on their Ph.D. degrees at Berkeley; H. Saito and his group at NTT – see below; to name but a few.

at large and searched for people within Bellcore interested in "taking a look" at the measured data. For me, their advertisement campaign and their "in-house" search came just at the right time.

I joined Bellcore Applied Research as a member of technical staff in the Computer and Communication Research Lab at the end of 1986, after finishing my Ph.D. thesis at Cornell University under the supervision of Murad S. Taqqu. Having Murad Taqqu, one of the foremost experts on the theory of self-similar processes as my advisor, I was exposed for four years to the basic concepts and latest developments in the area of self-similar stochastic processes. By listening to weekly seminars presented by the leading experts in the field, by taking special courses covering various aspects of the theory of self-similar processes and their applications, and by reading and starting to appreciate the numerous papers that Benoit Mandelbrot wrote in the 1960s and 1970s on topics related to self-similarity, I learned a lot about the field, without actually working on a particular problem. In fact, throughout my graduate studies, I was more interested and worked mainly in an area that became known as Mathematical Finance; that is, the application of mathematical techniques, especially from probability theory and stochastic calculus, to the study of financial markets. I continued working in this field during my first few years at Bellcore, but around 1990/91, the "writing on the wall" became clear and I was urged to work on problems that are less esoteric from Bellcore's perspective and are more directly related to the mission of Bellcore Applied Research of providing Bellcore's owner with fundamental research in networking- and communications-related areas. In my case, this meant a gradual re-focusing of my research, becoming acquainted with traditional teletraffic theory, learning about packet switched networking, ATM, and the Internet, and getting to know some of the pitfalls associated with the way many results from conventional queueing analysis and simulations were used and interpreted. During this process, I benefited tremendously from my colleague at Bellcore, V. Ramaswami, who got me interested in looking at traffic-related problems for packet networks and who taught me from the very beginning to take the existing packet traffic models with a grain of salt; the models tended to be mathematical constructs that depended heavily on the modelers' intuitive understanding of networking reality, they typically focused entirely on analytic tractability, and empirical validations against measured data were considered superfluous and unnecessary.

Equipped with this "unusual" appreciation for teletraffic theory and traffic modeling, and trained in the apparently completely unrelated and – at first sight – highly esoteric subject of self-similar processes, I first found out about Leland and Wilson's work on collecting Ethernet LAN traffic, about their initial findings, and their desperate search for someone to take a look at the data when I served on the Technical Program Committee for the 7th ITC Specialist Seminar on "Broadband Technologies: Architectures, Applications, Control and Performance" and handled Leland's paper [16]. In this paper and his other preprints with collaborators J. Fowler [12] and D. Wilson [17] that were circulating within Bellcore around that time, Leland described eloquently and in intuitive terms the surprising feature observed in the measurements, namely that the measured traffic exhibited burstiness over a wide range of time scales. To characterize this empirical observation, he used the metaphor *"traffic 'spikes' ride on longer-term 'ripples', that in turn ride on still longer-term 'swells',"*, and he supported his metaphor with two "similarly looking" plots of measured packet rates over hours and minutes, respectively. For me, his metaphor and the accompanying plots were just different ways of expressing the fact that the underlying measurements exhibit self-similar characteristics; that is, the packet rate process looks roughly the same, irrespective of whether it is measured over time units on the order of milliseconds, seconds, minutes or beyond. In any case, Leland and Wilson and I started to talk about the measurements in late 1990, and I introduced them to the concept of self-similarity shortly thereafter. The discussions continued and intensified in 1991 when I started a preliminary analysis of a few measured traffic traces, and a full-blown and mutually highly beneficial collaboration that included by now also Murad Taqqu was in high gear by 1992. This work resulted in the original paper on the self-similar nature of Ethernet LAN traffic presented at ACM/SIGCOMM'93 in San Francisco [18].[3]

3 Discovering 3D Putting the Pieces Together

Our empirical studies in the early 1990s at Bellcore that resulted in the finding that Ethernet LAN traffic is self-similar or fractal in nature serves as a reminder that new discoveries don't necessarily require new mathematical concepts, or novel statistical methodologies[4], or for that case, new networking technologies. Instead, the aspect of discovery often lies in applying a well-known mathematical concept (e.g., self-similar processes) in a new context (e.g., networking) where it does away with tradition (e.g., teletraffic theory) and hence provokes differences in opinions; advocates taking a new look at established theories; and invites exploring hitherto uncharted territories. However, the aspect of novelty has to go beyond stating the mere fact (e.g., LAN traffic is self-similar or fractal in nature) – it has to fully exploit the context within which the data have been collected in the first place (e.g., Ethernet local area network), and should take full advantage of the unique features of the available data (e.g., high-quality, high-volume, highly-structured).

As far as the underlying mathematical concepts are concerned, self-similar processes have been extensively studied by probabilists since the days of Kol-

[3] An extended version of this paper was subsequently published in *IEEE/ACM Transactions on Networking* [19] and was awarded the 1995 W.R. Bennett Prize from the IEEE Communication Society for the most outstanding paper reporting original work in the *IEEE/ACM Transactions on Networking* in 1994, and the 1996 IEEE W.R.G. Baker Prize from the IEEE Board of Directors for the most outstanding paper reporting original work in all of the IEEE publications in 1994.

[4] Note however, that the networking application motivated the recent development of new techniques for inferring scaling behaviors; for example, the emergence in the networking area of the highly effective and attractive wavelet-based methods for inferring self-similarity, introduced by Abry and Veitch [1].

mogorov [15]. During the 1960s and 1970s, they were brought to the attention of statisticians and applied scientists by Benoit Mandelbrot and his co-workers. Widely recognized as "the father of fractals," Mandelbrot focused on and popularized the essence behind self-similarity, namely the notion of "scale-invariance," and he demonstrated the relevance of scaling phenomena in a wide range of areas in the physical, social and biological sciences [22][5]. With regard to the problem of statistical inference for self-similar phenomena, a number of heuristic graphical methods had already been known and used for decades; for example, variance-time-type analysis by Cox and Townsend [4], R/S-analysis by Hurst [14] and studied extensively by Mandelbrot, and some periodogram-based techniques. Other less ad-hoc periodogram-based methods had just been studied analytically (e.g., [13,7,2]) and could be shown to have provably desirable statistical properties and to be computationally feasible [2]. Finally, as far as packet networks are concerned, they have been around since the early 1960s, and the research community had started to rely more and more on the rapidly expanding and increasingly popular Internet. In particular, since their development at around 1980, Ethernets had become one of the most successful and widely used LAN technology by 1990.

Despite the wide deployment of Ethernets, the traffic collection effort at Bellcore around 1990 was the first large-scale traffic measurement experiment performed on "live" Ethernet LANs that offered the potential for an in-depth look into the dynamics of Ethernet traffic at the level of individual packets. Simply put, the measurements collected by Leland and Wilson were the main reasons why our discovery of the self-similar nature of network traffic had such a pronounced impact on the networking, the applied probability and statistics communities, and beyond. As discussed in [31], it is difficult to think of any other area in the physical, social or biological sciences where the available data are so voluminous and provide such detailed information about so many different facets of behavior. To make the most of the unique opportunity of "mining" these first-of-their-kind data sets, I emphasized from the very beginning the need for the constant involvement of a range of researchers with very different backgrounds (e.g., networking, probability, statistics) in the analysis process. Examples that show that this insistence paid off right away and throughout our studies include (i) the way we went about dealing with the unheard of amounts of available high-quality data, (ii) our conscientious decision to present the results of our analysis in a visually intuitive manner rather than relying on some commonly accepted, abstract and non-intuitive (at least for non-statisticians) statistical formalism, and (iii) the ability to reduce the observed self-similarity phenomenon to a level where it could be explained and validated in simple networking terms.

[5] Although not related to data networking, Mandelbrot's paper [21] is one of the first applications of the self-similarity concept to communication systems.

4 Let the Data Do the Talking, or Know Your Audience

In terms of the measurements that Leland and Wilson collected at Bellcore and stored away on 8-mm tapes for "unspecified future" research purposes, the general sentiment in early the 1990s was that because of their heterogeneous nature (i.e., they were collected over a number of years, from different places in the network, and under quite different networking conditions), there would be little hope of finding any common features in the data. In the same spirit, though somewhat more optimistic, the overall feeling was that if there were to exist common features in these vast sets of measurements, the work involved to detect, identify and validate them across a representative subset of the collected data would be too time-consuming and extremely cumbersome and tedious, to say the least.

Not the least disturbed by this general skepticism about the potential of finding common hidden features in the data, my initial discussions with Will Leland about his "traffic spikes-ripples-swells" observation, my conjecture of a possible connection between his metaphor and the mathematical concept of self-similarity, and some ad-hoc testing of this conjecture using an initial supply of data sets extracted by Dan Wilson from the existing tapes showed convincingly that "scale-invariance" was something that the data did have in common. More importantly, it quickly dawned on us that this common feature could be visualized in a very simple way, making good use of the high time-resolution property of the measurements. Indeed, when plotting the traffic rate process (i.e. number of packets or bytes per time unit) at different levels of resolution (i.e., different choices of time units) ranging from hundreds of seconds to tens of milliseconds, it became quickly apparent by visually inspecting the resulting plots that Ethernet LAN traffic looked and behaved the same (i.e., had the same statistical properties), irrespective of the chosen time scale. Furthermore, when focusing on an arbitrary segment of the traffic rate process measured over a fixed time scale and investigating that segment under a "microscope" by zooming in on finer and finer resolution levels or time scales, the plots revealed a striking pattern that had all the features commonly associated with "fractals:" when viewed under this microscope, an apparent burst on one time scale is found to be made up of many little bursts, interspersed by less bursty periods, and each one of these little bursts consists of even smaller burst etc. In other words, moving from small to large time scales, *"traffic 'spikes' ride on longer-term 'ripples', that in turn ride on still longer-term 'swells',"* just as Leland pointed out in his early attempts to describe the "wild" type of burstiness he observed in the measured traffic traces.

Having succeeded in relating this "wildness" of the traffic to self-similarity (still only heuristically, though), we could start exploiting the mathematical and statistical framework provided by the theory of self-similar processes to put our heuristic finding on more solid grounds. That we were ultimately able to support our visual "proof" of the self-similar or fractal behavior of Ethernet LAN traffic with a combination of known graphical methods and appropriately modified rigorous statistical techniques that fully took into account the size of the available data, put "the icing on the cake." The resulting statistical analysis that kept me busy during most of 1992 involved an in-depth investigation of about 50–100 different 1 hour-long packet traces that were selected partly at random, partly by design (e.g., busy and non-busy periods) from the various continuous week-long measurements periods to form a representative cross-section of the available measurements. Even though the work was extremely time consuming and at times tedious and repetitive, doing the "homework" at this stage of the work helped me gain invaluable experience and paid off tremendously in the short and long term.

Although the large-scale analysis of the Bellcore Ethernet data was my responsibility, the overall effort was clearly the result of a mutually highly beneficial collaboration with researchers spanning the whole spectrum, from the very practical and networking-oriented to the highly theoretical and more mathematically-inclined. In particular, the involvement of the "in-house" networking experts Will Leland and Dan Wilson, the "parents" of these unique measurements, was crucial for the success of this work. For one, they knew the audience of networking researchers which we wanted to reach with our work and which was known to be highly critical of past traffic modeling attempts that generally ignored empirical evidence and relied instead on theoretical constructions that had little in common with networking reality. Thus, targeting this audience meant emphasizing networking intuition rather than statistical rigor[6]. To this end, Leland and Wilson served as "guinea pigs," and our experiments resulted, for example, in the "a picture is worth a thousand words" plot sequences in [19, Figure 4] that demonstrated how simple and easy it is to clearly distinguish between measured network traffic and synthetic traffic generated from the most popular and widely-used packet traffic models. Leland and Wilson's readiness to supply the necessary data and their willingness to put up with my often naive inquiries demonstrating ignorance on my side about networking in general and Ethernet LAN technologies in particular, also guaranteed that the often tedious analysis work always remained focused, never lost sight of the networking context in which it was performed, and never was in danger to turn into yet another data-fitting exercise.

Similarly, actively collaborating with experts on the probabilistic and statistical aspects of self-similar processes, namely with Murad Taqqu and – less frequently – with Jan Beran, ensured that the data analysis performed on the Ethernet LAN data made appropriate use of the known heuristic techniques for checking and testing for self-similar scaling behavior, with all their well-known and not so well-known pitfalls and shortcomings. Their expertise also enabled us to incorporate the latest methodologies (whose statistical properties had only recently been studied) into our analysis and to modify them appropriately to explicitly account for the uniqueness of the data at hand. It also demonstrated to the more mathematically inclined audience that the statistical work was solid,

[6] It is important to note that this did not mean we gave up on statistical rigor; it simply meant that while insisting on statistical rigor, we did not want to lose sight of the main message and hence tended to avoid technical jargon when presenting the final results.

that the mathematical concepts were sound and that the Bellcore Ethernet data were special and allowed for and motivated inference techniques for self-similar processes that would be inappropriate and to no avail if it were not the high-volume and high-quality measurements that motivated our work in the first place.[7]

5 Learning from the Physicists

Strictly speaking, all that our analysis of the Bellcore Ethernet data demonstrated was that the measurements were consistent with self-similar scaling over a wide range of time scales[8]. In particular, our analysis did not rule out the possibility of describing any one of the many 1 hour-long traces by some abstract and generally non-intuitive mathematical model that fit the data well in purely statistical terms.[9] To move beyond this potentially eternal philosophical discussion of interpreting the results of statistical analyses, two subsequent developments had a strong and ultimately decisive influence in favor of self-similar traffic models.

On the one hand, there was the speed and effort with which the networking community tried to replicate and repeat the measurement and analysis work we had done at Bellcore, but in very different networking environments and under very different conditions. The importance of this "reproducibility" effort is often overlooked (if not misunderstood) but cannot be emphasized enough in the context of understanding modern communication networks and the nature of the traffic that they carry. In fact, the idea of reproducibility offers a viable alternative to the commonly-employed model validation procedure advocated by traditional time series analysis. While the latter emphasizes the data-fitting philosophy that dominates much of the social sciences to date but is at a complete loss when it comes to dealing with the large number of large data sets collected from today's packet networks, the former has had a long and successful history in the physical sciences where it is viewed as an essential ingredient of any new discovery.

In the present context, one piece of "reproducibility" work stands out as one of the most important validations of our Ethernet analysis studies, namely the WAN traffic studies performed by Vern Paxson and Sally Floyd. Within one year of the original publication of our results in [18], Paxson and Floyd had analyzed packet traces from a number of different WANs and reported their results

[7] For an example of how working with the Bellcore Ethernet data motivated the development of new statistical methods for dealing with self-similar processes, see [3].

[8] Equivalently, based on our analysis, the hypothesis of no long-range dependence in the data had to be rejected.

[9] The fact that the same model typically performed badly when applied to a different 1 hour-long trace did not seem to bother the proponents of POTS-based data fitting approaches that have had a long tradition in traditional time series analysis.

at ACM/SIGCOMM'94 [24].[10] Their investigations set the standards for future WAN traffic studies, and their papers became landmark papers in this area. In their studies, Paxson and Floyd not only confirmed the self-similarity finding in the context of their Internet traffic traces, but in addition, they demonstrated that self-similarity comes in different "shades."[11] They also started to address the question that was already alluded to in [18] and that networking researchers were ultimately interested in, namely "Why is network traffic self-similar?" Another piece of work that has be mentioned in this context appeared right after the emergence of the Web in 1994 and the resulting explosive growth of WWW-related traffic on the Internet. In a paper at ACM/SIGMETRICS'96 [5] (see also [6]), Mark Crovella and Azer Bestavros presented results of their analysis of WWW traffic traces. By demonstrating that the emergence of a "killer application" such as the Web did not change the self-similar nature of Internet traffic at the packet level, they contributed to the present finding that self-similarity is an ubiquitous property of today's network traffic.

The second development that at the end convinced the networking community that self-similar traffic is for real and that set self-similar traffic models apart from the traditional traffic modeling work, was again in the true spirit of physical sciences research. It was the ability to explain self-similarity in simple networking terms that are intuitively appealing, coincide with engineering experience, agree with the measurements at the application level, and can be shown mathematically to cause exactly the same self-similar scaling behavior as has been observed in actual packet traces. To illustrate this physical-based explanation of self-similar network traffic, consider for example the LAN setting, where the aggregate traffic consists of a superposition of a large number of individual host-host packet traffic streams. It turns out that self-similarity of the aggregate flow of packets is caused by an "on-off" behavior of the individual host-host streams where during the "on" or burst-period, packets are sent at a constant rate, where no packets are sent during the "off" or idle-periods, and where, more importantly, the burst- or idle-periods exhibit extreme variability or equivalently, infinite variance.[12] This physical explanation can be pursued even further by relating, for example, the lengths of "on" periods to the sizes of files that reside on a typical file server and that a user reads to or writes from the file server, and by recalling that file size distributions are in general heavy-tailed with infinite variance. While some initial results and conjectures toward a physical explanation of the self-similar nature of network traffic can already be found in the original papers reporting on the discoveries of self-similarity in the LAN context [18] and WAN setting [24], we presented a complete explanation

[10] A more detailed version of this paper appeared subsequently in *IEEE/ACM Transactions on Networking* [25].

[11] While Ethernet LAN traffic over the time scales considered tends to be exactly self-similar, WAN traffic has been shown to be asymptotically self-similar; that is, it exhibits self-similar scaling for for a range of sufficiently large time scales.

[12] Mathematically speaking, we require the distributions of the burst/idle periods to be heavy-tailed with infinite variance.

consisting of the appropriate mathematical framework and corresponding empirical findings for the case of LANs at ACM/SIGCOMM'95 [28].[13] In the case of Internet WAN traffic, a similar, yet slightly different explanation holds and has been discussed in, for example, [5,20,30].

6 The Time Was Right

New discoveries or observations only rarely occur in isolation. Instead, they are often a response to changing conditions which put into question traditionally made (or previously validated) assumptions and are sufficiently interesting and challenging, both from a theoretical and practical perspective, so as to attract similarly-minded researchers in different parts of the world, with potentially very different backgrounds. In short, new discoveries often happen because the time is right: the overall level of interest in and awareness of the problem is sufficiently high, the ingredients needed to move beyond well-established boundaries are becoming available, and the theoretical groundwork has already been put in place.

In the case of self-similar traffic, its discovery at Bellcore turned out to coincide with three completely independent research activities, one in Japan, the other in Finland, and the third one – of all places – in a different part of Bellcore. In effect, all three of these activities resulted in the observation that packet traffic exhibits fractal-like characteristics and that in view of this finding, performance modeling for modern communication networks may have to be revisited or overhauled. However, in contrast to these activities, our discovery of self-similar traffic was supported by superb measurements, and more importantly, we used the available data to move beyond the descriptive stage to provide a physical understanding of the causes and effects of our finding.

The research effort in Japan was only recently brought to my attention (by Dr. Hiroshi Saito) and was carried out in the early 1990's by a graduate student, Shinsuke Shimogawa, at the NTT Telecommunication Network Laboratories, under the direction of Dr. Hiroshi Saito and advised by Dr. Hiroshi Yamada. Dissatisfied with the conventional models proposed for ATM cell streams, Shimogawa measured an ATM trace that was generated by a video application. Analyzing the observed cell loss process, he found characteristics consistent with fractal or self-similar behavior and discussed some implications of this finding for network performance. Unfortunately, the articles describing this work were published in hard-to-find places (even for Japanese researchers, e.g. [26,27]) and remained unknown outside of Japan.

In Finland, the research activity was carried out by Ilkka Norros, a mathematician working for VTT Information Technology. Based on a plot in the previously mentioned Fowler-Leland paper [12] that suggests that measured LAN traffic has a variance-time behavior consistent with a self-similar process, Norros proposed in 1993 a new traffic model based on fractional Brownian motion

[13] This work was done in collaboration with Murad Taqqu, Dan Wilson, and Robert Sherman; see also [29].

(FBM) that was capable of accounting for the empirically observed self-similar nature in measured LAN traffic. Subsequently, he published the original and widely cited paper on the FBM queueing model [23], demonstrating a very different queueing behavior for self-similar inputs to queues than was previously known for the traditional Markovian-based traffic processes. Norros' work appeared just in time to respond to one of the early criticisms and objections to self-similar traffic models, i.e., the "fact" that they defy conventional queueing methods and cannot be analyzed mathematically. Shortly thereafter, Nick Duffield and Neil O'Connell [8] did away with many of the remaining objections by obtaining and proving the large deviation principle for FBM.

A third independent approach for dealing with the problem of accurately and efficiently describing actual packet network traffic was pursued by another group of researchers at Bellcore around 1990. Fully aware of the pitfalls associated with relying on traditional models and with making them increasingly complex by adding more and more parameter to account for the tremendous variability inherent in observed packet traffic, (the late) R.P. Singh, Ashok Erramilli, and later on, Ashok's student, Parag Pruthi, set out to identify accurate and parsimonious new models of packet traffic that can be used in practice, i.e., by traffic engineers and network designers. Motivated by genuine engineering considerations, they demonstrated the feasibility of modeling packet traffic using deterministic nonlinear chaotic maps in such a way that the resulting models have a small number of parameters and are able to capture the observed bursty (or, as it became known later, "fractal") nature of packet traffic. As in the case of Leland and Wilson's measurements, I became aware of Erramilli and Singh's work through my involvement with the 7th ITC Specialist Seminar (see above), where they presented some initial findings of the chaotic map modeling approach and elaborated on its significance from the viewpoints of engineering and operating packet networks and of their performance evaluation [9].[14] It also marked the beginning of my extensive collaboration with Ashok Erramilli aimed at exploiting the fractal-like scaling behavior commonly observed in packet network traffic for the main purpose of developing measurement-based engineering methodologies to replace traditional POTS-based teletraffic theory whose failures have become all too apparent when applied to packet networks that are becoming faster, bigger, more complex, and more heterogeneous by the year.

7 Lessons for the Future

In light of our discovery of self-similar packet traffic, the general agreement that existed in the pre-self-similar times among the different groups involved in network-related research about the scientific value of checking how the myriad of existing packet traffic models would fare when compared to measured packet traffic quickly disappeared. It gave way to often lively discussions about the meaning of "comparing theoretical models and measured traffic," and provoked at times surprisingly strong negative reactions from proponents of some

[14] For a later more complete account of this work, see [10]).

of the more widely-used traditional models of packet traffic. On the one hand, the Internet research community fully shared in the excitement of our discovery and became a leading proponent of the work. Feeling partly vindicated for their critical assessment of past traffic modeling practice, the self-similarity finding supported the Internet researchers' "We told you so!"-response and allowed them to articulate in technical terms their first-hand experience of the "wildness" of actual Internet traffic. On the other hand, it is simply human nature that discoveries that question established theories and approaches are bound to cause strong reactions from the more tradition-minded segments of the research community – in our case from the proponents of teletraffic theory. At the same time, it is also in the spirit of science that new discoveries need to be fully exposed to criticisms, challenges and attacks. In fact, the course of science has shown again and again that new discoveries that cannot stand on their own in the presence of any sort of challenges and criticisms fade away and are quickly (and rightly) ignored. Although hard and at times unpleasant, researchers can and have to learn to live with constant criticisms if they want their work to have an impact.

In our case, learning how to best deal with the various challenges that arose in view of the self-similarity discovery consisted of gaining experience in judging what constitutes genuine and constructive criticism on the one hand and negativism that does not advance our understanding beyond what has been discussed and known for decades on the other hand. For example, I quickly learned that there was little value in discussing at length whether or not self-similarity can be approximated using conventional processes (of course, it can, but this approach offers no new insights into the nature of packet traffic and reduces the problem to a non-informative data fitting exercise!); whether or not certain statistical methods can be "fooled" into suggesting the presence of long-range dependence in the data when, in fact, no dependence structure exists at all (of course, there exist such methods, but by relying on different techniques, the problems can be avoided!); or whether or not self-similar processes are mathematical constructs that don't exist in reality (of course, they are, and of course, they don't, but we are talking here about mathematical abstractions of real-life phenomena!), etc.

In stark contrast, the Internet research community has provided the sort of constructive criticisms that has defined single-handedly my research agenda for the last few years. Not satisfied by our self-similarity finding and always aiming for a networking-based physical understanding of empirically observed phenomena in the data, they asked the pertinent questions such as "Why is packet traffic self-similar?" or "How do protocols such as TCP/IP impact the self-similarity behavior?" or "How can self-similarity be exploited for network engineering purposes?" etc. In fact, learning to listen to the "right' questions and attempting to solve them has led to new and exciting research opportunities and has improved our overall understanding of packet networks and packet traffic. Not surprisingly, I became quickly much more attuned to the reactions our work provoked within the Internet research community than to the type of criticism that argued for holding on to the past and relying on familiar concepts. As a result, since the discovery of self-similar traffic, our work has seen a steady influx of new theories and approaches (e.g., long-range dependence, heavy-tailed distributions, multi-fractals, wavelet-based analysis[15]) and has acquired many of the features that one generally associates with the physical sciences. In this sense, the development has been a natural reaction to the failure of traditional POTS-based approaches toward gaining a basic understanding of large-scale networks and of the complex interactions that exist within the network, among the users, between the network and the users, and across the different networking layers. It is safe to say that successful network performance modeling and evaluation work five years from now will have little in common with traditional teletraffic work. Teletraffic theory was highly successful in the homogeneous world of POTS but has been unable to account for and deal with the tremendous heterogeneity and complexity that are inherent in today's data networks. The self-similarity finding was just a first indication of how changing technologies affect the nature of research in areas ranging from data analysis to performance modeling and performance evaluation. New and more surprising discoveries are bound to happen, and to be part of these future developments, it will help to be at the right place, at the right time ... !

References

1. P. Abry and D. Veitch. Wavelet analysis of long-range dependent traffic, *IEEE Transactions on Information Theory* **44**, pp. 2–15, 1998.
2. J. Beran. *Statistics for Long-Memory Processes* Chapman & Hall, New York, 1994.
3. J. Beran and N. Terrin. Estimation of the long-memory parameter based on a multivariate central limit theorem, *J. Time Ser. Anal.* **15**, pp. 269–278, 1994.
4. D. R. Cox and M. W. H. Townsend. The use of the correlogram in measuring yarn irregularities, *Proc. Roy. Soc. Edinburgh Sec. A* **63**, pp. 290–311, 1947.
5. M. Crovella and A. Bestavros. Self-similarity in World Wide Web traffic – evidence and possible causes, *Proc. ACM/SIGMETRICS'96*, Philadelphia, PA, pp. 160–169, 1996.
6. M. Crovella and A. Bestavros. Self-similarity in World Wide Web traffic – evidence and possible causes, *IEEE/ACM Transactions on Networking* **5**, pp. 835–846, 1997.
7. R. Dahlhaus. Efficient parameter estimation of self-similar processes, *Ann. Statist.* **17**, pp. 1749–1766, 1989.
8. N. G. Duffield and N. O'Connell. Large deviations and overflow probabilities for the general single-server queue, with applications, *Mathematical Proceedings of the Cambridge Philosophical Society* **118**, pp. 363–374, 1995.
9. A. Erramilli and R. P. Singh. The application of deterministic chaotic maps to characterize traffic in broadband packet networks, *Proc. of the 7th ITC Specialist Seminar*, Morristown, NJ, October 1990.
10. A. Erramilli, R. P. Singh and P. Pruthi. An application of deterministic chaotic maps to model packet traffic, *Queueing Systems* **20**, pp. 171–206, 1995.
11. A. Feldmann, A. C. Gilbert and W. Willinger. Data networks as cascades: Investigating the multifractal nature of Internet WAN traffic, *Proc. of ACM/SIGCOMM'98*, Vancouver, Canada, September 1998, pp. 42–55, 1998.

[15] Recent work that illustrates the relevance of these theories in the networking area is discussed in [11] and involves a collaboration with Anja Feldmann and Anna Gilbert.

12. H. J. Fowler and W. E. Leland. Local area network traffic characteristics, with implications for broadband network congestion management, *IEEE Journal on Selected Areas in Communication* **9**, pp. 1139–1149, 1991.
13. C. W. J. Granger and R. Joyeux. An introduction to long-memory time series models and fractional differencing, *J. Time Ser. Anal.* **1**, pp. 15–29, 1981.
14. H. E. Hurst. Methods of using long-term storage in reservoirs, *Proc. Instit. Civil Eng. Part I* **5**, pp. 519–590, 1956.
15. A. N. Kolmogorov. The local structure of turbulence in incompressible viscous fluid for very large Reynolds numbers, *C. R. Acad. Sci. URSS (N.S.)* **30**, 1941. (Translation in *Turbulence* (S.K. Friedlander and L. Topper, Eds.), pp. 151-155, Interscience, New York, 1961.)
16. W. E. Leland. LAN traffic behavior from milliseconds to days, *Proc. of the 7th ITC Specialist Seminar*, Morristown, NJ, October 1990.
17. W. E. Leland and D. V. Wilson. High time-resolution measurements and analysis of LAN traffic: Implications for LAN interconnection, *Proc. of IEEE Infocom'91*, Bal Harbor, FL, April 1991.
18. W. E. Leland, M. S. Taqqu, W. Willinger, and D. V. Wilson. On the self-similar nature of Ethernet traffic, *Proc. of ACM/SIGCOMM'93*, San Francisco, CA, September 1993, pp. 183–193, 1993.
19. W. E. Leland, M. S. Taqqu, W. Willinger, and D. V. Wilson. On the self-similar nature of Ethernet traffic (Extended version), *IEEE/ACM Transactions on Networking* **2**, pp. 1–15, 1994.
20. T. G. Kurtz. Limit theorems for workload input models, in: *Stochastic Networks: Theory and Applications*, F.P. Kelly, S. Zachary and I. Ziedins (Eds.), Clarendon Press, 1996.
21. B. B. Mandelbrot. Self-similar error clusters in communication systems and the concept of conditional stationarity, *IEEE trans. Commun. Techn.* **COM-13**, pp. 71–90, 1995.
22. B. B. Mandelbrot. *The Fractal Geometry of Nature.* W.H. Freeman and Co., New York, 1983
23. I. Norros. A storage model with self-similar input, *Queueing Systems* **16**, pp. 387–396, 1994.
24. V. Paxson and S. Floyd. Wide-area traffic: The failure of Poisson modeling, *Proc. of ACM/SIGCOMM'94*, London, UK, September 1994, pp. 257–268, 1994.
25. V. Paxson and S. Floyd. Wide-area traffic: The failure of Poisson modeling, *IEEE/ACM Transactions on Networking* **3**, pp. 226–244, 1995.
26. S. Shimogawa, S. Nojo and T. Betchaku. A fractal property in an ATM video statistical multiplexing, *The 1992 Fall National Conference of ORSJ*, 1-C-6, 1992 (in Japanese).
27. S. Shimogawa, S. Nojo and T. Betchaku. Self-similar phenomena in an ATM video cell flow, *Proc. of Symp. for Performance Models in Information and Communication Networks*, M. Mori et a., (Eds.), Namazu, Japan, 1993.
28. W. Willinger, M. S. Taqqu, R. Sherman, and D. V. Wilson. Self-similarity through high-variability: Statistical analysis of Ethernet LAN traffic at the source level, *Proc. of ACM/SIGCOMM'95*, Cambridge, MA, August 1995, pp. 100–113, 1995.
29. W. Willinger, M. S. Taqqu, R. Sherman, and D. V. Wilson. Self-similarity through high-variability: Statistical analysis of Ethernet LAN traffic at the source level, *IEEE/ACM Transactions on Networking* **5**, pp. 71–86, 1997.

30. W. Willinger, V. Paxson and M. S. Taqqu. Self-similarity and heavy tails: Structural modeling of network traffic, in: *A Practical Guide to Heavy Tails: Statistical Techniques for Analyzing Heavy-Tailed Distributions*, R. Adler, R. Feldman and M.S. Taqqu (Eds.), Birkhauser Verlag, Boston, MA, pp. 27–53, 1998.
31. W. Willinger and V. Paxson. Where mathematics meets the Internet, *Notices of the AMS* **45**, pp. 961–970, 1998.

Author Index

Lecture Notes in Computer Science

For information about Vols. 1–1697
please contact your bookseller or Springer-Verlag

Vol. 1698: M. Felici, K. Kanoun, A. Pasquini (Eds.), Computer Safety, Reliability and Security. Proceedings, 1999. XVIII, 482 pages. 1999.

Vol. 1699: S. Albayrak (Ed.), Intelligent Agents for Telecommunication Applications. Proceedings, 1999. IX, 191 pages. 1999. (Subseries LNAI).

Vol. 1700: R. Stadler, B. Stiller (Eds.), Active Technologies for Network and Service Management. Proceedings, 1999. XII, 299 pages. 1999.

Vol. 1701: W. Burgard, T. Christaller, A.B. Cremers (Eds.), KI-99: Advances in Artificial Intelligence. Proceedings, 1999. XI, 311 pages. 1999. (Subseries LNAI).

Vol. 1702: G. Nadathur (Ed.), Principles and Practice of Declarative Programming. Proceedings, 1999. X, 434 pages. 1999.

Vol. 1703: L. Pierre, T. Kropf (Eds.), Correct Hardware Design and Verification Methods. Proceedings, 1999. XI, 366 pages. 1999.

Vol. 1704: Jan M. Żytkow, J. Rauch (Eds.), Principles of Data Mining and Knowledge Discovery. Proceedings, 1999. XIV, 593 pages. 1999. (Subseries LNAI).

Vol. 1705: H. Ganzinger, D. McAllester, A. Voronkov (Eds.), Logic for Programming and Automated Reasoning. Proceedings, 1999. XII, 397 pages. 1999. (Subseries LNAI).

Vol. 1706: J. Hatcliff, T. Æ. Mogensen, P. Thiemann (Eds.), Partial Evaluation – Practice and Theory. 1998. IX, 433 pages. 1999.

Vol. 1707: H.-W. Gellersen (Ed.), Handheld and Ubiquitous Computing. Proceedings, 1999. XII, 390 pages. 1999.

Vol. 1708: J.M. Wing, J. Woodcock, J. Davies (Eds.), FM'99 – Formal Methods. Proceedings Vol. I, 1999. XVIII, 937 pages. 1999.

Vol. 1709: J.M. Wing, J. Woodcock, J. Davies (Eds.), FM'99 – Formal Methods. Proceedings Vol. II, 1999. XVIII, 937 pages. 1999.

Vol. 1710: E.-R. Olderog, B. Steffen (Eds.), Correct System Design. XIV, 417 pages. 1999.

Vol. 1711: N. Zhong, A. Skowron, S. Ohsuga (Eds.), New Directions in Rough Sets, Data Mining, and Granular-Soft Computing. Proceedings, 1999. XIV, 558 pages. 1999. (Subseries LNAI).

Vol. 1712: H. Boley, A Tight, Practical Integration of Relations and Functions. XI, 169 pages. 1999. (Subseries LNAI).

Vol. 1713: J. Jaffar (Ed.), Principles and Practice of Constraint Programming – CP'99. Proceedings, 1999. XII, 493 pages. 1999.

Vol. 1714: M.T. Pazienza (Eds.), Information Extraction. IX, 165 pages. 1999. (Subseries LNAI).

Vol. 1715: P. Perner, M. Petrou (Eds.), Machine Learning and Data Mining in Pattern Recognition. Proceedings, 1999. VIII, 217 pages. 1999. (Subseries LNAI).

Vol. 1716: K.Y. Lam, E. Okamoto, C. Xing (Eds.), Advances in Cryptology – ASIACRYPT'99. Proceedings, 1999. XI, 414 pages. 1999.

Vol. 1717: Ç. K. Koç, C. Paar (Eds.), Cryptographic Hardware and Embedded Systems. Proceedings, 1999. XI, 353 pages. 1999.

Vol. 1718: M. Diaz, P. Owezarski, P. Sénac (Eds.), Interactive Distributed Multimedia Systems and Telecommunication Services. Proceedings, 1999. XI, 386 pages. 1999.

Vol. 1719: M. Fossorier, H. Imai, S. Lin, A. Poli (Eds.), Applied Algebra, Algebraic Algorithms and Error-Correcting Codes. Proceedings, 1999. XIII, 510 pages. 1999.

Vol. 1720: O. Watanabe, T. Yokomori (Eds.), Algorithmic Learning Theory. Proceedings, 1999. XI, 365 pages. 1999. (Subseries LNAI).

Vol. 1721: S. Arikawa, K. Furukawa (Eds.), Discovery Science. Proceedings, 1999. XI, 374 pages. 1999. (Subseries LNAI).

Vol. 1722: A. Middeldorp, T. Sato (Eds.), Functional and Logic Programming. Proceedings, 1999. X, 369 pages. 1999.

Vol. 1723: R. France, B. Rumpe (Eds.), UML'99 – The Unified Modeling Language. XVII, 724 pages. 1999.

Vol. 1724: H. I. Christensen, H. Bunke, H. Noltemeier (Eds.), Sensor Based Intelligent Robots. Proceedings, 1998. VIII, 327 pages. 1999 (Subseries LNAI).

Vol. 1725: J. Pavelka, G. Tel, M. Bartošek (Eds.), SOFSEM'99: Theory and Practice of Informatics. Proceedings, 1999. XIII, 498 pages. 1999.

Vol. 1726: V. Varadharajan, Y. Mu (Eds.), Information and Communication Security. Proceedings, 1999. XI, 325 pages. 1999.

Vol. 1727: P.P. Chen, D.W. Embley, J. Kouloumdjian, S.W. Liddle, J.F. Roddick (Eds.), Advances in Conceptual Modeling. Proceedings, 1999. XI, 389 pages. 1999.

Vol. 1728: J. Akoka, M. Bouzeghoub, I. Comyn-Wattiau, E. Métais (Eds.), Conceptual Modeling – ER '99. Proceedings, 1999. XIV, 540 pages. 1999.

Vol. 1729: M. Mambo, Y. Zheng (Eds.), Information Security. Proceedings, 1999. IX, 277 pages. 1999.

Vol. 1730: M. Gelfond, N. Leone, G. Pfeifer (Eds.), Logic Programming and Nonmonotonic Reasoning. Proceedings, 1999. XI, 391 pages. 1999. (Subseries LNAI).

Vol. 1731: J. Kratochvíl (Ed.), Graph Drawing. Proceedings, 1999. XIII, 422 pages. 1999.

Vol. 1732: S. Matsuoka, R.R. Oldehoeft, M. Tholburn (Eds.), Computing in Object-Oriented Parallel Environments. Proceedings, 1999. VIII, 205 pages. 1999.

Vol. 1733: H. Nakashima, C. Zhang (Eds.), Approaches to Intelligent Agents. Proceedings, 1999. XII, 241 pages. 1999. (Subseries LNAI).

Vol. 1734: H. Hellwagner, A. Reinefeld (Eds.), SCI: Scalable Coherent Interface. XXI, 490 pages. 1999.

Vol. 1564: M. Vazirgiannis, Interactive Multimedia Documents. XIII, 161 pages. 1999.

Vol. 1591: D.J. Duke, I. Herman, M.S. Marshall, PREMO: A Framework for Multimedia Middleware. XII, 254 pages. 1999.

Vol. 1624: J. A. Padget (Ed.), Collaboration between Human and Artificial Societies. XIV, 301 pages. 1999. (Subseries LNAI).

Vol. 1635: X. Tu, Artificial Animals for Computer Animation. XIV, 172 pages. 1999.

Vol. 1646: B. Westfechtel, Models and Tools for Managing Development Processes. XIV, 418 pages. 1999.

Vol. 1735: J.W. Amtrup, Incremental Speech Translation. XV, 200 pages. 1999. (Subseries LNAI).

Vol. 1736: L. Rizzo, S. Fdida (Eds.): Networked Group Communication. Proceedings, 1999. XIII, 339 pages. 1999.

Vol. 1737: P. Agouris, A. Stefanidis (Eds.), Integrated Spatial Databases. Proceedings, 1999. X, 317 pages. 1999.

Vol. 1738: C. Pandu Rangan, V. Raman, R. Ramanujam (Eds.), Foundations of Software Technology and Theoretical Computer Science. Proceedings, 1999. XII, 452 pages. 1999.

Vol. 1739: A. Braffort, R. Gherbi, S. Gibet, J. Richardson, D. Teil (Eds.), Gesture-Based Communication in Human-Computer Interaction. Proceedings, 1999. XI, 333 pages. 1999. (Subseries LNAI).

Vol. 1740: R. Baumgart (Ed.): Secure Networking – CQRE [Secure] '99. Proceedings, 1999. IX, 261 pages. 1999.

Vol. 1741: A. Aggarwal, C. Pandu Rangan (Eds.), Algorithms and Computation. Proceedings, 1999. XIII, 448 pages. 1999.

Vol. 1742: P.S. Thiagarajan, R. Yap (Eds.), Advances in Computing Science – ASIAN'99. Proceedings, 1999. XI, 397 pages. 1999.

Vol. 1743: A. Moreira, S. Demeyer (Eds.), Object-Oriented Technology. Proceedings, 1999. XVII, 389 pages. 1999.

Vol. 1744: S. Staab, Extracting Degree Information from Texts. X; 187 pages. 1999. (Subseries LNAI).

Vol. 1745: P. Banerjee, V.K. Prasanna, B.P. Sinha (Eds.), High Performance Computing – HiPC'99. Proceedings, 1999. XXII, 412 pages. 1999.

Vol. 1746: M. Walker (Ed.), Cryptography and Coding. Proceedings, 1999. IX, 313 pages. 1999.

Vol. 1747: N. Foo (Ed.), Adavanced Topics in Artificial Intelligence. Proceedings, 1999. XV, 500 pages. 1999. (Subseries LNAI).

Vol. 1748: H.V. Leong, W.-C. Lee, B. Li, L. Yin (Eds.), Mobile Data Access. Proceedings, 1999. X, 245 pages. 1999.

Vol. 1749: L. C.-K. Hui, D.L. Lee (Eds.), Internet Applications. Proceedings, 1999. XX, 518 pages. 1999.

Vol. 1750: D.E. Knuth, MMIXware. VIII, 550 pages. 1999.

Vol. 1751: H. Imai, Y. Zheng (Eds.), Public Key Cryptography. Proceedings, 2000. XI, 485 pages. 2000.

Vol. 1752: S. Krakowiak, S. Shrivastava (Eds.), Advances in Distributed Systems. VIII, 509 pages. 2000.

Vol. 1753: E. Pontelli, V. Santos Costa (Eds.), Practical Aspects of Declarative Languages. Proceedings, 2000. X, 327 pages. 2000.

Vol. 1754: J. Väänänen (Ed.), Generalized Quantifiers and Computation. Proceedings, 1997. VII, 139 pages. 1999.

Vol. 1755: D. Bjørner, M. Broy, A.V. Zamulin (Eds.), Perspectives of System Informatics. Proceedings, 1999. XII, 540 pages. 2000.

Vol. 1757: N.R. Jennings, Y. Lespérance (Eds.), Intelligent Agents VI. Proceedings, 1999. XII, 380 pages. 2000. (Subseries LNAI).

Vol. 1758: H. Heys, C. Adams (Eds.), Selected Areas in Cryptography. Proceedings, 1999. VIII, 243 pages. 2000.

Vol. 1759: M.J. Zaki, C.-T. Ho (Eds.), Large-Scale Parallel Data Mining. VIII, 261 pages. 2000. (Subseries LNAI).

Vol. 1760: J.-J. Ch. Meyer, P.-Y. Schobbens (Eds.), Formal Models of Agents. Poceedings. VIII, 253 pages. 1999. (Subseries LNAI).

Vol. 1761: R. Caferra, G. Salzer (Eds.), Automated Deduction in Classical and Non-Classical Logics. Proceedings. VIII, 299 pages. 2000. (Subseries LNAI).

Vol. 1762: K.-D. Schewe, B. Thalheim (Eds.), Foundations of Information and Knowledge Systems. Proceedings, 2000. X, 305 pages. 2000.

Vol. 1763: J. Akiyama, M. Kano, M. Urabe (Eds.), Discrete and Computational Geometry. Proceedings, 1998. VIII, 333 pages. 2000.

Vol. 1764: H. Ehrig, G. Engels, H.-J. Kreowski, G. Rozenberg (Eds.), Theory and Application of Graph Transformations. Proceedings, 1998. IX, 490 pages. 2000.

Vol. 1767: G. Bongiovanni, G. Gambosi, R. Petreschi (Eds.), Algorithms and Complexity. Proceedings, 2000. VIII, 317 pages. 2000.

Vol. 1768: A. Pfitzmann (Ed.), Information Hiding. Proceedings, 1999. IX, 492 pages. 2000.

Vol. 1769: G. Haring, C. Lindemann, M. Reiser (Eds.), Performance Evaluation: Origins and Directions. X, 529 pages. 2000.

Vol. 1770: H. Reichel, S. Tison (Eds.), STACS 2000. Proceedings, 2000. XIV, 662 pages. 2000.

Vol. 1771: P. Lambrix, Part-Whole Reasoning in an Object-Centered Framework. XII, 195 pages. 2000. (Subseries LNAI).

Vol. 1773: G. Saake, K. Schwarz, C. Türker (Eds.), Transactions and Database Dynamics. Proceedings, 1999. VIII, 247 pages. 2000.

Vol. 1774: J. Delgado, G.D. Stamoulis, A. Mullery, D. Prevedourou, K. Start (Eds.), Telecommunications and IT Convergence Towards Service E-volution. Proceedings, 2000. XIII, 350 pages. 2000.

Vol. 1780: R. Conradi (Ed.), Software Process Technology. Proceedings, 2000. IX, 249 pages. 2000.

9 783540 671930